IN SEARCH OF PROSPERITY

In Search of Prosperity

ANALYTIC NARRATIVES ON ECONOMIC GROWTH

Edited by

Dani Rodrik

PRINCETON UNIVERSITY PRESS   PRINCETON AND OXFORD

Copyright © 2003 by Princeton University Press

Published by Princeton University Press, 41 William Street,
Princeton, New Jersey 08540

In the United Kingdom: Princeton University Press, 3 Market Place,
Woodstock, Oxfordshire OX20 1SY

Library of Congress Cataloging-in-Publication Data

In search of prosperity : analytic narratives on economic
growth / Dani Rodrik, editor.
p.   cm.
Revisions of papers presented at a conference
held at Harvard University, 2001.
Includes bibliographical references and index.
ISBN 0-691-09268-0 (cl : alk. paper) — ISBN 0-691-09269-9 (pbk : alk. paper)
1. Economic development—Congresses.   2. Developing countries—
Economic conditions—Congresses.   I. Rodrik, Dani.
HD73 .I52 2003
338.9—dc21   2002072854

British Library Cataloging-in-Publication Data is available

This book has been composed in Times Roman
by Princeton Editorial Associates, Inc., Scottsdale, Arizona

Printed on acid-free paper. ∞
www.pupress.princeton.edu

Printed in the United States of America

5 7 9 10 8 6 4

ISBN-13: 978-0-691-09269-0

ISBN-10: 0-691-09269-9

Contents

Acknowledgments

EARLY versions of the chapters contained in this volume were (with one exception) first presented at the conference "Analytical Country Studies on Growth," held at the John F. Kennedy School of Government, Harvard University, April 20–21, 2001. I am tremendously grateful to the Ford Foundation for generous financial support that made this conference and the preparation of the country narratives possible. The Center for International Development at Harvard provided logistical support.

Even though their comments are not reproduced here, the discussants and other participants at the conference, some of whom came from very long distances, made a very important contribution to the quality of the final product. I thank in particular the assigned discussants for the individual chapters: Philippe Aghion, Abhijit Banerjee, Robert Barro, J. Edgardo Campos, Mauricio Cardenas, Alan Hirsch, Ishrat Hussain, Simon Johnson, J. Clark Leith, Benno Ndulu, Yung Chul Park, Urjit Patel, Lant Pritchett, and Ernesto Stein. Michele Kane handled the logistics for the conference with great skill. Zoë McLaren's editorial and administrative help was invaluable in the final stages of manuscript preparation.

List of Contributors

DARON ACEMOGLU
Department of Economics
MIT

MAITE CAREAGA
Stanford University

GREG CLARK
Department of Economics
University of California, Davis

J. BRADFORD DELONG
Department of Economics
University of California, Berkeley

GEORGES DE MENIL
Kennedy School of Government
Harvard University

WILLIAM EASTERLY
Development Research Group
The World Bank

RICARDO HAUSMANN
Kennedy School of Government
Harvard University

SIMON JOHNSON
Sloan School of Management
MIT

DANIEL KAUFMANN
The World Bank

MASSIMO MASTRUZZI
The World Bank

IAN MCLEAN
School of Economics
University of Adelaide

LANT PRITCHETT
Kennedy School of Government
Harvard University

YINGYI QIAN
Department of Economics
University of California, Berkeley

JAMES ROBINSON
Department of Political Science
University of California, Berkeley

DANI RODRIK
Kennedy School of Government
Harvard University

DEVESH ROY
The International Monetary Fund

ARVIND SUBRAMANIAN
The International Monetary Fund

ALAN M. TAYLOR
Department of Economics
University of California, Davis

JONATHAN TEMPLE
Department of Economics
University of Bristol

BARRY WEINGAST
Hoover Institution and Department
    of Political Science
Stanford University

SUSAN WOLCOTT
University of Mississippi

DIEGO ZAVALETA
The World Bank

IN SEARCH OF PROSPERITY

Introduction

WHAT DO WE LEARN FROM COUNTRY NARRATIVES?

DANI RODRIK

THE SPECTACULAR gap in incomes that separates the world's rich and poor nations is the central economic fact of our time. Average income in Sierra Leone, which is the poorest country in the world for which we have data, is almost one hundred times lower than that in Luxembourg, the world's richest country. Nearly two-thirds of the world's population lives in countries where average income is only one-tenth the U.S. level (fig. 1.1).[1] Since the starting points for all these countries were not so far apart prior to the Industrial Revolution, these disparities must be attributed almost entirely to differences in long-term growth rates of per capita income. The world is split sharply between countries that have managed to sustain economic growth over long periods of time and those that have not. How do we make sense of this?

The economics of growth has come a long way since it regained center stage for economists in the mid-1980s.[2] The early focus on theoretical models that generate self-sustaining growth and endogenous technological advance has been increasingly replaced with attempts to shed light on the diversity of experience with economic growth.[3] On the empirical front, the search for correlates of growth has gone beyond economic variables (such as physical and human capital, and price distortions) to examine "deeper" determinants of economic performance (such as geography and institutions).[4] Our understanding of the economic growth process has increased considerably as a result.

---

[1] These figures refer to per capita gross domestic product, adjusted for differences in purchasing power parity. The source is the World Bank's World Development Indicators 2001 CD-ROM.

[2] Solow 1956 is the landmark in the neoclassical analysis of economic growth. The resurgence of theoretical interest in growth in the 1980s can be traced to Romer's (1986) work on models with increasing returns to scale.

[3] Two book-length treatments of the theoretical literature on technological progress and growth are Grossman and Helpman 1991 and Aghion and Howitt 1998.

[4] See, among others, Barro 1991; Gallup and Sachs 1998; Hall and Jones 1999; and Acemoglu, Johnson, and Robinson 2001. Temple (1999) provides an excellent survey of the empirical growth literature.

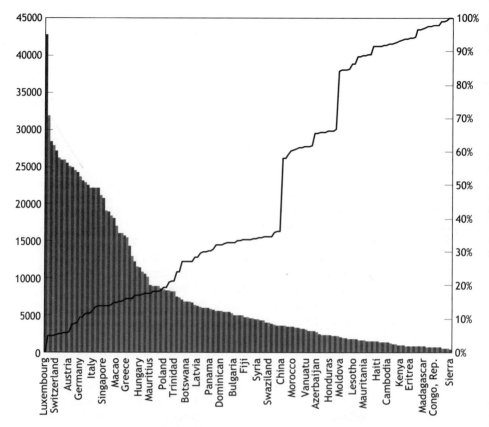

Figure 1.1. Global income distribution: GDP per capita in 1999 (PPP-adjusted, left axis) and cumulative percentage of world population (right axis)
Source: World Bank, World Development Indicators 2001

However, there remain serious gaps in the existing research. Consider some of the questions that come to mind after a cursory look at the cross-national record of the last few decades. How has China managed to grow so rapidly despite the absence of full-fledged private property rights? What happened in India after the early 1980s to lift its growth rate by approximately three percentage points? How have Mauritius and Botswana managed to avoid the problems that other countries in the rest of sub-Saharan Africa have succumbed to? Why did countries like Brazil, Mexico, or Venezuela do so well until the early 1980s and so poorly thereafter? How did Indonesia manage to grow over a 30-year period despite weak institutions and highly distorted microeconomic policies—and why did it collapse so spectacularly in the aftermath of the Asian financial crisis of 1997? Why do the Philippines and Bolivia continue to stagnate despite a sharp improvement in their "fundamentals" since the 1980s? What explains the very sharp divergence in the performance of the former socialist economies since the early 1990s? It would be fair to say that neither the cross-national growth literature nor existing country studies have made adequate progress in answering these and many other fundamental questions.

Of course, there is no shortage of country studies in the literature. But we have few examples that are explicitly informed and framed by the developments in recent growth theory or growth econometrics. Alwyn Young's (1992) work on Singapore and Hong Kong, Robert Lucas's (1993) quantitative exercise on South Korea, and Paul Romer's (1993) short discussion of Mauritius and Taiwan are rare exceptions.[5]

This volume begins to fill some of the holes. It offers a series of analytical country narratives that try to provide answers to selected growth puzzles—those that I have enumerated above as well as many others. These narratives explore the respective roles of microeconomic and macroeconomic policies, institutions, political economy, and initial conditions in driving patterns of technological convergence and accumulation in selected countries. Since the authors tend to be growth theorists and macroeconomists rather than country specialists, these are not country studies in the usual sense of the word. The strength of the chapters lies in drawing the connections between specific country experiences, on one side, and growth theory and cross-national empirics, on the other. The authors evaluate and extend our understanding of economic growth using the country narratives as a backdrop.

As the organizer of this collaboration and the editor of the volume, I must take full responsibility for the speculative nature of the efforts that resulted. I encouraged the authors to be bold and imaginative even if that meant going out on a limb. I even insisted that they take on countries about which they knew little, so that their vision and judgment would not be clouded by preconceptions. (I can now confess my amazement at how many of the contributors complied!) The compensating benefit, I hope, is that the authors have felt less restrained by conventional wisdom and more inclined to break new ground. They have formulated new insights for modelers to formalize, and new hypotheses for the econometricians to test. And if, as a by-product, they have ended up teaching us (and themselves) something about the individual countries, all the better!

SOME ORGANIZING PRINCIPLES

To organize our thinking about the economics of growth, it helps to distinguish between the "proximate" and "deep" determinants of growth. Figure 1.2 shows

[5] See also Rodrik 1995, which focuses on the growth transition of South Korea and Taiwan in the early 1960s and 1970s.

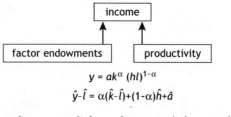

$$y = ak^{\alpha} (hl)^{1-\alpha}$$

$$\hat{y}\text{-}\hat{l} = \alpha(\hat{k}\text{-}\hat{l})+(1\text{-}\alpha)\hat{h}+\hat{a}$$

| per-capita GDP growth | = | capital deepening | + | human capital accumulation | + | productivity growth |

Figure 1.2. How economists think of income determination

the standard way in which economists think about the determination of income. The total output of an economy is a function of its *resource endowments* (labor, physical capital, human capital) and the *productivity* with which these endowments are deployed to produce a flow of goods and services (GDP). We can express this relationship in the form of an economy-wide production function, with *a* representing total factor productivity. Note that *a* captures not only the *technical* efficiency level of the economy, but also the *allocative* efficiency with which resource endowments are distributed across economic activities. The growth of per capita output can in turn be expressed in terms of three proximate determinants: *(a)* physical capital deepening; *(b)* human capital accumulation; and *(c)* productivity growth.

Conceptually, this is a straightforward decomposition, and it has given rise to a large literature on sources-of-growth accounting. But one has to be careful in interpreting such decompositions because accumulation and productivity growth are themselves endogenous. This prevents us from giving the sources-of-growth equation any structural interpretation. For example, observing that 80 percent of the growth is "accounted" for by accumulation and the rest by productivity does not tell us that growth would have been necessarily 80 percent as high in the absence of technological change; perhaps in the absence of productivity change, the incentive to accumulate would have been much lower and the resulting capital deepening significantly less. Indeed, to the extent that growth is driven by other fundamental determinants, not directly captured in the growth-accounting framework, the causality my well run backwards, from growth to accumulation and productivity instead of the other way around.

For these reasons it is best to think of accumulation and productivity change as proximate determinants of growth at best. The deeper determinants are shown in figure 1.3. While there is no shortage of candidates, I find a threefold taxonomy useful:

1. Geography
2. Integration (trade)
3. Institutions

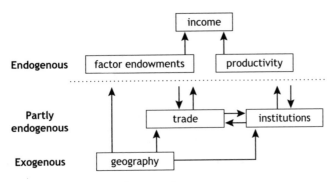

Figure 1.3. All of growth economics on one page

Geography relates to the advantages and disadvantages posed by a country's physical location (latitude, proximity to navigable waters, climate, and so on). Integration relates to market size, and the benefits (as well as costs) of participation in international trade in goods, services, capital, and possibly labor. Institutions refer to the quality of formal and informal sociopolitical arrangements—ranging from the legal system to broader political institutions—that play an important role in promoting or hindering economic performance.

Figures 1.4, 1.5, and 1.6 display some illustrative scatter plots, showing the relationship between each of these three factors and incomes. I use distance from the equator as the measure for "geography," the share of trade in GDP as the measure of integration, and a commonly employed subjective index for the quality of institutions. A first pass through the data indicates that all three are significantly correlated with per capita income. Such correlations are the stock-in-trade of the growth empiricist. The problem, however, is that neither trade nor the quality of institutions is truly endogenous, which creates severe difficulties when it comes to interpretation. I shall return to this issue below.

Geography

Geography plays a direct and obvious role in determining income because natural-resource endowments are shaped in large part by it. The quality of natural resources depends on geography. Commodities such as oil, diamonds, and copper are marketable resources that can be an important source of income. Soil quality and rainfall determine the productivity of land. Geography and climate determine the public-health environment (the inhabitants' proclivity to debilitating diseases such as malaria), and shape the quantity and quality of human capital.

Geography also influences growth via the other two factors. Geography is an important determinant of the extent to which a country can become integrated

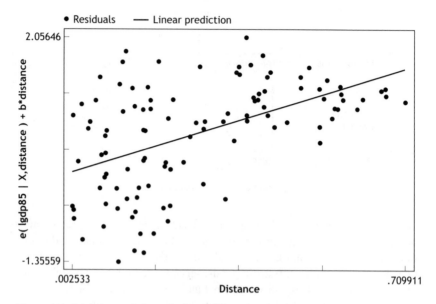

Figure 1.4. Partial association between income and distance from equator

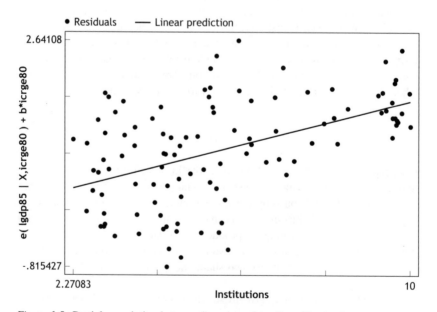

Figure 1.5. Partial association between income and quality of institutions

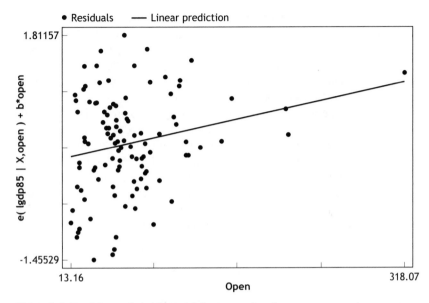

Figure 1.6. Partial association between income and trade

with world markets, regardless of the country's own trade policies. A distant, land-locked country faces greater costs of integration. Similarly, geography shapes institutions in a number of ways. The historical experience with colonialism has been a key factor in the institutional development (or lack thereof) of today's developing countries, and colonialism itself was driven in part by geopolitical considerations—consider the scramble for Africa during the 1880s. The natural-resource endowment bequeathed by a country's geography also shapes the quality of institutions. Natural-resource booms, for example, are often associated with the creation of rent-seeking and rent-distributing institutions—the so-called resource curse.

Geography is arguably the only exogenous factor in our threefold taxonomy. Trade and institutions are obviously endogenous and coevolve with economic performance. Nonetheless, it is useful to think of these as deep causal factors to the extent that they are not fully determined by incomes per se. Trade is obviously shaped in large part by a country's conscious choice of policies; and institutional development is at least partly a choice variable as well (or in any case can be determined by developments exogenous to the economy).

Trade

The significance of integration in the world economy as a driver of economic growth has been a persistent theme in the literatures on economic history and development economics. An influential article by Jeffrey Sachs and Andrew Warner (1995) went so far as to argue that countries that are open to trade (by the authors' definition) experience *unconditional* convergence to the income levels of the rich countries. Leading international policymakers from the World Bank, International Monetary Fund, World Trade Organization, and Organisation for Economic Cooperation and Development frequently make the case that integration into the world economy is the surest way to prosperity. The traditional theory of trade does not support such extravagant claims, as trade yields relatively small income gains that do not translate into persistently higher growth. However, it is possible to tweak endogenous growth models to generate large dynamic benefits from trade openness, provided technological externalities and learning effects go in the right direction. Capital flows can enhance the benefits further, as long as they go from rich countries to poor countries and come with externalities on the management and technology fronts.

Institutions

Institutions have received increasing attention in the growth literature as it has become clear that property rights, appropriate regulatory structures, the quality and independence of the judiciary, and bureaucratic capacity cannot be taken for granted in many settings and that they are of utmost importance to initiating and sustaining economic growth. The profession's priors have moved from an implicit assumption that these institutions arise endogenously and effortlessly as a by-product of economic growth to the view that they are essential preconditions and determinants of growth (North and Thomas 1973).

Once one moves beyond general statements of the kind that property rights are good for growth and corruption is bad, there is much that remains unclear. Which institutions demand priority? What are the specific institutional forms that are required? Do these differ across countries according to level of development, historical trajectory, and initial conditions?

Interrelationships

As the arrows in figure 1.3 indicate, the basic framework is rich with feedback effects, both from growth back to the "causal" factors, and among the "causal" factors. There are reasons to think, for example, that as countries get richer, they will trade more and acquire higher-quality institutions. Much of the cross-national empirical work on institutions has been plagued by the endogeneity of institutional quality: are rich countries rich because they have high-quality institutions, or the other way around? Only very recently has work by Acemoglu, Johnson, and Robinson (2001) provided convincing evidence that institutional quality is truly causal.[6] Similarly, there are hints in the empirical literature of a two-way interaction between trade and institutions: better institutions foster trade (Anderson and Marcouiller 1999), and more openness to trade begets higher-quality institutions (Wei 2000). These feedbacks make simple-minded empirical exercises of the type shown in figures 1.4–6 highly suspect. They require extreme care in laying out the hypotheses and in ascribing causality.[7] While case studies do not necessarily possess a methodological advantage here, they at least have the advantage of allowing a "thick" description of the interactions among geography, trade, and institutions.

Determinants of development such as institutions and geography change slowly, or hardly at all. Yet countries like China and India have gone through remarkable transformations during the last two decades in their economic performance, while many others have experienced sharp deteriorations. This suggests that moderate changes in country-specific circumstances (policies and institutional arrangements), often interacting with the external environment, can produce discontinuous changes in economic performances, which in turn set off virtuous or vicious cycles. In-depth country studies can highlight these important interactions in ways that cross-country empirics cannot.

THE QUESTIONS

Which are the arrows in figure 1.3 that matter most, and why? That is the central question of growth economics. The major debates in the literature on economic growth and development can be viewed as arguments about the relative strengths of the various arrows in figure 1.3. Those who stress the primacy of geography (climate, resources, and health) emphasize the arrows that emanate from that particular box—both to incomes (via endowments and productivity) and to trade and institutions. Those who view integration into the world economy as the key to growth emphasize the outward arrows from trade to incomes and institutions. The institutionalists emphasize the primacy of institution building, arguing that more trade and higher incomes are the result of better institutions.

Econometric results can be found to support any and all of these categories of arguments. However, very little of this econometric work survives close scrutiny (see the critique by Rodríguez and Rodrik 2001 of the literature on trade), or is able to sway the priors of anyone with strong convictions in other directions. Moreover, there is little reason to believe that the primary causal

[6] Acemoglu, Johnson, and Robinson (2001) rely on colonial legacy, in turn linked to variation in settler mortality, as an instrument for institutional quality.
[7] See Rodrik, Subramanian, and Trebbi 2002 for a recent attempt to sort out causality in the present framework.

channels are invariant to time period, initial conditions, or other aspects of a country's circumstances. There may not be universal rules about what makes countries grow. For a small country near major shipping routes, trade may indeed be the shortest route to economic salvation. For a large country located in a geographically disadvantaged region, a period of institution building may be the only way to escape poverty. Analytical country narratives, informed by growth theory and the cross-national evidence, can play a useful role in developing such contingent hypotheses and testing them (albeit informally).

It needs to be emphasized that case studies and cross-national econometrics are not substitutes for each other. They can be used in a complementary fashion to advance our understanding of the growth process. Ideally, case studies can generate novel hypotheses that in turn suggest new cross-national tests. A claim based on case studies that does not find support from cross-country regressions requires close scrutiny. By the same token, any cross-national empirical regularity that cannot be meaningfully verified on the basis of country studies should be regarded as suspect.

SOME ANSWERS FROM THE COUNTRY NARRATIVES

The country narratives are too rich to summarize in an introductory chapter, and I shall not attempt to do so. However, some themes that emerge are worth sketching out as a road map to the reader.

The quality of institutions is key.

Institutions that provide dependable property rights, manage conflict, maintain law and order, and align economic incentives with social costs and benefits are the foundation of long-term growth. This is the clearest message that comes across from the individual cases. China, Botswana, Mauritius, and Australia—four cases of success in our sample—all owe their performance to the presence (or creation) of institutions that have generated market-oriented incentives, protected the property rights of current and future investors, and enabled social and political instability.

Consider the case of Botswana, presented by Daron Acemoglu, Simon Johnson, and James Robinson. Per capita income in Botswana grew at 7.7 percent annually between 1965 and 1998. The proximate reasons for this outcome are easy to list. Law and order were maintained. Diamond revenues were managed exceptionally well. The bureaucracy was efficient and run along meritocratic lines. Hard budget constraints were the rule (and not the exception) in the public sector. There were large public investments in education, health, and infrastructure. The exchange rate was set at a competitive level. However, policies were not uniformly "good" in the conventional, Washington Consensus sense of that word. The government in Botswana has intervened massively in the economy, and the public sector accounts for a much larger share of the economy than is true on average in Africa. The key to Botswana, Acemoglu, Johnson, and Robinson argue, is that institutional arrangements have protected adequately the property rights of actual and potential investors. The authors provide a rich, textured account of the political and historical roots of these arrangements.

In the absence of good public institutions, growth has been difficult to achieve on a sustained basis. And when growth has taken place, it has either proved fragile (as in post-1997 Indonesia) or incapable of delivering high levels of social outcomes in areas such as health, education, or gender equality (as in Pakistan). In his chapter on Indonesia, Jonathan Temple describes the Indonesian implosion of 1997 as a case of outgrowing existing, weak institutions. Pakistan's failures in social development, despite respectable growth until very recently, are documented in painstaking detail in William Easterly's chapter. Easterly attributes this failure to the "roving bandit" syndrome (Olson 2000): State institutions dominated by a highly fragmented set of military and landed elites have had little incentive to produce public goods and therefore have not done so.

State institutions are not the only ones that matter. Social arrangements can have equally important and lasting consequences for economic growth. Gregory Clark and Susan Wolcott's discussion of Indian economic history illustrates this. They argue that India's backwardness is due in large part to the inability to *employ* technology, and not to an inadequate *diffusion* of technology per se. Their evidence from the textile industry shows that while identical machines were used in India and in Britain, these machines were operated much less profitably in the former. The problem in India is neither allocative inefficiency nor inadequate technology; the problem is low technical efficiency despite access to state-of-the-art technology. The authors speculate that the answer lies in the nature of the employment relationship and its variation across societies. In productive economies, workers exert more effort in the workplace than can be justified purely by monitoring or by direct financial incentives because they expect everyone else to act in that manner. India, the authors argue, is characterized by a mutual-shirking equilibrium, rather than a mutual gift-giving equilibrium. In this view, India's poverty is largely unconnected to government policy or public institutions.

Trade—or, more specifically, government policy toward trade—does not play nearly as important a role as the institutional setting.

All of the successful countries in our sample have benefited from trade and foreign investment. But as the narratives make clear, specific public policies that are directed at international economic integration or disintegration do not correlate very well with economic performance once one looks at the evidence carefully.

Take Australia, for example. Australia's relative decline vis-à-vis the United States or other rich countries is often attributed to the country's inward-looking policies. But as Ian McLean and Alan Taylor note, there is a timing problem in asserting this claim. While the Australian government sharply changed its policies towards integration in the first three decades of the 20th century (imposing higher tariffs, import licensing, and a stop to Asian immigration), Australia's relative decline compared to the United States and California took place largely before this change in "growth strategy."

Mauritius provides another illustration. According to Arvind Subramanian and Devesh Roy, the level of trade protection in Mauritius has long been among the highest even within sub-Saharan Africa and has come down appreciably only in the late 1990s—more than two decades after the onset of high economic growth. India was able to double its growth rate in the 1980s prior to the liberalization of its highly restrictive trade regime, which came a decade later (see below). Yingyi Qian argues that the impact of China's growing openness to trade and direct foreign investment came mainly through domestic institutional changes.

Geography is not destiny.

Consider Australia and Mauritius again. As McLean and Taylor stress, Australia is the only rich OECD economy that contains large areas of tropical land. Much of Australia is desert or arid, with low and highly variable rainfall. Soil quality is poor. Mauritius is a tropical country, with a high degree of dependence on an export commodity buffeted by terms-of-trade shocks. Botswana, which has the added disadvantage of being landlocked, has obviously not suffered greatly from being geographically disadvantaged either. Botswana and Mauritius both started out with extremely poor initial conditions. Good institutions, it appears, can overcome geographical constraints and lousy initial conditions.

Good institutions can be acquired, but doing so often requires experimentation, willingness to depart from orthodoxy, and attention to local conditions.

The narratives in this volume go beyond simply asserting that "institutions matter." Indeed, one advantage of case studies is that they can provide a richer account of where good institutions come from, the shape they take, and how they need to evolve to support long-term growth.

In Botswana's case, Acemoglu, Johnson, and Robinson speculate that the roots of Botswana's unusually good institutions lay in a combination of factors: tribal institutions that encouraged participation and imposed constraints on elite behavior; the limited effect of British colonization on these tribal institutions, as the colonizers had little interest in Botswana until relatively late; the relative power of rural interests, which created an overlap between Botswana's area of comparative advantage and the economic interests of the elites; and last but not least, the wise and foresighted leadership exhibited by postindependence political leaders. The final element in this list reminds us not to be too deterministic about the source of high-quality institutions. Choices made by political leaders make a big difference.

Perhaps nowhere has this been clearer than in China. Qian's discussion of China focuses on what he calls "transitional institutions"—institutions that can differ greatly from off-the-shelf, "best practice" institutions that are often the object of institutional reform in the developing world. Transitional institutions can have the virtue of being more suited to the realities on the ground on both economic efficiency and political feasibility grounds. Qian shows that the Chinese leadership experimented and purposefully crafted imperfect, but feasible institutional arrangements. He discusses four specific examples: dual-track reform, which liberalized prices at the margin while maintaining the "plan track" in place; township and village enterprises, which represented an intermediate form of ownership between private and state ownership; Chinese-style federalism, which left the regions with significant autonomy and created healthy economic competition among them; and anonymous banking, which allowed financial development while restraining the capacity of the state to expropriate large depositors. These "transitional institutions" succeeded because of their high ratio of economic benefits to political costs. They improved economic incentives without requiring a significant redistribution of income, large-scale (and risky) institutional reforms, or the expenditure of large amounts of political capital.

The Chinese example demonstrates that successful institutions often have heterodox elements. This is a lesson that comes across also from the narratives on Botswana and Mauritius. As noted before, Botswana mixed up market-friendly institutions with heavy state intervention and a large public sector. Mauritius combined its outward export-processing zone with centralized wage bargaining and (for a developing society) an unusually generous welfare state.

The country narratives suggest that "good" institutions—in the sense of institutions that promote and sustain growth—must often have elements that are highly specific to a country's circumstances. An approach to institutional reform that ignores the role of local variation and institutional innovation is at best inadequate, and at worse harmful. China, Mauritius, Botswana are examples of countries that have done very well over extended periods of time with a heterodox mix of institutional arrangements. In effect, these countries have combined orthodox elements with local heresies. As some of the other cases discussed in this volume demonstrate, property rights, sound money, and open trade in themselves do not always do the trick. For example, Clark and Wolcott note that preindependence (1873–1947) India's relative performance lagged despite institutional arrangements that would be regarded as ideal by many economists: secure property rights, free trade, open capital markets, and social and political stability. In his comparative analysis of Vietnam and Philippines, Lant Pritchett points to the paradox that the country whose policies and institutions best fit today's conventional wisdom (Philippines) is doing poorly, while the one with divergent institutions (Vietnam) does very well.

The experience of former socialist economies, discussed by Georges de Menil, further reinforces the role of local context. The three countries closest to western Europe (Poland Hungary, and the Czech Republic) have done very well. What seems to have been key for these countries, as de Menil emphasizes, is their relationship with the European Union (EU). The EU provided a plausible institutional model for these countries, in view of a common historical heritage and relatively short experience under Communism. Furthermore, this model was backed up with the carrot of eventual accession to the EU. Consequently, structural reform was effective and took hold relatively quickly in Poland, Hungary, and the Czech Republic. For countries further to the east, this same type of institutional reform proved to have worse "fit" and less political feasibility. Hence the finding that distance from Düsseldorf and the number of years under Communism together are the best predictors of a transition economy's relative economic performance.[8]

The narratives on Mexico and Bolivia complement these macro level analyses by providing more specific detail on how institutional arrangements matter to economic performance. Maite Careaga and Barry Weingast focus on fiscal federalism in Mexico. Their key point is that good institutions are those that provide public officials with the incentives to provide market-fostering public goods at least cost in terms of corruption and rent seeking. Thinking in such terms helps endogenize the concept of "good governance." The Mexican history with federalism provides a rich laboratory for studying the consequences of changes in legal provisions with respect to revenue sharing. Careaga and Weingast argue that greater dependence on locally generated revenues and greater electoral competition increase the provision of market-fostering public goods. They present evidence that is consistent with these expectations.

Bolivia has undertaken extensive macroeconomic reform, liberalization, and privatization since 1985. Yet economic performance has remained lackluster. Daniel Kaufmann, Massimo Mastruzzi, and Diego Zavaleta attempt to sort out the institutional reasons for this failure. Their main story is that the reform agenda has not been appropriately targeted on the most glaring trouble spots on the institutional front. Relying on a worldwide enterprise data set for benchmarking, they document the large variance in institutional quality that exists *within* Bolivia, with institutions relating to macroeconomic stability generally perceived as working much better than those relating to the rule of law. The authors identify petty corruption, uncertain property rights, and inadequate courts as the source of problems. Enterprises react to these by withhold-

---

[8] See Mukand and Rodrik 2002 for a formal model of institutional choice that accounts for this finding.

ing investments and taking shelter in the official economy. An important virtue of the data set and approach taken in this chapter is that the authors are able to unpack "institutional quality" and show how aggregate indices or country averages can be misleading. The clear implication of the Bolivia story is that institutional and governance shortcomings vary across national contexts, and that institutional reform agendas have to focus on the constraints that happen to bind the most locally.

The onset of economic growth does not require deep and extensive institutional reform.

This is one of the most important (and encouraging) lessons that emerge from the country narratives. It is also a lesson sharply at variance with conventional wisdom on institutional reforms, which holds that their complementary nature requires a long list of such reforms to be pursued simultaneously.

To appreciate the logic of the conventional wisdom, here is a thought experiment. Imagine a Western economist had been invited in 1978 to give advice on reform strategy to the Chinese leadership. How would she formulate her advice, in light of what we think we know today? Being a sensible economist, she would presumably know that the place to start would be agriculture, as the vast majority of the Chinese population lives in the countryside. Liberalization of crop prices would be number one item on the agenda. Cognizant that price incentives make little difference when farm incomes accrue to communes, she would immediately add that privatization of land must accompany price liberalization. Reminded that the obligatory delivery of crops to the state at controlled prices is an important implicit source of taxation, she would then add that tax reform is also required to make up for the loss in fiscal revenues. But another problem then arises: if the state cannot deliver food crops to urban areas at below-market prices, will urban workers not demand higher wages? Yes, that requires some reforms too. State enterprises need to be corporatized so they can set their wages and make hiring and firing decisions freely. (Privatization would be even better, of course.) But if state enterprises now have autonomy, will they not act as monopolies? Well, antitrust regulation, or trade liberalization as a shortcut, can take care of that problem. Who will provide finance to state enterprises as they try to restructure? Clearly, financial market reform is needed as well. What about the workers who get laid off from the state enterprises? Yes, that's why safety nets are an important component of any structural adjustment program. And so on.

The logic of the recommendations is impeccable, even if their practicality is questionable. The recipients of such advice would be excused if they reached the conclusion that this reform business is too hard to accomplish in one's own lifetime. Luckily, actual experience with successful reform provides a different lesson: an ambitious agenda of complementary institutional reforms is *not* needed to kick-start growth. As we know with hindsight, the Chinese reformers were able to take imaginative shortcuts that sidestepped the complementarities that might have otherwise ruined a partial and gradual approach. Dual-track price reform and the introduction of the household responsibility system enhanced agricultural production incentives at the margin without requiring ownership reform, undercutting fiscal revenues, and upsetting the social balance in urban areas. As Qian makes clear in his narrative, this may not have been an ideal reform by textbook standards, but it worked.

Is China a special case? Let's look at the world's next most populous country, India, which has recently managed to roughly double its rate of economic growth. How much reform did it take for India to leave behind its "Hindu rate of growth'" of 3 percent a year? J. Bradford DeLong shows that the conventional account of India, which emphasizes the liberalizing reforms of the early 1990s as the turning point, is wrong in many ways. He documents that growth took off not in the 1990s, but in the 1980s. What seems to have set off growth were some relatively minor reforms. Under Rajiv Gandhi, the government made some tentative moves to encourage capital-goods imports, relax industrial regulations, and rationalize the tax system. The consequence was an economic boom incommensurate with the modesty of the reforms. Furthermore, DeLong's back-of-the-envelope calculations suggest that the significantly more ambitious reforms of the 1990s actually had a smaller impact on India's long-run growth path. DeLong speculates that the change in official attitudes in the 1980s, towards encouraging rather than discouraging entrepreneurial activities and integration into the world economy, and a belief that the rules of the economic game had changed for good, may have had a bigger impact on growth than any specific policy reforms.

In short, the experiences of the world's largest two developing economies indicate that modest changes in institutional arrangements and in official attitudes towards the economy can produce huge growth payoffs. Deep and extensive institutional reform is not a prerequisite for a takeoff in growth. That is the good news. The bad news is that the required changes can be highly specific to the context. The "transitional institutions" of India and China, to use Qian's term, look very different. And for a good reason: the binding constraints on growth differed in the two countries. The mark of a successful reform is its ability to concentrate effort on the binding constraints.

Sustaining high growth in the face of adverse circumstances requires ever stronger institutions.

India and China are both very low-income countries. So is Vietnam, which has been growing quite rapidly under a Chinese-style strategy that defies conventional wisdom on institutional reform. Pritchett, who analyzes the Vietnamese record and compares it to the Philippines', suggests that countries that are in the process of escaping from low-level poverty traps may be fundamentally different from middle-income countries. The policies required to initiate a transition from a low-income equilibrium to a state of rapid growth may be qualitatively different from those required to reignite growth for a middle-income country. At low levels of income, with reasonable institutions and reasonable policies, it may be easy to achieve high growth up to semi-industrialization. But the institutional requirements of reigniting growth in a middle-income country can be significantly more demanding. Pritchett notes that per capita GDP in the Philippines remains lower than its level in 1982, even though institutional quality (with the transition to democracy after 1982) has increased significantly. Pritchett speculates that the trouble may be that uncertainty about the rules of the game has increased. In his words, "what trips countries up is the *transition* from one set of 'institutions' to another." The uncertainty over the rules of the game that accompanies comprehensive, but poorly managed, institutional change is a fundamental roadblock to sustained economic growth.

Indonesia provides an apt illustration of the dangers of letting institutional reform lag behind growth. Jonathan Temple describes Indonesia as a case of "growing into trouble." In his view, growth was not accompanied with the good fundamentals that would have provided the economy with the resilience to handle adverse shocks. Indonesia's economic performance since the mid-1960s has been facilitated by three fortuitous circumstances: oil, the green revolution, and high-growth neighbors. But rapid growth, Temple argues, made institutional weakness a great liability. Indonesia's political and economic institutions were unable to handle the adjustments required in the wake of the Asian financial crisis. The upshot is that Indonesia remains mired in a crisis that appears to have put a complete stop to its growth process. Perhaps what set countries like China and India (as well as South Korea or Taiwan) apart from Indonesia is that these countries have used economic growth as an opportunity to undertake further institutional reforms along the way.

The collapse of growth in the case of a country like Venezuela is much harder to explain on the basis of conventional indicators of institutional weakness. As Ricardo Hausmann explains in his narrative, Venezuela was seen as the most stable democracy in Latin America, with a strong party system, free press, and solid labor and business organizations to negotiate social conflicts. Yet Venezuela's growth rate, once Latin America's fastest at 6.4 percent per annum, has collapsed to the point where output per worker in the nonoil economy is almost half what it was in 1980. What happened? Hausmann focuses on two explanations. The neoclassical explanation is that the decline in the value of oil exports has reduced income and correspondingly (nontraded) output. But Hausmann's calculations suggest that this cannot account for more than half of the collapse. The second factor is a rise in country risk, reflected in Venezuela's country ratings and contractual interest rates, which has reduced the desired capital stock. What lies behind this, according to Hausmann, is the inability to settle distributive conflicts in the wake of a collapse in oil income. Venezuela has simply become a riskier environment, which in turn has eroded the quality of public institutions and their legitimacy. This argument is reminiscent of the importance Pritchett attaches to the rules of the game. It suggests that countries can trip even when their institutions appear strong by conventional yardsticks.

ORGANIZATION OF THE VOLUME

The country narratives that follow are organized under four headings. Part I is devoted to three chapters that take a longer historical perspective on economic growth: Australia (McLean and Taylor), India (Clark and Wolcott), and Botswana (Acemoglu, Johnson, and Robinson). Part II contains analyses of six cases of transitions in and out of growth: Vietnam and Philippines (Pritchett), Indonesia (Temple), India (DeLong), Mauritius (Subramanian and Roy), Venezuela (Hausmann), and Eastern Europe (de Menil). Part III covers three studies that take a closer look at institutions: China (Qian), Bolivia (Kaufmann, Mastruzzi, and Zavaleta), and Mexico (Careaga and Weingast). Part IV closes the volume with a case of growth without social development, Pakistan (Easterly), to remind us that economic growth is not all that matters.

REFERENCES

Acemoglu, Daron, Simon Johnson, and James A. Robinson. 2001. "The Colonial Origins of Comparative Development: An Empirical Investigation." *American Economic Review* 91: 1369–1401.

Aghion, Philippe, and Peter Howitt. 1998. *Endogenous Growth.* Cambridge: MIT Press.

Anderson, James E., and Douglas Marcouiller. 1999. "Trade, Insecurity, and Home Bias: An Empirical Investigation." NBER Working Paper No. 7000, March.

Barro, Robert J. 1991. "Economic Growth in a Cross Section of Countries." *Quarterly Journal of Economics* 106, no. 2: 407–43.

Gallup, John, and Jeffrey Sachs. 1998. "Geography and Economic Development." NBER Working Paper No. 6849, December.

Grossman, Gene, and Elhanan Helpman. 1991. *Innovation and Growth in the World Economy.* Cambridge: MIT Press.

Hall, Robert, and Charles Jones. 1999. "Why Do Some Countries Produce So Much More Output per Worker Than Others?" *Quarterly Journal of Economics* 114, no. 1: 83–116.

Lucas, Robert E. 1993. "Making a Miracle." *Econometrica* 61, no. 2: 251–72.

Mukand, Sharun, and Dani Rodrik. 2002. "In Search of the Holy Grail: Policy Convergence, Experimentation, and Economic Performance." January. Typescript.

North, Douglass C., and R. Thomas. 1973. *The Rise of the Western World: A New Economic History.* Cambridge: Cambridge University Press.

Olson, Mancur. 2000. *Power and Prosperity: Outgrowing Communist and Capitalist Dictatorships.* New York: Basic Books.

Rodríguez, Francisco, and Dani Rodrik. 2001. "Trade Policy and Economic Growth: A Skeptic's Guide to the Cross-National Literature." In *NBER Macroeconomics Annual 2000,* ed. Ben Bernanke and Kenneth S. Rogoff. Cambridge: MIT Press.

Rodrik, Dani. 1995. "Getting Interventions Right: How South Korea and Taiwan Grew Rich." *Economic Policy* 20:53–101.

Rodrik, Dani, Arvind Subramanian, and Francesco Trebbi. 2002. "Institutions Rule: The Primacy of Institutions over Geography and Integration in Economic Development." NBER Working Paper No. 9305.

Romer, Paul M. 1986. "Increasing Returns and Long Run Growth." *Journal of Political Economy* 94, no. 5: 1002–37.

———. 1993. "Two Strategies for Economic Development: Using Ideas and Producing Ideas." In *Proceedings of the World Bank Annual Conference on Development Economics, 1992.* Washington, D.C.: World Bank.

Sachs, Jeffrey, and Andrew Warner. 1995. "Economic Reform and the Process of Global Integration." *Brookings Papers on Economic Activity* 1995, no. 1: 1–118.

Solow, Robert. 1956. "A Contribution to the Theory of Economic Growth." *Quarterly Journal of Economics* 70, no. 1: 65–94.

Temple, Jonathan. 1999. "The New Growth Evidence." *Journal of Economic Literature* 37, no 1: 112–56.

Wei, Shang-Jin. 2000. "Natural Openness and Good Government." NBER Working Paper No. W7765, June.

Young, Alwyn. 1992. "A Tale of Two Cities: Factor Accumulation and Technical Change in Hong Kong and Singapore." In *NBER Macroeconomics Annual, 1992.* Cambridge: MIT Press.

Part I

HISTORICAL PERSPECTIVES ON ECONOMIC GROWTH

Australian Growth

A CALIFORNIA PERSPECTIVE

IAN W. MCLEAN   ALAN M. TAYLOR

THE AUSTRALIAN growth experience includes several challenges to growth economists—both theorists and policymakers. Australia is one of the few examples of an economy that has maintained living standards at or close to world-best levels for more than 150 years. Understanding how a small open economy achieved this despite major domestic shocks and dramatic shifts in international economic conditions should yield insights pertinent to the replication of similar outcomes elsewhere. In addition, Australia's high per capita income has been sustained in significant measure on the basis of the exploitation of its abundant natural resources. This contradicts one view in the growth literature that resource abundance is a curse rather than blessing. Further, for much of the twentieth century, Australia adopted what might be described as an inward-oriented development strategy. Yet, despite the consensus that such policies are inimical to sustained improvements in productivity and living standards, the Australian record is mixed as to whether a serious drag on growth resulted. Finally, Australia was formed by the federation of six colonies, and a colonial inheritance has frequently been offered as a fundamental cause of a disappointing subsequent growth. Yet at no time has the imperial legacy been invoked as seriously disadvantageous to the Australian economy.

To pursue these and related questions, we propose to examine the Australian growth experience partly through the prism of American experience, especially that of California. The United States is a useful benchmark against which to evaluate Australian growth not just because it is the standard used in most comparative studies. In addition, both societies inherited from Britain a number of

For their helpful comments we are grateful to Ricardo Hausmann, Alan Hirsch, Simon Johnson, Dani Rodrik, and participants at the conference "Analytical Country Studies on Growth," Center for International Development, Harvard University, April 2001. Research funding from the Ford Foundation is gratefully acknowledged. Alan Taylor thanks the Federal Reserve Bank of San Francisco for research support. We thank David Jacks, Timothy Nicolle, and David Norman for excellent research assistance, and Alan Olmstead and John Wallis for help and advice with data collection. The usual disclaimer applies.

cultural and institutional characteristics, both were (largely) European settler societies, and Australia and the continental United States are of similar area. Of course European settlement in the United States preceded that in Australia by more than 150 years, and they are now vastly different in total population and the aggregate size of their economies. Hence, for the analysis of other aspects of the growth record of Australia a more appropriate and illuminating comparison will be made with the state of California.

Neither Australia nor California has exhibited a marked economic failure: they hold the rare distinction of achieving sustained high and rising living standards for rapidly expanding populations since the mid–nineteenth century. But long-run success should not imply that there is nothing to learn from these economies. Their per capita growth trajectories have differed markedly in some subperiods, and over the longer term with respect to the growth in the size of their economies. They also serve as suitable comparators since in their early economic circumstances (such as during the mid-nineteenth-century gold rushes) they are quite similar. Most important, the comparison of an economy that remained a region in a much larger national economy with one that evolved into an independent political unit helps identify the role of several key policies. California—at least vis-à-vis its largest economic neighbor, the United States— had no independent monetary policy, or exchange rate, or controls over immigration or capital movements, or trade policy. Australia did—vis-à-vis the rest of the world—and after 1900 pursued an increasingly interventionist and inward-oriented development strategy until the 1970s. What difference did this make to long-run outcomes? And what other factors, exogenous and endogenous, account for the differences that have emerged between two economies that shared such similar initial conditions?[1]

Australia and California are both settler economies—regions of recent European settlement most often defined to include the United States, Canada, Australia, Argentina, and New Zealand, while some studies extend the coverage to Uruguay, Chile, South Africa, and even Siberia (e.g., Denoon 1983; Schedvin 1990). Since the focus is typically on the experience only from the nineteenth century, reference to the United States is often confined to the western regions settled at this time. The distinctive characteristics of these economies have frequently been noted to include all or most of the following. They occupied temperate zones containing extensive areas suitable for livestock and crop raising using (mainly) introduced plants, animals, and agricultural technology (Crosby 1986). They were sparsely populated at the time of European settlement, and the Europeans quickly became dominant—demographically, economically, politically—and re-created offshoots of European society. They tended

---

[1] A recently expanding subdiscipline of intranational economics has illustrated the benefits of taking a fresh look at the problems of international economics using within-country interregional economic interactions as a baseline, as in the volume by Hess and van Wincoop (2000).

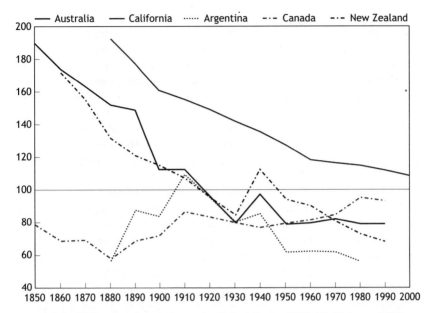

Figure 2.1. GDP per capita relative to the United States, 1850–98. Units are GDP per capita relative to the U.S. = 100.
Source: Maddison 1995; Mitchener and McLean 1999

to specialize early in the production of a small number of resource-intensive products for export.

As a result of their factor endowments, settler economies acquired from an early date incomes per capita that were high relative to those in the industrializing economies of Europe, attracting further large flows of European immigrants and accompanying large flows of foreign capital. Most important, the settler economies did not start out as peasant-agriculture societies that achieved rising incomes through shifting resources towards an expanding higher-productivity urban-industrial sector, the long-run growth path characteristic of most European and developing country experience. By contrast, the settler economies of the nineteenth century were born rich.[2]

To provide context to our analysis of Australia, figure 2.1 indicates the trends in per capita income for these settler economies, using the United States as the reference. This shows the well-known pattern of Australia starting above

---

[2] This is not to ignore the economic achievements of Aboriginal Australians prior to 1788, nor those of the pre-1848 inhabitants of California. So great was the transformation of both societies after these dates, that we follow the usual practice, beginning our narrative in the mid–nineteenth century.

the United States, being overtaken at the turn of the century, then stabilizing a little below. Canada begins a little below the United States, then converges on it. Argentina, comparable to Canada in the late nineteenth century, falls away dramatically in the interwar and postwar periods. New Zealand, initially above the United States and not far behind Australia, also falls away in the postwar period, though not as far as Argentina. Australians are aware that, by this measure of performance, they lost their early preeminence to the United States (and to Britain) about a century ago, then in the postwar period have been "overtaken" by perhaps a dozen other OECD economies. This secular relative decline in living standards is widely cited in Australia—it is one of the key "facts" of Australian history.

California is part of the United States West that satisfies the initial conditions of a settler economy of the nineteenth century, with the exception that it is a regional rather than national economy. In figure 2.1, California at the outset has a per capita income above even Australia, then steadily converges on the United States average, though remaining above it.[3] Clearly, had California been an independent state, Australia would not hold the distinction of having the highest per capita income in the late nineteenth century. One important question is, therefore, whether the factors lying behind the relatively high level of income in these two settler economies at this time were similar. Another feature of the figure is that Australian per capita incomes were about 80 percent of those in California in 1880, declining by 1900 to about 70 percent, since when they have retained a similar relative position—even as both have declined relative to that of the United States. Why did Australian relative economic performance deteriorate in the 1880–1900 period? More puzzling is why the very different policy conditions applying in the two economies produced similar per capita income growth over the following century. And why has the "level gap" between these two rich Pacific economies persisted? We take up each of these issues below.

A further feature of these two economies' historical record stands out in any comparison. At the end of the 1850s gold rushes, California's population was one-third that of Australia—380,000 compared to 1.1 million. Over the next four decades, the population of California grew only slightly faster than that of Australia. But after 1900, Australia's population growth was markedly slower. By 1940 California (6.9 million) had almost caught up to Australia (7.1 million), and by 2000, California's 33.9 million far outstripped Australia's 19.2 million. Thus, despite similar per capita economic performance since 1900, the aggregate economies had diverged greatly in size. Why?

In this chapter we draw on the growth experience of Australia in order to contribute to current debates within growth economics. Adopting a schematic arrangement common in that literature, our analytic narrative has the following

---

[3] The convergence of U.S. state incomes since 1880 has been widely studied (Barro and Sala-i-Martin 1992; Mitchener and McLean 1999).

structure. We first seek the explanation of the Australian success in terms of proximate and largely endogenous causes such as technology, endowments, and scale. We then consider the contribution of policies. Finally, we examine the role of several deeper determinants and largely exogenous factors—natural resources, institutions, and geography. And at several points we use the experience of either the United States or, more often, California as a mirror through which to assess aspects of the Australian story.

PROXIMATE CAUSES

We first examine some explanations for growth prominent in conventional analyses: the contributions of inputs and productivity improvement; some demographic influences; and the size of the domestic market.

Productivity

To what extent were there differences between Australia and the United States (or California) in the relative contributions to growth of factor accumulation and total factor productivity (TFP)? There is a levels dimension: comparing the initial levels of GDP per capita, we can ascertain whether the contributions of labor input per capita and productivity varied between the two economies. We turn to this in the next section. Here we will assess the familiar issue of the relative contributions of productivity and factor accumulation to growth over time.

For the United States as a whole, the story of the changing contribution of productivity to growth is well documented. Growth in the nineteenth century appears to have been primarily the result of accumulation of factors, with productivity improvement playing a small role. Around the turn of the century, the underlying relative sources of growth change, with productivity playing a much more prominent part (Abramovitz and David 1973).[4]

There is much less evidence on historical productivity trends and sources for Australia, but what exists suggests a different pattern. There are no aggregate studies of TFP for Australia in the nineteenth century, but it is difficult to believe its contribution would be any more significant than that of the United States at that time.[5] However, for the twentieth century, estimates indicate that,

---

[4] This accords with studies of the twentieth-century American economy (Solow 1956; Abramovitz 1956), which show the importance of technological change in explaining increases in output. More generally, advanced industrial societies are believed to owe their prosperity to the manifold forms of productivity improvement—difficult though they are to identify precisely.

[5] Indeed, growth and convergence internationally during this period appear to have been strongly driven by factor convergence (Taylor 1999).

unlike the U.S. experience, there was no fundamental shift in the sources of growth towards a markedly greater contribution from productivity—at least not before the very end of the century (Kaspura and Weldon 1980; Productivity Commission 1999). There is some evidence for Australia's having experienced in the last decade or so a fundamental shift in the contribution to growth from heightened efficiency. If so, it has occurred nearly a century after that in the United States. Put differently, Australia continued in the twentieth century with a nineteenth-century basis to its growth, being heavily reliant on factor accumulation rather than TFP. Why?

One explanation stresses the coincidence of a more open and less regulated economy since the 1980s and an improved productivity performance, the implication being that during the previous seven decades Australia's inward-oriented and more highly regulated economy could only deliver modest productivity gains. In this view the tariff (and associated policies) had depressed the scope for economy-wide efficiency gains from new technology by shifting resources from high-productivity export-oriented farming to lower-productivity import-substituting manufacturing. But the apparent lift in productivity growth in the 1990s is the subject of debate—whether it is just a by-product of the boom of that decade, or a delayed response to the wide-ranging economic reforms of the last 20 years.

An alternative view is that, unlike the United States, the fundamental laws of motion driving the Australian economy did not change at the beginning of the twentieth century. Australia continued to rely heavily on its highly efficient rural industries for its exports, and hence its overall prosperity. The service sector was already large, and the manufacturing sector was characterized by small-scale enterprises serving scattered local markets and was protected from import competition not just by rising tariffs but by natural barriers (wars, transport costs). Rapid technological change in agriculture and, after the 1950s, in the expanding minerals sector were the exceptions, not the rule. Hence, TFP made less of a contribution to overall growth in Australia than elsewhere in the OECD.

What of California? In the absence of data on sources of growth in the state through the twentieth century, we must speculate. First, there is evidence that structural change out of agriculture occurred later in Australia. The (declining) share of employment in agriculture had reached 20 percent in California by 1910 and 10 percent by 1940, whereas Australia had reduced its workforce in agriculture to these levels only three decades later—in 1940 and 1970 respectively. Second, the integration of the California and U.S. economies presumably gave California lower-cost access to a much larger "export" market than was available to Australian exporters. And third, California's inability to protect its producers from "import" competition from the rest of the United States provided a stimulus to efficiency and resource reallocation more bracing than that faced by their Australian counterparts—at least until recently.

Demography and the Labor Market

An important component to the high initial incomes per capita in both Australia and California was their high employment-to-population ratios (or labor input per capita), a characteristic of settler economies with high rates of immigration. That is, for a given level of labor productivity, per capita income will be higher the higher is labor input per capita. For example, in 1880 California had a labor input per capita of 0.435, 25 percent above the U.S. average of 0.347. Since California's estimated income per capita was 93 per cent above the U.S. average, a little over a quarter of that gap is accounted for by these demographic factors rather than any difference in labor productivity. The Australian situation is similar. Australian labor input per capita in 1880 was 0.413 (19 percent above the U.S. figure). Depending on the currency conversion employed, about a quarter of the margin between incomes in the United States and the higher incomes in Australia is also accounted for by the more favorable demographic and labor market characteristics in the latter.

This decomposition can be pushed a little further. Labor input per capita can be decomposed in various ways to reveal the influences on it of the masculinity ratio, age distribution, and workforce participation rate. Unsurprisingly, in small open economies experiencing high rates of immigration, the most important sources of the unusually high employment-to-population ratios is the high masculinity ratio and the favorable age distribution—favorable in that a high proportion of the population was of working age. By contrast, there is no evidence that the gender-specific workforce participation rates were unusually high in either economy. Over time, these favorable demographic and labor market characteristics in both Australia and California faded, relative to the U.S. average. Hence part of the story of their convergence lies in this rather than in any relative decline in productivity. For example, Australian GDP per capita relative to that of California in 1880 rises from 81.5 percent to 93.1 percent if California's labor input per capita is used. Thus only a little over one-third of the gap in income is due to a productivity advantage by California, and almost two-thirds to demographic and labor market characteristics.

Size of Market, or Smith versus Solow and Schumpeter

Adam Smith saw each nation's wealth originating in the division of labor, a process limited only by the size of the market. In most of the growth literature of the last decade or so, this idea has been unfashionable, even absent, with a few rare exceptions (Murphy, Shleifer, and Vishny 1989). In the world of A and k it has no place.[6]

---

[6] Following Ricardo and Schumpeter, one school of thought assigns the dominant source of long-run growth to A, the universal symbol for the level of technology (Dowrick and Nguyen 1989;

The Smithian counterattack has been a long time in coming, but there are early signs it may have begun. For example, even for the era of premodern growth, Kohn (2001) argues that preindustrial growth in Europe should be understood as a Smithian process. As for a more formal approach to testing the hypothesis in the era of modern economic growth, to distinguish the Smithian story from technological explanations of scale effects like increasing returns requires one to be adroit with the subtleties of each theory and deft when constructing an empirical test. Ades and Glaeser (1999) observe that looking at open versus closed economies can supply the needed identification. Increasing returns (in the form of a positive correlation of growth and scale) should show up in both cases, but Smithian effects only in the closed economy—since being open gives you the full extent of the global market anyway, and there is no effect that can operate.

As more evidence is adduced, we may discover that Smithian sources of growth deserve more attention, but in our analytic narrative, we think they find further support in the story of Australia and California. The former was a small economy, but not always open, either by dint of distance or policy, and the small size of the domestic market has long been held out as a major constraint on growth through the inability of firms to reap scale economies. The latter was always a very open economy, at least vis-à-vis the large market that comprised the rest of the United States, and in extensive terms it grew much more quickly over the long haul. At key junctures, this contrast between the two economies exposed very different Smithian forces and can potentially explain important differences in outcomes.[7]

A further aspect of size possibly influential to its growth performance is that the Australian domestic market has not just been relatively small throughout Australia's history, but also fragmented. Even today, none of the five major metropolitan markets (population over one million) is closer than four hundred

---

Rebelo 1991; Easterly and Levine 1999; Klenow and Rodriguez-Clare 1997; Hall and Jones 1999). This shorthand acknowledges a long historical tradition that gives center stage to invention and innovation (Mokyr 1992). On the other hand, the neoclassical revolution in growth following Robert Solow (1956) and Moses Abramovitz (1956), set its sights on k as the variable of interest, the capital-labor ratio. Including now human capital too, this theory stresses the capital-accumulation dynamics of the economy (Barro and Sala-i-Martin 1992; Mankiw, Romer, and Weil 1992).

[7] The comparison of a nation that is an island located far from the nearest potential trading partners or sources of factor inflows, and a region that is contiguous with other regional economies, blurs the easy definition of what constitutes the domestic market. There was a Greater California economy after the gold rushes, which certainly included Nevada but also stretched further into the mountain states and north to include, for some time, coastal British Columbia. Are these to be regarded as "foreign" markets, just as New Zealand was to Australia (but only because it chose to stay out of federation in 1901)?

miles from another, and one is fifteen hundred miles from its nearest neighbor. The area of California is only 5.3 percent that of Australia, yet its population is concentrated between San Diego and Sacramento—a distance of some five hundred miles. We shall return to the theme of the "tyranny of distance." But whether in a nineteenth-century world of expensive railroad communications, or a late-twentieth-century world where agglomeration economies are thought to be important sources of productivity, Australia has had to face possible disadvantages posed by its scattered population.

Under conventional agglomeration models (Krugman and Venables 1995) agglomeration can drive a strict separation of the world into haves and have-nots, or core and periphery, when all the increasing-returns industries end up at one location. But recent work indicates that such a scenario may not be inevitable if a plausible real-world antiagglomeration force is operating, namely technological diffusion or spillovers (Baldwin and Forslid 1999). We have reason to believe that the extent of such spillovers is conditioned by a great many factors economic and social (Abramovitz 1986). In particular, the ability of technological innovations to penetrate an economy (its openness to ideas) may be directly related to its openness to goods, capital, or people.[8]

Though empirically challenging, the applicability of these ideas in an intra-versus international context is appealing. California is open to the diffusion of ideas inward from the vast pool of innovative activity in the rest of the U.S. market, as well as from its own large pool of creative talent. Australia was not always so open with respect to such diffusion. The inflow of capital and people was certainly more muted, and closure in goods markets, to the extent that it inhibited the competitive pressure to adopt new technologies, might also have acted as a brake. We will consider below the role of trade policy on Australian growth but note here the dramatic decline in Australia's trade ratio from above 50 percent of GDP in the 1860s to around 30 percent in some years during the 1930s, 1950s, and 1960s, before gradually recovering to reach 50 percent again at the end of the 1990s (see fig. 2.2).

Fragmentation and agglomeration forces thus imply that pure Smithian size-of-market effects still might not be the only increasing-returns effects operating, and this is especially relevant in the California context. After all, the Golden State is home to two of the canonical examples of increasing-returns industries used so often in textbooks: Hollywood and Silicon Valley. Here again, the impact of openness on growth deserves to be studied more carefully, and the aforementioned industries may not be the only cases deserving scrutiny.

---

[8] Furthermore, if the rate of growth of ideas is proportional to population size, this, then, may be viewed as another quasi-Smithian force, by dint of the fact that open immigration can help expand the labor supply and reap the spillovers (Romer 1986; Kremer 1993).

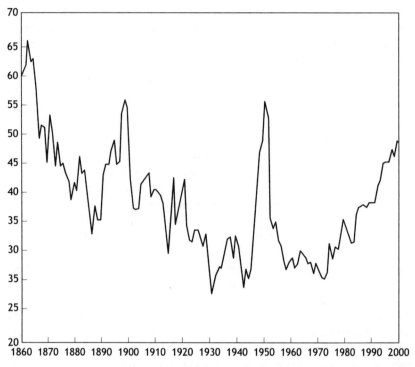

Figure 2.2. Australia: Trade Ratio, 1861–2000. Units are trade as a percentage of GDP. *Source:* Butlin 1962 for 1861–1900; Butlin 1977 for 1901 to 1974; Australian Bureau of Statistics for 1975 to 2000

ECONOMIC POLICY: GROWTH STRATEGY

Openness in Goods Markets

Dominating the discussion of Australia's long-run economic performance is the history of tariff protection of manufacturing (table 2.1). There is a consensus view that the rising level of insulation of the domestic economy in the early decades of the twentieth century was responsible for the (relative) decline in living standards at that time, and, symmetrically, that the increased productivity growth of the last few years results from the reopening of the domestic economy to international competitive influences that began in earnest in the 1980s.

The tariff may be at the center of the discussion, but both the initial turning inward and the recent outward reorientation were much broader in scope and effect. In the nineteenth century Australia had a relatively unregulated economy and was generally open to international flows of goods, immigrants, and invest-

TABLE 2.1

Australia, Nominal Average Manufacturing Tariffs, 1907–2000

	Panel A (1920 = 100)					
	1907	1914	1919	1929	1933	1940
Tariff index	82	99	84	126	225	210

		Panel B (1969 = 100)					
	1969	1975	1978	1984	1990	1996	2001
Tariff index	100	70	61	61	48	22	13

Sources: For 1907 to 1940, estimated by A. T. Carmody, cited in Anderson and Garnaut, 1987, 43. For 1969 to 2001, from Industry Commission, Trade, and Assistance review, various years.

Note: From 1919 onwards, rates are for financial years, prior to that for calendar years.

ment, even though the protective effect of tariffs was greater in some colonies (Victoria) than others (New South Wales remained free trade), and despite the colonial governments' prominence in developmental projects—such as construction and ownership of railroads.

After federation (1901) there occurred a dramatic shift in what may loosely be described as the country's growth strategy. The key objectives were to increase population via immigration; to expand employment in manufacturing (given the end to the spread of rural settlement and opportunities for employment growth in agriculture); to maintain the high level of real wages (especially for the unskilled) that had been achieved in the prosperous decades after the gold rushes; and to reduce the volatility in economic activity that was associated with exposure to the vagaries of international commodity and capital markets (as revealed in the depression of the 1890s), and associated also with dependence on a narrow economic base (in agriculture).

To achieve these objectives, the following policies gradually were implemented. In response to workers' fears of large-scale low-wage labor inflows, Asian immigration was effectively stopped—the so-called "White Australia" policy. To diversify the economic base away from the volatile commodity-producing sectors, manufacturing would be encouraged by tariff protection. Industrialization would also provide the needed employment opportunities for immigrants. To compensate for the higher cost structure resulting from the tariff, wage earners would have a guaranteed "living wage" (determined through a system of industrial courts), and exporters (farmers) would receive assistance in the form of state-subsidized production and marketing arrangements. The components of this inward-oriented strategy were introduced gradually between 1901 and the 1920s. Its maintenance during the 1930s is perhaps less surprising than its survival, even intensification, in the postwar decades. For example, Australia retained import-licensing schemes for industry until the 1960s.

The preceding discussion emphasizes protection and intervention as key differences between Australia and California, but in addition to being a function of distance, trade policies, and conditions in factor markets, the degree of integration is now increasingly being viewed as a function also of monetary and financial arrangements.[9] Here, Australia had its own currency, and for much of the twentieth century it floated. California, vis-à-vis its major trading partner, the United States, had not just monetary and exchange rate stability but a common currency, a device that might promote trade to an even greater extent (Rose 2000; Rose and van Wincoop 2001). It seems Australia had benefited from similar trade-boosting "common currency" features of the gold standard during the heyday of that monetary standard before 1914 (López-Córdova and Meissner 2000). But subsequently a floating currency introduced an element of risk into long-distance trade in goods, capital, and even perhaps to some migration decisions.

What was the effect of these barriers to trade on Australian long-run growth? The theoretical case has always favored the view that Australia sacrificed static efficiency and hence living standards for increased population and a more diversified economy via its induced industrialization policies. The policy debates go back to the 1860s (when Victoria turned protectionist). And there is a vast literature (Pomfret 1995). What can we add by viewing Australia's experience in the light of that of California?

In the context of long-run per capita incomes, the period in which Australia lost much of its favorable position relative to the United States and California lies before 1914 (see fig. 2.1). That is, the changed growth strategy followed the sharpest decline in Australia's relative economic performance (by this one measure), when, in the orthodox interpretation, the putative causation runs the other way. The view that Australia's decline in per capita ranking was due to protection must also be qualified by what happened after World War II. For two or three decades the protectionist measures remained at their highest levels, yet per capita performance relative to the United States did not vary significantly. Neither has it varied over the last 20 years, when Australia has undergone a substantial reorientation towards a more open and less regulated economy. At least in a comparison with the United States, and in the necessarily broad-brush approach adopted here, the big shifts in trade policy do not seem to have had the predicted outcomes. Of course, the counterfactual effects might still have had impacts consistent with theory, absent ceteris paribus. So what else is going on?

For one, the United States is not the only relevant comparison. In the post-1945 era of high protection, Australia's growth performance also appeared

---

[9] Specifically, monetary stability in the form of stable exchange rates might lower trading costs, cause prices to converge, and thus promote trade (Obstfeld and Taylor 1997).

poor in comparison with the OECD average. Concerns were raised that Australia was "falling behind," even taking "the Argentine road." In fact, use of the U.S. benchmark disguised the effect of the postwar catch-up of many OECD economies with both the U.S. and Australian levels of income (Dowrick and Nguyen 1988). Any claim that Australian living standards were in long-run relative decline must first allow for this convergence effect, and as suggested by figure 2.1, Australia has remained firmly in the OECD "club" throughout. On the other hand, there is no evidence of Australia's catching up to the United States and reversing the earlier overtaking episode. California, by contrast, though starting above the United States per capita income level has maintained a lead, albeit a shrinking one.

An alternative view is that the static efficiency costs of protection were accepted as a necessary cost to achieve the other objectives of reduced macroeconomic instability, a more diversified economic base, and a larger population. According to this view, the decline in GDP per capita relative to the U.S. benchmark after 1890 is not therefore an appropriate criterion for appraising the strategy. Rather, one might look at its effects on population levels and the growth and diversity of manufacturing. And, during the 1920s and again in the 1950s and 1960s, a case can be made for the policy's producing the desired outcomes. The share of the workforce in manufacturing peaked in the late 1960s at almost 30 percent. As expected, protection did succeed in reallocating resources toward manufacturing, albeit at some cost.

The subsequent problems in, and relative decline of, manufacturing do not negate the achievements to that time (indeed, this experience was common among industrialized countries during the 1970s and 1980s); it suggests rather that the restructuring that began in the 1980s was a decade or more overdue. However, in terms of population levels, the other policy objective, at least in comparison to California, the strategy was something of a failure. The population growth rate of the country was relatively slow in the twentieth century, after fast growth in earlier periods. This trajectory reveals something of the costs of the inward-looking strategy in an open economy, and we shall return to consider this issue in our conclusion.

Openness in Factor Markets

Openness and its effect on growth need not work solely via goods market effects. Open economies face world prices, but closed economies have relatively distorted prices. If these prices apply to capital goods, inputs in the growth and accumulation process, then Solovian growth can be retarded. There is ample evidence of this in postwar developing countries, including such well-known examples as Argentina or India (Jones 1994; Taylor 1994).

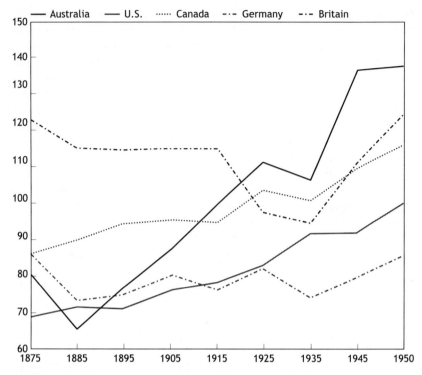

Figure 2.3. Relative price of capital, five countries, 1870–1950. Units are an index of investment prices relative to output prices, with U.S. = 100 in 1950.
Source: Collins and Williamson 2001

Have such effects played a role in earlier growth experience? California, as a regional appendage of the U.S. internal free trade area, has always had access to cutting-edge capital-goods technologies at essentially world market prices. Australia, especially after a more aggressive manufacturing tariff policy starting around 1910, has not.[10] Using late-nineteenth- and early-twentieth-century data on the relative price of capital, we can clearly see the price that was paid (fig. 2.3). Relative to the United States, always the low-cost region for capital goods in that era, Australia saw its capital-goods price rise from a level roughly equal to that of the United States circa 1870–90 to 140 percent of the U.S. level in 1950; or from being the lowest in the 1880s in this five-country sample to

---

[10] It is possible that Australia's reliance on Britain as the dominant source of capital-goods imports during the first half of the twentieth century, at a time when American technology had overtaken Britain in many fields, was a constraint on Australian productivity growth.

being the highest of all from the 1920s to the 1950s (Collins and Williamson 2001). A striking comparison can be made with the estimate of Díaz Alejandro (1970) that Argentina's capital inputs cost twice the U.S. level in the 1950s. Antipodean doomsayers of the 1970s considered the economic fortunes of Australia and Argentina as being on parallel paths (Duncan and Fogarty 1984). On most dimensions, and with the benefit of hindsight, this claim now looks overblown, but in one important dimension, this "tax" on capital accumulation, the analogy seems appropriate.

Openness in factor markets also marked a crucial difference between the Australian and California economies, but in itself could have provided a crucial source of their distinct Smithian trajectories. Market size is a function of national income, itself a function of factor endowments and factor prices. Both economies began as regions very open to the influx of capital and labor from beyond their borders, but in the early twentieth century Australia was to find itself behind barriers to both flows for a protracted time. These barriers were, in the case of labor, mostly self-inflicted and an expression of the notorious "White Australia" immigration policy (Pope 1981); in the case of capital, largely exogenous and a function of the implosion of global capital markets (Obstfeld and Taylor 2002).

California had no interruption at any time from such barriers, at least on its eastern and northern borders. Migrants, even in the depression years, have always flooded into the state. Access to the greater U.S. capital market has, similarly, always been assured both in terms of public and private investment funding. Moreover, in labor markets these were two-way doors for California; had shocks lowered wages, counterfactually below U.S. levels, there was ample scope to vent surplus labor. Again, due to world conditions, this was not as much of an option for Australia in the twentieth century.

Restricting immigration might, through conventional decreasing returns, have given Australians higher wages. But if the Smithian theory is correct, the overall net effect might have been adverse, with a lower population constraining the size of the market, the division of labor, and hence growth, at least during times of diminished openness—that is, during much of the middle decades of the twentieth century. Being reluctantly cut off from external capital flows might also have cost Australia, imposing a higher cost of capital on investment projects.

In a neoclassical world, open economies converge faster as factors migrate (Barro, Mankiw, and Sala-i-Martin 1995). Hence we should not be surprised to see the United States converge fairly rapidly up to the California level over the last century. But we should be surprised to see the United States converging faster on, and even "overtaking," Australia. This latter fact suggests that although California and Australia started off on parallel paths, some shock came along that put them, at least temporarily, on different trajectories.

The Developmental State and the Big Push

At first glance, one difference between the Australian and California economies stems from the greater capacity of the Australian government to influence the course of long-run development through trade or monetary policies, options that were unavailable to the state government in California. And this difference might be reinforced by the impression of a much greater regulatory and redistributive role being played by the state in Australian than in American history. It would be easy to conclude, therefore, that differences in long-run growth outcomes in California's favor might be in part attributed to the less fettered operation of market forces there. In fact, there might be less difference than generally believed.

The Australian story is well documented (e.g. Butlin 1959), but the myth of rugged individualism in the American West is countered by the "new" western history that stresses the greater dependence there than elsewhere in the United States on government (Limerick 1987, chap. 3). The history of water development is perhaps a good illustration. Further, the role of government in late-nineteenth-century development in Australia and California has many close parallels—such as in agriculture, including the establishment of departments of agriculture, and the promotion of land settlement, agricultural research and education, and irrigation schemes.

In the twentieth century, promotion of urban growth and employment opportunities, which in Australia were fostered through national policies to encourage immigration and industrialization, in California were encouraged by the state government with the more restricted set of policy instruments available to it. When World War II spread to the Pacific, the two economies' economic experiences were remarkably similar. War-related industries were rapidly expanded, and the skills and technologies acquired under wartime conditions were used by government as a basis for postwar industrial expansion.

Yet could these interventions, although very similar in scope, prove equally effective in both economies? The notion of a developmental state engaged in such activities ties into the idea of the "big push" as a scheme to overcome the barriers imposed by the size of market constraint, that is, to kick-start Smithian growth (Murphy, Shleifer, and Vishny 1989). As noted earlier, the simple form of the big push is likely to be more effective in a closed economy than in an open economy. An open economy already has access to the maximal market, so no push is needed, but a closed economy still labors under "too small" a domestic market.

This logic might lead us to conclude that major government intervention in big-push style might have benefited Australia more than California. Thus, should not initiatives of this type, especially in the mid-twentieth-century period, have enabled a rapid (and counterfactual) Australian catch-up? We see one major reason why not, and it depends on our earlier observation that a lack of openness in

Australia meant not only a small market size, but also price distortions. A big push in this context looks very different in its welfare consequences, as we know from, again, the Argentine experience. It is likely to be a push that reinforces a set of activities that already comprise an inefficient bundle.

Having drawn on theory to inform our narrative up to this point, we think this is one of the more interesting insights for theory offered by our narrative. Not all drives for the "big push" are the same, and we know from the theory of the second best that the same kind of push could be beneficial or harmful depending on the exact distortions present. We speculate that interactions between the degree of openness and the big push may lead an economy to higher or lower efficiency. We surmise that such a distinction helps us understand how after a big push in each economy before, during, and after World War II, California was catapulted to the leading edge of global technology and productivity, but Australia was not.

We turn now to the deeper determinants of economic performance, those exogenous forces that shape the proximate causes previously discussed.

NATURAL RESOURCES

Natural resources appear as a putatively exogenous feature that might be a blessing or a curse in terms of development. At first glance, a larger endowment of resources should not be immiserizing, but should rather push back an economy's growth constraint and raise welfare. However, that favorable conclusion can be overturned if political dynamics and property rights are malformed such that a resource discovery ends up being voraciously frittered away in directly unproductive activities. We now have models of such behavior and some suggestive evidence (Tornell and Lane 1998; Sachs and Warner 1995). It seems that for many developing countries, a larger than average resource endowment has been associated with slower growth, controlling for other attributes.

Set against this debate, once again Australia and California appear as examples that run counter to the conventional wisdom. For significant periods since 1850 both have seen growth driven by resource "windfalls" such as gold, oil, silver, and ores, or by the steady exploitation of a renewable resource, land in agricultural or pastoral use. Yet what was it about their political economy that allowed them to escape a wasteful misdirection of these resources?

Australia's early growth was based on a pastoral land boom that began in the 1820s, and was centered around the wool export industry. In the 1850s the gold rushes (mainly in Victoria) marked the second major resource shock. In the 1870s and 1880s the rural land boom resumed, based now on wheat as well as wool, while in the 1890s another gold rush (in Western Australia) occurred. Elsewhere in Australia the 1890s witnessed an economic collapse as severe as that of the 1930s—this being the period in which Australian per capita incomes decline relative to those in the United States and California. And for the next

TABLE 2.2
Australia, Wool, Gold, and Mineral Exports, 1861–1991
(Percentage of Total Exports)

Wool and Gold Exports, 1861–1911			Wool and Mineral Exports, 1947–1991		
Year	Wool	Gold	Year	Wool	Minerals
1861	27.0	48.9	1947	41.6	6.4
1871	41.5	32.7	1951	64.5	1.3
1881	48.0	23.3	1961	34.5	6.0
1891	56.1	15.8	1971	12.4	19.5
1901	28.3	31.9	1981	10.1	35.9
1911	34.2	13.6	1991	4.3	41.1

Source: Pinkstone, 1992.

half-century there were no further resource-based booms. The mineral industry faded to insignificance. And the agricultural sector was battered by droughts, wide fluctuations in world prices, the interruption to trade from two wars, and a world depression. It was not until the 1950s and 1960s that further mineral discoveries (iron ore, coal, copper, bauxite, oil, natural gas, uranium, etc.) underpinned the massive expansion of a sector that now accounts for 40 percent of Australia's export earnings (table 2.2).

The California story is in some respects similar. A series of resource-based booms followed the gold rushes (McLean 1993). Mineral discoveries elsewhere in the mountain states and British Columbia underpinned commercial activities in northern California as the gold rush there passed. Wheat exports boomed from the late 1860s. The spread of irrigation underpinned the expansion of horticulture in the following decades. But the fortunes of the two economies diverged after 1890. Although economic growth temporarily slowed in California in the 1890s, oil discoveries in the south of the state raised it to be the leading producer in the United States. Further, agricultural development in California continued, based substantially on the spread of irrigation. But the prime sources of growth shifted away from resource-intensive commodity production. Movies, aircraft production, and tourism flourished in the interwar period, manufacturing and defense-related activities took off in the 1940s, and the high-tech industries have underpinned growth in recent decades (Rhode 1990). Thus, California's succession of resource booms persisted as a major source of growth through the 1920s and 1930s, whereas Australia's resource-based growth faltered after the 1890s. And whereas the basis of California's economic growth became less reliant on resources, there was a revival of resource-based growth in Australia from the 1950s that has continued to the present.

Australia and California thus offer insights into another debate concerning resources, the argument over whether resources promote more rapid industrialization. There is certainly evidence that the United States developed its position as the world's leading manufacturing nation through a comparative advantage based on local resource endowments (Wright 1990; Irwin 2000). Yet this full gamut of resources did not reside within California itself, nor for that matter in Australia. Significantly, only one of these regions, California, became much more successful in the long run at establishing a high-productivity manufacturing sector with comparative advantage. This outcome suggests that we look again at the intranational versus international origins of productivity growth, where we must consider resources as a potentially traded input.

What are the implications of these observations for the debate about the role of natural resources in growth? First, for 150 years Australia and California have been among the world's richest societies, demonstrating that sustained growth can be achieved by economies that initially acquire their prosperity due to resource abundance. Some arguments to the contrary (e.g., Sachs and Warner 1995) appear to be based on an incomplete analysis of both the level and growth rate effects of starting out being resource rich. Second, neither economy experienced one-shot resource booms, but rather a succession of growth phases based on a range of resource industries. This may not be typical of developing countries. And the extent to which the later resource booms were endogenous, or were contingent events, remains unclear.[11] Third, the transition from resource-based growth to growth based primarily on other sources, which occurred earlier in California, was perhaps delayed in Australia at least in part for reasons of policy. The extensive protection afforded manufacturing may initially have encouraged the growth of domestic industrial production, but these firms remained internationally uncompetitive, and hence a drag on economy-wide productivity, until the recent reductions in the tariff. Manufacturing now accounts for around 20 percent of Australian exports.

GEOGRAPHY

Was Distance a Tyrant?

A major theme in the literature on Australia's history is the "tyranny of distance" (Blainey 1966). In its general form, "distance" embraces all the forces shaping society that arise both from the size of Australia itself, and also the remoteness of Australia from Europe, where lie its cultural, social, and political roots. In a narrower interpretation, the theme highlights the importance of transport and communication costs to the evolution and performance of the

---

[11] See David and Wright 1997 on the United States, McLean 1993 on California.

economy. And cross-country empirical growth analyses have indeed suggested that distance from the major centers of the world financial or economic system has had a negative impact on growth (Gallup, Sachs, and Mellinger 1999). But has distance mattered to growth in the Australian case, and, if so, when, in what form, and by how much?

Perhaps the most striking observation about distance and Australian economic growth is that in the nineteenth century a highly prosperous society was built on specialized production for markets on the other side of the world. Wool (from the 1820s) and gold (from the 1850s) dominated exports until the 1890s (table 2.2), and these exports went overwhelmingly to Britain. During the expansion phases of these export industries, British labor and capital flowed into Australia, sustaining high real wage levels, and increasing domestic market size—including the market for British manufactured goods. Establishing and sustaining this extraordinarily close set of economic relationships did not appear to be inhibited by distance.

Of course, wool and gold have certain characteristics that made long-distance trade profitable given prevailing costs and the technology of ocean shipping. They were nonperishable and had high ratios of value to weight (or bulk). Return freight rates on the British manufactured goods essential to Australian development cannot have been prohibitive, though it is noteworthy that Australia has long subsidized the passages of its "assisted" immigrants. The more interesting question is whether Australia would have acquired international competitiveness in other products had Britain (or Japan) been located nearby in the South Pacific.

Consider the California experience. Before gold, its exports (to the East Coast) were hides and tallow. After gold, there were new markets for a range of supplies in its neighborhood, as the mining frontier moved east into the mountain states and territories and north to British Columbia. The first commercial wheat exports in 1867 to Britain demonstrate that distance was no barrier here either.[12] Compared to Australia, the crucial differences in access to California's export markets were the population growth of nearby states in the West, the construction of transcontinental railroads, and the opening of the Panama Canal. We note that these events coincide with California's marked acceleration relative to Australia in intensive growth circa 1880–1900.

Soils, Water, and Climate

That geography and climate may determine output levels (or growth rates) remains a contentious claim. The correlation is certainly there in the data, whether

---

[12] By sea, San Francisco (absent the Panama Canal) is more remote from London than is Melbourne.

one takes a crude yardstick of tropical versus temperate climes as measured by latitude (Hall and Jones 1999) or a more refined mapping of climate zones (Sachs 2001).[13]

Though suggestive, this evidence does not pin down causality and may indeed be picking up other effects such as colonialism in the tropics. Evidence from studies of medicine and public health suggest that the disease environment of the tropics harbors larger and more persistent health threats, primarily due to a lack of frosts that disinfect as in temperate zones (Sachs 2001). Such a disease environment adds risk to economic activity and uncertainty to planning horizons, including not only investment but also the extent of life itself.[14]

In the context of this debate, Australia and California appear as curious exceptions. Australia is the only rich OECD economy that includes large areas of tropical land, amounting to 39 percent of the entire country. Yet if we take a broader view of what constitutes "tropical," the puzzle grows. Following Sachs (2001), we might prefer, for the epidemiological reasons just noted, to count as tropical any area where there are warm winters without the hard frosts that kill diseases. Such a criterion allows Sachs to reclassify India's low-income Gangetic plain, nominally a temperate zone, into the tropical zone, where it fits the hypothesis. Yet almost all of Australia exhibits a similar lack of winter frosts (excepting areas close to the small alpine region in the southeast), as does heavily populated coastal California and some of the Central Valley. That being the case, why were these regions able to escape the economic doldrums, a feat that has eluded most other warm climates?

Geography has other dimensions relevant to our study besides climate. There are few accounts of Australia's history, society, or economy that do not put considerable emphasis on the challenges posed by its physical environment. Much of Australia is desert, or arid, or semiarid, receiving very low rainfall. As significant as its low mean is the unusually high variability of rainfall across years, even decades, due, in particular, to the pronounced effects of the El Niño Southern Oscillation. For an economy generally classified as resource rich, there is one vital natural resource that is far from abundant—water. Australia has only 18 percent of the mean annual water runoff of the United States.

Further, the quality of Australian soil is generally poor and fragile. There are no extensive areas of deep, fertile soils as in the pampas or the Midwest, few river valleys, and only small pockets of volcanic soil. The interaction of climate and soil type means that land use in Australia is very different from that in western Europe or North America. Cropland comprises 20 percent of U.S. land use,

---

[13] And such correlations seem to survive even with additional controls for other putatively exogenous determinants of economic growth, such as measures of isolation from transport links.

[14] The explanation is thus at one with the older idea that the tropics lagged because such environmental factors held at bay one of the key ingredients of modern economic growth, the gradual scaling down of risk, noted by Eric Jones (1981).

TABLE 2.3
Land Utilization, United States and Australia

	United States	Australia
	Millions of Acres	Millions of Acres
Total area	1,904	1,891
	Percent	Percent
Cropland	21.0	2.5
Grassland pasture	27.6	3.3
Forest farmland	10.3	2.0
Other farmland	1.9	
Total farmland	60.8	7.8
Natural grazing land	18.5	61.7
Nonarid		17.8
Arid		43.8
Natural forest	12.5	3.5
Urban	4.6	1.0
Other uncultivated land	3.6	26.1
Total uncultivated	39.2	92.2

Sources: U. S. Department of Commerce 1975), series J50–65; McDonald 1989).

Note: For United States, figures are for 1954 and do not include Alaska or Hawaii. Cropland includes fallow land. Forest farmland includes Australian statistic for forestry. Natural forest includes wildlife sanctuaries.

but only 2 percent in Australia; improved pasture is 27 and 3 percent respectively. By contrast, land suitable only for natural grazing comprises 19 percent of the United States but 63 percent of Australia (table 2.3).

The economic significance of these observations about climate and soil quality for Australian growth have long been debated, most recently in the context of rising concern about the sustainability of agriculture, environmental damage, urban water quality and availability, and population pressure. Whereas population expansion was for long the paramount social objective, and the physical size of Australia was thought to be a good indicator of its population capacity, there has been a remarkable change in both expert and popular views. The new consensus is that the physical environment constrains Australia's ability to absorb a markedly greater population.

The importance of geography to Australian growth is well illustrated by comparison with California. Both have economies that have long faced serious problems of water supply. Some of the critical factors accounting for California's sustaining the much larger population at comparable living standards are the higher mean annual water runoff per capita, the capacity to redirect water within the state via diversion schemes, the ability to "import" large volumes of water from elsewhere, and the suitability of soils to irrigated agriculture close to where water is available. The conclusion is that differences in water availability, soil quality, and the variability of the climate (especially of rainfall) may account for much of the difference in past population growth rates, and current population sizes, in the two regions.

CULTURE, COLONIALISM, AND INSTITUTIONS

The long-term economic success of Australia and California is a reminder to ask whether geography, climate, and resource hurdles existed at all, and, if so, how they were overcome—for example, by policy choices. A complementary (and potentially rival) explanation would be to assert that such policies originated in the particular priorities of the developmental states established by new settlers in such regions—begging the question as to why such priorities were not imposed in other colonial ventures.

One explanation advanced for such unexpected outcomes in settler societies revolves around culture and colonialism (Acemoglu, Johnson, and Robinson 2000). It has never made sense to treat colonialism as a single entity, since at different times and in different corners of the globe it has taken many different forms. For example, why did colonial North America evolve into Canada and the United States, two rich OECD economies, whereas colonial Latin America evolved into a much poorer region of middle- and low-income economies (Engerman and Sokoloff 1997)? The claim of Acemoglu, Johnson, and Robinson is that beginning conditions could have pervasive long-term consequences. In some areas colonial masters sought purely the *ex ante* extraction of economic rents, though often without any such net gains materializing *ex post*. To minimize costs of extraction, investments in social infrastructure, like public health, would be of a lower priority if the gains from these investments spilled over, in small or large part, to locals. In other colonies, like settler regions, a mass migration of people from the colonizing region soon displaced or outnumbered the locals and set up a different dynamic, with a new class of locals whose welfare was of concern to the colonizing power. Such settlers would more likely be allowed to share in a dispersed set of private property rights to natural resources, to have political clout as regards public goods, and, as a result, to promote developmental spending. Mortality data seem to reveal stark contrasts between colonial administrations in such different kinds of regions, and in such divergent "initial conditions" might lie causes of long-run divergence.

The cases of Australia and California seem to fit one side of this description very well. Both soon revealed their extractive potential, but they also became more than simply "enclaves"—economies controlled by colonizers but operated by the colonized. Native people in both areas were soon outnumbered. If such colonies became identified as extensions of the colonizing country's economy, culture, and society—and not as "other"—then, so the argument goes, they were liable to benefit from a broader range of public investment activity.

Australia was formed in 1901 out of six British colonies that had had responsible self-government since the 1850s, so it inherited a legal system, language, and many of its cultural and social characteristics from Britain. Its political system is based on an amalgam of British and American influences. Parliamentary democracy and the rule of law have been unbroken. And there is no suggestion in the literature that these or other institutional arrangements were important brakes on long-run economic growth.[15] Even the colonial links with Britain are not generally thought to have been to the detriment of Australian economic development. If there were growth-limiting institutional arrangements in Australia, they must have been at some less general level. It is easier to note, in a comparative context, an example of institutional adaptation that avoided potential restraints on growth.

The method of allocating land during the settlement of a land-abundant region can have important long-run growth as well as distributional consequences. In comparisons of Australian and Argentine growth, much is made of the failure of the initial occupiers of large tracts of land in Australia (the "squatters") to obtain freehold. The beneficiaries of large land grants in Argentina did, hence locking-in an inequitable allocation of wealth that had long-lasting political effects. The large Australian pastoral holdings were held on lease only, and their breakup into smaller family farms in the 1860s to 1880s was accomplished peacefully. In California, the same transition was complicated by the inheritance of Mexican law, and the delay in the clarification of property rights in land in turn delayed the growth of agriculture in the years after the gold rush. In neither Australia nor California, however, is there any suggestion that institutional failure in land allocation had serious long-run economic consequences, whatever the short-run political fuss.[16]

---

[15] This is in striking contrast with, for example, writings on the economic history of Argentina, and especially in comparisons with Australia (Duncan and Fogarty 1984).

[16] An example of the role of dissimilar institutional arrangements accommodating similar economic imperatives is also to be found in a comparison of Australian and California gold-mining experience (La Croix 1992; Wright and Clay 1998). The Australian discoveries of alluvial (placer) gold were made in a region with a well-established legal system and (colonial) government, administering defined laws relating to the discovery of gold on unoccupied land (which belonged to

There is, however, considerable potential for growth-sapping corruption, rent seeking, and skewed distributional outcomes where economic development is based on natural-resource booms, as illustrated by the recent events in many developing countries, or by the history of Latin America. And there is evidence that corruption, rent seeking, and an unequal distribution of economic outcomes characterized the political and social histories of both Australia and California in the late nineteenth century. Why, in the latter two economies, was this not inimical to long-run growth?

We can only speculate on the explanation. One possibility is that, despite the concern with corruption at the time, it was less pervasive than in those societies that today suffer economically from endemic corruption. After all, both Australia and California had a free press and democratic institutions, so corruption was more likely to be exposed. A second possibility is that the corruption was of a form that was less corrosive of long-run growth. For example, many allegations of corrupt practice surround the construction of railroads in both Australia (by the state) and California (by railroad barons). In Australia the complaints were that they were built before there was warranted demand for them, or in a direction that suited a local politician; in California the complaints were about public subsidies underpinning the fortunes of private entrepreneurs. But the railroads at least were built, and they did form an essential component in the development of both economies.

It is safe to conclude that, in the broad-sweep perspective of this chapter, the many differences in institutional arrangements between California and Australia were not decisive in accounting for differences in their long-run growth outcomes. This lends support to attempts to seek a nuanced view of the role in growth of either corruption or a colonial inheritance.

SUMMARY: LESSONS FOR GROWTH ECONOMICS

Our reading of the economic histories of Australia and California leads to the following observations pertinent to current debates among growth economists. First, natural-resource abundance itself is not a barrier to sustained high levels of income or to high rates of growth. Most likely, these two economies escaped the growth-inhibiting problems associated with resource booms in some other economies for reasons related to their institutional and political conditions, especially those governing the growth-sustaining allocation of resource rents.

---

the Crown). By contrast, the California rushes occurred in a legal vacuum, with no effective government, so there occurred the well-known effort by miners to form their own laws and enforce property rights, with the rules varying between localities as conditions warranted. The two systems proved adaptable and to some degree convergent, nicely illustrating that more than one set of institutional arrangements may be compatible with very similar growth outcomes.

Distance from world markets seems not to have seriously impaired Australia's living standards over the long run. But other aspects of geography do seem to matter to the differences observed between Australia and California. In particular, rainfall, soil quality, and climate appear important in accounting for differences in the aggregate size of the two economies—or the populations able to be supported at high wages. For example, we have drawn attention to the small Australian domestic market's being also highly fragmented. This reflects in turn the few and scattered coastal areas having adequate and reliable water supplies to support high population densities.

The role of the state more generally in the growth of these two economies is difficult to summarize, but we see more similarities than differences. We particularly draw attention to the long-run economic impact of war. The postwar histories of both economies have been heavily influenced by decisions taken to develop industrial capacity during the Pacific War of 1941–45. It should be remembered that any resulting path dependency arose from large-scale government interventions in markets.

What can we learn about the link between tariffs and growth? The long period of inward-oriented industrial development in Australia from the 1920s to the 1970s is not associated with a decisive and sustained "falling behind" either California or the United States—as did occur in the case of Argentina. Australian per capita incomes slipped below that of the United States between 1890 and 1920—a period marked by severe depression, a major drought, and a world war that impacted negatively on economic activity. This occurred before trade policy was heavily protectionist. This correlation does not imply causation; that is, we cannot necessarily infer that inward-looking policies were beneficial for Australia, and for three important reasons where comparisons with California highlight the problems of inference.

First, although relative retardation of the Australian economy predates the rise of an aggressive tariff policy, that slowdown is in part attributable to other forces, such as the pronounced rural droughts of the 1890s. The failure to recover from these negative shocks may be the first sign that the growth dynamics of the Australian economy were adversely affected by the changes in commercial policy that began circa 1900 and continued to the present.

Second, and related to the persistence of this performance gap, it is possible that, absent the mineral discoveries and the growth of mineral exports in the last half-century, the postwar growth trajectory of Australia may have looked rather more like New Zealand. That is, the second great minerals boom in Australian history may have masked the drag on growth of the protected manufacturing industry, delaying until the 1980s the fundamental reorientation of the economy. No such distortion was possible in the California economy, of course.

Third, as our attention to the question of extensive growth has indicated throughout this chapter, the obsession of the growth literature with income per capita as the dependent variable, and the key barometer of performance, might be misplaced in this case. Regions like Australia and California have been extremely open throughout their histories to the immigration of labor. If labor supplies are thus elastic in the long run, the relevant measure of performance is population size, not output per capita. Why? As with the Malthusian dynamics of the preindustrial era (when elastic labor supplies were a result of demography, and not migration), in such economies all increases in income per capita due to productivity will, in the long run, be dissipated via the endogenous growth of population. Of course, the larger the positive technology shock, the larger the eventual population gain. In this respect the long-run population data (like the TFP data) seem to show that Australia and California, though on somewhat parallel paths in the nineteenth century, did diverge markedly in the twentieth century. This coincides with the decades of Australian industrial protection versus California's openness to the larger U.S. market for goods. Hence, if size is the right measure of performance—and, ironically, it was one of the Australian policymakers' key measures—then it could be argued that through productivity effects Australian tariff policy produced an entirely unintended outcome, and exactly the reverse of the one that policymakers had in mind.

REFERENCES

Abramovitz, Moses. 1956. "Resource and Output Trends in the United States since 1870." *American Economic Review* 46 (May): 5–23.

———. 1986. "Catching Up, Forging Ahead, and Falling Behind." *Journal of Economic History* 46 (June): 385–406.

Abramovitz, Moses, and Paul A. David. 1973. "Reinterpreting American Economic Growth: Parables and Realities." *American Economic Review* 63 (May): 428–37.

Acemoglu, Daron, Simon Johnson, and James A. Robinson. 2000. "The Colonial Origins of Comparative Development: An Empirical Investigation." NBER Working Paper No. 7771, June.

Ades, Alberto F., and Edward L. Glaeser. 1999. "Evidence on Growth, Increasing Returns, and the Extent of the Market." *Quarterly Journal of Economics* 114:1025–46.

Anderson, K., and R. Garnaut. 1987. *Australian Protectionism: Extent, Causes, and Effects.* Sydney: Allen and Unwin.

Australian Bureau of Statistics. Various issues. *National Accounts.* A. B. S. Catalogue #5302.0. Canberra.

Baldwin, Richard E., and Rikard Forslid. 1999. "The Core-Periphery Model and Endogenous Growth: Stabilising and De-stabilising Integration." NBER Working Paper No. 6899, January.

Barro, Robert J., N. G. Mankiw, and Xavier Sala-i-Martin. 1995. "Capital Mobility in Neoclassical Models of Growth." *American Economic Review* 85 (March): 103–15.

Barro, Robert J., and Xavier Sala-i-Martin. 1992. "Convergence." *Journal of Political Economy* 100 (April): 223–52.

Blainey, Geoffrey. 1966. *The Tyranny of Distance: How Distance Shaped Australia's History.* Sydney: Macmillan.

Butlin, M. W. 1977. "A Preliminary Annual Database 1900/01 to 1973/74." Research Discussion Paper No. 7701, Reserve Bank of Australia, May.

Butlin, Noel G. 1959. "Colonial Socialism in Australia, 1860–1900." In *The State and Economic Growth,* ed. Hugh G. J. Aitken. New York: Social Science Research Council.

———. 1962. *Australian Domestic Product, Investment, and Foreign Borrowing 1861– 1938/39.* Cambridge: Cambridge University Press,.

Collins, William J., and Jeffrey G. Williamson. 2001. "Capital Goods Prices and Investment, 1870–1950." *Journal of Economic History* 61 (March): 59–94.

Crosby, Alfred W. 1986. *Ecological Imperialism: The Biological Expansion of Europe, 900–1900.* Cambridge: Cambridge University Press.

David, Paul A., and Gavin Wright. 1997. "Increasing Returns and the Genesis of American Resource Abundance." *Industrial and Corporate Change* 6, no. 2: 203–45.

Denoon, D. 1983. *Settler Capitalism: The Dynamics of Dependent Development in the Southern Hemisphere.* Oxford: Oxford University Press.

Díaz Alejandro, Carlos F. 1970. *Essays on the Economic History of the Argentine Republic.* New Haven: Yale University Press.

Dowrick, Steven, and Duc-Tho Nguyen. 1988. "A Re-assessment of Australian Economic Growth in the Light of the Convergence Thesis." *Australian Economic Papers* 27:196–212.

———. 1989. "OECD Comparative Economic Growth, 1950–85: Catch-up and Convergence." *American Economic Review* 79 (December): 1010–30.

Duncan, Tim, and John Fogarty. 1984. *Argentina and Australia: On Parallel Paths.* Carlton, Victoria: Melbourne University Press.

Easterly, William, and Ross Levine. 1999. "It's Not Factor Accumulation: Stylized Facts and Growth Models." World Bank, October. Photocopy.

Engerman, Stanley L., and Kenneth L. Sokoloff. 1997. "Factor Endowments, Institutions, and Differential Paths of Growth among New World Economies: A View from Economic Historians of the United States." In *How Latin America Fell Behind: Essays on the Economic Histories of Brazil and Mexico, 1800–1914,* ed. Stephen Haber. Stanford, Calif.: Stanford University Press.

Gallup, John Luke, Jeffrey D. Sachs, and Andrew Mellinger. 1999. "Geography and Economic Development." Center for International Development Working Paper No. 1, Harvard University.

Hall, Robert E., and Charles I. Jones. 1999. "Why Do Some Countries Produce So Much More Output per Worker Than Others?" *Quarterly Journal of Economics* 114: 83–116.

Hess, Gregory D., and Eric Van Wincoop. 2000. *Intranational Macroeconomics.* Cambridge: Cambridge University Press.

Irwin, Douglas A. 2000. "How Did the United States Become a Net Exporter of Manufactured Goods?" NBER Working Paper No. 7638, April.

Jones, Charles I. 1994. "Economic Growth and the Relative Price of Capital." *Journal of Monetary Economics* 34:359–82.

Jones, Eric L. 1981. *The European Miracle.* Cambridge: Cambridge University Press.

Kaspura, Andre, and Geoff Weldon. 1980. "Productivity Trends in the Australian Economy, 1900–01 to 1978–79." Department of Productivity Working Paper No. 9, Canberra.

Klenow, Peter J., and Andres Rodriguez-Clare. 1997. "The Neoclassical Revival in Growth Economics: Has It Gone Too Far?" In *NBER Macroeconomics Annual, 1997*, ed. Ben S. Bernanke and Julio J. Rotemberg. Cambridge: MIT Press.

Kohn, Meir. 2001. "Trading Costs, the Expansion of Trade, and Economic Growth in Pre-industrial Europe." Dartmouth College, January. Photocopy.

Kremer, Michael. 1993. "Population Growth and Technological Change: One Million B.C. to 1990." *Quarterly Journal of Economics* 108:681–716.

Krugman, Paul, and Anthony J. Venables. 1995. "Globalization and the Inequality of Nations." *Quarterly Journal of Economics* 110:857–80.

La Croix, Sumner J. 1992. "Property Rights and Institutional Change during Australia's Gold Rush." *Explorations in Economic History* 29 (April): 204–27.

Limerick, Patricia Nelson. 1987. *The Legacy of Conquest: The Unbroken Past of the American West.* New York: W. W. Norton.

López-Córdova, J. Ernesto, and Chris Meissner. 2000. "Exchange-Rate Regimes and International Trade: Evidence from the Classical Gold Standard Era." University of California, Berkeley, August. Photocopy.

Maddison, Angus. 1995. *Monitoring the World Economy.* Paris: Organisation for Economic Cooperation and Development.

Mankiw, N. Gregory, David Romer, and David N. Weil. 1992. "A Contribution to the Empirics of Economic Growth." *Quarterly Journal of Economics* 107:407–37.

McDonald, G. T. 1989. "Rural Land-Use Planning in Australia." In *Rural Land-Use Planning in Developed Nations*, ed. Paul J. Cloke. London: Unwin Hyman.

McLean, Ian W. 1993. "No Flash in the Pan: Resource Abundance and Economic Growth in California, 1848–1910." Department of Economics, Adelaide University. Photocopy.

Mitchener, Kris J., and Ian W. McLean. 1999. "United States Regional Growth and Convergence, 1880—1980." *Journal of Economic History* 59 (December): 1016–42.

Mokyr, Joel. 1992. *The Lever of Riches.* Oxford: Oxford University Press.

Murphy, Kevin M., Andrei Shleifer, and Robert W. Vishny. 1989. "Industrialization and the Big Push." *Journal of Political Economy* 97 (October): 1003–26.

Obstfeld, Maurice, and Alan M. Taylor. 1997. "Nonlinear Aspects of Goods-Market Arbitrage and Adjustment: Heckscher's Commodity Points Revisited." *Journal of the Japanese and International Economies* 11 (December): 441–79.

———. 2002. *Global Capital Markets: Integration, Crisis, and Growth.* Japan–United States Center Sanwa Monographs on International Financial Markets. Cambridge: Cambridge University Press. In progress.

Pinkstone, B. 1992. *Global Connections: A History of Exports and the Australian Economy.* Canberra: Australian Government Publishing Service.

Pomfret, Richard, ed. 1995. *Australia's Trade Policies.* Melbourne: Oxford University Press.

Pope, David H. 1981. "Contours of Australian Immigration, 1901–30." *Australian Economic History Review* 21 (March): 29–52.

Productivity Commission. 1999. *The New Economy? A New Look at Australia's Productivity Performance.* Canberra: Commonwealth of Australia.

Rebelo, Sergio. 1991. "Long-Run Policy Analysis and Long-Run Growth." *Journal of Political Economy* 99 (June): 500–521.

Rhode, Paul W. 1990. "Growth in a High Wage Economy: California's Industrial Development, 1900–1960." Ph.D. diss., Stanford University.

Romer, Paul M. 1986. "Increasing Returns and Long-Run Growth." *Journal of Political Economy* 94 (October): 1002–37.

Rose, Andrew K. 2000. "One Money, One Market: The Effect of Common Currencies on Trade." *Economic Policy* 15 (April): 7–33.

Rose, Andrew K., and Eric van Wincoop. 2001. "National Money as a Barrier to Trade: The Real Case for Currency Union." University of California, Berkeley, January. Photocopy.

Sachs, Jeffrey D. 2001. "Tropical Underdevelopment." NBER Working Paper No. 8119, February.

Sachs, Jeffrey D., and Andrew M. Warner. 1995. "Natural Resources and Economic Growth." NBER Working Paper No. 5398, December.

Schedvin, C. B. 1990. "Staples and Regions of Pax Britannica." *Economic History Review* 20 (November): 533–59.

Solow, Robert M. 1956. "A Contribution to the Theory of Economic Growth." *Quarterly Journal of Economics* 70:65–94.

Taylor, Alan M. 1994. "Tres fases del crecimiento económico argentino." *Revista de Historia Económica* 12:649–83.

————. 1999. "Sources of Convergence in the Late Nineteenth Century." *European Economic Review* 43 (September): 1621–45.

Tornell, Aaron, and Philip R. Lane. 1998. "Voracity and Growth." NBER Working Paper No. 6498, April.

U.S. Department of Commerce. 1975. *Historical Statistics of the United States: Colonial Times to 1970.* Washington, D.C.: Government Printing Office.

Wright, Gavin. 1990. "The Origins of American Industrial Success, 1879–1940." *American Economic Review* 80 (September): 651–68.

Wright, Gavin, and K. Clay. 1998. "Property Rights and California Gold." Paper presented at the All-UC Conference on Economic History, Santa Clara University, March. Photocopy.

CHAPTER 3

One Polity, Many Countries

ECONOMIC GROWTH IN INDIA, 1873–2000

GREGORY CLARK   SUSAN WOLCOTT

INDIA is perhaps the most interesting of all economies for those interested in economic growth. It is one of the poorer countries of the world, and has even seen an erosion of its income per capita relative to the economically advanced economies such as the United States since we have the first reasonable data in 1873. But this relative decline has occurred in what has been for most of this period a very favorable institutional environment. Indeed from an economist's perspective the institutional environment in the colonialist years from 1873 to 1947—secure property rights, free trade, fixed exchange rates, and open capital markets—was close to ideal. So India captures the twentieth-century paradox of a world of ever more rapid and easy movement of information and goods combined with large and often increasing disparities in living conditions.

Figure 3.1 shows calculated GDP per capita in India from 1873 to 1998 measured relative to the United States and Britain. India did show a substantial increase in absolute GDP per capita over these years. Real incomes per capita in 1998 were 3.6 times those estimated for 1873. But relative to both Britain and the United States Indian income per person fell from 1873 to the mid-1980s, before rising from 1987 to the present. The rapid growth of Indian income per capita since 1987 has led some economists to optimistically predict that modest institutional reforms have provided a speedy remedy to India's problems, and that India is finally about to join the advanced economies (see DeLong, this volume).[1] But Indian income levels relative to the United States in 1998 were, at 8 percent, still below those of the early 1960s. And growth has been very uneven within the Indian economy, so that in some states income per capita has continued to decline relative to the United States. Income per capita in Bihar, with a population of over 100 million, is currently about 4 percent of that in the United States, and still falling relative to U.S. incomes. And since we have

---

[1] Since growth started under the Rajiv Gandhi administration, elected in late 1984, DeLong concludes that though the reforms were "hesitant," the "consequence of this first wave of reform was an economic boom."

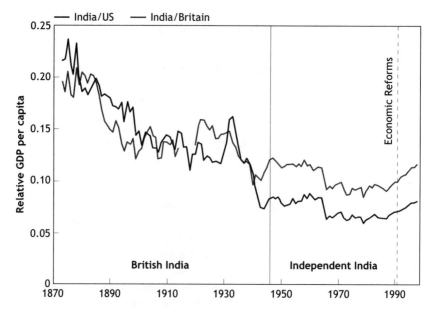

Figure 3.1. Indian GDP per capita relative to Britain and the U.S., 1873 to 1998
Source: India: Pre-1947, Heston 1983; 1950–80, Penn World Tables (PWT 5.6); 1981–98, Statesforum. U.S.: 1873–1929, Balke and Gordon 1992, *Economic Report of the President* 2001. United Kingdom/Britain: 1873–1965, Feinstein 1972; 1965–98, United Kingdom, National Statistical Office.

little understanding of what caused the erosion of India's economic position from 1873 to 1987, anyone who would confidently predict that economic reforms will ensure India will soon close the gap with the advanced economies forgets the lessons of its history.

Many other countries that have witnessed a declining relative income level have done so in circumstances where political and social institutions have suffered breakdowns. Thus, many of the countries of Africa that are now among the world's poorest have suffered from ethnic strife and the collapse of political institutions, since their independence. But the Indian economy experienced its decline in a long period of relative political and social stability, first under British colonial rule until 1947, and even after independence. Indeed the erosion of India's relative economic position has continued across three different political regimes. The accelerated economic growth since 1987 has been associated by many with the recent liberalization of the economy. But the era of reform properly dates only from 1991. Yet Indian income per capita rose 10 percent relative to the United States in 1987–91, compared to a 14 percent gain in 1991–98.[2]

Independence did create a substantial change in economic management. After 1947 there was a gradual move from a laissez-faire policy, with low taxation rates and taxation based heavily on lump-sum taxes on land rent, to an interventionist policy that relied more on taxes that could at some deadweight cost be evaded.[3] But India has remained a lightly taxed economy.

Table 3.1 shows the average state revenue as a percentage of income by province in British India in 1938–39, and in independent India in 1949–50 (before the formation of the modern Indian states) and 1998. Before independence a large share of tax revenue was generated by the land tax, which was in effect a lump-sum tax on land. Since then land taxes have steadily declined as a share of revenues, now constituting no more than 1 percent of national tax revenue. Land taxes have largely been replaced by sales taxes. Thus the form and incidence of taxation varies little across the modern Indian states.

India would seem also to have one great advantage relative to other underdeveloped economies: it is a political amalgam of countries—almost as diverse in religion, languages, and culture as is Europe—that was forged as the result of the accident of British colonial rule in the nineteenth century. In 1991, 44 years after independence, 11 languages were still spoken as the principle tongue by more than 20 million people in India. To achieve economic growth a country does not have to experience productivity gains in all sectors or all regions. As long as some industries and some localities can achieve productivity growth, gains can be transmitted to the economy as a whole through the migration of capital and labor to the successful locality, and through international trade the economy can specialize production in this sector. In the Industrial Revolution in Britain in 1760–1860 there was very little productivity growth in the southern half of the country, where two-thirds of the population lived in 1760. Most of the productivity growth in the north occurred in textiles. But through the twin forces of labor migration and international trade the success of Britain in this one sector was translated into widespread economic growth. Having so much internal diversity would seem to make India peculiarly fortunate relative to more homogenous underdeveloped countries such as its neighbor Bangladesh.

---

[2] The reforms had three important elements. The rupee became completely convertible in the current account, and restrictions on capital account were lessened. India joined the World Trade Organization and participated in the Uruguay Round of trade negotiations. The government has thus reduced though not eliminated trade restrictions. Finally, restrictions on foreign direct investment have been considerably weakened.

[3] This change was in part accidental. The land tax was fixed in nominal terms and the inflation of the war years severely eroded its real value.

TABLE 3.1

Taxation before and after Independence, by Province or State

Province	Revenue Income 1938–39 (%)	Revenue/ Income 1949–50 (%)	Land Revenue/ All Taxes 1938–39 (%)	State	State Taxes/ Income 1998 (%)	Land Revenue/ State Taxes 1998 (%)
Madras	4.3	3.5	44	Andhra Pradesh	7.6	2
Bombay	5.2	4.6	38	Bihar	4.7	1
Central provinces	3.0	3.0	65	Gujarat	8.0	1
United provinces	4.0	3.8	64	Haryana	8.0	0
Bihar	3.4	3.2	34	Karnataka	8.1	0
Assam	4.1	3.0	61	Kerala	7.9	1
Orissa	3.2	3.5	45	Madhya Pradesh	5.7	1
East Punjab	5.9	3.5	56	Maharashtra	5.8	1
West Bengal	4.4	8.2	31	Orissa	5.2	3
				Punjab	6.0	0
				Rajasthan	6.9	1
				Tamil Nadu	8.2	0
				Uttar Pradesh	4.7	1
				West Bengal	5.1	9
All India	4.0	4.2	46	India (all taxes)	8.3	1

Source: Natarajan 1949; Statesforum, www.statesforum.org.

THE SOURCES OF DIVERGENCE

Why did Indian income per capita decline relative to the advanced economies such as the United States until 1987? The overwhelming cause was a decline in the relative efficiency of utilization of technology in India. Conventional estimates report that about one-third of the difference in incomes per capita between countries comes from capital (conventionally measured), and the rest from efficiency (TFP) differences.[4] But this assumes that differences in

---

[4] See, for example, Easterly and Levine 2000.

TABLE 3.2
Rates of Return, Britain and India, circa 1910

Asset	Rate of Return in Britain (%)	Rate of Return in India (%)
Agricultural land, 1900–1914	2.83	4–6
Industrial capital, 1900–1914	8	7
Railway equity, 1870–1913	4.3	5.0
Railway debt, 1870–1913	3.7	3.7
Bank rate	4.3	5.4

Sources: Edelstein 1982; Goldsmith 1983; Clark 1987, 1998; Wolcott and Clark 1999, 402.

Note: Returns were lower on Indian than British railway bonds because the Indian government guaranteed the bonds of the railways as a way of promoting infrastructure investment.

capital per worker across countries, which are very highly correlated with differences in income per capita and measured TFP, are exogenous. In a world where capital can flow between economies, capital/worker should be regarded as an endogenous variable, and as *responding* to differences in the level of productivity across countries. Thus in the case of India by the late nineteenth century rates of return on capital were pretty close to those of England, as table 3.2 shows. The imperial connection removed all political risk for British investors.

Thus suppose the production function was Cobb-Douglas so that

$$Y = A\,K^\alpha\,L^\beta\,T^\gamma,$$

where T denotes land. Choosing units so that A, K, Y, and T are 1 in India, if the rental of capital were the same across countries, capital per worker in country i, relative to India, would be

$$(K/L)_i = A_i^{1/(1-\alpha)}\,(T/L)_i^{\gamma/(1-\alpha)} = (Y/L)_i.$$

The amount of capital employed would thus depend on the level of efficiency of the economy. The more efficient an economy, the more capital it would attract, which would have a second-round effect in increasing income per person. Capital per person in this Cobb-Douglas case would be just proportionate to output per person. If capital were exogenously chosen in each economy, then the efficiency (*TFP*) of other economies relative to India would be

$$TFP_i = A_i = (Y/L)_i\,(K/L)_i^{-\alpha}\,(T/L)_i^{-\gamma}.$$

But with capital endogenous and rates of return equalized across countries, then

$$(Y_i/L_i) = (A_i)^{1/(1-\alpha)} \, (T/L)_i^{-\gamma/(1-\alpha)}.$$

Also, the level of efficiency of any economy can be calculated as

$$A_i = (Y/L)_i^{1-\alpha} \, (T/L)_i^{-\gamma}.$$

Thus in this case we can calculate TFP for the United States and Britain relative to India from just the relative outputs per capita and the relative amount of land per person. That the share of land in national income, γ, has become very small in recent years (4) suggests that the sole significant cause of differences in income per capita between India and the United States and other advanced economies is differences in TFP. Table 3.3 shows the implied TFP of the United States and Britain relative to India assuming the share of capital in national income was 0.33, and that the share of land was 0.

After independence in 1947 the Government of India imposed a variety of restrictions on the free mobility of capital, so that the assumption of an equalized rate of return on capital is suspect. But the proportionality posited above between output per person and capital per person holds. U.S. output per person was 14.3 times output per person in India in 1992, while capital per person was 17.8 times greater. U.K. output per person was 10.5 times Indian output, and capital per person 10.9 times greater (Penn World Tables, version 5.6).

These differences in TFP could have two causes—slow diffusion of Western technology, or the inability to effectively employ Western technology. The evidence suggests that the latter explanation applies: since the late nineteenth century technology diffused rapidly to poor countries, and the low TFP of India comes in large part from an inability to effectively employ this new technology.

If we look at the industry with which we have expertise, cotton textiles, for example, we see that up to at least the 1940s there is no sign of any lag in the types of machinery India employed compared to the advanced economies. In the early nineteenth century a specialized machine-building sector developed within the Lancashire cotton industry. These machinery firms, some of which, such as Platts, were exporting at least 50 percent of their production as early as 1845–70, had an important role in exporting textile technology. They were able to provide a complete "package" of services to prospective foreign entrants to the textile industry, which included technical information, machinery, construction expertise, and managers and skilled operatives. By 1913 the six largest machine producers employed over thirty thousand workers (Bruland 1989, 5, 6, 34). These firms reduced the risks to foreign entrepreneurs by such practices as giving them machines on a trail basis and supplying skilled workers to train the local labor force. Similar capital-goods exporters developed in the rail sectors, and later in the United States in the boot and shoe industry. The sales records

TABLE 3.3
Calculated Relative TFP, USA and Britain (India = 1)

Year	USA TFP	Britain/UK TFP
1873–79	2.8	3.0
1906–14	3.8	3.8
1947	5.3	4.1
1987[a]	6.2	4.9
1991[a]	5.9	4.6
1998[a]	5.4	4.2

[a] For this year the assumption that the rate of return to capital was the same in India as the other countries is suspect because of government regulations in India on foreign investment.

of the English machine builders have survived along with detailed descriptions of the machines ordered by each customer. These show that Indian firms were buying Platts machinery of a description very similar to that used in the advanced economies.

The problem that limited the growth of the Indian industry was not machinery, then, but the low profits made by cotton mills in India, because of their inability to employ technology effectively. Low profits prevented the rapid industrialization of the country under the British despite India's great labor cost advantages. Table 3.4, for example, shows the gross profit rates of Bombay mills by quinquennia from 1905–9 to 1935–39, as well as the size of the Bombay industry and the output per worker in Bombay as an index with 1905–9 set at 100. As can be seen, profits were never great, but the industry grew substantially in the era of modest profits up to 1924.[5] Thereafter, however, profits collapsed (as a result of Japanese competition), and the Bombay industry soon began to contract. The last column in table 3.4 shows what was happening in Japan, where, using the same machinery purchased from England, output per worker increased greatly.

The inefficiency of operation of Indian mills shows up primarily in very low output per worker, rather than in low output per machine hour. Ever since India entered the factory cotton textile industry, output per worker-hour in the United States—using the same technology in spinning cotton yarn—has been many times the rate in India. In 1978, for example, output per worker-hour in cotton

[5] In comparison, banks charged a rate of 5.73 percent in 1905–9 and 5.44 percent in 1910–13 to discount commercial bills. See Goldsmith 1983, 6.

TABLE 3.4
The Bombay Industry, 1907–38

Year	Gross Profit Rate on Fixed Capital	Size of the Bombay Industry (m. spindle-equivalents)	Output per Worker in Bombay (index)	Output per Worker in Japan (index)
1905–9	0.09	3.09	100	100
1910–14	0.05	3.43	103	115
1915–19	0.07	3.68	99	135
1920–24	0.08	4.05	94	132
1925–29	–0.00	4.49	91	180
1930–34	0.00	4.40	104	249
1935–39	0.02	3.91	106	281

Source: Wolcott and Clark 1999.

Note: Profits and output per worker were calculable only for the mills listed in the *Investor's India Yearbook.*

spinning was 7.4 times greater in the United States in mills using substantially the same equipment. If there is substantial possibility of capital-labor substitution, then the odd pattern of the same output per spindle-hour but low output per labor-hour in India could still be the result of a generalized managerial inefficiency combined with a move to substitute labor for capital in Indian mills. But even in elements of the operation where the substitution possibilities are very limited, India has low output per worker. Thus in spinning, machines are stopped at regular intervals to remove the output packages, an operation called "doffing." Since the machines fill at a regular rate, doffing can be scheduled for the machines in rotation, and there is no issue of machine interference from changing the work assignment. Table 3.5 shows the number of packages doffed from spinning machines by workers in India, the United States, and England in a variety of years from 1907 on (data does not exist for the United States in more recent years because this operation was largely mechanized). As late as 1990 workers in southern India were completing an average of 230 doffs per hour, and worker productivity at this task in the Gujarat and Maharashtra centers of the industry was similar. This was less than one-quarter of the last recorded average U.S. performance of 1,000 doffs per hour, achieved thirty years earlier in 1959. Yet work study tests India suggest that, based on performance rates of Indian workers on the tasks doffers in India complete, a fully employed doffer would complete 863 doffs per hour. Thus, compared to both U.S. performance and what Indian workers can complete under work study

TABLE 3.5
Spindles Doffed per Worker per Hour

Year	USA	England	India
1921	728		118[a]
1944	606	354	124[b]
1946	770		
1949–50	933	570[c]	
1959	1,000		
1969		600[d]	
1978			160[e]
1990			230

Sources: Shirras 1923; Cotton Spinning Productivity Team 1951; Ratnam and Raja-manickam 1980; Doraiswamy 1983; SITRA 1990; Textile Council 1969.

Notes: [a] Bombay City and Island. Calculated from Shirras 1923 on the assumptions that there is one side per ring spinner (170 spindles), that output per spindle-hour averages 0.038 lbs., and that the weight of the doff package is 0.084 lbs (the same as Britain in 1949).
[b] India except the Bombay presidency.
[c] Lowest cost mills.
[d] Assumed performance in modernization study.
[e] South Indian mills. Doff package assumed to be 0.12 lbs.

conditions, the typical doffer in 1990 actually worked for only about 25 percent of their time in the factory.[6]

Thus the problem of the Indian economy is heavily associated with production inefficiency. This inefficiency is observed even when the same methods and machinery are employed as in the advanced economies. And this production inefficiency is associated in particular with an underutilization of the efforts of workers in the production process.

REGIONAL INCOME PER CAPITA IN INDIA, 1890–1998

While India as a whole has grown poorer relative to the advanced economies since 1873, there has always been considerable disparity between richer and

[6] Interestingly the SITRA (1990) pamphlet referred to above suggests that the worker assignments would be cost minimizing at only 440 spindle doffs per hour. But it does so on the assumption that (1) any increase in assignment would have to be accompanied by an increase in wages per worker, (2) given the "monotonous and repetitive nature" of doffing, it would be too much to expect more of workers, and (3) attempts at higher assignments would result in machine interference.

poorer regions within India, and this disparity has been growing in recent years. Consideration of regional growth in India is complicated by the changing boundaries of regions over time. The major administrative break was caused by the formation of the Republic of India in 1950. The new republic established 14 states and five union territories in 1956.[7] But new states were created by the subdivision of older ones in 1960 and 1966, and some union territories have been converted into states, so that there are now 25 states, the last created in 1991. Table 3.6 shows, for the 25 current states, their population in 1991, their principal languages, their rates of urbanization and literacy, and their income per person in 1991 in rupees of 1990. States were largely based on language groupings.

There is considerable variation in state real incomes per capita in 1991, even excluding the union territory of Delhi, which has the highest income of all. Incomes in the Punjab in 1991 were 3.2 times those in Bihar. Interestingly, the levels of income per capita have actually been diverging in India since at least 1961, despite the relative uniformity of institutional structure across states, as shown for example in the small variations in taxes as a share of income revealed in table 3.1.[8] Table 3.7, for example, shows the coefficient of variation of various measures of income per capita across Indian regions from 1890 on. In the earlier colonial period, with no variation in institutional structure across regions, and improving transport and communications, income variations were significant and relatively stable. Since independence the evidence is for steadily increasing income disparities, both before the economic liberalization of 1991 and since then. The fortunes of various states have also varied widely. In 1961, for example, West Bengal was the second richest of the 14 major states, with an income per capita very close to the richest, Maharashtra. By 1998 West Bengal ranked ninth in income per capita, and its income was less than one-half that of Maharashtra.

Figure 3.2 shows the state real income levels in 1998–99 compared to those of 1991–92 in rupees of 1993–94. Also shown is the predicted level of income per capita in 1998 based on 1991 when we assume all states' incomes increased

---

[7] States Reorganization Act of 1956.

[8] Aiyar (2001) and Cashin and Sahay (1996) claim to have found convergence in a cross section of Indian states. But they mean by convergence that they can find a regression specification under which the growth rate of income is associated negatively and statistically significantly with the initial level of income, not that actual incomes per capita are becoming less varied. Thus Cashin and Sahay (1996) only find evidence for convergence if they include the initial share of manufacturing in state GDP and the initial share of agriculture in their regressions, and if they divide the periods into decades. Aiyar (2001) finds convergence over the period 1971 to 1995 if he divides the period into five-year increments and includes for each period initial literacy and investment. Abler and Das (1998) included a measure of investment in their convergence regressions, which covered the entire period, 1961–90, and found no convergence, though they did find a statistically significant effect of investment.

TABLE 3.6
The Principal Indian States and Territories in 1991

State or Territory	Population 1991 (m.)	Principal Language	Urbanization (%)	Literacy (%)	Income/ Person (Rs) (1991)
Andhra Pradesh	43.5	Telagu	26	45	4,728
Assam	22.4	Assamese	11	53	4,014
Bihar	86.4	Hindi	13	38	2,655
Delhi[a]	9.42	Hindi	90	76	10,177
Gujarat	41.3	Gujarati	34	60	5,687
Haryana	16.5	Hindi	22	55	7,502
Himachal Pradesh	5.2	Hindi	9	63	4,790
Jammu & Kashmir	7.7	Urdu	24	27	3,872
Karnataka	45.0	Kannada	31	56	4,696
Kerala	29.1	Malayalam	26	91	4,207
Madhya Pradesh	66.2	Hindi	23	43	4,149
Maharashtra	78.9	Marathi	39	63	7,316
Orissa	31.7	Oriya	13	48	3,077
Punjab	20.3	Punjabi	30	57	8,373
Rajasthan	44.0	Rajasthani	23	39	4,113
Tamil Nadu	55.9	Tamil	34	64	5,047
Uttar Pradesh	139.1	Hindi	20	42	3,516
West Bengal	68.1	Bengali	27	58	4,753
All India	846.3				4,934

Source: Cashin and Sahay (1996).

[a] Union territory.

by the same proportion. The figure reveals clearly that in the 1990s the richest states improved their income levels faster than the poorer states. Gujarat had a growth rate of income per capita of 7.4 percent, while Bihar's was 1.0 percent. This despite the fact that measurement errors in the estimated state GDP per person in each year tend to produce an appearance of convergence. In 1991, for example, Bihar, the poorest of the 14 major states, had a GDP per capita of just

TABLE 3.7
Coefficient of Variation of Income per Person, India and Europe

Year	India (19 localities)	Imperial India (10 provinces)	India (19 states)	India (14 states)	Non-Communist Europe (18 countries)
1890	.30[a]				.23
1914	.26[a]				.21
1938		.29[b]			.27
1949		.28[b]			.25
1961			.22	.20	.38
1971	.35[c]				
1981				.28	
1991			.31	.31	.21
1998				.36	.17

Sources: Europe: 1890–1950, Prados de la Escosura 2000; 1950–98, OECD. India GDP: 1938, 1949, Nataraja 1949; 1961, Cashin and Sahay 1996; 1981, 1991, 1998, Statesforum, www.statesforum.org. India, Wages: 1890, 1914, Datta 1914; 1971, Lal 1988.

Note: Luxembourg was omitted from the list of European nations as an outlier. The earlier Indian data does not control for price level variations, but Collins found that the national coefficient of variation in real wages across Indian districts was .337 in 1873–79, and .355 in 1900–1906 (Collins 1999, table 2). Our uncorrected estimates are thus similar in magnitude.

[a] Carpenters.
[b] Excluding provinces that later fell in Pakistan.
[c] Rural wages only.

39 percent of the second richest state, Maharashtra. But by 1998 Bihar's GDP per capita was only 26 percent of Maharashtras, since income per capita in Bihar increased by only 7 percent in these seven years. Indeed, relative to the United States, the large northern Indian states of Bihar and Uttar Pradesh, with a combined population in 1998 of 277 million, both saw declining incomes per capita in the 1990s. Three out of the 14 major states, including these two, had slower growth rates of income per capita in the 1990s than in the 1980s.

India's experience since the 1960s contrasts sharply with that of western Europe and the United States. Table 3.7 shows, for example, for 18 non-Communist·countries in Europe the coefficient of variation of incomes back to 1890.[9] While in 1961 these European states showed much more variation in incomes

---

[9] Luxembourg was omitted. By 1999 it had the highest income per capita in the world.

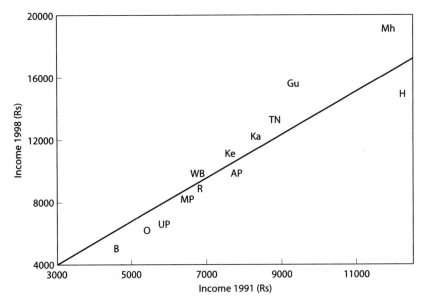

Figure 3.2. Income in 1998–99 as a function of 1991–92 (1993–94 rupees). Throughout in the figures we use the following symbols for states: AP, Andhra Pradesh, B, Bihar, G, Gujarat, H, Haryana, Ka, Karnataka, Ke, Kerala, MP, Madhya Pradesh, Mh, Maharashtra, O, Orissa, P, Punjab, R, Rajasthan, TN, Tamil Nadu, UP, Uttar Pradesh, WB, West Bengal. Rajasthan's income per capita is projected from 1997–98.
Source: Statesforum

per capita than did India, by 1998 the position had reversed, with European states showing dramatic convergence in income levels. The convergence of incomes per capita across the states of the United States is an oft-cited example of a supposedly general convergence tendency (Barro and Sala-i-Martin 1991, 1992). But the experience of the Indian states, and indeed also of provinces in China, suggests that the convergence witnessed in Europe and within the United States reveals no general growth law, but a contingent and accidental feature.[10]

EXPLAINING INCOME DIVERGENCE IN INDIA SINCE 1961

Just as the sources of India's decline in relative income compared to the advanced economies from 1873 onwards seems unconnected to government policy,

---

[10] China similarly has seen growing income disparities in the years 1978–98. Income per capita in Guangdong in 1998 was nearly three times that of Quinghai, even though Guangdong's per capita income slightly lagged that of Quinghai in 1978 (Démurger 2001).

TABLE 3.8
State Growth and State Policy Measures, 1991–98

Version	Adjusted R^2	Variable	Estimated Coefficient	Standard Error	p-value
1.	0.189	Log GDP/N, 1991	2.961	1.474	0.068
2.	0.380	Log GDP/N 1991	0.042	1.867	0.983
		Taxes as a share of state GDP, 1991 (%)	0.654	0.302	0.053
3.	0.233	Log GDP/N 1991	1.059	2.054	0.616
		Public education expenditure per 100 workers, 1991	0.015	0.012	0.222
4.	0.147	Log GDP/N 1991	2.604	1.641	0.135
		Public capital expenditures per 100 workers, 1991	0.006	0.010	0.540
6.	0.436	Log GDP/N, 1991	1.379	1.384	0.340
		% enrolled primary school, 1981	0.113	0.045	0.029
7.	0.146	Log GDP/N 1991	2.446	1.722	0.184
		% enrolled secondary school, 1981	0.049	0.078	0.544
8.	0.431	Log GDP/N 1991	6.716	1.958	0.006
		Phones per 100 workers, 1985	−1.906	0.771	0.031
10.	0.123	Log GDP/N 1991	2.923	1.539	0.084
		Km. Roads per 100 Workers, 1985	0.403	1.345	0.770

Sources: See appendix table 3.A1.

so the divergence of income per capita within India again seems largely un-connected with government policy. As table 3.1 shows, the burden of taxation across Indian states has varied little since independence, with the wealthier states if anything collecting a larger share of income in taxes. There are subtle elements of the regulatory climate in each state that the gross tax burden does not reveal, but for most important industries, such as textiles, the significant government policies were determined at the federal level, as with the excise tax on yarn and cloth, and the rights of workers in the mill sector.[11]

An investigation of the divergence of incomes in the reform era since 1991 shows no very promising signs of the effects of state policy. Table 3.8 shows the effects of some of the measurable dimensions of state policy, such as state taxes as a share of state GDP, public education expenditure per 100 workers, public capital expenditures per 100 workers, and the percentage of children en-

---

[11] Thus Misra, in his 1993 book on government policy and the textile sector, has no discussion of any effects of different state policies with regard to textiles.

rolled in primary and secondary education. In each case the variable is included as variable Z in a regression of the form

$$Growth\ Rate\ of\ GDP/N_{1991-98} = a + b(GDP/N)_{1991} + cZ + e$$

to control for the possible dependence of these Z variables on income per capita. Without any other variables included, the coefficient on $(GDP/N)_{1991}$ is strongly positive (though significant at only the 10 percent level). As can be seen, if state taxes as a share of income are included, then they are a much better predictor of growth than the current level of income. Higher state tax levels in 1991 are associated with faster growth. But if we look at what the states might do with this revenue to foster income growth, the picture is less clear. Both education expenditures per 100 workers in 1991 and capital expenditures per 100 workers show little sign of connection with economic growth. The percentage of children enrolled in primary school in 1981 does show a very strong connection with economic growth. But this is a variable only partially under the control of state governments. And before we get too excited about the possibilities in fostering economic growth through increased expenditures on education, notice that the percentage of children enrolled in secondary education in 1981 is not at all a predictor of growth in the 1990s.

We have two other measures of the states' potential success in developing infrastructure, the number of phones per 100 workers in 1985 and the number of kilometers of roads per 100 workers in 1985. Neither of these suggests much role for state actions. Phones per worker are statistically significantly associated with economic growth once we control for initial income. But the association is negative. And the amount of road infrastructure shows no connection. Thus if state policy was responsible for the divergence of incomes after 1991, it had to be through some very subtle measures.

Because the two high-income states in 1991 that did not perform so well in the ensuing years were Punjab and Haryana, which were still fairly agricultural and rural, it is possible to predict the growth rates in the 1990s fairly successfully using such measures as the urbanization rate in 1991 or the manufacturing share of output in 1991. Figure 3.3, for example, shows the income growth rates as a function of the urbanization rates in 1991. But this offers us little insight into the nature of the growth process. The internal variation in economic performance within India suggests that the role of institutional variations, the kind of thing on which economists can give advice, must be limited.

THE EMPLOYMENT RELATIONSHIP

We have seen that the obvious correlates economists have focused on in recent years to explain differences in income growth rates across economies are of

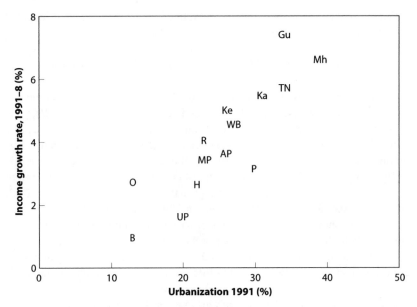

Figure 3.3. Income growth rates, 1991–98, and urbanization rates 1991
Source: Statesforum; Cashin and Sahay 1996

little help in explaining the changes in income per capita across states in post-independence India. We desperately lack a hypotheses that would explain the facts of India's peculiar economic path in the last 150 years. These facts are as follows.

1. A widening of the economic gap between India and the advanced economies up to 1980 that began sometime before 1873.

2. A deindustrialization in response to the industrialization of the advanced economies, even in the period of free trade. Thus by 1912 India was largely a raw material exporter. Why, at least in the era of free trade up till 1914, did India not only get poorer relative to the advanced economies, but also develop a comparative advantage in agriculture?

3. Wide differences in performance by different regions within the same institutional structures both under the British and after independence.

4. Low levels of performance by workers within India, but high levels of performance when these workers relocate to other economies such as Britain and the United States. Further, there is no indication that workers in India in such industries as textiles have any less aptitude than those in the United States in terms of the time taken to perform standard tasks.

The hypothesis we suggest, and it is a speculative one, is the following. The disadvantage India has relative to the advanced economies is in the *employment relationship*. This, to sound almost Marxist, is the bargain by which a worker sells his or her labor power for a set time to an employer. The Industrial Revolution in the West saw not only the development of new technology, but a greater reliance on the employment relationship as a way of producing output. In the preindustrial period most industrial workers were instead subcontractors. They sold output to employers in an arm's-length relationship. The arrival of the steam-powered factories in the 1770s also brought with it a new employment concept, "factory discipline." Under this new mode of employment the employer demanded regularity, punctuality, and sobriety from employees, as opposed to paying by results. The Industrial Revolution also brought a greater division of labor within production processes. Each employee specialized in some element of the process, and a complex hierarchy of employees supervising employees developed (see Clark 1994).

The employment relationship, as those who have participated in it know, is a peculiar one. In particular, fulfillment of the bargain to labor in exchange for wages is difficult to monitor. Workers vary in natural abilities, links between inputs and outputs are uncertain, and it is often too costly or technically impossible to measure individual outputs. Economists traditionally think of the employment relationship as being sustained by monitoring and by incentives the relationship establishes for rational, self-interested workers and employers. But at least as important is the complex human interplay among workers and bosses, and workers and workers, involving pride, notions of fairness, and gift exchanges. As Akerlof (1982) and others have stressed, workers give gifts to employers of more effort than is needed to avoid termination, and employers in return give gifts of higher wages than are needed to retain workers. Economists are tempted to reduce these arrangements to self-enforcing equilibria between completely rational self-interested agents. Such a reduction implies that the employment relationship must work identically in all countries, unless of course multiple equilibria are possible. Differences in relative prices and technology may influence the monitoring employers engage in and the "cheating" workers engage in, but otherwise the employment relationship will be structured similarly across economies and generate the same results everywhere.

But such a reduction seems doomed to fail to capture the nature of the employer-employee exchange. For example, anyone who has purchased services in modern America knows that workers often give gifts to customers that hurt the interests of their firms. A nonscientific survey of our colleagues suggests that many have at some time been the beneficiary of discounts they did not qualify for under a firm's price discrimination scheme, or recipients of more services than they paid the firm for. In this case there is no conceivable material benefit to workers. The relationship sustained between employers and workers, therefore, depends not just on a rational calculus between self-interested agents on the amount of effort to offer, and how much to monitor, but on a general attitude toward gift giving. Here in America we live in a gift-giving society. In most interactions we forebear to be opportunists—we gift the other party with more than we need do, and without benefit to ourselves. One case is letting a person into your lane on a congested highway. There is a cost—you are slowed down slightly—and no conceivable benefit. That is the nonrational calculator element. In part we do this because we have ourselves received many gifts. Others have done the same for us. This gift-giving exchange is an equilibrium, but not in the sense understood by economists. We receive from one and we give to another. Mutual gift giving thus constitutes a self-reinforcing social equilibrium. Its breakdown is also self-reinforcing. Various intermediate equilibria are also possible.

Suppose, however, that the employment relationship works well only in an environment of mutual gift giving. The unobservables in any employment relationship are such that only when the employed forebear to take advantage of the unobservability of outcomes will the relationship work well. Suppose also that in India the cultural equilibrium is for employment not to constitute the mutual exchange of gifts. Workers expect all other workers to take advantage of opportunities to shirk, and they adjust their own behavior accordingly. In this case technologies that rely for their implementation on the employment relationship will be handicapped. Employees will provide little for their wage. They will be protected by the knowledge that any potential replacements will provide little also. If all around you give nothing to the employer, then why should you give? Thus we can have several possible employment regimes, for example one where most workers voluntarily do more than they have to, and another where all workers act opportunistically. Since the mutual gift giving is sustained by observing that others do the same and by receiving gifts yourself, subtle changes in behavior can lead to a move to a very different equilibrium. Workers moving from one environment to another will change their behavior.

Our idea then would be that Indian employers extract little of the labor power they pay for from employees because of employees' unwillingness to give voluntarily what is costly to monitor. The opportunism displayed within the complex hierarchy of employees in modern production enterprises defeats employers.

What are the testable empirical implications of this hypothesis? First, if poor performance by labor in India attaches just to the employment relationship, then we should observe an adaptation to avoid this relationship in favor of self-employment and family employment.

India has seen an extraordinary maintenance in the textile-weaving sector, for example, of handlooms. By the 1830s in England handloom weaving of cottons was largely superseded by power looms in factories, even though the wages of handloom workers were only about half those of factory workers (see Bythell 1969). Yet 170 years later the handloom sector in India is still very large, particularly in cottons. Indeed the output of the handloom sector has grown steadily since 1900, when statistics were first gathered. In 1997, as table 3.9 shows, output of woven cloth from handlooms in India was about ten

TABLE 3.9
Cloth Production in India by Sector, 1997–98 (meters^2)

Year	Mill Production	Decentralized Powerloom Production	Decentralized Handloom Production
1900–1903	483	0	793
1936–39	3,630	0	1,420
1951	3,740		
1973	4,299		
1980–81	4,533	4,802	3,109
1997–98	1,948	20,951	7,603

Sources: Office of the Textile Commissioner 1997, 1998; Mazumdar 1984, 7, 36.

times as great as in 1900. In 1997–98, 25 percent of cloth production in India was still from handlooms.

Cloth in India is produced in three ways: the mill sector, consisting of large powerloom plants, as in the United States; the handloom sector consisting of looms in houses and workshops; and the "powerloom" sector, consisting of workshops of 1 to 50 powerlooms outside the formal regulation of the mill sector. The survival of the handloom industry is often attributed to government protection. Since independence the government has levied excise taxes on mill output while keeping the handloom sector tax-free. Thus even in 1997–98 most fabrics paid an excise duty of 10–20 percent, while handloom cloth was exempted. However, the informal powerloom sector has largely avoided paying these excise taxes (see Misra 1993, 89–119). The tax advantages explain why smaller powerloom operations can outcompete large mills. They do not explain why handlooms can still compete against untaxed powerloom operations. Powerlooms produce 2.5 times the output per hour handlooms do, and one weaver should be able to operate between four and eight powerlooms at a time, judging by labor requirements in Britain and the United States circa 1900. Day wages in the handloom and powerloom sectors are about the same, so powerloom weaving costs per meter of cloth should be 5–10 percent of handloom labor costs. Since capital costs for powerlooms per meter are estimated to be only about 20 percent higher than for handlooms, interest rates would have to be extraordinarily high before handlooms had any cost advantage. But in practice powerlooms in India require much more labor than machine-powered looms in England in the nineteenth century. Powerloom weavers typically supervise only 1.5 looms each (Mazumdar 1984, 93). This drastically reduces the labor cost advantages of the power loom. The high levels of staffing of power looms might be explained by the very low wages of the operatives, but Indian wages now are as high or higher than those in England in the 1830s, when a more primitive powerloom easily swept aside the competition of handlooms. The key factor here is that because of the capital requirements, powerlooms are operated with hired labor, while handlooms are placed in the homes of the workers, and the work is paid for on a piece-rate basis.

Another sector in which to test the hypothesis that the Indian economy works poorly because of the character of the employment relationship is agriculture. It should be structured with more use of land renting and less of wage labor than in European agriculture at a comparable state of mechanization. A second implication is that employment relations will be structured differently. If the relationship works because of mutual gift giving, then employers have an incentive to engage in repeated interactions with the same worker. They will prefer to hire the same workers even where there is no learning specific to the job since then it is easier to establish relationships based on mutual gifts. Employers will avoid casual labor markets where encounters between the same worker and employer would be infrequent. Thus we see in agricultural labor markets in preindustrial England a tendency for workers to be hired year-round by the same employers, and to work for the same employer year after year. Wages were finely calibrated to the individual worker. In modern rural labor markets in India, by contrast, workers are typically hired by employers on a casual, daily basis, with little sign of preference for the same workers by employers. Wage rates paid tend to be standardized, with little adjustment to individual productivities. Seemingly employers gain little from a connection with individual workers (see Datt 1996).

As noted above, this is a somewhat inchoate hypothesis. We are not sure that it is consistent with the details of Indian experience. But it would allow for differences in worker productivity—as created by different social equilibria in gift-giving behavior—within the different states that constitute India. It also implies that workers transferred from one social setting to another will change their behavior accordingly. Further, to explain the widening gap between India and the United States and other Western economies from 1873 to the 1980s, it would point to the increasing importance of the employment relationship in modern production systems.

POLICY IMPLICATIONS

We reach two conclusions above. First, government policy has had little impact on output per capita in India since 1873 because of the importance of differences in the efficiency of use of technology in explaining income disparities in general. And second, there has been a growing regional disparity in incomes per capita within India since at least 1961. In these circumstances what can the government do to foster growth, and in particular to foster growth in states like

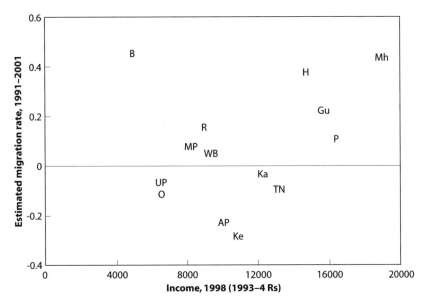

Figure 3.4. Estimated net migration per year, 1991–2001, versus state income per capita, 1998
Source: Census of India

Bihar and Uttar Pradesh, which have seen little impact even from the more rapid growth that began in the 1980s? Within both the United States and Europe movement of people from low-income regions to high-income regions has been an important force in increasing overall economic growth rates. But within India there has been little movement of people towards the higher-income states despite the very large disparities in income that emerged in the 1990s. Figure 3.4 shows the estimated net migration rate per year for the 14 major Indian states from 1991 to 2001 as a percentage of 1991 population as a function of state domestic income per capita in 1998. The net migration rate was estimated from the difference between actual populations in 2001 and those projected from populations in 1991 and state birth and death rates. With the notable exception of Bihar the states with high incomes in 1998 were clearly net recipients of migrants, while those with low incomes were net losers of people. But migration rates were very modest compared to the changes in population occurring through natural increase. Maharashtra, for example, now the richest Indian state, had a net gain of only 0.44 percent of the population in each year. But overall population growth in Maharashtra was about 2 percent per year, so that migration was a small factor in population change. Similarly outmigration from desperately poor Uttar Pradesh was estimated at only—0.07 percent per year, compared to a natural rate of population increase of 2.8 percent per year.

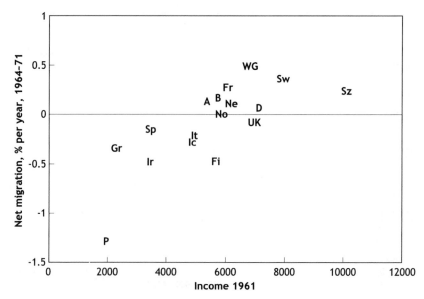

Figure 3.5. European net migration per year, 1964–71, versus national income per capita, 1961. A, Austria, B, Belgium, D, Denmark, Fi, Finland, Fr, France, WG, West Germany, Gr, Greece, Ic, Iceland, Ir, Ireland, It, Italy, Ne, Netherlands, No, Norway, P, Portugal, Sp, Spain, Sw, Sweden, Sz, Switzerland, UK, United Kingdom.
Source: United Nations 1991

These migration rates between Indian states, where there is no legal imped-iment to migration, are very modest compared even to migration rates across European nations in the 1960s, when there were significant legal impediments in many cases, and also if anything greater language barriers. Figure 3.5 shows net annual migration rates for non-Communist Europe in 1964–71 compared to income per capita in 1961. These net migration rates also include, however, migration to the Americas and Australasia. By 1970 after 20 years of con-strained postwar migration into Germany and France about 7 percent of the work-force was foreign-born in each country (Faini, de Melo, and Zimmermann 1999). Hatton and Williamson (1998) estimate that between 1870 and 1913 Europe lost 13 percent of its population through emigration to the New World, despite the transoceanic nature of this migration.

Within the United States, where the legal and language barriers do not exist, net migration rates between states are even higher. Figure 3.6 shows net annual internal migration rates for U.S. states for the years 1900–1999 compared to average annual pay for those employed in 1997 in dollars. For comparison, the

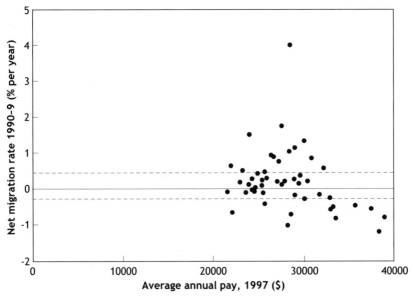

Figure 3.6. Net internal migration rates, 1990s, U.S. states
Source: U.S. Census Bureau

limits of state net migration rates in India in the 1990s are also shown. U.S. domestic net migration rates are many times greater than those in India, though the comparison may be influenced by the smaller average size of U.S. states. Interestingly U.S. migration has little on its face to do with differences in wage income per capita across states. The earnings reported here, however, make no allowance for differences in living costs across states. In addition, international migration into U.S. states is quantitatively important, and many of the high-income states losing internal migrants, such as California, New Jersey, and New York, are substantial net recipients of international migrants. Finally there is a significant component of life-cycle migration of the elderly in the United States to high-amenity states for retirement purposes. Barro and Sala-i-Martin (1991) estimate the relationship between relative state income and in-migration in the 1980s, controlling for some of these factors. They find that a 10 percent increase in a state's per capita income leads to a 0.26 percentage point increase in net migration per year. That responsiveness of migration to economic opportunity transferred to India would imply that a state like Maharashtra with an income per capita in 1998 85 percent greater than the rest of India would experience net migration equivalent to 2.2 percent of its population per year, five times the actual rate for the 1990s. Bihar equivalently, with 42 percent of the average income of the rest of India, would be losing about 1.5 percent of its population per year.[12] Had even 1 percent of the population of the lowest-income states in India, Bihar, Uttar Pradesh, and Orissa, moved to the highest-income states in each year in the 1990s the growth rate of income per capita in India would have been increased by 0.3 percent per year.[13] This is not huge, but it is a more substantial boost to income growth rates than any other feasible action Indian policymakers might take.

TABLE 3.A1
Data Sources Used in Regression Analysis

Variable	Source
State GDP per capita, 1991–92 and 1998–99	www.statesforum.org
Annual rate of population growth, 1961–91 and 1990–97	Indian Central Statistical Office, Basic Statistics (1980). www.censusindia.net
Adult literacy, 1991	www.censusindia.net
Percentage of 5- to 14-year olds enrolled in primary school	A Social and Economic Atlas of India 1987
Percentage of 10 to 19 year olds enrolled in secondary school	A Social and Economic Atlas of India 1987
Taxes as a share of state GDP, 1990–98	www.statesforum.org
Public capital expenditures per 100 workers, 1990–98[a]	www.statesforum.org; A Social and Economic Atlas of India 1987
Education expenditures per 100 workers, 1990–98[a]	www.statesforum.org; A Social and Economic Atlas of India 1987
Phones, km. Roads, and telephones per 100 workers, 1985	A Social and Economic Atlas of India 1987
Urbanization, 1961 and 1991	Indian Central Statistical Office, Basic Statistics (1980). www.censusindia.net

[a] Workers are defined as those 15 to 59 participating in the labor force.

[12] These rates are calculated for cases where the income disparities between states are much less than in India. The responsiveness in the United States to a change from a 50 percent income premium to a 60 percent premium might well be much greater than going from a 10 percent premium to a 20 percent premium.

[13] Assuming that the migration did not affect per capita incomes in the sending and receiving states. But this in the light of historical evidence seems a reasonable assumption.

REFERENCES

Data on nominal and real GDP for 14 of the major Indian states as well as state government capital and regular expenditure and revenue sources can be found at www. statesforum.org.

Abler, David G., and Jayanta Das. 1998. "The Determinants of the Speed of Convergence: The Case of India." *Applied Economics* 30, no. 12: 1595–1602.

Aiyar, Shekhar. 2001. "Growth Theory and Convergence across Indian States: A Panel Study." In *India at the Crossroads,* ed. Tim Callen, Patricia Reynolds, and Christopher Towe. Washington, D.C.: International Monetary Fund.

Akerlof, George A. 1982. "Labor Contracts as Partial Gift Exchange." *Quarterly Journal of Economics* 97, no. 4: 543–69.

Balke, Nathan S., and Robert J. Gordon. 1992. "The Estimation of Prewar Gross National Product: Methodology and New Evidence." *Journal of Political Economy* 97, no. 1: 38–92.

Barro, Robert J., and Xavier Sala-i-Martin. 1991. "Convergence across States and Regions." *Brookings Papers on Economic Activity* 1991, no. 1: 107–82.

———. 1992. "Convergence." *Journal of Political Economy* 100, no. 2: 223–51.

Bruland, Kristine. 1989. *British Technology and European Industrialization: The Norwegian Textile Industry in the Mid Nineteenth Century.* Cambridge: Cambridge University Press.

Bythell, Duncan. 1969. *The Handloom Weavers: A Study in the English Cotton Industry during the Industrial Revolution.* Cambridge: Cambridge University Press.

Cashin, Paul, and Ratna Sahay. 1996. "Internal Migration, Center-State Grants, and Economic Growth in the States of India." *IMF Staff Papers* 43, no. 1: 123–71.

Central Statistical Organisation. 1980. Dept. of Statistics, Ministry of Planning. *Basic Statistics Relating to the Indian Economy, 1950–51 to 1978–79.* Delhi.

Clark, Gregory. 1987. "Why Isn't the Whole World Developed? Lessons from the Cotton Mills." *Journal of Economic History* 47, no. 1: 141–73.

———. 1994. "Factory Discipline." *Journal of Economic History* 54, no. 1: 128–63.

———. 1998. "Land Hunger: Land as a Commodity and as a Status Good in England, 1500–1910." *Explorations in Economic History* 35, no. 1: 59–82.

Collins, William J. 1999. "Labor Mobility, Market Integration, and Wage Convergence in Late 19th Century India." *Explorations in Economic History* 36, no. 3: 246–77.

Cotton Spinning Productivity Team. 1951. *Cotton Spinning.* London: Anglo-American Council on Productivity.

Datt, Gaurav. 1996. *Bargaining Power, Wages, and Employment: An Analysis of Agricultural Labor Markets in India.* Thousand Oaks, Calif.: Sage.

Datta, Krishna Lal. 1914. *Report on the Enquiry into the Rise of Prices in India.* Calcutta: Superintendent of Government Printing.

DeLong, J. Bradford. 2003. "India since Independence: An Analytic Growth Narrative." In this volume.

Démurger, Sylvie. 2001. "Infrastructure Development and Economic Growth: An Explanation for Regional Disparities in China?" *Journal of Comparative Economics* 29: 95–117.

Doraiswamy, Indra. 1983. "Scope for Increasing Productivity in Spinning Mills." In *Resume of Papers, Twenty Fourth Technological Conference.* Ahmedabad Textile Industry Research Association, Bombay Textile Research Association, North India Textile Industry Research Association, and South India Textile Industry Research Association.

Easterly, William, and Ross Levine. 2000. "It's Not Factor Accumulation: Stylized Facts and Growth Models." World Bank and University of Minnesota. Typescript.

Economic Report of the President. 2001. Washington, D.C.: Government Printing Office.

Edelstein, Michael. 1982. *Overseas Investment in the Age of High Imperialism: The United Kingdom, 1850–1914.* New York: Columbia University Press.

Faini, Riccardo, Jaime de Melo, and Klaus F. Zimmermann, eds. 1999. *Migration: The Controversies and the Evidence.* Cambridge: Cambridge University Press.

Feinstein, C. H. 1972. *National Income, Expenditure, and Output of the United Kingdom, 1855–1965.* Cambridge: Cambridge University Press.

Goldsmith, Raymond. 1983. *The Financial Development of India, 1860–1977.* New Haven: Yale University Press.

Hatton, Timothy J., and Jeffrey G. Williamson. 1998. *The Age of Mass Migration.* Oxford: Oxford University Press.

Heston, Alan. 1983. "National Income." In *The Cambridge Economic History of India,* ed. Dharma Kumar and Meghnad Desai, vol. 2. Cambridge: Cambridge University Press.

Hurd, John. 1982. "Railways." In *The Cambridge Economic History of India,* ed. Dharma Kumar and Meghnad Desai, vol. 2. Cambridge: Cambridge University Press.

Lal, Deepak. 1988. "Trends in Real Wages in Rural India: 1880–1980." In *Rural Poverty in South Asia,* ed. T. N. Srinivasan and Pranab K. Bardhan. New York: Columbia University Press.

Mazumdar, Dipak. 1984. "The Issue of Small versus Large in the Indian Textile Industry: An Analytical and Historical Survey." World Bank Staff Working Paper No. 645, Washington, D.C.

Misra, Sanjiv. 1993. *India's Textile Sector: A Policy Analysis.* New Delhi: Sage.

Natarajan, B. 1949. *An Essay on National Income and Expenditure in India.* Madras: Economic Advisor to the Government of Madras.

Office of the Textile Commissioner, Mumbai. 1997. *Compendium of Textile Statistics, 1997.* Mumbai.

———. 1998. *Basic Textile Statistics for 1997–8.* Mumbai.

Prados de la Escosura, Leandro. 2000. "International Comparisons of Real Product, 1820–1990: An Alternative Data Set." *Explorations in Economic History* 37, no. 1: 1–41.

Ratnam, T. V., and R. Rajamanickam. 1980. "Productivity in Spinning: Growth and Prospects." In *Resume of Papers, Twenty First Technological Conference.* Ahmedabad Textile Industry Research Association, Bombay Textile Research Association, and South India Textile Industry Research Association.

Shirras, G. Findlay. 1923. *Report of an Enquiry into the Wages and Hours of Labour in the Cotton Mill Industry.* Bombay: Labour Office, Government of Bombay.

Southern India Textile Research Association (SITRA). 1990. "Doffing Boy Productivity in Ring Spinning." *SITRA Focus* 8, no. 3.

Summers, Robert, and Alan Heston. 1991. "The Penn World Table (Mark 5): An Expanded Set of International Comparisons." *Quarterly Journal of Economics* 106, no. 2: 327–68.

Textile Council. 1969. *Cotton and Allied Textiles.* Manchester.

A Social and Economic Atlas of India. 1987. Delhi: Oxford University Press.

United Nations. 1991. Dept. of International Economic and Social Affairs, Statistical Office. *Demographic Yearbook, 1989.* New York.

Wolcott, Susan, and Gregory Clark. 1999. "Why Nations Fail: Managerial Decisions and Performance in Indian Cotton Textiles, 1890–1938." *Journal of Economic History* 59, no. 2: 397–423.

CHAPTER 4

An African Success Story

BOTSWANA

DARON ACEMOGLU **SIMON JOHNSON**
JAMES A. ROBINSON

DESPITE some success stories in the 1960s and early 1970s, Africa is poor and getting poorer.[1] There is also an almost universally pessimistic consensus about its economic prospects. This consensus started to emerge in recent empirical work on the determinants of growth with Barro's (1991) discovery of a negative "African Dummy" and was summed up by Easterly and Levine's (1997) title, "Africa's Growth Tragedy." Table 4.1 collects some familiar comparative evidence on Africa's economic performance. The average sub-Saharan African country is poorer than the average low-income country and getting poorer. Indeed, the average growth rate has been negative since 1965, and there is approximately a 35-fold difference between the per capita income level of the average sub-Saharan country and the United States.

Against this background of poor performance, one African country, Botswana, has performed not only well, but better than any other country in the world in the last 35 years. In table 4.2 we examine the facts about Botswana in both an African and more general context. Botswana had a PPP-adjusted income per capita of $5,796 in 1998, almost four times the African average, and between 1965 and 1998, it grew at an annual rate of 7.7 percent.

Why has Botswana been so successful? Botswana did not start out with favorable initial conditions at independence. When the British left, there were 12 kilometers of paved road, 22 Batswana who had graduated from university and 100

We are indebted to many people who gave generously of their time and expert knowledge to help us undertake this project. Our greatest debt is to Clark Leith who helped open many doors in Gaborone and who provided many helpful suggestions. We also learned from discussions with Chris Adam, Michael Kevane, René Lemarchand, David Leonard, Steven Lewis Jr., Robert Price. In Gaborone we would like to thank Ken Good, Charles Harvey, Keith Jefferis, Zibani Maundeni, Mpho Molomo, Clara Olson, Neil Parsons, and Thomas Tlou for their patient and expert advice.

[1] Henceforth *Africa* always refers to sub-Saharan Africa.

TABLE 4.1

Comparative Development

	GDP per Capita, 1998 (U.S. $)	GDP per Capita, 1998 (PPP $)	Average Growth Rate GDP per Capita 1965–98	% Labor Force in Agriculture, 1990	% Total Population Urban, 1998	Primary Enrollment Rate, 1997	Secondary Enrollment Rate, 1997	Life Expectancy at Birth, 1997
World	4,890	6,300	1.4	49	46	87.6	65.4	66.7
Sub-Saharan Africa	510	1,440	-0.3	68	33	56.2	41.4	48.9
Low-income Countries[a]	520	2,170	3.7	68	30	60.4	31.2	51.7
East Asia and Pacific[b]	990	3,280	5.7	68	34	97.8	58.3	70.0
Latin America and Caribbean	3,860	6,340	1.3	25	75	93.3	65.3	69.5

Sources: Columns 1–5, World Development Indicators 2000, Columns 6–8 Human Development Report 1999.

[a] In this case low income is the LDCs.
[b] Southeast Asia and Pacific.

TABLE 4.2
Botswana in Comparative Perspective

	GDP per Capita, 1998 (U.S. $)	GDP per Capita, 1998 (PPP $)	Average Growth Rate of GDP per Capita 1965–98	% Labor Force in Agriculture, 1990	% Total Population Urban, 1970	% Total Population Urban, 1998	Primary Enrollment Rate, 1997	Secondary Enrollment Rate, 1997	Life Expectancy at Birth, 1997
Botswana	3,070	5,796	7.7	46	8	49	80	89	47
Zaire	110	733	-3.8	68	30	30	58	37	51
Côte d'Ivoire	700	1,484	-0.8	60	27	45	58	34	47
Ethiopia	100	566	-0.5	86	9	17	35	25	43
Ghana	390	1,735	-0.8	59	29	37	43		60
Lesotho	570	2,194	3.1	40	9	26	68	73	56
Zambia	330	678	-2.0	75	30	39	72	42	40
South Korea	8,600	13,286	6.6	18	41	80	99	99	72
Mauritius	3,730	8,236	3.8	17	42	41	96	68	71
Singapore	30,170	25,295	6.4	0	100	100	91	75	77

Sources: Columns 1–6, World Development Indicators 2000; columns 7–9, Human Development Report 1999.

from secondary school.[2] Botswana is a predominantly tropical, landlocked country (which many economists see as a disadvantage, e.g., Bloom and Sachs 1998). It is true that diamonds have been important for growth in Botswana, and currently account for around 40 percent of the country's output. Yet in many other countries, natural-resource abundance appears to be a curse rather than a blessing (e.g., Sachs and Warner 1995). So how did Botswana do it?

There is almost complete agreement that Botswana achieved this spectacular growth performance because it adopted good policies.[3] The basic system of law and contract worked reasonably well. State and private predation have been quite limited. The large revenues from diamonds have not induced domestic political instability or conflict over control of this resource. The government sustained the minimal public service structure that it inherited from the British and developed it into a meritocratic, relatively noncorrupt and efficient bureaucracy. The parastatal sector has never been large and, to the extent that it has existed, has faced hard budget constraints. Although there was a government marketing board, usually an institution employed by the urban interests to exploit farmers (e.g., Bates 1981), in Botswana the board was not used to extract resources from the rural sector. Moreover, the government invested heavily in infrastructure, education, and health. Fiscal policy has been prudent in the extreme and the exchange rate has remained closely tied to fundamentals.

Not everything in Botswana is rosy. Though the statistics are not fully reliable, Botswana has one of the highest adult incidences of AIDS in the world with perhaps 25–30 percent of adults being HIV positive.[4] This probably represents, above else, a serious public policy failure. Although economic growth has been rapid, inequality is remarkably high and has not decreased. The unemployment rate, especially of migrant workers from rural areas, is very high. Moreover, while Botswana has had freely contested democratic elections since independence, one party has always won, and there has never been a credible opposition. There is also evidence that the government has treated minorities such as the San quite ruthlessly and has what some describe as "soft authoritarian" tendencies (for example, Good 1997). It therefore remains to be seen whether Botswana's institutions will continue to be effective in fostering future economic growth, as well as deal with unemployment and persistent inequality, and most importantly, with the demographic crisis created by the AIDS epidemic. Nevertheless, despite these important caveats, the evidence suggests that there is something distinctly successful about Botswana's economic policy.

---

[2] There was no university in Botswana at independence, and most of those who acquired even a secondary education were the children of chiefs who attended schools for Africans in South Africa such as the famous Fort Hare College, where Nelson Mandela also studied.

[3] See the comprehensive survey of the evidence in Harvey and Lewis 1990; Good 1992; and Leith 2000; or in the earlier book by Colclough and McCarthy (1980).

[4] See, for example, the WHO's assessment: http://www.who.int/emc-hiv/fact_sheets/pdfs/botswana_EN.pdf, September 4, 2002.

In this chapter, we argue that Botswana's good economic policies, and therefore its economic success, reflect its institutions, or what we call *institutions of private property* (Acemoglu, Johnson, and Robinson 2001b). Such institutions protect the property rights of actual and potential investors, provide political stability, and ensure that the political elites are constrained by the political system and the participation of a broad cross-section of the society.

The puzzle is why Botswana ended up with such good institutions, especially when compared with other African countries. There is relatively little research on this topic, and a satisfactory answer requires a detailed analysis of Botswana's history and comparison with other African experiences. Although we are not Africanists, we undertake a preliminary attempt at such a study to generate some conjectures about the relative success of Botswana in building institutions of private property.

Our conjecture is that Botswana's institutions reflect a combination of factors. These include tribal institutions that encouraged broad-based participation and constraints on political leaders during the precolonial period; only limited effect of British colonization on these precolonial institutions because of the peripheral nature of Botswana to the British Empire; the fact that upon independence, the most important rural interests, chiefs and cattle owners, were politically powerful; the income from diamonds, which generated enough rents for the main political actors to increase the opportunity cost of further rent seeking; and finally, a number of important and farsighted decisions by the post-independence political leaders, in particular Seretse Khama and Quett Masire.

Because many of these factors are difficult to measure, and even more difficult to compare across countries, we are unable to test our conjecture using statistical methods. Nevertheless, both our reading of Botswana's history and our comparison of Botswana with a number of other African countries are consistent with this conjecture.

The chapter proceeds as follows. In the next section, we outline what we mean by good institutions and provide statistical evidence that the relative success of Botswana appears to be related to its institutions. We also undertake a brief analysis of the statistical determinants of these institutions, which reiterates the conclusion that the standard structural features do not account well for why Botswana ended up with relatively good institutions. This motivates our more detailed look at Botswana's political history. In section 2, we provide an outline of Botswana's political and economic history, showing how the current state emerged out of the experiences of both its precolonial past and British colonialism. In the light of this history, in section 3 we provide an analysis of the exceptionality of Botswana. It is difficult to assess this explanation without putting it into a comparative context, and we attempt to do this in section 4, where we compare the hypotheses about Botswana with the experiences of some other African countries. Section 5 concludes.

1. BOTSWANA'S ECONOMIC SUCCESS AND INSTITUTIONS

There is almost complete consensus that Botswana achieved rapid growth because it managed to adopt good policies. Diamonds no doubt helped in the rapid
growth. Yet it is striking that, contrary to other African countries with abundant
natural resources, such as Angola, Zaire (Congo), Sierra Leone, or Nigeria, in
Botswana there has been no civil war or intense infighting to control the revenues from diamonds.

What explains the good economic policies pursued in Botswana? After all,
in the rest of Africa, good economics is often bad politics—that is, good economic policies often do not generate enough rents for politicians, or they make
it more likely that the government will be overthrown. In contrast, in Botswana,
the government appears to have pursued relatively sound economic policies, and
there is little evidence of infighting across different tribes or groups for control
of the state apparatus.

Therefore, in Botswana good economics appears to have been good politics.
Why? It is useful to first consider a number of possible explanations that do not
appear to explain why good policies were chosen.

First, perhaps policies have been better in Botswana because it is more
"equal" (Alesina and Rodrik 1994; Persson and Tabellini 1994; Benabou
2000)? The difficulty with this explanation is that inequality, both of assets (primarily cattle) and income, is extremely high in Botswana, indeed as high as in
South Africa and on a par with Latin American countries such as Brazil and
Colombia. Comprehensive data on inequality in Botswana was collected in
1985–86 and 1993–94 and suggest a Gini coefficient of 0.56 and 0.54 for the
two periods.[5]

Second, perhaps good economic policies are just a reflection of the fact that
government intervention in Botswana has been limited (e.g., Krueger 1993)?
The actual circumstances contradict this suggestion as well, for there has been
massive intervention in the economy, with detailed planning, and central government expenditure is now around 40 percent of GDP, well above average for
Africa.

Institutions

The most plausible cause of relatively good economic policies therefore appears
to be that the underlying institutions in Botswana, both political and economic,

---

[5] This inequality of income appears to stem importantly from the severe inequality in the ownership of cattle (see Leith 2000, 29–30, table 7).

are "good." What do we mean by good institutions? Here we follow our earlier paper, Acemoglu, Johnson, and Robinson 2001b, and define good institutions as corresponding to a social organization that ensures that a broad cross-section of the society has *effective property rights*.[6] We refer to this cluster as *institutions of private property*. Such institutions contrast with extractive institutions, where the majority of the population faces a high risk of expropriation by the government, the ruling elite, or other agents.

Two requirements are implicit in our definition of institutions of private property. First, institutions should provide secure property rights, so that those with productive opportunities expect to receive returns from their investments. The second requirement is embedded in our emphasis on an opportunity to invest for "a broad cross-section of the society." A society in which a very small fraction of the population, for example a class of landowners, holds all the wealth and political power is not the ideal environment for investment, even if the property rights of this elite are secure. In such a society, many of the agents with investment opportunities and the entrepreneurial human capital may be those without the effective property rights protection. In particular, the concentration of political and social power in the hands of a small elite implies that the majority of the population does not have secure property rights, and probably risks being *held up* by the powerful elite.

Institutions of private property, therefore, require effective property rights for a large segment of the society, against both state expropriation and predation by private agents; relative political stability to ensure continuity in these property rights; and effective constraints on rulers and political elites to limit arbitrary and extractive behavior.

Institutions and Economic Performance

Do institutions of private property matter for economic performance? Although it is difficult to map our notions of institutions of private property to empirical measures, in Acemoglu, Johnson, and Robinson 2001a, 2001b, we used two plausible ones: protection against expropriation risk between 1985 and 1995 from Political and Risk Services, which approximates how secure property rights are, and constraints on the executive from Gurr's Polity IV data set, which can be thought of as a proxy for how concentrated power is in the hands of ruling

---

[6] Clearly enforcement of property rights may be viewed as yet another policy rather than a measure of underlying institutions. By institutions of private property, we do not simply mean the policy of enforcing property rights, but a set (cluster) of institutions that will support and ensure the enforcement of property rights.

groups. We documented that both of these measures are strongly correlated with economic performance, in particular, with income per capita today.

But such correlation is difficult to interpret. It is quite likely that rich economies choose or can afford better institutions. Economies that are different for a variety of reasons will also differ both in their institutions and in their income per capita. Therefore, to demonstrate that institutions are a first-order determinant of economic performance, we need a source of exogenous variation in institutions.

In Acemoglu, Johnson, and Robinson 2001a, we exploited differences in the mortality rates faced by European colonialists to estimate the effect of institutions on economic performance. We documented that Europeans adopted very different colonization policies in different colonies, with different associated institutions. The choice of colonization strategy was in turn at least partly determined by whether Europeans could settle in the colony. In places where Europeans faced high mortality rates, they could not settle, and they were more likely to set up extractive institutions. These early institutions have persisted to the present.

Exploiting differences in mortality rates faced by soldiers, bishops, and sailors in the colonies as an instrument for current institutions, we estimated large effects of institutions on income per capita. It is especially noteworthy that our estimates imply that changes in institutions can close as much as three-quarters of the income gap between the nations with the best institutions and worst institutions. Moreover, we found that once we control for the effect of institutions, countries in Africa do not have lower incomes. Therefore, our institutional hypothesis could account both for a large fraction of the income differences across countries and for why most African nations are so poor relative to the rest of the world.

Can this institutional hypothesis also explain the success of Botswana? Although we did not have data for settler mortality for Botswana in Acemoglu, Johnson, and Robinson 2001a, we believe the answer is yes. To see why, note that the baseline Instrumental Variables (IV) estimate in Acemoglu, Johnson, and Robinson 2001a implies that

Log GDP1995 = 1.91 + 0.94*Protection Against Expropriation Risk.

We can then investigate whether, given this predicted relationship between property rights enforcement and income, Botswana is an outlier. It turns out that the answer is no. Botswana is rich because it has good institutions. Figure 4.1 shows a scatter plot of income per capita in 1995 among former European colonies against the protection against expropriation risk measure, with the above empirical relationship plotted as a solid line. Botswana is very close to the predicted relationship, showing that its economic success largely reflects

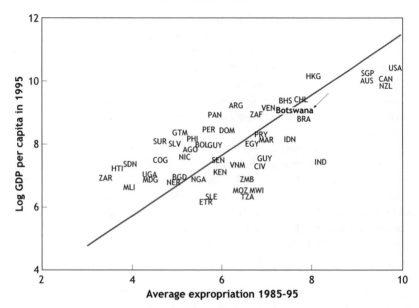

Figure 4.1. Average expropriation, 1985–95 vs. log GDP per capita in 1995 (KM: these are the two axes for the figure, which has no title.)
Note: See table 4.A1 for data.

its good institutions (and by extension, this success is not an immediate consequence of its natural-resource wealth).

Similarly, the IV estimate of the relationship between income and institutions using the constraints of the executive measure for 1990 is

Log GDP1995 = 5.76 + 0.56*Constraints on the Executive 1990.

Figure 4.2 shows this predicted relationship and Botswana's position. Botswana is now not on the regression line, but also not too far from it.

The cross-country evidence is therefore consistent with the idea that Botswana was successful because it has good institutions. But, at some level, this is only a proximate answer to the question of why Botswana is so successful. The underlying, deeper question is why Botswana has such good institutions, especially compared to other countries in Africa.

Explaining Botswana's Institutions

Why does Botswana have such good institutions? In table 4.3, we make a first attempt to answer this question by looking at whether standard structural variables provide an explanation.

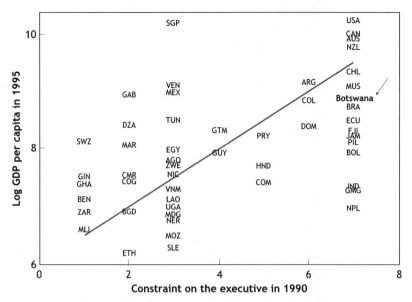

Figure 4.2. Constraint on the executive in 1990 vs. log GDP per capita in 1995. (KM: these are the two axes for the figure, which has no title.)
Note: See table 4.A1 for data.

Following the hypothesis in Acemoglu, Johnson, and Robinson 2001a, we look at whether colonial origins, in particular, patterns of European settlements, account for good institutions in Botswana (the comparison group being all countries colonized by European powers).[7] We also follow Acemoglu, Johnson, and Robinson 2001b and look at the effect of population density. The argument advanced in that paper is that a large population made it profitable for the Europeans to set up extractive institutions, with political power concentrated in the hands of a small elite. High population density, for example, meant a large supply of labor that the Europeans could force to work in mines or plantations, or tax heavily by taking over existing tribute systems. Furthermore, high population density made it less attractive for Europeans to settle and because, as argued above, Europeans were more likely to set up extractive institutions in places they did not settle, high population density also made the development of institutions of private property less likely.

In this table, we also control for potential determinants of institutional differences that other authors have emphasized, including geographic characteristics of Botswana (as implied by the emphasis in Bloom and Sachs 1998),

_____

[7] We cannot look at settler mortality directly since, as we noted above, we do not have data for settler mortality for Botswana.

TABLE 4.3
Determinants of Institutions

	All Former Colonies (1)	All Former Colonies (2)	All Former Colonies (3)	All Former Colonies (4)	All Former Colonies (5)	All Former Colonies (6)	All Former Colonies (7)	All Former Colonies (8)	All Former Colonies (9)	All Former Colonies (10)
	Panel A: Dependent Variable Is Constraint on the Executive in 1970					Panel B: Dependent Variable Is Constraint on the Executive in 1990				
Botswana dummy	4.85 (1.88)	5.56 (1.95)	5.66 (1.96)	5.41 (1.98)	5.57 (2.00)	4.12 (1.90)	4.43 (1.98)	5.01 (1.72)	5.30 (1.73)	5.68 (1.70)
European settlements in 1900	0.04 (0.01)	0.05 (0.01)	0.05 (0.01)	0.04 (0.02)	0.04 (0.02)	0.06 (0.01)	0.06 (0.01)	0.04 (0.01)	0.05 (0.01)	0.05 (0.01)
Log population density in 1500		0.23 (0.17)	0.22 (0.17)	0.19 (0.18)	0.21 (0.18)		0.10 (0.18)	0.05 (0.15)	0.08 (0.15)	0.13 (0.15)
Africa dummy			-0.38 (0.47)	-0.41 (0.47)	-0.57 (0.52)			-2.15 (0.41)	-2.12 (0.41)	-2.49 (0.44)
Latitude				1.70 (2.03)	2.00 (2.09)				-1.98 (1.77)	-1.17 (1.78)
Ethnolinguistic fragmentation					0.60 (0.80)					1.46 (0.68)
R^2	0.24	0.26	0.27	0.27	0.28	0.36	0.37	0.53	0.54	0.56
Number of observations	82	82	82	82	82	83	83	83	83	83

Panel C: Dependent Variable Is Constraint on the Executive in First Year of Independence

Years since independence	-0.02 (0.004)	-0.02 (0.004)	-0.03 (0.005)	-0.03 (0.005)	-0.03 (0.005)
Botswana dummy	3.08 (2.09)	3.25 (2.19)	3.67 (2.10)	3.52 (2.13)	3.36 (2.15)
European settlements in 1900	0.05 (0.01)	0.05 (0.02)	0.04 (0.02)	0.04 (0.02)	0.04 (0.01)
Log population density in 1500		0.06 (0.20)	0.07 (0.19)	0.05 (0.19)	0.04 (0.19)
Africa dummy			-1.59 (0.55)	-1.63 (0.56)	-1.51 (0.59)
Latitude				1.07 (2.21)	0.80 (2.25)
Ethnolinguistic fragmentation					-0.60 (0.87)
R^2	0.26	0.26	0.33	0.33	0.34
Number of observations	83	83	83	83	83

Panel D: Dependent Variable Is Average Protection against Expropriation Risk, 1985–95

Years since independence					
Botswana dummy	1.82 (1.26)	1.64 (1.32)	1.84 (1.33)	1.60 (1.36)	1.86 (0.14)
European settlements in 1900	0.03 (0.01)	0.03 (0.01)	0.03 (0.01)	0.02 (0.01)	0.02 (0.01)
Log population density in 1500		-0.06 (0.12)	-0.05 (0.12)	-0.08 (0.13)	-0.05 (0.13)
Africa dummy			-0.40 (0.33)	-0.43 (0.33)	-0.73 (0.39)
Latitude				1.30 (1.57)	1.98 (1.61)
Ethnolinguistic fragmentation					0.91 (0.61)
R^2	0.31	0.31	0.32	0.33	0.35
Number of observations	74	74	74	74	74

Note: OLS regressions. Dependent variable is institutions, with precise measure indicated at the head of each panel (from Polity III and Political Risk Services). Independent variables are a dummy for Botswana, European population as a percentage of total population in 1900, the log of population density in 1500, a dummy for Africa, latitude (the absolute value of distance from the equator), and ethnolinguistic fragmentation. For detailed sources and descriptions see appendix table 1 in Acemoglu, Johnson, and Robinson 2000, except for population density, for which see Acemoglu, Johnson, and Robinson 2001.

ethnolinguistic fragmentation (as emphasized by Easterly and Levine 1997), and an Africa dummy that is often found to be significant in this type of regression.

We use four different measures of institutions: protection against expropriation risk from Political and Risk Services and constraints on the executive in 1990, 1970, and in the first year of independence, from Gurr's Polity IV data set. In all specifications, we report the Botswana dummy. If this dummy is significant, it implies that Botswana is an outlier in this relationship. In different columns, we control for a variety of factors that could, directly or indirectly, influence institutions. In all specifications, the Botswana dummy is economically large, and in most of them it is statistically significant. For example, the coefficient of 4.85 on the Botswana dummy in column 1 of panel A in table 4.3 is highly significant and corresponds to a difference in protection against expropriation risk greater than the difference between the United States and Ethiopia or Sierra Leone.

This result implies that aggregate cross-country variables do not adequately explain why Botswana has relatively good institutions. We therefore need a more detailed analysis of the case of Botswana to develop different conjectures or explanations.

2. A BRIEF POLITICAL HISTORY OF BOTSWANA

Botswana is a landlocked country surrounded to the south by the Republic of South Africa, to the west and north by Namibia, and to the east by Zimbabwe. It borders Zambia at a single point (Kazungula on the Zambezi River) in the northeast. It comprises 220,000 square miles (570,000 square kilometers) about the size of France, Kenya, or Texas. The environment is mostly arid, and 84 percent of the country is Kalahari sand, supporting thornbush savanna vegetation. Eighty percent of the population lives in a long strip in the east of the country along the line of rail that links South Africa with Zimbabwe and was originally built by Cecil Rhodes's British South Africa Company (BSAC). Most of the usable arable land is here. About 4 percent of all the land can be easily cultivated; the bulk of it, including the desert areas, is rangeland only suitable for seasonal grazing (see Parson 1984, 4).

The ancestors of the modern Tswana tribes[8] migrated into the area of modern-day Botswana[9] in the eighteenth century from the southeast (modern South Africa) and are closely related to the Basotho of modern-day Lesotho (anthro-

---

[8] There are eight main Tswana tribes: the Bangwato (Seretse Khama's tribe), Batawana, Bangwaketse, Bakwena, Balete, Bakgatla, Barolong, and Batlokwa. A tribe is known as a *merafe*.

[9] The country is Botswana, which comes from the root word *Tswana*. A single Tswana person is a *Motswana*, two or more *Batswana*. Tswana language and culture is referred to as *Setswana*.

pologists refer to Tswana-Sotho language and culture).[10] They conquered the indigenous San and other tribes, who were basically amalgamated into the Tswana. By 1800 several related Tswana societies were established, and over time new ones were created as groups broke away from the existing ones. For instance, the Bangwato resulted from a split in the Bakwena, and the Batawana was created as a result of a split in the Bangwato.

Several features of Tswana political and economic organization stand out.[11] The chief was the central political figure in these societies with power to allocate land for grazing crops and for residences. His authority was exercised through a hierarchy of relatives and officials and ward headmen. A special type of ward was for outsiders whom the Tswana amalgamated into their tribal structures. Alongside this hierarchy was a series of public forums. The *kgotla* was an assembly of adult males in which issues of public interest were discussed. Both wards and the whole society itself had *kgotlas*. Even though they were supposed to be advisory, they seem to have been an effective way for commoners to criticize the king. They also were the venue where the king heard court cases and law was dispensed.

Although one might imagine that these features were characteristic of all precolonial African societies, this is not the case. Schapera (1967, 64) noted that "the governmental system also provides for consultation between the chief and some form of popular assembly; this feature is far more characteristic of Sotho, and especially Tswana, than any other Bantu." He shows that "among the Sotho, and especially Tswana, almost all matters of public concern are discussed finally at a popular assembly . . . which ordinary tribesmen are also expected to attend . . . Tribal assemblies are also known among Nguni and Tsonga . . . but they are usually held only on great ceremonial occasions. Consequently they are not nearly as important in the system of government, there is seldom any public discussion of policy" (43–44).[12]

While land was collectively owned, cattle were privately owned, and the chief and aristocracy were large owners. "Herds were divided up among a large

---

[10] See Schapera 1938; Parsons 1977, 1999; Tlou 1985; Wilmsen 1989; Tlou and Campbell 1997; and Tlou 1998.

[11] Fortunately, there is a long and distinguished history of study of the comparative political organization of the Tswana tribes: see Fortes and Evans-Pritchard 1940; Schapera 1956; Stevenson 1968; with a very useful comparative perspective coming from Vansina (1966).

[12] There is no consensus in the anthropological literature about the origins of these differences and why Tswana political institutions evolved the way they did. Schapera (1956) speculates that this was because of different settlement patterns. The Tswana, despite an economy based on cattle, tended to live in large concentrated settlements, whereas other Bantu tribes, such as the Zulu, lived in more dispersed hamlets. This, according to Schapera, made it easier to hold regular political meetings in a Tswana tribe. However, since nothing appears to be known about the historical timing, one might just as well argue that the causality was the other way round, with the political institutions a cause of the differential settlement patterns.

number of clients who had the use of the cattle (as well as some of the meat and milk). In return for the use of the cattle, non-cattleowners were expected to provide political support for the officials" (Parson 1984, 16-17).

The relatively integrative nature of Tswana institutions and the lack of colonialism seems to account for the current relative homogeneity of Botswana. Scholarly literature tends to emphasize the endogeneity of ethnic identities in Africa, and particularly how they were formed by the colonial state. Lonsdale (1981, 151) notes that "it is difficult to imagine an aroused ethnicity prior to the state. It is a response to state power, even a condition for its successful exercise, in providing the categories between which men divide in order to rule." This literature emphasizes not just divide and rule, but also how ethnic groups come into being within the colonial period as colonial powers exploited the existing structure of institutions and incentives.[13] Despite appearances, as the research of Schapera (1952) and Parsons (1999) shows, probably no more than 50 percent of Batswana are actually Tswana. Although 85 percent of the population speak Setswana (the only language taught in public schools along with English), there is rather a large amount of underlying *ethnic* if not *linguistic* diversity. The Tswana tribes did traditionally attempt to integrate other groups into their institutional structure (though there were often tributary elements in this), and even after independence, this promotion of homogeneity continued in Botswana. Unlike the Ga or Ewe in Ghana, the San or Kalanga in Botswana do not have a separate historiography and experience of "stateness" but were rather integrated into Tswana society.

The early nineteenth century was tumultuous for the Tswana tribes. Starting in 1818 and lasting into the 1830s is the period known as the *difaqane,* when widespread migrations and conflicts occurred as a result of the expansion of the Zulu kingdom under Shaka. The Batswana had to fight to protect their lands and consolidate their hold on Botswana. As this period of fighting subsided, they began to interact with the spread of colonialism. Clashes with Afrikaners began from the 1830s onwards (the Boer "Great Trek" occurred in 1835) and even before that the effects of the European occupation of South Africa began to be felt. The movement of the Boers into Tswana territory was halted, however, by the success of the Tswana at the battle of Dimawe in 1852. An interesting feature of these wars is the extent of cooperation between the tribes in the face of a common enemy. Tlou and Campbell (1997, 170) note that "perhaps the most important result of the wars was the uniting of the Batswana against a common enemy. This was to lay the foundations for a future Republic of Botswana, in which merafe recognize a common unity."

---

[13] See for instance Horowitz's (1985) discussion of the Ibo in colonial Nigeria, Ranger's (1985) fascinating analysis of the origins of the distinction between the Shona and the Ndebele in Zimbabwe, and the essays in Vail 1991.

Even before these wars and as early as 1805 the Bangwaketse were trading ivory as far as the Orange River in South Africa, and European traders ventured into Botswana after 1810. These seem to have been welcomed by the Tswana chiefs, who saw trade as a way to acquire important goods, particularly guns. The London Missionary Society (LMS) founded its first mission in Botswana in 1817,[14] and David Livingstone traveled widely there in the 1840s. Khama III, chief of the Bangwato, converted to Christianity in 1860.

Just as there seems to have been an unusual structure of cooperation within the Tswana states, there was also to be a unique interaction between the states and the British. As early as 1853, long before the "scramble for Africa" started, Sechele, chief of the Bakwena, had traveled to Capetown to persuade the British to offer the Batswana protection from the Boers. The British basically ignored such pleas, including those from the LMS on behalf of the Batswana, until 1885. Gradually, the views of the British about the importance of Botswana changed. Diamonds were discovered in Kimberly in 1867 and gold on the Witwatersrand in 1884–85. In 1884 Germany annexed South West Africa (now Namibia), the Berlin Conference that formalized the scramble for Africa took place in 1885, and the British began to look inwards from the Cape Colony towards central Africa. Suddenly Botswana occupied an important strategic position blocking German South West Africa on one side and the Boer states on the other. Britain declared the creation of a crown colony in British Bechuanaland[15] in 1885 and creation of the Bechuanaland Protectorate in 1885.[16] Both were to be administered from Vryburg and then Mafeking in British Bechuanaland. British Bechuanaland become part of the Cape Colony in 1895 and is now part of Cape Province in the Republic of South Africa. The Bechuanaland Protectorate, now Botswana, was administered from South Africa until the hasty transfer to Gaborone in 1962 in the transition to independence.

The Tswana tribes were amalgamated into the British Empire mostly because of the strategic location of their territory, not because the territory was thought to be particularly valuable or attractive in itself. The protectorate served both to contain German and Boer expansionism and guarantee Britain and later Rhodes's BSAC (founded in 1889) a route into the interior. Right from the beginning, the idea was that the protectorate would be relatively quickly amalgamated with South Africa. This seems to have been an important factor that accounts for the failure of the British to impose indirect rule. The Act of Union of 1910 that created South Africa provided for the amalgamation of the three British protectorates—Bechuanaland, Basutholand, which is modern Lesotho, and Swaziland—into South Africa.

---

[14] They produced a rudimentary spelling book in Setswana in 1819 as a prelude to producing a Bible, and this was probably the first written Setswana (Tlou and Campbell 1997, 188).

[15] *Bechuanaland* is an archaic form of *Botswana;* the Batswana were known as the *Bechuana.*

[16] Historians stress that what were to be "protected" were not the Batswana but rather British interests.

As a result of the way in which Botswana entered the empire, and because of the putative amalgamation with South Africa, colonialism was very light. In 1885 the high commissioner defined the role of the British government as follows (quoted in Picard 1987, 36): "We have no interest in the country to the north of the Molope [the Bechuanaland Protectorate], except as a road to the interior; we might therefore confine ourselves for the present to preventing that part of the Protectorate being occupied by either filibusters or foreign powers doing as little in the way of administration or settlement as possible." During the colonial period 75 percent of the expenditures of the administration went toward "administrative costs" (Parson 1984, 22). Little was spent for investment or development of any kind.

Almost immediately after the creation of the protectorate, Rhodes and the BSAC lobbied intensively to take control of it. In 1895 three Tswana chiefs, Khama III of the Bangwato, Batheon of the Bangwaketse, and Sebele of the Bakwena went to Britain to see Queen Victoria and pled with her for Britain and not Rhodes to control the protectorate (see Parsons 1998 for a brilliant reconstruction of this visit). They succeeded, helped by the fiasco of the Jameson Raid.[17] In the face of external threats, and in contrast to many other precolonial African states, the Tswana states again showed an amazing ability to cooperate.[18]

Colonialism had important effects on the structure of the economy. In 1899 a hut tax of one pound payable in money was introduced, and this was increased by the addition of a three shillings "native tax" in 1919. The effect of these taxes, as in many places in colonial Africa, was to force Africans into the labor market to earn money to pay them (see Arrighi 1973). In the case of the Batswana, the relevant labor market was that of the Witwatersrand. In 1930, 4,012 Batswana were employed in South Africa, and by 1943 nearly half of all males between the ages of 15 and 44 were working away from the protectorate (Schapera 1947, 32, 39, 115).

After neglecting the protectorate for nearly 50 years, British policy changed from 1934 onwards, and there was a more sustained attempt by the British administration to "once and for all establish its authority over the chiefs in the tribal territories" (Parson 1984, 27). However, these measures were challenged in the courts by two chiefs, Tshekedi Khama (of the Bangwato), one of the sons of Khama III acting as regent for the young chief Seretse Khama, and Bathoen (of the Bangwaketse).[19] Though they lost the formal case, the united opposition of the chiefs and World War II essentially blocked the imposition of the new policies.

---

[17] Leander Jameson was the BSAC's agent in the protectorate, and in December 1895 he led an unsuccessful armed attack, essentially a coup, against the Boer Republic of the Transvaal.

[18] Contrast this with the extent to which most other African tribes succumbed to the divide-and-rule strategies of the British and French colonial powers (Robinson 1977).

[19] See Wylie 1984 for an analysis of Tshekedi Khama and his era.

Following the war, and particularly the rise of National Party in South Africa after 1948, the amalgamation of the protectorate into South Africa seemed less and less feasible to the British, though it was only formally abandoned as a goal in 1961. In 1948 Seretse Khama, who had been studying in Britain and married a white Englishwoman, was banned by the British from returning to the protectorate to take up his chieftanship.[20] The ban was to placate enraged South African reaction to the interracial marriage. He remained in exile until 1956, when both he and his uncle, Tshekedi, renounced their claims to the chieftanship. Seretse returned to the protectorate and began to take an active part in the Joint Advisory Council that the British had formed in 1951 by amalgamating formerly separate European and African councils. In 1960 the British announced the creation of a Legislative Council and at the same time the first political party, the Bechuanaland People's Party (later the Botswana People's Party [BPP]) was founded.

The BPP adopted a radical anticolonial stance and took inspiration from the antiapartheid struggle in South Africa.[21] In response to this Seretse Khama and others founded the Bechuanaland Democratic Party (later the Botswana Democratic Party [BDP]). While the BPP initially appealed to urban groups and workers, this was a very narrow political base in the early 1960s. In contrast the BDP integrated within it not only an emerging educated elite of teachers and civil servants, but also the traditional chiefs (see Cohen 1979). Seretse Khama bridged this gap, being both the hereditary leader of the largest Tswana state and European educated. The particular political strength of the BDP coalition was that they could integrate within the party the traditional rural structures of loyalty between commoners and chiefs. This structure of traditional loyalty was cemented by the continuation of clientelistic practices such as the lending of cattle, the *mafisa* system noted above (Parson 1984, 85).

As a result, the BDP easily won the first elections held in 1965. As tables 4.4 and 4.5 show, the BDP has won every election ever since and has always maintained a commanding majority in the National Assembly.[22] Seretse Khama maintained the presidency until his death in 1980, after which it fell to Quett Masire, who had been his deputy from 1966 on. Masire retired in 1998 and was succeeded by Festus Mogae. During this period there is no evidence of electoral fraud.

While the only daily newspaper is government run, there are several weekly papers that freely criticize the government and any instances of mismanagement. Though the BPP was initially the strongest opposition party, by the 1969

---

[20] The definitive biography of Seretse Khama is Parsons, Tlou, and Henderson 1997.

[21] Two of the early leaders, P. G. Matante and Motsamai Mpho, had worked and become politicized in South Africa. Ramsay and Parsons (1998) overview this period.

[22] The turnout in elections has varied between a low of 31 percent in 1974 to a high of 58 percent in 1965 (see Molutsi 1998, 369).

TABLE 4.4
Percentage of Popular Vote, by Party, 1965–99

	1965	1969	1974	1979	1984	1989	1994	1999
BDP	80.4	68.4	76.6	75.2	67.9	64.7	54.5	54.2
BNF		13.5	11.5	12.9	20.5	26.9	37.3	24.6
BPP	14.2	12.1	6.6	7.4	6.6	4.5	4.1	
BIP/IFP	4.6	6.0	4.8	4.3	3.0	2.4	3.6	
Others	0.8	0.0	0.5	0.2	2.0	1.5	0.5	11.3[a]

Note: BCP: Botswana Congress Party. BIP: Botswana Independence Party. IFP: Independence Freedom Party.
[a] Includes BCP.

election the Botswana National Front (BNF), founded by Kenneth Koma, had become the strongest opposition. Their electoral success in 1969, where they won three seats in the National Assembly, was primarily due to an unlikely coalition between Koma, a radical, and Batheon, former chief of the Bangwaketse who resigned his chieftancy and ran for the assembly. In doing so, he defeated Masire in the 1969 election.[23] By siding with the BNF Batheon switched the voters in his tribal area to the BNF. His main motivation was to try to build a coalition to restore power to the chiefs (an agenda completely different from Koma's). This outcome clearly indicates the strength of tribal affiliations.

Even though the BDP has ruled continuously, there is evidence that they have been responsive to the threat of losing power. For instance, before the 1974 election and after the shock of 1969, the Accelerated Rural Development Programme, which involved extensive investment in infrastructure in the rural areas, was launched. The primary aim of this program was to show to its supporters that the BDP was doing its job. It is notable, however, that even if politically motivated, this redistribution took a basically efficient form. Another example of political responsiveness is that after losing ground in the 1994 election the BDP responded by introducing popular reforms such as reducing the voting age from 21 to 18 and allowing Batswana outside the country to vote (particularly important given the large number still employed in South Africa).

Although the composition of the BDP goes a long way to explain its electoral success, there was a crucial tension between the nature of the party and the political strategy of Seretse Khama in the period leading up to independ-

---

[23] Masire was returned to the assembly as one of the members nominated by the president.

TABLE 4.5

Number of National Assembly Seats Held by Each Party, 1965–99

	1965	1969	1974	1979	1984	1989	1994	1999
BDP	28	24	27	29	28	31	31	33
BNF		3	2	2	5	3	13	6
BPP	3	3	2	1	1	0	0	
BIP/IFP BCP in 1999	0	1	1	0	0	0	0	1

Source: Molutsi 1998.

Note: The National Assembly had 31 seats in 1965 and 1969, 32 in 1974 and 1979, 34 in 1984 and 1989, 44 in 1994, and 47 in 1999.

BCP: Botswana Congress Party. BIP: Botswana Independence Party. IFP: Independence Freedom Party.

ence.[24] In particular, despite being himself a traditional chief, Khama seems to have been intent on constructing a strong central state that would not be impeded by the powers of traditional rulers. To achieve this, he successfully controlled the constitutional negotiations with the British. The National Assembly that emerged from the constitutional negotiations initially consisted of the speaker, the attorney general (who has no voting rights), 31 elected members, and 4 specially appointed members chosen by the president. Executive power resides with the president, who is chosen by the vote in the National Assembly. Assembly constituencies are British-style "first-past-the-post" constituencies, and candidates must declare which presidential candidate they support during the elections. After 1970 the president no longer had to run for the assembly.

In addition to the assembly, the constitutions created a House of Chiefs that consists of the eight chiefs of the eight Tswana tribes, four representatives of other subchiefs (from minor ethnic groups), and three members selected by the House of Chiefs. Members of the House of Chiefs cannot sit in the assembly. Seretse Khama ensured that the House of Chiefs became a talking shop that gave the chiefs no real power over legislation. Once in power the BDP passed legislation that progressively stripped the chiefs of their residual powers, for example over the allocation of lands. Particularly important were the Chieftancy Act of 1965 and the Chieftancy Amendment Act of 1970 (see Proctor 1968; Somolakae and Lekorwe 1998). These essentially gave the president the ability to remove a chief. These steps were crucial in the construction of the state.

One of the most crucial decisions was the passing in 1967 of the Mines and Minerals Act that vested subsoil mineral rights in the national government.

---

[24] See Edwards 1967 and Fawcus and Tilbury 2000 for this period.

Before this the rights accrued to the tribes. This decision is particularly interesting given that the main diamond mines were under the lands of the Bangwato, of whom Seretse Khama was the chief. It now seems likely (Parsons, Tlou, and Henderson 1995, 255) that De Beers and Seretse knew of the likelihood of diamonds and their location even before independence.

At independence in 1966, Botswana was a very poor country with few assets and little infrastructure. Though in 1954 an abattoir had been opened in Lobatse, enabling beef to be sold beyond the region for the first time, this was about the only industry in the country. Harvey and Lewis (1990, chap. 2) survey the dreadful initial conditions. In 1966 there were only two secondary schools in the country that offered full five-year courses and only 80 Batswana in the final year. In contrast, Zambia had 10 times as many secondary school graduates, and Uganda 70 times! The quality of education was uniformly poor with large class sizes and a high failure rate. The lack of education was reflected in the make-up of the civil service with only a quarter of 1,023 civil servants in 1965 being Batswana (Harvey and Lewis 1990, table 2.4, 21). Given the poor agricultural conditions in the country, imports of food were also large (about 10 percent of GDP in 1965) and most analysts wrote Botswana off as a dependent underdeveloped labor reserve for South Africa. Indeed, it was regarded as little different from the Bantustans such as the Transkei and Bophutatswana that the apartheid regime was then constructing. In addition, 50 percent of government expenditures upon independence had to be financed by transfers from Britain. Like Lesotho and Swaziland, Botswana was also part of the South African Customs Union and used the South African rand as its currency. As Harvey and Lewis (1990, 25) comment, "it was about as bad a start as could be imagined."

To solve this problem the BDP adopted several highly successful strategies. First, they renegotiated the customs union with South Africa in 1969, securing for themselves a greater share of the revenues. They also encouraged mining companies to explore the country. As a result, copper and nickel deposits were quickly found at Selebi-Phikwe and coal at Marupule. Most crucially, kimberlite diamond pipes containing diamonds of industrial and gem quality were discovered at Orapa and Letlhakane and later at Jwaneng. Moreover, in 1975, once it became clear how productive these mines were, the government invoked a clause in the original mining agreement with De Beers and renegotiated the diamond-mining agreement. As a result the government received a 50 percent share of diamond profits.

From independence the BDP adopted and implemented a consistent series of development plans emphasizing investment in infrastructure, health, and education. These plans have been run from the Ministry of Finance and Development Planning (see Samatar 1999, chap. 3). In stark contrast to most other African countries after independence, the BDP resisted all calls to "indigenize" the bureaucracy until suitably qualified Batswana were available. Thus they kept in place expatriate workers and freely used international advisers and consultants. The initial development plan of 1966 conservatively imagined phasing out all expatriate staff by 1991 (Samatar 1999, 64), a target that has not yet been achieved. As Parson (1984, 10) put it, in the Botswanan bureaucracy "probity, relative autonomy and competency have been nurtured and sustained." This was clearly a conscious choice by the BDP. In his first speech as president Seretse Khama announced, "My Government is deeply conscious of the dangers inherent in localizing the public service too quickly. Precipitate or reckless action in this field could have disastrous effects on the whole programme of services and development of the Government" (quoted in Parsons, Tlou, and Henderson 1995, 253).

In the absence of any other sector to develop, the early development plans focused on the rural sector—basically cattle ranching. Building infrastructure and developing this sector was entirely in the interests of the BDP political elites. Good (1992, 73) notes "a rising rural capitalist class . . . made a successful transition from political power in precolonial societies to the new nation state. . . . such direct engagement in agricultural production is similar to that of the settler political elites in Rhodesia, where government by farmer-politicians was something of a norm. But it is quite unlike the common situation in contemporary Africa." Samatar (1999, 69–70) shows that as many as two-thirds of members of the National Assembly in the early years were "large or medium size cattle owners."

Immediately upon independence the abattoir at Lobatse was nationalized (the government ultimately built two more, one at Maun and one at Francistown) and the Botswana Meat Commission (BMC) was founded (Samatar 1999, chap. 4). The BMC is a traditional type of marketing board that is a monopsony purchaser of cattle from ranchers. It sets the prices and sells the beef on regional and world markets. The BMC has been largely controlled by cattle interests and aided the development of the industry. Indeed, the government has heavily subsidized veterinary services and the distribution of vaccines and extension services and built over five thousand kilometers of cattle fences to maintain the health of the stock. Under the auspices of the Lome convention, the BMC (with the direct intervention of Seretse Khama) also negotiated access to the lucrative EEC market, gaining prices far above world levels.

By the mid-1970s the government budget was in surplus and the diamond income began to accrue. Right from the beginning the income was managed in an intertemporally efficient manner with the rents being allocated to investment in the government budget (see Jefferis 1998 for an excellent discussion of all aspects of the diamond economy). The best evidence of this is in the early 1980s, when in an attempt to maintain the market price for diamonds Botswana was unable to sell any diamonds for six months. This led to no cuts in expenditure, as the government was able to optimally smooth expenditures relative to income. Botswana diamonds now represent about one-third of the diamonds sold by the De Beers cartel, and Botswana has benefited enormously from this successful attempt to maintain high diamond prices.

While the government stayed within the South African Customs Union, in 1976 they introduced their own currency, the pula,[25] which has been essentially pegged against the rand.

To stimulate industry, the government introduced in 1970 the Botswana Development Corporation and in 1982 they created the Financial Assistance Policy to subsidize industrial ventures. Though these have not led to large-scale industrialization, it is significant that manufacturing has stayed at around 5 percent of GDP, which is quite an achievement given the dominance of resources in the economy. As Leith (2000, 4) notes, "the growth of the Botswana economy is not simply a story of a mineral enclave with an ever growing Government, attached to a stagnating traditional economy."

In general nearly every aspect of Botswana economic performance is spectacular. Inflation has rarely been above 10 percent, investment has been between 20 percent and 30 percent of GDP, and there has been significant investment in human capital. The balance of payments has typically been in surplus, there are large accumulated reserves, and government has not needed any structural adjustment loans. Although diamonds have clearly fueled Botswana's growth path, these resources rents have been invested rather than squandered.

3. THE POLITICAL ECONOMY OF BOTSWANA: THE HYPOTHESES

We can draw the following conclusions from the last section: the economic success of Botswana since independence has been due to sound economic policy. While diamonds have played the driving role, the government maximized the benefits from the gems in its negotiations with De Beers and exploited the resource in a socially efficient way by investing the rents. It also ensured that the set of institutional restrictions on different tribes and interest groups made it unattractive for these actors to fight for the control of the resources rents.

Although one can certainly point to instances of corruption in Botswana (Good 1994), the bureaucracy has been on the whole meritocratic and noncorrupt. Despite the mineral wealth, the exchange rate has not become overvalued, while monetary and fiscal policy has been prudent, and the government invested heavily in public goods, such as infrastructure, health, and education.

We now attempt to use the evidence presented so far to build a story that can help to explain Botswana. We see the above discussion of good policies and institutions as outcomes, not causes, and seek the fundamental determinants of these good policies and institutions.

---

[25] *Pula* means "rain" and is also a greeting in Setswana.

There are a number of (structural) features that appear potentially relevant to understanding its institutional and economic performance:

1. Botswana is very rich in natural-resource wealth.

2. It had unusual precolonial political institutions allowing commoners to make suggestions and criticize chiefs. The institutions therefore enabled an unusual degree of participation in the political process and placed restrictions on the political power of the elites.

3. British colonial rule in Botswana was limited. This allowed the precolonial institutions to survive to the independence era.

4. Exploiting the comparative advantage of the nation after 1966 directly increased the incomes of the members of the elite.

5. The political leadership of the BDP, and particularly of Seretse Khama, inherited the legitimacy of these institutions, and this gave it a broad political base.

How did these various features of Botswana's history and political situation affect the design of its institutions? To answer this question, we first have to note that institutions are ultimately the endogenous creation of individuals. Institution building, therefore, has to be analyzed within the context of the interests of the actors and the constraints facing them. In particular, here we emphasize three factors:

Economic interests. A good institutional setup will lead to outcomes that are in the interest of the politically powerful agents. For example, institutions that restrict state predation will not be in the interest of a ruler who wants to appropriate assets in the future. Yet this strategy may be in interest of a ruler who recognizes that only such guarantees will encourage citizens to undertake substantial investments, or will protect his own rents. They will also be in the interest of the major groups that can undertake investment in production activities in the future.

Political losers. The issue here is whether institutional development will destabilize the system, making it less likely that elites will remain in power after reforms (see Acemoglu and Robinson 2000). An institutional setup encouraging investment and adoption of new technologies may be blocked by elites when they fear that this process of growth and social change will make it more likely that they will be replaced by other interests—that they will be "political losers." Elites that are relatively secure in their position will be less afraid of change, and may therefore be less likely to block such change. Similarly, a stable political system where the elites are not threatened is less likely to encourage inefficient methods of redistribution as a way of maintaining power.

Constraints. When institutions limit the powers of rulers and the range of distortionary policies that they can pursue, good policies are more likely to arise (see Acemoglu and Robinson 1999). Constraints on political elites are also useful through two indirect channels. First, they reduce the political stakes and contribute to political stability, since, with such constraints in place, it becomes less attractive to fight to take control of the state apparatus. Second, these constraints also imply that other groups have less reason to fear expropriation by the elites and are more willing to delegate power to the state.

In light of this simple framework, we can discuss how the particular features of the Botswana case might have contributed to the development of institutions of private property in this country.

The first point to note is that in the aftermath of independence, well-enforced property rights were, to a large extent, in the interests of Botswana's political elites, making the first factor, *economic interests,* stack the cards in favor of good institutions. After independence, cattle owners were the most important economic interest group, and they were politically influential. As many scholars have recognized, the close connection between the cattle owners and the BDP has played a key role in Botswana's development. Harvey and Lewis (1990, 9) echo the majority opinion when they argue that "Botswana's government was largely a government of cattlemen." At independence the only real prospect for a sector of the economy to develop was ranching. This was done successfully by exploiting the EEC market, and a great deal of the infrastructure development had the effect of increasing ranching incomes. Moreover, the fact that the elite was invested in the main export sector explains why the marketing board (the BMC) gave the ranchers a good deal and also why the exchange rate was not overvalued, which contrasts with the experiences of many African countries. The political elites were therefore enriched by the developmental policies that were adopted from 1966. They benefited from membership of the custom union with South Africa, and they also benefited from the heavy investment in infrastructure throughout the country. Picard (1987, 264) argues that "the primary beneficiaries of government policy in the areas of economic and rural development have been the organizational elites, bureaucratic, professional, and political, who dominate the system."

The economic interest of the elites in development appears to be only part of the story, however. As discussed in more detail in the next section, this is true in a number of other countries in Africa, yet there is only one Botswana. Moreover, by the mid-1970s the income from diamonds swamped the income from ranching, so one needs to account for why this did not induce the political elite to change its strategy and expropriate the revenues from diamonds. To build a convincing account of Botswana's development, we therefore need to appeal to the other two factors we emphasized.

First, it was important that political elites did not oppose or feel threatened by the process of growth—they did not fear becoming *political losers.* The political security of the elites was to some degree an outcome of the relatively developed institutions that Botswana inherited from its precolonial period, which ensured some degree of political stability. It was also an outcome of Seretse Khama's legitimacy as a leader, which resulted both from his position as the hereditary chief of the Bangwato and from the relatively broad coalition he formed within the BDP, including the tribal chiefs and cattle owners. In this context, the limited impact of colonial rule in Botswana, as compared to the experiences of many other nations in Africa, South America, or the Caribbean, may have been quite important. Limited colonial rule allowed the continuity of the precolonial institutions, which provided the legitimacy to Sertese Khama and enabled him to form a broad-based coalition. The relative security of elites in Botswana contrasts with the situation in many postindependence African countries, where developmental policies appear to have undermined the power base of traditional political institutions such as chiefs, destabilizing the power of existing elites.

Second, the underlying structure of institutions may have also been important in restricting the range of options, in particular distortionary policies, available to the political leadership—that is, political elites faced effective *constraints*. For example, political institutions such as the *kgotla* ensured a certain degree of accountability of political elites.[26] The constraints placed by these institutions may help to explain why, while the cattle owners clearly preferred their own property rights to be enforced, they did not use their political power in order to expropriate the revenue from diamonds starting in the 1970s.[27] The indirect benefits from the presence of these political constraints may have also been quite important: there was no political instability in Botswana, and Sertese Khama could build a relatively effective bureaucracy without the majority of economic groups fearing future expropriation.[28] Here again, the limited nature of colonial rule may have been important. Contrary to many other countries in Africa, colonial rule did not strengthen Botswana's chiefs and did not destroy the *kgotla* and other related institutions, nor did it introduce indirect rule with substantial power delegated to the political elites representing the British Empire (see for example, Ashton 1947; and Migdal 1988).

Finally, it is important to recognize the contribution of diamonds to the consolidation of the institutions of private property in Botswana. Botswana got off onto the right track at independence, and by the time the diamonds came on stream, the country had already started to build a relatively democratic polity and efficient institutions. The surge of wealth likely reinforced this. Because of the breadth of the BDP coalition, diamond rents were widely distributed, and the extent of this wealth increased the opportunity cost of undermining the good

[26] There is controversy about the importance of the *kgotla* today, with some scholars seeing it as a "rubber stamp" on elite policies rather than an institution with significant power (e.g. van Binsbergen 1995; see Holm 1988 and Holm and Molutsi 1992 for overviews of different arguments).

[27] See Maundeni 2000, 2001 for the idea that unique features of Tswana political culture were crucial in allowing the Botswana state to promote development.

[28] This may have also been important in ensuring that Sertese Khama and the BDP did not need to use inefficient methods of redistribution to ensure support for their policies.

institutional path—no group wanted to fight to expand its rents at the expense of "rocking the boat."

Our reading of the evidence is that none of these key factors, by itself, appears to explain Botswana's institutions. So what explains Botswana's success? Our conjecture is that it is not any of these key factors by itself, but the juxtaposition of them that has been important in Botswana. We believe that Botswana was able to adopt good policies and institutions because they were in the interests of the political elites, which included the cattle owners and powerful tribal actors. But it wasn't simply that cattle owners were politically powerful. Instead, they inherited a set of institutional prerequisites that ensured that they would keep their political power by pursuing good policies and placed restrictions on infighting among themselves over political rents.

It is noteworthy that our account de-emphasizes the fact that Botswana is homogeneous from an ethnolinguistic point of view. As we discussed earlier, to the extent that this is true, it appears to be more of an outcome of Botswana's political institutions than an independent cause. Moreover, it is clear that political elites have studiously avoided exacerbating any underlying ethnic tensions in Botswana.[29]

Our hypotheses stress structural factors, which we believe to have been important. But we do not rule out that "agency" may have been significant. Key decisions made by Batswana leaders, particularly Seretse Khama and Quett Masire, appear to have been crucial. Although these individuals operated in a relatively helpful institutional environment, they probably also made a big difference. Seretse Khama's handling of the independence negotiations and constitutional convention, minerals policy, and generally political issues ensured that political stakes remained low, contributing to political stability and an environment with secure property rights. For example, it appears plausible that had Seretse Khama not transferred the property rights over subsoil diamonds away from his own tribe, the Bangwato, to the government, there could have been much greater conflict among tribes over the control of the wealth from diamonds. Or had he not reduced the political powers of tribal chiefs shortly after independence, tribal cleavages may have been more important.

It is also significant that when the BDP's political power was threatened, for example in the early 1970s and late 1990s, their response was to change their policies to make themselves more popular. Contrast this with the response of the Basutoland National Party in Lesotho led by Chief Lebua Jonathan, who mounted a coup after losing an election. Although we argue in the next section that one reason for this may have been the greater political stakes and relative lack of constraints in Lesotho, at some level a decision to mount a coup or respond demo-

---

[29] Both Somalia and Lesotho are more homogeneous than Botswana, and neither has succeeded economically. Moreover, Lesotho has a linguistic, cultural, and institutional inheritance that is identical to Botswana's, ruling out simple cultural explanations of the exceptionality of Botswana.

cratically must be taken by individuals. In Botswana, Seretse Khama and subsequent leaders consistently chose to take the democratic path.[30]

4. A COMPARATIVE PERSPECTIVE

The arguments we have presented in the last section provide a possible explanation for the success of Botswana. They explain why it managed to sustain a political equilibrium of a nature that no other African country could. To check the plausibility of these different arguments it is important to evaluate them in comparison with the experience of other countries. We do this not by estimating regressions but rather by undertaking case studies to help to evaluate the casual connections we have stressed. This is motivated by the fact that many of the factors that appear important in the success of Botswana are hard to measure or understand without a detailed investigation, making a comparative analysis of a few cases more fruitful. Our focus is selective—we concentrate for the most part on comparing Botswana to four other countries; Somalia, Lesotho, Ghana, and the Côte d'Ivoire. We argue that this comparative evidence shows that it is the juxtaposition (or perhaps even the interaction) of these factors we have stressed that is important.

We argued that Botswana had a state that benefited from a precolonial institutional inheritance that was not perverted by colonialism. Somalia suggests the importance of Tswana state institutions. Despite being a relatively homogeneous nation, Somalia suffers from its inheritance of highly dysfunctional precolonial political institutions.

Lesotho, on the other hand, is culturally identical to Botswana and had the same precolonial institutions. Yet these institutions were affected differently by warfare in the nineteenth century and colonialism. In particular, the powers of chiefs were strengthened, and a single paramount chief emerged with far fewer constraints than in Botswana. This resulted in a greater vested interest in the status quo, higher political stakes, and greater political instability.

The evidence from Ghana and the Côte d'Ivoire supports our emphasis on the crucial nature of the political coalition integrated into the BDP and institutional constraints on postindependence political power. The fact that the BDP represented the majority of the traditional political elites in Botswana gave them a broad and stable coalition with little to fear from abandoning the status quo and promoting development. Moreover, the relatively limited nature of

---

[30] Another revealing incident in Botswana came after the death of Seretse Khama in 1980. He was succeeded as president by Masire, who, unlike Khama, was neither a Bangwato nor from royal descent. When his picture was printed on national banknotes, large protests erupted in the Bangwato tribal area. Rather than exploiting the protests in order to increase their political power, the Bangwato leaders joined with others in order to defuse this potentially explosive situation.

political power meant that the BDP was not too threatening to potential opponents. This reduced political instability.

In Ghana, Nkrumah and his Convention People's Party (CPP) lacked such a coalition and, in the absence of institutional limits, posed a threat to other groups. The CPP therefore quickly became locked into an antagonistic relationship with other tribes, particularly the Ashanti. The resulting political instability led to the collapse of democracy and highly inefficient income redistribution. Our reading of this suggests that the lack of economic interest of Nkrumah and the CPP in promoting development (as emphasized by Bates 1981) was less crucial than this political instability, which was exacerbated by the long divisive impact of the Atlantic slave trade and colonialism on indigenous political institutions.

In line with this, in the Côte d'Ivoire, postindependence political elites did have strong interests in coffee and cocoa production but, as with the CPP, had a narrow political base. This narrow base of support is likely to have made political elites feel threatened by economic and social change (i.e., they feared becoming "political losers"), and the absence of effective constraints on political elites enabled them to pursue distortionary policies and inefficient redistribution to maintain power. As a result, despite the alignment of the economic interests of the governing elite with development in the Côte d'Ivoire, many distortionary policies were adopted, and economic performance has been poor.

We now briefly discuss the experiences of Somalia, Lesotho, Ghana, and the Côte d'Ivoire in more detail to substantiate these points.

Somalia

The continuity of institutions from precolonial times to independence appears to be important in understanding Botswana's success. In this context, the comparison with Somalia is interesting. Of all the countries in Africa, Somalia was not just a state, it was a nation. Clapham (1986, 255) states, "The dynamic of Somali nationhood differs from . . . the inherited colonial statism of most of the rest of Africa. Alone among African states, the Somali republic is derived from the sense of self-identity of a single people who possess a common history, culture, religion, and language (but who have never been governed by common political institutions)."

Moreover, British colonial rule had minimal effect on the structure of Somali society. As in Botswana, the motivation for the creation of a British colony in the Horn of Africa was strategic since Somalia commanded the sea-lanes between the Suez Canal and the Red Sea and India and the Far East. Lewis (1980, 104–5) notes that nothing happened in the colonial period to the basic political institutions of the clans because the British "administration's aims were extremely modest, and restricted in fact to little more than the maintenance of effective law and order. . . . [there was no pervasive system of indigenous chiefs and consequently no basis for a true system of indirect rule."

Despite these similarities with Botswana, Somalia has had a dismal economic record, has been unable to sustain democratic politics, and has suffered a high degree of political instability. An investigation of the nature of postindependence politics in Somalia suggests that the precolonial institutions may have contributed to political instability rather than helped the creation of institutions of private property. Clapham (1986, 273) argues that "these peculiarities [of the Somali case] reside in the structure of a nomadic society, in which shared identities of culture, language, and religion nevertheless coexist with intense factional conflict resulting from the perennial competition over very scarce resources. This dichotomy is symbolized in the Somali national genealogy, which, on the one hand, traces the descent of all Somalis from a common ancestor (Somal) and on the other, divides them into clans that provide a natural base for political factions."

What explains the difference between Botswana and Somalia? We conjecture that this difference reflects the importance of the form of political institutions that the Tswana tribes developed. These not only integrated *disparate* ethnic groups, thus creating the homogeneity we observe today, but also allowed the Tswana to create a political culture of intertribe cooperation very different from the Somali experience. Despite ethnic, cultural, and linguistic homogeneity, the political structure of the Somali clans was therefore highly divisive, and institutions placing constraints on political elites were absent. This increased the stakes in controlling the state apparatus and encouraged political elites to fight each other, forming coalitions along clan lines. In fact, after independence in 1960 and the unification of British Somaliland and (former) Italian Somaliland into the state of Somalia, clan loyalty dominated politics, even after the military takeover in October 1969. Parties formed along clan lines or were subject to complex internal battles along clan lines.[31] Laitin and Samatar (1987, 155) conclude that "one can scarcely think of a significant domestic or foreign development in Somali politics since independence that was not influenced to a large degree by an underlying clan consideration."

The Somali example therefore suggests that it is not the limited effect of colonialism itself that promotes the building of good institutions, but the interaction of this limited colonial rule with precolonial institutions placing effective constraints on political elites.

Lesotho

Lesotho is a small country, about the size of Maryland, completely surrounded by South Africa. The Sotho are culturally and linguistically very closely related

---

[31] The 1969 elections were contested by 62 parties.

to the Tswana, and Sotho-speaking tribes were established in the area of modern Lesotho at the start of the *difaqane*.[32] As for the Tswana, the 1820s were a period of endless conflict and, most importantly, several of the Sotho tribes united under the chieftainship of Moshoeshoe to protect themselves.[33] "By the mid-1830's . . . Moshoeshoe's small and insignificant . . . chiefdom had been transformed into a kingdom, the largest and most powerful in the region. His own preeminence was increasingly recognized through the title by which he was commonly addressed: Chief of the Basotho." Despite Moshoeshoe's role, the political institutions of the Basotho resembled those of the Tswana right down to the role of the *kgotla*. Moreover, they adopted similar strategies of incorporating strangers into their tribal structures and attempting to use foreign missionaries to stave off the threat of the approaching Boers.

So why did the political experiences of Botswana and Lesotho diverge?[34] We conjecture that this divergence reflects the effects of a series of wars with the Boers and of British colonialism on the political institutions in Lesotho. Both of these experiences contributed to the centralization of political power in the hands of the elites and undermined the institutions, such as the *kgotla,* that constrained political leaders. Relative to Botswana, this increased the value of controlling political power and led to greater political instability.

A brief look at Lesotho's political history explains how this centralization of political power took place. As early as 1841 Moshoeshoe appealed to the British for help against the Boers (Bardill and Cobbe 1985, 12) and in 1843 signed a treaty with Sir George Napier, the governor of the Cape, which recognized a significant proportion of his claim to territory. Unfortunately for the Basotho, the British reneged on their treaty in 1849, and tensions finally gave way to a series of wars with the Boers between 1865 to 1868. Finally, reacting to the Boer expansionism, the British decided to annex Basotho in 1868 under the name of Basutoland. In 1871 the Cape Colony took over direct responsibility for running Basutoland, and there followed 13 chaotic years of inconsistent policies and conflict leading to the Gun War of 1880–81 and the Crown's taking direct control

---

[32] The common root *sotho* is found in the name of the country, *Lesotho,* the language, *Sesotho,* a person, *Mosotho,* and the people, *Basotho.*

[33] Thompson 1975 is the seminal biography of the great chief. See Parsons 1983 for an overview of the historical experience.

[34] Although economic performance has been quite good over the independence period, this is due mostly to increases in real wages of migrant workers in South Africa (classed as resident in Lesotho). The government has done little to aid the economy. Bardill and Cobbe note, "having identified the broad objectives of development . . . the government has failed to provide a comprehensive and systematic strategy through which these might be realized" (1985, 150), and "perhaps the worst obstacle to the effective utilization of personnel, however, has been the government's tendency to subordinate professionalism to political loyalty" (152). Thus in Lesotho, political competition survived for only five years, and the country has also experienced severe violence and attempted coups since.

in 1884. It appears that this series of wars with the Boers is important in understanding why institutions that gave greater powers to the chiefs in general, and to the paramount chief in particular, emerged in Lesotho, but not in Botswana.

As with Botswana the British invested practically nothing in Lesotho. However, the British did make a concerted attempt to foster the power of the paramount chief. To this end they created the Basutoland Council in 1910, which was dominated by the paramount and other chiefs as well as the members appointed by the British. This policy seems to have undercut significantly the role of institutions such as the *kgotla*, further contributing to divergence in political institutions between Lesotho and Botswana.

This difference in political institutions between the two countries appears to explain why the stakes in politics were higher and there were no effective constraints on political elites in Lesotho. As a result, unlike in Botswana, in the postindependence era the chiefs had important legislative powers. More importantly, Chief Lebua Jonathan, after narrowly winning the first election with the traditionally based Basutoland National Party (BNP), mounted a coup following his defeat in the 1970 election.

Ghana and the Côte d'Ivoire

After independence had been secured from the British, the anticolonial coalition in Ghana crumbled. Pellow and Chazan (1986, 30) note that "by 1951, with the British agreement in principle to grant independence to the colony, this stage of decolonization gave way to a period of domestic struggles for power on the eve of independence. At this junction, the internal tensions that had been somewhat in check erupted into an open clash over the control of the colonial state."

Kwame Nkrumah (who was from a minor Akan ethnic group, the Nzima) and his Convention People's Party (CPP) were left with a very precarious political base. To compensate for this, Nkrumah engaged in a "divide and rule" strategy with respect to the Ashanti (whose chiefs were one of his strongest opponents) by attempting to set different factions of commoners against the chiefs. The chiefs and their National Liberation Movement (NLM) "met the nationalist appeal of the CPP with a rival nationalism of its own, through an impassionate demand for recognition of the traditional unity of the Ashanti nation" (Austin 1964, 250).[35]

This political strategy ensured Nkrumah's power at independence in 1957. After the departure of the British, he moved to suppress the opposition and ultimately to declare a one-party state. Despite the announced objectives of modernization, the need to stabilize political power seems to be the key determinant

---

[35] Apter 1972 is a classic study of the politics of this period. See Leith and Lofchie 1993 and Leith and Söderling 2000 for integrated analyses of the political economy of development in Ghana.

of economic policies.[36] Pellow and Chazan (1986) argue that by 1964 the CPP had "reduced the role of the state to that of a dispenser of patronage. By advocating the construction of a ramified bureaucracy, Nkrumah established a new social stratum directly dependent on the state. By curtailing the freedom of movement of these state functionaries through the diversion of administrative tasks to political ends, the regime contributed directly to undermining their effective performance." The disastrous economic impact of the CPP's policies have been well analyzed by Bates (1981).

In contrast to Ghana, the ability of political elites in Botswana to build institutions and to refrain from politically motivated redistribution was important. This ability in turn appears to have stemmed from the fact that the BDP enjoyed a large and stable majority in the National Assembly, did not fear losing its position as a result of social and economic change, and operated within a set of institutions that constrained the range of distortionary policies the leaders could pursue. This difference in institutions led to less underlying political instability and distortionary policies in Botswana than in Ghana.

The experience of Ghana is interesting because it is the archetype of a state where decisive political elites had little direct interest in export agriculture (Bates 1981). So it also emphasizes the importance of economic interests. Yet we believe that it is not only economic interests, but also the constraints placed by the institutions that are important. This is illustrated by the experience of the Côte d'Ivoire, where, as in Botswana, political elites were invested in the productive sectors of the economy. Widner (1994, 137), for example, argues that in the Côte d'Ivoire "the ability of senior decision makers to capture some of the benefits that flow from improved agricultural performance provides an inducement to them to support pro-farmer policies" (see also Widner 1993; Boone 1998; and Lofchie 1989). Yet economic interests of the political elites were not sufficient to ensure development in the Côte d'Ivoire. Why? It appears that this was due, as in Ghana, primarily to the precarious positions of political elites, who feared that promoting development would mobilize political opposition against them and functioned in environment without effective constraints on their behavior (see Cohen 1973 on the Côte d'Ivoire; and van der Walle 1993 for a related argument about Cameroon).[37]

5. CONCLUDING REMARKS

The success of Botswana is most plausibly due to its adoption of good policies. These have promoted rapid accumulation, investment, and the socially efficient

[36] There is some controversy on this issue, with different interpretations of attempts to industrialize under Nkrumah. Some (e.g., Killick 1978; Bates 1981) see government promotion of industry as essentially well-meaning if misguided. Others, such as Price (1984) and Owusu (1970), see it simply as a method for redistributing income to supporters.

[37] Indeed it is clear that the economic interests of the political elite in the Côte d'Ivoire did not

exploitation of resource rents. Consistent with our previous cross-country empirical work (Acemoglu, Johnson, and Robinson 2001a, 2001b), these policies resulted from an underlying set of institutions—institutions of private property—that encouraged investment and economic development.

We discussed the factors that could account for the distinct institutional equilibrium that emerged in Botswana after 1966. We conjectured that Botswana's institutions of private property reflect a combination of factors:

1. Botswana possessed precolonial tribal institutions that encouraged broad-based participation and placed constraints on political elites.

2. British colonization had a limited effect on these precolonial institutions because of the peripheral nature of Botswana to the British Empire.

3. Upon independence, the most important rural interests, chiefs and cattle owners, were politically powerful, and it was in their economic interest to enforce property rights.

4. The revenues from diamonds generated enough rents for the main political actors, increasing the opportunity cost of, and discouraging, further rent seeking.

5. Finally, the postindependence political leaders, in particular Seretse Khama and Quett Masire, made a number of sensible decisions.

We suggest Botswana as an optimistic example of what can be done with the appropriate actions towards institutional design, even starting with unfavorable initial economic conditions. Many, if not most, African countries are well endowed with natural resources and mineral wealth. Botswana was able to grow rapidly because it possessed the right institutions and got good policies in place. Despite being a small, agriculturally marginal, predominantly tropical, landlocked nation, in a very precarious geopolitical situation, Botswana experienced rapid development. We think this shows what can be done with the right institutions. In Botswana's case, these institutions emerged in part as a result of a unique juxtaposition of a historical conditions and political factors, which obviously cannot be duplicated. However, to the extent that individual actions have been important, similar institution-building may be helpful in other African nations.

We end with a note of caution. While the economic achievements of Botswana have been impressive, there remain serious problems, particularly the incidence of AIDS, the persistence of inequality, and high urban unemployment. It remains to be seen if Botswana's institutions will be strong enough to address these issues and sustain growth.

---

engender the type of institution building so crucial to the Botswana experience. Indeed, Fauré (1989, 69–70) notes that "studies of the Ivorian political society entirely confirm the good health of the patrimonial system . . . one observes behaviour whereby public resources give way to quasi-private appropriation . . . the majority of the administrative and parapublic positions that carry any weight are allocated according to only vaguely meritocratic criteria." Thus it seems that in order to consolidate their political power, the Ivorian elite adopted the same political strategy as elsewhere in Africa with the same adverse effects on economic performance.

TABLE 4.A1

Data Used in Figures 4.1 and 4.2

Name of Country	Abbreviation	Log GDP per Capita in 1995	Average Expropriation 1985–95	Constraint on Executive in 1990
Angola	AGO	7.770645	5.363636	3
Argentina	ARG	9.133459	6.386364	6
Australia	AUS	9.897972	9.318182	7
Burundi	BDI	6.565265	—	1
Benin	BEN	7.090077	—	1
Burkina Faso	BFA	6.84588	4.454545	1
Bangladesh	BGD	6.877296	5.136364	2
Bahamas	BHS	9.285448	7.5	.
Bolivia	BOL	7.926602	5.636364	7
Brazil	BRA	8.727454	7.909091	7
Botswana	BWA	8.855093	7.727273	7
Central African Federation	CAF	7.192934	—	1
Canada	CAN	9.986449	9.727273	7
Chile	CHL	9.336092	7.818182	7
Cote d'Ivoire	CIV	7.444249	7	2
Cameroon	CMR	7.501082	6.454545	2
Congo	COG	7.420579	4.681818	2
Colombia	COL	8.809863	7.318182	6
Comoros	COM	7.383989	—	5
Costa Rica	CRI	8.794825	7.045455	7
Dominican Republic	DOM	8.364042	6.181818	6
Algeria	DZA	8.389359	6.5	2
Ecuador	ECU	8.470101	6.545455	7
Egypt	EGY	7.95156	6.772727	3
Ethiopia	ETH	6.109248	5.727273	2
Fiji	FJI	8.301521	—	7
Gabon	GAB	8.907883	7.818182	2
Ghana	GHA	7.36518	6.272727	1
Guinea	GIN	7.489971	6.545455	1
Gambia	GMB	7.272398	8.272727	7
Guatemala	GTM	8.294049	5.136364	4
Guyana	GUY	7.904704	5.886364	4
Hong Kong	HKG	10.04975	8.136364	.
Honduras	HND	7.68708	5.318182	5
Haiti	HTI	7.146772	3.727273	1
Indonesia	IDN	8.070906	7.590909	2
India	IND	7.326	8.272727	7
Jamaica	JAM	8.188689	7.090909	7
Kenya	KEN	7.056175	6.045455	3
Laos	LAO	7.090077	—	3
Sri Lanka	LKA	7.731931	6.045455	5

(continued)

TABLE 4.A1 *(Continued)*

Name of Country	Abbreviation	Log GDP per Capita in 1995	Average Expropriation 1985–95	Constraint on Executive in 1990
Lesotho	LSO	7.306531	—	1
Morocco	MAR	8.042378	7.090909	2
Madagascar	MDG	6.835185	4.454545	3
Mexico	MEX	8.943768	7.5	3
Mali	MLI	6.565265	4	1
Mozambique	MOZ	6.461468	6.5	3
Mauritania	MRT	7.414573	—	3
Mauritius	MUS	9.053686	—	7
Malawi	MWI	6.461468	6.818182	1
Malaysia	MYS	8.894258	7.954545	7
Namibia	NAM	8.515191	—	3
Niger	NER	6.733402	5	3
Nigeria	NGA	6.813445	5.545455	1
Nicaragua	NIC	7.544332	5.227273	3
Nepal	NPL	6.937314	—	7
New Zealand	NZL	9.756147	9.727273	7
Pakistan	PAK	7.352441	6.045455	3
Panama	PAN	8.836374	5.909091	7
Peru	PER	8.396154	5.772727	7
Philippines	PHL	8.098643	5.454545	7
Paraguay	PRY	8.207947	6.954545	5
Rwanda	RWA	6.476973	—	1
Sudan	SDN	7.306531	4	1
Senegal	SEN	7.402452	6	3
Singapore	SGP	10.14643	9.318182	3
Sierra Leone	SLE	6.253829	5.818182	3
El Salvador	SLV	7.948032	5	.
Suriname	SUR	8.01	4.681818	.
Swaziland	SWZ	8.10772	—	1
Chad	TCD	6.835185	—	1
Togo	TGO	7.222566	6.909091	1
Trinidad and Tobago	TTO	8.76873	7.454545	7
Tunisia	TUN	8.482602	6.454545	3
Tanzania	TZA	6.253829	6.636364	3
Uganda	UGA	6.966024	4.454545	3
Uruguary	URY	9.031214	7	3
USA	USA	10.21574	10	7
Venezuela	VEN	9.071078	7.136364	3
Vietnam	VNM	7.279319	6.409091	3
South Africa	ZAF	8.885994	6.863636	7
Zaire	ZAR	6.866933	3.5	1
Zambia	ZMB	6.813445	6.636364	1
Zimbabwe	ZWE	7.696213	6	3

REFERENCES

Acemoglu, Daron, Simon Johnson, and James A. Robinson. 2001a. "The Colonial Origins of Comparative Development: An Empirical Investigation." *American Economic Review* 91: 1369–1401.

———. 2001b. "Reversal of Fortune: Geography and Institutions in the Making of the Modern World Income Distribution." Typescript.

Acemoglu, Daron, and James A. Robinson. 1999. "The Political Economy of Institutions and Development." Background paper prepared for the World Bank's World Development Report 2001.

———. 2000. "Political Losers as a Barrier to Economic Development." *American Economic Review* 90:126–30.

Alesina, Alberto, and Dani Rodrik. 1994. "Distributive Politics and Economic Growth." *Quarterly Journal of Economics* 109:465–90.

Apter, David E. 1972. *Ghana in Transition.* Princeton: Princeton University Press.

Arrighi, Giovanni. 1973. "Labour Supplies in Historical Perspective: A Study of the Proletarianization of the African Peasantry in Rhodesia." In *Essays in the Political Economy of Africa,* ed. Giovanni Arrighi and John S. Saul. New York: Monthly Review Press.

Ashton, Edward H. 1947. "Democracy and Indirect Rule." *Africa* 27:235–51.

Austin, Dennis. 1964. *Politics in Ghana, 1947–1960.* Oxford: Oxford University Press.

Bardill, John E., and James H. Cobbe. 1985. *Lesotho: Dilemmas of Dependence in Southern Africa.* Boulder, Colo.: Westview Press.

Barro, Robert J. 1991. "Economic Growth in a Cross Section of Countries." *Quarterly Journal of Economics* 106:407–33.

Bates, Robert H. 1981. *Markets and States in Tropical Africa.* Berkeley and Los Angeles: University of California Press.

Benabou, Roland. 2000. "Unequal Societies: Income Distribution and the Social Contract." *American Economic Review* 90:96–129.

Bloom, David E., and Jeffrey D. Sachs. 1998. "Geography, Demography, and Economic Growth in Africa." *Brookings Papers on Economic Activity* 1998, no. 2: 207–95.

Boone, Catherine. 1998. "State Building in the African Countryside: Structure and Politics at the Grassroots." *Journal of Development Studies* 34:1–15.

Clapham, Christopher. 1986. "The Horn of Africa." In *Politics and Government in African States, 1960–1985,* ed. Peter Duignan and Robert H. Jackson. London: Croon Helm.

Cohen, Dennis L. 1979. "The Botswana Political Elite: Evidence from the 1974 General Election." *Journal of Southern African Affairs* 4:347–70.

Cohen, Michael A. 1973. "The Myth of the Expanding Centre—Politics in the Ivory Coast." *Journal of Modern African Studies* 11:227–46.

Colclough, Christopher, and Stephen McCarthy. 1980. *The Political Economy of Botswana: A Study of Growth and Income Distribution.* Oxford: Oxford University Press.

Easterly, William, and Ross Levine. 1997. "Africa's Growth Tragedy: Policies and Ethnic Divisions." *Quarterly Journal of Economics* 112:1203–50.

Edwards, Robert H. 1967. "Political and Constitutional Change in the Bechuanaland Protectorate." In *Transition in African Politics,* ed. J. Butler and A. A. Castagno. New York: Praeger.

Evans-Pritchard, Edward E. 1940. *The Nuer: A Description of the Modes of Livelihood and Political Institutions of a Nilotic People*. Oxford: Clarendon Press.

Fauré, Yves A. 1989. "Côte d'Ivoire: Analysing the Crisis." In *Contemporary West African States*, ed. Donald B. Cruise O'Brien, John Dunn, and Richard Ratherbon. Cambridge: Cambridge University Press.

Fawcus, Peter, with Alan Tilbury. 2000. *Botswana: The Road to Independence*. Gaborone: Pula Press.

Fortes, Meyer, and Edward E. Evans-Pritchard. 1940. *African Political Systems*. Oxford: Oxford University Press.

Good, Kenneth. 1992. "Interpreting the Exceptionality of Botswana." *Journal of Modern African Studies* 30:69–95.

———. 1994. "Corruption and Mismanagement in Botswana: A Best-Case Example?" *Journal of Modern African Studies* 32:499–521.

———. 1997. *Realizing Democracy in Botswana, Namibia, and South Africa*. Pretoria: Africa Institute of South Africa.

Harries-Jones, Peter. 1975. *Freedom and Labour: Mobilization and Political Control on the Zambian Copper Belt*. New York: St. Martin's Press.

Harvey, Charles, and Stephen Lewis Jr. 1990. *Policy Choice and Development Performance in Botswana*. London: Macmillan.

Holm, John D. 1988. "Botswana: A Paternalist Democracy." In *Democracy in Developing Countries: Africa*, ed. Larry Diamond, Juan J. Linz, and Seymour Martin Lipset. Boulder, Colo.: Lynne Rienner.

Holm, John D., and Patrick Molutsi. 1992. "State-Society Relations in Botswana: Beginning Liberalization." In *Governance and Politics in Africa*, ed. Goran Hyden and Michael Bratton. Boulder, Colo.: Lynne Rienner.

Horowitz, Donald L. 1985. *Ethnic Groups in Conflict*. Berkeley and Los Angeles: University of California Press.

Jefferis, Keith. 1998. "Botswana and Diamond-Dependent Development." In *Botswana: Politics and Society*, ed. Wayne A. Edge and Mogopodi H. Lekorwe. Pretoria: J. L. van Schaik.

Killick, Tony. 1978. *Development Economics in Action: A Study of Economic Policies in Ghana*. London: Heineman.

Krueger, Anne O. 1993. *Political Economy of Policy Reform in Developing Countries*. Cambridge: MIT Press.

Laitin, David D., and Said S. Samatar. 1987. *Somalia: Nation in Search of a State*. Boulder, Colo.: Westview Press.

Leith, J. Clark. 2000. "Why Botswana Prospered." Department of Economics, University of Western Ontario. Typescript.

Leith, J. Clark, and Michael F. Lofchie. 1993. "The Political Economy of Structural Adjustment in Ghana." In *Political and Economic Interactions in Economics Policy Reform: Evidence from Eight Countries*, ed. Robert H. Bates and Anne O. Krueger. Cambridge, Mass.: Basil Blackwell.

Leith, J. Clark, and Ludvig Söderling. 2000. "Ghana: Long-Term Growth, Atrophy, and Recovery." Report prepared for the OECD Development Centre.

Lewis, Ioan M. 1980. *A Modern History of Somalia: Nation and State in the Horn of Africa*. London: Longman.

Lofchie, Michael F. 1989. *The Policy Factor: Agricultural Performance in Kenya and Tanzania.* Boulder, Colo.: Lynn Rienner,

Lonsdale, John. 1981. "States and Social Processes in Africa: A Historiographical Survey." *African Studies Review* 24:139–225.

Maundeni, Zibani. 2000. "State Culture and the Botswana Developmental State." Forthcoming in the *Review of African Political Economy.*

———. 2001. "The Origin of the Zimbabwean Non-developmental State." Department of Political and Administrative Studies, University of Botswana. Typescript.

Migdal, Joel S. 1988. *Strong States, Weak Societies.* Princeton: Princeton University Press.

Molutsi, Patrick P. 1998. "Elections and Electoral Experience in Botswana." In *Botswana: Politics and Society,* ed. Wayne A. Edge and Mogopodi H. Lekorwe. Pretoria: J. L. van Schaik.

Owusu, Maxwell. 1970. *Use and Abuses of Power: A Case Study of Continuity and Change in the Politics of Ghana.* Chicago: University of Chicago Press.

Parson, Jack. 1984. *Botswana: Liberal Democracy and the Labor Reserve in Southern Africa.* Boulder, Colo.: Westview Press.

Parsons, Neil. 1977. "The Economic History of Khama's Country in Botswana, 1844–1930." In *The Roots of Rural Poverty in Central and Southern Africa,* ed. Neil Parsons and Robin Palmer. Berkeley and Los Angeles: University of California Press.

———. 1983. *A New History of Southern Africa.* New York: Holmes and Meier.

———. 1998. *King Khama, Emperor Joe, and the Great White Queen.* Chicago: University of Chicago Press.

———. 1999. *Botswana History Index.* Department of History, University of Botswana. http://ubh.tripod.com/bw/index.html.

Parsons, Neil, Thomas Tlou, and Willie Henderson. 1995. *Seretse Khama, 1921–1980.* Bloemfontein: Macmillan.

Pellow, Deborah, and Naomi Chazan. 1986. *Ghana: Coping with Uncertainty.* Boulder, Colo.: Westview Press.

Persson, Torsten, and Guido Tabellini. 1994. "Is Inequality Harmful for Growth?" *American Economic Review* 84:600–621.

Picard, Louis A. 1987. *The Politics of Development in Botswana: A Model for Success?* Boulder, Colo.: Lynne Rienner.

Price, Robert M. 1984. "Neo-colonialism and Ghana's Decline: A Critical Assessment." *Canadian Journal of African Studies* 18:163–93.

Proctor, J. H. 1968. "The House of Chiefs and the Political Development of Botswana." *Journal of Modern African Studies* 6:59–79.

Ramsay, Jeffrey, and Neil Parsons. 1998. "The Emergence of Political Parties in Botswana." In *Botswana: Politics and Society,* ed. Wayne A. Edge and Mogopodi H. Lekorwe. Pretoria: J. L. van Schaik.

Ranger, Terence. 1985. *The Invention of Tribalism in Zimbabwe.* Harare: Mambo Press.

Robinson, Ronald. 1977. "British Imperialism and Indigenous Reactions in British West Africa 1880–1914." In *Expansion and Reaction: Essays on European Expansion and Reactions in Asia and Africa,* ed. H. L. Wesserling. Leiden: University of Leiden Press.

Sachs, Jeffrey D., and Andrew Warner. 1995. "Natural Resource Abundance and Economic Growth." NBER Working Paper No. 5398.

Samatar, Abdi Ismail. 1999. *An African Miracle: State and Class Leadership and Colonial Legacy in Botswana Development.* Portsmouth, N.H.: Heinemann.

Schapera, Isaac. 1938. *A Handbook of Tswana Law and Custom.* London: Macmillan.

————. 1947. *Migrant Labour and Tribal Life: A Study of Conditions in the Bechua-naland Protectorate.* Oxford: Oxford University Press.

————. 1952. *The Ethnic Composition of Tswana Tribes.* London: Macmillan.

————. 1956. *Government and Politics in Tribal Societies.* New York: Schocken.

Somolakae, Gloria M., and Mogopodi H. Lekorwe. 1998. "The Chieftancy System and Politics in Botswana, 1966–1995." In *Botswana: Politics and Society,* ed. Wayne A. Edge and Mogopodi H. Lekorwe. Pretoria: J. L. van Schaik.

Stevenson, Robert F. 1968. *Population and Political Systems in Tropical Africa.* New York: Columbia University Press.

Thompson, Leonard. 1975. *Survival in Two Worlds: Moshoeshoe of Lesotho, 1786–1870.* Oxford: Oxford University Press.

Tlou, Thomas. 1985. *A History of Ngamiland, 1750 to 1906: The Formation of an African State.* Gaborone: Macmillan.

————. 1998. "The Nature of Batswana States: Towards a Theory of Batswana Tradi-tional Government—the Batawana Case." In *Botswana: Politics and Society,* ed. Wayne A. Edge and Mogopodi H. Lekorwe. Pretoria: J. L. van Schaik.

Tlou, Thomas, and Alec Campbell. 1997. *A History of Botswana.* Gaborone: Macmillan.

van Binsbergen, Wim. 1995. "Aspects of Democracy and Democratization in Zambia and Botswana: Exploring African Political Culture at the Grassroots." *Journal of Contemporary African Studies* 13:3–33.

van der Walle, Nicholas. 1993. "The Politics of Non-reform in the Cameroon." In *Hemmed In: Responses to Africa's Economic Decline,* ed. Thomas M. Callaghy and John Ravenhill. New York: Columbia University Press.

Vail, Leroy, ed. 1991. *The Creation of Tribalism in Southern Africa.* Berkeley and Los Angeles: University of California Press.

Vansina, Jan. 1966. *Kingdoms of the Savanna.* Madison: University of Wisconsin Press.

Widner, Jennifer A. 1993. "The Origins of Agricultural Policy in Ivory Coast, 1960–1986." *Journal of Development Studies* 29:25–60.

————. 1994. "Single Party States and Agricultural Policies: The Cases of Ivory Coast and Kenya." *Comparative Politics* 26:127–48.

Wilmsen, Edwin N. 1989. *Land Filled with Flies: A Political History of the Kalahari.* Chicago: University of Chicago Press.

Wylie, Diana. 1984. *A Little God: The Twilight of Patriarchy in a Southern African Chiefdom.* Hanover, N.H.: University of New England Press.

Part II

TRANSITIONS INTO AND OUT OF GROWTH

A Toy Collection, a Socialist Star, and a Democratic Dud?

GROWTH THEORY, VIETNAM, AND THE PHILIPPINES

LANT PRITCHETT

> Growth Theory (as we shall understand it) has no
> particular bearing on underdevelopment economics,
> nor has the underdevelopment interest played
> any essential part in its development.
> —John Hicks, *Capital and Growth*, 1965

ROBERT SOLOW often refers affectionately to his famous namesake model as a "parable" (in print) or verbally as a "toy" model. Being a toy does not mean that the model is not serious, but rather that in the interests of clarity it is stripped to its barest essentials. The toy model eliminates complexity to illuminate a few key relationships in the clearest possible way. The sacrifice for this clarity is generality. The Solow model explains the "broad facts about the growth of advanced industrialized economies" (Solow 1970, 3), and he has never maintained that it is applicable to developing countries. He opens his exposition of growth theory with the concern that "there are areas where it [the simplified model] appears to throw light but on which it actually propagates error" (Solow 1970). The "new growth theory" that blossomed in the 1980s following the seminal work of Romer (1986, 1990) and others is primarily a competing toy for explaining the OECD experience. At times toys can be compared head to head in the hope that one provides the "best" explanation, that is, can illuminate the phenomena of interest clearly with least loss of verisimilitude in the applicable range.

But John Hicks's sentiment that the "economics of underdevelopment" has played no essential role in the evolution of growth theory holds nearly as true for many of the developments in the last two decades as in its original flowering.

Understanding the diversity of growth experiences of developing countries requires not a toy *model* but a toy *collection*. Each one of many toy models covers part of the range of phenomena to be understood but no one model is "best." The question is not whether a top is a superior to a Slinky, but the circumstances and purposes to which each is best adapted.

In attempting to apply recent "growth theory" to particular country episodes of growth one could go one of three routes. One could choose a particular toy model (such as the Solow model) with its associated set of determinants and ask: "How much of this country's experience in this time period do the phenomena illuminated by this particular toy capture?" Or one could use the country experience as a horse race with an eye to choosing one toy over another. Which of a pair of toy models (e.g., "exogenous" versus "endogenous" growth models) fits the country experience "better"?

The third route, which I will pursue, is to play with all the toys. I begin with an encompassing approach that treats "growth theory" as a set of models applicable to different circumstances. In particular, I distinguish between models that attempt to illuminate differences in the rate of growth within a given growth "state" (e.g., models that seek to explain the relative rate of growth of two advanced industrial economies) and models that attempt to explain transitions between growth "states" (e.g., why do some countries shift from low to explosive growth, such as Korea in the 1960s or China in the 1980s or India in the 1990s) and why do other countries shift from growth to implosion such as Africa (in the 1970s and 1980s) or eastern Europe (in the 1990s).

It is conceivable there is a generic answer to the question, "What policies are best to promote economic growth?"—but it seems much more plausible that the answer is, "It depends." Is one giving policy advice about growth to a mature economy near the global leaders (e.g., United States or Germany)? To a booming, rapidly industrializing country trying to prevent stalling on a plateau (e.g., Korea, Taiwan, or Chile)? To a once rapidly growing and at least semi-industrialized country trying to initiate another episode of rapid growth (e.g., Brazil or Mexico or the Philippines)? To a country just launched into rapid growth from a very low level of income per head (e.g., Vietnam, India)? To a country still trying to take off into sustained growth (e.g., Tanzania or Myanmar or Haiti)? The appropriate policies for economic growth need to be taken within a set of models that allow for application to circumstances.

With this approach I move to the experience of Vietnam and the Philippines and see which of the toys in the box works the best in these cases, and what it might teach us about the rules of the game for growth theorizing. I argue that Vietnam's rapid growth in the 1990s is a classic "escape from poverty trap" burst occasioned by a credible shift in economic policies. This was not a shift to "good" policies in an absolute sense. Vietnam shifted *from* policies that reinforced a poverty trap (exchange rate overvaluation, hyperinflation, lack of incentives in the rural sector, reliance on Soviet aid for investment, severe limitations on the private sector in both rural and urban areas) *to* a set of policies that could support a substantially higher level of economic activity. This can create an extended boom. But the duration of the boom depends critically on policies and institutions and investments (infrastructure, human capital) keeping potentially supportable levels of income far ahead of actual income.

In contrast, the Philippines is an example of a failed shift in policies and institutions, where at an already quite high level of income the Marcos regime failed to keep potential income ahead of actual, and so growth slowed, then stalled. The democratic governments since have not been able to create a credible alternative set of policies and institutions that would kick off a growth boom to a higher level of income.

GROWTH THEORY: A TOY COLLECTION

This section does four things. First, it explicitly expands the range of phenomena to be covered by growth theory from just the facts of steady states in advanced industrial countries (Kaldor's "six facts") to the growth booms, busts, and poverty traps observed throughout the developing world. Second, it lays out seven stylized facts about the behavior of growth rates over the long and medium run. Third, it discusses what a growth theory toy box might be full of. Fourth, it shows how a simulated "toy collection" can replicate the range of stylized facts.

What Is Growth Theory a Theory Of?

There is much potential confusion created by the complete disjunction between the common and professional uses of the word *growth* as applied to national economies. For most people *growth* is about the short run—what is "growth" going to be next quarter or next year or, at the outside, what are prospects for "growth" in the next five years. In contrast the standard interpretation of "growth" theory in economics ignores all those concerns, dealing only in comparative equilibrium dynamics: differences in steady state growth rates.

While the words *economic growth* in their broadest sense could be made to cover all changes in aggregate output (e.g., GDP) between any two periods—whether over the past quarter or past quarter-century—I would like to classify "growth theories" into three horizons.

First, there are theories of the long-run growth of potential output. The key question for these theories is: What determines the equilibrium steady state rate of growth of an economy's productive potential?

Second, there is "macroeconomics" as conventionally understood—what determines the actual outcomes of the economic aggregates at any point in time? Output could be either above or below the equilibrium productive potential due to a combination of either transitory shocks (on demand or supply side) or policy actions and the less-than-instantaneous adjustment to disequilibria in the goods, labor, or money markets.

The third time horizon is medium-run growth. This "growth" is neither a change in the equilibrium rate of growth nor a temporary deviation of output from its current potential. Rather it is the dynamic adjustment process to a change in the *level* of potential output. Any policy reform that raises potential output, no matter how slightly, creates a period in which the economy, to move from the lower to the higher level of output at a given equilibrium steady state rate of growth, must "grow" faster. When the change in output level is substantial, this can result in an extended period of potentially very rapid "growth" (or decline) as part of the dynamic adjustment process.

Suppose that a single, discrete technological innovation raises the productivity in a poor country's staple crop by 50 percent. This is going to have direct effects on agricultural output that will play out as the innovation is adopted. In addition to the direct effects there will be indirect effects of increased demand for other agricultural and nonagricultural goods, which will induce investments in other industries (both capital and consumer goods). The direct and induced impacts of a single technological innovation will themselves play out over the course of several years or several decades. During this period "growth" will be more rapid than the steady state level in this country as the country makes the transition from the lower to the higher level of potential output.

Similarly, "policy" or "institutional reform" can change the level of potential output, perhaps substantially. In discrete cases—such as the unification of East and Western Germany—this is easy to see. The potential output of East Germany shifted dramatically, but it will take decades for the direct and indirect impacts of this shift to be observed.

While it is conceivable that a single "growth" theory could capture all three elements of growth of aggregate output, economics much more commonly prefers relatively simple models of the phenomena individually, with these models competing amongst themselves as the preferred model of "long-run growth" or the "business cycle" or "growth between levels." In this sense there is a collection of "growth theories" that inform particular issues.

An adequate collection of growth theories would be a *mutually consistent* set of models that can handle the basic facts about economic growth and address basic policy questions. While we can accept that no single theory addresses growth at all frequencies, if we need to invoke logically inconsistent "growth theories" about the same dimension of growth to explain different facts, this is an unacceptable state of theorizing.

Seven Stylized Facts about "Growth"

The collection of growth theories should be capable of addressing at least the following facts that have emerged from empirical research.

1. *Since 1870 there has been a massive divergence in absolute and relative incomes between the "leaders" and the "laggards."* The average absolute gap between the richest country and all other countries has grown by at least an order of magnitude since 1870, from P$1,200 to over P$12,000. The absolute difference in income between the leading country and the least developed in 1870 was, at most, around P$2,000—about the difference today between the Philippines and Vietnam (World Bank 2001), and yet the difference now between the United States and a country like Ethiopia is over P$20,000 (Pritchett 1997).

2. *Very steady growth of the "leading country" (United States) since 1870.* A truly remarkable fact is that if a single logarithmic trend estimated only using data through 1930 is used to predict income 58 years ahead to 1988 the prediction error is only 2.4 percent. Whatever forces there have been to raise or lower steady state growth, they remained nearly balanced for more than a century (Jones 1995).

3. *A set of "leading" countries has had nearly equal growth rates over the long haul.* Among the countries that were the economic leaders in 1870 growth rates have remained within a quite narrow range over the long run, with some mild (Baumol 1986) and period specific tendencies to convergence (Taylor and Williamson 1997).

4. *The poorest countries have had historically very low (near zero) growth rates.* A point made very early on by Kuznets (1956) was that, since there is a lower bound to what output per head could have been even in the far distant past, one can infer from the present level the maximum growth rate. While historically there may have been periods of progress and regress, if a country is poor today, its "beginning of history to today" growth rate has been significantly lower than the growth rates of the leading countries.

5. *Some countries that began poor in 1960 have had episodes of extremely rapid sustained growth.* Fourteen of the 107 countries with 25 or more years of data in the Penn World Tables 5.6 had GDP per capita growth rates over the entire period 1960–92 of more than 4 percent per annum—far more rapid than the historical or present OECD experience.

6. *The growth rates over the 1960–92 period have varied enormously across developing countries.* While some developing economies were booming, others were stagnating. The range of developing country growth rates over the 1960 to 1992 period is more than four times as large as for the developed economies—a whopping 9.6 percentage points. Korea and Mozambique went from roughly the same level of GDPPC in 1960 to levels different by an *order of magnitude* (over P$7,000 in Korea and under P$700 in Mozambique).

7. *Growth has been enormously variable within developing countries, and there is little persistence of economic growth rates.* The variation of growth rates within countries over time has also been more than twice as large for developing countries. The average change in growth rates (in absolute value) in developing countries from one decade to the next is a full 3 percentage points (Pritchett 2000). Some countries have had growth accelerate enormously: Indonesia's GDP per capita growth rate was 0.57 from 1960 to 1970, 5.08 percent since. Others have had rapid growth rates come to a complete halt: Brazil's GDPPC grew 5 percent per year until 1980, and only 0.06 percent yearly until 1992. Mexico's GDPPC grew 3.8 percent per year until 1981 and 0.05 per year from 1981 to 1992. Still others have seen growth punctuated with huge falls in output (e.g., Chile's GDP per capita fell 23 percent from 1972 to 1976 and 22 percent from 1981 to 1983). The cross-country correlation of growth rates is very low, even over fairly extended periods, such as 10 or 15 years. Using the data since 1960 one finds that, if one excludes the Four Asian Dragons and Japan, the correlation of growth rates over the beginning and end periods of the sample is only .17 (Easterly et al. 1993).

An Encompassing Model of Economic Growth Theories

No one toy model of economic growth is going to be able to generate all of the observed facts about "growth." Let me be clear by what I mean by that. Take a simple complete growth model that has all these features: a production function, a specification of the equilibrium capital stock (we'll aggregate human capital in for now), an adjustment dynamics to that capital stock, a specification of the country-specific productivity, and an adjustment dynamics for productivity. So a long-run growth model would be a system of equations like these:

Production function:
$$y_t^j = A_t^j * f(k_t^j)$$

Equilibrium capital stock:
$$k_t^{j*} = k(Z_k, \Theta_k)$$

Capital stock dynamics:
$$\dot{k}_t^j = \alpha_k(Z_k, \Theta_k, k_t^j - k_t^{j*})$$

Evolution of productivity frontier:
$$\dot{A}^W = A^W(Z_{AW}, \Theta_{AW})$$

Evolution of country productivity:
$$\dot{A}_t^j = \alpha_A(Z_A, \Theta_A, A_t^W - A_t^j)$$

One could argue that this system of equations is a sufficiently general single growth model capable of generating whatever growth dynamics might be observed. However, what makes a general model into a toy model is specification. The equations above are not yet a model, and several of the elements—capital stock dynamics or technological diffusion—have many intriguing contributions and suggestive directions but no canonical model (Aghion and Howitt 1998; King and Rebelo 1989).

Simplification is a necessary and desirable feature of model specification that aids in understanding individual causal mechanisms. However, this simplification usually involves three steps that limit the range of applicability: parsimony, homogeneity, and linearity. *Parsimony* is the selection of one or few variables that become the driving force. The savings rate, R&D, education are some of the choices for the "intermediate" variable with each in turn driven by some one or few variables—uncertainty, discount rates, scope of the market. *Homogeneity* is embedded in the above equations in the restriction that all countries share the same functional form—the same set of "Z's" and the same parameters determine the equilibrium capital stock in Tanzania as in Albania as in Argentina. Nearly always the equations are specified such that history doesn't matter, institutions don't matter, the level of socioeconomic development doesn't matter. The ultimate simplification, usually driven by analytic convenience or empirical specification is *linearity*.[1] These toy models are explicitly rejected by the fact that in linear regressions the constancy of coefficients is rejected soundly when tested: regression coefficients are not stable over time, across sets of countries, or with respect to interaction effects. This parameter instability demonstrates that, while the models have their uses in exposition and for illustration of simple points, they are far from adequate in their empirical performance.

The feasible project is not to construct a single growth model, but rather to put the various models into a collection in a way that their relationship to one another and to their range of applicability is clear.

My preferred encompassing model of economic growth would have two sets of models. One set consists of different models to explain the growth rates of countries in the same "state." The second set of models would explain transitions between growth "states."

Growth states. I propose an encompassing growth model with six possible states (see table 5.1): (1) advanced industrial country steady growth, (2) low-level poverty trap, (3) self-sustaining moderate growth or non-converging follower, (4) rapid growth, (5) implosion, (6) non-poverty-trap zero (or very low) growth. In each state, growth is determined according to the determinants and dynamics of the model appropriate to that state. Why six states? I believe this is the minimum necessary to encompass the facts.

---

[1] What would it take to create a model with a linear specification between the observed growth rate between period t and $t-n$ and some other variable Z over that same period? To even begin to list the conditions is to see how improbable they are: *(a)* the parameterization of each of the equations is linear, *(b)* all parameters are time invariant, *(c)* all parameters are invariant across levels of income and institutions (e.g., no interaction effects), *(d)* the dynamic adjustments are all exactly the same across all countries (so that a lagged level variable can capture the disequilibrium dynamics for all variables), *(e)* the variable of interest must either enter only one of the equations or it must enter all of them exactly the same.

Countries like the United States or Germany or Sweden are all in the "state" of "advanced industrial countries." The important features of the medium- and long-run growth dynamics of all countries in this state could perhaps be illuminated by the equations of motion of a single growth model. Perhaps the Solow model is the best model for countries in this state. Perhaps a newer, endogenous growth model, along the lines of Romer (1986) is better. But in either case some model has to be able to explain *(a)* the extremely steady growth of the United States and *(b)* the existence of a "convergence club" of a group of the more technologically advanced countries that have grown at relatively steady rates (on average) for more than a century.

But countries like Senegal or Nepal or Laos are not in the state of "advanced industrial economies." Rather, these countries are in the growth "state" called something like a "low-level poverty trap." The equations of motion for this "state" would be determined by a model of a poverty trap. There are a number of candidates for such a model, Aziardis and Drazen 1990, Easterly 1994, or even perhaps one of the older "underdevelopment" models of Lewis (1955). The medium- and long-run growth dynamics are not well understood if they are assumed to be governed by the same equations of motion as the United States (whether that be Solow or an endogenous growth variant). Some model is necessary to explain why some countries have essentially never had an extended period of long-run growth even at the speed of the advanced industrial economies (no less a period of rapid convergence).

A third state accommodates those countries that are neither technological leaders nor advanced industrial countries and are not in a poverty trap. What is the model that captures the behavior of the nonzero but nonconverging growth rates of countries like Colombia or Tunisia? Perhaps they can be understood with a Solow model of endogenous growth with imperfectly diffusing technological knowledge. Perhaps not. There is something of a puzzle in the standard model: why do countries not have quite rapid convergence to the leaders in the absence of growth impediments?

Along with the "leader" and the "poverty trap" and "nonconverging follower" as models of steady state growth there must be at least three other states. Any model of steady state long-run growth will have difficulties with the observed extremes of the growth experience. Both very fast and negative growth episodes are impossible to explain as alternative steady state equilibriums (Bernard 2001).

The fourth state is "rapid growth." The very rapid growth episodes of the East Asian Tigers (or of the Latin American "Miracle" countries before them) cannot be understood as being rapid steady state growth or, I would argue, as transitional dynamics within a Solow model (King and Rebelo 1989). Rather, these rapid growth episodes may represent medium-run dynamics in the form of transition to a new, much, much higher level of output driven causally by large shifts in the level of supportable income. The speed of the adjustment to that new level of output must be determined by the equations of motion of a theory of dynamics of disequilibrium that can accommodate periods of extremely rapid growth mediated primarily by rapid expansions in investments.

A fifth state is a country in an extended period of negative growth, which must be explained by its own equations of motion, apart from those determining the long-run level and growth rate for the obvious reason that negative growth cannot be a steady state. Nevertheless there are obviously episodes in which countries sustained negative growth rates for a decade or more (Madagascar, Guyana). The recent enormously large collapses in output of the "transition" countries are another set of examples of negative growth. Some model in the collection has to be able to accommodate these non-steady-state transitions of output from a higher to a lower level. Perhaps there is a solution in models along the lines of the "disorganization" models of Blanchard and Kremer (1997) or a model of shifting fundamentals.

Finally, there must be a state of zero growth outside of a poverty trap. Argentina, for instance, has experienced extended episodes of zero or near zero growth but is far from existing at levels of income, human capital, or anything that could be characterized as a "poverty trap." Similarly, many Latin American countries have been in extended periods of stagnation following the crises of the 1980s.

Economic growth within states. In each state S the growth rate of a given country i in period t would be given by the growth model M^S particular to that state. Within a given model M, growth is determined by factors Z and parameters (Θ).

$$g_{i,t}^S(M^S(Z_{i,t}^M, \Theta^M)) \tag{1}$$

For example in the state of "advanced industrial country" the chosen model may be the "Solow" model (extended so as to include human capital) so that per capita growth rates depend only on steady state TFP and transitional dynamics (where the transitional dynamics are responses of deviations of actual from long-run capital stocks).

$$g_{i,t}^{AIC} = TFP + transitional\ dynamics \tag{2}$$

The other growth states are more difficult to characterize, as the models of transitional dynamics are much less well developed than of steady states.

For instance, the state of "rapid growth" may include some TFP growth but is dominated by the medium-run dynamics of adjusting from one level of income to a new, much higher level.[2] Suppose a country moves from an existing

---

[2] So for instance in the case of the East Asian tigers a great deal of the growth was accompanied by rapid growth of physical and human capital stocks (as well as expansion in the labor force participation rate). While TFP growth was not inconsequential, it did not account for the major fraction of the rapid growth.

TABLE 5.1
A Possible Typology of Growth "States"

Growth State	Defining Empirical Characteristics	Possible Country Examples	Models
Steady growth at levels of income near world leaders	Productivity level at or near leader	Western Europe and areas of settlement	Solow (and variants), Engogenous growth theories of TFP
Poverty trap	Growth at or near zero at levels of income at or near subsistence	Senegal, Chad, Congo (Zaire), Myanmar, Cambodia, North Korea	Aziardis and Drazen (threshold externalities), Easterly (policy thresholds)
Nonconverging steady growth	Productivity not near subsistence but growth neither rapid nor near zero (between 1 and 5 percent)	Colombia, Pakistan, India (pre-1991)	
Rapid growth	Sustained growth (>five years) are very rapid rates (5 percent per capita)	South Korea, Indonesia (1967–97), Brazil (1964–79), Japan (pre-WWII), Vietnam (post-1989)	
Growth implosion	Either negative growth rates for >10 years or drop in per capita level of >20 percent	Countries of former USSR, Guyana, Madagasar, Côte d'Ivoire (post-1974), Venezuela (post-1980)	Blanchard and Kremer
Non–poverty trap stagnation	Near zero growth for extended period at levels of productivity substantially above subsistence	Brazil (post-1980), Bolivia (post-1986), Philippines (post-1993)	

set of policies (P) and institutions (I) to a new set that sustains a much higher level of income. How rapid the growth is between those states is likely a function of the magnitude of the gap between the new equilibrium income and existing income and another set of factors that determine the speed for any given gap, such as the availability and flexibility of finance to invest to create the new, higher capital stock consistent with the new level of income (denoted as Z). In this case growth would be some function of underlying TFP growth plus transitional dynamics.

$$g_{i,t}^{RG} = TFP + \Psi(y^*(Policies, Institutions) - y_{i,t}, Z) \qquad (3)$$

Or, in a "poverty trap" state the growth rate could be zero across a large range of variables within a threshold and then jump to some positive level above the threshold.

$$g_{i,t}^{PT} = \begin{array}{l} 0 \; \textit{if } \beta^*Z < \textit{Threshold} \\ \alpha \; \textit{if } \beta^*Z \geq \textit{Threshold} \end{array} \qquad (4)$$

The most difficult growth states to characterize are the nonconverging growth, non–poverty trap stagnation, and growth implosions. While there are some models of why a country would get trapped at subsistence levels of income— what leads a country like Brazil that had been growing very rapidly and does have investment capacity to get stuck at a level of income substantially below that of the OECD? Even worse, what leads to sustained contractions in the level of output—even when factors of production exist?

Transitions between states. The encompassing approach to a broader theory of growth requires not only individual models of growth within states but also explanations for country transitions between states. The simplest way to characterize this is a matrix of transition probabilities between various states (table 5.2). Since the growth states are characterized by levels of productivity and growth, it is only possible to make the transition from some states to others (as instantaneous changes in level are not possible). But a set of models that explain transitions (or persistence in the same state) is necessary to understand why some countries initiate episodes of rapid growth, while others after extended growth begin to stagnate.

These models of transition will not be easy, as often countries subject to apparently equivalent shocks show substantially different transition behavior so that the same exogenous shock pushes some countries into extended periods of stagnation (or implosion) while others continue to grow (Rodrik 2000).

As a general specification in each year a country finds itself at some level of income, some accumulated level of "capitals," with a set of policies and institutions, and in some growth state. Each of these then play a role in determining the growth state to which the country makes the transition in the next period (and not all states are possible from any given state—one cannot move immediately from "poverty trap" to "technological leader").

$$\pi_{i,t}^{S,S'} = \Pi(Initial\ conditions,\ History,\ Policies,\ S,\ S') \qquad (5)$$

By now of course the reader will see that aggregating this collection of models is not parsimonious, homogeneous, or linear. There is no reason why these theories of transition should be symmetric: it is logically possible, and in my mind quite plausible, that the correct policies to initiate a transition from a growth

TABLE 5.2

Transitions between States

	Technological Leader and Close Followers	Low-Level Poverty Trap	Self-sustaining Moderate Growth	Rapid Growth	Growth Implosion	Low Growth (non–poverty trap)
Technological leader(s)	$\pi_{TL,TL}$	0	0	0	0	$\pi_{TL,ZG}$
Low-level poverty trap	0	$\pi_{PT,PT}$	$\pi_{PT,MG}$	$\pi_{PT,RG}$	0	0
Self-sustaining moderate growth	0	$\pi_{MG,PT}$	$\pi_{MG,MG}$	$\pi_{MG,RG}$	$\pi_{MG,GI}$	$\pi_{MG,ZG}$
Rapid growth	$\pi_{RG,TL}$	0	$\pi_{RG,MG}$	$\pi_{RG,RG}$	$\pi_{RG,GI}$	$\pi_{RG,ZG}$
Growth implosion	0	$\pi_{GI,PT}$	$\pi_{GI,MG}$	$\pi_{GI,RG}$	$\pi_{GI,GI}$	$\pi_{GI,ZG}$
Non–poverty trap low or zero growth	0	0	$\pi_{ZG,MG}$	$\pi_{ZG,RG}$	$\pi_{ZG,GI}$	$\pi_{ZG,ZG}$

implosion to a state of rapid growth are not just the policies to move from rapid growth to a growth implosion with the sign reversed. So there must be at least six different *classes* of models (not just models) that would explain transitions from various states to various states. So one class of models might explain the transitions from poverty trap (and include the persistence in a poverty trap). Another class of models might explain transitions from rapid growth (again, including the possibility of remaining in rapid growth). Within these six classes it may even be that the same toy model of transition is not applicable to transitions into different states—the same factors that propel a transition from zero to rapid growth may not be simply the reverse of the factors that determine a transition from zero growth to growth implosion.

Simulations with an Encompassing Model

Before moving to the individual examples of Vietnam and Philippines, I will offer a brief demonstration of the ability of the encompassing model to replicate the basic "stylized facts" of growth laid out above by simulating GDP from

1870. I use the simplest possible model in which both growth within states and transition probabilities between states are fixed.

The mathematical model is based on simulating a GDP per capita series (y) for each of n countries ($n = 117$) over t periods based on cumulating a series from a starting date.

$$y_t^n = y_{t-1}^n * (1 + g_t^n) \qquad (6)$$

The set of countries is divided into two, the "rich" countries and the "developing" countries. In the simulations there are 14 rich countries and 103 developing countries.

For the 14 rich countries the model is simple. The initial GDPPC in 1870 was drawn from a uniform distribution with minimum of P\$1,700 and maximum of P\$2,050. The rich countries grew in every period at 1.8 percent, and the transition probability of transition into any other state is zero.

The 103 developing countries were more complicated (but not quite as complicated as above). The initial GDPPC in 1870 was drawn from a uniform distribution with a minimum of P\$250 and a maximum P\$950. In each period the growth rate (g) for each country in each period t is decided stochastically to be in one of four states. There is a "low growth" state with growth of 0.5 percent per annum; a self-sustaining growth at the same rate as the "leaders," $g = 1.8$ percent. There is a "rapid growth" state where the growth rate is proportional to the gap between the country's current output and that of the leader,

$$g = (1.8) * (rich\ country\ income^t)/y_n^t).$$

This creates booms with extremely rapid growth, but which eventually settles down to the "rich" country rate. Finally, there is an "implosion" period in which

$$g = -1.8 * (y_n^t - 250)/y_n^t),$$

which creates the possibility of large recessions (especially for poorer countries) but with no country going below the minimum level of income (so growth slows eventually to zero). All poor countries begin the simulation in the same state, which in this instance corresponds to a "poverty trap."

The matrix of transition probabilities between the various stages is exogenous and is given in table 5.3. All of these probabilities are simple constants across all simulations except that for the transition from stagnation to growth. This transition is in two stages, first, from stagnation where there is a probability of transition from stagnation to growth (of 1.5 percent in each period), and then, conditional on shifting to growth, either "nonconverging" growth (probability .7) or a boom (with probability .3).

TABLE 5.3

Matrix of Transition Probabilities between Various Growth Rate States in Simulations

To	From			
	Stagnation	Implosion	Plateau	Boom
Stagnation	.885	.4	.1	0
Implosion	.1	.6	0	0
Plateau	.7	0	.8	.1
	.015			
Boom	.3	0	.1	.9

The structure of the model and the transition probabilities were chosen so as generate approximately the observed magnitude of divergence and to roughly reflect the seven facts about growth rates. The 1870 to 1995 figures show absolute divergence of approximately the right magnitude. By obvious construction there are a set of leader countries with steady growth. Given the high probability of remaining in the "poverty trap," a significant number of countries remain at or near subsistence. In addition, if after running the simulation one calculates the statistics about the growth rates over the last 30 years, one also gets several features any standard model would have difficulty generating: the huge range of growth rates in developing countries and the low degree of persistence in growth rates over time (table 5.4).

COUNTRY STUDIES WITHIN AN ENCOMPASSING "GROWTH THEORY": VIETNAM AND THE PHILIPPINES

All of this is background for addressing the question of Vietnam and the Philippines. For both of these countries the growth theories relevant to "advanced industrial countries" are of little interest. The question is, how can we understand

TABLE 5.4

Summary Statistics of Growth Rates Over the Last 30 years of a 125-Year Simulation Using Growth States and Transition Probabilities

Mean of growth rates	1.77
Standard deviation of "developing" country growth rates	2.3
Range of "developing" country growth rates	8.8 (8.02 to −0.76)
Correlation of growth rates of "developing" countries between first and last half of the period	.12

their experiences and how do the various theories help? With Vietnam, I think the right story is twofold: a basic "escape from poverty" trap transition followed by a "Tarzan of the Jungle" (a non-multicultural reference to be explained below) series of growth episodes—in which Vietnam has, until now, been able to maintain rapid growth by staying on the series of transitions necessary.

The Philippines in contrast, is an example of a "George of the Jungle" (another culturally specific reference) failed transition.

A Tarzan or George of the Jungle Theory of Medium-Run Growth

Understanding medium-run growth episodes is hampered by the lack of a well-accepted theory of any of three necessary features: *(a)* transitions between growth episodes, *(b)* transitional dynamics of levels of output within episodes of large changes in the supportable level of output, or *(c)* (and this is controversial) a determination of the level of supportable output. Let me start from the latter and work back to the former in a simple formalization.

I propose that for any given level of "policies" and "institutions" there is a level of output determined by the supportable level of physical and human capital associated with those policies and institutions and the supportable level of productivity at which those stocks of productive factors are used. I use the odd word *supportable* to avoid three confusions. First, this is not necessarily an "equilibrium" level of physical capital in any market sense. For instance, in the Leninist/Stalinist period of the Soviet Union there was in fact a large and rapid increase in physical capital that was "supportable" given policies and institutions. This supportable level of capital was by no means an "equilibrium" of the market (or for that matter voluntary) but, given the coercive ability of the existing institutions, the necessary investable surpluses could be created and sustained. Second, I use the word *supportable* to avoid the word *sustainable,* which is precisely what many of the episodes of rapid growth and even levels of income were not. Third, supportable income is not current potential output; rather, supportable output is the maximum potential output once all processes of accumulation have run their course.

So, without specifying any particular functional form, supportable output in country j at time t is

$$y_t^{jS} = y^S(P, I, H). \tag{7}$$

Now suppose some change in policies or institutions creates a clear gap between current output and supportable output. This creates the potential for upward (or downward) movement in output. How rapidly these changes in output are realized depends, arithmetically, on how much of the change is due to productivity, conditional on accumulated factors, how rapidly those gains can be realized,

a.

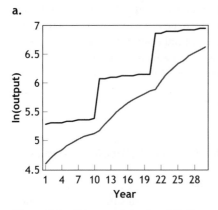

b.

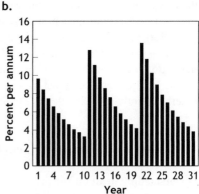

Figure 5.1a. "Tarzan of the Jungle": Supportable output doubles each 10 years, rapid transition

Figure 5.1b. Per annum growth rates with "Tarzan of the Jungle" evolution of output

how much of the change is to be realized through accumulation of factors, and how rapidly that factor accumulation can be realized.

Now suppose that clear-cut changes in policies and institutions that cause substantial revisions in supportable output happen only periodically. That is, in most periods the revisions in policies are relatively minor but there are discrete episodes of shifts that are recognized by all actors as a discrete shift in economic regime. What kind of growth dynamics will that generate?

Let me present some simple simulations of possible 30-year evolutions of output to illustrate the types of rich medium-run growth dynamics this simple setup can generate.

Suppose that every *N* (I'll use 10) years there is a regime shift and supportable output can increase, decrease, or stay the same. Given the shift in supportable output, the dynamics can be fixed by specifying how many years it would take to eliminate the gap between current and supportable income. In these simulations the growth rate in each year is set such that if growth were to continue at that rate, it would eliminate the gap between actual and supportable output in *X* years. Finally, I add that, for any given level of policies and institutions, supportable income grows at 1 percent per year (to mimic the movement in the "world" frontier).

Tarzan of the Jungle. In the first example in figure 5.1 and columns 1–3 of table 5.5 there is sustained rapid growth. Each 10 years the supportable level of output doubles, and the growth dynamics are such that this growth differential would be eliminated in 10 years of current growth (it is not in fact eliminated in 10 years, as in the next period the gap is smaller, so growth is slower, etc). Growth comes in waves as each jump in supportable income causes an

TABLE 5.5
Tarzan of the Jungle: Bursts of Rapid Growth as "Supportable Output"
Increases ahead of Actual Output

Year	Supportable Output	Transition Speed[a]		
		10 Years	7.5 Years	20 Years
1	200.0			
2	202.0	7.18%	9.68%	3.53%
3	204.0	6.54%	8.48%	3.40%
4	206.1	5.98%	7.45%	3.28%
5	208.1	5.47%	6.57%	3.16%
6	210.2	5.01%	5.81%	3.05%
7	212.3	4.60%	5.16%	2.95%
8	214.4	4.24%	4.59%	2.85%
9	216.6	3.91%	4.11%	2.76%
10	218.7	3.61%	3.69%	2.67%
11	437.5	3.35%	3.32%	2.59%
12	441.8	10.40%	12.84%	6.07%
13	446.3	9.42%	11.18%	5.81%
14	450.7	8.55%	9.77%	5.56%
15	455.2	7.77%	8.55%	5.33%
16	459.8	7.07%	7.52%	5.11%
17	464.4	6.45%	6.62%	4.90%
18	469.0	5.89%	5.86%	4.70%
19	473.7	5.39%	5.19%	4.51%
20	478.5	4.95%	4.63%	4.33%
21	956.9	4.54%	4.13%	4.16%
22	966.5	11.55%	13.60%	7.62%
23	976.2	10.45%	11.84%	7.28%
24	985.9	9.46%	10.33%	6.95%
25	995.8	8.59%	9.03%	6.65%
26	1005.7	7.80%	7.93%	6.36%
27	1015.8	7.10%	6.98%	6.08%
28	1025.9	6.48%	6.16%	5.82%
29	1036.2	5.92%	5.46%	5.58%
30	1046.6	5.41%	4.85%	5.34%
31	1057.0	4.96%	4.33%	5.12%

Note: In this simulation, supportable output increases 100 percent each 10 years plus 1 percent per annum growth.

[a] Period over which existing gap would be eliminated if annual growth rate maintained.

a.

b.

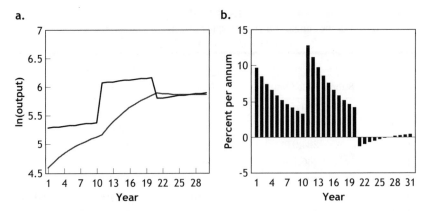

Figure 5.2a. "George of the Jungle": Supportable output doubles twice, then falls 30 percent rapid transition

Figure 5.2b. Per annum growth rates with "George of the Jungle" evolution of output

acceleration in growth, and growth gradually then decelerates as actual approaches supportable. I call this the "Tarzan of the Jungle" model of medium-run growth because Tarzan would swing through the jungle from vine to vine. Each vine gave him a maximum amount of forward progress on that vine, which would come with first a rapid acceleration followed by a slowing. If, before his forward progress was completely halted, he managed to grab a new vine, then this cycle was repeated and his rapid forward motion could be sustained indefinitely through a series of discrete episodes.

The second and third examples show the same evolution of supportable output, but with different transitional dynamics. In the second example, the dynamics are faster such that the gap would be eliminated in 7.5 years. This is perhaps because more of the gains are achievable with productivity gains (if, for instance, the regulatory environment had positively inhibited output, a burst of output is possible early on), or if higher rates of investment are possible (given higher savings, either domestic or foreign) such that the new level of capital is reached more quickly. In this case the growth rates are obviously even more rapid. In contrast, if the adjustment period is lengthened to 20 years, then growth is less rapid and the bursts of acceleration around each episode of policy and institutional reform less pronounced.

George of the Jungle. George of the Jungle was a parody on Tarzan, being just as strong, but much less bright. The trademark cry of George's friends was "Watch out for that tree!" Unlike Tarzan's graceful conveyance, George's rapid forward progress is arrested by a large obstacle. I simulate a George of the Jungle growth path by replicating the first two increases in supportable output, but then in the third period, supportable output instead of rising by 100 percent falls by 30 percent (fig. 5.2 and table 5.6). In this case, the growth dynamics

TABLE 5.6

George of the Jungle: Bursts of Rapid Growth as "Supportable Output"
Increases ahead of Actual Output, followed by a Large Shock

Year	Supportable Output	Transition Speed[a]		
		10 Years	7.5 Years	20 Years
1	200.0			
2	202.0	7.18%	9.68%	3.53%
3	204.0	6.54%	8.48%	3.40%
4	206.1	5.98%	7.45%	3.28%
5	208.1	5.47%	6.57%	3.16%
6	210.2	5.01%	5.81%	3.05%
7	212.3	4.60%	5.16%	2.95%
8	214.4	4.24%	4.59%	2.85%
9	216.6	3.91%	4.11%	2.76%
10	218.7	3.61%	3.69%	2.67%
11	437.5	3.35%	3.32%	2.59%
12	441.8	10.40%	12.84%	6.07%
13	446.3	9.42%	11.18%	5.81%
14	450.7	8.55%	9.77%	5.56%
15	455.2	7.77%	8.55%	5.33%
16	459.8	7.07%	7.52%	5.11%
17	464.4	6.45%	6.62%	4.90%
18	469.0	5.89%	5.86%	4.70%
19	473.7	5.39%	5.19%	4.51%
20	478.5	4.95%	4.63%	4.33%
21	334.9	4.54%	4.13%	4.16%
22	338.3	0.43%	−1.24%	2.11%
23	341.7	0.49%	−0.94%	2.06%
24	345.1	0.54%	−0.68%	2.01%
25	348.5	0.59%	−0.46%	1.96%
26	352.0	0.63%	−0.27%	1.91%
27	355.5	0.67%	−0.10%	1.86%
28	359.1	0.70%	0.05%	1.82%
29	362.7	0.73%	0.17%	1.78%
30	366.3	0.76%	0.28%	1.74%
31	370.0	0.78%	0.38%	1.70%

Note: In this simulation, supportable output increases 100 percent each 10 years plus 1 percent p.a. growth, followed by a 30 percent decrease in supportable output in year 20.

[a] Period over which existing gap would be eliminated if annual growth rate maintained.

depend on the speed of adjustment. Under rapid adjustment (7.5 years) the economy turns very rapidly from a boom to bust following the shock to supportable output: growth turns from over 4 percent to *negative* 1.2 percent from one year to the next.

If on the other hand the adjustment was slow in any case (20 years), then the output slowdown is much less visible—just as at the shock to supportable GDP it still substantially exceeds actual GDP, so there is a much more gradual slowing—gradually slowing from 4 to positive 2.1 percent(to approach the underlying growth rate of 1 percent).

In both of these cases one can see how a combination of discrete shifts in the level of income combined with simple adjustment dynamics produces very rich dynamics in the growth rates. Only now do we turn to the two countries at hand.

Vietnam: Booming out of a Poverty Trap

Table 5.7 and figure 5.3 show the actual growth experience of Vietnam from 1976 (the first full year of unification after the United States withdrew) to 1999 (see also table 5.A1). I break the policy experience up into five periods, as described in table 5.7.[3] From 1976 to 1982 the policy was roughly one of "War Communism"—a rapid administrative unification of the country after the war and a continuation of strict centralized planning in the North and attempts at imposing the same system in the South. Typical is the episode in March 1978 in which a surprise raid was carried out on private businesses throughout former South Vietnam to nationalize nearly all private activity. Because of the devastation of the war (both physical and human) and the rigidity of the regime, the supportable income given policies and institutions was as low as supportable income can be and remain demographically sustainable (perhaps somewhat lower).

These efforts at immediate "socialism" created a severe economic crisis. Policies were relaxed somewhat on a piecemeal basis, but without any clear shift in policy direction, as the hardliners in the government did not want to concede any fundamental changes. Nevertheless, compared to the completely coercive policies of the earlier period, even this modest relaxation of controls allowed some growth.[4]

---

[3] For the narrative of Vietnam's basic political transitions and economic policy reforms I drew on various sources: the World Bank's country economic memorandum, particularly Dollar 1993; the reports in the Economist Intelligence Unit for Vietnam; Forbes et al. 1991; Duiker 1995, Harvie and van Hoa 1997; and Hiebert 1996.

[4] As a newcomer to reading postwar Vietnamese economic policies I was struck by an almost perverse desire of the Vietnamese to relive not just the successes but also the failures of Lenin. Why would people aware of Russian economic history choose to relive it rather than skip straight to the New Economic Policy? One suspects that for all its horrific consequences for output the interim period of "war communism" serves some political purpose (perhaps confiscating large amounts of property to reward loyal soldiers?).

TABLE 5.7
Economic Growth in Vietnam over Various Periods, 1976–99

Period	Policy Environment	Per annum Growth of per Capita GDP during the Period
1976–81	Unification of the country, "war communism" nationalization of private industry, trading, collectivization of farms in the south.	−0.67%
1981–86	Second Five Year Plan, some relaxation of controls in rural areas, introduction of "contract system," but no announced reform path	5.86%
1986–88	*Doi moi,* prestabilization: Reforms were announced in 1986, but proceed slowly.	1.97%
1988–97	*Doi moi,* with macroeconomic stabilization: a major stabilization in 1989 includes exchange rate unification, abolition of dual price system, reducing quotas and tariffs, and others.	5.85%
1997–99	East Asia Crisis: Spillover effects dampen growth.	3.40%

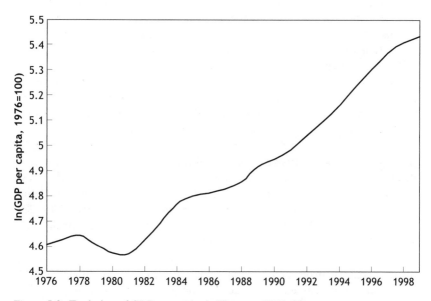

Figure 5.3. Evolution of GDP per capita in Vietnam, 1976–99

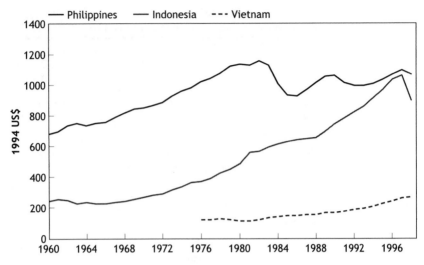

Figure 5.4. GDP per capita in 1994 U.S.$

However, this growth petered out, and in 1986 the Sixth Congress, while remaining committed to a transition to socialism, announced a new direction that allowed for a "multisectoral" (e.g., mix of public and private sectors) approach. Implementation of these reforms was weak, and it was not until an agricultural crisis in 1988 and the collapse of the Soviet Union in 1989 that the government addressed the growing macroeconomic crisis through aggressive reform.

This reform was enormously successful, creating rapid growth until the effects of the East Asian crisis began to show in 1997.

Three points about the Vietnamese experience are salient.

First, Vietnam has had very rapid growth, but from a very, very low level. While international comparisons in output levels are hard to make because of fluctuating exchange rates and the lack of a solidly based PPP estimate for Vietnam, it is clear that Vietnam has yet to reach the levels reached by other East Asian economies in the early 1970s. For instance, figure 5.4 shows the level of GDP per capita in dollars at 1994 exchange rates for a set of East Asian countries. In this figure all of the features of acceleration and deceleration of growth so evident in figure 5.3 are lost, as the level of output is so low that in absolute terms, even with the boom, Vietnam is where Indonesia was in the early 1970s. This suggests that it should not be difficult to maintain reform momentum and keep supportable output ahead of actual output for a long and sustained boom.

The second point is about the timing of the output boom versus the timing of any increase in investment or capital stock. The growth was initiated in 1989, when domestic investment and especially domestic savings were very low. This suggests, as is plausible, that there were still enormous gains in productivity available simply from freeing up and providing incentives for the existing factors of production. However, at the same time the boom created a remarkable turnaround in domestic savings. From a level of domestic savings of *negative* 2.4 percent in 1988 domestic savings rose to 10.1 percent of GDP in 1991—just three years later. This ability to mobilize domestic savings is not a cause of the expansion of GDP but is a key element in the rapid transition.

Third, an important point in understanding the growth experience of the socialist countries (and for the Philippines, as I argue below) is that there has never been any serious threat to political control—there has been enormous political and "institutional" continuity. The economic policy transitions have been from one set of economic policies to set of policies capable of sustaining a much higher (but absolutely low) level—within the same political and institutional regime. There has been very little uncertainty about who the government is and, broadly speaking, what it intends to do or whether, again roughly speaking, it can carry out what it intends to do.

Philippines: Failed Transition

The puzzle of the Philippines is why, 12 years and four presidents after the departure of Marcos and a transition to democracy, the country's GDP per capita is *lower* than it was in the last "precrisis" year 1982 two decades ago.[5] Not only have the democratic governments following the "People Power" uprising that overthrew Marcos not been able to achieve the rapid, East Asian–style growth seemingly enjoyed by all their neighbors (at least precrisis)—they have not even been able to restore the level of output per capita to its bad old dictatorship days.

Examining figure 5.5, one sees that from 1970 to 1982 the Thai and Philippine economies grew at very similar rates: while Thailand grew at 3.1 percent, the Philippines was not far behind at 2.6 percent. However, since then, the Philippines' GDP per capita has fallen to only 92 percent of its 1982 level, while Thailand's output has doubled. At least prior to its crisis, Indonesia had overtaken the Philippines.

It is not easy to explain the continued stagnation in the Philippines either in terms of the standard "policy" or "institutional" variables or even as a result of a shift in factor accumulation. Perhaps shocks can explain its poor performance—as it has received its share—but even there countries with equivalent or larger shocks have adapted without the growth stagnation.

Policies. Two policies often pointed to as causes of growth failures are an excessive appreciation of the exchange rate (as a proxy for competitiveness in export markets and potential macroeconomic disequilbria) and a budget deficit

---

[5] For the political and economic policy history in the Philippines I drew on the World Bank country economic memorandum; Economist Intelligence Unit reports; Boyce 1993; and Vos and Yap 1996.

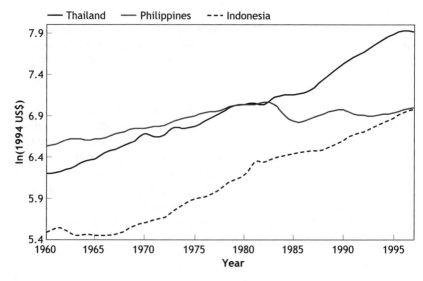

Figure 5.5. GDP per capita in 1994 U.S.$ in Philippines, Thailand, Indonesia

(as a proxy for fiscal imbalance and failure of government control). While the "optimal" budget deficit and real exchange rates are complex responses to existing conditions and history, the raw numbers do not suggest for either of these indicators a policy deterioration in the democratic period versus the precrisis period capable of explaining the significant growth slowdown (table 5.8).

Shocks. Contemporary policy narratives can point to shocks that might explain Philippine stagnation, as the new governments were not blessed with favorable circumstances internationally or with a cooperative mother nature.

TABLE 5.8
Politics, Policy, and Growth in the Philippines

Years	Description	GDP per Capita Growth	Budget Deficit	Real Exchange Rate
1965–82	Marcos, precrisis	2.57%	−2.60%	129.3
1982–86	Crisis and end of Marcos era (Feb 1986)	−5.38%	−2.73%	112.7
1986–88	Democratic Bounce	4.49%	−2.52%	87.7
1988–98	Decade of democracy	0.53%	−1.02%	93.8

Source: IMF International Financial Statistics.

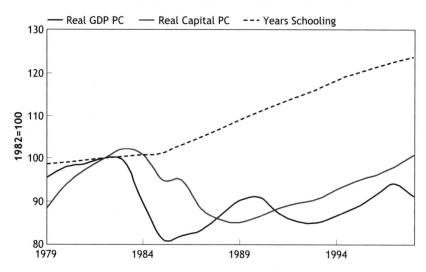

Figure 5.6. Factor accumulation and growth, 1979–98

The Philippines inherited a debt problem from Marcos, and the Aquino government negotiated a debt rescheduling. However, negotiations over withdrawal of U.S. forces caused disruption in political support from the United States, export prices dropped, and of all things, a volcano eruption caused widespread damage. While one can point to this event or that as a proximate cause of trouble, however, this is neither theoretically or empirically satisfying. If other countries buffeted by similar shocks continued to have rapid growth, then not shocks but failure to respond adequately to them is the explanation of slowed growth, and the analytic question is why the Philippines failed to weather the shocks as well as it could.

Factor accumulation. Growth stagnation in the Philippines cannot be attributed to a failure in human capital, as the country has always been far ahead of its more rapidly growing neighbors in the stock of education. The years of schooling of the potential labor force (population over age 15) continued to grow after the overthrow of Marcos, and if anything, accelerated. Physical capital accumulation slowed and then rebounded, but the timing suggests that the fall in capital was a consequence, not cause, as the fall in GDP began well before and was much steeper than the fall in physical capital per worker. Investment rates and hence physical capital growth recovered after 1988, and growth in capital has been faster and steadier than output growth (fig. 5.6).

Institutions. By many currently popular standards, institutions in the Philippines improved dramatically after Marcos. There were free and reasonably fair elections, with an orderly transfer of power from Aquino to Ramos to Estrada (initially).[6] There are more civil rights, the press is freer, and one would guess "transparency" and "accountability" have improved. The blatant crony corruption of the Marcos days was eliminated. It would seem this improvement in institutions should be rewarded with faster growth.

However, my conjecture is that although in some ways "institutions" may have improved under democracy, "institutional uncertainty" has increased. This increase in institutional uncertainty—the reliability with which economic actors can anticipate the rules of the game (no matter how good or bad those rules might be)—may account for a stagnation in the level of supportable output that accounts for the Philippines' growth dynamics.

Under a regime that has reasonable institutional stability and is not completely dysfunctional, a rapidly increasing level of GDP per capita is possible up to semi-industrialization. The fact that Indonesia (precrisis) under Soeharto had reached the Philippines' level of per capita income implies that one does not in fact need a great deal of "institutional capacity" to achieve that level of income. However, what trips countries up is the *transition* from one set of "institutions" to another. That is, under a Marcos or a Soeharto (or a stable corporate person, such as under the Communist Party in Vietnam) there is, as long as one expects those regimes to have a reasonable prospect for the future, a rough and ready system for enforcing contracts and providing for stability of investors' expectations. Moreover, at their best, these types of regimes, while they tolerate high levels of corruption, also demand some performance such that the corruption does not become absolutely "disorganized" (Shleifer and Vishny 1993). In this case, the level of supportable output even with corruption can be quite high (and can support quite rapid growth if beginning from a low base).

Countries can easily slip in the transition from one regime to another. A country can begin with a supportable level of income under a system of policymaking and contract enforcement (in the broadest sense) that is corrupt and personalistic but predictable. In the transition to a new, better set of policies and institutions—that if they functioned well could support a much higher level of income—one can create deep uncertainty among both past and future investors. Investors under the old regime will be leery and under siege for having made corrupt deals and hence will be reluctant to create substantial new investments. Recent empirical studies have shown that the *predictability* of corruption, over and above its level, matters for investment (Wei 1997; Campos, Lien, and Pradhan 1999). New investors will be reluctant to come in until the stability of the property rights regime is fully established. In this case the supportable level of output is potentially substantially *lower* in the new "better" but uncertain regime than in the bad old days.

---

[6] Depending on one's point of view, the recent transfer of power was either a perfectly legitimate democratic exercise in removing a corrupt leader by political pressures or a quasi coup in which a populist leader was forced from power.

After this low growth persists for an extended period, then it is not clear how one escapes this "non–poverty trap, low or zero growth" state back into a rapid (or at least moderate) growth. If the problem is systemic uncertainty—that is, uncertainty about economic prospects and performance under the system of institutions as operating—it is not clear that individual, piecemeal economic reforms, even cumulated, can shift the growth state.

CONCLUSION

The conclusion is that to understand the growth experiences of particular countries one needs not one simple model but an array of models. Within the array of models of growth some are now well understood and have many variants. Missing, however, are two key features for developing countries. One is a theory of transitions from state to state. The second is a well-articulated theory of determination of the level of income with factors and productivity endogenized and particularly, a theory of dynamics within a transition. I have attempted to make some progress, not in producing such a model, a task for another day, but in producing what such a model will produce—in a set of simulations both of cross-national and of individual country experience.

TABLE 5.A1
Vietnam GDP Data

Year	GDP per Capita 1994$	GDP per Capita (1976 = 100)	Growth GDP per Capita
1976	121.90	100	
1977	124.58	102.2	2.20%
1978	126.85	104.06	1.83%
1979	122.03	100.10	−3.80%
1980	118.17	96.94	−3.16%
1981	117.85	96.67	−0.28%
1982	124.01	101.73	5.23%
1983	133.02	109.12	7.26%
1984	143.17	117.44	7.63%
1985	148.01	121.41	3.38%
1986	149.88	122.95	1.27%

(continued)

TABLE 5.A1 *(Continued)*

Year	GDP per Capita 1994$	GDP per Capita (1976 = 100)	Growth GDP per Capita
1987	152.38	125.00	1.67%
1988	156.93	128.74	2.99%
1989	166.72	136.76	6.23%
1990	171.80	140.93	3.05%
1991	177.90	145.93	3.55%
1992	188.74	154.83	6.09%
1993	199.32	163.51	5.61%
1994	212.50	174.32	6.61%
1995	228.20	187.20	7.39%
1996	244.90	200.90	7.32%
1997	261.76	214.73	6.88%
1998	272.04	223.16	3.93%
1999	279.83	229.55	2.86%

REFERENCES

Aghion, Philippe, and Peter Howitt. 1998. *Endogenous Growth Theory.* Cambridge: MIT Press.

Aziardis, Costas, and Allan Drazen. 1990. "Threshold Externalities in Economic Development." *Quarterly Journal of Economics* 105:501–26.

Baumol, William J. 1986. "Productivity Growth, Convergence, and Welfare: What the Long-Run Data Show." *American Economic Review* 76:1072–85.

Bernard, Andrew. 2001. "Trends and Transitions in the Long-Run Growth of Nations." Tuck School of Business, Dartmouth. Photocopy.

Blanchard, Olivier, and Michael Kremer. 1997. "Disorganization." *Quarterly Journal of Economics* 112:1091–1126.

Boyce, James K. 1993. *The Philippines: The Political Economy of Growth and Impoverishment in the Marcos Era.* Honolulu: University of Hawaii Press in association with OECD Development Centre.

Campos, J. Edgardo, Donald Lien, and Sanjay Pradhan. 1999. "The Impact of Corruption on Investment: Predictability Matters." *World Development* 27, no. 6: 1059–67.

Dollar, David. 1993. *Vietnam: Transition to the Market.* Washington, D.C.: World Bank.

Duiker, William J. 1995. *Vietnam: Revolution in Transition.* 2d ed. Boulder, Colo.: Westview Press.

Easterly, William. 1994. "Economic Stagnation, Fixed Factors, and Policy Thresholds." *Journal of Monetary Economics* 33, no. 3: 525–57.

Easterly, William, Michael Kremer, Lant Pritchett, and Lawrence Summers. 1993. "Good Policy or Good Luck? Country Growth Performance and Temporary Shocks." *Journal of Monetary Economics* 32, no. 3: 459–83.

Forbes, D. K., T. Hull, D. Marr, and B. Brogan, eds. 1991. *Doi Moi: Vietnam's Renovation Policy and Performance.* Canberra: Australian National University Press.

Harvie, Charles, and Tran Van Hoa. 1997. *Vietnam's Reforms and Economic Growth.* Houndmills: Macmillan; New York: St. Martin's Press.

Hicks, John. 1965. *Capital and Growth.* Oxford: Oxford University Press.

Hiebert, Murray. 1996. *Chasing the Tigers: A Portrait of the New Vietnam.* New York: Kodansha International.

Jones, Charles. 1995. "R&D Based Models of Economic Growth." *Journal of Political Economy* 103:759–84.

King, Robert, and Sergio Rebelo. 1993. "Transitional Dynamics and Economic Growth in the Neoclassical Model." *American Economic Review* 83:908–31.

Kuznets, Simon. 1956. *Quantitative Aspects of the Growth of Nations.* Chicago: University of Chicago Press.

Lewis, W. Arthur. 1955. *The Theory of Economic Growth.* London: George Allen and Unwin.

Pritchett, Lant. 1997. "Divergence, Big Time." *Journal of Economic Perspectives* 11, no. 3: 3–17.

———. 2000. "Understanding Patterns of Economic Growth: Searching for Hills among Plateaus, Mountains, and Plains." *World Bank Economic Review* 14, no. 2: 221–50.

Rodrik, Dani. 2000. "Where Did All the Growth Go?" *Journal of Economic Growth.*

Romer, Paul. 1986. "Increasing Returns and Long-Run Growth." *Journal of Political Economy* 94:1002–37.

———. 1990. "Endogenous Technical Change." *Journal of Political Economy* 98, no. 5, pt. 2: 71–102.

Shleifer, Andrei, and Robert W. Vishny. 1993. "Corruption." *Quarterly Journal of Economics* 108:599–618.

Solow, Robert. 1970. *Growth Theory: An Exposition.* Oxford: Oxford University Press.

Taylor, Alan, and Jeffrey Williamson. 1997. "Convergence in the Era of Mass Migration." *European Review of Economic History* 1, no. 1: 153–90.

Vos, Rob, and Josef T. Yap. 1996. *The Philippine Economy: East Asia's Stray Cat?* New York: St. Martin's Press in association with Institute of Social Studies.

Wei, Shang-Jin. 1997. "Why Is Corruption So Much More Taxing Than Tax? Arbitrariness Kills." NBER Working Paper No. 6255.

World Bank. 2001. *World Development Report 2000/2001: Attacking Poverty.* Oxford: Oxford University Press.

CHAPTER 6

Growing into Trouble

INDONESIA AFTER 1966

JONATHAN TEMPLE

FEW COUNTRIES have experienced reversals in economic fortune and reputation as dramatic as those of Indonesia. In the early 1960s, one influential commentator described the country as a "chronic dropout" and "the number one failure among the major underdeveloped countries."[1] By 1996, the picture looked very different: under Suharto, the country had grown rapidly for most of the previous thirty years, living standards had significantly improved, and the incidence of poverty had been sharply reduced. Although its record was by no means one of consistent success, Indonesia was increasingly regarded as yet another East Asian example of sound policy and strong growth.

Then in 1997–98 there was another sharp reversal in its fortunes. Of all the countries affected by the Asian financial crisis, Indonesia has fared much the worst. The year 1998 saw a fall in GDP of 13 percent. Political instability and institutional weaknesses, combined with internal tensions, have led to a swift reassessment of the country's prospects, and increasing gloom. As tensions increase, some are even predicting that the country will not survive in its current form.

There are many reasons to study this turbulent history. First and most obviously, Indonesia is home to more than 200 million people. Second, its record is of a kind that may offer important wider lessons. In sharp contrast to the genuine development "dropouts" of the last forty years, Indonesia's long period of success might tell us something about a set of sufficient conditions for fast growth. Yet there is also enough variation over time to offer some insight into the factors that initiate growth, and those that could bring it to an end.

In exploring these issues, this chapter will take a somewhat idiosyncratic approach. It provides a brief overview of Indonesian economic development and

I am grateful to the discussant, Lant Pritchett, and to Bryan Graham, Steve Redding, Jim Robinson, Dani Rodrik, and the conference participants for comments and discussion. Any errors are my responsibility.

[1] These quotations are from Benjamin Higgins, as cited in Hill 2000a. Much of the background material in this chapter has been drawn from Hill's excellent book.

the recent crisis, but one that is far from comprehensive.[2] Several excellent accounts are already available, notably Bevan, Collier, and Gunning 1999 and Hill 2000a. Rather than summarize their work, one aim of this chapter is to see where analysis of Indonesia's record might be informed by recent empirical and theoretical work on economic growth. A second aim is to contribute to our wider understanding of the growth process.

In thinking about wider implications, the case of Indonesia raises a number of interesting puzzles. The central open question is easily identified. How did Indonesia grow so quickly for so long, despite unfavorable initial conditions, some weak institutions, and flawed microeconomic policies? The answer lies in a number of mutually reinforcing factors, but especially political stability, unusually competent macroeconomic policy, and some important instances of good fortune.

One message of this chapter, and that of earlier observers like Bevan, Collier, and Gunning (1999), is that Indonesia's achievements have been precarious ones. The risk of failure was probably never far away, and Indonesia's rapid growth was partly sustained by favorable external shocks. The chapter emphasizes and analyzes three. As a predominantly agricultural economy in the 1960s, the country stood much to gain from the introduction of new crop varieties and other agricultural innovations, often better suited to Indonesia than developing countries elsewhere. Second, as an oil exporter, Indonesia benefited greatly from the two oil shocks of the 1970s. Finally, and probably of lesser importance, Indonesia's geographic neighbors and trade partners are among the world's fastest-growing countries. The emerging literature on international economic geography suggests that this should have hastened the process of industrialization.

These gifts were not returned unopened, and Indonesia made much of its new opportunities. This makes it essential to understand the origins of the superior policy outcomes. Why did Suharto promote economic development rather than simply ransacking the economy? Why was macroeconomic policymaking more adept than elsewhere? Why did the regime give a higher priority to the agricultural sector than other developing country governments? It has become a truism to say that the origins of economic success or failure can be traced to political factors, but the case of Indonesia has much to offer in thinking about these issues.

Although growth was rapid, a dynamic manufacturing sector was slow to emerge, and Indonesia is often grouped with Malaysia and Thailand as one of the Southeast Asian "latecomers" to industrial transformation. With this in view, the chapter will also investigate why Indonesia has lagged behind other East Asian countries in developing its manufacturing sector. Was this due to the

---

[2] Among the more important omissions are the regional dimension, the record on poverty and equity, and management of the environment. All these topics are discussed by Hill (2000a).

flawed microeconomic policies of the Suharto era, and the initial lack of impetus behind reform? Or should it be related to other factors, such as unfavorable initial conditions and the abundance of natural resources?

A final question is more speculative, gives the chapter its title, and relates to the recent crisis. The events of 1997–98 have led to a sweeping reassessment of the underlying health of the Indonesian economy and its institutions, on the part of investors and economists alike. The chapter will not provide a complete account, but it will investigate whether rapid growth laid some of the foundations for the severity of the crisis. Olson (1963) argued that rapid growth could be a profoundly destabilizing force. The Indonesian case does not fit his arguments exactly, but perhaps offers some other ways in which a country could be said to "grow into trouble."

The chapter has the following structure. Section 1 gives a brief overview of Indonesian economic development, and particularly the New Order period from 1966 onwards. Section 2 will examine the nature and political economy of policy under Suharto, before discussing the complementary role of good luck. Section 3 considers the role of agriculture and structural change in Indonesia's growth. Sections 4 and 5 explore the effects of the 1970s oil boom and the regional growth takeoff, respectively. Section 6 draws on this discussion to analyze the microeconomic reforms of the 1980s. Finally, section 7 asks whether Indonesia grew into trouble, before section 8 concludes.

1. INDONESIA'S GROWTH: AN OVERVIEW

In the mid-1960s, Indonesia was among the poorest economies in the world. Some evidence for this can be seen in table 6.1. Its GDP per capita compared on a PPP basis was less than 60 percent of that in other East Asian countries, lower than for many sub-Saharan African countries, and much lower than in Latin America.

Indonesia was then led by Sukarno, a charismatic figure who had been central in the battles for independence from the Dutch. Throughout the 1950s he had been faced with difficult circumstances in attempting to build a stable government in the aftermath of colonial rule. Political instability and the lack of a coherent economic policy, together with a large adverse shock to the terms of trade, led to economic collapse in the early 1960s. By this time the attempts at expansion and central planning had failed. The government budget deficit escalated ever higher, and inflation reached almost 600 percent in 1965. By December of that year, the country could no longer meet its debt service obligations, and its economic future seemed bleak.

As Sukarno's popular support ebbed away, the military intervened. General Suharto assumed formal executive authority in March 1966, instituting the New Order and a grip on power that would last more than thirty years. This military

TABLE 6.1
GDP, Trade, and Agriculture in Indonesia and Other Asian Countries, 1965

	Population (millions)	GDP per Capita	Trade Share (% of GDP)[b]	Agriculture (% of GDP)
Indonesia	104	608	24	53
South Korea	29	1058	27	36
Malaysia	9	1671	80	29
Taiwan	13	1660	41	24
Thailand	31	1136	35	32
Regional medians[c]				
South Asia	32	889	21	40
Sub-Saharan Africa	4	736	43	39
Latin America	4	2014	36	21

Source: Global Development Network database, World Bank.

Note: The trade share and agriculture share are 3-year averages (1964–66) when sufficient data are available.

[a] GDP per capita is PPP adjusted and measured in international dollars (1985 base year).

[b] Imports plus exports as a share of GDP.

[c] Regional medians exclude countries with fewer than one million people.

regime was a repressive and at times murderous one, but here I concentrate on its economic record. The extent of the transformation in performance can be seen in figure 6.1, which shows growth in GDP per capita between 1961 and the crisis years of 1997–98. In most years the economy grew rapidly, and over the whole period, GDP per capita rose more than fourfold. The incidence of poverty declined, and there has been undisputed improvement in other welfare indicators such as infant mortality rates (Booth 2000).

The extent of the turnaround can be seen not only in the growth statistics, but also in those for investment and structural change. Gross domestic investment as a proportion of GDP climbed throughout the period, rising particularly quickly in the late 1960s, as the quality of economic management improved (fig. 6.2). Structural change has seen agriculture's share of employment fall from about 75 percent to nearer 50 percent, still high by the standards of East Asia, but a striking development nevertheless. As one might expect, the structural change has been accompanied by rapid urbanization. In 1965, on one definition 16 percent of the population lived in urban areas. By 1996, this figure was around 40 percent.

Another important aspect of Indonesia's development has been rising educational attainment, from inauspicious beginnings. In 1960, literacy rates and primary enrollment compared quite favorably with countries at a similar level of

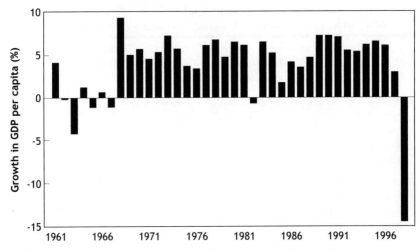

Figure 6.1. Growth in GDP per capita, Indonesia, 1961–98
Source: World Development Indicators 2000

development, but were lower than elsewhere in East Asia (Rodrik 1996, table 4).
Since then, average years of schooling in the population have steadily increased
for both men and women, from 1.5 years to 5 years. The greater extent of schooling is reflected in a rising literacy rate. By 1997, only 15 percent of the population were classified as illiterate, compared with more than 40 percent in 1970.

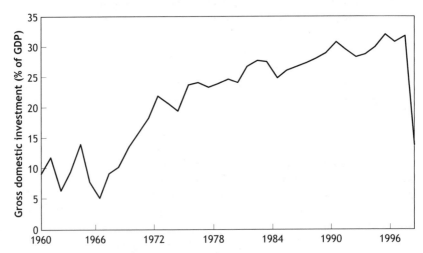

Figure 6.2. Gross domestic investment (% of GDP), 1960–98
Source: World Development Indicators 2000

TABLE 6.2
Social Conditions in Indonesia and Other Asian Countries, 1965

	Urban %	Ethnic Diversity	Adelman-Morris	Primary Enrollment	Secondary Enrollment	Life Expectancy
Indonesia	0.16	0.76	−0.40	0.72	0.12	43
South Korea	0.32	0	0.85	1.01	0.35	55
Malaysia	0.30	0.72		0.90	0.28	56
Taiwan	0.60	0.42	1.05	0.97	0.38	66
Thailand	0.13	0.66	0.50	0.78	0.14	54
Regional medians[b]						
South Asia	0.14	0.67	−0.28	0.45	0.13	43
Sub-Saharan Africa	0.13	0.73	−1.22	0.40	0.04	40
Latin America	0.44	0.17	0.79	0.97	0.18	58

Sources: Global Development Network database, World Bank; Adelman and Morris 1967.

[a] Regional medians exclude countries with fewer than one million people.

[b] The Adelman-Morris index is not available for Malaysia.

So far, this overview suggests that Indonesia has followed a course familiar from other East Asian countries, namely strong growth driven by capital accumulation and rising educational attainment. As for other countries in the region, there is some debate about the relative importance of growth in total factor productivity (TFP). Although measured TFP growth is often found to have been low for Indonesia, the counterfactual simulations of Robertson (2000) suggest that it played a key role.

It is also interesting to look at ways in which the experience of Indonesia differs from other countries in the region, and especially South Korea and Taiwan. Some of the most interesting differences are found in the initial conditions that faced the respective countries. Indeed, the transformation under Suharto looks all the more impressive when one considers that some of Indonesia's initial conditions did not augur well. In the mid-1960s, the country was a predominantly rural, agricultural society, in which life expectancy was lower than elsewhere in East Asia. As noted previously, educational provision lagged behind some of the other countries in the region (see table 6.2, and Booth 1999).

The empirical growth literature has drawn attention to several other aspects of initial conditions. In a widely cited paper, Easterly and Levine (1997) argued that high levels of ethnolinguistic diversity may have adverse effects on growth. Indonesia's extent of diversity is high compared to that of South Korea and Taiwan (see table 6.2), and ethnic tensions have been a recurring theme of recent Indonesian history. This has included discontent with the prominent role of ethnic Chinese in business, particularly in boom periods such as the mid-1970s and early 1990s.

Some recent work on growth has also emphasized the extent of socioeconomic development. Arguably the most useful summary measure is that compiled by Adelman and Morris (1967), and subsequently highlighted by Rodrik (1995) and Temple and Johnson (1998). The measure provides a snapshot of social arrangements for the early 1960s, derived from a factor analysis of a number of components, based on survey evidence and interviews with country experts.

As table 6.2 shows, again Indonesia compares somewhat unfavorably with East Asian neighbors. The reasons for Indonesia's low score on the index, relative to other East Asian countries, can be inferred from the individual components listed in Adelman and Morris 1967. The low score is driven by the extent of dualism; the limited role for an indigenous middle class; low social mobility; a low adult literacy rate; the limited spread of mass communications; and a lack of "modernization of outlook."[3] We can use the results in Temple and Johnson 1998 to illustrate the potential consequences. Conditional on initial income, the difference between Indonesia's Adelman-Morris index (−0.40) and Thailand's (0.50) implies an annual growth rate 1.6 percentage points higher in Thailand, over 25 years.

Five more features of Indonesia are central to an understanding of its development, and important to discussion later in the chapter. First, Indonesia is unusual among East Asian countries in its relative abundance of natural resources. The most obvious and important manifestation of this is the country's role as an oil exporter, sometimes accounting for around 7 percent of OPEC output (Warr 1986). The fluctuations in oil prices of the 1970s and 1980s, including the huge windfall gains associated with the 1973 oil shock, presented Indonesia with particular challenges.

A second and related feature of the country's development is that a large industrial sector has been much slower to emerge than in South Korea and Taiwan. As noted earlier, even by the mid-1990s, agriculture still accounted for nearly half of total employment. The structure of exports is also revealing. In the early 1980s, manufactured goods were less than 5 percent of total merchandise exports, in sharp contrast to the early specialization in manufacturing of the tiger economies further north.

A third difference lies in the economic role of the state. One legacy of the Sukarno era and its nationalization programs, never quite shaken off, has been a major role for state enterprise, and ambivalence towards capitalism. It was only in the 1980s that Indonesia began to see the rise of a large independent capitalist class, the "rise of capital" identified by Robison (1986). Although

---

[3] Some of these variables are clearly endogenous to the level of income per capita, and it should therefore be acknowledged that Indonesia's low score for the Adelman-Morris index is partly explained by Indonesia's economic underdevelopment at the time of the study.

ownership definitions are often blurred, Hill (2000a) estimates that even by the late 1980s government entities accounted for about 30 percent of GDP, and almost 40 percent of nonagricultural GDP.

Fourth, Indonesia has been unusual in the concentration of political power in its president. A key feature of the Suharto regime was that, despite the nominal presence of an electoral process, organized interest groups, a legislature, and a judiciary, these institutions were all arranged in such a way that Suharto effectively wielded something very close to absolute power (MacIntyre 1999a).

The fifth and final aspect of Indonesia under Suharto is perhaps the best known: the unusually pervasive corruption, associated with state involvement in the economy and the centralization of political power. To gauge the extent of the problem, the indices reported in Wei 2000 allow formal comparisons with other countries. Those indices suggest that Indonesia under Suharto was rather more corrupt than the median countries of sub-Saharan Africa and Latin America, more corrupt than South Korea and Taiwan, but roughly on a par with Thailand and the Philippines.

2. THE ORIGINS OF GOOD POLICY

Perhaps the most important lesson to be drawn from the Indonesian record is also the most obvious, namely the critical role of macroeconomic stability. It is surely no coincidence that the rapid growth achieved under Suharto coincided with relatively tight control of inflation and budget deficits, and a generally cautious approach to macroeconomic management.

The contrast with the previous regime and the benefits of the new approach became clear early on, nowhere more so than in the response to inflation. In the aftermath of Sukarno's rule, inflation peaked at an annual rate of almost 1,500 percent in mid-1966. In what is sometimes regarded as one of the most successful instances of inflation control in the twentieth century, the new government ensured that inflation was stabilized and brought down to a rate of 15 percent by 1969, without any sustained contraction in output.

The introduction of greater stability was not a fleeting achievement. Although the economy sometimes ran into difficulties, notably with the fading of the second oil boom in the early 1980s, the Suharto regime often responded quickly and effectively when needed. For the most part, macroeconomic stability was maintained. As in other East Asian countries, it appears to have played a key role in enabling Indonesia's rapid growth.

For the broader picture, it is worth quoting Hill (2000a, 9–10) at length:

> Much of the Indonesian record since 1966 is a confirmation of the principles of orthodoxy . . . the recipe of success is no great secret. A new, orthodox and pragmatic regime of economic management after 1966 signalled a decisive change in

direction. The government provided a stable economic and political environment, property rights were respected, Indonesia re-entered the international community, prices—especially the exchange rate—reflected conditions of demand and supply, and the provision of public goods such as physical and social infrastructure began to increase substantially.

Hill's emphasis on the contribution of orthodox policies is unlikely to be controversial. The remaining challenge is to identify the reasons why these policies were chosen, and why the economic outcomes were so much better than elsewhere.

The simplest answer is to argue that the Suharto government was an example of a "strong state" insulated from democratic pressures and organized interests, in a way that allowed tough and decisive action when necessary. Yet we know from the records of autocracies elsewhere that economic success is by no means a foregone conclusion, and that leaders of such regimes have often chosen to ransack their economies rather than promote development. A satisfactory explanation of Indonesia's growth ultimately needs to explain why Suharto appears to have sought rapid growth as well as personal gain.

Suharto's choices look all the more remarkable given the context in which he came to power. Political stability appeared unlikely, as the experience under Sukarno had shown. Indonesia had all four of the characteristics that Robinson (2000) identifies as risk factors for predatory behavior by the state, namely large benefits to holding power, an abundance of natural resources, low endowments of factors complementary to public investment, and intrinsic instability.

Why did Indonesia take a different course? Muller (1998) draws attention to the role of the army, which saw itself as acting in the interests of the country as a whole. The military government not only ensured political stability, but also redefined the country's goals, with economic growth seen as a priority, and foreign policy redirected towards economic needs. Economic policy was increasingly driven by pragmatism rather than ideology. As Muller acknowledges, however, it is hard to explain why the New Order gave rise to better economic outcomes than military rule in other countries, although it is possible that the drive for economic development was given greater urgency by the threat of a communist uprising.

Another explanation would be to follow Overland et al. (2000) in arguing that a dictator's hold on power is likely to depend on the state of the economy—more specifically, in their model, on the capital stock. For example, other things equal, a dictator in an economy with a larger capital stock will find it easier to buy off potential opponents. This means that rapid growth is potentially in the interests of a dictator or elite group: not only does it provide the regime with a degree of legitimacy, but it may also help to secure its grip on power through less innocent means. Conversely, if the regime presides over an economy that begins with a low capital stock, political stability will also be low. This encourages the regime to ransack the economy, leading to a vicious circle of corruption, poor economic performance and increasing political instability.

The overall story does not fit Indonesia exactly, since the country was relatively poor and unstable when Suharto took control, suggesting that a vicious circle was the most likely outcome. Yet Suharto quickly established an unusually secure grip on power and may have calculated that economic growth would help to maintain it. Later in the chapter, I will discuss the ways in which Suharto was able to use his control of a rapidly growing economy to eliminate political competition, consistent with some of the ideas of Overland et al. (2000).

Macroeconomic stability and growth may have contributed to political stability, but it is also possible to point to reinforcing effects in the other direction. For those developing countries where political stability is absent, the risk of losing power may be an important reason that governments sometimes act myopically and choose bad policies. In contrast, Suharto's secure grip on power enabled a long-term view and an unusual degree of continuity in policymaking.

This by itself would not guarantee success, but in seeking growth, Suharto's early decisions often turned out well. On taking power, he appointed a team of economic advisers drawn from the Faculty of Economics of the University of Indonesia. Three of the five academics appointed were fairly recent Berkeley Ph.D.s, and they became known as the "Berkeley Mafia" or "technocrats," broadly in favor of markets and foreign capital. Their influence, and that of later advisers, appears to have been a major factor behind the generally high quality of macroeconomic policy for more than two decades.

The early influence of the Berkeley Mafia is perhaps not surprising, because the state of the economy in the mid-1960s was such that the new government had little choice but to accept the prescriptions of the IMF and World Bank. Perhaps more of a puzzle is why subsequent macroeconomic policies followed orthodoxy so closely. In this respect, discussions of Indonesian economic policy often draw attention to the open capital account. Unusually, the account was almost completely open as early as 1970, and this is said to have provided useful discipline for economic policy, in particular guarding against exchange rate overvaluation.[4] This is an important claim, and one area of Indonesia's macroeconomic policies that would repay detailed study.

In discussing economic policy, it is also worth noting that Indonesia did not get everything right, in the sense of adhering to textbook prescriptions. The technocrats appear to have had little influence on microeconomic policy, and could not halt a shift towards import substitution, and ever more widespread state intervention, in the 1970s. This approach was eventually reversed in the mid-1980s, but it should be emphasized that Indonesia's record has not been a uniformly straightforward application of orthodoxy.

---

[4] See for example Bevan, Collier, and Gunning 1999, 421; and Hill 2000a.

Given the failings of microeconomic policy and the unfavorable initial conditions, a common reading of Indonesia's success is that it also owed much to good fortune. This idea has especial interest in the light of Easterly et al. 1993. They pointed out that relatively few countries have achieved sustained growth, suggesting that the differences between "economic disasters" and "economic miracles" may be partly a matter of luck. This argument is similar to the idea that Rabin (2000) has called "fictitious variation," namely the common tendency for observers of relative performance to exaggerate the role played by fundamentals, and underestimate the role of chance. In the growth context, this view acquired greater resonance with the Asian crisis of 1997, a dramatic interruption to growth of the kind common elsewhere in the world, but previously rare in East Asia.

In the case of Indonesia, the role of historical accident can be seen in the fluctuating influence of the technocrats. Memories of the high inflation of the mid-1960s, and its highly successful stabilization, seem to have strengthened the hand of those committed to orthodox macroeconomic policies, as later did the scale of the financial problems associated with the giant state-owned energy company Pertamina in the mid-1970s.[5]

To develop the "good luck" story further requires one to identify favorable external shocks, or other events that can plausibly be attributed to historical accident. The next sections of the chapter will analyze three important and favorable shocks that have aided Indonesia's growth at different times and complemented good macroeconomic policy. These shocks, in roughly the order that they occurred, are the green revolution in agriculture, the 1970s oil boom, and the regional growth takeoff, all of which presented new opportunities and challenges.

3. THE ROLE OF AGRICULTURE

This section examines the contribution made to Indonesia's economic development by the agricultural sector. There is general agreement that technical progress in agriculture played a key role in the growth of the 1970s, and also in poverty reduction. Yet this was not simply an exogenous productivity shock, because in contrast with many developing country governments elsewhere, the Suharto regime did much to make agriculture a priority, raising some interesting questions in political economy.

---

[5] Observers of Indonesia agree that the Pertamina scandal was one of the most important and remarkable events of the 1970s. After the company failed to meet its debt obligations in 1975, a government report revealed that Pertamina had accumulated external debt equivalent to almost 30 percent of Indonesian GDP. Sjahrir and Brown (1992) describe the company president's approach to financial management as "unorthodox."

As in other poor countries, Indonesia's agricultural sector accounted for around three-quarters of total employment in the early 1960s. This implies that, in the early phases of development, growth in labor productivity would be strongly related to agricultural performance. One way to see this is to note that aggregate labor productivity can be written as a weighted average of labor productivity in each sector, where the weights are the shares of each sector in total employment. If agriculture accounts for a high share of employment, growth in GDP per capita requires either respectable productivity growth in agriculture, or breakneck expansion elsewhere in the economy.

In this respect, analysis of a country like Indonesia may have some important lessons for the empirical modeling of growth. Cross-country empirical work rarely acknowledges the predominant role of agriculture in many of the countries being studied. Analyzing the role of agriculture is an area in which case studies have much to contribute, and where these studies could inform future empirical work. Once again Indonesia stands out as a useful laboratory, since agricultural development was a stated priority of the New Order, even if some of its policies discriminated against the sector.[6]

Before discussing these issues in more detail, I want to point out a common fallacy in analyzing the performance of a particular sector, which might be called the "enclave fallacy." Writers assessing the performance of a sector often proceed as if the sector were a self-contained economy or enclave, and then compare growth in sectoral output and labor productivity across countries. The problem here is that in general equilibrium, changes in agricultural output and labor productivity typically depend not only on agricultural performance, but also on the performance of other sectors.

This type of result can be derived from very simple general equilibrium models of production, of a form often used in trade theory and described in the appendix to this chapter. The appendix also shows how to calibrate one such model, in order to confirm that a productivity gain in agriculture can have a major impact on overall output. The particular examples considered are based on an initial employment share for agriculture of 75 percent, Indonesia's position in the 1960s. Depending on the technology parameters, a doubling of agricultural total factor productivity raises overall output by roughly 80 percent.

With all this in mind, we can now return to the Indonesian example, to assess the New Order's agricultural policies and their implications for development. In practical terms, the emphasis on agriculture was reflected in large subsidies for inputs (fertilizers, pesticides), stabilization of rice prices, and investments in rural infrastructure (irrigation, roads, and schools). The early attempts to raise agricultural productivity were not particularly successful, but the regime had learned from some of these mistakes by the time of the oil boom

---

[6] For more on urban versus rural bias in Indonesia, see Timmer 1993 and Garcia Garcia 2000.

of the 1970s, which greatly increased the resources available for spending on rural development and food policy.

Combined with the introduction of high-yielding crop varieties—the green revolution—the results have been genuinely impressive. Perhaps the best index of this success is provided by measures of crop yields (weight/hectare). Yields of the major crops have all risen strongly. The principal crop to examine is rice, which dominates the Indonesian diet. Rice yields showed particularly strong growth in the late 1970s and early 1980s, as the government raised fertilizer subsidies and sought to accelerate the spread of high-yielding varieties, measures that were funded with oil revenues. The striking achievement was to move Indonesia from a position where it imported almost a third of the world's traded rice in some years, to self-sufficiency by 1985, a goal that had been thought unattainable by informed commentators (Hill 2000a, 131).

Such emphasis on agriculture is unusual among developing countries. This raises an interesting question of political economy: what was different about Indonesia that led the New Order to see rural development as a key priority? Gelb and Glassburner (1988) imply that part of the reason was the country's predominantly rural nature. Policies that favored the urban sector and hence encouraged rural-urban migration would have put great pressure on the cities. Another explanation sometimes given is Suharto's own rural background.

A more cynical view is that, given the predominance of rice in the Indonesian diet and its importance to Javanese agriculture, the regime's policies to help rice farmers were motivated by Suharto's desire for self-preservation, and the need to maintain his power base in Java. The unrest during the rice shortage of late 1972, after prices doubled in a matter of months, illustrated the potential dangers to the regime of neglecting food policy. Part of the background is that under the previous leader, Sukarno, the Indonesian state had appeared committed to the interests of ordinary people, creating expectations that later became a constraint on Suharto, and that help to explain his emphasis on poverty alleviation (Bevan, Collier, and Gunning 1999, 420). The regime was also aware that many rural farmers had given strong support to the Communist Party in the 1960s; any return to this political radicalism in rural areas would have been highly destabilizing (MacIntyre 2001c).

Another open question is the extent to which the emphasis on rural development contributed to overall industrialization. In this respect, it is worth pointing out that Indonesia's productivity gains had significant opportunity costs. The drive for self-sufficiency in rice required high subsidies for inputs, especially fertilizer. Nor was the strategy to promote rural development uniformly successful, with notable policy failures in the promotion of cash crops such as palm oil, and in the production of natural rubber (Muller 1998).

There is also some theoretical ambiguity in the relation between agricultural improvement and long-run development. In a closed economy, improved productivity in agriculture will raise the steady-state level of income almost inevitably, both directly and perhaps also through market size effects. Matsuyama (1992) pointed out that things are more complex in an open economy, however. Given a positive shock to agricultural productivity, comparative advantage shifts against nonagriculture. If there are significant externalities or learning effects in nonagriculture, the economy as a whole may grow more slowly in the long run.[7] Such ambiguity can also be found in models with multiple equilibria, for instance when there are a number of nontraded intermediate inputs produced with fixed costs. Overall, these considerations mean that identifying the net benefits of the New Order's agricultural policies is potentially a complex task.

Given that Indonesia was a poor, rural economy in the 1960s, any movement in the direction of rapid capital accumulation and higher productivity was likely to generate substantial structural change. The remainder of the section will analyze this process, partly to cast some light on Indonesia's status as a latecomer to industrialization.

Orthodox explanations of structural change are based on varying income elasticities of demand, differential rates of productivity growth, or changes in comparative advantage brought about by technical change and/or shifts in factor endowments. At first glance, trade theory seems to offer some remarkably strong predictions. In a model with two goods and two factors, the Rybczynski theorem implies that a rising capital-labor ratio should prompt an increase in the relative output of the capital-intensive good. At least on a conventional view of capital intensities, Indonesia's shift out of agriculture could then be explained by its high rates of investment, as in the empirical analysis of Martin and Warr (1993).

Yet from a theoretical perspective, this kind of account is not wholly satisfactory. One problem is that the Rybczynski theorem is among those that do not generalize in a straightforward way to an economy with more than two goods. Even if we retain the 2×2 version of Heckscher-Ohlin trade theory, this has the limiting implication that factor prices will be independent of factor supplies.[8] If it is capital accumulation driving structural change, rather than technical progress, then wages and returns to capital will be constant.

The solution of Leamer (1987) to this problem is to introduce a third factor, land or natural-resource abundance. One advantage of this approach is that there are now several distinct paths of development, depending upon where a country initially stands in its relative endowments of capital, labor and natural resources. In the case of intermediate resource abundance, a country will eventually shift towards exporting manufactures, but manufacturing specialization will only emerge relatively late in the development process compared to resource-scarce countries, where this pattern is found at lower levels of capital intensity.

---

[7] This may not be a good argument against promoting agricultural productivity, since an economy that specializes in agriculture may have a relatively high standard of living.

[8] This statement should be qualified somewhat, since factor prices will only be independent of factor endowments while the economy remains incompletely specialized.

The relevance to Indonesia's development is clear, given its traditional specialization in resource-based exports. More recently, indices of relative comparative advantage show a marked shift in export specialization, beginning in the early 1980s, towards resource-based manufacturing, and increasingly towards labor-intensive manufacturing (Hill 2000a). Hill suggests that "Indonesia is following the well-trodden path of labor-intensive, outward orientation of the East Asian economies, albeit a good deal later than most" (83). The delay can be attributed at least partly to resource abundance, as in Leamer's analysis, and need not be interpreted in a negative light. The next section will reinforce this argument, by drawing attention to the general equilibrium effects of the oil windfall.

4. THE OIL WINDFALL

An account of economic performance under Suharto would be seriously incomplete without some consideration of the 1970s oil boom, and Indonesia's distinctive and effective policy response. This section provides a discussion of the "Dutch disease," and the extent to which the patient resisted the usual symptoms. The potential importance of this analysis can be seen by examining the structure of Indonesia's exports and government revenues. By the peak of the oil boom, oil accounted for around three-quarters of export earnings, and more than 60 percent of government revenues (Warr 1986).

The quadrupling of oil prices in 1973 represented a windfall gain for Indonesia, raising real income almost overnight. Yet we know from the experience of other oil exporters that such a windfall has often been a mixed blessing. Swings in oil prices have been accompanied by fiscal deficits and macroeconomic instability, while the new government revenues were often wasted (Gelb and Associates 1988). More generally, newly valuable endowments of natural resources have often been associated with predatory states or political instability, as opposing groups compete for a share of the associated rents.

Theoretical work on resource windfalls has provided a good understanding of their general equilibrium effects. The windfall means an increase in real income. Since the price of traded goods is set on world markets, the effect of the increase in demand is to put upward pressure on the relative price of nontraded goods (the "spending effect"). Production of nontraded goods increases, and the nonoil traded sector typically has to contract, at least in relative terms, as a real appreciation takes place.[9]

---

[9] See for example Neary and van Wijnbergen 1986. In the case of a country like Indonesia, committed to a fixed exchange rate for most of the 1970s, the appreciation must be achieved by inflation rates that are high relative to those of trading partners.

There is more to the Dutch disease than short-run reallocation, however. The reason is that contraction of the nonoil traded sector may work against long-run industrialization. If learning effects are important in industry, or if nontraded intermediate inputs are produced under increasing returns to scale, or if industrial productivity depends on other agglomeration effects and externalities, any contraction of the nonoil traded sector could retard industrialization and growth.

The importance of these considerations could easily be exaggerated, not least because the high oil prices were a temporary phenomenon. For most countries, it appears to have been the adjustment to the end of the oil boom, rather than the Dutch disease effects, that became a crucial determinant of economic performance. Here, Indonesia scored highly. When the current account moved sharply into deficit over 1980–82, the government responded quickly with a series of measures designed to restore stability. Of the six oil exporters studied by Gelb and Associates (1988), Indonesia was the only one to follow a determined policy that combined expenditure reduction with exchange rate realignment. Although growth weakened in the early 1980s, a more dramatic crisis was avoided, due to swift adjustment and an initial debt burden that was lower than elsewhere.

Indonesia had also performed well on another criterion, namely the allocation of the massive new government revenues created by the oil boom. As we have seen, the New Order pursued a relatively broad development strategy, which emphasized infrastructure, education and agriculture, as well as capital-intensive industry. An unusually high proportion of government spending was allocated to agriculture. In this way, the oil boom contributed to the long-term success of other sectors, limiting the extent of Dutch disease effects.

In sharp contrast, other governments appear to have wasted a large part of their oil revenues on overambitious and risky investments in resource-based industry. That Indonesia did not follow suit was partly a matter of historical accident: the government's own plans in this direction were fortunately delayed by the Pertamina crisis. This meant that when oil prices declined in the early 1980s, there was still time to postpone or cancel many of the planned investments. As elsewhere in the story of Indonesia's development, a combination of historical accident and the government's pragmatism served the economy well.

5. THE GEOGRAPHY OF INDUSTRIALIZATION

So far, we have examined two instances of good fortune for Indonesia, namely the effects of the green revolution on agriculture, and the oil boom of the 1970s. In this section, I will consider a third and final external shock: the rapid growth of Indonesia's geographic neighbors and trade partners. This change in the external environment has taken on greater importance over time, and the consequences for trade and investment patterns have been especially clear since the late 1980s.

One reason to emphasize this development is that, for most of its recent history, Indonesia has been remote from large markets. If we look at the Great Circle distance between Jakarta and other capital cities, the United States is more than 16,000 km away, Western Europe about 11,000 km away, and even Canberra in Australia is 5,400 km distant. By contrast, Jakarta is relatively close to Singapore, Malaysia, Thailand, Hong Kong, and Taiwan (all under 4,000 km) while China, Korea, and Japan are all about 5,000 km away.[10]

In the 1960s, the East Asian markets were small relative to those of Europe and the United States. As a result, the indices constructed by Redding and Venables (2000) show that the extent of Indonesia's access to international markets, relative to that of other countries, has been intermediate at best. Another measure of isolation can be derived from using geographic variables to predict bilateral trade flows. Even for 1985, an exercise of this kind predicts a low trade share for Indonesia, below 10 percent (Frankel and Romer 1999).

To understand why a country like Indonesia might benefit from proximity to newly fast-growing markets, we need to go beyond the world of the trade theory textbooks. In the simpler models of international trade, rapid growth in Japan, China, and the newly industrializing countries of East Asia would have no more consequence for Indonesia than for Nigeria or Brazil.

This presumption is overturned by the emerging literature on international economic geography.[11] The starting point of these models is a simple hypothesis, namely that increasing returns to scale are central to the spatial distribution of production. If returns to scale were constant, firms would supply local markets with many small plants, given the presence of transport costs. In contrast, with increasing returns, firms will choose to produce in relatively few locations, and the outcome is agglomeration. Importantly, this agglomeration involves "cumulative causation" or feedback effects that reinforce the process over time.

The ideas and models of economic geography can be used to understand differences in economic outcomes across countries. For example, Puga and Venables (1999) model the spread of agglomeration from country to country. With increasing world demand for manufactured goods, the wage gap will tend to widen between industrialized countries and those that are less developed. As this process continues, the widening wage gap encourages increased production in low-wage countries. Yet not all countries will benefit at once, since the forces for agglomeration imply that firms gain by producing in a country where other firms are also active, or becoming established. Given the potential importance of the feedback effects, any country that gets slightly ahead may pull away.

---

[10] These data are taken from Jon Haveman's website at http://www.eiit.org/.

[11] The following discussion draws heavily on Henderson, Shalizi, and Venables 2000.

TABLE 6.3
Per capita GDP Growth
of Trading Partners, 1965–98

Indonesia	3.62
South Korea	2.82
Malaysia	3.65
Taiwan	2.76
Thailand	3.28
Regional medians	
South Asia	2.50
Sub-Saharan Africa	2.28
Latin America	2.02

Source: Global Development Network database, World Bank.

Given Indonesia's initial isolation, together with proximity to some unusually fast-growing markets, it seems to be a very good testing ground for the predictions of the economic geography literature. We can start by identifying trade partners. As one might expect, Indonesia trades relatively intensely with Japan, Singapore, and the other developing countries of northeast Asia, including China (see Hill 2000a). By using a measure of per capita growth rates of trading partners, weighted by trade shares, we can measure the extent to which Indonesia's trading partners have expanded rapidly, compared to the partners of other countries. Table 6.3 shows that GDP per capita of trading partners has grown more rapidly for Indonesia than for the median countries in South Asia, sub-Saharan Africa, and Latin America. The differences in growth rates imply substantial divergence of GDP per capita of trading partners over time.

Given the rapid growth of Indonesia's trade partners, the importance of trade should have increased over time. There has certainly been an upwards trend in the trade share since the early 1970s, although the oil boom and trade reform must also be part of the explanation. Another prediction is more tightly related to the economic geography literature. One might expect the other newly industrializing countries of East Asia to have invested increasingly heavily in Indonesia, since as wages rose in the NICs, the incentives to relocate production increased. Exactly this process does seem to have taken place in the 1980s. Firms from the NICs did shift some of their labor-intensive manufacturing production into Indonesia, and East Asia's importance as a foreign investor in Indonesia rose dramatically (Thee 1991).

It would be easy to exaggerate the importance of foreign direct investment (FDI), since inward FDI flows accounted for only 9 percent of total fixed investment in Indonesia even at their 1996 peak (Ramstetter 2000). More generally, it is not clear that Indonesia has made the most of the regional growth takeoff. As noted earlier, industrialization occurred relatively late, with rapid growth in labor-intensive manufacturing exports not emerging until the 1980s. If Suharto had originally followed an export-promoting strategy, rather than import substitution, it is possible that Indonesia would have benefited earlier from the rapid growth of its trading partners, even in the presence of the oil boom.

6. THE 1980s REFORMS

From a policy perspective, the 1980s are one of the most interesting periods in Indonesia's development. Over the decade, there were several rounds of wide-ranging microeconomic reform. Some of these reforms represented a change in overall strategy, from import substitution towards export promotion. The reforms were followed by a dramatic increase in the growth of manufacturing exports, and a marked improvement in the TFP performance of the manufacturing sector. The analysis of this section forms a reminder that Indonesia's economic success has not been simply a matter of sound macroeconomic policy and good fortune. Microeconomic intervention and reform are also part of the story.

The background to the reforms is that microeconomic intervention by the Indonesian government had steadily increased for much of the 1970s.[12] The banking system was dominated by state-owned banks. Credit was subsidized and favored the politically powerful. The government took an increasing role in investment, acting through state-owned companies and increasing its equity holdings. The various objectives of industrial policy, including the desire for regional dispersion of development and a greater economic role for indigenous ethnic groups, led to complex regulations. There was an increase in barriers to imports, partly in response to demands for protection from the nonoil traded sector, increasingly being hurt by the real appreciation associated with the oil boom.

The reform process began in the early 1980s, apparently precipitated by declining oil prices and a sharp rise in the current account deficit, which was over 7 percent of GDP by 1983. The initial response to the deficit was a devaluation in March 1983, followed by another in September 1986. Accompanying this was a series of microeconomic reforms, encouraged by concern that Indonesia had become a "high cost economy," with many industries that would be uncompetitive if required to trade at world prices. The banking sector was reformed in 1983 and 1988, with entry barriers and most credit subsidies removed. In an interesting example of successful institutional reform, the tasks of the corrupt and inefficient customs service were contracted out to a Swiss company from 1985.

---

[12] The discussion here draws on Aswicahyono, Bird, and Hill 1996.

In May 1986, a degree of import liberalization was introduced for exporters, based on a duty draw-back scheme that was implemented efficiently and without corruption. Starting later that year, quantitative restrictions and other nontariff barriers were gradually dismantled, with a shift towards tariffs as the preferred tool of trade policy.

The response was dramatic. Between 1983 and 1992, the share of manufactures in total merchandise exports rose from 7 percent to almost 50 percent. A naive interpretation of this shift is that it was entirely due to the policy reforms, but the explanation is more complex. Part of the change in export shares was due to falling world prices for oil and rubber, and to the 1980 export ban on unprocessed logs, which raised exports of plywood. Hill nevertheless suggests that the boom in exports of manufactured goods "represents a watershed in Indonesia's modern economic development" (2000a, 84). Among other things, it created for the first time a sizable export lobby in the manufacturing sector and momentum for further reform.

The change in export specialization happened so quickly that one might indeed regard it as an outcome of successful structural reform, and hence something of a watershed in the country's industrialization. But it can also be seen, in part, as the effect of the Dutch disease in reverse, as world oil prices started to decline in the early 1980s, with sharp falls in 1985–86. The lower oil prices implied a reduction in national income, and adjustment to this required the relative price of nontraded goods to fall and the nonoil traded goods sector to expand. This process of adjustment implies a real depreciation, carried out by Indonesia with the two large devaluations of 1983 and 1986. The changes in the real exchange rate are likely to have played an important role in the manufacturing export boom.

One consequence is that it is difficult to disentangle the relative contribution of structural reforms from the fall in oil prices. Yet in thinking about the oil price effects, one point of interest is that the export growth of the 1980s was in manufacturing rather than export crops. This may reflect a shift of comparative advantage away from agriculture from the early 1970s onwards, due to productivity growth and capital accumulation. When oil prices fell in the 1980s, the effect was to create rapid growth in manufacturing exports, something that might have been observed much earlier, and perhaps less dramatically, in the absence of the oil boom.

Given the general equilibrium considerations associated with the Dutch disease and also with agricultural development, the most informative way to assess the structural reforms is to examine changes in total factor productivity. Timmer (1999) presents estimates for the manufacturing sector for 1975–95. As he notes, the degree of uncertainty is considerable, and previous estimates differ widely. His own work shows a sharp contrast between 1975–86, for which annual TFP growth is just 0.3 percent, and 1986–95, for which the figure is 4.8 percent. These figures tend to support the idea that the microeconomic reforms were highly effective, although the comparison may overstate the change in underlying performance, given the recession of the early 1980s.

What motivated the reforms, and should they have been carried out earlier? There is no doubt that the ending of the oil boom was a major factor and was regarded by some officials as "a blessing in disguise" precisely because it created a political climate allowing reform (Booth 1992). MacIntyre (1992) provides an account of the reform process that also emphasizes political changes, including growing influence for business groups, and changing social attitudes towards capitalism. Earlier liberalization, for example in the 1970s, would have been greeted by hostility and suspicion, reflecting a deep-seated ambivalence towards free markets. The government was careful to present the 1980s reforms as pragmatic, to avoid discussions of overall development strategy that would have quickly polarized opinion.[13] All this suggests that while earlier microeconomic reform may have been desirable, it would have been difficult to implement.

7. GROWING INTO TROUBLE?

To summarize the arguments so far, Indonesia grew rapidly after 1966 for a number of reasons, including political stability, unusually competent macroeconomic policy, rapid productivity improvement in agriculture, and an effective response to the oil windfall. A shift towards manufacturing took place later than in some of the other high-performing East Asian economies, but this can probably be attributed at least partly to natural-resource abundance, and especially the effect of the oil boom on the structure of production and exports. When oil prices fell and the Dutch disease was reversed, manufacturing exports in the 1980s grew dramatically. At this time, TFP growth was unusually rapid, suggesting that the microeconomic reforms of the mid-1980s also played a central role.

If I had been writing this chapter in 1996, the above summary of Indonesia's performance would have led me to sound a note of cautious optimism about the country's economic prospects. The crisis of 1997–98, however, has cast a shadow over such predictions, and also over the historical record. While the economy was growing rapidly, some of its latent problems could be regarded as worrying, but perhaps not critical. In the aftermath of an economic collapse as severe as Indonesia's, one of the swiftest reversals of postwar history, the foundations naturally tend to appear rather insecure. The undeniable achievements of the past 30 years now look less than inevitable and more like a precarious balancing act. Perhaps some degree of failure was never far away.

When it came, the crisis saw "everything going wrong at once" (Hill 2000b). As elsewhere, it seems likely that institutional weaknesses are a large part of

---

[13] This point is made by Soesastro (1989), quoted in Hill 2000a, 117.

the explanation (see for example Johnson et al. 2000). This section of the chapter adds to existing accounts by asking whether rapid growth itself made an indirect contribution to the severity of the crisis. This inquiry is in the tradition of Olson (1963), who argued that growth could be a destabilizing force. His central argument is that rapid growth is associated with social dislocation and hence political instability. Time has not necessarily been kind to this hypothesis, but Indonesia may offer some support for the broader theme.

This section will argue that in the case of Indonesia, fast growth interacted with weak institutions in a way that gradually undermined the country's capacity to withstand an adverse shock. In particular, it will discuss the connections between growth and the highly centralized form of corruption that was integral to the functioning of Suharto's government. The extent of corruption was one of the key factors in his failure to respond effectively to the crisis, and in his subsequent downfall.

The nature of Suharto's rule was almost monarchical. Cassing (2000) argues that the observed patterns of regulation, rent seeking, and corruption can be largely explained by Suharto's desire to eliminate political competition. The lack of competition allowed him to engineer streams of rents that were not only lucrative but also largely free of risk and could then be used to enrich politically important allies and even family members. This highlights a key feature of Indonesia's corruption problem: Suharto's grip on power was sufficiently secure that he had no incentive to compromise in his policies and interventions. In particular, there were few mechanisms by which the extent of corruption could be restrained. In the circumstances, it is perhaps all the more remarkable that Indonesia grew so rapidly for so long, and that the state was not more predatory.[14]

The form of corruption was connected to the high degree of state involvement in the economy, or what some discussions refer to as the politicization of economic activity. This process dates back to the nationalizations under Sukarno, and even though the state gradually started to disengage from business in the 1980s, it was partly replaced by private conglomerates that were often associated with political patronage. Hence growth and structural change, including the increased importance of private industry, contributed further to the prominence of rent seeking and "crony capitalism."

When resource allocation depends on political influence as much as commercial acumen, distortions and deadweight losses are inevitable. But there have also been more important adverse effects, on social cohesion and the prospects for political stability and economic reform. Some of the main beneficiaries of growth have been conglomerates strongly associated with Sino-Indonesian entrepreneurs rather than indigenous ethnic groups, and their increasing visibility

---

[14] The seemingly paradoxical coexistence of Indonesia's rapid growth with a high degree of centralized corruption is analyzed by MacIntyre (2000, 2001a).

and economic dominance has contributed to social tensions (Hill 2000a). One side effect is that the government has remained committed to a large state enterprise sector and resisted other reforms that might benefit the private conglomerates, in order to placate restless indigenous groups. Meanwhile, support for privatizing at least some state enterprises has not always been forthcoming from the expected quarters, partly because of fears that attempts at such reform would quickly be undermined by corruption.

The unchecked authority of Suharto, and the centralized nature of corruption, may also be part of the explanation of the severity of the crisis in Indonesia's financial sector. Cole and Slade (1998) argue that the crisis had political origins. Although it exposed problems in financial supervision, these were not always due to a lack of expertise or awareness on the part of regulators, but to the obstacle that political connections sometimes placed in the way of effective supervision. Cole and Slade point out that some prominent officials tried and failed to apply prudential rules to financial institutions or transactions connected with the Suharto regime. Increasingly, connections to Suharto became seen as a guarantee or collateral, sometimes the only kind underpinning enterprises and financial institutions, notably in banking.

Partly due to these considerations, the financial sector was ill prepared for the events of 1997. The initiating factor was Thailand's devaluation, which led to a reassessment of exchange rate valuations across the region. McLeod (1998) argues that this reassessment was the straw that broke the camel's back: with a new awareness of exchange rate risk, the depreciation of the rupiah became a self-fulfilling prophecy. The depreciation, combined with a series of policy mistakes, particularly the sudden closure of sixteen failing banks, contributed to a swift collapse of confidence in the financial sector. The financial crisis led to astonishingly steep declines in investment and output, and Indonesia's economic miracle unraveled amidst growing social disorder and internal tensions.

In summary, the long period of rapid growth under Suharto may have interacted with institutional weaknesses in a way that partly explains the severity of the crisis. Structural change and growth created new and highly lucrative opportunities for rent seeking and centralized corruption. The increasing visibility of "crony capitalism" undermined Suharto's legitimacy, an important event in a country where urbanization and mass education have begun to change the social and political context. Meanwhile, the effects of corruption, and the politicization of economic activity, started to threaten the security of the financial system.

These institutional weaknesses suggest that, by the late 1990s, Indonesia may have lacked resilience in the face of shocks. Over the course of 1997–98, everything went wrong at once. As Hill (2000b) argues, corruption certainly did not precipitate the crisis, but its form and the wider nature of the political system may explain why Suharto was unwilling, and perhaps unable, to respond effectively. The public perception that Suharto was intent on protecting his commercial interests, perhaps at all costs, undermined faith in the regime, and the crisis began to feed on itself. Once Suharto lost the support of the Indonesian elite, his fall from power was inevitable.

Hill writes that "it is hard to think of a regime which, having achieved so much over a quarter of a century, ended so abruptly and ignominiously" (Hill 2000b, 135). The case that rapid growth contributed to this ignominious end could easily be overstated. Many of the institutional weaknesses would have emerged as problematic in the absence of growth, structural change, and urbanization. If the Suharto regime had not delivered in economic terms, it is likely that popular discontent would have emerged much earlier, with uncertain consequences. It is also the case, as Hill points out, that bad luck played a role in the depth of the crisis.

Whether or not one regards economic growth as indirectly contributing to the crisis, it seems likely that Indonesia was destined for trouble. The experience of 1997–98 draws attention to the ways in which even an autocracy as long-lived as Suharto's may be vulnerable to events, and this raises the question of whether the crisis would have been less severe under an alternative set of political institutions.

The central importance of institutions for sustaining growth in the face of external shocks has been emphasized by Rodrik (1999a). He argues that shocks are more likely to be problematic in countries with latent social conflict and weak institutions for managing conflict. Both conditions seem to apply to Indonesia. The unbalanced nature of growth, unevenly spread among regions and ethnic groups, has worsened long-standing tensions. Meanwhile the country's political institutions, which imposed few constraints on Suharto, meant that the scope for decisive action was also accompanied by the potential for arbitrary, destabilizing measures and swift policy reversals, of the kind seen during the unfolding of the crisis (MacIntyre 1999b, 2001b).

Would a democracy have fared any better? In examining the East Asian crisis and how policy responses varied across the countries involved, Rodrik (1999b) has pointed to three advantages of democratic institutions in managing a crisis. First, there is the handling of leadership transitions. A democratic tradition in Indonesia might have allowed a smoother transfer of power from the discredited Suharto to new leaders. Instead, his attempts to retain power and influence, and to a lesser extent his failing health, contributed to the worsening of the crisis. Second, the democratic process may allow the fashioning of consensus about the policies needed in the face of an external shock, important in a divided country like Indonesia. Third, a democracy should allow opposition to be voiced through recognized channels, undermining the perceived legitimacy of direct protest through riots or other social disorder.

The issues here are complex, because even if Indonesia's existing political institutions were badly suited to handling the crisis of 1997–98, that is not necessarily true of earlier times. One can point to occasions when the authoritarian regime almost certainly achieved better outcomes than would have been possible under democracy. One obvious example would be in 1974, when inflation was rising and deflationary measures were needed, while at the same time political pressure mounted to spend the huge increases in oil revenues. More generally, it is possible that Indonesia's abundance of natural resources would have persistently undermined democracy, because of the political advantage that the availability of rents is likely to confer on incumbents.[15]

Yet the Indonesian example does clarify the lurking dangers of authoritarian regimes in which power is as tightly concentrated as it was under Suharto. The regime delivered long-term political and economic stability, but such a political system is only as effective as its current leader. Concerns about the failure of Suharto to groom an appropriate successor had been expressed before the crisis. As support for him diminished, together with any belief that he would act in the national interest, it became increasingly clear that Indonesia was destined for a period of considerable political turmoil at exactly the wrong time. As a result, one of the central lessons of Indonesia's recent past is that even a long-lived and economically successful autocracy cannot guarantee an effective response to adverse shocks and, at least eventually, may even preclude it.

8. CONCLUSIONS

Most recent work by economists on Indonesia has been focused, quite naturally, on the deep crisis of 1997–98. This chapter has taken a longer view, and I hope to have shown that Indonesia's experience under Suharto is likely to be of lasting interest. I will first discuss some possible implications for future growth research, and then consider the more immediate lessons for other countries.

There is general agreement that research on growth, and especially empirical research, has been more successful at identifying interesting associations than at providing a clear view of the forces and mechanisms behind success or failure. An example of this would be the much-discussed negative correlation between resource abundance and growth. Analyzing a case like Indonesia allows a more nuanced view. Resource abundance is not destiny, and as one might expect, its consequences turn on the policy response. The distinctive features of Indonesia's response were the use of oil revenues to fund agricultural improvements, followed by successful adjustment to the end of the oil boom, through exchange rate management, expenditure reduction, and microeconomic reform. This adjustment seems to have been a more important determinant of growth outcomes than any long-run Dutch disease effects, and therefore helps us to understand more fully why resource booms might have undermined growth elsewhere.

---

[15] Wantchekon (2000) analyzes the observed relationship between resource abundance and autocracy along these lines.

Indonesia's experience can also alert us to some possible omissions in much research on growth. Many accounts draw attention to the importance of the New Order's agricultural policies, and this perhaps confirms that cross-country empirical work should probably give more attention to agricultural performance and its determinants, as development economists have frequently pointed out. Equally, given that the changing pattern of Indonesia's access to markets appears to have had effects on industrial growth, it is possible that future empirical research should give more attention to economic geography, as in Redding and Venables (2000).

More fundamentally, almost any case study is likely to draw our attention, once again, to the centrality of political economy in explaining development outcomes. In cross-country empirical work, it is difficult to assess or explain the origins of good policy in a satisfactory way, yet perhaps nothing is more important. The chapter has tried to offer some thoughts on why policy outcomes were so much better in Indonesia than elsewhere, but the account is far from complete, and a great deal remains to be done.

These questions are urgent, because Indonesia's record may have wider lessons. Most obviously, it shows what can be achieved despite unfavorable initial conditions, some weak institutions, and flawed microeconomic policies. Given that the country grew rapidly for three decades, so that per capita GDP rose more than fourfold, it is clear that the necessary conditions for successful economic development are not quite as demanding as often suggested.

Less optimistically, if Indonesia's road to development has been the one less traveled, it may also be a difficult one for others to follow. To a large extent, the rapid growth under Suharto can be seen as the outcome of two mutually reinforcing factors, political stability and macroeconomic stability. Neither is easily achieved, and neither was anywhere near inevitable given Indonesia's institutions, as the record before 1966 makes clear.

This point is worth emphasizing, as a qualification to the analysis above. There is a danger in any historical case study, particularly of a single country, of seeing the past as fully determined. It is worth remembering that a different leader might have emerged in 1966, for better or worse. Suharto might have been Marcos, and the economic history of Indonesia could have been that of the Philippines. Even if we take Suharto's ascent to power as a given, his task was made easier by some instances of good fortune. The recent crisis adds to this chapter's case that Indonesia's remarkable achievements have been precariously balanced.

What does this imply for the country's future prospects? I leave detailed thoughts on this to more expert observers, but there seems little doubt that almost everything depends on the political developments of the next few years. The universal obstacles to establishing democracy are accompanied in Indonesia's case by a history of corruption and institutional weaknesses, as in the legal framework, which will only make the task even more difficult. Long-standing regional and ethnic tensions suggest that the stakes are high.

APPENDIX

This appendix shows how simple general equilibrium models of production, of the form often used in trade theory, can offer insight into growth and structural change in an economy like that of Indonesia. In particular, the models demonstrate that labor productivity is likely to be an inadequate measure of sectoral performance.

Consider a small open economy with two sectors, agriculture (subscript a) and nonagriculture (subscript m). The agricultural good is the numeraire. Outputs of both sectors are tradable, so that world prices tie down the relative price of the nonagricultural good, denoted by p. Under this assumption, a simple model might start from the following four equations:

$$Y_a = A_a L_a$$
$$Y_m = A_m F(K, L_m)$$
$$Y = Y_a + p Y_m$$
$$L = L_a + L_m,$$

where Y is total output, L is total employment, Y_a and Y_m are outputs of the two sectors, L_a and L_m are employment in the two sectors, K is the capital stock, A_a and A_m are productivity parameters, and $F(.)$ is a constant returns to scale production function.

If we assume that labor is paid its marginal product in both sectors, and labor movements between the two sectors bring about equality in wages, then the level of real wages is determined entirely by the exogenous level of productivity in agriculture, A_a. Hence this model yields a very strong conclusion, which is that while specialization is incomplete, wages in both sectors will only rise to the extent that agricultural productivity increases. Another implication of this framework is that simple measures of labor productivity are a good yardstick by which to judge performance in agriculture.

Yet these implications are clearly far from general, at least in the long run. A more conventional model would allow for the possibility of substitution in agriculture between labor and other inputs, as in the two-good, specific factors model of trade theory. That is, we would have

$$Y_a = A_a G(R, L_a),$$

where R is a factor, perhaps land, specific to agriculture. Now it is clear that wages in each sector, and by implication labor productivity, will depend on what is happening in both sectors. One corollary is that in the long run, raising agricultural productivity is not necessarily the only way to help the rural poor, at least if rural and urban labor markets are well integrated.

We can use a model of this form to analyze the increase in output associated with an increase in agricultural total factor productivity. The simplest interesting case is provided by Cobb-Douglas production functions in labor and two specific factors:

$$Y_a = A_a R^\beta L_a^{1-\beta}$$
$$Y_m = A_m K^\gamma L_m^{1-\gamma}.$$

Labor is the only mobile factor, and labor market equilibrium implies

$$(1 - \beta) \frac{Y_a}{L_a} = (1 - \gamma) \frac{pY_m}{L_m}$$

$$(1 - \beta) A_a \left(\frac{R}{L_a} \right)^\beta = (1 - \gamma) pA_m \left(\frac{K}{L_m} \right)^\gamma.$$

What happens if agricultural TFP is raised by a factor θ? We can write down a new labor market equilibrium condition similar to that above, and dividing one by the other and simplifying yields

$$\theta = \left(\frac{1-b}{1-b} \right)^\gamma \left(\frac{b}{a} \right)^\beta,$$

which implicitly defines the new agricultural employment share, b, as a function of the initial share a, the productivity increase θ, and the two technology parameters, β and γ.

We can then calculate the ratio of new output to old, Λ, as follows:

$$\Lambda = \frac{Y_a' + pY_m'}{Y_a + pY_m} = \frac{pY_m'}{pY_m} \left[\frac{\dfrac{Y_a'}{pY_m'} + 1}{\dfrac{Y_a}{pY_m} + 1} \right],$$

where an apostrophe (') indicates the new values of output in agriculture and nonagriculture. Using the old and new labor market equilibrium conditions, this can be rewritten as

$$\Lambda = \left(\frac{1-a}{1-b} \right)^\gamma \left[\frac{1 - \beta - b(\gamma - \beta)}{1 - \beta - a(\gamma - \beta)} \right].$$

We can now calculate the effect of a rise in agricultural TFP on overall output. Taking the case where the initial employment share is $a = 0.75$, the effect of

TABLE 6.A1
Effects of Agricultural TFP Increases on Total Output

γ	0.1	0.2	0.3	0.4
0.2	1.89	1.89	1.90	1.90
0.3	1.83	1.84	1.85	1.87
0.4	1.78	1.79	1.81	1.82
0.5	1.72	1.73	1.75	1.78

Note: The entries show the ratio of new total output to old total output in the wake of a doubling of TFP in the agricultural sector, calculated for different values of the technology parameters β and γ.

doubling agricultural total factor productivity is shown in table 6.A1, for a variety of assumptions about the technology parameters.

These calculations show that the aggregate effects of higher agricultural TFP can be substantial, but they should be seen as only illustrative. In particular, the assumptions made on β and γ are inconsistent with the observed data on agriculture's share of output unless there is a wage differential across sectors. In turn, a fixed wage differential has implications for the output gain. If the marginal product of labor is higher in nonagriculture than in agriculture, the effects of a rise in agricultural TFP will be less than those shown in table 6.4, because labor will be reallocated to a sector in which it has lower marginal productivity.

REFERENCES

Adelman, Irma, and Cynthia Taft Morris. 1967. *Society, Politics, and Economic Development.* Baltimore: Johns Hopkins University Press.

Aswicahyono, H. H., Kelly Bird, and Hal Hill. 1996. "What Happens to Industrial Structure When Countries Liberalise? Indonesia since the Mid-1980s." *Journal of Development Studies* 32, no. 3: 340–63.

Bevan, David L., Paul Collier, and Jan Willem Gunning. 1999. *Nigeria and Indonesia.* Oxford: Oxford University Press.

Booth, Anne. 1999. "Initial Conditions and Miraculous Growth: Why Is South East Asia Different from Taiwan and South Korea?" *World Development* 27, no. 2: 301–21.

———. 2000. "Poverty and Inequality in the Suharto Era: An Assessment." *Bulletin of Indonesian Economic Studies* 36, no. 1: 73–104.

———, ed. 1992. *The Oil Boom and After: Indonesian Economic Policy and Performance in the Soeharto Era.* Oxford: Oxford University Press.

Cassing, James H. 2000. "Economic Policy and Political Culture in Indonesia." *European Journal of Political Economy* 16, no. 1: 159–71.

Cole, David C., and Betty F. Slade. 1998. "Why Has Indonesia's Financial Crisis Been So Bad?" *Bulletin of Indonesian Economic Studies* 34, no. 2: 61–66.

Easterly, William, Michael Kremer, Lant Pritchett, and Lawrence H. Summers. 1993. "Good Policy or Good Luck? Country Growth Performance and Temporary Shocks." *Journal of Monetary Economics* 32, no. 3: 459–83.

Easterly, William, and Ross Levine. 1997. "Africa's Growth Tragedy: Policies and Ethnic Divisions." *Quarterly Journal of Economics* 112, no. 4: 1203–50.

Frankel, Jeffrey A., and David Romer. 1999. "Does Trade Cause Growth?" *American Economic Review* 89, no. 3: 379–99.

Garcia Garcia, Jorge. 2000. "Indonesia's Trade and Price Interventions: Pro-Java and Pro-Urban." *Bulletin of Indonesian Economic Studies* 36, no. 3: 93–112.

Gelb, Alan, and Associates. 1988. *Oil Windfalls: Blessing or Curse?* Oxford: Oxford University Press.

Gelb, Alan, and Bruce Glassburner. 1988. "Indonesia: Windfalls in a Poor Rural Economy." In Alan Gelb and Associates, *Oil Windfalls: Blessing or Curse?* Oxford: Oxford University Press.

Henderson, J. Vernon, Zmarak Shalizi, and Anthony J. Venables. 2000. "Geography and Development." World Bank Working Paper No. 2456.

Hill, Hal. 2000a. *The Indonesian Economy.* 2d ed. Cambridge: Cambridge University Press.

———. 2000b. "Indonesia: The Strange and Sudden Death of a Tiger Economy." *Oxford Development Studies* 28, no. 2: 117–39.

Johnson, Simon, Peter Boone, Alidair Breach, and Eric Friedman. 2000. "Corporate Governance in the Asian Financial Crisis." *Journal of Financial Economics* 58:141–86.

Leamer, Edward E. 1987. "Paths of Development in the Three-Factor, *n*-good General Equilibrium Model." *Journal of Political Economy* 95, no. 5: 961–99.

MacIntyre, Andrew J. 1992. "Politics and the Reorientation of Economic Policy in Indonesia." In *The Dynamics of Economic Policy Reform in South-east Asia and the South-west Pacific,* ed. Andrew J. MacIntyre and Kanishka Jayasuriya. Oxford: Oxford University Press.

———. 1999a. "Political Parties, Accountability, and Economic Governance in Indonesia." In *Democracy, Governance, and Economic Performance: East and Southeast Asia,* ed. Jean Blondel, Takashi Inoguchi, and Ian Marsh. Tokyo: United Nations University Press.

———. 1999b. "Political Institutions and the Economic Crisis in Thailand and Indonesia." In *The Politics of the Asian Financial Crisis,* ed. T. J. Pempel. Ithaca, N.Y.: Cornell University Press.

———. 2000. "Funny Money: Fiscal Policy, Rent-Seeking, and Economic Performance in Indonesia." In *Rents, Rent-Seeking, and Economic Development: Theory and Evidence in Asia,* ed. Kwame Sundaram Jomo and Mushtaq Khan. Cambridge: Cambridge University Press.

———. 2001a. "Investment, Property Rights, and Corruption in Indonesia." In *Corruption: The Boom and Bust of East Asia,* ed. J. E. Campos. Quezon City: Ateneo de Manila University Press.

———. 2001b. "Institutions and Investors: The Politics of the Economic Crisis in Southeast Asia." *International Organization* 55, no. 1: 81–122.

———. 2001c. "Rethinking the Politics of Agricultural Policy Making: The Importance of Institutions." In *The Evolving Roles of State, Private, and Local Actors in Asian Rural Development,* ed. Ammar Siamwalla. Oxford: Oxford University Press.

Martin, Will, and Peter G. Warr. 1993. "Explaining the Relative Decline of Agriculture: A Supply-Side Analysis for Indonesia." *World Bank Economic Review* 7, no. 3: 381–401.

Matsuyama, Kiminori. 1992. "Agricultural Productivity, Comparative Advantage, and Economic Growth." *Journal of Economic Theory* 58, no. 2: 317–34.

McLeod, Ross H. 1998. "From Crisis to Cataclysm? The Mismanagement of Indonesia's Economic Ailments." *World Economy* 21, no. 7: 913–30.

Muller, A. L. 1998. "The Indonesian Economy since 1966." Review article. *South African Journal of Economics* 66, no. 1: 130–44.

Neary, J. Peter, and Sweder van Wijnbergen. 1986. "Natural Resources and the Macroeconomy: A Theoretical Framework." In *Natural Resources and the Macroeconomy,* ed. J. Peter Neary and Sweder van Wijnbergen. Oxford: Basil Blackwell.

Olson, Mancur. 1963. "Rapid Growth as a Destabilizing Force." *Journal of Economic History* 23, no. 4: 529–52.

Overland, Jody, Kenneth Simons, and Michael Spagat. 2000. "Political Instability and Growth in Dictatorships." CEPR Discussion Paper No. 2653.

Puga, D., and Anthony J. Venables. 1999. "Agglomeration and Economic Development: Import Substitution vs. Trade Liberalisation." *Economic Journal* 109:292–311.

Rabin, Matthew. 2000. "Inference by Believers in the Law of Small Numbers." University of California, Berkeley, January. Typescript.

Ramstetter, Eric D. 2000. "Survey of Recent Developments." *Bulletin of Indonesian Economic Studies* 36, no. 3: 3–45.

Redding, Stephen J., and Anthony J. Venables. 2000. "Economic Geography and International Trade." CEPR Discussion Paper No. 2568.

Robertson, Peter E. 2000. "Diminished Returns? Growth and Investment in East Asia." *Economic Record* 76:343–53.

Robinson, James A. 2000. "When Is a State Predatory?" University of California, Berkeley, May. Typescript.

Robison, R. 1986. *Indonesia: The Rise of Capital.* Sydney: Allen and Unwin.

Rodrik, Dani. 1995. "Getting Interventions Right: How South Korea and Taiwan Grew Rich." *Economic Policy* 20:53–108.

———. 1996. "Understanding Economic Policy Reform." *Journal of Economic Literature* 34, no. 1: 9–41.

———. 1999a. "Where Did All the Growth Go? External Shocks, Social Conflict, and Growth Collapses." *Journal of Economic Growth* 4, no. 4: 385–412.

———. 1999b. "The Asian Financial Crisis and the Virtues of Democracy." *Challenge* 42, no. 4: 44–59.

Sjahrir and Colin Brown. 1992. "Indonesian Financial and Trade Policy Deregulation: Reform and Response." In *The Dynamics of Economic Policy Reform in South-east Asia and the South-west Pacific,* ed. Andrew J. MacIntyre and Kanishka Jayasuriya. Oxford: Oxford University Press.

Soesastro, M. H. 1989. "The Political Economy of Deregulation in Indonesia." *Asian Survey* 29, no. 9: 853–68.

Temple, Jonathan R. W., and Paul A. Johnson. 1998. "Social Capability and Economic Growth." *Quarterly Journal of Economics* 113, no. 3: 965–90.

Thee, K. W. 1991. "The Surge of Asian NIC Investment into Indonesia." *Bulletin of Indonesian Economic Studies* 27, no. 3: 55–89.

Timmer, C. Peter. 1993. "Rural Bias in the East and South-east Asian Rice Economy: Indonesia in Comparative Perspective." *Journal of Development Studies* 29:149–76.

Timmer, Marcel P. 1999. "Indonesia's Ascent on the Technology Ladder: Capital Stock and Total Factor Productivity in Indonesian Manufacturing, 1975–95." *Bulletin of Indonesian Economic Studies* 35, no. 1: 75–97.

Wantchekon, Leonard. 2000. "Why Do Resource Dependent Countries Have Authoritarian Governments?" Yale University, February. Typescript.

Warr, Peter G. 1986. "Indonesia's Other Dutch Disease: Economic Effects of the Petroleum Boom." In *Natural Resources and the Macroeconomy,* ed. J. Peter Neary and Sweder van Wijnbergen. Oxford: Basil Blackwell.

Wei, Shang-Jin. 2000. "Local Corruption and Global Capital Flows." *Brookings Papers on Economic Activity* 2000, no. 2: 303–46.

CHAPTER 7

India since Independence

AN ANALYTIC GROWTH NARRATIVE

J. BRADFORD DELONG

How USEFUL is the modern theory of economic growth? Does it provide a satisfactory framework for analyzing the wealth and poverty of nations? This chapter investigates this question by applying modern growth theory to the case of the economic development of India over the past half-century. Whether growth theory turns out to be useful—whether valid, interesting, and nonobvious insights are generated—is left as an exercise to the reader.

I should note at the start that this is a hazardous exercise: I know a fair amount about growth theory, but I know relatively little about India. The general rule is that one should try to write about subjects where one is knowledgeable, rather than about subjects where one is not. Whether the exercise I undertake in this chapter yields useful insights is not for me to judge.

The conventional narrative of India's post–World War II economic history begins with a disastrous wrong turn by India's first prime minister, Jawaharlal Nehru, toward Fabian socialism, central planning, and an unbelievable quantity of bureaucratic red tape. This "license raj" strangled the private sector and led to rampant corruption and massive inefficiency. As a result, India stagnated until bold neoliberal economic reforms triggered by the currency crisis of 1991, and implemented by the government of Prime Minister Narasimha Rao and Finance Minister Manmohan Singh, unleashed its current wave of rapid economic growth—growth at a pace that promises to double average productivity levels and living standards in India every sixteen years (table 7.1).

Yet if you look at the growth performance of India during its first postindependence generation under the Nehru dynasty in the context of the general cross-country pattern, India does not appear to be an exceptional country. Its rate of economic growth appears average. Moreover, its values of the proximate determinants of growth appear average as well.

Simple growth theory tells us that the proximate determinants of growth are *(a)* the share of investment in GDP (to capture the effort being made to build up the capital stock), *(b)* the rate of population growth (to capture how much of investment effort has to be devoted to simply equipping a larger population with the infrastructure and other capital needed to maintain the current level of

TABLE 7.1
Indian Rates of Economic Growth, 1950–2000

	1950–80	1980–90	1990–2000
Annual real GDP growth	3.7%	5.9%	6.2%
Annual real GDP per capita growth	1.5%	3.8%	4.4%

Source: IMF.

productivity, and *(c)* the gap between output per worker and the world's best practice (to capture the gap between the country's current status and its steady-state growth path, and also to capture the magnitude of the productivity gains possible through acquisition of the world's best-practice technologies). Neither India's investment share nor its rate of population growth are in any sense unusually poor for an economy in India's relative position as of independence.

The fact that pre-1990 India appears "normal," at least as far as the typical pattern of post–World War II economic growth is concerned, places limits on the size of the damage done to Indian economic growth since World War II by the Nehru dynasty's attraction to Fabian socialism and central planning. India between independence and 1990 was not East Asia as far as economic growth was concerned, to be sure. But it was not Africa either.

One possibility is that the constraints placed on growth by the inefficiencies of the Nehru dynasty's "license raj" were simply par for the course in the post–World War II world: perhaps only exceptional countries were able to avoid inefficiencies like those of the license raj. A second possibility is that the failure of economic policies in promoting efficiency was in large part offset by successes in mobilizing resources: India in the first decades after World War II had a relatively high savings rate for a country in its development position.

Yet a third possibility is that the destructive effects of inefficiency-generating policies were offset by powerful advantages—a large chunk of the population literate in what was rapidly becoming the world's lingua franca, cultural patterns that placed a high value on education, the benefits of democracy in promoting accountability and focusing politicians' attention on their constituents' welfare, or some other factors—that should and would with better policies have made India one of the fastest-growing economies of the world not just in the 1990s but in previous decades as well.

If Indian economic growth before the past decade appears more or less ordinary, no one believes that Indian economic growth in the past decade and a half is anything like ordinary. In the 1990s India was one of the fastest-growing economies in the world. At the growth pace of the 1990s, Indian average productivity levels double every sixteen years. If the current pace of growth can be maintained, sixty-six years will bring India to the real GDP per capita level of the United States today. The contrast between the pace of growth in the 1990s and the pace of growth before 1980—with a doubling time of fifty years, and an expected approach to America's current GDP per capita level not in 2066 but in 2250—is extraordinary.

Moreover, this acceleration in Indian economic growth has not been "immiserizing." Poverty has not fallen as fast as anyone would wish, and regional and other dimensions of inequality have grown in the 1990s. But it is not the case that India's economic growth miracle is being fueled by the further absolute impoverishment of India's poor. Ahluwalia (1999) quotes Tendulkar (1997) as finding a 7 percent decline in the urban and a 20 percent decline in the rural poverty gap[1] between 1983 and 1988, followed by a further 20 percent decline in both the urban and rural poverty gaps between 1988 and 1994. According to the Indian Planning Commission, the years between 1994 and 1999 saw a further 20 percent decline in the nation's poverty gap, leaving the best estimate of the proportional poverty gap today at 54 percent of its value back in 1983.

What are the sources of India's recent acceleration in economic growth? Conventional wisdom traces them to policy reforms at the start of the 1990s. In the words of Das (2000), the miracle began with a bang:

> In July 1991 . . . the announcement of sweeping liberalization by the minority government of P. V. Narasimha Rao . . . opened the economy . . . dismantled import controls, lowered customs duties, and devalued the currency . . . virtually abolished licensing controls on private investment, dropped tax rates, and broke public sector monopolies. . . . [W]e felt as though our second independence had arrived: we were going to be free from a rapacious and domineering state.

Yet the aggregate growth data tells us that the acceleration of economic growth began earlier, in the early or mid-1980s, long before the exchange crisis of 1991 and the shift of the government of Narasimha Rao and Manmohan Singh toward neoliberal economic reforms.

Thus apparently the policy changes in the mid- and late-1980s under the last governments of the Nehru dynasty were sufficient to start the acceleration of growth, small as those policy reforms appear in retrospect. Would they have just produced a short-lived flash in the pan—a decade or so of fast growth followed by a slowdown—in the absence of the further reforms of the 1990s? My hunch is that the answer is yes. In the absence of the second wave of reforms in the 1990s it is unlikely that the rapid growth of the second half of the 1980s could be sustained. But hard evidence to support such a strong counterfactual judgment is lacking.

---

[1] The percentage gap between the expenditure levels of all poor households, and what the expenditure levels of all poor households would be if they were pulled up to the poverty line.

PRE-1990 ECONOMIC GROWTH

Simple Growth Theory

The simplest of the theoretical approaches to understanding economic growth derived from Solow (1956) begins with an aggregate production function:

$$\frac{Y_t}{L_t} = \left(\frac{K_t}{L_t}\right)^a (E_t)^{1-a}.$$

Real GDP per worker (Y/L) is equal to the product of two terms. The first term is the economy's average capital-labor ratio (K/L) raised to the power less than one, α, that parameterizes how rapidly diminishing returns to investment set in. The second term is the economy's level of total factor productivity, written for convenience as the efficiency of labor E raised to the $(1 - \alpha)$ power.

In this approach, there are three factors that are proximate determinants of economic growth. The first, labeled s, is the share of the economy's output devoted to building up its capital stock: the investment-to-GDP ratio. Higher shares of investment in GDP increase the speed with which the economy's capital stock grows, and raise productivity by increasing the economy's capital-labor ratio. (Moreover, in more complicated models in which technology is embodied in capital or in which learning-by-doing is an important source of productivity growth, higher investment raises output by more than just the private marginal product of capital. See DeLong and Summers 1991.)

The second proximate determinant, labeled n, is the population growth rate. A higher rate of growth of population means that more of the economy's resources must be devoted to infrastructure and capital accumulation just to stay in the same place. It is expensive to equip each additional worker with the economy's current average level of capital per worker, and to provide the extra infrastructure to connect him or her with the economy. In an economy with a disembodied efficiency-of-labor growth rate g and a rate of depreciation of capital equipment δ over time the capital-output ratio will tend to head for its steady state value κ^* of

$$\kappa^* = \frac{s}{n + g + \delta}.$$

At this value of the capital-output ratio, the proportional rate of growth of the capital stock $g(k)$ is

$$g(k) = \frac{s}{\kappa^*} - \delta = \frac{s}{(s/(n + g + \delta))} - \delta = n + g$$

and is equal to the proportional growth rate of output $g(y)$, so once the capital-output ratio is at its steady-state value, it will remain there.

Thus a higher level of the population growth rate n reduces the steady-state value of the capital-output ratio. It makes the economy less capital intensive and poorer because a greater share of investment is going to equip an enlarged workforce, and less remains to support capital deepening.

The third of the proximate determinants of economic growth is the economy's initial level of output per worker. The initial level captures how far the economy is away from its steady-state growth path, and thus what are the prospects for rapid catch-up growth as the economy converges to its steady-state growth path. (In more sophisticated models, the initial level of output per worker also captures the technology gap vis-à-vis the world's potential best practice. It thus indicates the scope for growth driven by the successful transfer of technology from outside to the economy.)

Under the approximations set out by Mankiw, Romer, and Weil (1992), the economy's average growth rate of output per worker, $g(y/l)$, over a period from some initial year 0 to year t will be given by

$$\Delta g(y/l) = \frac{(1 - e^{-\lambda t})}{t(1 - \alpha)} \times \frac{\Delta s}{\bar{s}} - \frac{(1 - e^{-\lambda t})}{t(1 - \alpha)} \times \frac{\Delta n}{n + \bar{g} + \delta}$$
$$- \frac{(1 - e^{-\lambda t})}{t} \times \Delta \ln(Y_0/L_0),$$

where capital Δ's indicate deviations from the world's average values, where lines over variables indicate that they are world average values, and where λ is a function of the other parameters of the model given by

$$\lambda = (1 - \alpha)(n + g + \delta).$$

Thus this simple growth theory suggests an obvious regression to investigate the worldwide pattern of economic growth. In the cross-country sample, simply regress the average growth rate of output per worker ($g(y/l)$) on the share of investment in GDP (s), on the population growth rate (n), and on the log of output per worker in 1960 ($\ln(Y_0/L_0)$). Such a regression run for 85 economies in the Summers-Heston Penn World Table database for which data from 1960 to 1992 are available produces the estimated equation:[2]

$$g(y/l) = + 0.149\, s \quad - \quad 0.406\, n \quad - \quad 0.007 \ln(Y_0/L_0)$$
$$\qquad\quad (0.023) \qquad\quad (0.204) \qquad\quad (0.002)$$

$$\text{SEE} = 0.012 \qquad n = 85 \qquad R^2 = 0.431.$$

[2] Regression run using the Heston and Summers Penn World Table, version 5.6; data file at http://www.j-bradford-delong.net/Econ_Articles/India/Data-india_growth.jmp. See Summers and Heston 1991.

The coefficients on these variables have natural interpretations as composed of terms—like $(1 - e^{-\lambda\tau})/t$—that capture the theoretical prediction that differences in growth rates diminish over time as countries converge to their Solow steady-state growth paths, and terms—like $1/((1 - \alpha)s)$—that capture the immediate output-boosting benefit of that factor. This estimated equation accounts for more than 40 percent of the variance in 1960–92 growth rates for these 85 countries with just three simple proximate determinants of growth.

It is, however, not possible to have confidence that this equation captures a "structural" relationship. The population growth rate n is determined by where the country is in the demographic transition, and is thus highly likely to be unaffected by any growth-influencing omitted variables or residual disturbances (see Livi-Bacci 1996). But omitted variables that slow down growth will also lead to a low level of initial output per worker: omitted variables will thus reduce the absolute value of the coefficient on initial output per worker below its "structural" value. And there is little reason to believe that the investment share is exogenous: it may be functioning as much as an indicator for residual factors left out of the regression as a direct booster of production via a higher capital stock.[3]

Average India?

However, the nonstructural nature of this regression is not disturbing. For our purposes the most interesting factor is that from the perspective of the regression above there is very little that appears unusual about India's economic growth between independence and the late 1980s. In cross-country growth experience of 85 countries from 1960 to 1992, India lies smack in the middle of the scatter of world growth rate, as figure 7.1 shows.

Moreover, it is not just that India's actual rate of growth of output per worker has been very close to the average across the world's nations. The rate of growth predicted for India from its initial level of log output per worker, its share of investment in GDP, and its population growth rate was also very close to the world's average. Conditional on the values of the other right-hand side variables, the proximate determinants of growth in India take on unsurprising values. The investment-to-GDP share is just what one would expect for a country with India's rate of population growth and output per worker level in 1960. The rate of population growth is just what one would expect for a country with India's initial output per worker level and investment share of GDP. As figure 7.2 shows, leverage plots—diagrams that show the partial scatters of the variables in a multivariate regression—find nothing unusual in India's proximate determinants

---

[3] However, for an argument that investment shares are close to exogenous in practice even if not in theory—that shifts in investment have powerful effects on growth no matter what their causes— see DeLong and Summers 1991.

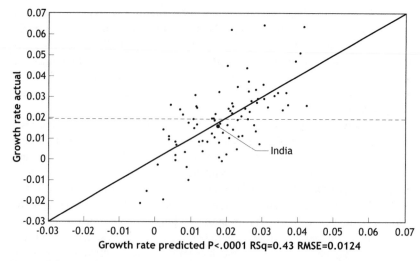

Figure 7.1. Actual and predicted 1960–92 output per worker growth

of economic growth over 1960–92. For none of the three right-hand side variables is India an outlier, nor does it contribute any significant identifying variance to the cross-country regression. India's 1960–92 growth experience appears ordinary.

Implications of "Average" India

The conventional wisdom today is that India's first prime minister, Jawaharlal Nehru, took it down the wrong road as far as economic development was concerned, and so wasted nearly half a century in economic stagnation. Nehru was impressed with what he (and many others at the time) saw as the successful mobilization of resources for development by the Soviet Union. In the shadow of the Great Depression only a decade past, it seemed naive to believe that the private sector could successfully and reliably generate the investment that a growing economy needed. And in a country as desperately poor as India, the government needed to put its thumb on the scales to insure that economic growth produced widely distributed income gains. It could not afford to have increased productivity channeled into the fortunes of a small slice of the population made up of merchant and industrial princes.

As Gurchuran Das (2000) puts it, the desire to make sure that private industrial development conformed to social needs led to

> a nightmare. . . . An untrained army of underpaid engineers . . . operating . . . without clear-cut criteria, vetted thousands of applications on an ad-hoc basis . . . months

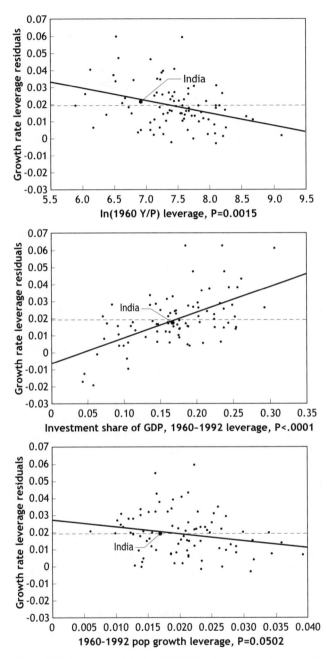

Figure 7.2. Leverage plots for 1960–92 output per worker growth

in . . . futile micro review . . . again lost months reviewing the same data . . . [The] interministerial licensing committee . . . equally ignorant of entrepreneurial realities . . . also operat[ing] upon ad hoc criteria in the absence of well-ordered priorities. . . . [sought] approval for the import of machinery from the capital goods licensing committee . . . foreign agreements committee . . . state financial institutions. The result was enormous delays [of] years . . . with staggering opportunities for corruption.

Moreover, established business houses learned how to game the system with "parallel bureaucracies in Delhi to follow up on their files, organize bribes, and win licenses." Established businesses could use the first-come, first-served nature of the licensing process to foreclose competition: apply for your competitor's license before they did, watch their application be rejected because enough capacity had already been licensed in that industry and the government did not want to see overinvestment, and then simply sit on the license without using it to build any capacity.

Thus the consensus view among economists is that of Bhagwati (2000), who describes Indian growth before the reforms of the early 1990s as having been "stuck at a drastically low level" during "nearly three decades of illiberal and autarkic policies." He endorses Lal (1998), who attributes the failures of economic growth to two factors, the first and less important "cultural"[4] and the second and more important "political." As Bhagwati summarizes Lal, India's bane is

the professional "povertywallas": the politicians who have incessantly mouthed slogans such as "garibi hathao" . . . [Indira Gandhi is meant here: that was the major slogan of her 1971 election campaign] and the economists who write continually about "abysmal poverty." Both have generally espoused policies, such as defending public sector enterprises at any cost, discounting and even opposing liberal reforms, promoting white-elephant style projects that use capital-intensive techniques on unrealistic grounds such as that they would create profits and savings when in fact they have drained the economy through losses. (2000, 28).

The rhetoric seems to suggest that India has suffered a unique series of disasters caused by bad judgment on the part of Jawharlal Nehru in being overimpressed with the Soviet Union's resource mobilization, bad company being kept by Indian colonial elites who listened too much to British Fabian socialists, and malevolent bad judgment exercised by politicians (chief among them Nehru's

---

[4] A deeply held distrust over centuries of the commercial classes and preference for dirigisme reinforced by the colonial elite's English education in Fabianist socialism. Anyone who makes any firm and bold statements about culture and economic growth is braver than I. Consider that while there is much to admire in Weber's (1976) *Protestant Ethic and the Spirit of Capitalism,* Weber also was certain that East Asia was doomed to centuries of economic stagnation because of the deep incompatibility of Hindu, Buddhist, and Confucian values with the requirements of modern economic rationality.

daughter Indira Gandhi) who saw India's poverty not as a problem to be solved through economic growth but as an interest group to be appeased in an attempt to seize and maintain political power.

Yet as was pointed out above, the extraordinary thing about India's post–World War II growth is how ordinary and average it seemed to be—up until the end of the 1980s. It is not nearly as bad as growth performance in Africa (see Dumont 1965; Bates 1984). It is not nearly as good as growth performance in East Asia (see World Bank 1994). It is average—suggesting either that India's poor growth-management policies were not *that* damaging, or rather that they were par for the course in the post–World War II world.

There are three ways to reconcile the widespread belief that the inefficiencies of the Nehru dynasty's license raj were very destructive for pre-1990 India. The first is to argue that the inefficiencies created by the Nehru dynasty were paralleled by similar mistakes of economic management in most of the countries of the world. If true, this would suggest that a different mode of explanation is needed to account for Indian economic policy and its failures in the first generation after World War II. It is possible to attribute mistakes in economic policy to bad ideology or bad judgment if such mistakes are exceptional. But if it is indeed the case that the same growth-retarding policy biases found in India were found throughout most of the world, then a different, more structural mode of explanation is called for. Why were governments attracted to an inward-looking, import-substituting path rather than an outward-looking, export-promoting one? What were the political benefits seen from a massive and monopolistic—and inefficient—publicly owned enterprise sector? Why the fear of foreign capital and foreign technology?

At the ideological level, I believe we understand very well where the attachment to planning and near-autarky came from. But as an economist I believe that in almost all cases ideologies can become powerful and effective only if they reflect (in distorted fashion, perhaps) the material interests of politically powerful groups. And here I do not think I understand the political strength of the interest groups that supported policies of overregulation and hostility to foreign trade, either in India or elsewhere.

A second possibility is that the failure of economic policies in terms of promoting efficiency was in large part offset by successes in mobilizing resources. For example, India in the first decades after World War II maintained a relatively high savings rate for a country in its development position. Total private savings as a share of national product were about 6 percent of GDP in the early 1950s, but rapidly rose to 15 percent of GDP in the early 1960s, and by the 1980s averaged 23 percent of income. As Jones (1994) pointed out, however, over most of the post–World War II period India's relatively high savings effort as a share of GDP translated into relatively low increases in the real capital stock because the price of capital goods was relatively high in India. A high price of capital goods means that a given amount of expenditure on investment buys little real capital.

Under this interpretation, the conventional wisdom about Nehru dynasty economic policies is too pessimistic because it sees only the efficiency costs, and does not see the potential gains from resource mobilization, of which a high savings rate would be one. This line of argument would be more convincing, however, if more Indians were literate. The failure of Indian governments to approach universal literacy, and the failures of Indian public health, suggest that the view that Indian central planning and public investment had massive benefits overlooked by economists' current conventional wisdom cannot bear too much weight.

Yet a third possibility is that the license raj was very destructive, destructive enough to cripple what would otherwise have been a true growth miracle along the lines of those seen in East Asia over the past two generations. It is plausible to speculate that in the long run India *must* have powerful growth advantages. For millennia it has had a culture that places a high value on formal education and literacy. One of the legacies of the British Empire is a large chunk of the population literate in what is rapidly becoming the world's lingua franca. People who can process English-language information may well become one of the world's production bottlenecks over the next generation. India is very well placed to take advantage of high demand for readers, speakers, and writers of English. Add to these the likely benefits of democracy in promoting accountability and focusing politicians' attention on their constituents' welfare, and a case can be made that India ought to have been one of the fastest-growing economies of the world not just in the 1990s but in previous decades as well.

To my mind, all three of these ways of assessing Indian economic growth in the first postindependence generation are still live possibilities. I do not yet have the information I need to think that I can establish that the weight of probability lies on any particular one of them.

Nevertheless, the central point is clear: India's economic growth failure in the first generation after independence was absolute, not relative. It is not that India fell far behind the benchmark established by the average performance of other developing economies. It is that Indian growth was much slower than one could reasonably have hoped, and much slower than the benchmark established by the performance of the fastest-growing developing economies.

THE INDIAN GROWTH MIRACLE

The Value of India's Example

The fact that India's growth performance seemed too *ordinary* in world context for the first three postindependence decades makes India's acceleration of economic growth since then much more exciting. With other countries that have experienced growth miracles, it is very difficult to imagine how to translate their experience into lessons for other developing countries. How is a country that seeks to emulate the Italian growth miracle to reproduce the close transport and trade links with the northwest European core? How is a country that seeks to repeat the growth miracle of Taiwan to attain the initial condition of an astonishingly equal distribution of land? How is a country that seeks to follow the Japanese model to assemble—in Japan's case, more than one hundred years ago—the national consensus for structural transformation and economic development that obtained among those who ruled in the name of Emperor Meiji?

It cannot be done. That is why the Indian case is so interesting, because it shows an example of an economy that was relatively stagnant and suffered from mammoth growth blockages yet managed to turn all that around, and in a short period of time.

Structural Breaks

To the extent that we trust aggregate national-level income accounts, it is clear that by 1985 Indian aggregate economic growth had undergone a structural break (fig. 7.3). Whether we should look for key causes of India's growth acceleration in the years immediately before 1985 depends on how we conceptualize that structural break. Was it the result of a once-and-for-all change that put the economy on a new, different path? Or when we say "structural change," are we referring to an ongoing process of waves of reform, each of which requires that the political coalition behind reform be reassembled, each of which could fail—with that failure capable of returning Indian growth to its pre-1980 pace?

Depending on how you answer this question, you focus on one of two time periods. If you seek a single structural break, you look at the last years of Indira Gandhi's rule and at Rajiv Gandhi's administration, the years when economic reform and economic liberalization became ideologically respectable within the Indian government along with policies that a development-seeking government ought to pursue to some degree.

If you wish to identify ongoing waves of reform, each of them debated and debatable, then you are more likely to focus on the early 1990s—when the exchange crisis served as a trigger for larger-scale reforms by the government of Narasimha Rao than had been previously contemplated—and today, when one key item on the table is reform of India's budget, so that claims on social resources in excess of production do not lead to an inflation crisis.

The Last Nehru-Gandhi Government

Rajiv Gandhi's Congress party won 77 percent of the seats in the Lok Sabha in the election that followed his mother's assassination by her bodyguards. Party

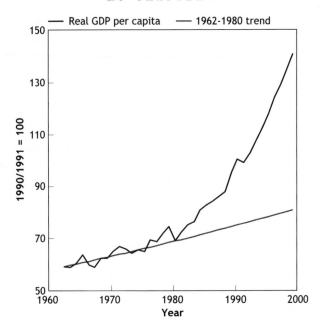

Figure 7.3. Indian real GDP per capita level and 1962–80 trend
Source: International Monetary Fund

discipline was not overwhelmingly strong, but the magnitude of the majority—and the association of most members of parliament with Rajiv—meant that a relatively underdeveloped apparatus for enforcing party discipline did not matter. During Rajiv Gandhi's administration India came as close to an *elected* dictatorship as it has ever been. And as the visible representative of a new Indian generation—uncorrupt, interested in reform, focused on applying modern managerial techniques—this last Nehru-Gandhi government ought to have had the power to carry out whatever plans of reform its leader could decide on.

Winning 48 percent of the national vote in the December 1984 election, and with 415 out of 545 seats in the Lok Sabha, this last government of the Nehru dynasty had the overwhelming majority needed for substantial reform. Moreover, the fact that Rajiv Gandhi himself was a new politician with his own circle of advisors and his own priorities meant that his government met the preconditions for a strong reforming executive: his government had the "relative autonomy" needed for it to have a good chance to transform the economy, rather than—as is usually the case—finding itself pulled back to the "political mainstream" by the standard pressures of politics.[5]

---

[5] This is Varshney's (1999) judgment, relying on the typology of economic reform set out by Haggard and Webb (1994).

For the first time, private industry executives found it easy to move into powerful ministerial positions in an Indian government. Prime Minister Rajiv Gandhi himself spoke of how his government would pursue "deregulation, import liberalization, and . . . access to foreign technology" and invoked the example of Japan, which had in less than a generation moved from a country whose products were "synonymous with shoddy goods" to "a byword for the best available" (see Varshney 1999). The first budget of the Rajiv Gandhi government sought to reduce marginal tax rates, reduce tariffs, make restrictions on imports transparent by replacing quotas with tariffs, remove restrictions on large firms that had been imposed in 1969 as part of India's antitrust policy, and begin the process of eliminating license restrictions on manufacturing industries.[6]

The economic reform program that Rajiv Gandhi's government decided upon focused on *(a)* encouraging capital imports and commodity exports, *(b)* a modest degree of industrial deregulation, and *(c)* a modest degree of tax system rationalization. In the government's first year it eliminated quantitative controls on imports of industrial machinery and cut tariffs on imports of capital goods by 60 percent. (I know: it is hard to think of a reason for a country like India to have any tariffs or restrictions on imports of capital goods whatsoever. But you have to crawl before you can walk.) Taxes on profits from exports were halved as well. Subsidies were reduced (arousing bitter political opposition: Varshney (1999) cites Kothari (1986) as an example). The government reduced the number of industries subject to government capacity licensing from 77 to 27 in 1988. And—although only in its last days—the government began to end price controls on industrial materials like cement and aluminum.

Yet somehow, somewhat paradoxically, the political power of Rajiv Gandhi's government was not transformed into rapid structural reform. Factions within the Congress Party seemed not to believe that their interests were bound up with the success of their leader and his policies, but were instead threatened by the potential backlash against an administration that was concerned with the prosperity of the rich rather than alleviating poverty: the Rajiv Gandhi regime had, after all, tried to increase the profits of businesses and cut marginal tax rates on food, kerosene, and fertilizer. Thus the reform plans carried out under Rajiv Gandhi were less bold than one would have expected given the rhetoric of his initial speeches.

The consequence of this first wave of economic reform was an economic boom. Real GDP growth averaged 5.6 percent per year over the Rajiv Gandhi government, while real rupee exports grew at 15 percent per year. By the end of the 1980s Indian aggregate labor productivity was one-third higher than a simple extrapolation of the pre-1980 trend would have predicted.

---

[6] The requirements that businesses obtain government licenses before they could build a plant or expand their capacity.

Using Growth Theory to Assess India's Growth Acceleration

The lens of growth theory provides a natural interpretation of the sustained three percentage point per year acceleration in economic growth under the Rajiv Gandhi government. The first starts with the equation for the speed of an economy's convergence to its steady-state growth path. As Mankiw, Romer, and Weil (1991) showed, an economy closes approximately λ percent of the gap to its steady-state growth path each year, where λ is given by

$$\lambda = (1 - \alpha)(n + g + \delta),$$

with α being the capital share in the production function, n being the population growth rate, g being the long-run trend growth rate of the efficiency of labor, and δ being the capital depreciation rate. The latter three variables sum up in the case of India to approximately 8 percent. α is unknown: it could—for narrow definitions of "capital"—be as low as 0.3; it could—for views of the growth process closer to those of endogenous growth theorists, or of DeLong and Summers (1991)—be as high as 0.8. Thus estimates of λ lie in the range between 0.016 and 0.056.

Thus today's standard simple growth theory predicts, in the presence of reforms that raise the economy's long-run steady-state growth path, that economic growth will accelerate in the short run by an amount equal to $\lambda \times \Delta y$, where Δy is the proportional change in the economy's long-run steady-state growth path produced by the reforms. In the longer run, as the economy closes in on its new long-run steady-state growth path and the gap between its current position and the steady-state path narrows, this "convergence" component of annual economic growth will shrink. A large acceleration in economic growth can only be produced by a change in economic policy or in the economic environment that causes a large upward jump in the economy's steady-state growth path. The fact that growth accelerated so rapidly in the mid-1980s suggests that the 1980s saw structural changes that did indeed have an enormous effect on India's long-run economic destiny.

If we model the effect of economic reform as a one-time once-and-for-all upward jump in the economy's steady-state growth path, then the 3 percent per year acceleration of growth that followed the beginnings of economic reform is the result of convergence—at the rate λ above—to the new, higher steady-state growth path. For a value of λ equal to 1.6 percent, this means that the Rajiv Gandhi government's change in policies boosted the economy's long-run steady-state growth path by 186 percent. For a value of λ equal to 5.6 percent, this means that the Rajiv Gandhi government's changes in policies boosted the economy's long-run steady-state growth path by 54 percent. In either case, this is an extremely large long-run effect for what seemed at the time to be relatively small changes in economic policy.

Much conventional wisdom claims that the boom created by Rajiv Gandhi's reforms was "unsustainable" and in some way "fictitious" because the late-1980s boom ended in an exchange rate crisis. The country's net capital import bill rose to 3 percent of GDP by the end of the 1980s. This growing foreign indebtedness—more than a quarter of exports were going to pay international debt service by the end of the 1980s—set the stage for the exchange crisis of 1991. Nevertheless, it is hard to argue that India would have been better off in the 1980s had it not borrowed from abroad. (It is easy to argue that it would have been better off had it followed a more realistic exchange rate policy in 1989 and 1990.) With limited exports, foreign borrowing is an extremely valuable way to finance capital-goods imports. If Lee (1995) is correct in arguing that such capital-goods imports are extraordinarily productive sources of technology transfer, then even extreme vulnerability to international financial crises as a result of foreign borrowing is a cost that weighs lightly in the balance relative to the benefits of one's firms being able to buy more foreign-made capital on the world market.

Standard simple growth theory would predict that over time after reform the speed of growth would slow as the economy closed in on its new, higher steady-state growth path. After a decade the "convergence" component of economic growth should be between .85 and .60 of its initial, immediate postreform value. This would suggest a slowing of growth by the late 1990s of between 0.6 and 1.4 percentage points relative to the second half of the 1980s, if Rajiv Gandhi's reforms were the only powerful change in the economy's long-run growth prospects.

However growth did not slow in the 1990s. Further, larger waves of reform washed over the economy in the 1990s. Economic growth accelerated by at least one further percentage point per year in the 1990s.

How large were the effects of these subsequent waves of reform, at least according to standard growth theory? Performing the same kinds of calculations then suggests that the second wave of reforms—those undertaken by the government of Narasimha Rao and Manmohan Singh—had effects on the country's long-run steady-state growth path between two-thirds and five-sixths as large as those of the first wave of reforms. Moreover, there has been a third wave of reforms undertaken in recent years by the Bharatiya Janata Party (BJP) government. It is as of yet too early to use growth theory to assess the impact of this latest wave of reform on the economy's long-run steady-state growth path.

The Narasimha Rao Government

The fact that simple growth theory suggests that the effects of the Rao government's policies on growth were less than the effect of the Rajiv Gandhi government's is both interesting and puzzling. It is puzzling because the Rao era economic reforms seem much more comprehensive and significant. It raises the possibility that the particular reforms undertaken by the Rajiv Gandhi government had an extraordinarily high payoff.

Narasimha Rao's Congress Party won only 43 percent of the seats in the Lok Sabha in the 1991 election. For five years, however, he maintained his hold on the prime ministership and a narrow working majority. Varshney (2000) points out that in some respects the failure of the Congress Party to achieve a majority in the Lok Sabha in 1991 is deceptive and understates the strength of Rao's government. By 1991 the Hindu nationalist BJP had come to prominence in Indian national politics (see Hansen 1999). It was the second largest party in the Lok Sabha after the 1991 election. All of the other minor parties—the Janata Dal, the Communist Party of India (Marxist) (CPI(M)), and so forth—had to reckon that upsetting the Rao government and the Congress Party might well lead to the coming to power of the BJP, which was not to any of their tastes. Challenging any of the decisions of the Rao government might bring it down. Hence, as Echeverri-Gent (1998) puts it, because it was so weak—because it was a minority government—the Rao government could be very strong.

Under the Rao government, tariffs were reduced from an average of 85 percent to 25 percent of import value. The rupee became convertible. By the mid-1990s total foreign trade—imports plus exports—amounted to more than 20 percent of GDP. Foreign direct investment was encouraged and grew from effectively zero in the 1980s to $5 billion a year by the mid-1990s. The government walked rapidly down the path of reform that Rajiv Gandhi's government had tiptoed cautiously onto.

On the macroeconomic side, attention was focused on limiting money growth and thus controlling inflation. The government attempted—unsuccessfully—to erase the extremely high budget deficits of the past. And the government attempted—successfully—to build up its foreign exchange reserves.

The Rao government took the steps that the Rajiv Gandhi government had proposed to encourage foreign investment: it provided automatic government approval for FDI joint ventures in which foreigners held up to 51 percent of the equity; it provided automatic government approval for agreements licensing foreign technology as long as royalty payments to foreigners were kept at or below 5 percent of total sales.

And the Rao government carried through to completion a number of initiatives begun during the Rajiv Gandhi government to replace quantitative restrictions on imports by tariffs, to lower tariffs, to reduce the scope of licensing, and to attempt to reduce the scope of publicly owned monopolies.

Given that all of these reforms surely add up to much more than did the Rajiv Gandhi's government, it is interesting that the simple applications of growth theory above suggest that their effect on the economy's long-run steady-state growth path was smaller. Two possibilities suggest themselves: first, that simple growth theory is in fact not very useful considered as a lens to understand the process of economic growth in different countries; second, that in some way the reforms undertaken by the Rajiv Gandhi administration were strategic—that they had a uniquely high benefit-cost ratio, a uniquely high social product.

The Vajpayee Government

The governments that succeeded the Rao government have, in a move that many commentators found somewhat surprising, continued the reform process. After the Rao government, reform had become politically popular—indeed, inescapable for governments that wanted to take their share of credit for India's relatively rapid economic growth.

Most recently the BJP-led government of Prime Minister Vajpayee has removed capacity-licensing restrictions from the fossil-fuel and oil-cracking industries, from bulk pharmaceuticals, and from the sugar industry. The government has attempted to make sure that the remains of its old-fashioned industrial policy do not hobble the rapidly expanding Indian information technology industry. The government has gingerly taken steps toward establishing private industry and competition in electricity and telecommunications. The process by which licensing restrictions are removed from imports has continued. And further steps have been taken to try to rationalize the tax system.

The net effect of all of these reform policies has been a decade and a half of growth at the "new Hindu rate of growth" of 6 percent per year for overall real GDP, and of 3.5–4 percent per year for labor productivity. Such a pace of growth has made India one of the world's fastest-growing large economies— behind only China.

Reforms have had an effect not only on the policies notionally followed by the government, but on how those policies are implemented—on the amount of red tape and inefficiency generated by the government. The *Economist* reports that the head of General Electric's Indian subsidiaries, Scott Bayman, tells its reporters that the proportion of his time he spends in government offices has fallen from 70 percent to less than 5 percent.

CONCLUSION

What comes next for India? The governments that followed the Rao government—first the United Front and now the BJP-led coalition—have continued reform and liberalization, albeit not as rapidly as one might have hoped given the pace of economic reform in the first half of the 1990s. But the amount that is still left to be done is staggering.

For example, consider the electricity sector. The State Electricity Boards generate electricity and distribute it to consumers. Many consumers, including farmers and the politically favored, pay virtually nothing for their electricity. Many others steal it: losses in transmission and distribution amount to 35 percent of all electricity generated. The State Electricity Boards finance their operations by overcharging industrial and commercial consumers—giving them an incentive not to use higher-productivity electricity-intensive means of production. The rest of the State Electricity Boards' funding comes from the government. According to the *Economist,* the year-2000 losses of State Electricity Boards amounted to more than 1 percent of GDP, and accounted for 12 percent of the total public sector deficit. And the electricity provided is of miserable quality, with frequent blackouts and voltage spikes that have driven a third of industrial consumers to establish their own—small-scale, technically inefficient—private electricity generation facilities.

For another example, consider that India still has internal customs barriers. Trucks making a 500-mile journey may well have to pay internal tariffs at three different stops.

Moreover, India's government is a federal government. Much red-tape reduction needs to be accomplished not at the national but at the provincial level. And there are many provinces with huge populations and large shares of India's poor—Uttar Pradesh, Bihar, Orissa—in which the political establishment does not believe that increased governmental efficiency and reduced red tape should be a priority.

In the second half of the 1990s, India's governments have failed to make progress in bringing social claims on output into balance with productivity. The total deficits of the public sector—state and local governments, national government, and state-owned enterprises together—now amount to more than 10 percent of GDP. Unless this budget deficit is reduced and the rate of growth of the debt-to-GDP ratio brought under control, an inflation crisis at some point in the future seems likely once potential lenders to the Indian government decide that its debt-to-GDP ratio has risen too high for comfort.

Whether Indian real economic growth continues at the rapid pace of the past decade even if reform slows down and government budget deficits continue will tell us much about the resiliency of the growth process.

If Indian real economic growth does continue to be rapid even in the face of erratic public-sector performance, that will suggest to us that the most important factors were those that changed in India in the 1980s. What changed in the 1980s were three things. The first was a shift toward integration with the world economy—both the encouragement of exports, and the recognition that foreign investment and foreign-made capital goods had enormous potential as carriers of new and improved technology. The second was a shift in entrepreneurial attitudes: the fact that Rajiv Gandhi had not spent his life as a politician and the fact that his powerful ministers included ex-businessmen may have functioned as the Indian equivalent of Deng Xiaping's catch-phrase: "To get rich is glorious!" The third was a belief that the old Nehru dynasty order had come to an end, and that the rules of the economic game had changed. It may well be that these deeper changes had more importance for Indian growth than did individual policy moves.

On the other hand, if reform stagnates—or even continues at its current not very rapid pace—it may well be that Indian real growth will slow over the next decade. If so, that will suggest that the potential benefits in terms of higher growth from each act of policy liberalization are quickly taken up and exhausted. In that case successful reform will require not just that reformers be strong at one moment but that they institutionalize the reform and liberalization process over generations.

In either case, the world's economists now have an example of an economy that did *not* have remarkably favorable initial conditions but that has sustained rapid economic growth over two decades. To those for whom the East Asian miracle seemed out of reach—for whom the advice to emulate South Korea seemed so unattainable as to lead to despair—advice to emulate India may well prove more useful.

REFERENCES

Ahluwalia, Montek. 1999. "India's Economic Reform: An Appraisal." In *India in the Era of Economic Reforms,* ed. Jeffrey Sachs, Ashutosh Varshney, and Nirupam Bajpai. New Delhi: Oxford University Press.

Bates, Robert. 1984. *Markets and States in Tropical Africa.* Berkeley and Los Angeles: University of California Press.

Bhagwati, Jagdish. 2000. "Roses Carry Thorns: A Review of Sachs-Varshney-Bajpai and Lal." *Times Literary Supplement,* March 31, 2000, 28.

Das, Gurcharan. 2000. *India Unbound: A Personal Account of a Social and Economic Revolution.* New York: Knopf.

DeLong, J. Bradford, and Lawrence H. Summers. 1991. "Equipment Investment and Economic Growth." *Quarterly Journal of Economics* 106:445–502.

Dumont, Rene. 1965. *False Start in Africa.* New York: W. W. Norton.

Echeverri-Gent, John. 1998. "Weak State, Strong Reforms: Globalization, Partisan Competition, and the Paradoxes of Indian Economic Reform." University of Virginia. Typescript.

Haggard, Stephan, and Steven Webb, eds. 1994. *Voting for Reform.* Oxford: Oxford University Press.

Hansen, Thomas Blom. 1999. *The Saffron Wave: Democracy and Hindu Nationalism in Modern India.* Princeton: Princeton University Press.

Jones, Charles. 1994. "Economic Growth and the Relative Price of Capital." *Journal of Monetary Economics* 34:359–82.

Kothari, Rajni. 1986. "The Flight into the Twenty-first Century: Millions Will Be Left Behind." *Times of India,* April 27, 1986.

Lal, Deepak. 1998. *Unfinished Business: India in the World Economy.* Oxford: Oxford University Press.

Lee, Jong-Wha. 1995. "Capital Goods Imports and Long-Run Growth." *Journal of Development Economics* 48:91–110.

Livi-Bacci, Massimo. 1996. *A Concise History of World Population.* Oxford: Oxford University Press.

Mankiw, N. Gregory, David Romer, and David Weil. 1992. "A Contribution to the Empirics of Economic Growth." *Quarterly Journal of Economics* 107:407–37.

Solow, Robert M. 1956. "A Contribution to the Theory of Economic Growth." *Quarterly Journal of Economics* 70:65–94.

Summers, Robert, and Alan Heston. 1991. "The Penn World Table (Mark 5). An Expanded Set of International Comparisons, 1950–1988." *Quarterly Journal of Economics* 106:327–68.

Tendulkar, S. 1997. "Indian Economic Policy Reform and Poverty." In *India's Economic Reforms and Development: Essays for Manmohan Singh,* ed. I. J. Ahluwalia and I. M. D. Little. Oxford: Oxford University Press.

Varshney, Ashutoth. 1999. "India's Economic Reforms in Comparative Perspective." In *India in the Era of Economic Reforms,* ed. Jeffrey Sachs, Ashutosh Varshney, and Nirupam Bajpai. New Delhi: Oxford University Press.

———. 2000. "Mass Politics or Elite Politics? India's Economic Reforms in Comparative Perspective." In *India in the Era of Economic Reforms,* ed. Jeffrey Sachs, Ashutosh Varshney, and Nirupam Bajpai. New Delhi: Oxford University Press.

Weber, Max. 1976. *The Protestant Ethic and the Spirit of Capitalism.* Trans. Talcott Parsons. New York: Scribner.

World Bank. 1994. *The East Asian Miracle.* Oxford: Oxford University Press.

Who Can Explain the Mauritian Miracle?

MEADE, ROMER, SACHS, OR RODRIK?

ARVIND SUBRAMANIAN   DEVESH ROY

IN THE postwar period, few sub-Saharan African countries have made the transition to high standards of living for their population. The record of sustained economic performance in sub-Saharan Africa (hereafter Africa) is not heartening. It is not that there have not been periods of sustained growth: as table 8.1 shows, sixteen African countries, at various points in time, achieved high rates of growth. Sadly, however, very few such episodes have been long and sustained enough to lead to high levels of income and standards of living.[1] In 1998, only two African countries ranked among the top 50 countries in the world in terms of per capita GDP (calculated on a PPP basis), and none ranked among the top 50 on the UN's Human Development Index.[2] This is surprising, especially in an era of rapid globalization, which should have led to significant catch-up by Africa relative to the rest of the world. After all, globalization is the vehicle par excellence for catch-up because it is supposed to facilitate the transmission of capital, ideas, and technology, which are the determinants of growth (see Coe, Helpman, and Hoffmaister 1997). And yet, instead of convergence of global incomes, we see "divergence big time."

But Africa is not without its successes. At the very top of this admittedly short list of accomplishments is Mauritius. Yet it did not have to be Mauritius that succeeded. Indeed, we had it on the highest authority—Nobel Prize winner James Meade's—that Mauritius was, if anything, a strong candidate for failure because it was a typical African economy: monocrop; prone to terms-of-trade shocks; growing rapidly in population; and susceptible to ethnic tensions.

> Heavy population pressure must inevitably reduce real income per head below what it might otherwise be. That surely is bad enough in a community that is full of political conflict. But if in addition, in the absence of other remedies, it must lead either to unemployment (exacerbating the scramble for jobs between Indians

---

[1] In many cases, growth decelerated or ground to a halt around the time of the oil and debt crises, which Rodrik (1999b) refers to as the growth collapse.

[2] These assessments exclude the Seychelles.

TABLE 8.1
Sustained Growth in Africa, 1960–98

Country	Start	End	Length in Years	Average Growth Rate	PPP GNP per Capita (U.S. dollars, 1998)	Rank (out of 174)
South Africa	1960	1974	14	5.1	8,296	49
Mauritius	1980		18+	5.4	8,236	50
Gabon	1965	1976	11	13.1	5,615	63
Botswana	1965		33+	9.1	5,796	65
Namibia	1961	1979	18	6.4	5,280	75
Ghana	1983		15+	4.7	1,735	129
Lesotho	1970	1982	12	9.9	2,194	133
Cote d'Ivoire	1960	1978	18	9.5	1,484	134
Cameroon	1967	1986	19	7	1,395	138
Togo	1960	1974	14	6.8	1,352	145
Uganda	1986		10+	6.1	1,072	152
Kenya	1961	1981	20	6.7	964	156
Mozambique	1986		12+	7.1	740	162
Ethiopia	1960	1972	12	4.5	566	170
Malawi	1964	1979	15	6.6	551	172
Tanzania	1961	1975	14	5.7	483	173
Sub-Saharan Africa					1,607	

Sources: Berthelemy and Soderling 2001; United Nations 2000.

and Creoles) or to even greater inequalities (stocking up still more the envy felt by the Indian and Creole underdog for the Franco-Mauritian top dog), *the outlook for peaceful development is poor.* (Meade et al. 1961; emphasis added)

History, or rather Mauritius, proved Meade's dire prognostication, made in 1961, famously wrong. This chapter seeks to understand this failed prediction in terms of three explanations of long-run growth performance: initial conditions, openness, and institutions. Section 1 provides a brief political and economic history of the country, highlighting the economic achievements. Section 2 describes the various aspects of the initial conditions in Mauritius. Section 3 then analyzes three aspects of Mauritius's openness strategy, articulated by Sachs and Warner (1995, 1997), Romer (1993), and Rodrik (1999a) respectively. Section 4 discusses the role played by institutions in Mauritian economic performance. Section 5 presents econometric results that shed light on the different explanations. Finally, Section 6 offers some concluding observations.

1. POLITICAL HISTORY AND ECONOMIC ACCOMPLISHMENTS

Political History

In the years leading up to independence in 1968, Mauritius experienced intense political activity, including some sporadic outbursts of violence. At issue was the fear by the minority communities (mainly the Franco-Mauritian, the Creole, and the Muslim) that the Hindu majority, which was consistently demanding early independence from Britain, would use its majority power against the numerically weaker groups. To allay these fears, the constitutional conference of 1965, which paved the way for independence, agreed on a unique political compromise aimed at protecting minority rights. The 34-member Legislative Council, which was created under British rule in 1947 and included 21 elected seats, would be replaced by a larger National Assembly that would have 62 elected plus 8 so-called best loser seats; the latter would be awarded to the four communities (Hindu; "General Population," which comprised the Franco-Mauritian and Creole communities; Muslim; and Chinese) that were underrepresented in the main election, provided that the balance of power was not changed.

Notwithstanding these provisions, the support for independence itself was far from unanimous. An alliance favoring independence, which was led by the moderately socialist Mauritian Labor Party (LP), and included parties representing the poor rural Hindu and parts of the Muslim communities, won only about 55 percent of the popular vote in the August 1967 elections, securing 39 of the 62 elected seats. A broad alliance of Franco-Mauritians, Creoles, Chinese, Muslims, and Tamils, which was led by the conservative Parti Mauricien Social Democrate (PMSD) and had openly opposed independence favoring instead a "free association" with the United Kingdom, won about 43 percent of the popular vote. Following the August 1967 elections, the new constitution was formally adopted, and in March 1968 Mauritius gained independence from the United Kingdom, while remaining within the Commonwealth.[3] The leader of the LP and first prime minister, Sir Seewoosagur Ramgoolam, presided over

---

[3] In 1992 Mauritius became a republic, and the queen was replaced as official head of state by a president who is elected by the National Assembly.

four governments from 1967 to 1982. His long tenure contributed greatly to establishing and adapting constitutional democracy to the needs of Mauritius's fragmented multiethnic society.

Even though the Franco-Mauritian community was in a minority, it played an important role in the decision-making process both at the political and the economic levels through its influence in the PMSD and various business organizations such as the powerful Sugar Producers' Association. Soon after loosing to the LP, the PMSD, by displacing a smaller coalition partner, joined the LP to form a government of national unity in 1969. The PMSD continued as a junior partner in a number of governments through the late-1980s.

Two more political parties have played an important role in Mauritian politics and indeed form the current government. The Mouvement Militant Mauricien (MMM) was founded in 1969 as an ultra-left-wing party that attacked the existing parties for encouraging "ethnic politics" and challenged the LP's grip on the labor movement by organizing rival and more radical trade unions, notably in the transportation, sugar, and electricity sectors. In late-1971 Mauritius was swept by a wave of MMM-supported strikes that severely disrupted economic activity and led to shortages of essential foods. The LP-led government that had earlier delayed the national elections, which were due in 1972, to 1976, responded by using newly enacted emergency powers to declare a state of emergency, close down a number of trade unions, and arrest more than a hundred union and MMM leaders. Not until 1974 did the government start to relax restrictions on trade union and political activities, and in 1976 it lifted the state of emergency. In its first contested general election in December 1976, the MMM gained 34 of the 70 seats, yet it was kept out of power by the LP/PMSD coalition. The MMM has since moderated its ideology and moved to the mainstream of Mauritian politics, and its current leader is Mr. Paul R. Bérenger, the deputy prime minister and minister of finance.

The Mouvement Socialist Militant (MSM) was formed in 1983, when a breakaway group led by the then–prime minister Sir Anerood Jugnauth left the MMM and joined members of the junior coalition partner, the Parti Socialiste Mauricien (PSM), to form a new party. Only a year earlier, Sir Anerood Jugnauth had decisively defeated Sir Seewoosagur Ramgoolam to become Mauritius's second prime minister. Since then, Sir Anerood Jugnauth has remained as prime minister except for a five-year interval during 1995–2000, when Dr. Navin Ramgoolam (the late Sir Seewoosagur Ramgoolam's son) led an LP government.

With the exception of some communal fighting and disruptive industrial action in the early years after independence, Mauritius has experienced over the past three decades a remarkable and enviable era of highly inclusive democratic participation. The Mauritian democracy has been marked not only by a genuine consensus among the major political parties on the rules of attaining, exercising, and relinquishing power, but also by an intense and combative, yet peaceful, political debate among opponents, supported by a free and widely read print media. While party alliances have been formed, broken, and regrouped in all imaginable combinations, the political system has remained surprisingly stable, with only three prime ministers having held power since 1968: Sir Seewoosagur Ramgoolam (1968–82); Sir Anerood Jugnauth (1982–95; and 2000–present); and Mr. Navin Ramgoolam (1995–2000).

Economic Accomplishments

Between 1973 and 1999, real GDP in Mauritius grew on average by 5.9 percent per year compared with 2.4 percent in Africa. In per capita terms the corresponding numbers are 3.25 percent and about 0.7 percent. The magic of compounding means that the income of the average Mauritian has increased three and a half times over a 40-year period, while that of the average African increased by 32 percent. In terms of the chronology of the growth performance, Mauritius started with a reasonable but low (2.5–3 percent) growth rate in the 1970s, and it was in the late 1970s and the beginning of the 1980s that the Mauritian transition to very high growth rates occurred. The Mauritian economy maintained high levels of growth in the 1990s, apparently resilient to the depressed global conditions in the early 1990s and to the financial crises in Asia and other places later in the decade.

The economy, once reliant on sugarcane, got a boost in the 1980s through the export boom of the textile and apparel sector. The process of diversification of economy was furthered by the policy thrust that favored new sectors like tourism and financial services. However, sugarcane occupies nearly 90 percent of the cultivated land area and continues to account for roughly one-fifth of export earnings, but manufacturing accounts for the largest portion of national output.

The export processing zone (EPZ) was established in 1970 with the purpose of diversifying exports into manufactures. Although the setting up of the EPZs was conceived as a way of developing a range of manufacturing enterprises, in practice, the EPZ became synonymous with the textiles and clothing industry. Some 80 percent of investment and exports and 90 percent of employment in the EPZ sector are from the textiles and clothing industry. The period 1970–75 was one of moderate growth of the EPZs. The period of growth started with the signing of the Lome Convention in 1975. The number of textile and clothing firms increased from 8 in the beginning of 1971 to 45 by 1976; employment in the textiles and clothing industry rose by 35.6 percent to 19,400. The momentum of EPZ activity slowed down in the period 1976–80. A rising real exchange rate tended to reduce considerably Mauritius's international competitiveness. After 1980 the performance of the EPZs improved through technological change and to some extent by outsourcing. The growth rate of investment (constant prices) had dropped to –0.7 percent in the period 1976–80. It touched 4.5 percent in the period 1981–86, even higher than the investment in 1971–75 (2.8 percent).

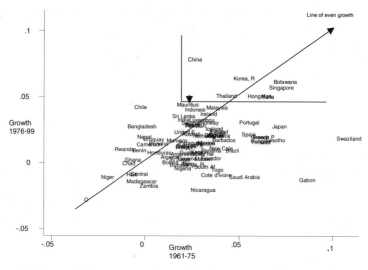

Figure 8.1. Per capita income growth rate: 1976–99 versus 1961–75

The growth rate of exports in real terms (32.4 percent) was nearly as high as in 1971–75. The number of firms reached an all time high, crossing the 400 mark. During this period, employment in the EPZ grew from approximately 21,000 to almost 90,000.

The golden period of the EPZ was undoubtedly the decade beginning 1980. During the early 1990s the growth of investment, employment, and exports slowed down due to an increase in the number of closures of both small and large firms. Inefficient firms had to close down owing to labor shortages. EPZ firms are coping by shifting to higher value-added segments and shifting their hardware bases in labor surplus areas like Mozambique and Madagascar.

Figure 8.1 depicts the comparative growth performance for a cross section of countries over two periods, 1961–75 and 1976–99. The 45° line represents the locus of points of equal growth in the two periods. Countries above the line grew faster in the later period, and vice versa for the countries below the line. Countries are mostly clustered below the line, confirming the characterization due to Rodrik (1999b) of the growth collapse after the first oil shock. Mauritius defied this trend, its per capita growth rate of 4.2 percent in the later period being about one and a half percentage points above that in the earlier period. In terms of growth performance, moreover, very few countries outperformed Mauritius in both periods (in the figure, very few countries lie to the northeast of Mauritius). This group comprises the East Asian tigers and Botswana, the only African country to have registered high rates of growth.

Improvements in human development indicators have been equally impressive. Life expectancy at birth increased from 61 years in 1965 to 71 in 1996; primary

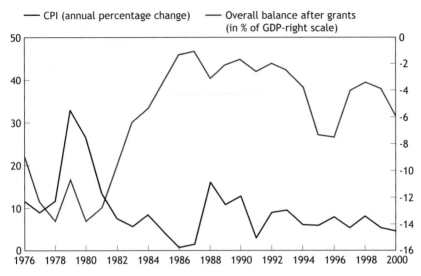

Figure 8.2. Mauritius: Budget deficit and inflation, 1976–2000

enrollment increased from 93 to 107 between 1980 and 1996 compared with 78 and 75, respectively in Africa. Income inequality has also seen impressive improvements: the Gini coefficient declined from 0.5 in 1962 to 0.42 in 1975 and 0.37 in 1986–87.

High growth rates have been delivered along with macroeconomic stability. Between 1973 and 2000, consumer price inflation averaged 7.8 percent per annum, compared with over 25 percent in Africa (fig. 8.2). Although subject to episodic spikes, the variability of inflation has also been well below that for Africa as a whole. For example, the standard deviation of inflation in Mauritius (2.4 percent) has been half of that in Africa.

As interesting as the cross-sectional comparison is the temporal evolution in Mauritius's economic performance. A growth accounting framework analysis highlights the contrasting performance between the 1980s and 1990s (table 8.2). In the former period (1982–90), economic growth was intensive; that is, it was motored predominantly by the growth of inputs—capital and labor—which together accounted for 90 percent of the annual average rate of GDP growth of 6.2 percent. It is worth noting the stellar performance of employment growth in this period, which averaged 5.2 percent a year, reflected in a sharp decline in the unemployment rate from nearly 20 percent in 1983 to 3 percent in the late 1980s (see fig. 8.3).

In contrast, economic growth in the 1990s was driven to a greater extent by productivity growth. As wages started to climb, firms economized on the use of labor, focusing instead on sustaining growth through higher productivity (see

TABLE 8.2
Sources of Growth: Mauritius and Other Developing Countries

	GDP per Worker	Total Factor Productivity
Mauritius		
1982–99	2.5	0.7
1982–90	1.0	0.6
1991–99	3.5	1.4
Other developing countries (1984–94)		
East Asia	4.4	1.6
Latin America	0.1	−0.4
Middle East	−1.1	−1.5
South Asia	2.7	1.5
Sub-Saharan Africa	−0.6	−0.4

Sources: Authors' estimates for Mauritius; Collins and Bosworth 1996 for other developing countries.

fig. 8.3). TFP growth during this period averaged 1.4 percent a year and accounted for a full 25 percent of total growth. This improvement in TFP performance, which compares favorably with that of Asia (see Collins and Bosworth 1996), also augurs well for the future as Mauritius runs into labor shortages and limits to capital deepening.

Figure 8.3. Mauritius: Real product wage, factor productivity, and unemployment rate

Finally, it is worth mentioning that Mauritian economic performance has been sustained by OECD-type social protection. This has taken several forms: a large and active presence of trade unions with centralized wage bargaining; price controls especially on a number of socially sensitive items; and generous social security, particularly for the elderly and civil servants. Unlike the OECD countries, however, generous social protection has thus far not necessitated high taxes, reflecting both strong growth and a favorable demographic structure with a high proportion of the population being of working age.[4] The OECD affliction of a changing demographic structure, with rising number of dependents, however, looms large for Mauritius in the coming years.

2. MEADE AND THE MIXED INHERITANCE OF MAURITIUS

Meade's prophecy of doom for Mauritius was based on his reading of what he saw as the country's very adverse inheritance, primarily the impending population explosion. Imbued as he was by the prevailing labor surplus doctrine, he saw little prospect for expanding the traditional agricultural sector and was equally pessimistic about the possibilities in manufacturing. In his view, there was little technical know-how in manufactures and little experience outside the sugar factories in the conduct of the industry; there was scarcity of capital; there were few raw materials available within boundaries, and the domestic market was miniscule. Meade moreover noted that the Mauritian society was highly fragmented on all lines—ethnic, economic, and political—which made the task of progress much more difficult than elsewhere.[5]

But was Meade's reading of an adverse inheritance correct? A retrospective answer to this question can be offered based on the indicators that the current growth literature suggests as being important for long-run growth. Table 8.3 depicts how Mauritius scores on these indicators both in absolute terms and in comparison with three other groups of countries. These indicators are selected from Sachs and Warner (1997) and are supplemented with a few others considered important for long-run growth.

One of the most important of these indicators relates to the phenomenon of catch-up or convergence. Conditional on other determinants of growth, the higher the per capita income at the beginning of the growth process, the slower will be the subsequent rate of growth. As the scatter plot in figure 8.4 for a selected group of countries shows, Mauritius had the highest per capita income

---

[4] The tax-to-GDP ratio for Mauritius was high in the 1970s and the 1980s (0.26 and 0.24 compared to 0.21 and 0.19 for the countries at comparable levels of per capita GDP). In the 1990s, the ratio for Mauritius (0.20) was very close to that of developing countries (0.21).

[5] Meade's development strategy hence proposed wage restraint, agricultural diversification, a rapid change in industry structure, overseas welfare assistance, a system of welfare benefits for the unemployed, emigration of workers to other British colonies, and an effective family planning system.

TABLE 8.3
Inheritance: Mauritius versus Africa, Fast-Growing Economies,
and Other Developing Economies

	Mauritius	Africa	Fast-Growing Economies[a]	All Other Developing Economies
Inheritance				
Catch-up[b]	8.72	7.29	7.90	7.85
Life expectancy in years (circa 1970) (human capital)	60.40	41.60	57.10	51.9
Ethnolinguistic fractionalization[c]	0.58	0.64	0.42	0.32
Population growth[d]	0.97	−0.09	0.82	0.33
Share of primary exports in total exports	0.29	0.18	0.09	0.12
Geography				
Fraction of area in tropical climate	1.00	0.89	0.69	0.59
Landlocked[e]	0	0.33	0	0.11
Remoteness (km)[f]	11,249	9,183	9,464	8,633

Sources: Authors' calculations; and Sachs and Warner 1997.

[a] The fast-growing countries include Thailand, Malaysia, Indonesia, China, Hong Kong SAR, and Singapore.

[b] Log of real GDP per economically active population in 1965.

[c] Probability that two randomly selected people from a country will not belong to the same ethnic or linguistic group.

[d] Growth of working age population minus growth of total population between 1965 and 1990.

[e] Score 1 if landlocked, 0 if not. For a group it depicts the fraction of countries landlocked.

[f] Average distance to trading partners, weighted by their share in the world GDP.

in 1960 and hence was likely to witness slower growth rates than other African countries on this count (see also table 8.3).

One variable on which Mauritius scores highly is human capital: for example, life expectancy at birth (60.4 years) in the early 1970s was substantially higher in Mauritius than even in the fast-growing economies of Asia. On most of the other variables, however, Mauritius fares either more poorly than other African economies or at least no better than them. For example, on geography, although Mauritius is not landlocked, it does have a fully tropical climate (score of 1 on the tropics variable), and in terms of its remoteness from world markets, Mauritius fares the worst, being about 25 percent farther away from the world's

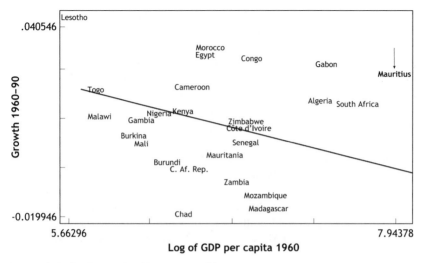

Figure 8.4. Catch-up: Mauritius versus Africa

economic center of gravity than the average African country and 30 percent farther than the average developing country.

Two other points about Mauritius's inheritance are worth highlighting. First,
the empirical growth literature increasingly points to the adverse effects of
being commodity dependent (see Dalmazzo and de Blasio 2001). They stem
not just from the secular decline or increased variability associated with commodity prices but also from the rent seeking and corruption to which they give
rise. Mauritius actually fares much worse than the average African economy in
terms of commodity dependence. In 1970, the share of exports accounted for
by commodities was nearly 30 percent, compared with 18 percent for the average of the African economy.

But is it possible that Mauritius was nevertheless less susceptible to commodity dependence because sugar (Mauritius's main export) fared better than
other commodities? It is certainly true that Mauritius's terms of trade have been
less variable than for the average country, but this may be a misleading indicator of the adverse impact of commodity dependence. The reason is that Mauritian sugar *production* has been subject to a series of cyclone- and drought-
related shocks that have imparted great variability to the export earnings derived
from sugar. The importance of production shocks, indeed the greater impact of
these shocks for Mauritius compared with the average commodity-exporting
countries, is suggested by an interesting result in Cashin and Patillo 2000. According to their results, shocks to Mauritius's terms of trade have been less persistent than for the average commodity-exporting country, but the shocks to

Mauritius's income terms of trade (terms of trade multiplied by exports) have indeed been far more persistent than for the average country.

Ironically, Meade's greatest fear, rapid population growth, proved to be a blessing for Mauritius. Mauritius's demographic inheritance was extremely favorable, even more so than in the fast-growing economies, with the growth in labor force outpacing the growth in the overall population. The rapid job creation in the last two decades—indeed to the extent that it now imports substantial amounts of labor—has meant that Mauritius is now a labor-scarce rather than labor-surplus economy.[6]

Thus, the overall conclusion is that Mauritius's excellent growth performance since the late 1970s cannot be attributed to favorable initial conditions, as Mauritius fares worse than the average African economy. Meade was therefore not entirely wrong on the facts: although he misread the demographic inheritance and missed the very favorable initial stock of human capital, he was broadly correct in the assessment that Mauritius's overall inheritance was unfavorable.

3. MAURITIUS'S OPENNESS STRATEGY

Perhaps the most interesting aspect of the Mauritian development experience has been its openness strategy (defined broadly as its openness to trade and foreign investment [FDI]). Different economists read into this experience their own interpretation. But a proper understanding of this experience is interesting if not controversial.

Openness Outcomes

At one level, the Mauritian experience can be advanced as a showpiece for the prescription associated with the Bretton Woods Institutions (the so-called Washington consensus) that openness is unambiguously beneficial. Figure 8.5 illustrates this. Since the mid-1980s, the volume of imports and exports of goods has grown quite rapidly, at a rate of 8.7 percent and 5.4 percent, respectively, per year; the openness ratio (the ratio of trade in goods to GDP) increased from about 70 percent to 100 percent over this period, compared with an openness ratio for Africa that stagnated around 45 percent. Particularly strong was the growth in manufacturing exports, originating predominantly from the export processing zone (EPZ).[7]

---

[6] It is estimated that over 30 percent of the labor force in the textile and clothing sector is imported.

[7] However, Mauritius has been considerably less open than the fast-growing countries of East Asia, whose openness ratio increased from 85 percent to 180 percent between 1973 and 2000.

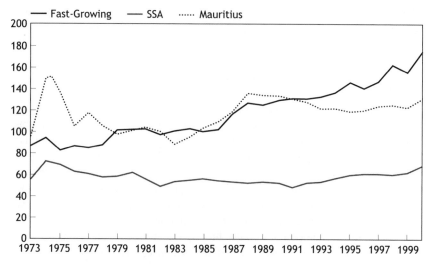

Figure 8.5. Mauritius: Sub-Saharan Africa and the fast-growing economies: openness ratio, 1973–2000 (exports plus imports of goods and services in % of GDP)
Source: World Economic Outlook

This trade performance, especially in contrast to its African neighbors, merits an explanation or explanations. To say that Mauritius's growth performance was due to the rapid growth of its trade begs the next obvious question: why did trade grow as much as it did? Three explanations have been offered. The first, due to Sachs and Warner, is that Mauritian trade policy was open. The second, due to Rodrik (1999a), is that Mauritian trade policy was heterodox, involving segmentation with imports being "closed" and exports relatively open. The third is due to Romer (1993), who emphasizes Mauritius's openness to FDI and its favorable consequences. We shall examine each in turn.

Trade Policies

Trade policies clearly affect trade. One of the most important insights of trade theory due to Abba Lerner is that a restrictive import regime imposes a tax not just on imports but also on exports and hence on trade as a whole. Thus, quantitative restrictions and high tariffs reduce the size of a country's total trade. An import tax reduces exports by raising the cost of inputs that make exports less competitive in world markets. In a more fundamental sense, however, import taxes increase the attractiveness of domestic production of import-competing goods, hence diverting resources away from sectors where a country has comparative advantage, namely the export sector. Empirical results for Africa show that on average if trade taxes go down by one percentage point, the trade-to-GDP ratio increases by about an equivalent amount (Rodrik 1999a).

The Sachs-Warner Assessment

Trade policies affect not only trade, but also long-run economic growth. In two papers, Sachs and Warner (1995, 1997) argued that one of the key determinants of long-run growth is a country's trade *policies*. Using an elaborate scheme for classifying various aspects of trade policies, they computed a binary measure for determining whether a country was open or closed. According to that measure, 18 countries in Africa were classified as closed in 1980, and only 7 countries were classified as open.[8] Their estimates indicated that, if a country moved from being closed to open, its long-run growth rate would increase by 2.2 percentage points. Trade policies could thus significantly affect a country's standard of living. Mauritius was one of the countries that Sachs and Warner classified as being open or following liberal trade policies. But this categorization of Mauritius as an open economy was misleading, even incorrect. Tables 8.4 and 8.5 provide estimates of the restrictiveness of Mauritius's trade policy regime. During the 1970s and 1980s, Mauritius remained a highly protected economy: the average rate of protection was high and dispersed. In 1980, the average effective protection exceeded 100 percent, and although this diminished by the end of the 1980s, it was still very high (65 percent). Moreover until the 1980s, there were also extensive quantitative restrictions in the form of import licensing, covering nearly 60 percent of imports.

An alternative scheme of classification that has been devised in the International Monetary Fund ranked Mauritius as one of the most protected economies in the early 1990s: Mauritius elicited a rating of 10, the highest possible category of policy restrictiveness. It is only in the late 1990s, that conventional measures of trade protection began to decline: by 1998, Mauritius obtained a rating of 7 on the Fund's index, still amongst the highest in the world and in Africa (Subramanian et al. 2000). A more recent study by Hinkle and Herrou-Aragon (2001) comes to even stronger conclusion (table 8.5). On nearly every indicator of trade policy Mauritius fares worse than the average African economy.

The conclusion that we draw is the following. It may well have been that Mauritius in some broad sense (examined below) was indeed open, but certainly not on the basis of indicators of import policies of Sachs and Warner (1995). On the contrary, it was a highly restricted economy during much of the 1970s, 1980s, and the early 1990s. More specifically, the data suggest that Mauritius

---

[8] The Sachs and Warner (1995) results have been criticized on a number of grounds and in particular by Rodriguez and Rodrik (1999). But that is not really relevant to the argument made below.

TABLE 8.4

Mauritius: Estimates of Effective Protection, 1980 and 1990
(in percent)

	1980	1990
Beverages and tobacco	123	182
Textile yarn/fabrics	77	11
Apparel	99	4
Leather products	269	8
Footwear	158	88
Wood products	191	38
Furniture	130	241
Paper products	131	57
Printing/publishing	75	7
Chemical products	38	21
Rubber products	125	144
Plastic products	89	59
Nonmetallic products	77	48
Iron/steel	154	73
Fabricated metal products	156	48
Machinery	62	3
Electrical machinery	179	181
Transport equipment	23	4
Optical goods, etc.	266	9
Average	127	65
Share of imports under licenses	57	

Source: Milner and McKay 1996.

TABLE 8.5
Openness of Mauritius and Africa

Criterion	Mauritius	Africa Average
Parallel market premia (index of foreign exchange restrictions) (1996)	4.0	2.8
Discrimination against imports in excise taxes (average rate of taxation) (1996)	219.0	27.4
Maximum trade taxes on imports (includes statutory tariff rates plus surtaxes and the ad valorem equivalents of specific duties)	80.0	78.3
Exemptions as percentage of dutiable imports	13.2	18.9
Unweighted average tariff rate	26.4	17.2
Import weighted average tariff rate	20.3	12.4
Tariff collections as percent of GDP	6.0	2.6
Import weighted average tariff on consumer goods	25.2	19.7
Unweighted average import tariff on inputs	19.3	11.0
Unweighted average import tariff on capital goods	15.9	7.7
Indicators of effective protection in agriculture	19.5	18.2
Indicators of effective protection in manufacturing	150.2	82.7

Source: Hinkle and Herrou-Aragon 2001.

would not have met two of the criteria—relating to average tariffs and coverage of quantitative restrictions—that Sachs and Warner (1997) deemed necessary for classifying a country as open.

Heterodox Opening (Rodrik)

Clearly, by the most usual measures for determining trade policy openness, Mauritius is not the poster boy for the Washington consensus. Mauritius had a highly restrictive trade regime. But why did this not translate into an export tax and hence a tax on all trade? According to Rodrik (1999a), Mauritius chose a strategy of trade liberalization that was unusual and that effectively segmented the export and import-competing sectors. Through a policy of heterodox opening Mauritius ensured that the returns to the export sector were high, effectively segmenting its export sector from the rest of the economy and preventing a restrictive trade regime from spilling over to this sector. This combination ensured that the returns to the export sector remained high, and high enough to prevent domestic resources from being diverted to its inefficient import-competing sector.

The institutional mechanism for achieving the segregation of the exporting sector from the importing sector was the creation of the export processing zone (see below), but the policy instruments that were deployed were the following:

First, duty-free access was provided to all imported inputs. This ensured that the export sector's competitiveness on world markets was not undermined by domestic taxes that could have raised the cost of inputs used in export production.[9]

Second, a variety of tax incentives was provided to firms operating in the export processing zones, which had the effect of *subsidizing* exports.[10] This subsidization was a key element helping to offset the impact of the implicit tax on exports created by the restrictive trade regime.

Most importantly, the labor market for the export sector was effectively segmented from the rest of the economy (and in particular the import-competing sector). Different labor market conditions prevailed at least until the mid-to-late 1980s. Employers had greater flexibility in discharging workers in the EPZ sector (for example, no severance allowances had to be paid before retrenching workers and advance notification of retrenchment to a statutory body was not required), and the conditions of overtime work were more flexible. Most importantly, although legal minimum wages were the same in the EPZ sector as in the rest of the economy, minimum wages for women were fixed at lower levels (Hein 1988; Wellisz and Saw 1993). And since EPZs employed disproportionate amounts of female workers (in 1990 for instance the EPZ workforce comprised 60,372 females and 27,886 males), these labor market measures also acted as an implicit subsidy for exports, as they increased the incentive to produce in the export- than in the import-competing sector. Figure 8.6 illustrates the wage differential between the EPZ and the rest of the economy in the 1980s and 1990s.[11] EPZ wages were about 36–40 percent lower in the 1980s, with the differential narrowing to between 7 percent and 20 percent in the 1990s.

Thus, according to Rodrik (1999a, 46),

The creation of the EPZ generated new opportunities of trade and of employment (for women), without taking protection away from the import-substituting groups

---

[9] Note that duty drawbacks and equivalent schemes do not entail export subsidization, they merely offset the bias from restrictive import policies.

[10] The main incentives included a 10-year tax holiday on retained earnings, and a partial tax holiday for periods beyond that; free repatriation of capital and profits; and preferential interest rates for firms in the EPZ.

[11] For example, in 1984, 79 percent of total employment in the EPZs was female, compared with 31 percent in the rest of the economy (Hein 1988).

Figure 8.6. EPZ wage in Mauritius compared to other wages

and from privileged male workers. The segmentation of labor markets was particularly crucial, as it prevented the expansion of the EPZ from driving wages up in the rest of the economy, and thereby disadvantaging import-substituting industries. New profit opportunities were created at the margin, while leaving old opportunities undisturbed. There were no identifiable losers.

To summarize these arguments, Mauritius managed to maintain neutrality of incentives between the export and import-competing sectors. The neutrality of incentives was achieved through a high dose of intervention on both imports and exports ("heterodox opening"). On the one hand, imports were restricted through high trade barriers; on the other, to offset this intervention, extensive and selective intervention occurred on the export side. In this sense, it appeared to follow the dirigiste approach of Korea, Taiwan, and Japan rather than that of Singapore and Hong Kong SAR.

Heterodox Opening: The Role of Preferential Access

The argument made by Rodrik is plausible but needs to be augmented to empirically strengthen the argument that neutrality of incentives between export and import-competing sectors was achieved. For example, table 8.4 indicates that effective protection for the import-competing sector averaged about 125 percent in the 1980s and about 65 percent in the 1990s. At the same time, figure 8.6

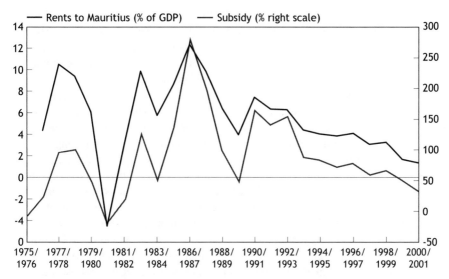

Figure 8.7. Mauritius: Benefits from preferential access to EU sugar market
Source: IMF staff calculations

indicates that the de facto subsidization through the labor market was closer to 25–30 percent, even less if EPZ wages are compared with those in the import-competing sector. Even allowing for favorable tax breaks, it seems that hetero-dox opening and intervention (in the form of subsidies in the export sector) did not offset completely the antiexport bias of the restrictive import regime.[12] There is a missing piece, and that is the preferential access to the export markets enjoyed by Mauritius.

The policy of heterodox opening would probably not have been a success, or at least not to the same extent, without the policies of Mauritius's trading partners, which played an important role in ensuring the profitability of the export sector. Mauritius has enjoyed preferential access to the markets of the major trading partners—the United States and especially Europe. This access has affected two main products that have together accounted for over 90 percent of Mauritian exports.

First, since independence in 1968, Mauritius has been guaranteed a certain volume of exports of sugar to the European Union. Moreover, these quotas are at a guaranteed price that has been above the market price by about 90 percent on average (fig. 8.7) between 1977 and 2000. The resulting rents to Mauritius have amounted to a hefty 5.4 percent of GDP on average each year, and up to

---

[12] The impact of the corporate tax incentives on exports could not have been large because most non-EPZ manufacturing firms also benefited from the numerous tax concessions.

13 percent in some years.[13] Effectively, this preferential arrangement in the sugar sector increased the return to the export sector and acted like a subsidy to domestic production of sugar. Unlike a domestic subsidy, subsidies received through the preferential access were a transfer from consumers in the importing country to producers (and taxpayers) in Mauritius.

Mauritius has also enjoyed preferential access on its exports of textiles and clothing. Foreign investment into the clothing sector, which originated largely in Hong Kong SAR, was motivated in part by the need to circumvent the quotas on textiles and clothing that was constraining clothing exports from Hong Kong SAR. The international regime in place, known as the Multi-Fiber Arrangement (MFA)—was an attempt by the United States and the European Union (EU) to limit imports into their own markets. These limits were achieved by awarding country-specific quotas for the different textile and apparel exporting countries. One of the effects of these quotas was to redistribute production between exporting countries—away from low-cost toward high-cost sources of production. Thus, high-cost producing countries gained an advantage relative to low-cost producers, resulting in higher production than would otherwise have taken place.

Table 8.6 provides quota rents for Mauritius in the apparel segment under the MFA arrangement as a percentage of the GDP.[14] The substantial rents accruing to exports ensured that resources were not diverted away despite the attractiveness of the protected import-competing sector. From a macroeconomic perspective, moreover, these rents played a crucial role in sustaining high levels of investment and explain the fact that during the growth boom in Mauritius, domestic rather than foreign savings have financed domestic investment. Our calculations suggest that rents in Mauritius from preferential access in sugar and clothing together amounted to about 7 percent of the GDP in the 1980s and to about 4.5 percent of GDP in the 1990s.

Preferential access made an enormous contribution to offsetting the bias of import policies. The de facto subsidization of the two key export sectors amounted to about 50 percent. This, combined with export subsidization through domestic policies, would have been about 90 percent, very close to the tax stemming from import restrictiveness. Quantitatively, preferential access contributed more

---

[13] Most, but not all, of these rents accrued to producers because of the export tax on sugar, which averaged about 12 percent between 1975 and 1995. The sugar rents contributed to sizable levels of domestic savings and financed investment in the EPZ sector. Sugar barons have substantial interests in the EPZ sector. A majority of the EPZ firms were either directly owned by the sugar barons or through a complex web of corporate businesses. In fact the sugar barons have also used their privileged corporate links with the largest Mauritian-owned commercial bank to obtain credits for investment in both the EPZ and the tourism sectors. The bulk of commercial banks' credit to the EPZ are underwritten by the state-owned development bank of Mauritius. The commercial banks therefore do not hesitate to lend to the EPZ sector.

[14] The quota rents are actually an upper bound under the assumption of perfectly elastic export supply.

TABLE 8.6
Rents to Mauritius from Apparel Exports

	1984				1996				1999			
	EU		USA		EU		USA		EU		USA	
	ETE	Rent	ETE	Rent	ETE	Rent	ETE	Rent	ETE	Rent	ETE	Rent
Shirt knitted	3	0.01	15	0.00	28.3	3.40	57.8	2.55	18.1	4.33	37.6	4.88
T-shirts knitted	3	0.02	17	0.00	28.3	40.95	0.8	0.29	14.7	45.31	7.6	0.97
Shirts not knitted	5	0.09	27	0.29	12.6	9.54	50.8	27.77	10.6	6.95	42.9	36.62
Trousers	20	0.79	20	1.41	9	9.85	31.6	19.81	11.6	9.81	25.7	23.56
Ladies' blouses etc.	10	0.18	17	0.62	4.4	0.62	8.4	0.35	9.9	1.05	12.1	1.30
Jerseys, pullovers, cardigans etc.	3.1	0.20	25.6	1.39	1.8	3.07	1.6	0.10	8	12.20	12.7	1.62
Total rent	1.29		3.71		67.44		50.87		79.65		68.96	
Rent/GDP (%)	0.49%				2.91%				3.54%			

Note: The percent of apparel exports covered for the European and United States for the three time periods are 45 and 68, 93 and 84 and 80 and 94 percent, respectively. Rents are in millions of current U.S. dollars. Export tax equivalents (ETE) are in percentages.

TABLE 8.7
Import Tax and Offsetting Export Subsidies
(in percent)

| | | Export Subsidy | | | | | | |
| | | From Domestic Policy[b] | | From Preferential Access | | | Total | |
Period	Import Protection[a]	Case A	Case B	Sugar	Apparel	Total	Case A	Case B
1980s	127	32	39	108	15	52	84	91
1990s	65	7	20	98	28	47	54	66

[a] To capture the resource allocation effects, protection is measured in effective rather than nominal terms.

[b] Refers to the difference between the EPZ wage and the wage in non-EPZ manufacturing (case A) and in the entire economy (case B).

to offsetting the antiexport bias of the import regime than domestic export subsidization policies (table 8.7).

In sum, Mauritius benefited enormously from the policies of its trading partners who granted preferential access to Mauritius. An alternative way of stating this is that Mauritius benefited from the protectionist policies of the United States and EU in the sugar and textile and clothing sectors. Had these industrial countries liberalized their markets, it is quite likely that the Mauritian trade performance would have been quite different. It is therefore no secret that Mauritius has not been enthusiastic about dismantling protection in world agricultural and clothing markets.

Trading Rules

Another less well known aspect of the international trading regime is relevant in analyzing Mauritian trade policies. Under the WTO, developing countries have generally been exempted from undertaking obligations to rein in protectionist trade policy. This favorable treatment of developing countries has, until the Uruguay Round, extended to export subsidies. The Mauritian regime for export processing zones, particularly the favorable tax treatment of firms in EPZs, could not have flourished had the prohibition of export subsidies by developed countries also been applied to developing countries. The international regime was therefore indulgent toward Mauritius in this respect as well.[15]

---

[15] Interestingly, the WTO rules do not treat differential labor regulations between the export and other sectors as a subsidy.

TABLE 8.8
Total Factor Productivity in EPZ Sector in Mauritius

	%GDP	%K	%L	Labor Share	TFP
1982–99	10.2%	9.5%	5.4%	0.69	3.5%
1982–90	19.0%	24.1%	17.5%	0.67	−0.8%
1991–99	5.7%	0.7%	0.0%	0.71	5.4%

Export Processing Zones: FDI and Ideas (Romer)

By any conventional measure, the EPZ experiment in Mauritius has been a resounding success: it has literally helped transform the Mauritian economy. Since 1982, output has grown by 19 percent per annum on average, employment by 24 percent, and exports by about 11 percent. The EPZ sector from a base of zero in 1971 now accounts for 26 percent of GDP, 36 percent of employment, 19 percent of capital stock, and 66 percent of exports.

It could be argued that this performance is a reflection of the various financial incentives provided to firms operating in EPZs and that a proper economic evaluation that incorporates the social costs of these incentives might portray a different picture. To test this proposition, a growth accounting analysis was conducted for the EPZ sector and compared with that for the economy as a whole. The results are striking. For the period 1983–99, productivity growth in the EPZs has averaged about 3.5 percent compared with 1.4 percent in the economy as a whole. For the 1990s, EPZ productivity growth was spectacular, averaging 5.4 percent per annum, a level not matched even in the fast-growing countries of East Asia (see table 8.8). As wage costs have risen in Mauritius, firms have economized on their use of inputs and improved their efficiency in order to sustain growth.

Does the performance of the EPZ reflect the benefits of FDI? Romer (1992) has strongly argued that the Mauritian experiment is a vindication of a strategy of importing ideas and allowing the economy to generate high rates of growth based on them. The conceptualization of ideas in Romer (1992) as a public good has the policy implication that the government needs to subsidize the *use/ production* of ideas. According to Romer "The only obvious candidate for explaining the success of Mauritius is the policy of supporting an EPZ, which made investment attractive to foreigners." Beginning with Meade, who took a narrow view of Mauritian entrepreneurial expertise, Romer's story explains well that foreign entrepreneurs brought an array of ideas in a new line of activity, that is, textiles and apparel. Ideas, which are useful, are expected to be reflected in rising productivity, and the experience of the EPZ sector in Mauritius does confirm this prediction.

Openness: What to Conclude?

Of the three explanations, the one due to Sachs and Warner does not appear to square with the facts. Mauritius was simply not a liberal economy in import policy terms. The explanation due to Romer encounters two problems. While it may have been true that the initial wave of investments that triggered the growth in EPZ output was largely foreign, the Mauritian EPZ sector, unlike that in many countries, had a substantial local presence. For example, in 1984, only 12 percent of the total employment in the EPZ was accounted for by wholly foreign-owned operations, compared with 72, 42, and 64 percent respectively in Korea, the Philippines, and Malaysia. It is estimated that about 50 percent of the total equity of firms in the EPZ was owned by Mauritian nationals. In other words, ownership figures do not provide unambiguous support for the notion that ideas originated from abroad and were mediated through foreign direct investment.[16]

A second problem is more general. True, the Mauritian government did support the export processing zones, but was it unique to Mauritius? Apart from Mauritius, EPZ facilities and the attendant incentives were provided by a host of other African countries, such as Zimbabwe, Senegal, Madagascar, and Cameroon. Hinkle and Herrou-Aragon (2001) rated countries like Zimbabwe and Senegal at par with countries without the EPZs, for the reason that these countries implemented the arrangements so poorly that they were judged no better off than African countries without the EPZs. Other countries like Cameroon, which tried the same experiment, had only moderate success. The EPZ experiment failed in almost all these countries. Put differently, while Romer's insight on the successful use of ideas (mediated through FDI) by Mauritius may be valid, the question of why FDI flowed to Mauritius rather than to others that attempted to similarly attract FDI remains unanswered.

This poor performance elsewhere in Africa was not limited to the EPZs alone. In fact, reviewing the system of export incentives in 13 African countries, Hinkle and Herrou-Aragon conclude that no sample country came anywhere close to international best practice for export incentives. They attribute this unambiguous failure to fiscal constraints and limited administrative capacity, the latter resulting in leakage of commodities benefiting from the incentives to the domestic market, favoring import-competing rather than export-oriented activities. There seems to be more to the EPZ experience of Mauritius than the import of ideas through subsidies.

The heterodox opening argument due to Rodrik points in a promising direction. When supplemented with the role played by trading partners, it appears to

---

[16] Of course, given the public good nature of ideas, even very small initial amounts imported from abroad could have subsequently been adopted by domestic firms. Thus, substantial domestic ownership of the EPZ firms need not invalidate the Romer insight.

explain why the trade regime was at least neutral between the export and import-competing sectors. But again this explanation appears to be a proximate one. Other African countries established EPZs and enjoyed preferential access to foreign export markets without comparable success. There seems to be more to the Mauritian experiment than interventionist policies at home and generosity abroad.

4. THE ROLE OF INSTITUTIONS

The role of efficient and properly functioning institutions as a precondition to investment, entrepreneurship, and innovation and hence long-run growth is increasingly emphasized in the growth literature. Institutions have been argued to confer two types of benefits. First, they enhance long-run growth (Collier and Gunning 1999; Acemoglu, Johnson, and Robinson 2000), and second, they impart resilience to an economy, allowing it to adjust to exogenous shocks (Rodrik 1999b).

As is evident from the partial scatter plot in figure 8.8, fast growers have on average better institutions.[17] In reality, though, it is difficult to identify all the attributes of the capital called institutions. There is social capital in the form of trust, work ethics, and religious and ethnic tolerance, and civic capital in the form of infrastructure (not all of which can be captured in the form of trade costs), legal and judicial systems, and so on. In practice, different institutions embodying these varying attributes tend to be highly correlated, and cross-country evidence on growth has tended to be robust across different indices.[18]

Collier and Gunning (1999) argue that the long-run growth process itself is directly related to the quality of domestic institutions. Public social capital consists of government institutions that facilitate private activity, such as well-functioning courts that ensure contract enforcement and respect of property rights. This reduces the risks of private investment, leading to larger quantities of it. Public social capital also ensures that government policy is not dominated by any single favored groups whose interests are at variance from the community as a whole. The expansion of the public sector and import substitution and the taxation of agriculture witnessed in Africa have resulted in part from the lack of mechanisms for inclusiveness in policymaking. Finally, poor social capital has led to a high incidence of corruption.

---

[17] The measure of institutional quality is due to Acemoglu, Johnson, and Robinson (2000). The index of institutional quality is in fact the fitted value from the first stage of the 2SLS regressions. The measure captures the protection against the risk of expropriation of property.

[18] For our sample, the correlation between the ICRGE index and democracy and the ICRGE index and the index of participation are, respectively, 0.71 and 0.72. The correlation between democracy and the participation index is 0.95.

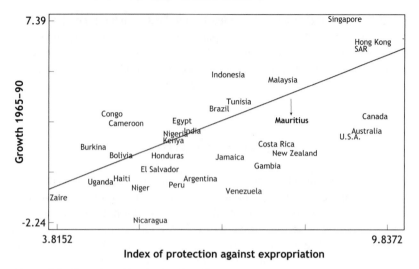

Figure 8.8. Growth and institutional quality

The most compelling empirical evidence on the importance of institutions is due to Acemoglu, Johnson, and Robinson (2000), who show that there is a strong systematic relationship between institutions and economic performance. The European colonizers developed and sustained better institutions in those places where the mortality rates were lower and consequently settlements rates were higher, such as the United States, Australia, New Zealand, and so on. One important result is that, after controlling for institutions properly, geography does not matter (Acemoglu, Johnson, and Robinson 2000). In other words, institutions might well be the most critical determinant of economic performance.

Rodrik (1999b) has argued very strongly that the postwar growth experience, notably the slowdown of economic growth after the first oil shock, needs to be explained in terms of the ability of governments to adjust their macroeconomic policies to exogenous shocks. In his view, the key determinant of this ability is the quality of domestic institutions. The point here is that macroeconomic responses to exogenous shocks have serious domestic distributional implications. Take the standard example of an oil shock that creates a balance of payments problem. The IMF and textbook recommendation is for countries to implement policies to reduce domestic absorption (mainly by tightening fiscal policies) and to switch expenditure from foreign goods to domestic goods.

But which ones and how? Should fiscal tightening take the form of tax increases or expenditure reductions? If the latter, should cuts fall on defense, capital projects, health, or education? Should expenditure switching be accompanied by an incomes policy? Each of these actions has very different distributional implications. If the inevitable distributional conflict can be managed,

TABLE 8.9

Mauritius and Other Countries with Respect to Indices of Institutions

Institutional Quality Index	Mauritius[a]	Africa	Fast-Growing Countries	Other Developing Countries
ICRGE[b]	7.23	4.54	6.86	4.29
Protection against Expropriation[c]	8.06	5.75	8.54	6.47
Democracy[d]	0.75	0.25	0.47	0.51
Participation index[d]	0.80	0.30	0.49	0.44

[a] For ICRGE and Protection against Risk of Expropriation, Mauritius has fitted values.

[b] ICRGE (International Country Risk Guide) index is a measure of institutional quality that contains aspects of government that affect property rights or the ability to carry out business. It is published by a private firm that provides consulting services to international investors.

[c] For ICRGE index and index of protection against the risk of expropriation the scale is between 0 and 10, with higher values indicating better institutional quality.

[d] Participation measures the extent of competitiveness of political participation. This index is taken from the Polity III data set of Jaggers and Gurr (1995), who define it as the "extent to which non-elites are able to access institutional structures for political expression" (it is rescaled to range from 0 to 1 in Rodrik 1999. The democracy index also ranges from 0 to 1.

the impact of the shock can be mitigated. If not, the economic shocks get amplified by the shocks emanating from the domestic social and political conflicts creating long-run damage for the economy. What robust domestic institutions do is to allow these conflicts to be handled at least possible cost (Rodrik 1999b provides evidence in support).

That institutions might be important in explaining Mauritian economic performance is suggested by the high quality of its institutions. Mauritius ranks well above the average African country on all indices of institutional quality, political as well as economic (table 8.9) and also above the fast-growing economies on most indices. The role of institutions in Mauritian growth and development is illustrated by at least three examples.

Gulhati and Nallari (1990) have argued that Mauritius's success in overcoming its macroeconomic imbalances in the early 1980s owes to domestic institutions. Macroeconomic adjustment was in fact implemented by three different governments of apparently divergent ideological persuasions: this presupposed consultation and a recognition of the need to evolve a national consensus in favor of the adjustment. Further, a culture of transparency and participatory politics ensured that early warning signals and feedback mechanisms were in place, allowing emerging economic problems to be tackled at an early stage.

A second illustration of the role of institutions relates to the success of the EPZs in Mauritius compared with the rest of Africa. EPZs have failed in most countries because institutions and governance have not been able to manage the rent seeking, corruption, and inefficiency that accompany the high degree of selective interventionism embodied in EPZs. It is likely that the well-paid civil service (which was part of the political bargain between the political and economic elites) contributed to lower levels of corruption and inefficiency and hence to lower costs of doing business in Mauritius.

The example of the success of the sugar sector in Mauritius also highlights the role of institutions in Mauritian economic performance. Sugar is the prime agricultural product in Mauritius. Like most other African countries, its dependence on the primary product has been high. Where Mauritius differs from the rest of Africa is that it has nurtured and developed the sugar sector rather than taxed it. While the rest of Africa killed its cash cow, Mauritian sugar industry has thrived. The role of institutions in achieving this result is elaborated in greater detail in the concluding section.

5. AN ECONOMETRIC INVESTIGATION OF THE MAURITIAN GROWTH EXPERIENCE

In this section, we test econometrically the validity and relative importance of the different explanations of the Mauritian growth experience. To do this, we use as the benchmark two widely cited cross-country-growth studies: the first due to Sachs and Warner (1997), which seeks to explain long-run growth performance and the second due to Rodrik (1999b), which seeks to explain the *change* in the growth performance since the oil crises of the 1970s and the debt crisis of the early 1980s.

The explanatory variables in Sachs and Warner 1997 can be placed in four broad categories: initial conditions; geography; policy, including openness; and institutions. Given our priors—that institutions could potentially be an important determinant of growth performance in Mauritius—it is essential to draw attention to our treatment of this variable before we elaborate on our results.

Much of the literature on cross-country growth uses a few or a common set of institutional variables. The most commonly used variable is due to the International Country Risk Guide (ICRGE), which captures aspects of the government that directly affect property rights or the ability to carry out business transactions. Knack and Keefer (1995) have compiled information on these aspects of the government from the International Country Risk Guide, a publication by a private firm that provides consulting services to international investors. The problem, however, is that there is a two-way relationship between institutions and growth. While institutions clearly influence growth, higher incomes increase the demand for participation, accountability and transparency and also provide the public resources that can be devoted to improving them. Thus much of the existing literature uses a variable for institutions that is prone to endo-geneity bias.[19]

To address this problem, we drew upon the results of Acemoglu, Johnson, and Robinson (2000), who use settler's mortality data in the former colonies as an instrument for the variable that captures institutional quality.[20] Table 8.10 presents the results based on the Sachs and Warner regressions, while table 8.13 presents those based on Rodrik 1999b. Table 8.11 lists the estimated deviation in Mauritian growth from the different groups of countries based on the basic Sachs-Warner regressions.

Given our discussions earlier about Mauritius's trade policy, we chose to cat-egorize it as closed rather than open economy. On this basis, we ran the original SW regression (column 1) as well as an augmented one with the instrumented institutional variable due to Acemoglu, Johnson, and Robinson (2000). The fitted values for institutional quality used in the second stage have been obtained by regressing the index of protection against expropriation on historical settler's mortality and a host of geography and other exogenous variables. The dummy for Mauritius is significant and positive. In other words the cross-country growth regression is inadequate in explaining Mauritian growth performance.[21]

The openness issue for Mauritius as raised in this chapter is likely to be con-troversial. The assessment of Mauritius as a closed economy seems in con-formity with the data, but to explore further Mauritius's trade performance, we estimated a gravity model based on Subramanian and Tamirisa 2001 to check whether Mauritius was an exceptional trader. The results presented in table 8.12 are interesting. The results indicate that Mauritius has simply been an average

[19] Ideally one should recognize the two-way relationship between institutions and economic growth. Several attempts have been made to deal with the endogeneity of institutions by using an instrumental variables approach. Mauro's (1995) instrument for corruption is ethnolinguistic frac-tionalization, which is not such a good instrument after all if growth is accompanied with emer-gence of a centralized state and integration via markets. Moreover, as Easterly and Levine (1997) argue, the further problem with ethnolinguistic fractionalization is that it can directly affect per-formance by causing political instability. Hall and Jones (1999) use distance from equator as an instrument since the distance from equator proxies "Western influence." Acemoglu, Johnson, and Robinson (2000) critique Hall and Jones on empirical grounds: that it is not easy to argue that West-ern influence led to better institutions. They cite as an example the Belgian influence in the Congo. To our knowledge, Acemoglu, Johnson, and Robinson 2000 appears to be the best attempt at get-ting the right instrument for institutional quality.

[20] Acemoglu, Johnson, and Robinson's (2000) instrument for institutional quality in an equation with the log of income per capita (rather than growth of this variable).

[21] The interesting result from a general perspective is that instrumenting for institutions *trumps* openness. The openness variable in the SW regressions is no longer significant once the 2SLS methodology is adopted, nor are the geography variables. In fact the central message of the Ace-moglu et al. paper is that once institutions are controlled for, geography does not matter. Sachs and McArthur (2001) contest this result.

TABLE 8.10

Cross-Country Growth Regression as in Sachs-Warner (1997)

Dependent Variable: Growth Rate 1965–90	OLS	2SLS
Log of initial GDP	−1.44*** (−6.45)	−1.79*** (−5.73)
Openness × log of GDP	−1.18*** (−3.5)	−0.27 (−0.57)
Openness (fraction of years open according to Sachs and Warner 1995)	11.85*** (4.25)	3.21 (0.79)
Landlocked dummy variable	−0.61*** (−2.71)	0.39 (0.38)
Log life expectancy circa 1970	45.47*** (2.71)	111.14* (1.82)
Square of log life expectancy	−5.37** (−2.32)	−13.81* (−1.79)
Central government saving 1970–90	0.11*** (5.17)	0.11** (2.31)
Dummy for tropical climate	−0.82*** (−2.92)	0.52 (0.66)
Institutional Quality Index (ICRGE)	0.34*** (4.14)	
Expropriation index instrumented		1.41* (1.72)
Natural resource exports/GDP 1970	−3.82*** (−3.97)	−5.64*** (−3.94)
Growth in economically active population—population growth	0.74** (2.16)	−0.46 (−0.38)
Mauritian dummy	1.46** (1.94)	1.89** (1.88)
Constant	−83.26** (−2.46)	−216.43* (−1.76)
R^2	0.87	0.83
Adj R^3	0.85	0.78
Number of observations	85	52

Note: Figures in brackets represent *t* ratios.

* significant at 99%.   ** significant at 95%.   *** significant at 99%.

TABLE 8.11
Breakdown of Mauritian Growth

Explanatory Variable	Difference in Mauritian Growth from Baseline Growth of		
	Africa	Fast-Growing Countries	Other Developing Countries
Catch-up[a]	−2.33	−1.33	−1.41
Life expectancy	1.51	0.29	0.68
Landlocked	0.19	0	0.06
Tropical climate	−0.09	−0.26	−0.34
Natural resource abundance	−0.35	−0.65	−0.55
Etholinguistic reactionalization[a]	0.01	−0.03	−0.05
Total inheritance	−1.06	−1.98	−1.61
Openness[b]	−0.20	−1.93	−0.47
Central government savings	−0.43	−0.53	−0.08
Average national savings ratio	−0.001	−0.02	−0.006
Institutional quality	0.75	0.10	0.82

Note: Estimates are based on the Sachs and Warner (1997) basic regression.

[a] Inheritance variable.
[b] Policy variable.

rather than an exceptional trader. The Mauritian dummy in the regressions for the early 1980s and the late 1990s is not statistically different from zero. This is in contrast with the vast majority of African countries that are typically undertraders and the tigers of East Asia that are consistent overtraders. The inference therefore is that exceptional growth performance was not the result of an exceptional trade performance.

The same results, namely the uniqueness of the Mauritian growth record, hold for Mauritius in the Rodrik regressions. The significance of the Mauritian dummy is robust to alternative measures of institutional quality (table 8.13), including the Acemoglu variation. The results are stronger on the uniqueness of Mauritius because the Rodrik regressions are aimed at explaining performance of the post-1975 period relative to the pre-1975 period, and it is in the latter that Mauritian growth accelerated. Relative to most other countries in Africa and in

TABLE 8.12
Undertraders, Average Traders, and Supertraders
(coefficient on country dummies
in a gravity model)

Country	1997–98
Angola	0.975
Burundi	−1.804**
Congo	−1.617**
Ethiopia	−1.650**
Kenya	−1.103**
Madagascar	−0.945*
Malawi	−1.361**
Mauritius	0.252
Mozambique	−1.654**
Rwanda	−1.939**
Seychelles	−0.325
Tanzania	−1.901**
Uganda	−2.066**
Zambia	−1.416**
Zimbabwe	−0.974**
Indonesia	0.086
Malaysia	1.569**
Thailand	0.819**
China, Hong Kong SAR	1.505**
Korea	0.764**
Singapore	1.852**
Taiwan	1.292**

Note: A negative and significant coefficient implies under trader, while a positive and significant coefficient implies overtrade.

* Significant at 10% level.   ** Significant at 5% level.

TABLE 8.13
Cross-Country Regressions of Change in Growth
(Rodrik 1999b)

East Asia dummy	2.41***	2.11***	
		(−3.26)	(−3.06)
Latin America dummy	−2.16***	−1.77**	
	(−4.56)	(−3.7)	
SSA dummy	−2.11***	−2.09**	
	(−3.38)	(−3.6)	
Growth 1960–75	−0.77***	−0.72**	−0.83**
	(−7.11)	(−6.41)	(−5.41)
Log GDP/capita 1975	−0.90***	−0.87**	−2.03**
	(−3.02)	(−2.91)	(−4.54)
External shocks	−0.03	−0.07**	−(0.04)
	(−1.05)	(−2.84)	(−1.26)
Democracy	1.73**		
	(2.18)		
Institutional quality (instrumented for index			1.85*
of protection against risk of expropriation)			(5.41)
Index of participation		2.02***	
		(2.57)	
Ethnolinguistic fractionalization	−1.65***		
	(−2.38)		
Dummy for Mauritius	3.68**	4.30***	3.91**
	(2.19)	(2.49)	(2.29)
Constant	8.55***	(3.11)	(1.98)
	(3.94)	(3.11)	(1.98)
R^2	0.6039	0.6051	0.54
Adjusted R^2	0.5629	0.5741	0.49
Number of observations	97	97	59

** significant at 95% level.   *** significant at 99% level.

Latin America, Mauritius enjoyed a sustained boom, while others suffered a growth collapse.[22]

6. CONCLUDING OBSERVATIONS: WHAT MIGHT BE UNIQUE ABOUT MAURITIUS

The foregoing discussion can be summarized as follows: first, the Mauritian growth performance between 1960 and 1990, and especially since the 1970s, has been exceptional. In standard cross-country growth regression models, Mauritius is an outlier, implying that conventional determinants of growth do not fully capture the country's performance.

Second, initial conditions have had an ambiguous, and on balance a negative, impact on subsequent growth performance. Its initial inheritance of human capital and demographic characteristics were favorable, but its higher level of initial income, commodity dependence, and unfavorable geography have exerted a drag on growth. Certainly, in the growth race, Mauritius did not receive a stagger, relative at least to countries in Africa. Table 8.11 indicates that the initial conditions disadvantaged Mauritius relative to all groups of developing countries. Mauritius's inheritance implied a drag on growth of about 1 percentage point relative to the average African country and close to 2 percentage points relative to the fast growers.

Third, Mauritius adopted a distinctive approach to openness. It has not had an open trade regime in any conventional sense; on the contrary, its import regime for much of the 1970s, 1980s, and 1990s has been highly restrictive. The distinctiveness has been how Mauritius prevented an import tax from becoming an export and trade tax. Through a mixture of segmentation of the import-competing and export sectors, and heavy intervention to promote the latter, initially though more liberal labor market policies but also through the tax system, part of the antiexport bias was offset.[23] The institutional distinctiveness—which gave effect to segmentation—was the creation of EPZs. These were the heterodox aspects of Mauritius's openness strategy. However, it is the preferential access provided by Mauritius's trading partners, in sugar and textiles and clothing, and the resulting implicit export subsidization, that has allowed the antiexport bias to be fully offset. Thus, while there are shades of East

---

[22] Because of the high coefficient of the initial growth rate (between 1960 and 1975), the Rodrik regressions come very close to being a conventional growth regression for the period 1975–89 rather than a "change in growth" regression.

[23] Technically speaking the term *antiexport bias* is defined for the given terms of trade. Our perspective here is to compare the profitability in the export sector versus the import-competing sector, and this calculation requires looking at both the role of domestic policy and policies of the trading partners that affect the terms of trade.

Asian–style (particularly Korea and Taiwan) interventionism in Mauritius's trade and development strategy, a substantial role was played by trading partners (to a much greater extent than in the case of East Asia) in boosting trade performance. The emphasis on heterodox policies by Rodrik (1999a) therefore needs to be qualified.

But it should be underscored that while Mauritian policy offset the antiexport bias, neutrality rather than a protrade bias was achieved. In other words, Mauritian trade performance was average, not exceptional, as in the case of the tigers of East Asia. Thus, Mauritian trade performance cannot explain Mauritius's exceptional growth performance. It was a supergrower but not a supertrader.[24]

But these are proximate rather than underlying causes of Mauritian growth success because the favorable trade environment and the creation of EPZs were not unique to Mauritius. Other developing countries had similar trade opportunities and adopted similar policies but failed where Mauritius succeeded. To some considerable extent, strong domestic institutions have contributed substantially to Mauritian success and are a good candidate for underlying explanations of the Mauritian miracle. Compared with many developing countries, Mauritius has since independence been a democracy and developed strong participatory institutions.

The econometric results, however, suggest that even after accounting for the role of institutions there is a sizable unexplained component to Mauritian growth. Cross-country growth models, by definition, cannot capture country-specific idiosyncratic effects. In Mauritius, there were many. But one particularly important one, ironically, appears to be the very diversity and ethnic fragmentation that Meade lamented as a curse.

Diversity had three important benefits: it was a repository of communities (or diasporas) that turned out to have important linkages with the rest of the world, creating positive externalities for the country; it forced the need for economic balance that explains the preservation of the cash cow, namely the sugar sector; and third, it forced the need for participatory political institutions that were important in maintaining stability, law and order, rule of law, and mediating conflict.

First, the role of business and social networks in promoting trade and investment has attracted increased research interest in recent years. Casella and Rauch (1999) develop a model of trade that reflects the difficulty of introducing one's product in a foreign market. Access to local sources that can provide information about the market then facilitate entry, and one prominent source of

---

[24] Another factor that needs to be taken into account in explaining trade performance is the role of the services sector in Mauritius. Africa is afflicted by high trade costs. Despite its geographical remoteness, Mauritius has been able to keep transaction costs under control. Ports have been well managed and have rendered efficient service, the financial sector is well developed, and telecommunications are fairly efficient.

information transmission is coethnicity. A well-known example of the role of ethnic networks in trade is provided by the overseas Chinese who have created formal or informal societies that help in information flows and even at times in enforcement of contracts. Head, Ries, and Wagner (1997) find that immigrants significantly increase trade between Canada and the source countries. Rauch (1999) presents evidence that common language and colonial ties play an important role in international trade.

Just as business and social networks are important for trade, they are conceivably important for investment, owing to similar mechanisms. Mauritius has a small Chinese population that played an important role in attracting the first wave of foreign direct investment flows from Hong Kong SAR. Entrepreneurs from Hong Kong SAR chose Mauritius as an investment location to circumvent the quotas on exports of textiles and clothing from Hong Kong SAR. In a similar vein, the offshore financial sector has grown because of the Indian diaspora, which led to the signing of a double taxation treaty between Mauritius and India. As a result, Mauritian offshore centers have mediated large financial flows to India, and Mauritius has become the largest investor in India.

Diversity had other important consequences. Here, one should emphasize a distinctive element of Mauritian diversity. There was a nice, almost symbiotic separation of economic and political power in Mauritius. Compared to resource-rich countries in Africa (for instance Ghana and Nigeria, where the economic power and political power were vested in the same authority), Mauritius did not have a ruling elite that derived economic power from the control over resources. Economic power was vested in the minority French community.

This had one important consequence: Mauritius avoided one of the major mistakes made in most of resource-rich Africa, killing the cash cow. Thus, agriculture and the resource sector were taxed in much of Africa (Ghana, Kenya, Tanzania). In part, this was induced by ideology—the push toward import-substituting industrialization. But the newly independent government in Mauritius—of a distinctly socialist persuasion—was just as susceptible to this siren call.[25] Yet the call was resisted. Political economy played an important role. The sugar sector was owned predominantly by the minority French community. On the one hand, it was farsighted of the majority Indian community not to have nationalized or heavily taxed this sector. Equally, the economic elite—the French—exercised their clout and ensured that an outcome adverse to them did not result. The cleavage between the economic elite (a political minority) and the political elite and the need to achieve balance between the two in a newly independent state thus ensured the fortunes of the sugar sector.

---

[25] The first prime minister, Sir Seewoosagur Ramgoolam, was a Fabian socialist and wedded ideologically to a socialist model of development.

In return for guaranteeing the rights of the sugar owners, the political majority did implicitly extract a compromise in terms of transferring some of the rents from sugar to itself. One important aspect of this transfer was a large, relatively well paid civil service (staffed predominantly by the majority Indian community) and a generous system of social protection, particularly related to pensions. The success of the sugar industry in Mauritius can thus be seen as an example of optimal rent sharing between the political (predominantly Indian) and economic elites (predominantly non-Indian).

Diversity also had important political consequences. To some extent, Mauritius had no choice but to evolve such institutions. Just prior to independence, in a referendum on this question, 44 percent of the population (virtually the entire non-Indian population) rejected independence and wished to stay as a British colony. Assuaging the misgivings of such a large section of the population made participatory politics in the postindependence era a necessity.[26] These institutions have ensured free and fair elections, the rule of law, a vibrant and independent press, and respect for property rights, all of which have made Mauritius an attractive investment location.

Thus, both politics and economics were shaped by the diversity of the population and the need to accommodate it in the face of large fissures. Another less well known choice made by Mauritius, which in retrospect seems a farsighted one, is related to the sugar quota. Mauritius in the 1970s was offered the choice between access at the then high world price with limited quotas and access at a lower domestic EU price but with higher guaranteed quotas. Many countries chose the former, attracted by the high price prevailing at that time. Mauritius chose the latter. The larger quantitative access, combined with the pressure from the domestic EU producer's lobby that raised domestic EU prices, handed Mauritius huge rents, which proved to be vital in financing private investment and generating growth.

One clear message is that attempting to replicate the Mauritian experiment might be hazardous for other countries, in part because the trading environment is now less favorable. Preferential margins for African countries will slowly but inevitably decline as global liberalization proceeds apace. Perhaps, more importantly, it may be difficult for other countries to replicate the key elements of the Mauritian globalization strategy—heavy intervention, extensive subsidization, and targeting, including through the creation of EPZs—because the preconditions for ensuring that an interventionist strategy succeeds, notably, high-quality domestic institutions and political processes, may not be in place.

---

[26] The extraordinary effort devoted to assuaging minority interests is reflected in the "best loser" system discussed above.

REFERENCES

Acemoglu, D., S. Johnson, and J. A. Robinson. 2000. "The Colonial Origins of Comparative Development: An Empirical Investigation." NBER Working Paper No. WP/00/7771.

Berthelemy, J. C., and L. Soderling. 2001. "Will There Be New Emerging Markets in Africa by the Year 2020?" OECD Development Centre. Photocopy.

Casella, A., and J. Rauch. 1999. "Anonymous Market and Group Ties in International Trade." Columbia University. Photocopy.

Cashin, P., and C. Patillo. 2000. "Terms of Trade Shocks in Africa: Are they Short-Lived or Long-Lived." International Monetary Fund Working Paper No. WP/00/72.

Coe, D., E. Helpman, and A. Hoffmaister. 1997. "North-South R&D Spillovers." *Economic Journal* 107:134–49.

Collier, P., and W. Gunning. 1999. "Explaining African Economic Performance." *Journal of Economic Literature* 37:64–111.

Collins, S., and B. Bosworth. 1996. "Economic Growth in East Asia: Accumulation versus Assimilation." *Brookings Papers on Economic Activity* 1996, no. 2:135–91.

Dalmazzo, A., and G. de Blasio. 2001. "Resources and Incentives to Reform: A Model and Some Evidence on Sub-Saharan African Countries." International Monetary Fund Working Paper, WP/01/86.

Easterly, W., and R. Levine. 1997. "Africa's Growth Tragedy: Policies and Ethnic Divisions." *Quarterly Journal of Economics* 112:1203–50.

Gulhati, R., and R. Nallari. 1990. *Successful Stabilization and Recovery in Mauritius.* EDI Development Policy Case Series. Washington, D.C.: World Bank.

Hall, R. E., and C. I. Jones. 1999. "Why Do Some Countries Produce So Much More Output per Worker Than Others?" *Quarterly Journal of Economics* 114:83–116.

Head, K., J. Ries, and D. Wagner. 1997. "Immigrants as Trade Catalysts." In *The People Link: Human Resource Linkages across the Pacific,* ed. W. Dobson and A. E. Safarian. Hong Kong Bank of Canada Papers on Asia, vol. 3. Toronto: University of Toronto Press.

Hein, C. 1988. "Multinational Enterprises and Employment in the Mauritian Export Processing Zone." International Labor Office Working Paper No. 52, Geneva.

Hinkle, L. E., and A. Herrou-Aragon. 2001. "How Far Did Africa's First Generation Trade Reforms Go?" World Bank. Photocopy.

Jaggers, K., and T. R. Gurr. 1995. "Tracking Democracy's Third Wave with Polity III Data." *Journal of Peace Research* 32:469–82.

Knack, S., and P. Keefer. 1995. "Institutions and Economic Performance: Cross-Country Tests Using Alternative Institutional Measures." *Economics and Politics* 7 (November): 207–27.

Mauro, P. 1995. "Corruption and Growth." *Quarterly Journal of Economics* 110:681–712.

Meade, J. E., et al. 1961. *The Economics and Social Structure of Mauritius—Report to the Government of Mauritius.* London: Methuen.

Milner, C., and A. McKay. 1996. "Real Exchange Rate Measures of Trade Liberalization: Some Evidence for Mauritius." *Journal of African Economies* 5, no. 1: 69–91.

Rauch, J. 1999. "Networks versus Markets in International Trade." *Journal of International Economics* 48:7–35.

Rodriguez, F., and D. Rodrik. 1999. "Trade Policy and Economic Growth: A Skeptic's Guide to Cross-National Evidence." NBER Working Paper No. WP/99/7081.

Rodrik, D. 1999a. *The New Global Economy and Developing Countries: Making Openness Work.* London: Overseas Development Council.

———. 1999b. "Where Did All the Growth Go? External Shocks, Social Conflict, and Growth Collapses." *Journal of Economic Growth* 4:385–412.

Romer, P. 1992. "Two Strategies for Economic Development: Using Ideas and Producing Ideas." In *World Bank Annual Conference on Development Economics, 1992.* Washington, D.C.: World Bank.

———. 1993. "Idea Gaps and Object Gaps in Economic Development. *Journal of Monetary Economics* 32, no. 3: 543–73.

Sachs, J. D., and A. Warner. 1995. "Economic Reform and the Process of Global Integration." *Brookings Papers on Economic Activity* 1995, no. 1: 1–118.

———. 1997. "Sources of Slow Growth in African Economies." *Journal of African Economies* 6:335–76.

Sachs, J. D., and J. W. McArthur. 2001. "Institutions and Geography: Comment on Acemoglu, Johnson and Robinson (2000)." NBER Working Paper No. WP/01/8114.

Subramanian, A., E. Gelbard, R. Harmsen, K. Elborgh-Woytek, and P. Nagy. 2000. "Trade and Trade Polices in Eastern and Southern Africa." International Monetary Fund Occasional Paper No. 196, Washington, D.C.

Subramanian, A., and N. Tamirisa. 2001. "Africa's Trade Revisited." International Monetary Fund Working Paper No. WP01/33.

United Nations. 2000. *Human Development Report.* New York.

Wellisz, S., and P. L. S. Saw. 1993. "Mauritius." In *The Political Economy of Poverty, Equity, and Growth,* ed. R. Findlay and S. Wellisz. Oxford: Oxford University Press.

Venezuela's Growth Implosion

A NEOCLASSICAL STORY?

RICARDO HAUSMANN

A WITCH HUNT

ONCE UPON a time there was a prosperous village. Life was good and people were happy. One year the crops failed and living conditions deteriorated. When the same thing happened the following year, the town elders met and decided that such a second occurrence could not be a coincidence: it had to be the work of the devil, acting through some witch whose soul he had possessed. The problem had to be dealt with.

The elders decided to establish an inquisitorial committee to search for witches and burn them at the stake. They had scientific means of identifying them: since the soul of the devil was less dense than that of a good Christian, possessed individuals would tend to float abnormally when in water. Thus, they had a clear mechanism to establish guilt.[1] The committee quickly identified seven witches, all of them elderly women with patently strange behavior. After burning them at the stake in the central square, the committee concluded that they had rid the village of evil spirits and prayed for a better crop next year.

Next year came and the crops were better than the previous catastrophic year, but still not as good as usual. The committee debated what to do: one group, who called themselves the doves, argued that they should allow more time for nature to recover. Another group, appropriately named the hawks, suggested that they should search for more witches. The doves won the debate and the village anxiously waited for the following year's crop. It was an utter disaster: the crops failed again! The hawks, while saddened by the misery of the village, felt confirmed in their wisdom: they had been right all along. The doves had appeased the devil and caused the current disaster. The issue was clear: more witches needed to be found and summarily burnt at the stake. Compassion had no role when dealing with the devil.

---

[1] During the three hundred–odd years in which the witch-hunts took place, this was a common practice (Robinson 1992). Unfortunately, osteoporosis has a similar effect on buoyancy, increasing the likelihood that older women would get identified as witches.

The inquisition labored hard in order to thoroughly identify all the witches in the village and the surrounding valley. After much hard work they had put to death almost 80 elderly ladies, reigning in the opposition from relatives who could not come to understand that the soul residing in those women was not that of their loved ones, but instead, that of the devil. While the process was traumatic, the village was relieved when the crops improved the following year, although not to the levels of years past.

The story could continue, but we can leave it here. Once the relationship between crops and witches has been established, the question is how many old women should be burned at the stake. If enough possessed souls have been destroyed, the situation should improve. But one never knows how much is enough. Deteriorations are an indication that more needs to be done. Once the paradigm has been established, it is very hard to find it wanting. If witches actually do not exist, or if, while existing, they do not deal in crops, the village will never find out. There are too few observations and too much fluctuation from year to year for the village scientist to prove the proposition one way or the other. But society cannot afford not to take a view on such a central matter.

The tragedy of growth collapses—or of disappointing growth in general—generates this kind of situation. If the belief is that the problem with growth is insufficient reform, then more privatizations or new financial regulations are needed to burn the witches. And if it does not work, more must be required. If the conviction is that corruption is the relevant witch, then throwing the rascals out in the next election and starting a "witch-hunt" of former public officials should improve matters. And if it does not, then it must be that the new guys are still stealing and consequently more changes of government and new crackdowns are in order. If by any chance corruption, inefficient public enterprises, or high tariffs are not central to the growth problems of a country, societies will have trouble finding that out.

This chapter is about finding the witch that destroyed the prosperity of Venezuela. As we shall see, Venezuela, at 6.4 percent per annum, was the fastest growing of the major Latin American countries between 1920 and 1980. Its output per worker in the nonoil economy declined to almost half in the following 20 years.

To a large extent, Venezuela is a strange candidate for a growth implosion. It did not have a civil war like El Salvador or Nicaragua, or a political-economic transition like eastern Europe. In fact, it was perceived at the time its growth collapse started as the most stable democracy in Latin America. Unlike Mexico, there were two main parties that competed fiercely for power. Unlike Colombia, their membership reached into the millions and voter turnout was in excess of 90 percent. There was a carefully crafted balance of powers so that the opposition had important attributions in the Congress, the Supreme Court, the appointment of justices, the comptroller general and the attorney general. There were very strong labor and business institutions to negotiate social conflicts. Political competition and a free press created important checks and balances on the government. There was no history of inflation. In fact, of all the countries in the International Financial Statistics of the IMF, Venezuela experienced the lowest inflation rate between 1950 and 1980. As late as 1980, the country had a credit rating of AAA. Twenty years later, none of these things were true.

What happened? The Venezuelan public is convinced that the core explanation is corruption and has been kicking out whoever is in power. Growth has yet to resume. International agencies favor the assumption of insufficient structural reforms or poor institutions. Whichever explanation one chooses needs to account for the fact that the past 20 years were preceded by 60 remarkable years of growth, with probably similar institutions and degrees of corruption.

The academic literature has a few additional hints as to what may have happened. Some of the explanations start with the role of natural resources. Matsuyama (1992) argues that if industries intensive in natural resources exhibit fewer growth externalities such as learning by doing, then static comparative advantage will lead to specialization away from sectors such as manufacturing that may be more dynamic over time. Corroborating this, Sachs and Warner (1995) find that countries rich in natural resources tend to grow more slowly. This logic cannot possibly explain the Venezuelan experience. First, as we shall see, Venezuela's growth collapse took place after 60 years of expansion, fueled by oil. If oil explains slow growth, what explains the previous fast growth? Moreover, the growth collapse happened when oil revenues were declining, so that the Dutch disease should have operated in reverse, facilitating the growth of output in nonoil tradables: it did not happen.

Other papers emphasize the political economy of oil rents. Tornell and Lane (1998) argue that oil booms may be problematic: overspending may result as different constituencies fight over the rights to appropriate a growing common pool of resources. While this logic may explain some dynamics around booms, it makes busts less problematic. Moreover, it does not explain a 20-year growth collapse.

Rodríguez and Sachs (1999) argue that the drop in growth is caused by the declining importance of oil income. Their argument is based on the idea that since oil resources are exhaustible, any optimal extraction plan will imply zero oil income in some distant future. They show that if there is a home bias in investment, countries will see their level of income and capital per worker overshoot the long-term steady state. Countries will approach the long run from above, by growing below trend. This argument has two main complications. First, the large and increasing volume of oil reserves makes arguments about exhaustion less compelling as a determinant of current trends. Second, the assumption of a home bias in investment implies that residents must be investing domestically at rates of return below those of the world, but decide to keep their savings at home anyway. While limits on borrowing can be explained as the consequence of problems of contract enforcement or sovereign risk, it is much harder to argue that overinvestment is caused by limits to capital outward capital mobility. Moreover, there is scant evidence that profit rates were unusually low during the boom years.

Rodrik (1998) argues that the problem originates from the interaction between external shocks, latent social conflict, and conflict management institutions such as democracy and the rule of law. The idea is that if a country gets a bad shock to which it must react, latent conflict and weak institutions may make it difficult to arrive at a politically viable solution. Adjustment may be delayed as constituencies fight over who will bear the burden, as in Alesina and Drazen 1991. While this explanation seems plausible in general, it is not a good explanation of the Venezuelan case. As we shall see, Venezuela did get a large external shock expressed in a large decline of oil rents. However, Venezuela—at the time in which the growth collapse started—had as strong a democratic political system as can be found in any developing country. A stable system of political parties, dominated by two main organizations, was able to garner massive support in terms of party membership and turnout at elections. In addition, both labor and business organizations each formed large national organizations to negotiate the interests of the membership with the government. Moreover, for the first decade of the collapse, while the system was not able to stop the decline, it did do a remarkable job at maintaining social peace and political participation.[2]

All this did change over time. Society became much more conflictual, and institutions did loose legitimacy. Nevertheless, this can best be understood as a consequence rather than a cause of the economic implosion.

Finally, other authors emphasize the impact of oil revenues on the state's political capacities. For example, Naím and Pinango (1984) argue that the presence of oil created mechanisms for conflict resolution based on redistribution of the oil rent. These mechanisms break down when oil revenues dwindle, making shocks harder to manage. Karl (1997) argues that in oil-producing economies the political system is based on redistribution of petroleum rents, leaving the political system with no tradition of justifying the state's use of general taxation. This makes such oil-dependent societies less able to deal with revenue shortfalls.

---

[2] In any case, Venezuela's growth collapse is an outlier in Rodrik's paper. In his data set, Venezuela appears as having a growth decline of only 3 percent. Three of his five main equations predict growth declines of about 1 percent. In our data set, the growth puzzle is closer to 5 percent. These results are due to the fact that Venezuela appears as having low latent social conflict, as measured either by inequality, ethnolinguistic fragmentation, or the proportion of the population that does not speak the main language. Moreover, Venezuela scores relatively high on measures of democracy and rule of law.

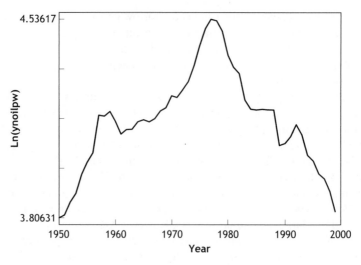

Figure 9.1. Venezuela: GDP per worker, excluding oil sector, in logs

VENEZUELA'S GROWTH IMPLOSION: SOME STYLIZED FACTS

Figure 9.1 shows the evolution of output per worker in the economy excluding the oil sector. The nonoil economy hires about 99 percent of the labor force and generates around 80 percent of national income. We concentrate on it in order to focus our attention on a variable that is not itself directly impacted by oil discoveries, sudden changes in oil prices or output. It is more readily understandable in terms of traditional factors of production such as labor, physical and human capital, and productivity.

The graph shows the Venezuelan drama. Between 1950 and 1980 (peaking in 1978) output per worker increased at an annual rate of 2 percent (about 80 percent cumulative). Employment grew by 3.7 percent, meaning that output expanded at about 5.8 percent. However, in the following 20 years, output per worker fell at a rate of about 3 percent per year, reaching again the levels of the early 1950s. As growth collapses go, this one is relatively big and follows what could arguably be called a growth miracle: 60 years of per capita growth in the nonoil economy of just under 4 percent: an enviable record. In fact, according to Maddison (1995, 156–57) Venezuela's 6.4 percent per annum total GDP growth rate between 1920 and 1980 was the fastest of the seven Latin American countries whose GDP he reports. This compares with 5.5 for Brazil, 4.8 for Peru and Mexico, 4.7 for Colombia, 3.4 for Argentina, and 3.3 for Chile.[3]

---

[3] For Mexico the data starts in 1921 and for Colombia in 1925.

TABLE 9.1

The Venezuelan Growth Experience, 1920–1999

(Annual rates of growth in percent)

	Nonoil GDP	Population	Nonoil Employment	Nonoil GDP per Capita	Nonoil GDP per Worker	Total GDP per Capita	Total GDP per Worker
1920–80	6.7	2.7		3.9		4.3	
1920–50	7.5	1.7		5.7		7.1	
1950–80	5.8	3.7	3.7	2.1	2.0	1.6	1.5
1950–70	5.9	3.9	3.6	2.0	2.3	2.2	2.5
1970–80	5.6	3.2	4.0	2.3	1.5	0.3	−0.4
1980–99	0.44	2.51	3.52	−2.02	−2.98	−1.58	−2.54
1920–30	10.6	1.0		9.5		13.7	
1930–40	2.5	1.3		1.2		0.5	
1940–50	9.7	2.8		6.6		7.5	
1950–60	6.5	4.1	2.7	2.3	3.6	2.1	3.5
1960–70	5.4	3.7	4.4	1.7	0.9	2.2	1.5
1970–80	5.6	3.2	4.0	2.3	1.5	0.3	−0.4
1980–90	0.0	2.9	3.3	−2.8	−3.2	−2.6	−3.0
1990–99	0.9	2.1	3.8	−1.2	−2.7	−0.4	−2.0

Source: Baptista 2002.

The fact that a 20-year-long growth collapse was preceded by a 60-year growth miracle implies that factors that are constant throughout the 80-year period will not be able to account for both subperiods. For example, the supposed deleterious growth effects of natural resources or the origin of the legal code could not simultaneously explain miracle and collapse. Notice also in table 9.1 the onset of the demographic transition in the decade of the 1940s. The growth collapse coincides with a period of declining dependency ratios, which usually makes growth easier.

Nor can the decline in output per worker be explained by inadequate accumulation of human capital. On the contrary, Venezuela exhibited very rapid improvements in social indicators. For example, between 1960 and 1990 life expectancy increased from 55 years to 71 years. Years of schooling of the female population over 25 jumped from two in 1950 to five in 1985 (fig. 9.2). Thus,

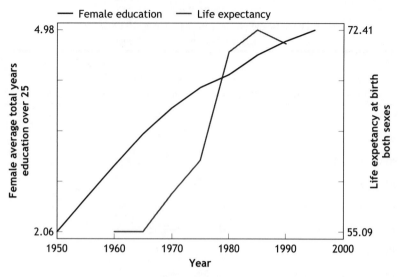

Figure 9.2. Venezuelan progress in health and education: Life expectancy and average years of schooling of females over 25
Source: World Bank

current Venezuelan workers have a similar output per capita as the workers of 1950, in spite of the fact that they are now endowed with much more human capital. How is it that after 50 years of technological progress at the global level, a more educated, healthier, and more urban labor force can only produce as much output per worker as in 1950?

While measures of human capital per worker have been trending up, physical capital per worker has been declining (see fig. 9.3). Panel 3a shows four distinct periods: a rapid process of capital deepening in the 1950s, followed by a deceleration in the 1960s, a rapid acceleration during the oil boom of the 1970s and a decline in the last 20 years. Notice that while output per worker is back to levels circa 1950, capital per worker is not.

Panel 4b plots the scattergram of output per worker versus capital per worker. The graph is interesting in that it essentially shows a break in the quite linear relationship between the two variables. The period prior to 1978 exhibits a much higher production per worker per unit of capital per worker. This starts telling us a story. Capital deepening has been reversed. However, the reversal has been accompanied by a reduction in total factor productivity. To gauge how big the effect could be, we conduct the analysis in two forms. First, we ran a regression between output and capital per worker in the nonoil economy, including a trend and a dummy for the period 1983–99. To see how sensitive the

a.

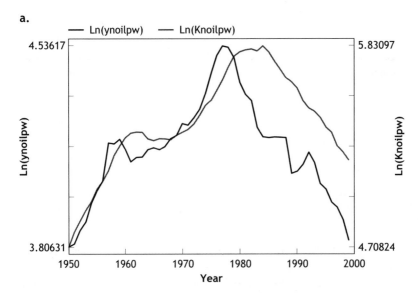

b.

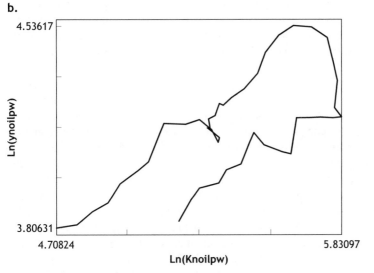

Figure 9.3 (a and b). GDP and physical capital per worker 1950–99

break is to the dates chosen, we estimated the equation with and without taking into account the period between 1977 and 1982 inclusive. We find a very high elasticity of output to capital per worker. In fact, the point estimates, between 0.57 and 0.62, must be contrasted with the estimated share of capital income in the nonoil economy, which was about 0.3 in the 1950s and has been trending

TABLE 9.2
The Collapse in Output in the Nonoil Economy
Dependent Variable: GDP per Worker

Capital per worker	0.57	0.62
	(12.30)	(16.20)
Trend	0.02	0.03
	(1.40)	(2.90)
Dummy 1983–99	−0.28	−0.34
	(7.70)	(10.00)
Years	1950–99	excludes 1977–82

Note: t-statistics in parenthesis.

up to about 0.45. This is consistent with the hypothesis that productivity growth has been correlated with capital deepening.[4]

Table 9.2 also shows that, controlling for capital per worker, GDP per worker in the nonoil economy has been about 30 percent lower in the implosion period of 1983–99 compared to the 1950–77 expansion.[5] If we follow Pritchett (2000) in arguing that traditional estimates of capital based on cumulative depreciated investment (which is what our source, Baptista 1997, uses) is not a good measure, because capital can become obsolete or wasted, then the decline in output of 0.3 is equivalent to a disappearance of half of the capital stock. Using the estimated elasticity of output with respect to capital of 0.6, this figure is equivalent to a reduction in the previously existing capital stock of 40 percent.

Table 9.3 decomposes growth in the traditional fashion. The decline in growth of GDP per worker between 1950–80 and 1980–99 is 5 percent per annum. The decomposition attributes about 2.8 percent to the reversal in capital deepening and 2.2 percent to the decline in total factor productivity trends. Obviously, both factors can be caused by the same phenomenon. If something lowers the overall productivity of the economy, then capital per worker and the Solow residual would be affected. Starting from a long-run steady state, lower returns would prompt a reduction in the desired stock of capital. If technology is embodied in machines, this would lead to a decline in the rate of productivity growth.

It is important to point out that this decomposition does not take account of the rising level of human capital during this time period. Including this factor would lead to even bigger decline in total factor productivity growth.

---

[4] If productivity and capital deepening are correlated, the estimated term of the contribution of capital to growth will be overestimated and the estimated productivity trend will be underestimated.
[5] We estimate the equation with and without including the 1977–82 transition between miracle and implosion.

TABLE 9.3

Venezuela: Growth Decomposition, 1950–99

	GDP per Worker	Capital per Worker	Capital Share 1	Capital Share 2	Capital Contribution 1	Capital Contribution 2	TFP 1	TFP 2
1950–60	3.6%	6.3%	0.330	0.400	2.1%	2.5%	1.5%	1.1%
1960–70	0.9%	0.3%	0.343	0.400	0.1%	0.1%	0.8%	0.8%
1970–80	1.5%	4.6%	0.385	0.400	1.8%	1.8%	−0.3%	−0.3%
1980–90	−3.2%	−2.0%	0.462	0.400	−0.9%	−0.8%	−2.3%	−2.4%
1990–99	−2.7%	−4.4%	0.480	0.400	−2.1%	−1.7%	−0.6%	−1.0%
1950–80	2.0%	3.7%	0.353	0.400	1.3%	1.5%	0.7%	0.5%
1980–99	−3.0%	−3.1%	0.471	0.400	−1.5%	−1.3%	−1.5%	−1.7%

Note: Capital shares were calculated from actual national accounts using Banco Central de Venezuela (1990). However, there are three distinct base years for these accounts (1957, 1968, and 1984). In each successive system, the capital share rises discontinuously with the change in the base year. I use both a period specific share and a common share for all periods.

OIL REVENUES AND NONOIL GROWTH

We now turn to the relationship between growth and oil revenues. We again focus on the nonoil economy as our measure of growth in order to clarify the issues. We take as the relevant measure of the oil sector the value of its exports in terms of importables. Hence, we are indifferent between changes in the value of exports caused by movements in volumes or in the relative price of oil. Figure 9.4a shows these values in per capita terms. Figure 9.4b shows the GDP per worker in the nonoil economy and real oil exports per worker in the economy as a whole. Table 9.4 shows summary statistics of related information.

The broader picture is one of great comovement between oil revenues and the nonoil economy. Oil revenues have gone through several distinct phases. There was a huge boom in production in the 1920s, when Venezuela started production and by 1929 became the largest oil exporter in the world. Then came the Great Depression with declining prices and low volume growth. In 1942 Venezuela reformed and extended its oil concessions, leading to a new boom in production and prices that lasted until the boom of 1956–57 associated with the Suez Canal war. In 1958 three important things happened: prices declined, a democratic movement took over political power, and oil policy became less encouraging of foreign investment. Oil revenues dropped and kept a declining trend until 1970. Revenues started to increase in the early 1970s and boomed during the first (1973–74) and second (1979–80) oil shocks. After 1982 revenues declined.

GDP per capita in the nonoil economy broadly follows these trends. There was a dramatic boom in the 1920s, stagnation in the 1930s, and another boom

a.

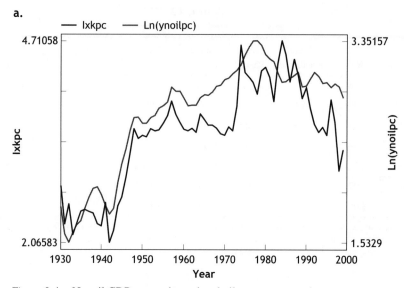

Figure 9.4a. Nonoil GDP per capita and real oil exports per capita

b.

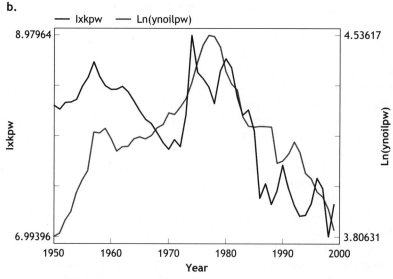

Figure 9.4b. Nonoil GDP per worker and real oil exports per worker

in the 1942–57 period, followed by a period of slower growth in the 1960s. Growth accelerated in the 1970s and collapsed in the 1980s. Two important points are in order. In the 1960s, the economy kept on growing in spite of the decline in oil revenues. Second, growth collapsed around 1978 before the second oil shock. Oil revenues only collapsed after 1982. These two periods make

TABLE 9.4
Nonoil GDP Growth and Real Oil Exports

	Nonoil GDP per Capita		Real Oil Exports per Capita (US$ 1990 prices)			Capital per Worker in the Nonoil Sector	
	Mean Growth	SD	Mean Level	Mean Growth	SD	Mean Growth	SD
1920–80	3.9%	9.1%		17.6%	43.5%		
1920–50	5.7%	11.6%		26.4%	52.4%		
1950–80	2.1%	4.9%	1,263	9.8%	29.9%	3.7%	3.1%
1950–70	2.0%	4.9%	1,172	3.8%	8.1%	3.3%	3.5%
1970–80	2.3%	5.1%	1,387	22.7%	46.8%	4.6%	2.0%
1980–99	−2.02%	5.5%	792	−0.4%	24.2%	−3.1%	2.8%
1920–30	9.5%	11.5%		71.0%	61.1%		
1930–40	1.2%	10.2%		−0.6%	28.1%		
1940–50	6.6%	12.5%		22.4%	29.7%		
1950–60	2.3%	5.8%	1,331	6.6%	10.3%	6.3%	1.5%
1960–70	1.7%	4.4%	1,019	1.1%	3.0%	0.3%	2.2%
1970–80	2.3%	5.1%	1,387	22.7%	46.8%	4.6%	2.0%
1980–90	−2.8%	5.6%	1,000	−2.6%	25.5%	−2.0%	2.9%
1990–99	−1.2%	5.3%	555	2.1%	25.1%	−4.4%	1.7%
1920–29	11.1%	11.0%		82.4%	57.2%		
1929–42	−0.8%	10.0%		−0.5%	31.9%		
1942–57	7.9%	9.2%		21.0%	23.4%		
1950–57	4.7%	5.6%	1,330	12.4%	7.0%	6.3%	1.3%
1957–70	0.5%	5.4%	1,075	−0.5%	8.0%	1.7%	3.3%
1970–78	4.5%	2.8%	1,290	17.6%	50.9%	4.6%	2.0%
1978–99	−2.4%	5.3%	855	3.2%	25.9%	−2.4%	3.9%
1978–82			1,604				
1983–99			634				

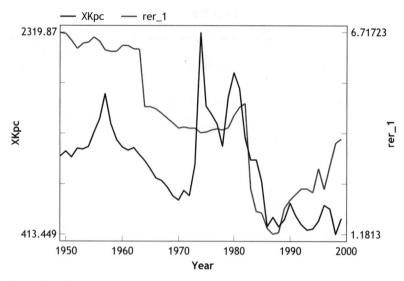

Figure 9.5. Real exchange rate and real oil exports per capita

the relationship between oil revenues and overall growth less sharp. The experience of the 1960s is associated with a real depreciation and the adoption of import substitution policies, while the second can be related to the overexpansion of the economy in the 1974–78 period. The broad characteristics of the periods and economic policies are described in appendix table 9.A1.

The real exchange rate (fig. 9.5) exhibited a remarkable stability until 1983. The nominal exchange rate was devalued in 1960, in response to the balance of payments crisis that followed the fall in oil exports of 1958. The devaluation translated into a permanent movement of the real exchange rate, which in fact kept on depreciating until the mid-1970s. Notice that the oil booms of the 1970s lead to remarkably little real appreciation. The period after the collapse of oil revenues in 1983 is characterized by dramatic shifts in relative prices.[6] Between 1982 and 1989 there was a massive real depreciation. In the 1990s the overall pattern exhibits the opposite trend, in spite of the fact that oil revenues did not recover much. This is a fact that needs explaining.

It is important to note that it was the private sector, not the public sector, that drove the dynamics of investment and disinvestment in Venezuela. As figure 9.6 shows, fluctuations in private investment per worker dwarfed movements in public investment. Hence, the evolution of investment is not a fiscal story with investment being simply influenced by changes in government revenue. It is a

[6] During 1983–88 and 1994–96 there were multiple exchange rate. Figure 5 shows the real exchange rate calculated at the parallel rate.

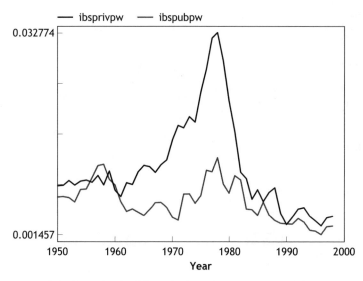

Figure 9.6. Gross fixed public and private investment per worker

private reaction to changing market signals. Interestingly, if we look only at the private, nonoil sector, figures 9.7a and 9.7b tell exactly the same story as figures 9.3a and 9.3b. The collapse of output and investment and the apparent fall in productivity, or alternatively the destruction in the stock of capital, is mainly a private sector phenomenon. So arguments about the wastefulness of public investment, although possibly true, are not central to the story.

Finally, it is important to point out that in spite of the speed of the collapse in investment after 1978, capital per worker kept rising until 1983.

THE SIMPLEST POSSIBLE MODEL

Much of the literature on resource-rich countries focuses on the Dutch disease effect.[7] The idea is that a boom in the resource-based tradable sector, such as oil, will cause a real appreciation and a fall in output in the non-resource-based tradable sector such as agriculture or manufacturing. Hence, oil booms should be bad for nonoil tradable growth. If these are more capable of sustaining endogenous growth, then oil booms should be bad for growth. By contrast, oil busts should be good. This obviously is the opposite of the Venezuelan experience. To generate a model that has a fighting chance of illuminating the issues,

---

[7] See for example Corden 1984; Corden and Neary 1982; Gelb 1988.

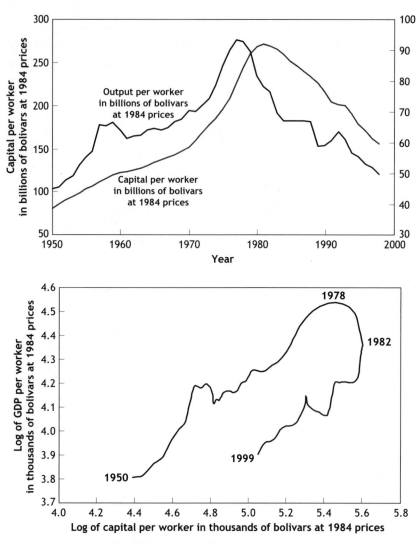

Figure 9.7 (a and b). Private capital and output per worker in the nonoil economy

it is better to focus on a model where nonoil production is essentially nontradable. It boils down to assuming that there is no nonoil tradable sector in the economy. This can be interpreted as there being such a large oil-induced Dutch disease that no other tradable sector survives.[8]

---

[8] It is important to point out that nonoil exports of Venezuela amount to about 4 percent of GDP and are dominated by capital-intensive, resource-intensive industries such as steel, aluminum, and

For this reason, we assume an economy that has only two sectors. The first sector, z, is constituted by oil, which is manna from heaven. The rest of the economy produces nontradables x with capital and labor. Capital is composed purely of tradables. Since we are concerned about long-run equilibria, we assume that capital adjusts to equalize international returns. Labor is constant and we normalize it to 1.

$$x = Ak^\alpha. \tag{1}$$

Households have a Cobb-Douglas utility function over tradables (which are imported) and nontradables.

$$U = C_T^{1-\beta} C_N^\beta. \tag{2}$$

National income in units of tradables is given by

$$y = z + w + r^* \bar{k}, \tag{3}$$

where we assume that the only endogenous variable is w. $\bar{k}$ is the stock of capital owned by residents, which may be indistinctly held at home or abroad. It does not equal the capital invested in the nontradable sector.

Profit maximization implies that

$$k = \left(\frac{\alpha A q}{r^*}\right)^{\frac{1}{1-\alpha}}$$

$$x = A^{\frac{1}{1-\alpha}} \left(\frac{\alpha q}{r^*}\right)^{\frac{\alpha}{1-\alpha}}$$

$$w = (1 - \alpha) q x.$$

Demand for nontradables is given by

$$C_N = \frac{\beta y}{q} = \frac{\beta(z + w + r^* \bar{k})}{q} = \frac{\beta(z + r^* \bar{k} + (1 - \alpha)qx)}{q}. \tag{4}$$

Equilibrium in the market for nontradables is determined by

$$x = \frac{\beta(z + r^* \bar{k} + (1 - \alpha)qx)}{q}$$

$$x = \frac{\beta(z + r^* \bar{k})}{\alpha q} = A^{\frac{1}{1-\alpha}} \left(\frac{\alpha q}{r^*}\right)^{\frac{\alpha}{1-\alpha}}.$$

petrochemicals. These sectors were developed during the oil boom as part of a diversification strategy. No significant new exports have emerged since the collapse of the real exchange rate in 1983.

Therefore, the whole system is described by the relative price of nontradables q:

$$q = \frac{r^{*\alpha}(\beta(z + r^*\bar{k}))^{1-\alpha}}{A\alpha} \tag{5}$$

$$x = \frac{A(\beta(z + r^*\bar{k}))^{\alpha}}{r^{*\alpha}}. \tag{6}$$

Under such a system, a collapse in real oil exports would lead to a decline in output in nontradables. To see how this works, assume that you start from an equilibrium position in which the return to capital in the nontraded sector is equal to the world interest rate. A decline in oil income leads to a fall in the demand for the nontraded good. This will cause a fall in the relative price q, which will imply that the return to capital in that sector falls below the international level, leading to a reduction in the stock of capital invested. If capital is initially fixed and can only be adjusted gradually, then there will be a period in which returns to capital are below world levels, and net private disinvestment will take place. Notice that the real exchange rate will overshoot its long-run level: at the beginning of the decline, the excess capital in the nontradable sector implies a high supply of goods and hence a low relative price. As the disinvestments process proceeds, supply contracts and the relative price recovers partially. This would explain the sharp real depreciation in the 1980s and the sharp appreciation in the 1990s.

EXPLAINING THE GROWTH IMPLOSION

Can the collapse in oil revenues explain the growth implosion? To give oil a maximum chance of explaining the fall, let us assume that there is no private sector capital wealth ($r^*k = 0$). Using equation (6) above, the decline in z will be reflected in a fall in x with an elasticity of α. As shown in table 9.4, oil exports per capita at 1990 prices declined from a peak of US$1,600 in the 1978–82 period to about US$600 in the 1983–99 period (see table 9.4). As table 9.5 shows, this decline in oil income underpredicts the fall in output that actually took place by some 30 percent. If instead, we make the more reasonable assumption that r^*k takes on a value in line with the capital share of nonoil income circa 1978, then the equation underpredicts the fall by about 67 percent.

These calculations indicate that the decline in the value of oil exports alone cannot explain the magnitude of the collapse in output. Note that the model we use, by not including a nonoil tradable sector that could expand in the context of a fall in oil income, gives oil the best possible chance to explain the growth performance.

Now, within the confines of this narrow model, can an explanation be found? One important variable is the interest rate r^*. A rise in the interest rate in the

TABLE 9.5
Can the Decline in Oil Income Alone Explain the Growth Collapse?

	Capital Owned by Residents	
	None	Large
Peak oil income	1600	1600
$r*k$	0	1600
Recent average oil income	600	600
Recent/peak	37.5%	68.8%
α	40.0%	40.0%
Predicted recent/max nonoil GDP per worker	67.5%	86.1%
Actual recent/peak	51.4%	51.4%
Underprediction	31.4%	67.5%

Note: The first column assumes no capital owned by residents, and the second column assumes a very large stock of capital owned by residents.

context of our simple model would cause the required rate of return in the nonoil economy to go up and hence the equilibrium stock of capital to decline. As equation (6) above shows, an increase in the interest rate can have a powerful impact on the long-run level of output. A doubling of the interest rate could explain a drop in output of 25 percent if α is 0.4. So a mix of a decline in the price of oil and a major increase in the interest rate could do it. But did such an increase actually take place?

In 1978, as mentioned above, Venezuela was rated AAA. By early 1983, in the context of the decline in oil prices, it defaulted on its foreign debt. It regained market access only after the Brady plan was renegotiated in August 1990. At present the country is rated B–. Table 9.6 shows recent spreads of the Emerging Markets Bond Index for the major Latin American countries. Venezuela is consistently one of the weakest credits among the major Latin American countries. The table shows data for July 1998, before the Russian crisis but at a time when the price of oil was very low and for January 2001, when the price of oil had recovered quite significantly. The table shows spreads for Venezuela on the order of 800 bp. This is equivalent to a real interest rate of the order of 11–12 percent. Hence a massive rise in the interest rates on foreign dollar-denominated borrowing did take place.

Is this the relevant rate to look at? When considering the cost of capital in Venezuela should we use the international riskless interest rate or should we correct for country risk? After all, is it not the case that a risk-neutral investor

TABLE 9.6
Recent Latin American Spreads and the Price of Oil

	July 31, 1998	January 31, 2001
Argentina	444	603
Brazil	565	673
Colombia	426	666
Mexico	401	366
Uruguay	189	275
Venezuela	794	808
Average	470	565
Oil ($/b)	11.05	26.5

expects only to get the riskless rate in expected terms and the spread only compensates him for the states of nature in which he would receive a smaller amount? This depends on whether the risks that are considered are endogenous or exogenous to the project in which the capital is invested. If the risk is endogenous, then on average the project need only pay the riskless rate in expected terms. However, if the risks are exogenous to the project, it is the contractual interest rate that matters. To see this, assume that a project is riskless and that the factors that impede payment are exogenous to the project, such as expropriation risk. In this case, only projects that can generate an excess return above the riskless rate would be undertaken. This requires a higher marginal product of capital and a lower capital stock. Hence, for the rise in the contractual interest rate to matter, we need to assume that the associated risks are mainly exogenous to projects.

Table 9.7 asks whether our simple model can account for the Venezuelan collapse using only the fall in oil revenues and the increase in the interest rate. The table shows that the predicted fall is broadly in line with the actual decline. Hence, within the context of our very simple model, we can account for the collapse in output, broadly speaking, by making reference to two variables: the decline in oil export revenues and the increase in the interest rate.

WHERE DID THE INTEREST RATE INCREASE COME FROM?

Does this mean that we have a neoclassical story of a growth collapse? Does the fact that we can account for Venezuela's growth collapse by making reference only to the fall in oil income and the interest rate mean that we can do

TABLE 9.7

Can the Decline in Oil Revenues and the Increase in Real Interest Rates
Explain the Collapse in Output?

| | Capital Owned by Residents | |
	None	Large
Peak oil income	1600	1600
$r*k$	0	1600
Recent average	600	600
Recent/peak	37.5%	68.8%
α	40.0%	40.0%
Real interest at peak	4.0%	4.0%
Recent real rates	12.0%	12.0%
Ratio peak/recent interest rates	33.3%	33.3%
Predicted recent GDP per worker (peak = 100%)	43.5%	55.5%
Actual recent/peak	51.4%	51.4%
Proportional difference	−15.3%	7.9%

away with political-economy considerations? The decline in oil revenues can be taken, to a very significant extent, as an exogenous factor determined mainly by the decline in international prices. However, the interest rate we have used includes country risk, a quite endogenous variable. Hence, the answer to the question depends on what interpretation is given to the increase in the interest rates.

We have already argued that in order to use this particular interest rate and not the riskless rate, we need to assume that risks are somehow exogenous to projects. This points us away from representative-agent (neoclassical) models, since it implies that problems arise in the aggregation, not in the individual projects themselves.

Moreover, in the neoclassical world defined in the simple model used in this chapter, a permanent decline in oil income would not lead to a change in the return to capital, given the assumption of perfect capital mobility. If instead we assume that capital is fixed in the short run, then a permanent fall in oil revenues would cause an immediate decline in the rate of return. If capital was contracted in the form of debt, such a fall could lead to returns below the contractual interest rate, causing defaults. This may well have taken place in Venezuela. However,

TABLE 9.8
Average Current Account Balance

	Average Current Account
1960–70	2.0%
1970–80	1.6%
1980–90	1.1%
1990–99	3.2%
1960–72	1.5%
1973–82	1.9%
1983–99	2.3%

this is only a transitional dynamic. Why would the interest rate remain high after 20 years?

The puzzle of the Venezuelan interest rate is even deeper. The country is a net creditor vis-à-vis the rest of the world. Table 9.8 shows the evolution of the current account in Venezuela. It indicates that the country accumulated surpluses during all periods, before and after the collapse in oil revenues. In fact, surpluses were even higher after oil income fell in 1983 than during the oil boom of the 1970s and early 1980s.[9] So a representative agent would not have any risk of defaulting, as she could use her international assets as collateral. In reality, the net assets are in private hands, while the public sector has a net foreign debt, suggesting that political-economy considerations are behind the higher interest rate.

Moreover, Venezuela's low credit rating and high spreads stand out in international comparisons, given the fact that it exhibits much stronger financial ratios than other emerging markets with better credit ratings. Table 9.9 shows the debt-to-export ratios of selected Latin American countries for 2000. In the case of Venezuela, the ratio was also calculated for 1998, the year with the lowest oil prices since 1986. The picture is quite clear. Venezuela's debt-to-export ratio is lower than that of investment-grade countries such as Chile, Uruguay, and Colombia.[10] It is a fraction of that of Brazil and Argentina, two countries that exhibit spreads smaller than Venezuela's, as shown in table 9.6. In fact, Venezuela's spread has remained high even after the dramatic recovery in the

---

[9] This is consistent with our model, as it indicates that after the fall, the demand for capital in the country declines, leading to disinvestment.

[10] The ratio for Mexico is distorted by the importance of low-value-added *maquila* exports in the denominator.

TABLE 9.9
Total External Debt to Exports of Goods,
Services, and External Income, 2000

Country	Debt-to-Export Ratio
Mexico	85.163
Venezuela	88.732
Chile	168.232
Panama	169.138
Colombia	224.229
Ecuador	231.372
Uruguay	315.038
Brazil	324.602
Peru	340.425
Bolivia	354.381
Argentina	384.321

Source: International Institute of Finance.

price of oil in 2000. Venezuela's structural current account surplus, its net creditor position, its high level of international reserves, and its low debt ratio suggest that its low credit rating and high country risk are not determined by ability-to-pay factors, but reflect instead willingness-to-pay problems. This argues in favor of a distributive conflict surrounding the allocation of the decline in oil revenues.

One indication of distributive conflicts is the very high real exchange rate volatility exhibited after the collapse in the fixed exchange rate regime in 1983. This balance of payments crisis was followed by the adoption of at least four different regimes and the occurrence of six currency crises. As table 9.10 shows, this increase in real exchange rate volatility cannot be associated with a rise in the volatility of changes in real oil revenue. In fact, the volatility of per capita real oil exports remained relatively stable after 1950 and if anything declined somewhat after 1983. The volatility of the real exchange rate shot up by a factor of five in the period after 1983 compared to the 33 prior years. So the increased real exchange rate volatility cannot be accounted for by the greater importance of real shocks. Instead, it points to the inability to settle distributive conflicts.

Movements in the real exchange rate have complicated distributive implications. On the one hand, the real exchange rate is the relative price at which the

TABLE 9.10
Volatility of the Annual Rate of Change of Oil Revenues
and the Real Exchange Rate

	Real Exchange Rate	Real Exports
1950–82	6.3%	25.6%
1950–82[a]	2.5%	25.6%
1964–82	2.9%	34.0%
1983–99	30.1%	23.6%
1983–89	41.1%	22.9%
1990–99	13.6%	24.1%

[a] Excludes the nominal depreciation of 1963.

public sector exchanges its oil surplus for nontraded goods: it is the relative price of teachers in terms of oil dollars. On the other hand, it changes the relative price of foreign assets and liabilities in terms of nontraded goods. In addition, unanticipated changes in the nominal exchange rate affect the value of nominal assets and liabilities. This nominal dimension has been an important aspect of the problem, as the post-1983 period has been characterized by highly negative average interest rates, which have eroded the real value of monetary assets, as shown in figure 9.8. Since uncovered interest parity implies that ex ante real interest rates cannot be negative, this indicates the important role of exchange rate and inflationary surprises in the post-1983 period.

Thus, all these factors point to a political-economy interpretation of the rise in the cost of capital. The data is consistent with the perception of higher risks, exogenous to individual projects and associated with more macro factors. The higher international interest rate cannot be accounted for through measures of external solvency and credit fundamentals, given that the country is a net creditor and that the gross debt is small relative to better-rated comparators. Real exchange rates have been unusually volatile, although real oil income volatility has not increased. Real interest rates have been on average highly negative, consistent with the idea that inflation and exchange rate surprises have been very important.

CONCLUDING REMARKS

Venezuela suffered a major growth collapse over the last two decades after six decades of remarkable growth. This collapse implies that today's nonoil sector workers have levels of productivity similar to those of 1950 in spite of major

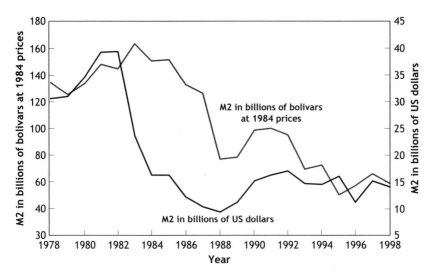

Figure 9.8. The collapse in nominal assets. M2 in constant U.S.$ and in constant local currency prices

improvements in their human capital endowment and in the technologies available in the world. We explain this collapse as caused by two principal factors: the decline in oil revenues and the rise in the relevant interest rate.

First, the decline in oil revenues lowered the demand for the nontraded outputs of the economy. In a neoclassical framework with perfect capital mobility, this is also consistent with a decline in the capital per worker and the output per worker in that sector. However, quantitatively, this effect can only account for about half the decline in output per worker. Second, a major rise in the external interest rate would explain further declines in capital and output per worker, as projects would need higher marginal returns on capital.

It is hard to make the rise in interest rates consistent with a representative agent, neoclassical story. The country is a net foreign creditor, so it should be able to pay all its external debts in the aggregate. In addition, indicators of ability to pay are superior to better-rated neighboring countries that pay smaller spreads. This points to willingness-to-pay problems that call into question the protection of property rights. In addition, the country exhibits a very volatile real exchange rate, which cannot be explained by an increase in the importance of real shocks, and has experienced strongly negative real interest rates, which have eroded the value of nominal assets.

All this points to the notion that distributive conflicts are part of the story of the growth collapse. However, we suggest that the mechanism through which this conflict affects growth is its impact on the cost of capital, leading to declines in output and capital per worker. In the Venezuelan case, accommodating this increase has gone along with larger current account surpluses in spite of the decline in oil revenues.

Rodrik (1998) explains growth collapses as determined by the magnitude of the external shock and the quality of the conflict management institutions. This chapter suggests that the intermediate variable through which the political economy effects may take place is the external interest rate, even if the country is not dependent on attracting foreign capital. This rate will affect the required marginal product of capital, determining declines in output and capital per worker over and above those caused by the loss of external income.

REFERENCES

Alesina, Alberto, and Allan Drazen. 1991. "Why Are Stabilizations Delayed?" *American Economic Review* 81, no. 5: 1170–88.

Banco Central de Venezuela. 1990. *Series Estadísticas de Venezuela de los últimos cincuenta años.* Caracas: Ediciones Banco Central de Venezuela.

Baptista, Asdrubal. 1997. *Bases cuantitativas de la economia venezolana, 1830–1995.* Caracas: Fundacion Polar.

———. 2002. "Un buen número = una buena palabra." In *Venezuela siglo XX: Visiones y testimonios,* ed. Asdrúbal Baptista. Caracas: Fundación Polar.

Corden, Max. 1984. "Booming Sector and Dutch Disease Economics: Survey and Consolidation." *Oxford Economic Papers* 36:359–80.

Corden, Max, and Peter Neary. 1982. "Booming Sector and Deindustrialization in a Small Open Economy." *Economic Journal* 92:825–48.

Gelb, A. 1988. *Oil Windfalls: Blessing or Curse?* Oxford: Oxford University Press.

Karl, Terry Lynn. 1997. *The Paradox of Plenty: Oil Booms and Petro-States.* Berkeley and Los Angeles: University of California Press.

Maddison, Angus. 1995. *Explaining the Economic Performance of Nations: Essays in Time and Space.* Aldershot, England: Edward Elgar.

Matsuyama, Kiminori. 1992. "A Simple Model of Sectoral Adjustment." *Review of Economic Studies* 59, no. 2: 375–87.

Naím, Moises, and Ramon Pinango. 1984. *El caso Venezuela: Una ilusion de armonia.* Caracas: Ediciones IESA.

Pritchett, Lant. 2000. "The Tyranny of Concepts. CUDIE (Cumulated, Depreciated Investment Effort) Is Not Capital." World Bank Working Paper No. 2341.

Robinson, Enders A. 1992. *Salem Witchcraft and Hawthorne's "House of the Seven Gables."* Bowie, Md.: Heritage Books.

Rodríguez, Francisco, and Jeffrey D. Sachs. 1999. "Natural Resources and Economic Growth: A Quantitative Exploration." Harvard Institute for International Development.

Rodrik, Dani. 1998. "Why Do More Open Economies Have Bigger Governments?" *Journal of Political Economy* 106, no. 5: 997–1032.

Sachs, Jeffrey D., and Andrew Warner. 1995. "Economic Reform and the Process of Global Integration." *Brookings Papers on Economic Activity* 1995, no. 1: 1–95.

Tornell, Aaron, and Philip R. Lane. 1998. "Voracity and Growth." NBER Working Paper No. 6498.

TABLE 9.A1
A Short Overview of Policy Events

Period	External Situation	Policy Orientation	Principal Results
1964–73	Stagnant oil income	1. Fixed unified exchange rates 2. Fiscal discipline 3. Import-substitution industrialization	1. High but falling rate of growth (average 6.8%) 2. Very low inflation (1.7%) 3. External balance
1974–76	1. First oil shock 2. Higher world inflation	1. Expansionary fiscal policy 2. Emphasis on publicly owned basic industries 3. Nationalizations and restrictions on foreign investment	1. Acceleration in growth (9%) 2. Higher inflation but lower than world levels (9%) 3. Large and declining surpluses in fiscal and accounts Balance achieved in 1976.
1977–78	Declining oil income	1. Increase in public spending mainly in state enterprises 2. Some attempts to cut back spending and credit	1. Decline in growth (3. 5% in 1978) 2. Major external and fiscal deficits 3. Extensive supply bottlenecks: labor and installed capacity
1979–80	1. Second oil shock 2. Jump in world interest rates	1. Strong fiscal contraction (mainly in imports) 2. Price liberalization 3. Wage increase law 4. Some trade liberalization 5. Interest ceilings do not adjust fully for the rise in world rates	1. Growth falls to zero 2. Unemployment grows slowly 3. Inflation accelerates to record levels (21% in 1980) 4. Real exchange rate appreciates strongly 5. External and fiscal balance achieved 6. Capital outflows begin
1981–82	Oil income very high, starts to fall	1. Fiscal expansion in public works 2. Interest rates are freed but monetary policy is expansionary 3. Large deficits in public enterprise sector financed through foreign borrowing	1. Mediocre growth (1%) 2. High but falling inflation (16%) 3. Large current account deficit and massive capital outflow (US$8 bn. in 1982)
1983	1. Fall in oil income 2. Start of debt crisis	1. Adoption of a multiple exchange rate regime, average devaluation 30% 2. Import controls 3. Contractionary fiscal policy 4. Monetary policy expansionary 5. Generalized price controls are adopted	1. GDP falls 5% 2. Inflation kept at 7%. 3. Large balance of payments surplus (US$4 bn.) 4. Still important fiscal deficit 5. Large expansion in money supply 6. Floating rate depreciates over 200%

(continued)

TABLE 9.A1 *(Continued)*

Period	External Situation	Policy Orientation	Principal Results
1984–85	Oil income stable at lower level (US$13bn.)	1. Devaluation of official rate 2. Maintenance of import controls 3. Fiscal cuts 4. Interest rate controls adopted 5. Price controls are relaxed 6. Debt strategy: simple rescheduling	1. After an additional contraction in 1984 (−2%), economy starts to grow in 1985 (3.5%); unemployment reaches peak 2. Inflation increases to moderate levels (15%) 3. Large fiscal and balance of payments surpluses
1986–88	1. Oil income collapses (US$8 bn.) 2. No adjustment	1. Fiscal expansion adopted 2. Forced financing of imports 3. Major devaluation when situation becomes untenable 4. No change in interest rate ceilings	1. Economy grows at 5% average; unemployment falls back to 7% 2. Major balance of payments and fiscal deficit 3. Acceleration of inflation to over 3% 4. Floating rate depreciates by almost 200% over the period
1989–93	The day of reckoning	1. Exchange rate system unified in a floating arrangement 2. Interest rates and prices freed 3. Trade and foreign investment liberalized 4. Subsidies cut, public sector prices increased	1. GDP drops by almost 10% in 1989 and recovers quickly 2. Inflation exceeds 80% and falls back to 30% 3. Exchange rate unified close to parallel rate and then crawls 4. Rapid initial current account adjustment followed by capital inflows 5. Bank credit boom 6. Political turmoil: two military coup attempts in 1992 and a presidential impeachment in 1993
1994–96	Unstable and low income	1. Banking crisis 2. Readoption of multiple exchange regimes 3. Structural reform stopped	1. Severe economic contraction 2. Inflation accelerates 3. Current account surplus and capital flight resumes
1996–98	Oil prices collapse again	1. Exchange rate unified in a massive real depreciation 2. Economic liberalization resumes 3. Opening of oil industry to private investment	1. Initial enthusiasm followed by a contraction when oil collapsed 2. Inflation jumps to over 100 percent and starts to decline 3. Massive real depreciation followed by rapid appreciation

CHAPTER 10

History, Policy, and Performance in Two Transition Economies

POLAND AND ROMANIA

GEORGES DE MENIL

THE GROWTH of the formerly Communist countries of Europe since 1990 is a study in contrasts: A small group of countries—notably Poland, Hungary, and the two parts of Czechoslovakia—recovered early from an initial drop of output (common to all the countries in the region) and achieved sustainable and consistently high rates of growth (4–8 percent) with moderate inflation. In others—in the former Soviet Union, or in southeastern Europe—output continued to fall until the end of the century, or recovered and then fell again. Some of these low-performance countries suffered bouts of high inflation. But the most damning aspect of their experience was the stagnation of output.

To what degree are these differences due to differences in the policies pursued, and to what degree are they due to differences in initial conditions? There exists a substantial literature of cross-sectional statistical studies that seeks to answer this question.[1] Many of the studies analyze panels consisting of annual observations on growth and its determinants in each of the transition countries.

Though the specifics vary, the studies all come, by and large, to similar conclusions:[2] The growth has been greater (or decline less) in countries that have stabilized early, and that have implemented deep structural reforms. There are

This chapter grew out of comments on a presentation by Philippe Aghion at the conference "Analytical Country Studies on Growth," organized by Dani Rodrik, at the Kennedy School of Government, April 20–21, 2001. The research assistance of Christian Ponce de Leon and Yosuke Tada and the excellent typing of Laura Medeiros are gratefully acknowledged. The author benefited from conversations with Daniel Daianu and Wojtek Maliszewski.

[1] None of these studies compares European transition experiences with Asian transition experiences. The consensus is that it is not meaningful to compare the transitions of these highly industrialized countries with weak Communist Party structures to that of a predominantly agricultural economy with a strong Party structure, like that of China. See Sachs and Woo 1994.

[2] See Aslund, Boone, and Johnson 1996; Berg et al. 1999; de Melo, Cevdet, and Gelb 1996; Hernandez-Cata 1997; Fischer, Sahay, and Vegh 1998; Havrylyshyn, Izvorski, and van Rooden 1998; Falcetti, Raiser, and Sanfey 2000; Wyplosz 1999; and World Bank 1996.

very few countries with high inflation in which output has increased. Among the structural reforms, internal price liberalization and external trade liberalization are the most highly correlated with growth. Small and medium-scale enterprise (SME) privatization contributed significantly to growth. But large-scale privatization per se has not been as important as the introduction of hard budget constraints. The development of the legal and institutional infrastructure for markets has also contributed importantly to growth. There are only a few countries (Belarus and Uzbekistan)[3] that have experienced growth without liberalization and stabilization. No country that has implemented deep structural reforms and maintained budgetary discipline has not grown.

However, the authors of several of these studies also conclude that it is difficult to distinguish between these policy effects and the effects of geography and history. Equations that relate growth results exclusively to variables such as the number of years under Communism, or the distance from the capital to Düsseldorf, provide explanations that are almost statistically indistinguishable from equations that relate growth to liberalization indices and the reduction of inflation. The countries that stabilized and implemented deep structural reforms are also the countries that are furthest west and had a relatively shorter experience with Communism. None of the countries that had been in the Soviet Union since the 1930s both rapidly liberalized and quickly enforced hard budget constraints.[4]

The evidence is clearly that policy mattered. What is less clear is why some countries enacted reform policies and others did not. Initial conditions, context, and history seem to have been important. The promarket, reform agenda received more support in countries that were closer to the West, and in which there were people active in 1990 with personal memory of the economy and polity that preceded Communism.

This chapter will use a case study approach and examine how economic policies were formed in two countries in the region, Poland and Romania. Getting into the narrative will allow one to focus on the influence of specific institutional factors. It will make it possible to understand better the interplay between history, geography, and policy. Poland and Romania are natural choices for a comparison. In some ways, they have many things in common. They are the largest of the European transition countries outside of the former Soviet Union,

---

[3] Belarus presents the surprising anomaly of a nonreformed country with extensive controls, which has nonetheless had high rates of growth. One possible explanation is its proximity to and special relationship with Russia. What makes Uzbekistan a special case may be its low degree of industrialization, energy sufficiency and specialization in cotton. See Fischer and Sahay 2000, sec. 4A.

[4] Falcetti, Raiser, and Sanfey (2000) use instrumental variables to estimate the contribution to growth of reform efforts in excess of those that were predictable on the basis of geography and history alone. They conclude that the correlation between more-than-predictable reform and growth is only marginal.

which both of them border. Both were heavily overindustrialized in 1989. In both countries, agriculture also provided a large share of employment. But the policies they followed after 1990 were radically different. There is no greater difference to be found between the transition policies of two former European satellite countries than that which exists between Poland and Romania.[5] Valerie Bunce (1995, 1998) has argued that these two countries epitomize the extremes of peacetime policy response to transition in Communist Europe west of the Soviet Union. Her interpretation of those differences is similar to the one that is proposed in this chapter.

In what follows, first for Poland, then for Romania, I will summarize the strategy pursued, discuss its consequences, and ask how the recent history of each country contributed to the choices that were made.

But first, I will review a common factor that affected both Poland and Romania, and their immediate neighbors in important ways: the engagement of the European Union, and its eventual decision to invite most of them to become candidates for accession. This will lead me to touch upon issues of intellectual and political climate, similar to those to which I shall return in the discussion of Poland and Romania.

THE ENGAGEMENT OF THE EUROPEAN UNION

For the transition countries furthest to the West, Europe was, from the beginning, the objective. Sachs (1993) describes the way in which the vision of "returning to Europe" mobilized the political and popular forces in Poland. It corresponded at one and the same time to a deep national aspiration, and offered a ready-made answer to otherwise complex questions about the ideal vision of society and the economy.[6]

The European Union, conscious of the significance of developments so close to its borders, soon engaged several of the transition countries in formal negotiations aimed at producing trade and cooperation agreements. The first wave of these "Europe Agreements" was signed in December 1991, with Czechoslovakia, Hungary, and Poland. Subsequently, similar agreements were also reached

---

[5] One can find greater policy differences if one compares longtime members of the former Soviet Union (such as Ukraine or Tajikistan) with former satellite countries (such as Poland, Hungary, or Czechoslovakia). But the longtime members of the Soviet are in a class apart. The historical, institutional, and intellectual legacy of 60 to 70 years of Communism raises complex questions that are best treated separately.

[6] In a country like Ukraine, which had never been a part of Europe in the same way, political leaders lacked a clear vision of where they wanted to go (see Aslund and de Menil 2000). The resulting confusion contributed to the slow pace of reform there, and in those of the other new independent states that had long been members of the Soviet Union.

with Bulgaria, Estonia, Latvia, Lithuania, Romania, and Slovenia. These agreements provided for progressive trade liberalization, leading eventually to the near elimination, not only of quotas, but also of customs duties. ("Sensitive" areas, including agriculture, were exempted.)

Six years later, in its Agenda 2000, the European Commission recommended that negotiations for full accession begin with a subset of the above countries—namely the Czech Republic, Estonia, Hungary, Poland, and Slovenia. Romania, Bulgaria, Latvia, Lithuania, and Slovakia were added to the list of eastern European countries formally invited to negotiate accession, at the Helsinki Summit, December 1999.

The obligation, as potential EU members, to eventually adopt the *acquis communautaire* provides each of these countries with a full and exhaustive agenda of legal, institutional, and economic reforms. The multiyear process of negotiating accession has become for each of them a forceful framework and road map for their national reform strategies. The necessary consistency and comprehensive nature of the measures to be taken have strengthened the reform process.

In addition, the fact that reform has come to be embedded in the accession process has given it a weight and credibility that it could only with great difficulty have had on its own. The enhanced credibility has been important both internally and externally. Internally, it has placed the most important aspects of the reform program in a consensual space, protected from the intensity of political conflict and rivalry. This has strengthened the hand of the partisans of reform. Their efforts have been enhanced by the sense that their objective has a high probability of succeeding. Externally, the prospect of accession has also acted as a signal to foreign investors of a country's commitment to reform. This has encouraged foreign capital inflow, and particularly foreign direct investment.[7]

The enlargement of NATO has been an additional, important integrating factor, which has benefited a select number of the eastern European countries. Though logically independent, NATO and EU enlargement have nonetheless influenced one another in indirect ways. NATO invited the Czech Republic, Hungary, and Poland to join the alliance at its Madrid summit, in July 1997, shortly before the European Commission released its Agenda 2000. The three officially entered the alliance in March 1999. Their membership in NATO has been an important and visible manifestation of the political commitment of the Atlantic powers to their future. It has strengthened support for continuing reform in all three countries.

---

[7] Obviously, the countries that are not likely to join the European Union have not enjoyed the advantages of the accession dynamic that the candidate countries have. Prior to 2000, that group consisted of the new independent states (all of the Soviet Union except the Baltics), what remained of the Federal Republic of Yugoslavia, and perhaps Bosnia-Herzegovina. It is a collection of countries that also corresponds to those that have been the most laggard in reform.

In summary, the promise of integration in Euro-Atlantic structures has been an important source of support for the forces of reform in the former Soviet satellite countries of Europe. The support of the European Union has not been dramatically different from country to country; the second wave of invitations to enter into accession negotiations followed on the first by only two years. Membership in NATO has been more discriminatory: Poland, Hungary, and the Czech Republic were invited in 1997. Romania and others are waiting. However, there are many other, more important differences between Poland and Romania. To these, we now shall turn.

POLAND

Poland has been by far the most successful of the European transition countries.[8] This despite the fact that the last year of the Communist regime, 1989, was one of grave macroeconomic disorders; Poland ended the year in hyperinflation, with very substantial external debt.[9] In the course of the first two years, the new government, supported by the Solidarity movement, stopped hyperinflation, negotiated substantial debt reduction, and put into effect policies that, over time, led to a profound restructuring of the economy. From the end of the transition recession in 1992 through 2000, GDP per employed person grew at an average rate of 5.5 percent per year. By 1998, GDP per employed person was 20 percent above its preform, 1989 level. In 1998, Poland, with a population of less than 40 million people, had a GDP that, at market exchange rates, was nearly half that of the Russian Federation. Inflation has also progressively declined and was less than 10 percent per year in each of the three last years of the 1990s (fig. 10.1).

Poland's success is, in some sense, all the more remarkable in that it has neither precluded nor been blocked by a number of important, persistent economic problems. The unemployment rate in Poland is one of the highest in the region. Restructuring in certain key sectors, and privatization in general, has been slow. Poland continues to be marked by a large, traditional, and inefficient agricultural sector.[10] The Polish success story is not a storybook tale of perfection.

What, then, has made the difference?

The central and most important feature of Poland's recovery is that it is a supply side story. The fact that unemployment has risen during the Polish expansion suggests strongly that it has not been demand driven. Technical studies of

---

[8] This section draws on OECD 1992, 1994, 1997, 2000, 2001; and IMF 2000, 2001b.

[9] The debt, $45 billion, was 46 percent of GDP at purchasing power parity exchange rates, and 74 percent of GDP at current exchange rates. (See World Bank 2000.)

[10] See OECD 2001 for a discussion of each of these problem areas.

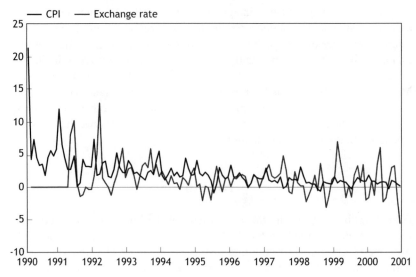

Figure 10.1. Poland: CPI and USD exchange rate, monthly rates of change

the relationship between actual and potential output, and of the determinants of the growth of potential output, support this evaluation (De Broeckand Koen 2000 and OECD 2001, annex 1). Growth in Poland has also been the antithesis of what growth was, when it was not illusory, in Soviet times. It has not been the result either of massive transfers from agriculture to industry, or of capital deepening. Productivity improvement has been the principal, and almost exclusive, source of growth during Poland's recovery. Of the 5.8 percent average annual rate of growth of potential output, from 1994 to 1999, the OECD estimates that 4.4 percent has been due to the growth of total factor productivity. Employment has remained stagnant, and investment, though important, is deemed essentially to have replaced obsolete capital, thus not to have been very capital deepening, and not to have contributed to an important degree to the expansion of capacity (OECD 2001, 130).

What lies behind this growth of total factor productivity? The rising rate of unemployment partly tells the story. Enterprises in all of the principal nonagricultural sectors—with the exception of mining and transportation—have been reorganized. Polish enterprises across the board have adopted Western principles of management and standards of efficiency. The first step in their transformation has entailed shedding substantial amounts of labor. A substantial portion of the labor released from old enterprises has found employment in new enterprises in the private sector (see table 10.2).

What triggered this large-scale reorganization and reallocation of labor?

In principle, the productivity gains could have been a spillover effect of foreign direct investment. At the end of the decade, FDI did become an important potential motor of further productivity improvement. However, in the first years of the transition, the gains materialized before the investment came.[11]

It is a well-established feature of growth in Poland that a majority of the productivity gains on which it has been based occurred in state-owned enterprises (Pinto, Belka, and Krajewski 1993; Belka et al. 1994). Formal privatization proceeded more slowly than it did in many other European transition countries. The enterprises where the largest cuts in employment were made were often still owned by the state at the time of their restructuring. What spurred the managers of these enterprises to take the restructuring decisions they did?

The answer appears to be that the managers were motivated by both a carrot and a stick. The carrot was a credible, early commitment to reasonably orderly privatization. What was important was the early realization that state-owned assets would not be given wholesale to insiders, but assigned to new owners through a process in which efficient managers could expect to benefit. The stick was a credible commitment neither to protect nor to continue subsidizing loss-making enterprises.

The stick was clearer than the carrot. In a variety of ways, the new Polish leadership opted at the very outset for openness to trade externally and hard budget constraints internally. Both commitments confronted state managers with the prospect of losing their enterprises if they did not adapt. Intense foreign competition from imports meant that an enterprise that did not improve its efficiency was likely to end up loosing money rapidly. Hard budget constraints implied that loss-making enterprises would not survive.

In neither case was the policy to which an initial commitment had been made immune from backsliding.

Openness to Trade

The first round of trade liberalization was more radical and rapid than any other instance of trade liberalization in the post–World War II period. Exchange controls were eliminated, and the zloty rendered effectively convertible on current account from day one. Within six months, state trade monopolies had been

---

[11] Net direct foreign investment was still only $542 million in 1994. By 1998, it had become $4.966 billion, and the following year was over $7 billion. See IMF 2000, table 29. The FDI attracted by Poland's early success, and the growing prospect of entry in the EU, became an independent source of productivity growth (through knowledge and technical spillovers), by the second half of the 1990s.

TABLE 10.1
Poland, Macroeconomic Performance

	1990	1991	1992	1993	1994	1995	1996	1997	1998
Rate of growth of real GDP	−4.9	−5.5	3.1	4.3	5.1	7.0	6.0	6.8	4.8
Rate of growth of real exports	79.9	−1.7	10.8	3.2	13.1	22.8	12.0	12.2	
Rate of growth of real gross domestic investment	−6.7	−2.6	3.6	4.3	8.3	16.5	19.7	21.7	14.5
Current account surplus (deficit) as %GDP	5.0	−2.7	−3.5	−6.3	1.0	0.7	−2.3	−4.0	−4.4
Annual rate of inflation	555.4	76.7	45.3	36.9	33.3	26.8	20.2	15.9	11.7

dismantled, almost all quotas abolished, and almost all customs duties reduced to zero. External observers commented that in the middle of 1990, Poland had the most liberal trade regime of any country in Europe (see de Menil 1997). The comparison with western Europe's gradual and protracted move to current account convertibility and relatively free trade after World War II is striking.[12]

Before the year was out, Poland began to backslide on its commitment to very low import duties. The evolution of the average rate of import duties in table 10.1 tells the story. In part the backsliding was a response to political pressure. But it corresponded also, in part, to an effort on the part of the Polish authorities to enhance their bargaining position in negotiations leading to the Europe Agreement Poland signed in December 1991. If Poland's import duties had remained close to zero, it would have been in a poor position to extract concessions that would improve access for its exports to European markets. As it turned out, the pace of subsequent tariff reduction written into the Europe Agreement was very gradual. It was not until 1998 that Poland returned to its almost tariff-free status in 1990. Nonetheless, the agreement, and subsequently the EU accession process, expressed a clear and unambiguous commitment to the medium-term objective of free trade with the EU. Any Polish businessman with foresight knew that the days of protection were limited.

The pressure for cost reduction coming from international competition is also evident in the rising real exchange rate implied by figure 10.2. After an initial devaluation of over 50 percent on January 1, 1990 (which followed even greater depreciation in 1989), the Polish authorities used a fixed, and then crawling, peg

---

[12] The currencies of western Europe remained inconvertible until 1958, twelve years after the end of the war. During that time, intra-European payments were effected through the Western European Payments Union.

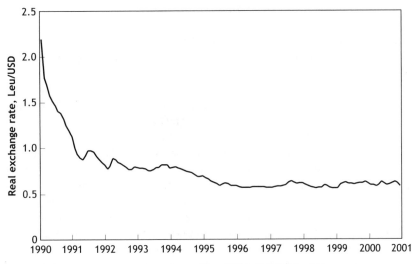

Figure 10.2. Poland, real exchange rate, Zloty/USD (1991.01 = 1.0)

as a nominal anchor in their inflation reduction strategy. This resulted in a continuous real appreciation, which lasted until the end of 1995. Whereas the devaluation had stimulated exports and restricted imports, the appreciation increased competitive pressure on domestic production.

It is worth emphasizing that the argument presented here is that the causal chain linking trade openness to growth is not essentially a Keynesian demand-pull linkage. To the extent that growth in Poland was supply constrained, the important question is what the influence of trade openness was on productivity and aggregate supply. I have argued that the international competition produced by trade openness contributed to restructuring and labor shedding by state-owned enterprises. The way in which aggregate demand absorbed the increased supply is a different aspect of the story. Export growth may, indeed, have been a significant feature of that aspect of the story. As Rodrik (1995) has pointed out, the Keynesian link between export growth and the growth of aggregate demand depends on the share of exports in GDP, and the magnitude of the export multiplier. In an economy such as that of Poland, in which exports are approximately 25 percent of GDP, a 10 percent real growth of exports can, if the multiplier is 2.0, generate a 5 percent growth of aggregate demand. A linkage of this sort may contribute to an explanation of the growth of aggregate demand in Poland. But the demand growth would not have been realized if different, structural processes had not generated at least as large an increase in aggregate supply.

Hard Budget Constraints

The enforcement of budgetary discipline also went through a sequential process in which constraints imposed in one area were undermined by laxity in another, until all of the leaks had essentially been plugged.

The first phase of what was to be a protracted effort to impose budgetary discipline consisted in cutting government subsidies to enterprises. These were slashed from more than 16 percent of GDP in 1986 to 3.3 percent of GDP in 1992 (see OECD 1992).

As the subsidies disappeared, and the economy entered the transition recession of 1990–91, state-owned enterprises turned for working capital to the nine state-owned commercial banks. Short-term credit supplied by these banks multiplied manyfold, and much of it became nonperforming. "The number of problem debtors owing money to state-owned banks increased six-fold between 1989 and 1990, five-fold again in the next year, and twice again in 1992" (Gray and Halle 1996, 3). By the end of 1991, this recently incurred debt exceeded old loans incurred under socialism in many state-owned enterprises (Gray and Halle 1996, 2).

It took more than a year for the government to devise an effective response, but by February 1993, it had put into place a comprehensive Enterprise and Bank Restructuring Program designed to put a stop to these soft credits, and to turn the state banks from facilitators of laxity into instruments of restructuring. The program included a firm commitment to progressive privatization of all the state commercial banks (four had been privatized by the end of 1995), new procedures for work-outs of existing claims, and compensation schemes, which gave management strong incentives to exercise prudence in their lending policies (see Gray and Halle 1996; Montes-Negret and Papi 1996). As a result, the percentage of total domestic credit going to state-owned enterprises, which had been 80 percent in 1989, and was still 73.5 percent in 1993, dropped in 1994 and subsequent years (see Montes-Negret and Papi 1996, 19, table 4; World Bank 2000, table 5.8).

Even as the flow of soft credits was being curtailed, enterprises began accumulating arrears, to one another, to the state budget, and to the social security budget. The government's response was to enact procedures allowing the Ministry of Finance, and the Social Security Fund, to impound assets and execute payment.

Each of the government's successive steps to contain the pressures for subsidies and credits had an immediate impact and contributed over the decade to the increasing effectiveness of state budgetary constraints. Each provided increasing incentives for state and other enterprises to restructure in order to reduce costs and increase sales.

TABLE 10.2
Structural Change in Poland, 1990–99

	1990	1991	1992	1993	1994	1995	1996	1997	1998	1999[a]
Private sector's share										
GDP	30.9	41.7	45.2	47.9	45.5	52.8	54.5	58.7	60.9	
Employment[b]	45.1	50.2	53.7	56.8	59.4	61.9	64.1	68.1	70.7	
Industrial Output[c]	18.5	24.8	28.2	34.6	39.4	45.2	52.4	64.2	69.1	
Profitability of enterprises[d]										
Total	22.0	4.6	2.2	2.8	4.1	4.2	3.4	3.6	2.0	1.6
Public			3.0	3.7	5.2	4.8	3.1	3.5	0.7	0.6
Private			0.0	1.1	2.1	3.3	3.7	3.6	2.6	2.2
Direction of trade,[e] total customs exports										
Former CMEA[f]	28.6	26.5	23.7	22.9	23.8	25.5	22.4	25.6	12.8	
EU	44.3	55.6	58.0	63.2	62.7	70.0	66.2	64.0	68.3	
Other	32.5	27.6	26.6	23.5	22.8	12.7	13.3	10.4	18.9	
Shares of exports in GDP[g]	28.6	23.5	23.7	23.0	23.8	25.5	24.4	25.7	25.4	
Average tariff rate[h]	5.5	18.4	18.4	19.0	19.0	9.4	8.0	6.3	4.8	3.5
Share of administered prices in CPI basket[i]	11.0	11.0	11.0	10.6	12.0	12.0	11.6	13.6	14.1	14.2
Share of private banks										
Assetts				13.0	18.6	26.9	28.9	46.2	49.7	
Capital[j]				26.4	27.7	32.2	50.6	69.5	76.6	
Pensions expenditure as a share of GDP[k]			14.6	14.6	14.5	13.6	13.4	13.6	13.2	13.3
Number of private businesses (in thousands)	1,171	1,473	1,698	1,944	2,071	2,061	2,356	2,540	2,773	2,905

Sources: Central Statistical Office, Ministry of Finance, and National Bank of Poland's own estimates.

[a] I-VII 1999
[b] Annual average employment, including agriculture.
[c] Industrial output sold; since 1993 excluding VAT
[d] Defined as gross profit to total income (in 1992, gross profit to total cost)
[e] Share of exports to country groups in total exports: customs statistics (shipment basis).
[f] Data for 1998 onwards includes CEFTA, the Baltic countries, Belarus, Russia, and Ukraine only. In 1977 these accounted for 90 percent of total exports to former CMEA countries.
[g] Estimates based on balance of payments statistics; 1990–95 shares recalculated at 1996 real effective exchange rate.
[h] Including suspended tariffs, free trade agreements, and tariffs on duty-free tariff quotas
[i] Prices directly controlled by the government; end-year weights. Includes prices monitored by government agencies from 1997.
[j] Data for 1996 onwards includes dispersed holdings.
[k] Totals for Social Insurance Fund (FUS) and Farmer's Social Insurance Fund (of FRUS). Data for 1999 is preliminary.

Political Commitment

One of the most important aspects of the carrot and stick policy that Poland pursued from 1990 through the end of the decade was the degree to which it was broadly supported by majority coalitions of both the Right and the Left. During the period, Poland experienced two parliamentary elections, and two presidential ones. Both parliamentary elections and one of the presidential ones led to a reversal of majorities. These changes not withstanding, the overall thrust of economic policy remained stable. During their tenure in government, the Socialists, backed by the former Communist Party, basically continued and implemented the reform strategy initiated by Leszek Balcerowicz, when he was finance minister of the first democratically elected government, of center-right persuasion. The relative consistency and predictability of Poland's economic strategy undoubtedly enhanced its effectiveness in promoting the growth of productivity.

The Anatomy of Political Will

We turn now to a more difficult question. Why did Poland succeed? What was it about the reformers, and about the circumstances surrounding their program, that enabled them to overcome the natural opposition of vested interests, to forgo short-run political advantage, and to push through the painful adjustments required to achieve their long-run objectives?

The first thing to note, in answer, is that success was not a foregone conclusion. When, in February 1989, the Communist Party convened a roundtable with the previously outlawed Solidarity Movement, no one imagined that the outcome would be a parliamentary democracy and free markets. Events moved very quickly. The first non-Communist prime minister of postwar Poland, Tadeusz Mazowiecki, was installed August 24, six months later.

The story of the events separating February and August has already been well told (Sachs 1993, chap. 2). What is important is that, at the end of the day, a government backed by a broad, democratic movement, and supported by the population at large, came to office with the explicit mandate to dismantle the previous regime. Prime Minister Mazowiecki and Deputy Prime Minister Leszek Balcerowicz, the architect of the economic program, knew what they wanted—a "jump to the market." They rejected, as a mirage that they had seen repeatedly fail in the previous decade, the vision of a third way, of an objective intermediate between socialism and capitalism.

Further, during the months that followed the beginning of the program, a time Balcerowicz has described as a period of "exceptional politics," the leadership acted with determination and resolve and did not compromise its long-term objective. In short, a clear vision, determination in its implementation, and broad popular support were central ingredients of its success.

ROMANIA

The dominant impression that the record of the first ten years of transition in Romania makes on an outside observer is one of difficulty.[13] The period was marked by a succession of crises, and at the end of the decade, Romania remained one of the poorest countries of eastern Europe, a country with weak growth and high inflation. On strictly macroeconomic terms, Romania entered its transition in much better health than Poland.

Thanks to a draconian compression of demand in the previous decade, in 1989 Romania had no foreign debt and was running a budget surplus and a current account surplus. But in the course of the succeeding years, Romania rapidly dissipated this potential advantage, experienced several years of inflation in excess of 100 percent per year, and had to confront more than half a dozen foreign exchange crises.[14] Why?

The Play of Political Forces

It is hard not to start a review of Romania's transition with an account of political developments that had a determining influence on the course of economic policy.

The full identity of the forces at play in the dramatic overthrow of Ceauşescu in December 1989 remain a mystery. In hindsight, it appears that the December Revolution was manipulated by a reform faction in the Communist Party, led by Ion Iliescu, a former head of the youth movement of the Communist Party, and onetime protégé of Ceauşescu. In any event, Iliescu emerged as the leader of the National Salvation Front, the revolutionary committee, which took control after the execution of the dictator. The NSF was able, through popular measures enacted in the first months of 1990, and through forceful, extralegal

---

[13] This section draws heavily on Demekas and Khan 1991; OECD 1993, 1998; Daianu 1996; IMF 2000; and the author's experience as advisor to Romania's three prime ministers from 1997 through 2000.

[14] The recurrent foreign exchange crises, and the episodes of high inflation, are visible in figure 10.3, which plots the record of monthly inflation and depreciation in Romania. What one sees, by comparison, in the Polish case, is a large initial devaluation and jump in prices, followed by a gradual but continuous reduction of inflation and steady appreciation of the real value of the currency (see fig. 10.1). Tables 10.1 and 10.3 also describe the overall macroeconomic performance of the two countries.

obstruction of the "historical parties" (which predated World War II, and had been suppressed by the Communist regime), to position itself to win elections announced for May 1990. (Coal miners were called into Bucharest from the Western Carpathians four times between February 1990 and September 1991 to harass and intimidate prodemocracy demonstrators.) The result of the May elections was that the National Salvation Front became the dominant force in the new transitional parliament, and Iliescu was elected president. Iliescu and a government drawn from the NSF oversaw the writing of a new constitution and managed the affairs of the country for the two years that preceded the first national elections under the new constitution, in September 1992. As we shall see, the economic policies followed from January 1990 to September 1992 had a decisive effect on the course of events for the rest of the decade.

In September 1992, the reformed wing of the former Communist Party, restructured and renamed the Democratic Socialist Party of Romania (PDSR), won a large victory at the polls, and President Iliescu was reelected. In the elections of November 1996, after seven years of Iliescu leadership, both the president and his party were defeated. The new president, Emil Constantinescu, formed a government led by the Democratic Convention of Romania (a coalition of "historical " parties and prodemocracy activists) and supported by the Social Democratic Union and the Hungarian Democratic Federation.

Economic Policies

The economic policies followed by Romania's successive governments from January 1990 through December 1996 could not have been more different from those followed by Poland's governments in the same period. Where the emphasis in Poland had been on opening the economy, both internationally and domestically, and on imposing hard budget constraints, the thrust in Romania was populist with little attention given to imposing market discipline. The account that follows divides the seven years into two periods.

From the December Revolution to the First Elections under the New Constitution

The first three years of transition were decisively important in Romania, as, in a different way, in Poland. They both laid the groundwork, in practical terms, and established expectations for what was to follow.

The biggest difference between the two countries relates to budgetary discipline. In the first year, Poland's budget switched from deficit to surplus, as the government made deep cuts in preexisting subsidies. In the first year, Romania's budget switched from surplus to deficit, as the government expanded social se-

TABLE 10.3

Romania, Macroeconomic Performance

	1990	1991	1992	1993	1994	1995	1996	1997	1998
Rate of growth of real GDP	−5.7	−12.9	−8.8	1.5	3.9	7.1	3.9	−6.6	−7.5
Rate of growth of real exports	−39.8	−17.9	2.9	11.1	19.0	17.0	0.2	2.1	2.5
Rate of growth of real gross domestic investment	−35.6	−31.6	11.0	8.3	20.7	6.9	3.9	−15.9	−19.2
Current account surplus (deficit) as % GDP	−8.5	−3.5	−6.0	−4.5	−1.5	−5.4	−8.2	−6.1	−7.6
Annual rate of inflation		230.6	211.2	255.2	136.8	32.2	38.8	154.8	59.1

curity provisions for early retirement, disability, and sick leave and enacted five-day workweek legislation.

In Poland, as the effects of massive devaluation in 1989 worked their way through the economy, budgetary contraction and tight money (real interest rates were immediately raised to positive levels, on a forward-looking basis) also led to a compression of domestic absorption. The two forces together produced a switch in the current account, from deficit in 1989 to surplus in 1990. In Romania, the authorities expanded demand and allocated credit at negative real interest rates. The result was another turnaround of the current account, but this one from positive to negative. (Compare table 10.3 and table 10.1.) Not only did Romania's balance go from a surplus of $2.9 billion to a deficit of $1.7 billion, but in the process the foreign currency reserves, which had been painfully accumulated over the preceding years of austerity, were almost entirely exhausted.

The contrast in the treatment in the two countries of foreign exchange controls and price controls is similarly striking.[15] On January 1, 1990, the first day of its new program, the Polish authorities permanently dismantled previous controls covering 80 percent of prices, and both enacted and committed themselves to maintaining current account convertibility of the exchange rate. The Romanian authorities waited until after the election of May 1990 to lift 50 percent of preexisting price controls and kept existing foreign exchange controls in full force. Devaluations of 43 percent against the U.S. dollar in February 1990, and 75 percent in November of the same year, left the exchange rate still overvalued and controlled. Controls and overvaluation of the exchange rate were to remain a central feature and a critical vulnerability of the Romanian economy, with only one brief interruption, until February 1997.

The treatment of banks' nonperforming loans provides still a further symptomatic contrast. In November 1990, the Romanian authorities conducted an

---

[15] Compare figures 10.3 and 10.1.

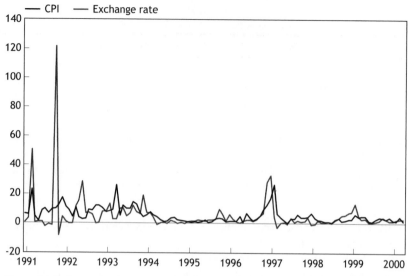

Figure 10.3. Romania: CPI and USD exchange rate, monthly rates of change

economy-wide cancellation of debts, the centerpiece of which was a write-off, for all enterprises, of all of their debts to banks and to the state. The deposits of the state at the National Bank were simply transferred to the banks to offset their losses. An operation more undermining of budgetary discipline would be hard to imagine. At roughly the same time, in Poland, the Ministry of Finance was struggling to stem the flow of new credits to nonperforming debtors. Those efforts led eventually to the Polish Bank Restructuring Act of 1993.

It is obvious, but should be emphasized, that the objective of Romania's first Post-1989 governments was not to return to a command economy with quantity controls. One of the first acts of the National Salvation Front was to abolish centralized control by national ministries over state enterprises. Nor did it intend to close the country's borders and keep out all foreign competition. Romania's relative political autonomy in the Soviet system had permitted it to develop substantial trade relations with non-Comecon partners. Its intent was rather to maintain those ties and encourage an influx of foreign goods, to satisfy massive pent-up domestic demand.

The leaders of the governments of 1990 to 2000 were closer in spirit to the reformed communism of Gorbachev or Jaruzelski than to the Stalinist principles of Ceauşescu's regime. In fact, they experienced, in more moderate form, some of the same difficulties as did Gorbachev and Jaruzelski. One of these was an inability to restrain real wage increases in a situation in which enterprise authority has been decentralized, but the disciplines of private ownership did not yet exist. Another characteristic was the need for expansionary policies and generous transfers to generate political support, which might otherwise have been provided by democratic legitimacy.[16]

1992–96

The second phase of Romania's transition corresponds to the first government under the new constitution, the first government to last for the duration of a four-year legislature. In this phase, macroeconomic policy was more structured. During 1993, the authorities made a significant attempt at macroeconomic stabilization. But very little was done in the way of microeconomic restructuring.

Privatization of large-scale industrial and mining enterprises remained almost nonexistent.[17] An early voucher scheme for giving citizens minority interests in enterprises that would remain state-controlled had been introduced, but was stillborn in 1991. It was transformed and revived in 1995, but in a form so complex that it was almost guaranteed not to have any effect on corporate governance. An additional list of large, loss-making enterprises was withheld from sale to strategic investors, in order to allow time for these enterprises to be restructured first. Subsidies were paid, already soft budgets were thereby further loosened, and the restructuring did not occur.

In the meantime, the central bank continued to make extensive use of directed credits to support politically connected activities in industry and agriculture. The channel through which this aid flowed was the loan desk of the state-owned banks. These remained dominant in the banking system (see table 10.4) and continued to make large, subsidized loans to loss-making enterprises in heavy industry and agro-industry, as well as directly to individuals connected to the political parties. Since these loans were by their nature nonperforming, the banks, in turn, sought to make themselves whole by obtaining refinancing aid from the central bank. (See table 10.5.)

With the exception of an interlude in 1993 itself, the exchange rate remained substantially overvalued (and controlled) through the period. (See fig. 10.4.) Foreign exchange accumulated at artificially low exchange rates was allocated to state-owned, heavy energy consuming industries, in order to subsidize their purchases of oil on world markets.

---

[16] The policies of these governments bear some similarity to the Latin American "macroeconomic populism" that Dornbusch (1990) describes.

[17] This is reflected by the low degree of privatization in industry reported in table 10.4. (The high level of privatization in agriculture reported in that table is misleading. Though the land formerly in cooperatives was in principle distributed to the farmers, they did not have title for many years, and they remained dependent on state-owned channels for marketing and supplies.)

TABLE 10.4
Romania's Structural Change, 1990–99

	1990	1991	1992	1993	1994	1995	1996	1997	1998	1999[a]
Share of private ownership:										
Agriculture				83.5	89.3	89.0	90.1	96.8	95.9	97.2
Industry				17.4	23.3	29.9	38.5	42.1	45.6	48.7
Construction				26.8	51.6	57.8	69.3	76.6	77.9	78.0
Services				29.3	39.1	58.1	66.7	71.5	72.7	73.0
Share of adminis-tered prices in CPI basket[a]	52.0	52.0	52.0	33.0	33.3	33.3	33.3	16.1	10.6	13.2
Direction of trade Share of EU in total exports	33.9	36.9	35.2	41.4	48.2	54.1	56.5	56.6	64.5	65.5
Share of EU in total imports	21.8	28.7	41.3	45.3	48.2	50.5	52.3	52.5	57.7	55.1
Share of exports in GDP	16.7	17.6	27.8	23.0	24.9	27.6	28.4	29.7	23.7	30.1
Role of the 5 major state banks in the banking system										
Share of total credit to non-government					81.3	76.1	76.0	73.0	67.5	53.3
Share of total deposits					73.9	71.3	72.8	70.3	68.9	59.8

Sources: IMF (2000); National Statistics Commission; National Bank of Romania; and author's calculations.

[a] Prices directly controlled or monitored by government end-of-year weights. Estimated by applying applicable laws and regulations to CPI categories.

The macrostabilization effort of 1993 began in April with a second step in price liberalization, in which the scope of goods and services whose price was administered dropped from 50 percent of the CPI to 33 percent of the CPI. (See table 10.4.) It continued with a decision on the part of the central bank, in October, to raise real interest rates on its refinancing and on bank loan rates themselves (which had been highly negative during the preceding years) to positive levels. Paradoxically, the economy responded to this dose of monetary austerity, with increased real growth and moderating inflation. A supportive international environment (of recovery from the Gulf War recession), and offsetting, expansionary fiscal policy were part of the explanation. Nonetheless, during 1994 and 1995, it looked as if Romania had achieved high rates of real growth and low inflation without microeconomic restructuring. In fact, microeconomic distortions and a growing current account imbalance (amplified by preelectoral largesse in the run-up to the 1996 elections) eventually led to another foreign exchange crisis at the end of 1996. (See figs. 10.3 and 10.5.)

TABLE 10.5

Romania: National Bank of Romania Refinancing Practices, 1994–99

	Total Refinancing Credits (billions of Lei)[a]	Total Refinancing Credits (% of NBR assets)[a]	Shares in Total Refinancing (in percent)				
			Directed Lines[b]	Auction	Overdraft	Troubled Banks[c]	Directed Credit to Agriculture
1992							
March	409	99					
June	302	83					
Sept.	328	75					
Dec.	350	58					
1993							
March	377	56					
June	534	73					
Sept.	1226	121					
Dec.	1541	119					
1994							
Q1	1891		70.9	36.0	8.4	0.0	40.8
Q2	2026		82.1	40.5	0.0	0.0	42.7
Q3	2064		88.3	34.5	0.0	0.0	57.3
Q4	2331	25.1	92.4	34.3	0.0	1.5	71.7
1995							
Q1	2074		93.5	38.1	0.0	0.0	72.4
Q2	2146		74.6	38.5	8.7	0.7	54.3
Q3	2790		70.6	37.6	14.3	0.0	59.2
Q4	3679	28.8	54.0	27.5	7.8	23.8	51.3
1996							
Q1	3707		53.8	25.6	2.0	36.2	48.9
Q2	4413		49.8	11.0	5.8	39.3	39.6
Q3	5029		57.3	7.6	0.0	37.1	45.6
Q4	8024	50.2	54.0	28.9	0.0	23.3	46.0
1997							
Q1	5429		39.3	5.5	0.0	34.5	48.1
Q2	3801		48.6	0.0	0.0	49.6	49.1
Q3	2720		28.7	0.0	0.0	69.3	28.8
Q4	2517	7	23.0	0.0	0.0	74.9	23.0
1998							
Q1	586		100.0	0.0	0.0	0.0	91.1
Q2	556		100.0	0.0	0.0	0.0	90.6
Q3	556		100.0	0.0	0.0	0.0	90.6
Q4	556	1.3	100.0	0.0	0.0	0.0	90.6
1999							
Q1	5237		10.6	0.0	0.0	89.4	9.6
Q2	5678		9.8	0.0	0.0	90.2	8.9
Q3	516		100.0	0.0	0.0	0.0	97.5
Q4	2433	3.5	20.7	0.0	0.0	79.3	20.7

Sources: National Bank of Romania; IMFstaff estimates; IMF 2000, table 26.

[a] Monthly data, 1992–93, from Daianu 1996, are not strictly comparable with subsequent quarterly data, from IMF 2000.

[b] Directed lines for various sectors of the economy, at subsidized interest rates.

[c] NBR special credits to banks with problems.

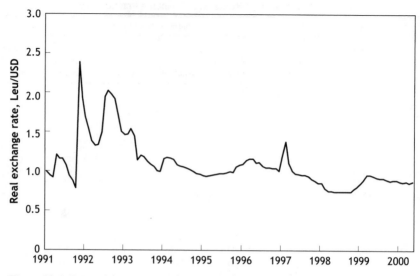

Figure 10.4. Romania, real exchange rate, Leu/USD (91.01 = 1.0)

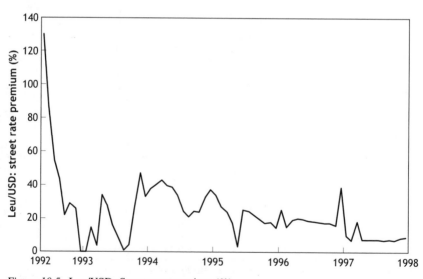

Figure 10.5. Leu/USD: Street rate premium (%)
Source: The "street rate" is a "parallel/black or free market" rate supplies by Wojtek Mal-iszewski, and obtained from Global Currency Report, a publication of Currency Data and Intelligence.

1997–2000

The election, in November and December 1996, of a government and president (Emil Constantinescu) supported by the Democratic Convention of Romania led to a significant change in the thrust of economic policy. In January and February 1997, the new government ended most price controls (freeing all but 16 percent of the CPI basket), increased publicly administered energy prices to world market levels and indexed them to world prices, and established definitive, full current account convertibility for the exchange rate. Monetary and fiscal policy were both tightened in order to forestall a lasting increase of inflation. As direct result of these measures, Romania entered a second transition recession, which did not end until 2000.

In the months and years that followed February 1997, the government also launched a series of microeconomic restructuring measures. It privatized the national telephone monopoly, the major national automobile company, several major banks, and a number of other large enterprises. It closed half of the coal mines in the Carpathians (but did little to alleviate the attendant social problems). It progressively put a halt to the directed credit activities of the major state banks and the national bank. (See table 10.3.) The decisive steps in this process were the closure of the largest state bank, and the privatization (begun in 2000 and finished in 2001) of the state agricultural bank.

However, the program soon ran into the opposition of entrenched special interests and eventually fell prey to political battles within the governing coalition. These power struggles, sometimes supported by groups wanting to stop reform, forced the resignation of two successive prime ministers and caused the coalition's program to fall badly behind schedule. In the process, IMF and World Bank support, which had been secured in April 1997, was canceled once, renewed, and then canceled again. This, and a series of unfavorable external shocks, meant that by the time of the 2000 elections, the country had experienced all pain and no gain. The consequence was that the Democratic Convention of Romania badly lost those elections, and Iliescu and the PDSR returned as president and as governing party. Nonetheless, the liberalization and restructuring of the previous four years, combined with a significant real exchange rate depreciation in the spring of 1999, laid the ground for a modest recovery in 2000, which has continued since. By early 2002, Romania had reached a position that was qualitatively similar to that of Poland ten years earlier.

The Political Dynamic of a Difficult Transition

Why did it prove so difficult for the Democratic Convention to pursue reform? At least part of the answer was related to the opportunity for radical reform that had been lost a decade earlier. Years of delay had given ample time to special interests to constitute themselves, and to learn effectively to oppose the liberalizing measures that risked undermining their position. The counterpart of that was that the forces of reform themselves lacked decisiveness and fell easily prey to political infighting.

What was important about Romania's attempts at reform was not that they came from the Right rather than the Left. We have seen that in Poland, both Right and Left pursued the course that had been set in the first two years. What proved to be decisive was that, by delaying reform at the outset, the first governments of the country provided the nomenclatura with opportunities to appropriate economic rents, whose expropriation through liberalization it then resisted with determination.

Why was Romania's journey to the market as faulted as it was in the first decade of transition? An important part of the answer is that the revolution of 1989 was taken over by the nomenclatura of the previous regime in the very first days. Given its background, the principal priority of the top leadership of the first government was not to create markets, but to stay in power. To that end, it pursued populist macroeconomic policies and refrained from submitting the major industrial structures of the economy to the cold shower of privatization and competition.

CONCLUSION

Our comparison of economic transition in Poland and Romania is consistent with the principal conclusions of the statistical studies, which were summarized at the beginning of this chapter: Policy choices have a determining effect on outcomes, and they themselves are influenced by initial conditions. There is a stark contrast between Poland's supply side policies, in which openness and hard budget constraints forced productivity gains, and Romania's policies, characterized by soft budget constraints and intermittent phases of populist demand expansion. That contrast was largely responsible for the high rate of growth that Poland enjoyed after its transition recession, and for the stop-and-go cycles and high inflation that characterized Romania during the same period.

In these two cases, our accounts have also shown that the first years, indeed the first months, were decisively important. Balcerowicz had set the course and established policy expectations by the summer of 1990. In Romania, by the end of 1990, the stage had been set for a continuing series of retreats from confrontation with hard budget constraints.

Finally, our accounts point to the critical importance of the balance of political forces in those first months. Poland's first, post-1989 government wrested its authority from the Communist regime in a democratic confrontation. In Romania, the National Salvation Front and its successor governments were dominated by important segments of the nomenclatura of the previous regime.

This distinction goes a long way to explaining the difference between the rapidity with which structural change was implemented in Poland, and the ability of vested interests to block the same changes for protracted periods of time in Romania.

Our accounts also raise as many questions as they answer. Why was a democratic opposition to Communism able to emerge in Poland and not in Romania? The speed of events in the decisive first months surprised all participants in both countries. But the Solidarity Movement was able to take the upper hand in Poland. No similar movement existed in Romania. Taking a somewhat longer view, one is led to ask why the Soviet regime took such a harsh and extreme form in Romania, and why it eventually proved more porous, and open to outside influences, in Poland. Answers to those questions lie perhaps in the legacy of geography, culture, and earlier history.

REFERENCES

Aslund, A., P. Boone, and S. Johnson. 1996. "How to Stabilize: Lessons from Post-Communist Countries." *Brookings Papers on Economic Activity* 1996, no. 1: 217–313.

Aslund, A., and G. de Menil, eds. 2000. *Economic Reform in Ukraine: The Unfinished Agenda.* New York: M. E. Sharpe.

Belka, M., S. Estrin, M. E. Schaffer, and I. J. Singh. 1994. "Enterprise Adjustment in Poland: Evidence from a Survey of 200 Private, Privatized, and State Owned Firms." Paper presented at the World Bank Workshop on Enterprise Adjustment in Eastern Europe.

Berg, A., E. Borensztein, R. Sahay, and J. Zettelmeyer. 1999. "The Evolution of Output in Transition Economies." International Monetary Fund Working Paper No. 99/73.

Budina, N., W. Maliszewski, G. de Menil, and G. Turlea. 2000. "Money, Inflation, and Output in Romania, 1993–1999." October 10. Typescript.

Bunce, V. 1995. "Sequencing of Political and Economic Reforms." In *East-Central European Economies in Transition,* ed. J. Hardt and R. Kaufman. New York: M. E. Sharpe.

———. 1998. "Regional Differences in Democratization: The East versus the South." *Post-Soviet Affairs* 14, no. 3: 187–211.

Daianu, D. 1996. "Stabilization and Exchange Rate Policy in Romania." *Economics of Transition* 4, no. 1: 229–48.

De Broeck, M., and V. Koen. 2000. "The 'Soaring Eagle'—Anatomy of the Polish Take-off in the 1990's." International Monetary Fund Working Paper No. WP/00/06.

Demekas, D., and M. Khan. 1991. *The Romanian Economic Reform Program.* International Monetary Fund Occasional Paper No. 89, December.

de Melo, M., D. Cevdet, and A. Gelb. 1996. "From Plan to Market: Patterns of Transition." *World Bank Economic Review* 10:397–424.

de Menil, G. 1997. "Trade Policies in Transition Economies: A Comparison of European and Asian Experiences." In *Economies in Transition: Comparing Asia and Eastern Europe,* ed. W. T. Woo, S. Parker, and J. Sachs. Cambridge: MIT Press.

Dornbusch, R., and S. Edwards. 1990. "Microeconomic Populism" *Journal of Development Economics* 32, no. 2: 247–77.

Falcetti, E., M. Raiser, and P. Sanfey. 2000. "Defying the Odds: Initial Conditions, Reforms, and Growth in the First Decade of Transition." EBRD Working Paper No. 55, July.

Fischer, S., and R. Sahay. 2000. "The Transition Economies after Ten Years." International Monetary Fund Working Paper No. 00/30.

Fischer, S., R. Sahay, and C. Vegh. 1998. "From Transition to Market: Evidence and Growth Prospects." International Monetary Fund Working Paper No. 98/52.

Gray, C., and A. Halle. 1996. "Bank-Led Restructuring in Poland (I): An Empirical Look at the Bank Conciliation Process." World Bank, September.

Havrylyshyn, O., I. Izvorksi, and R. van Rooden. 1998. "Recovery and Growth in Transition Economies, 1990–97: A Stylized Regression Approach." International Monetary Fund Working Paper No. 98/141.

Hernandez-Cata, E. 1997. "Liberalization and the Behavior of Output during the Transition from Plan to Market." International Monetary Fund Working Paper No. 97/53.

International Monetary Fund (IMF). 2000. "Republic of Poland: Statistical Appendix." Staff Country Report No. 00/61, April.

———. 2001a. "Romania: Selected Issues and Statistical Appendix." Staff Country Report No. 01/16, January.

———. 2001b. "Republic of Poland: 2000 Article IV Consultation." Staff Country Report No. 01/56, April.

Montes-Negret, F., and L. Papi. 1996. "The Polish Experience in Bank and Enterprise Restructuring." World Bank, November.

Organisation for Economic Cooperation and Development (OECD). 1992. *OECD Economic Surveys: Poland.* Paris: OECD.

———. 1993. *Romania: An Economic Assessment.* Paris: OECD.

———. 1994. *OECD Economic Surveys: Poland.* Paris: OECD.

———. 1997. *OECD Economic Surveys: Poland.* Paris: OECD.

———. 1998. *OECD Economic Surveys: Romania.* Paris: OECD.

———. 2000. *OECD Economic Surveys: Poland.* Paris: OECD.

———. 2001. *OECD Economic Surveys: Poland.* Paris: OECD.

Pinto, B., M. Belka, and S. Krajewski. 1993. "Transforming State Enterprises in Poland: Evidence on Adjustment by Manufacturing Firms." *Brookings Papers on Economic Activity* 1993, no. 1: 213–55.

Rodrik, D. 1995. "Getting Interventions Right: How South Korea and Taiwan Grew Rich." *Growth Policy* 20:55–107.

Sachs, J. 1993. *Poland's Jump to the Market Economy.* Cambridge: MIT Press.

Sachs, J., and W. T. Woo. 1994. "Structural Factors in the Economic Reforms of China, Eastern Europe, and the Former Soviet Union." *Economic Policy* 18:101–45.

Scarpetta, S., A. Bassanini, D. Pilat, and P. Schreyer. 2000. "Economic Growth in the OECD Area: Recent Trends at the Aggregate and Sectoral Level." OECD Economics Department Working Paper No. 248.

World Bank. 1996. *From Plan to Market: World Development Report, 1996.* Oxford: Oxford University Press.

———. 2000. *World Bank Development Indicators.* Oxford: Oxford University Press.

Wyplosz, C. 1999. "The Years of Transformation: Macroeconomic Lessons." Paper prepared for the Annual World Bank ABCDE Conference, April 28–30, Washington, D.C.

Part III

INSTITUTIONS IN DETAIL

How Reform Worked in China

YINGYI QIAN

A PUZZLING REFORM THAT WORKED

IN THE LAST 22 years of the 20th century, China transformed itself from a poor, centrally planned economy to a lower-middle-income, emerging market economy. With total gross domestic product (GDP) growing at an average annual rate of about 9 percent, China's per capita GDP more than quadrupled during this period. The benefits of growth were also shared by the people on a broad basis: the number of people living in absolute poverty was substantially reduced from over 250 million to about 50 million, a decline from a one-third to a twenty-fifth of its population; and life expectancy increased from 64 in the 1970s to over 70 in the late 1990s. Both the formal statistics and casual tourist impressions tell the same story: China's growth is real. Two decades ago, few economists would have bet on the outcome in China today. At the time, coming out of the disastrous decade of the Cultural Revolution, China was poor, over-populated, short of human capital and natural resources, and was constrained by an ideology hostile toward markets and opposed to radical reform. Growth of this kind under such initial conditions is a surprise.

China's phenomenal growth is not just another successful growth story because China is not a "typical" country, although in cross-country regressions China can only represent one data point, the same as Singapore or Ireland or Botswana. China is the largest transition and developing economy. As an economy in transition from plan to market, China has a population three times greater than all other transition economies combined, including the 15 former Soviet Republics. In 2000, its $1 trillion economy was already bigger than all other transition economies combined. As a developing economy, China has a population almost three times that of all eight high-performing East Asian economies of Japan, South Korea, Taiwan, Hong Kong, Singapore, Malaysia, Thailand, and Indonesia. It has managed to match the growth record of these economies during their heyday, but with a much larger population. The cumulative effects of the two decades' growth are significant when comparing China with its two largest neighbors: in total GDP terms, in 1988 China was less than half of Russia, but ten years later Russia was less than half of China. On per capita basis, two decades ago China and India were about equal, but now China is about twice as rich as India.

China's growth is unlikely to end any time soon. In the first half of 2001, China's economy ignored the global slowdown and continued to grow at an annual rate of about 8 percent. Defying the perception that China has reached a plateau of growth, more and more economists are starting to believe that the best part of China's growth has not come yet. With entry into the World Trade Organization (WTO), they suspect that China's economy is on the verge of the next boom.

According to Maddison's (1998) calculation, China might overtake the United States in total GDP in terms of "purchasing power parity" by 2015.[1] If Maddison is right, China would be the only economy, excluding the European Union, capable of surpassing the U.S. economy (in purchasing power parity) within the next two decades. And this would make China the largest economy in the world, regaining the historical position that it lost in the middle of the nineteenth century. No wonder Lawrence Summers speculated in the early 1990s: "It may be that when the history of the late 20th century is written in a hundred years the most significant event will be the revolutionary change in China" (1992, 7).

On the ground of economic growth and improving living standard, there is no question that China's reform has worked. But this reform is puzzling. In the early 1990s, the economics profession and policymakers reached a striking degree of unanimity on the recipe for transition from plan to market. Simply put, it calls for stabilization, liberalization, and privatization, following political democratization. Although many economists may not consider this recipe sufficient, few would question its necessity. Theoretically, it is difficult to imagine how a reform would work without these essential ingredients. Empirically, the fresh memory of the frustrated reform experience in Hungary, Poland, and the former Soviet Union prior to 1990 suggests that a reform will fail if it does not follow these recommendations.

The Chinese path of reform and its associated rapid growth is puzzling because it seems to defy this conventional wisdom. Although China has adopted many of the policies advocated by economists—such as being open to trade and foreign investment and sensitive to macroeconomic stability—violations of the standard prescriptions are striking. For the most part of the past two decades, China's reform succeeded without complete liberalization, without privatization, and without democratization. One might have reasoned that coexistence of the

---

[1] In terms of purchasing power parity, China's per capita GDP in 1995 was about 11 percent of that of the United States. Because China had a population approximately 4.5 times as large as the United States, China's total GDP, in terms of purchasing power parity, was about one-half that of the United States in 1995. If China continues to grow four percentage points faster than the United States annually, then China's total GDP will be larger than that of the United States in 20 years.

planning mechanism with partial liberalization would only cause more distortion and become a source of disruption, not growth. Without privatization and secure private property rights, how could there be genuine market incentives? Without democracy, economic reform lacks a political basis and commitment to a market and thus is vulnerable. The actual performance of the Chinese reform provides a striking contrast to these expectations. Why has China grown so fast, ask Blanchard and Fischer (1993), when conditions thought to be necessary for growth were absent?

It is not surprising that China's reform has been viewed as an anomaly and thus has been unappreciated by mainstream economists. For example, *From Plan to Market: World Development Report 1996* on transition economies (World Bank 1996) gave China short shrift because it couldn't figure out where to put China on the various measurement parameters. China simply does not fit into the general description of the report.

Those who do not find China's reform puzzling often misunderstand it. Two types of misperceptions of China's economic success are common. The first is to regard foreign direct investment (FDI) and exports as the driving force for China's success. In this connection the roles of overseas Chinese and of Hong Kong and Taiwan are often emphasized. The simplicity of the argument adds to its power, and the tacit message—it is the foreigners and foreign markets that made China grow—finds an appreciative audience outside China. However, the argument loses its plausibility as soon as one considers a parallel experience in Germany. If Hong Kong or Taiwan could play such a powerful role in mainland China, West Germany should have been even more effective in East Germany, given that West Germany is much larger and stronger than Taiwan and Hong Kong combined, and East Germany is much smaller than mainland China.

The role of FDI in China is vastly overstated in the press. For the entire 1980s, FDI in China was tiny. FDI only started to increase substantially in 1993, and at its peak it accounted for about 10 percent of total investment. On per capita basis, China's FDI was not high by international standards. It is true that China's exports expanded very fast, but that cannot be the main story. The direct contribution of foreign trade and investment to large countries cannot be quantitatively as important as to small countries.

Like FDI, China's exports were very concentrated in coastal provinces. However, contrary to a popular perception, China's growth was not just a phenomenon of coastal provinces—it is across the board, both coastal and inland. Inland provinces are growing fast, though coastal provinces are growing faster. Anyone who has traveled to inland cities such as Xi'an or Guiyang cannot fail to notice their vibrant local economies. Indeed, if each China's provinces were counted as a distinct economy, about 20 out of the top 30 growth regions in the world in the past two decades would be provinces in China, many of which did not receive much foreign investment and did not depend on exports. Table 11.1

TABLE 11.1
GDP Growth Rates by Province
(percent)

Province	1978–90	1978–95	Province	1978–90	1978–95
Beijing	9.0	9.8	Henan	12.6	10.9
Tianjin	7.7	8.9	Hubei	9.4	10.5
Hebei	8.5	10.2	Hunan	7.7	8.7
Shanxi	8.2	8.8	Guangdong	12.3	14.2
Inner Mongolia	9.8	13.0	Guangxi	7.2	9.9
Liaoning	8.1	8.8	Hainan	10.1	12.3
Jilin	8.9	9.5	Sichuan	8.6	9.5
Heilongjiang	4.9	4.8	Guizhou	9.2	9.1
Shanghai	7.4	9.1	Yunan	9.7	9.9
Jiangsu	11.0	12.8	Tibet	7.7	8.3
Zhejiang	11.7	13.8	Shaanxi	9.0	9.1
Anhui	9.3	10.7	Gansu	8.2	8.6
Fujian	11.5	13.7	Qinghai	6.5	6.8
Jiangxi	9.0	10.4	Ningxia	9.2	8.9
Shangdong	10.0	11.9	Xinjiang	10.8	11.1

Source: China Statistical Yearbook.

shows GDP growth by province in China and refutes the perception that growth in China is only coastal.

If focusing on FDI and foreign trade tends to downplay the entire reform process and the role of indigenous institutions, then a simple-minded view on trade and foreign investment creates obstacles to the understanding of growth in any country. This is because the effect of openness has to work through corresponding internal changes. Russia became very open after reform, more so than China, but neither higher growth nor more FDI ensued. Even in small East Asian countries, an export-oriented policy worked through domestic changes in investment and human capital accumulation. Therefore, it could well be the case that it is not exports that drive growth, but that the same forces of domestic change drive both exports and domestic growth.

The second common misperception about China's success is to attribute it exclusively to the agricultural reform in the early 1980s. To be sure, China's agricultural reform was a huge success. And the reason for it is pretty much a standard story of family farming plus market liberalization, although research has shown that the story is more complicated than that. For example, there seemed to be significant contributions from the rural R&D and infrastructure investments made in the 1970s toward the agriculture productivity growth in the 1980s (Huang and Rozelle 1996); and the state institutions for marketing also played important roles in rural development (Rozelle 1996). Nevertheless, economists are generally comfortable with the Chinese agriculture reform because it fits their models of the world.

This way of thinking becomes a myth when one regards agricultural reform as the only successful reform in China. Often it carries two implicit messages: China did not do well in nonagricultural sectors because it did not follow the conventional advice, and China did well in agriculture reform because it was—and still is—a poor, agricultural country. The truth is that the agricultural reform was the first reform success in China, but its bigger achievements lie elsewhere. At the outset of reform in the late 1970s, over 70 percent of China's labor force was employed in agriculture. By 2000, China's agriculture labor force had already declined to below the 50 percent mark, which is impossible without successful development outside the agriculture sector. In the late 1990s, the agricultural share of China's GDP was at 16 percent, about the same level as in Poland and the Soviet Union in the early 1980s. Table 11.2 provides evidence showing that most of China's growth came from the nonagricultural sector—the industrial and tertiary sectors.

The agricultural sector can have important indirect effects on nonagricultural sectors. For example, successful agricultural reform provides sources of savings and labor to boost industrialization. But in order for this mechanism to work, reform of the nonagricultural sector is necessary. The fact that today China is no longer a poor, agricultural country demonstrates that the main success of China's reform lies outside agriculture.

One cannot understand China's growth without understanding how its reform worked in the domestic, nonagriculture sector, which is the focus of this chapter.

PERSPECTIVES ON INSTITUTIONS

In their standard way of thinking, economists consider labor, physical capital, human capital, and productivity as the proximate determinants of growth. But factor accumulation and productivity changes are endogenous, depending on improvement in technology, allocative efficiency, and incentives, which in turn are shaped by institutions. The advocates of new institutional economics (Coase 1992; North 1997; Williamson 1994) recognize that a good market economy requires not only "getting prices right," but also "getting property rights right"

TABLE 11.2
Growth Rates of GDP and GDP Components
(percent)

Year	GDP	Agriculture	Industry	Tertiary
1979	7.6	6.1	8.2	7.8
1980	7.8	−1.5	13.6	5.9
1981	5.5	7.0	1.9	10.4
1982	9.1	11.5	5.6	13.0
1983	10.9	8.3	10.4	15.2
1984	15.2	12.9	14.5	19.4
1985	13.5	1.8	18.6	18.3
1986	8.8	3.3	10.2	12.1
1987	11.6	4.7	13.7	14.4
1988	11.3	2.5	14.5	13.2
1989	4.1	3.1	3.8	5.4
1990	3.8	7.3	3.2	2.3
1991	9.2	2.4	13.9	8.8
1992	14.2	4.7	21.2	12.4
1993	13.5	4.7	19.9	10.7
1994	12.6	4.0	18.4	9.6
1995	10.5	5.0	14.1	8.0

Source: China Statistical Yearbook.

Note: Data on industry includes construction.

and "getting institutions right." This is because property rights, and institutions in general, set the rules that affect the behavior of economic agents.

The institutional economists thus regard the conventional wisdom on transition, focusing on stabilization, liberalization, and privatization, as inadequate because it misses the institutional dimension. To these economists, a set of institutions is critical for sustained growth, including secure private property rights protected by the rule of law, impartial enforcement of contracts through an independent judiciary, appropriate government regulations to foster market competition, effective corporate governance, transparent financial systems, and so on. The fact that all of them can be readily found in the developed economies, especially in the United States, implies that they are "best practice" institutions.

Economists then use these institutions as a benchmark to judge transition and developing economies, and often find huge institutional gaps. These findings then serve three purposes. First, they generate a diagnosis of the deficiency of institutions in developing and transition economies. Second, they are used to explain why these economies perform poorly, confirming the central hypothesis that institutions matter. Third, they lead to recommendations for institution building: If the economy has weak property rights, clarify them. A weak financial system? Strengthen it. A bad law? Change it. A corrupt legal system? Clean it up.

This "menu perspective" on institutions is useful in providing a benchmark of best-practice institutions with which today's most advanced economies have pushed the development frontier. But this perspective does not provide enough intellectual power for investigations of how reform worked (or did not work) in many developing and transition economies. Compare China with Russia for the last decade. Neither of them had rule of law, secure private property rights, effective corporate governance, or strong financial system. But the two exhibited a huge differences in performance, which obviously cannot be attributed to the presence or absence of the best-practice institutions.

The same kind of problem arises from the cross-country regressions incorporating institutional development indices. For example, the World Bank study *Beyond Washington Consensus: Institutions Matter* (Burki and Perry 1998) gets serious on institutions. It compiles a "composite institutional development index" for each country, using a menu of institutions that includes the rule of law, financial institutions, ownership, public administration, and so on. The study carries out cross-country growth regressions using this index to find positive associations between economic growth and institutional development. While the cross-country regressions are useful in estimating the magnitudes of the effects of explanatory variables on growth, they only do this right when the latter are correctly measured and truly exogenous. Otherwise they lead to biased estimations or leave large residuals unexplained. Indeed, China, together with Taiwan and Chile, is an outlier in the regression showing the relationship between institutional development and economic growth (Burki and Perry 1998, fig. 1.1.a). China is again an outlier in the more refined regression of the "true" partial coefficient between institutional development and growth (Burki and Perry 1998, fig. 1.1.b), together with Thailand, Indonesia, and Korea. In all these cross-country regressions, China's performance is too high relative to its index value of institutional development. This is not surprising because the measurement of the institutional development index is imprecise and the underlying variable is likely not exogenous.

Recognizing the importance of institutions is only a beginning. A major problem in the study of reform in developing and transition economies is not that a neglect of institutions. Not any more. The problem is a naive perspective on institutions. The naive perspective often confuses the goal (i.e., where to finish) with the process (i.e., how to get there) and thus tends to ignore the intriguing issues of transition paths connecting the starting point and the goal. It is like neglecting the "transition equations" (or "equations of motion") and the "initial conditions" in dynamic programming. Although building best-practice institutions is a desirable goal, getting institutions right is a process involving incessant changes interacting with initial conditions. The difference between China and Russia is not at all that China has established best-practice institutions and that Russia has not. The difference lies in the institutions in transition.

To understand how reforms work in developing and transition economies, we need to broaden our perspective on institutions. It is not enough to study the forms of institutions found in the most developed economies as a desirable goal; it is also essential to study the variety of unfamiliar forms of institutions in transition. The distinction between the conventional, best-practice institutions and the transitional institutions is important. Gerschenkron (1962) made a crucial point in his studies of economic development of latecomers such as Germany in the nineteenth century: the latecomers need to make special arrangements to compensate for their backwardness, and they can find ways to do so. In parallel, the broadened perspective on institutions takes a dynamic, not static, view on institutions. It recognizes that the real challenge of reform facing transition and developing countries is not so much knowing where to end up, but searching for a feasible path toward the goal. Therefore, it focuses on transitional institutions, not best-practice institutions. In mountain climbing, the peak offers the best view, but mountaineers enjoy a better and better view along the path toward it. The challenge is not the study of the peak, but the search for a feasible path toward it. Like Shleifer and Treisman's (1999) investigation of the Russian transition, this study of China's transition is not about what is desirable, but what is feasible.

Compared to the developed economies, the backwardness resulting from the initial institutional conditions in transition and developing economies can be both disadvantageous and advantageous for growth. On the one hand, the immediate effects of the initial institutional conditions are generally not hospitable to growth in most transition and developing economies. Although these countries can take advantage of being latecomers to shorten the time of change, they may not be able to complete all the changes in a short period of time. This is disadvantageous for growth. On the other hand, because the adverse initial institutions create myriad distortions, these economies usually enjoy great growth potential once institutions are changed to remove these distortions. In this regard the most striking examples are former centrally planned economies. These economies started reform from an extremely inefficient status quo. They operated not only far away from the Pareto frontier due to the enormous allocative distortions, but also deep inside the production possibility set because of poor incentives. Huge room existed for improved efficiency, which might generate great growth opportunity not seen in the developed economies. Thus the central question for many transition and developing countries is how to make institutional changes to realize the great growth potential when the initial condition has multiple distortions.

Underlying China's reform is a series of institutional changes in the novel form of transitional institutions. These institutions work because they achieve two objectives at the same time—they improve economic efficiency on the one hand, and make the reform compatible for those in power on the other. They also take into consideration China's specific initial conditions. At one level, one could argue that China's transitional institutions merely unleashed the standard forces of incentives, hard budget constraints, and competition. This is true, but such an economic rationale is inadequate. The transitional institutions are not created solely for increasing the size of a pie, they are also created to reflect the distributional concerns of how the enlarged pie is divided and the political concerns of how the interests of those in power are served. Rudimentary political logic readily predicts the existence of inefficiency, but it has difficulties in explaining why inefficient institutions are replaced by more efficient ones. China's reform shows that when the growth potential is large, with intelligence and will reformers can devise efficiency-improving institutional reforms to benefit all, including and especially those in power. There is apparently more room than we thought for institutional innovations to address both economic and political concerns, that is, for reforms to improve efficiency while remaining compatible with the interests of those in power.

The general principle of efficiency-improving and interest-compatible institutional change is simple, but the specific forms and mechanisms of transitional institutions often are not. Successful institutional reforms usually are not a straightforward copy of best-practice institutions. They need not be and sometimes should not be. They need not be because room exists for efficiency improvement that does not require fine tuning at the beginning. They should not be because the initial conditions are country- and context-specific, requiring special arrangements. Therefore, inevitably, transitional institutions display a variety of nonstandard forms. Furthermore, because these institutions are often responses to the initial institutional distortions, the mechanisms of their functioning can be intricate. Understanding these mechanisms sometimes needs an appeal to the counter-intuitive "second-best argument," which states that removing one distortion may be counterproductive in the presence of another distortion. For all these reasons, studying institutions in transition requires careful, and sometimes imaginative, analysis.

In this chapter I study the general principle and the specific mechanisms underlying China's transitional institutions through the analysis of four successful reforms and one failure. Together, these five examples cover a broad spectrum of institutional reforms of the market, firms, and the government.

The first example is market liberalization through the so-called dual-track approach under which prices were liberalized at the margin while inframarginal plan prices and quotas were maintained. This approach is unconventional but shows in the simplest way how a reform can simultaneously improve efficiency and protect existing rents. The dual track reveals both the economic and political rationale, and also illustrates how a market-oriented reform can utilize existing institutions, which were designed for central planning.

The second example concerns an innovative form of ownership of firms—local government ownership in general and rural township-village enterprises (TVEs) in particular. This form is not standard, neither private nor state (i.e., national government) ownership. Yet TVEs were China's growth engine until the mid-1990s. The nonstandard ownership form worked to improve efficiency in an adverse environment characterized by insecure private property rights. At the same time, the equity stake of local governments served the interests of both local and national governments by giving them a higher share of revenue relative to the standard private ownership form.

The third example is one of making fiscal federalism productive. China's fiscal contracting between the central and local governments has worked to provide the incentives for local governments to pursue economic prosperity. By granting high marginal retention rates, this innovative arrangement has aligned the interests of local governments with local business, and played a fundamental role in turning local governments into "helping hands" for local business. Local governments responded to incentives by supporting productive nonstate enterprises and reforming nonproductive state enterprises.

The fourth example demonstrates a way to constrain the government in order to protect private incentives in the absence of rule of law. The institution of anonymous banking is not only unconventional but also contrary to the principle of transparency. But it has an economic logic: when other institutional means are not working, it limits government predation by reducing the amount of information available to it. The government accepts such a constraint because it benefits from the revenue out of the banking system through its control over interest rates and capital flow. Although such a practice of financial repression violates usual policy recommendations, it plays a crucial role in inducing the government to give up discretionary taxes on individuals.

Not all China's reforms worked. One miserable failure is the reform of large-scale state-owned enterprises (SOEs). After many experiments, no reforms of SOEs have been found to improve economic efficiency in a fashion compatible with the interests of those in power. The institution of Party appointment of top managers is a key obstacle. This failure reform is very costly to China. But fortunately it is not fatal, as SOEs now account for less than one-quarter of the entire economy, and their role is diminishing.

CREATING THE MARKET:
A DUAL-TRACK APPROACH TO LIBERALIZATION

The simplest way to demonstrate how China's reform worked is through an illustration of the dual-track approach to market liberalization (Lau, Qian, and Roland 2000). It highlights the general principle underlying this innovative, transitional institution: reform must improve efficiency and yet be compatible with important interests. It also shows that initial conditions, including existing institutions, play a role in the implementation of reform.

It is well known that the essential building block of a market system is allocating resources according to free market prices. An essential ingredient of any market-oriented reform involves price liberalization. The eastern European experience has shown two alternative approaches. In the first approach, practiced in Hungary for example, after its 1968 reform, bureaucrats set prices administratively, supposedly in accordance with market supply and demand. But in reality, prices were set through bureaucratic bargaining, often to serve the political objectives of bureaucrats, such as keeping state firms afloat (Kornai 1986). Such reform satisfies bureaucrats' interests, but does not improve efficiency in any significant way because prices are not really determined by the market. This approach proved a failure. After 1990, eastern European countries have adopted a standard approach: prices are freed in one stroke and determined solely by the market.

China adopted a third, unconventional approach to market liberalization, the dual-track approach. Its basic principle is as follows. On one track, economic agents are assigned rights to, and obligations for, fixed quantities of goods at fixed planned prices as specified in the preexisting plan. At the same time, a market track is introduced under which economic agents participate in the market at free market prices, provided that they fulfill their obligations under the preexisting plan. In essence, prices were liberalized at the margin while inframarginal plan prices and quotas were maintained for some time before being phased out. Clearly this approach differed from the two approaches experienced by the eastern European countries: it differs from their experience prior to 1990 because real market prices and markets as a resource allocation institution were created immediately. It was also different from their experience after 1990 because of the continued plan track.

The first implication of the dual-track approach is political: it represents a mechanism for the implementation of a reform without creating losers. The introduction of the market track provides the opportunity for economic agents who participate in it to be better off, whereas the maintenance of the plan track provides implicit transfers to compensate potential losers from the market liberalization by protecting the status quo rents under the preexisting plan. This can be seen easily from the special case of efficient rationing and efficient planned supply; that is, the planned output is allocated to users with the highest willingness to pay and the planned supply is delivered by suppliers with the lowest marginal costs. Dual-track liberalization means that planned quantity continues to be delivered at planned price, but any additional quantity can be sold freely in the market. With the dual track, the surpluses of the rationed users and the planned suppliers remain exactly the same. At the same time the new users and suppliers outside the plan are together better off. In comparison, the single-track approach to liberalization in general has distributional consequences that cannot guarantee an outcome without losers.

The second implication of the dual-track approach is economical: it always improves efficiency. Moreover, as the compensatory transfers are inframarginal, the dual-track approach may achieve allocative efficiency too. This can be seen most obviously in the special case of efficient rationing and efficient planned supply. In this case, because there is no inefficiency under the planned track by assumption, the efficient market track matching the residual demand and supply then implies the efficiency of the overall allocation. In a more general case of inefficient rationing and/or inefficient planned supply, the kind of market liberalization as described above cannot achieve efficiency, although it always improves efficiency. However, efficiency can still be achieved with full market liberalization, under which market resales of plan-allocated goods and market purchases by planned suppliers for fulfilling planned delivery quotas are permitted after the fulfillment of the obligations of planned suppliers and rationed users under the plan (Lau, Qian, and Roland 2000). This type of transaction takes many common forms in practice, for example, subcontracting by inefficient planned suppliers to more efficient nonplanned suppliers, and labor reallocation when workers in inefficient enterprises keep housing while taking a new job in more efficient firms. In both examples, after fulfilling the obligations under the plan (planned delivery of supply and welfare support through housing subsidies, respectively), the market track functions to undo the inefficiency of the plan track.

The dual-track approach to market liberalization is an example of reform making best use of existing institutions. First, it utilizes efficiently the existing information embedded in the original plan (i.e., existing rents distribution) and thus its implementation does not require additional information. Second, it enforces the plan through the existing plan institutions and does not need additional institutions. Enforcement of the plan track is crucial for preserving the preexisting rents. However, contrary to common understanding of the relationship between state power and reform, state enforcement power is needed here not to implement an unpopular reform, but to carry out one that creates only winners, no losers.

Agricultural market liberalization followed the dual-track approach. The commune (and later the households) was assigned the obligation to sell a fixed quantity of output to the state procurement agency as previously mandated under the plan at predetermined plan prices and to pay a fixed tax to the government.

TABLE 11.3
Dual-Track Market Liberalization

	1978	1988
Grain (millions of tons)		
State procurement at plan price	47.8	50.5
State procurement at market price	near 0	43.8
Total domestic production	304.8	394.1
	1981	1990
Steel (millions of tons)		
Plan quota	13.91	15.58
Domestic production	26.70	51.53
Plan/production	0.52	0.30
	1978	1994
Labor (millions of employees)		
State permanent	74.51	83.61
State contract	0	28.53
Nonstate	48.9	204.85
State permanent/total	0.60	0.26

Source: Lau, Qian, and Roland 2000.

It also had the right to receive a fixed quantity of inputs, principally chemical fertilizers, from state-owned suppliers at predetermined plan prices. Subject to fulfilling these conditions, the commune was free to produce and sell whatever it considered profitable, and to retain any profit. Moreover, the commune and households could purchase grain (or other) outputs from the market for resale to the state to fulfill its responsibility. As table 11.3 shows, under the dual track, the state procurement of domestically produced grains between 1978 and 1988 remained essentially fixed, with 47.8 million tons in 1978 and 50.5 million tons in 1988, while total domestic grain production increased from 304.8 million tons to 394.1 million tons, almost a one-third increase.

Industrial market liberalization also shows how markets could grow out of plans (Byrd 1991; Naughton 1995). For coal, China's principal energy source, the planned delivery was increased somewhat from 329 million tons in 1981 to 427 million tons in 1989 (mainly because new state coal mines were opened), but the market track increased dramatically from 293 million tons to 628 million tons in the same period. The increments came mainly from small rural coal mines run by individuals and TVEs. For steel, another one of China's major industrial materials, the plan track was quite stable in absolute terms, but the share of plan allocation fell from 52 percent in 1981 to 30 percent in 1990. Unlike coal, the supply response in steel came mainly from large SOEs rather than small nonstate firms. In the cases of both coal and steel, because the plan track was basically "frozen," the economy was able to grow out of the plan on the basis of the market track expansion by state or nonstate firms.

Labor market development follows a similar pattern. Table 11.3 shows that employment in the nonstate sector increased from 48.9 million to 204.9 million in 1994. In contrast, total employment in the state sector, including civil servants in government agencies and nonprofit organizations, increased only from 74.5 million to 112.1 million. Furthermore, within the state sector, there are two tracks as well. Beginning in 1980, while preexisting employees maintained their permanent employment status, most new hires in the state sector were made under the more flexible contract system. Employment in the plan track has been virtually stationary—it went from 74.51 million in 1978 to 83.61 million in 1994.

DEVELOPING FIRMS: THE NONCONVENTIONAL OWNERSHIP FORM OF TOWNSHIP-VILLAGE ENTERPRISES

Ownership reform of firms is a central issue in transition to a market economy. The eastern European experience in ownership transformation has the following pattern. In the earlier reforms (prior to 1990), there was a lack of development of nonstate enterprises and a lack of privatization of state-owned enterprises; both were thought responsible for the reform failure. In the post-1990 transition, mass privatization of state enterprises became the cornerstone of the reform, and in many cases, it was a political mandate. Evidence shows that new entry private firms, rather than privatized state firms, have been the driving force for recovery and growth.

New entry firms have been also the driving force behind China's growth. But China differs from eastern Europe and most other developing economies in an important aspect: in the first 15 years of reform between 1979 and 1993, most new entry Chinese firms were neither private firms nor state firms (i.e., national government firms), but local government firms. As table 11.3 shows, private enterprises played only a minor role: in 1993 they contributed less than 15 percent of the national industrial output. In contrast, in the same year local government firms contributed 42 percent of the national industrial output (table 11.4).

The most important segment of local government firms are township-village enterprises (TVEs) in rural areas, which numbered 1.5 million with employment of 52 million in 1993. The TVE shares of output and employment in rural industry were 72 percent and 58 percent respectively, the rest being private shares. Although TVEs were being privatized and private firms became the engine of growth in the late 1990s, China's performance would look very different without the early contributions of TVEs. Thus, in order to understand how reform worked in China, one has to understand TVEs.

TABLE 11.4
Industrial Output Share by Ownership
(percentage of total)

	1978	1993
State firms	78%	43%
Nonstate firms	22%	57%
Local government firms	22%	42%
Private and other types firms	0%	15%

Source: China Statistical Yearbook.

The crucial feature of TVEs is the local community (i.e., township or village) government control of firms, in contrast with private or national government control (Chang and Wang 1994; Li 1996; Che and Qian 1998a). Given the obvious costs associated with government intervention, what are the comparative advantages of community government ownership over private ownership?

One of the most salient institutional features in China (and in many developing countries as well) is the absence of rule of law to protect private property rights. Along with a strong anti–private property ideology inherited from the central planning era, private property rights, both cash flow and control over assets, are not secure. Indeed, the state has attacked private enterprises during several general political crackdowns after the reform, which include the "anti-spiritual-pollution campaign" of 1983, the "anti-bourgeois-liberalization campaign" of 1987, and most recently, after the Tiananmen Square demonstrations of 1989. Therefore it is not surprising that private firms were underdeveloped because of the absence of legal protection of private property rights.

In such an institutional environment the property rights of local government-owned firms, such as TVEs, can be more secure than those of private enterprises because of the protection of community governments. In some countries the national government relies on local governments for votes. The political support provided by local governments makes them useful to the national government, which can use them as the basis of its power. But under the China's political system rural community governments do not vote or elect the national government. Their support for the national government takes a different form— providing local public goods, such as maintaining order, building roads, providing water and irrigation systems, and implementing family planning. These local public goods have both political and economic dimensions. For example, maintaining order provides political support to the national government; at the same time it is conducive to local business development.

Because the local community government provides local public goods, the interests of the national government are potentially more aligned with those of local governments than with those of owners of private enterprises. Indeed, when the local government controls TVEs, it becomes more useful to the national government than private owners. The following arguments show that, as a result, the national government may be more friendly toward TVEs than toward private enterprises, and therefore, property rights of TVEs become endogenously more secure than those of private enterprises in the absence of rule of law (Che and Qian 1998b).

Ownership of firms provides owners with control over firms' books and accounts, which allows the owner to hide a portion of revenues. This provides the owner with incentives when revenue-based contracts are credible in the absence of rule of law. In the case of private ownership it is the manager who has the control rights and receives unobservable revenue. Worrying about the possibility of government predation, private owners rationally hide excessive revenue by choosing short-term or liquid projects. This provides incentives to managers but also incurs revenue-hiding costs. When the manager has the control rights over firms, the local government loses control. Then the local government does not have incentives to provide local public goods because it cannot be sure it can reap the future benefits.

In the case of local government ownership it is the local government that has control rights and receives unobservable revenue. When the local government runs a business, ownership and control rights interact with government activities and generate two effects that are absent under private ownership. First, the local government has higher incentives in providing local public goods because its ownership rights give it access to the future revenue in a credible way. Second, anticipating this, the national government would leave a bigger budget to the local government and thus optimally prey less on TVEs than on private enterprises. This in turn makes the local government less worried about revenue confiscation and reduces TVE revenue hiding. Both effects improve efficiency.

Both economic and political rationales work in the ownership form of TVEs. TVEs not only contribute to growth, but also serve the interests of national and local governments. The crucial linkage is the role of local government in providing local public goods. There is evidence suggesting such a linkage. The national government has stipulated that the TVE after-tax profits should be essentially used for two purposes: reinvestment and provision of local public goods. Nationwide in 1985 about 46 percent of the after-tax profits of TVEs were reinvested, and 49 percent were used for local public expenditure. In 1992, 59 percent of the after-tax profits of TVEs were reinvested, and 40 percent were used for local public expenditure (*Statistical Survey of China* 1992, 1993).

Does the TVE ownership, relative to private ownership, better serve the interests of the national and local community governments in terms of tax revenue? From the panel data of 28 provinces between 1986 and 1993, the relationship between ownership forms and fiscal revenues of local and national governments has been estimated (Jin and Qian 1998). The main findings are that, in rural China, the share of TVEs relative to private enterprises in a province has a positive association with the revenue shares of the national, and especially the township and village, government, after controlling for the level of per capita income and other geographic variables. Specifically, a 10 percentage point increase in the share of TVEs relative to private enterprises in the total rural nonagriculture employment (i.e., TVEs plus private enterprises) is associated with a 1.1 percentage point increase in the revenue share to the national government. Considering that the mean of the national share is 7.3 percent, the national government benefits significantly from TVE ownership in terms of fiscal revenue. Moreover, a 10 percentage point increase in the share of TVEs is associated with a 2.4 percentage point increase in the revenue share to township and village governments. This is an even more significant effect, given that the mean of township and village government revenue share is 8.2 percent. These results indicate that local government ownership not only provides higher revenues to both the national and the township and village governments, but also makes proportionally more revenue stay in rural areas.

From the perspective of fiscal institutions, the above results reveal other interesting implications of TVE ownership. One of the common institutional problems in developing and transition countries is an inadequate system for generating tax revenue for the government and a poor fiscal system for using it. On the revenue side, all transitional economies have been experiencing sharp government revenue shortfalls because of the erosion of monopoly profits from SOEs and the greater difficulty in taxing new private firms. In a centrally planned economy, taxation is simple: the government uses distorted prices to concentrate most surpluses in the final industrial sectors and extracts revenues from them. After the liberalization of prices and ownership, profits are more equally distributed among different sectors and the government loses revenue bases, especially in enterprises it does not control (McKinnon 1993). The ensuing fiscal collapse is one of the major reasons behind the recent Russian crisis. On the expenditure side, governments in developing countries often bias the use of revenue toward certain groups in urban areas for political reasons (Bates 1987). After revenue is collected, the government is often unable to spend it on local public goods in rural areas because of political lobbying from urban elites.

Both problems hurt rural industrialization and development. Local government ownership of TVEs can mitigate both problems. With the ownership and control rights over firms, the local government has a less costly way to extract revenues from these firms than from private firms because the latter control their own financial accounts. For the same reason, when local governments control firms, it is harder for the central government to extract revenue from them, and thus revenue is more likely to stay in the local areas. The above evidence shows that the role of TVE ownership to some extent substitutes for the problematic fiscal system: on the revenue side, it allows for some revenue extraction despite the lack of an effective taxation system at the time of general tax revenue decline; on the expenditure side, it keeps a large proportion of revenue in rural areas, avoiding redistribution by the national government to the urban areas.

TVEs are an example of how existing institutions can be modified to serve the new purpose of development. The root of TVE organization is the agricultural commune system initiated in 1958. The commune system was a huge failure in agriculture production, responsible for more than 20 million deaths in the early 1960s in the greatest famine in human history. The same organizational structure of the commune also bred the commune and brigade enterprises, the predecessor of TVEs. They were the driving force for the first wave of rural industrialization in 1958, but were no success in and of themselves. Operating on the fringe of the central planning, they were a moderate success in the second wave of rural industrialization in the 1970s. Commune and brigade enterprises were renamed as TVEs in the 1980s and became the engine of growth and the driving force for market-oriented reform. This illustrates the complexity of institutional development. Local government ownership became something phenomenal only under particular circumstances, with complementary changes elsewhere in the economy. The fact that TVEs were being privatized in the 1990s is another reminder that one should not take a static view of institutional reforms. There is no foolproof way of designing a particular institution.

REFORMING THE GOVERNMENT:
PRODUCTIVE FISCAL FEDERALISM

Economists working on transition used to focus on the trilogy of stabilization, liberalization, and privatization. But they increasingly realized that an important missing component in this menu was the government. Even in an economy that has been stabilized, liberalized, and privatized, there is no guarantee that growth will ensue. A crucial determinant of growth is the behavior of government, especially that of local governments, which often have direct regulatory authority over new small enterprises. In one way, local governments can be a "grabbing hand" vis-à-vis private enterprises; in another way, they can be a "helping hand" (Shleifer 1997). To some extent, whether local governments play "grabbing hands" or "helping hands" depends on their incentives. The incentives of local government officials can be structured in many ways. One aspect that has important bearing on the incentives of local governments is their fiscal relationships with higher-level government.

A comparison between China and Russia is relevant. Both are large countries, and thus the central-local relationship is an important issue for reform, which is quite different from smaller transition countries like Poland and Hungary. Arguably, Russia has implemented more reforms in the areas of price and trade liberalization and privatization than China. Nevertheless local governments in Russia are often obstacles to local development. In contrast, local governments in China have been very enthusiastic in supporting local development and helping local businesses. Why the difference? It cannot be attributed to China's better rule of law. One plausible explanation is the local government's fiscal incentives.

An important innovation in China has been a fiscal reform of central-local relations, beginning as early as 1980. Before the reform, the shares of local government expenditure in total government expenditure were 46 percent during 1971–75 and 50 percent during 1976–80. After the reform, the shares were 51 percent during 1981–85 and 60 percent during 1986–90. After excluding price subsidies during 1986–90 to make the data comparable to previous periods, the shares of local spending come down to about 50 percent. Therefore, the aggregate local-central spending ratio has been basically the same before and after the reform. However, for two reasons the share of local government expenditure itself does not capture the important elements of reform and decentralization in China. First, prior to the reforms, local governments had no authority over the structure of their expenditures. After the reforms, local governments acquired authority within a broad set of guidelines set by the central government. Provinces also gained the authority to decide on the fiscal arrangements with the subprovincial governments within them.

Second, China's decentralization involved more than just the devolution of government authority. It also involved changes introduced between 1980 and 1993 in the fiscal incentives for local governments through the so-called fiscal contracting system. Government revenue in China falls into three categories: budgetary funds, extrabudgetary funds, and off-budget funds. The off-budget funds are not recorded, so little can be said about them. Extrabudgetary revenue consists of tax surcharges and user fees levied by the central and local governments' agencies as well as earnings from SOEs. The extrabudgetary local revenues are not subject to sharing with the central government, but the budgetary revenues are. Up to 1994, all budgetary revenues except custom's duties were collected by local governments. In 1980, a new fiscal system was put into place, known as "eating from separate kitchens." This system represents a dramatic departure from the previous system of "unified revenue collection and unified spending," that is, "eating from one big pot."

Under the new system, the central and provincial budgetary revenue and expenditures were determined in the following way (Wong 1997). First, central fixed revenue was defined to include custom's duties, direct taxes or profit remittances from central-government-supervised SOEs, and some other taxes. All other revenue falls under the heading of local revenue. Second, local revenue was divided between the central and provincial governments according to predetermined sharing schemes. In one such scheme, for example, between 1980 and 1987 Guangdong province would remit a fixed amount of 1 billion yuan per year; and between 1988 and 1993, it would remit a fixed amount per year, which

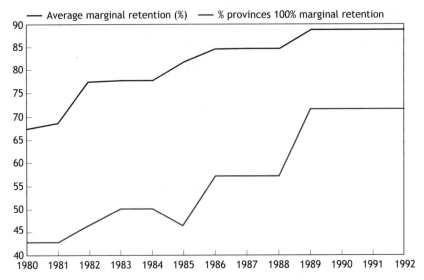

Figure 11.1. Provincial marginal revenue retention rates (1980–92). The upper line is the average of marginal retention rates. The lower line is the share of the provinces with 100 percent marginal retention rates.
Source: Jin, Qian, and Weingast 2001

increased by 9 percent per year. Guizhou province would receive fixed subsidies that increased by 10 percent per year. On the other hand, Jiangsu province would remit a fixed share of revenue to the central government. Over time, many provincial governments retained 100 percent of the total local revenue at the margin, which effectively made them residual claimants. Figure 11.1 displays the average of the provincial marginal revenue retention rates and the share of provinces with 100 percent marginal retention rates. It shows that in the early 1990s, provinces retained nearly 90 percent of local revenues on average, and about 70 percent of provinces became "residual claimants" because they retained 100 percent of local revenue at the margin.

What are the motivations for introducing the fiscal contracting system? There are two stated purposes (Oksenberg and Tong 1991). First, the central government intended to guarantee itself a certain flow of revenue from provincial governments. Second, the central government also wanted to provide provincial governments with incentives to build up local economies and their own revenue bases. High fixed remission amounts and high marginal local revenue retention rates apparently serve both purposes.

Two issues are relevant in examining how this reform worked in practice. First, to what extent had the provincial governments' fiscal incentives been strengthened as the result of this reform? Second, how did provincial governments respond to the fiscal incentives?

TABLE 11.5
The Correlations between Local Revenue and Expenditure

	1982–91		1970–79	
Fixed Effect	β	R^2	β	R^2
Budgetary expenditure on budgetary revenue	0.752 (19.73)	0.968	0.172 (6.172)	0.930
Extrabudgetary expenditure on extrabudgetary revenue	0.971 (32.25)	0.991		

Source: Jin, Qian, and Weingast 2001.

Notes: Each regression includes a full set of year dummies. Huber-White robust *t*-statistics are in parentheses.

Jin, Qian, and Weingast (2001) have used the panel data from 28 provinces between 1982 and 1992 to answer these two questions. Through an examination of the correlation between local governments' revenue generated and their expenditures, one can gauge the marginal fiscal incentives of provincial governments. As table 11.5 shows, during the reform period between 1982 and 1991, the correlation coefficient between the provincial budgetary revenue and budgetary expenditure is, on average, .75, and that for the extrabudgetary revenue and expenditure is as high as .97. These numbers imply that a one-yuan increase in provincial budgetary revenue results in about three-quarters of a yuan of provincial budgetary expenditure, and the relationship becomes almost one to one for extrabudgetary revenue and expenditure. In comparison, during the prereform 1970–79 period, the corresponding coefficient between the budgetary revenue and expenditure is, on average, .17. It indicates that prior to the reform the central government, on average, extracted over 80 percent of any increase in provincial revenues. Comparing the postreform and prereform results, we find that the fiscal contracting system represents a drastic departure from the past by allowing provinces to keep the lion's share of increases in revenue at the margin. Therefore, the new fiscal system indeed substantially enhanced the fiscal incentives for local governments.

A comparison of these findings with parallel investigations in Russia is also revealing. Zhuravskaya (2000) examined the fiscal incentives of city governments in the region-city fiscal relationship in postreform Russia (city is one level below region, which in turn is one level below the federal government). Using the data of 35 cities for the period 1992–97, and by regressing the change in "shared revenues" between local and regional governments on the change of "own revenue," she found that the coefficient was—.90. This estimation means that increases in a city's own revenue are almost entirely offset by decreases in shared revenues from the region to the city. The resulting near-zero incentives in postreform Russia look similar to the prereform China but stand in sharp contrast to postreform China.

The incentive theory tells us that if the central government takes away all the locally generated revenue, the local government has no incentive to support productive local businesses because it cannot benefit from such an effort. Conversely, if local governments' expenditures are closely linked to the revenue they generate, local governments are more likely to support productive local businesses, as they benefit directly from their efforts. The empirical evidence found by Jin, Qian, and Weingast (2001) reveals that such incentive effects do exist and are significant. An increase in the marginal fiscal revenue retention rate in a province by 10 percentage points is associated with an increase of 1 percentage point in the growth rate of employment by nonstate enterprises in that province. This result holds when "nonstate enterprises" are measured by rural enterprises only and by all nonagriculture-nonstate enterprises, rural and urban. Quantitatively these numbers are quite significant because the mean of the growth rates of rural enterprise employment is 6 percent, and that of all non-agriculture-nonstate employment is 9 percent. Similar results are found for some reform measurements in state-owned enterprises. A 10 percentage point increase in the marginal revenue retention rate in a province is associated with a 0.5 percentage point increase in the share of contract workers (as opposed to permanent workers), where the mean is 9 percent. As for the change of the share of bonuses in total employee wages, a 10 percentage point increase in the marginal revenue retention rate is associated with a 0.15 percentage point increase in the share of contract workers, where the mean is 15 percent. These results imply that local fiscal incentives are an important inducement for local economic development and reform, more so for the former.

CONSTRAINING THE GOVERNMENT
WITHOUT REDUCING ITS REVENUE

One of the fundamental institutional obstacles to economic development, according to economic historians such as North, is the lack of institutional constraint on the powerful, discretionary state. When the state is not constrained, it faces a fundamental commitment problem, that is, how to credibly commit not to prey on private gains or intrude on private economic activities despite the great temptation to do so. The lack of such commitment often results in an excessive discretionary marginal tax rate that is detrimental to private incentives. Moreover, the state itself also suffers from its lack of commitment: when the discretionary marginal tax rate is too high, the state is only able to grab little revenue because it is on the downward-sloping part of the Laffer curve. While the rule of law is an effective way of constraining the state in developed countries, China does not yet have it.

But there are other institutional arrangements that perform the function of constraining the government to protect private incentives. It may be possible to reduce the effectiveness of state power by reducing the information available it. Bai et al. (1999) suggest that reducing information available to the state has played an important role in constraining the government in China. These practices of concealment include anonymous business transactions through the use of cash and anonymous financial assets through the use of anonymous bank deposits.

In China there was very tight control over the use of cash for business transactions before the reform. Any transaction of more than 30 yuan (about U.S.$20) had to go through a state bank. During the reform, government controls were relaxed. The ratio of cash in circulation to GDP was less than 6 percent at the eve of reform in 1978, but increased to more than 13 percent in the 1990s. When a transaction is conducted in cash rather than through a state bank, the state obtains no information about the actual income earned through business transactions.

Cash is not only useful for anonymous transactions but also for storing value in an anonymous way. Yet there is a more efficient way of accumulating wealth anonymously: the use of anonymous household bank deposits. In China, individuals making bank deposits need not present personal IDs or register their real names. As a result, the state banks cannot find out in any way which deposits belong to whom. As such, the state does not have the information about individual's financial wealth in the forms of cash and bank deposits.

The use of anonymous transactions and financial assets leads to a combination of hidden income and hidden wealth, which in turn sets credible limits to government taxation and thus preserves private incentives. The theoretical argument goes as follows. Consider first the benchmark case of information centralization under which the state observes all income generated in the economy. For ease of argument, suppose an extreme case prevails in which the state cannot make any credible commitment in the absence of the rule of law. Then a discretionary ex post marginal tax rate of 100 percent will be imposed on all individuals' income because the state has perfect information. When individuals anticipate that the state is going to undertake such discretionary taxation, and given that all revenues are observable to the state, individuals will have no private incentives to work or invest. The result is a very low-efficiency equilibrium.

In contrast, under the regime of anonymous transaction and anonymous bank deposits as described above, the state does not observe individual incomes or savings but only aggregate savings deposits. This implies that the state cannot target particular individuals and thus can only levy a flat tax on savings deposits. Consider that even an autocratic government faces at least one constraint—the fear of rebellion from the poor and needy, and the government maximizes revenue minus the cost associated with probable revolt. However, the fear of rebellion itself is not sufficient to constrain the state under good information, because the state can still avoid rebellion from the poor by taxing at a 100 percent marginal rate only on the rich. With anonymous transactions and financial assets, the state is forced to tax the rich and the poor at the same flat rate. Then there is a maximum amount the state can levy beyond which the needy may starve and revolt. As a result, anonymous transactions and financial assets would impose an upper bound of taxation on savings deposits. In this way, even in the absence of any institution to explicitly constrain government power, limiting the information available about an individual's transactions and savings can credibly limit government predation. This mechanism can enhance secure private property rights that would otherwise not be possible.

The above analysis shows how reducing information available to the state improves economic efficiency. It is clear that this is in the interest of private entrepreneurs, but less clear how this is also in the interest of the state. Conceivably it could be against the interests of the state if the state cannot tax anything. The government could benefit from anonymous transactions and financial assets by controlling international capital flow and imposing restrictions on domestic interest rates. Then the government is able to collect "quasi-fiscal" revenues from the state banking system, despite the fact that it may well lose fiscal revenue in terms of income taxes. Through this type of financial repression, the government also benefits from information opaqueness.

In summary, opaqueness of information, together with financial repression, achieves two goals at the same time: improved efficiency and compatibility with interests. Foremost, it credibly limits government predation by imposing upper bounds on explicit taxation on outputs and implicit taxation on bank deposits. This fosters private incentives. Second, it implies that the lower bound on the implicit taxation on bank deposits is greater than zero so that the government can collect some revenues from the state banking system. This suits the government's own interests. Together, the institution of anonymous transactions and financial assets, together with a mild financial repression, can limit government predation without reducing its revenue. While it does not reduce government revenue in absolute amounts, it does reduce the average tax rate because of the expansion of the pie of the economy as a result of improved private incentives.

Evidence from China reveals a general trend of fiscal decline together with financial deepening after the reform. The total (consolidated) government budgetary revenue as a percentage of GDP declined sharply from 31 percent in 1978 to only 11 percent in 1996. If one includes extrabudgetary revenue and off-budgetary revenue, then the total government fiscal revenue as a percentage of GDP declined from about 40 percent in 1978 to 17 percent in 1996. Notice, however, that the absolute amount of fiscal revenue has been rising in real terms because of the fast growth of the economy. More precisely, real government budgetary revenue almost doubled in 20 years when the economy expanded almost fivefold. An important reason for the decline of the government's fiscal revenue as a percentage of GDP is the formal reduction of tax rates, but rather

TABLE 11.6
Currency Seigniorage and Implicit Taxation on Bank Deposits
(percentage of GDP)

	Currency Seigniorage			Implicit Tax on Bank Deposits
	Inflation Tax	Real Expansion	Currency Seigniorage[a]	Implicit Tax on Bank Deposits[b]
1986	0.7	1.5	2.2	1.33
1987	1.1	0.7	1.8	3.07
1988	0.9	3.9	4.8	1.12
1989	0.8	0.5	1.3	−0.09
1990	0.7	−0.7	−0.0	−1.11
1991	1.0	1.5	2.5	0.70
1992	1.7	3.0	4.7	5.61
1993	2.0	3.6	5.6	4.40
1994	1.9	3.3	5.2	4.43
Average 1986–94	1.2	1.8	3.0	2.10

Source: Bai et al. 1999.

[a] Equal to sum of two preceding columns.

[b] A zero real interest rate is assumed as opportunity cost of capital. Inflation compensation for household term deposits maturing in over three years is not taken in to account.

the inability of the government to collect taxes, which is mainly due to hiding private revenue from government observation.

However, government's fiscal revenue is only a partial story, because the government has another important "quasi-fiscal" revenue source from the state banking system. Accompanying the fiscal decline, there was an impressive financial deepening in China when individuals voluntarily held cash and deposited money in the state banking system. The ratio of household bank deposits to GDP was merely 6 percent in 1978. It went up to 56 percent in 1996 and further to more than 65 percent in 1998. This impressive financial build-up benefited the government in two ways: it collected revenue from both currency seigniorage and from implicit taxes on savings deposits when interest rates were set below the market rate. According to table 11.6, between 1986 and 1994 currency seigniorage averaged about 3 percent of GDP each year, where about 1.2 percent was inflationary but 1.8 percent was due to the expansion of real money balance. Implicit taxes on bank deposits were about 2 percent of GDP each year on average, assuming a zero interest rate as the opportunity cost of capital. Then total quasi-fiscal revenue from the state banking system (the central bank and state commercial banks) was over 5 percent of GDP each year. Combining the fiscal and the quasi-fiscal revenues, total government revenue was more than 22 percent of GDP in the mid-1990s. This may well be substantially less than in the prereform period, but does not represent a collapse of government revenue.

It is interesting to compare China again with Russia in this regard. In both countries, government fiscal revenue as shares of GDP declined dramatically, even more so in China than in Russia. In both countries individual economic agents engaged in revenue hiding, but in Russia individuals engaged in barter transactions, while in China cash transactions were more common. In Russia, there was high inflation, and the government collected only a low level of seigniorage. In fact, because of the extensive use of U.S. dollars and free international capital flow, the seigniorage in Russia went into the Treasury Department in Washington and capital flew to Swiss banks. In contrast, the Chinese government was able to control inflation at a modest level and collected sizable seigniorage revenue through capital control and interest rate control.

Anonymous household bank deposits existed even before the reform. It not so much that a new institution is created but that an existing institution finds its new use in a new environment. Because private economic activities were prohibited before the reform, private savings were very low and the role of anonymous bank deposits in protecting private incentives was limited at best. Anonymous bank deposits become an important institution to protect private interests only after the reform when the ban on private businesses was lifted and the use of cash for business transaction became legal. In fact, China learned about anonymous bank deposits from the Soviet Union. But unlike China, Russia abandoned them after the reform in order to follow international "common practice." As a result, the mafia, colluding with the banks, was able to obtain information about the depositors' wealth. This is an important difference between China's local government, which does not have information about depositors, and Russia's mafia, which has this information.

FROM TRANSITIONAL INSTITUTIONS
TO BEST-PRACTICE INSTITUTIONS

During the transition from central planning to a market economy, markets need to be created and expanded, firms needs to be developed, and the government needs to be transformed. The previous four sections have provided four examples from China's experience showing how innovative institutional reforms improve efficiency, benefit major decision makers, and complement existing institutions. In the dual-track market liberalization, efficiency improves because market prices play a role in resource allocation and reform is interest-compatible because existing rents are protected by the planned track. In the example of TVEs, efficiency improves because of more secure property rights for local government–owned firms and local governments have more incentives to provide more local public goods. Both the national and the local governments' interests are better served because TVEs provide more revenue, as compared with private enterprises, to both. Under the fiscal contracting system, the closer link between local revenue generated and local government expenditures enhances the incentives of local governments, which in turn helps the development of local nonstate enterprises and the reform of state-owned enterprises. In the final example, in the absence of the rule of law, anonymous transaction and financial assets improve efficiency because they credibly constrain the state's discretionary behavior to better protect private incentives. The state itself also benefits from the improved private incentives when it is able to extract quasi-fiscal revenues from the state banking system through a mild financial repression.

However, the institutional forms in all the above four examples are better understood as transitional institutions. They are transitional because they incur higher costs and generate lower benefits than some alternative institutions if other complementary institutions are in place. The costs of the dual-track liberalization include the cost of enforcing the planned track, the consequence of failed enforcement such as supply diversion, and the possibility of ratcheting up the scope of the planned track. The weak managerial incentives, together with costly government intervention in TVEs, make them uncompetitive in the market place in the long run. The fiscal contracting system suffers from the renegotiation problem and perhaps makes macroeconomic stability more difficult to achieve. The information opaqueness resulting from anonymous transaction and banking often facilitates corruption, detrimental to corporate governance, and makes it harder to introduce modern taxation. Therefore, these institutions should not be viewed as permanent and should eventually be replaced by more conventional, best-practice institutions when the underlying environment improves.

The fact that best-practice institutions are more efficient than transitional institutions does not imply that the former should always prevail. To the contrary, theoretical arguments and empirical evidence from other countries show the opposite. Specifically, vested interests who benefit from transitional institutions may block their replacement, leading to a possible "partial reform trap." Hellman (1998) emphasized this possibility and provided some evidence from eastern Europe and Russia showing that it was the interim winners, not the losers, of partial reform who blocked further reform. However, this is only one of two possibilities. Dewatripont and Roland (1992, 1995) and Wei (1997) demonstrated another, more optimistic possibility in which a sequential reform strategy has the important advantages of building constituencies as well as momentum, at the interim stage of reform, for further reform. China's experience has demonstrated that this latter possibility can hold and that the new vested interests do not necessarily block further reforms. Three factors seem to facilitate the effects of building up constituencies and momentum: the nature of early reforms, the potential gains from further reforms, and the compensation schemes for potential losers. In what follows we examine each of the four examples above.

From the early 1990s, the planned track of the dual track in product markets was gradually phased out. By 1996, the plan track was reduced to 16.6 percent in agricultural goods, 14.7 percent in industrial producer goods, and only 7.2 percent in total retail sales of consumer goods. These numbers became even smaller in the late 1990s, and the planned track in those markets almost ceased to exist. On January 1, 1994, planed allocation of foreign exchange was completely abolished, and the planned track and the market track were merged into a single market track. Two direct factors have contributed to the smooth transition to a single track market.

First, because of the fast growth of the market track, the planned track became less significant as compared to the market track. For example, table 11.3 shows that steel production under the planned track dropped to 30 percent in 1990 from the level of 52 percent in 1981. Similarly, In 1978, 97 percent of total retail sales were under the planned track, but only 31 percent in 1989. In the foreign exchange markets, at the time when the planned track of the foreign exchange was finally abolished in January 1994, the share of centrally allocated foreign exchange had already fallen to less than 20 percent of the total. With rapid growth, the plan track becomes a matter of little consequence to most potential losers, which in turn reduces the cost required for compensating them.

Second, when the plan track was abolished, potential losers were explicitly compensated. For example, although consumers have been able to buy foodstuffs in the market since 1980, urban food coupons (for purchasing grain, meat, oil, etc.) were finally removed only in the early 1990s. Guangzhou completed the removal of the above coupons in 1992 and spent on average 103 yuan in 1988, 113 yuan in 1990, and 43 yuan in 1992 per urban resident for compensation *(Guangzhou Statistical Yearbook)*. Beijing also spent 182 yuan in 1990, 185 yuan in 1991, and 123 yuan in 1994 per head before eliminating the coupons *(Beijing Statistical Yearbook)*. At the time of abolishment of the central allocation of foreign exchange in 1994, annual lump-sum subsidies sufficient to enable the purchase of the prereform allocation of foreign exchange were offered for a period of three years for those organizations that used to receive cheap foreign exchange.

After reaching the peak in the early 1990s, TVEs were being privatized throughout the 1990s. Privatization of TVEs accelerated in 1998 after the Chinese constitution was amended to regard the private sector as "an important component" of the economy. Wuxi in southern Jiangxu province was often regarded as the model for TVEs for the whole country, and it was the subject of almost all major studies on TVEs, including the important one by the World Bank (Byrd and Lin 1990). Until mid-1990s, TVEs were dominant in Wuxi, and private enterprises were almost nonexistent. Correspondingly, the income from TVEs was the chief revenue source for the township and village governments there. However, throughout the late 1990s, TVEs were being privatized in all the three counties in Wuxi, and by the year 2000 over 90 percent of TVEs had been privatized (author's interview, March 2001).

Three changes have played significant roles in increasing the gains from privatization of TVEs or the costs for the local government to continue to run TVEs. First, an important benefit of TVE ownership is the political protection of local government in order to secure property rights. In the late 1990s, private ownership of enterprises gained more legitimacy, as evidenced by the aforementioned constitutional amendment and the increased share of the private sector in the economy. Therefore, the benefit of TVEs in terms of more secure property right decreased. Second, the cost of TVE ownership, mainly the lack of managerial incentives, became more important as the economy became increasingly marketized and both product and labor market competition intensified. In the product market, fast entry of firms changed the previous seller's market to a buyer's market, eroding the profit margins TVEs enjoyed in the 1980s as early starters. Indeed, in the 1990s, the profitability of many TVEs deteriorated, while private enterprises started to boom in the same location. In the labor market, TVEs also started to lose good managers to foreign and joint venture firms when the latter gave the managers high salaries or even company shares. Third, the reforms in the monetary and banking systems made local bank branches more independent of local governments. TVEs found more difficulty in obtaining credit from the banking system.

The potential social gains from privatization will not automatically lead to privatization unless the local governments have the incentives to do it. As shown above, the significant benefits of TVE ownership to local governments are the tax revenues they extract from TVEs. After privatization, the township and village governments were able to keep all the privatization revenue They were also able to continue to levy fees on all local private firms, usually 1.5 percent of total sales. This "local tax" is not shared with the higher level government; instead, township and village governments usually pay a fixed amount. Therefore, local governments support, rather than oppose, privatization out of their own interests.

China's fiscal contracting system played a positive role of providing fiscal incentives for local governments. But the fiscal contracting was an ad hoc arrangement and was not rule-based. On January 1, 1994, China introduced major tax and fiscal reforms that are more aligned with international best practices. Previously, China had never had a national tax bureau; there was no need because all taxes were collected by local governments and shared with the central government. The 1994 reform established formal fiscal federalism by introducing a clear distinction between national and local taxes and by establishing a national tax bureau and local tax bureaus, each responsible for its own tax collection. The reform also set up fixed rules between the national and local governments. For example, under the new system, the value-added tax is shared by the national and local government at a fixed ratio of 75:25.

Although the new tax and fiscal institutions are more in line with international best practice, they might hurt the interests of some local governments, which kept larger marginal shares of revenue under the previous fiscal contracting system. Why did the local governments accept such a change? Although some local governments (such as Guangdong province) benefited tremendously from the earlier fiscal contracting system, they also recognized that the ad hoc nature of the contracting system created many uncertainties and that the political pressures from other provinces had increased. The potential gain by moving to a rule-based tax system instead of the ad hoc contracting system is in their long-term interests. Moreover, the central government compensated the local governments for their potential revenue losses in the short run in the following way: Local government expenditures in the subsequent three years would be guaranteed to stay at the 1993 levels. This is why in the fourth quarter of 1993 local expenditure exploded because local governments wanted to increase the base for compensation. The move from the fiscal contracting system to fiscal federalism turned out to be quite successful.

On April 1, 2000, China introduced "real name" household deposits under which all the bank deposits require a depositor's ID. This is an important step in moving from anonymous banking to real-name banking, an international practice. As in Korea, this change was not designed to increase tax revenue but to reduce political corruption by making the flow of money transparent. What is interesting is the particular way China introduced real-name banking: It followed a dual-track approach. The real-name policy only applies to new deposits made after April 1, 2000. Withdrawals from existing deposits, which amounted to about 6 trillion yuan (or more than 60 percent of China's GDP), continued to be anonymous. This drastically reduced opposition to this reform. By following the dual-track approach, the existing bank deposits were "grandfathered" and thus protected, and only the new deposits were required to follow the new rule.

The Chinese experience of institutional changes shows that transitional institutions can be superseded by conventional best-practice institutions when more development and reform take place. Transitional institutions do not necessarily lead to a partial reform trap, and incremental reforms do not always create obstacles to further reforms. However, China's experience also shows that this pattern will not develop automatically. It depends on the nature of early reforms, future gains, and especially, compensation schemes.

AN EXAMPLE OF FAILURE:
REFORM OF LARGE STATE-OWNED ENTERPRISES

The above sections analyzed how reforms worked in China through four examples of success. These reforms worked precisely because they found ways to improve economic efficiency and at the same time to divide the pie to benefit all, especially those in power. In one notable area reform has not worked in China. This is the reform of large-scale state-owned enterprises. In this section we examine the troubled path of this reform, showing how efficiency-improving and interest-compatible solutions failed to emerge.

Reforming state-owned enterprises has always been a priority in China. In fact, SOE reform started in Sichuan province in October 1978, even before agriculture reform, in an experiment of expanding enterprise autonomy and introducing profit retention. But the most successful SOE reforms to date are perhaps privatization of small SOEs and layoffs of redundant employees in the mid-1990s. Privatization of small SOEs was started by local governments as an experiment, first in a few provinces such as Shandong, Guangdong, and Sichuan as early as in 1992 (Cao, Qian, and Weingast 1999). Later, the central government endorsed these privatizations under the policy of "grasping the large and releasing the small." Since 1995, millions of redundant SOE workers have also been laid off. After reaching a peak in 1995, the total state employment in China (including both civil servants and SOE employees) started to shrink. By the late 1990s, it had dropped to below 100 million, the level of the late 1980s.

However, the core of the SOE sector—the large-scaled state-owned enterprises—remains a problem spot. Many reforms were implemented, but they did not work well. In the 1980s, the "managerial contract responsibility system" was introduced to provide profit incentives for managers. It had limited success by some measurements, for example, in increasing productivity (Groves et al. 1994). But the financial performance (i.e., profitability) of these enterprises continued to decline. On average, profits and taxes per unit of net capital stock and working capital in state industrial enterprises fell from 24.2 percent in 1978 to 12.4 percent in 1990 and further to 6.5 percent in 1996 (*China Statistical Yearbook* 1997). In the late 1990s, more than one-third of SOEs were in the red.

In the 1990s, the focus of SOE reform shifted to ownership and governance issues, but still saw no breakthroughs. Several failed attempts in the late 1990s were quite revealing. Some large SOEs were corporatized, including those already listed on China's two stock exchanges. But they often suffered from the conflict between the so-called three old committees (i.e., the Party committee, the employee representative committee, and the workers union) and the "three new meetings (i.e., the meeting of shareholders, the meeting of the board of directors, and the meeting of the supervisory committee). In some cases, the conflict between the Party secretary and the CEO is so severe that it interferes with an enterprise's normal operation. In response, some enterprises opted to place the same person in both positions. But this leads to another problem of insider's control. To address this problem, starting 1998, hundreds of external "special inspectors" were sent by the central government to large SOEs to supervise their operations. However, these inspectors were mostly retired high-level bureaucrats who had no knowledge about business operation and financial accounting. Not surprisingly, they could not play any constructive role in addressing the corporate governance problem. Then the government came up another solution by setting up a "Large Enterprise Working Committee" within the Party's Central Committee to be responsible for making appointments of top managers in large SOEs directly instead of going through different levels of bureaucracy.

So what is the problem? The key problem is the Party's control over the appointment of SOE managers (Qian 1996). Although the past SOE reform adopted various reform policies, the fundamental principle of the so-called Party control personnel remained unchallenged. It is not uncommon for the Party to make political appointments for administrative posts. But the Party in China not only appoints cadres to administrative posts but also all the managers of state-owned enterprises. The Party has exercised control over the selection and dismissal of SOE managers through its organization departments at different levels. For example, the Central Party Organization Department has the authority over appointments of the top managers of very large SOEs (the level of minister or deputy minister), as does the Provincial or Municipality Party Organization Department for most large and medium-sized SOEs (the level of bureau chief or deputy bureau chief). This authority applies to joint-stock companies as long as the state has the majority share, even if they are listed on the stock market or are located in the special economic zones. The appointment and dismissal process represents the most important channel of political influence over enterprises by the Party.

Under the Party control personnel system, SOE managers, like mayors, ministers, and Politburo members, are political appointees of the Party. This political process of managerial appointments has serious problems. First, besides being politicized, the appointment process is secretive and complicated. When the Party selects both managers and politicians at the same time, it may not choose the people who are the right managers. Second, selection and evaluation methods are based on information obtained through bureaucratic rather than market channels, such as the stock market, rating companies, and investment banks. Third, the Party bureaucrats have neither the ability nor the incentives to make the right decisions on managerial selection according to business criteria. It is interesting to compare SOEs with TVEs in this regard. Although TVE managers are appointed by township or village governments, they do not go through the higher-level Party apparatus because they are not "state cadres." Therefore, they are not subject to the same political process as SOE managers.

With the Party acting as a "superowner," corporate governance is hard to establish. Corporate governance is a set of institutional arrangements governing the relationships among investors (shareholders and creditors), managers, and workers. The structure of corporate governance concerns (1) how control rights are allocated and exercised; (2) how boards of directors and top managers are selected and monitored; and (3) how incentives are designed and enforced. In other developed economies, major issues of corporate governance concern legal rules limiting the agency problems, protecting shareholders and creditors, and providing room for managerial initiatives. The same problems arise in China, but with a special concern about the role of the state as a large stakeholder. Unless the state, institutional investors, and individual investors are put on an equal footing, political intervention by the powerful government and the Party will continue to plague the performance of these firms.

The SOE sector in China now accounts for about one-quarter of industrial output, but more in such services as wholesale commerce, transportation, communication, and banking. Large-scaled SOEs still constitute the backbone of the economy. The state sector continues to place a disproportionately large claim on economic resources. For instance, SOEs' share of bank lending remained at near 60 percent by the end of 1998. Although SOEs remain the main revenue source for the government (they account for more than one-half of total government revenue), they also represent a big financial burden. The poor financial performance of SOEs is responsible for China's banking sector problem. Total nonperforming loans may have reached as high as 50 percent of GDP in 1999 before some of them were removed from the banks' balance sheets to the newly created "assets management companies."

Fortunately for China, the vibrant nonstate sector has grown so fast that the problem of the state sector becomes less critical. Things would have been different 20 years ago when the state sector constituted about 80 percent of total national industrial output. But will China's reform of large-scaled SOEs (including privatizing them) eventually work? The most recent government policy on SOE reform adopted in September 1999 intended to jump-start the stalled reform (*China Daily,* September 27, 1999). The first, and perhaps most important, new policy is "readjustment of the layout of the state economy" to narrow down its scope dramatically. SOEs are operating in almost all sectors of the economy, ranging from fighter plane production to hotel operation, from book selling to toymaking. Committing the government to withdrawing from most industrial and service sectors is a significant and encouraging step forward in transforming the state sector in the economy. The second new policy calls for the diversification of ownership structure for those enterprises over which the state still wants to maintain control. Except for a few enterprises in which the state intends to retain 100 percent ownership, all other enterprises will become joint stock companies with multiple owners. These new owners can be either domestic private investors or foreign investors, and the companies can be listed on the domestic or foreign stock markets. Examples include PetroChina, listed on the New York Stock Exchange, and China Telecom (Hong Kong), listed on the Hong Kong Stock Exchange.

Will the reform work this time? As for the Party's role in corporate governance, the recent policy on SOE reform sent out a mixed signal. On the one hand, the government intends to follow the international common practice in hiring, empowering, and rewarding top managers for its enterprises, including giving them stocks. On the other hand, the policy reiterated the fundamental principle of "Party control personnel," although it also mentioned that the "control method" will improve. Party control gives the enterprise Party committee extraordinary power in making strategic decisions, and thus presents a fundamental problem in corporate governance. In the coming years we will not be surprised to see frustrating contradictions at every turn in corporate governance reforms.

CONCLUDING REMARKS

This chapter has demonstrated how novel transitional institutions of market, firms, and government worked in China. The institutional reforms achieved two objectives at the same time: they are both efficiency-enhancing and interest-compatible. The real challenge of reform facing transition and developing countries is not so much knowing where to end up but finding a feasible path toward the goal. To understand how reform works in a country, it is not enough to study best-practice institutions as a desirable goal. One should also study how feasible, imperfect institutions fit the economic and political reality and function as stepping stones in the transition toward the goal. The good news is that in these economies room usually exists for efficiency improvement (that is why they need reforms in the first place). China's experience has shown that there will be a time period in which impressive growth does not require perfect institutions, and imperfect but sensible institutions can perform. On the other hand, China's success in unconventional institutions does not constitute an argument against fostering best-practice institutions such as rule of law, private ownership of firms, and transparent government. It is an argument against simplistic and naive views on institutional reform.

As a whole, China's reform experience is unique among developing and transition economies. However, each component of China's reform may find analogues in other countries. For instance, all schemes involving various forms of "grandfathering" have a resemblance to the Chinese dual-track approach. The two-tier wage system with lower wages for newly hired employees and higher wages for existing employees has been used in some industries, such as the U.S. airline industry. The dual track also worked in the export zones in Mauritius, as documented by Rodrik (1999). Although the huge scale of TVEs is unique to China, successful firms in developing and transition economies in which the government holds equity stakes are not unusual. Moscow firms controlled by its mayor or Indonesian firms in which the Suharto family holds substantial shares all enjoy the comparative advantage of political protection. Giving equity stakes to the government does not guarantee growth, but it does align the interests of the government with growth and sometimes helps growth in an environment that lacks a rule of law. Anonymous banking is not unique to

China. Korea, and even some developed countries in Europe such as Austria, had it for a long time, not to mention Switzerland, where the entire banking industry is built upon it.

The thrust of the arguments in this chapter—that is, institutional development needs to fit initial conditions and to be made compatible with the interests of ruling groups—also finds parallels in other successful experiences, such as Botswana. In contrast to most African countries, where institutions were imported and were significantly at odds with the indigenous political culture and the political ambitions of the most powerful people, Botswana's imported institutions were largely consistent with the political ambitions of the powerful. The success of Botswana is much due to the fact that good economics was also good politics (see Acemoglu, Johnson, and Robinson 2003). This is the common ground between China and Botswana, despite the huge differences between the two successful growth experiences.

The country study of China's growth experience highlights the context-specificity of what worked and what did not, which may not be exposed in cross-country regressions. It allows us to use a richer set of information to bring out the diverse paths of good transition and development. China's path of reform is filled with seemingly frustrating contradictions. Starting from misaligned prices, unproductive firms, and an overreaching government, the inefficient economy had a large scope for improvement. Unconventional solutions applicable to developing and transition economies usually come from the people who have a stake in the economy and have information about its own initial conditions and history.

Our study does not predict the eventual success of China's transition, but it does question the prognosis that China's reform is doomed to fail because it did not follow the conventional wisdom. Whether China 's present short march to a market economy muddles through or ends like Indonesia of the late 1990s is still an unknown. But nothing on this scale and within such short a time period has ever been attempted in the history of the world.

REFERENCES

Acemoglu, Daron, Simon Johnson, and James A. Robinson. 2003. "An African Success Story: Botswana." Chapter 4 in this volume.

Bai, Chong-En, David D. Li, Yingyi Qian, and Yijiang Wang. 1999. "Anonymous Banking and Financial Repression: How Does China's Reform Limit Government Predation without Reducing Its Revenue?" Stanford University. Photocopy.

Bates, Robert. 1987. *Essays on the Political Economy of Rural Africa*. Berkeley and Los Angeles: University of California Press.

Beijing Statistical Yearbook. Various years. Beijing: China Statistical Publishing House.

Blanchard, Olivier, and Stanley Fischer. 1993. Editorial. *NBER Macroeconomics Annual, 1993*. Cambridge: MIT Press.

Burki, Shahid Javed, and Guillermo E. Perry. 1998. *Beyond the Washington Consensus: Institutions Matter.* World Bank Latin American and Caribbean Studies. Washington, D.C.: World Bank.

Byrd, William. 1991. *The Market Mechanism and Economic Reforms in China.* New York: M. E. Sharpe.

Byrd, William, and Qingsong Lin, eds. 1990. *China's Rural Industry: Structure, Development, and Reform.* Oxford: Oxford University Press.

Cao, Yuanzheng, Yingyi Qian, and Barry R. Weingast. 1999. "From Federalism, Chinese Style, to Privatization, Chinese Style." *Economics of Transition* 7, no. 1: 103–31.

Chang, Chun, and Yijiang Wang. 1994. "The Nature of the Township Enterprises." *Journal of Comparative Economics* 19:434–52.

Che, Jiahua, and Yingyi Qian. 1998a. "Institutional Environment, Community Government, and Corporate Governance: Understanding China's Township-Village Enterprises." *Journal of Law, Economics, and Organization* 14, no. 1: 1–23.

———. 1998b. "Insecure Property Rights and Government Ownership of Firms." *Quarterly Journal of Economics* 113:467–96.

China Statistical Yearbook. Various years. Beijing: China Statistical Publishing House.

Coase, Ronald. 1992. "The Institutional Structure of Production." *American Economic Review* 82:713–19.

Dewatripont, Mathias, and Gérard Roland. 1992. "Economic Reform and Dynamic Political Constraints." *Review of Economic Studies* 59:703–30.

———. 1995. "The Design of Reform Packages under Uncertainty." *American Economic Review* 83:1207–23.

Gerschenkron, Alexander. 1962. *Economic Backwardness in Historical Perspective: A Book of Essays.* Cambridge: Harvard University Press.

Groves, Theodore, Yongmiao Hong, John McMillan, and Barry Naughton. 1994. "Autonomy and Incentives in Chinese State Enterprises." *Quarterly Journal of Economics* 109:183–209.

Guangzhou Statistical Yearbook. Various years. Beijing: China Statistical Publishing House.

Hellman, Joel S. 1998. "Winners Take All: The Politics of Partial Reform in Postcommunist Transitions." *World Politics* 50 (January): 203–34.

Huang, Jikun, and Scott Rozelle. 1996. "Technological Change: Rediscovery of the Engine of Productivity Growth in China's Rural Economy." *Journal of Development Economics* 49:337–69.

Jin, Hehui, and Yingyi Qian. 1998. "Public vs. Private Ownership of Firms: Evidence from Rural China." *Quarterly Journal of Economics* 113:773–808.

Jin, Hehui, Yingyi Qian, and Barry R. Weingast. 2001. "Regional Decentralization and Fiscal Incentives: Federalism, Chinese Style." Stanford University. Photocopy.

Kornai, Janos. 1986. "The Hungarian Reform Process: Visions, Hopes, and Reality." *Journal of Economic Literature* 24:1687–1737.

Lau, Lawrence, Yingyi Qian, and Gérard Roland. 2000. "Reform without Losers: An Interpretation of China's Dual-Track Approach to Transition." *Journal of Political Economy* 108, no. 1: 120–43.

Li, David D. 1996. "A Theory of Ambiguous Property Rights in Transition Economies: The Case of the Chinese Non-state Sector." *Journal of Comparative Economics* 23, no. 1: 1–19.

Maddison, Angus. 1998. *Chinese Economic Performance in the Long Run.* Paris: OECD Development Centre.

McKinnon, Ronald. 1993. *The Order of Economic Liberalization: Financial Control in the Transition to a Market Economy.* 2d ed. Baltimore: Johns Hopkins University Press.

Naughton, Barry. 1995. *Growing out of the Plan.* Cambridge University Press.

North, Douglass. 1997. "The Contribution of the New Institutional Economics to an Understanding of the Transition Problem." WIDER Annual Lecture, Helsinki, March.

Oksenberg, Michel, and Tong, James. 1991. "The Evolution of Central-Provincial Fiscal Relations in China, 1971–1984: The Formal System." *China Quarterly* 125:1–32.

Qian, Yingyi. 1996. "Enterprise Reform in China: Agency Problems and Political Control." *Economics of Transition* 4, no. 2: 427–47.

Rodrik, Dani. 1999. "Institutions for High-Quality Growth: What They Are and How to Acquire Them." Harvard University. Photocopy.

Rozelle, Scott. 1996. "Gradual Reform and Institutional Development: The Keys to Success of China's Rural Reforms." In *Reforming Asian Socialism: The Growth of Market Institutions,* ed. John McMillan and Barry Naughton. Ann Arbor: University of Michigan Press.

Shleifer, Andrei. 1997. "Government in Transition." *European Economic Review* 41: 385–410.

Shleifer, Andrei, and Daniel Treisman. 1999. *Without a Map: Political Tactics and Economic Reform in Russia.* Cambridge: MIT Press.

Statistical Survey of China. 1992. Beijing: Statistical Publishing House, 1992.

———. 1993. Beijing: Statistical Publishing House, 1993.

Summers, Lawrence. 1992. "The Rise of China." *Transition Newsletter* (World Bank), 3, no. 6: 7.

Wei, Shang-Jin. 1997. "Gradualism versus Big Bang: Speed and Sustainability of Reforms." *Canadian Journal of Economics* 30, no. 4: 1234–47.

Williamson, Oliver. 1994. "Institutions and Economic Organization: The Governance Perspective." Presented at the World Bank Conference on Development Economics.

Wong, Christine P. W., ed. 1997. *Financing Local Government in the People's Republic of China.* Hong Kong: Oxford University Press.

World Bank. 1996. *From Plan to Market: World Development Report, 1996.* Oxford: Oxford University Press.

Zhuravskaya, Ekaterina V. 2000. "Incentives to Provide Local Public Goods: Fiscal Federalism, Russian Style." *Journal of Public Economics* 76, no. 3: 337–68.

CHAPTER 12

Sustained Macroeconomic Reforms, Tepid Growth

A GOVERNANCE PUZZLE IN BOLIVIA?

DANIEL KAUFMANN   MASSIMO MASTRUZZI
DIEGO ZAVALETA

1. BACKGROUND

WE ARE cognizant of the limits to large cross-country empirical studies in trying to understand in depth a particular country reality, in ways useful for advice. At the same time, merely relying on a single country account at a particular point in time ignores the historical and comparative cross-country perspective. Worse, an in-depth investigation of a single issue within a country begs the question of whether the particular issue is fundamental for the country's growth and development relative to other determinants, or not. Further, there are drawbacks in excessive reliance on narrow empirical approaches, or on mere qualitative narrative.

Consequently, the approach undertaken here, based on the case of Bolivia, is of an integrated nature, combining the following strands: (1) a *historical* perspective from the twin standpoints of the evolution of the *enterprise* and *government sectors* over the past half-century; (2) a *review of the literature* on explanations of Bolivia's performance; (3) an empirical analysis of the country's enterprise sector performance on the basis of a detailed *firm-level survey* conducted recently in 80 countries, and, (4) a comparative empirical analysis of

This chapter was originally prepared for the conference "Analytical Country Studies on Growth" at the Kennedy School of Government, April 20–21, 2001. We are grateful for the excellent feedback from the conference's commentator on the presented paper, Simon Johnson, from its convener, Dani Rodrik, and from the conference participatns. Our appreciation also goes to Tugrul Gurgur, Pablo Alonso, Carlos Mollinedo-Trujillo, Maria Gonzalez de Asis, Isabel Guerrero, Yasuhiko Matsuda, Keta Ruiz, and Aart Kraay for valuable inputs and insights. Erin Farnand effectively assisted in processing. This research has also benefited from official World Bank reports on Bolivia. Any errors remain the authors' responsibility, and the views presented here do not necessarily reflect those of the institution or its executive directors.

Bolivia's public agencies based on a *survey of public officials* in Bolivia working in over 100 institutions. To provide an additional element of comparability, we also utilize *cross-country governance* indicators.

The historical background sections provide a simplified account of the evolution of Bolivia's political economy, in turn framing key hypotheses tested in the subsequent econometric analysis. In particular, a salient hypothesis in this chapter, resulting from the historical account, and tested subsequently with the new data sets, is the ascent and entrenchment of "unofficialdom" in Bolivia: both the enterprise sector and the public sector are characterized by substantial unofficial and informal behavior, and these are related. In the public sector it is linked to politics of patronage, of "clientelism" and of corruption, while in the enterprise sector it relates to the lack of a level playing field and high costs of formality—only the elite benefiting from staying in the formal sector. Thus, central to this probe is the role that misgovernance in Bolivia has played in framing the dynamics linking the public and private sectors and the underperformance of formal institutions.

In turn, the extent of "unofficialdom" and misgovernance in Bolivia has had adverse consequences for the country's growth performance. Consequently, a key tenet in this work is that the potentially much higher growth rate that Bolivia could have enjoyed in the aftermath of ambitious macroeconomic reforms boldly launched in the mid-1980s has been thwarted by inefficient progress on the governance front. In undertaking this approach to our inquiry, with its stated hypotheses, a number of conventions are challenged—such as the notion that broad macroeconomic reforms can *suffice* to attain high growth rates. Instead we highlight the potentially key role that may be played by nontraditional institutional factors such as misgovernance, corruption, and "unofficialdom." The empirical approach permits us to quantify at the microeconomic level the effects of "soft" variables usually not subject to measurement, such as extent of politicization of public agencies, the degree of "voice" afforded to enterprise and public service users, and the effectiveness of protection of its property rights. Further, within the exploration of the effects of misgovernance on enterprise behavior and performance, we also test hypotheses such as whether there is a beneficial "grease" role of corruption, as claimed in earlier writings.

More broadly, the methodological approach questions the limits of concentrating on *country aggregates* as a relevant unit of empirical observation. The empirical evidence in this chapter attests to the large variance in performance and governance across *institutions,* and also on the variance across policy and institutional *factors*—within a country. This challenges the tendency to rely solely on single summary indicators, ignoring the within-country variance and thus masking the strengths and weaknesses that institutions in the country may have—in turn clouding the need to provide prioritized and focused policy advice at the country level.

2. INTRODUCTION

The Calderón-Vargas family have been members of Bolivia's upper middle class for generations. Over the last two generations, the family has alternated its residence between La Paz, the seat of government, and Santa Cruz, the entrepreneurial center. Don Ramiro Calderón, nowadays the family elder statesman, lived much of his life in Santa Cruz with his spouse, Marta Vargas de Calderón, a historian by training. Ramiro Calderón Sr. was a moderately successful and highly respected businessman, eventually becoming the elected head of the country's industrialist's association in the early 1980s. At that point he passed on the management of his family business to his daughter, Patricia Calderón-Vargas, and, through a high-level contact in the party currently in power, secured his spouse Marta a midlevel position in the Ministry of Development. Thus, both parents, Ramiro and Marta, moved to La Paz, with their son, Jose Calderón Jr., who was still in high school—while Patricia stayed in Santa Cruz in charge of the family business. In La Paz, after graduating from the university with a degree in public policy in 1993, and through the recommendation of his mother, young Jose joined the Ministry of Finance in a technical position.

Eight years later, at the turn of the new millennium, Ramiro Sr. was in full retirement, Marta was in her last year in government, and their son, Jose, had ascended to the post of undersecretary of the budget. Meanwhile, in Santa Cruz, Jose's sister Patricia was adroitly weathering the depressed environment faced by her business, carrying out downsizing measures that, coupled with some creative accounting, lowered substantially the firm's tax burden, enhancing the chances of survival of the firm.

Over the Christmas weekend recess in Santa Cruz at the end of the year 2000, with her parents and brother visiting from La Paz, the conversation turned to Patricia's account of the managerial challenges of the business, and her concern at the plight of some of the dismissed workers—one of whom she had seen the previous week peddling wares informally in the sidewalk of the main street in the center of town, with one child at his side. More generally, she was also troubled about a number of recent dramatic episodes of social unrest the country had experienced, the result of economic hardships by many who felt disenfranchised and also due to unpopular tariff hikes for public services. She voiced her view that Bolivia had already awkwardly entered the globalized twenty-first century with unclear prospects; a country with a seemingly perennial per capita income hovering around only US$1,000 per year, with about one-half of the population living at less than two dollars a day, and with a dormant enterprise sector.

"But it is not as if recent governments have sat idly," her brother Jose protested, adding, "in fact we should put our challenge in perspective and consider the scope of what has been achieved since the mideighties. Following decades of political and economic chaos, political stability was restored within a democratic framework, and since then there have been fifteen years of resolute economic reforms." Unimpressed, Patricia retorted: "Then, how come there is so little to show for it?" Their mother Marta intervened, referencing her readings of the literature, which pointed to a such a multiplicity of different potential obstacles to high growth in Bolivia—which had averaged virtually zero in annual per capita terms since the mideighties. With her erudition, she alluded to the many writings about Bolivia and Latin America (as summarized in the bibliographic summary review table 12.1), where virtually the full gamut of obstacles to growth has been emphasized.

Upon reviewing the "multifaceted" picture that emerges from a review of the existing literature—which in their view does not focus on the priority factors for Bolivia's growth nowadays—during that Christmas evening the four members of the family decided to devote some of their free time over the next few months to investigating the question: why is it that in the aftermath of bold and sustained reforms for 15 years, the economy had grown so tepidly?[1] They were aware of the costs due to the landlocked nature of Bolivia, and of its topography as well as the vagaries of the terms of trade, yet they agreed that there was much more that needed to be understood.

With his vast entrepreneurial experience for half a century, Ramiro Sr. would provide a historical perspective from the enterprise's vantage point (section 3), while Marta Calderón, with her historical background, erudition in political economy, and public sector experience, would provide a historical account of the politics of the public sector (section 4). The younger generation would complement the perspective of their parents, with Patricia undertaking to analyze current empirical evidence on the obstacles to the firm's operating officially and to vigorous enterprise growth—relying on a very large survey of enterprises worldwide that included Bolivia (section 5), while her brother Jose would suggest a framework and analyze empirically the determinants of public sector performance, in turn based on an in-depth survey of public officials in Bolivia (section 6). The four of them agreed that they would meet in a few months to discuss and attempt to integrate their accounts and draw implications from this exercise (concluding section 7).

3. THE ENTREPRENEURIAL HISTORICAL CONTEXT: SEVERE OBSTACLES TO ENTERPRISE DEVELOPMENT, RESULTING IN THE RISE OF UNOFFICIALDOM

Mr. Ramiro Calderón Sr., with his uncanny memory, can recall in enormous detail the travails that the Bolivian private sector has gone through in the last

---

[1] The Calderón-Vargas "family" is a narrative construct, and as such is fictitious, yet their personalities, experiences, and insights attempt to capture elements of Bolivia's reality. By contrast, none of the data and evidence presented in this work is fictitious, and any other named persons (other than the Calderón-Vargas family) are real.

TABLE 12.1

What Are the Main Obstacles to Bolivia's Growth? A Synthesis of Bibliography Review

Study	Period Covered	Macroeconomic Mismanagement	Trade Policies/ Taxation	Political Obstacle	Institutional Obstacle	Infrastructure	Entrepreneurship/ Labor/ Skills	Finance	External Factors	Geography	Ethnicity	Non-diversified Economic Structure (mono-producer)
							Main Cause of Low Growth					
1. Barrera and Lora 1997	1983–1995	xx	xx				xx	xx				
2. Cámara Nacional de Industrias	various years in 1990s				xx	xx	xx	xx		xx		
3. Chavez 1997	1990s						xx					xx
4. Easterly, Loayza, and Montiel 1996	1960–93	xx	xx		xx			xx				
5. Eder 1968	1950–60	xx										x
6. Fundación Milenio (various)	1990s				xx	xx	xx	xx	xx	x		xx
7. Gallup, Sachs, and Mellinger 1999	Multiple periods to 1990s	xx	xx							xx		
8. Grebe 1999	1990				xx		xx					
9. IDB 1997	1980–90				xx	xx	xx			x		

10. IMF 1998 Country report	1950–90	xx	x			xx		xx	xx
11. Montano and Villegas 1993	1950–90		xx	xx	xx	xx	x		xx
12. Morales and Pacheco 1999	1900–90	xx	xx	x	xx	xx	x		xx
13. OECEI 1969	1920–67	xx	xx	x	xx	xx	x		xx
14. Rodriguez Ostria 1999	1900–90		xx	xx	xx	xx	x		xx
15. Sachs and Morales 1990	1950–80	xx	xx	x	x	xx	x		xx
16. United Nations 1958	1940–58			xx	xx	xx	xx		xx
17. Whitehead 1991	1930–80		xx	xx		xx	xx	x	xx
18. World Bank 1994. Structural adjustment	1980–1990s	xx	xx	xx	xx	xx	xx		
19. World Bank 2001	1990s		xx	xx	xx	xx			
20. World Bank 2000	1990s	xx	xx			xx			

Note: Two *xx*'s signifies that particular prominence is given by the study to the factor identified in that column, while one *x* indicates that while there was treatment of such obstacle to growth in the study, it is not given primary prominence. An empty cell signals absence of treatment of such factor in the study. These evaluations are based on the authors' review of bibliography, and as such there is an element of subjectivity.

50 years, where most often the entrepreneurial segment faced a hostile business environment. He has witnessed dramatic political changes: from a revolution that transformed the country into a "modern" nation, to the attempt at a "state capitalist" model (Morales and Sachs 1990), to two major inflation episodes,[2] to the implementation of a far-reaching economic reform in recent decades. The latter has transformed the country into one of the most privatized economies in Latin America; yet paradoxically the climate for enterprise is still subpar. The private sector has developed under political and constitutional instability, within arbitrary and changing sets of rules, coping with uncompetitive practices by those who have privileged interactions with the state, and facing insecure property rights. This set of factors, in turn, has been associated with a large and entrenched unofficial economy.

Before the 1952 revolution, the Bolivian economy essentially relied on the production of tin and a very rudimentary agricultural system. The mining industry was composed of three major private firms, Patiño, Hochschild, and Aramayo, which, by providing most of the state's revenues,[3] exerted extraordinary political and economic influence, akin to "state capture"—defined as the capacity of firms to shape the state's basic rules of the game (including its policies, laws and regulations). The extent of the capture by these firms led to the label of the "Mining Superstate," signaling the enormous influence they wielded.[4] At the time, the agricultural system was based on large land holdings in the hands of the few, with an archaic quasi-feudal production structure, resulting in very low productivity of the sector—a net importer.[5]

Industry concentration was also marked, with very few producers of food processing, beverages, textiles, and confections products, a pattern that has not changed dramatically until today (United Nations 1958; Rodriguez Ostria 1999), as seen in figure 12.1. Industrial and agricultural development was affected by the high profitability of the mining industry, and its concomitant "Dutch disease" effect through an exchange rate that was overvalued in terms of promoting the development of the nonmining sectors.

In 1952 a violent revolution brought the National Revolutionary Movement (MNR) to power. The MNR was formed by middle-class professionals and veterans from the Chaco war against Paraguay. The main ideology of the party was the creation of a national state and the overthrow of the mining-landlords oli-

---

[2] The second hyperinflation, which peaked in 1985 at an impressive 25,000 percent a year, has been the major hyperinflation not caused by war.

[3] Morales and Pacheco (1999) estimate that taxes on mining production and international trade represented 66.8 percent of the total revenues of the Bolivian state in 1940.

[4] In Hellman, Jones, and Kaufmann 2000, the notion of state capture is developed and analyzed empirically for modern-day transition economies of the former socialist states, and it is found that about one-half of the economies in transition exhibit high levels of state capture by the elite enterprise sector.

[5] For a good overview of the Bolivian economy before 1952 see Morales and Pacheco 1999.

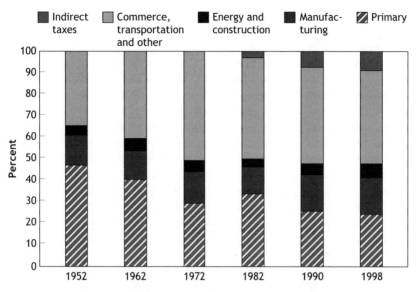

Figure 12.1. Evolution of the composition of GDP in Bolivia (1952–98)
Source: Based on figures in Morales and Sachs 1990; World Bank 2001

garchy. The mines were nationalized and its management unified into a large corporation—the Bolivian Mining Corporation (COMIBOL). Land reforms were carried out. A new economic model was implemented, "state capitalism," whereby import substitution and large public investments in infrastructure were emphasized. Large resources were transferred to the agro-industrial and manufacturing sector, and institutions to promote industrial development were created or strengthened.

The government set up a complex set of incentives and sanctions to influence the private sector's production and investment decisions, relying on heavily subsidized credit, financed by the use of differential exchange rates, and tax incentives. Protective barriers were also set in place,[6] and an increasingly interventionist state in the enterprise sector became a reality.

Within such a growing role of the state in the operations of the enterprise sector, political realities were ripe for the development of an elaborated system of job "patronage" vis-à-vis the government-owned enterprises (SOEs), that is, the use of such enterprises as political tools to hire supporters of the regime. Political imperatives, coupled with the weakness of the judiciary, also gave place to "clientelism"—the use of governmental (or SOE) public contracts to

---

[6] The new regime inherited a complex tariff structure that was composed of thousands of different rates.

garner support from specific individuals or groups. The main employer became the public sector, a situation that was to remain for another forty years, until the mid-1990s.[7]

A competitive private enterprise sector was not encouraged by this statist strategy, which politicized the sector and affected the relationship with the business community. For the new administration the public sector was to be a main engine of growth. Prominent businessmen associated with the former regime were discredited; they were replaced by new insiders with connections to the incoming regime, who benefited from the incentives offered by the state. The supply response was tepid, since the complex system of interventions undermined business confidence. There was uncertainty over property rights, after land reform and nationalization, and corrupt and illegal influence schemes by insiders led to a noncompetitive economic structure of the market. Major resource misallocation took place in agriculture and industry and growth rates turned negative, while overspending by the government sector, complemented by an expansionary monetary stance, resulted in annual inflation rates exceeding 100 percent per year in 1956–57.[8]

By the late fifties, a stabilization plan was put in place as a response (emulated decades later in the 1985 stabilization plan), featuring price liberalization, exchange rate unification, and a drastic reduction in the fiscal deficit through the elimination of subsidies and specially targeted benefits. Trade openness, coupled with a disciplined fiscal stance, exposed the inefficiencies of much of the enterprise sector: of 1,556 firms registered in 1955 only 878 survived by 1958 (OECEI 1969). These measures were kept in place until 1965, when barriers to trade were reintroduced. This period also witnessed the beginning of a period of military rulers (interspersed by very short-lived democratic administrations), which was to last until 1982 (see table 12.2). Following the military coup of 1964, the state capitalism ideology remained as the basic economic model, and consistent with it, the nationalization of the Gulf Oil Company took place.[9]

---

[7] For a good overview see Morales and Sachs 1990, where inter alia the misgovernance manifestations of "patronage" and "clientelism" are addressed. Clientelism is defined by them as "the use of public contracts to maintain support from specific individuals or groups—in public contracts and purchases—from both government and State Owned Enterprises," while patronage is "the use of public enterprises to hire supporters of the regime." According to *Merriam-Webster's Ninth New Collegiate Dictionary,* patronage is "the power to make appointments to public sector jobs specially for political advantage." Among political scientists, clientelism in Latin America is also often seen as the exchange of votes from blocks of voters in return to access to resources by the politician when in power (Rehren 2001).

[8] George Jackson Eder was the leader of the Technical Assistance Mission of the U.S. government that supported the government of Bolivia with the stabilization plan of 1957. For an overview of the mission, see Eder 1968.

[9] Grebe 2001; Morales and Sachs 1990; Montano and Villegas 1993. In Bolivia the conventional import substitution industrialization (ISI) strategy was never aggressively pursued as in other Latin

Growth resumed by the late sixties, at a time when the economy benefited from favorable international commodity prices, the rapid development of the eastern part of the country and its commercial agriculture, and growth of the hydrocarbons industry as a result of previous investments. Large influxes of foreign aid funds, particularly from international agencies, resulted from Kennedy's Alliance for Progress initiative. The practices of patronage and clientelism governing the relations between the state and enterprise did not change from one regime to another, however. The use of jobs for political payoffs and of public contracts awards to derive political benefit were part of the political system, and were associated with corrupt behavior.

Hugo Banzer came to power in 1971 through a violent coup; his dictatorship lasted until 1978, a period of relatively high growth (table 12.2; see also fig. 12.2), when the economy benefited from high commodity prices, a boom in the production of gas, and large influxes of capital financed through heavy borrowing. Bolivian external debt exploded during these years from U.S.\$480 million in 1970—Bolivia had essentially been cut off from international financing since 1931—to U.S.\$2,228 million in 1980 (Morales and Sachs 1990). The economic expansion also benefited from the emerging cocaine industry (valued then at about U.S.\$400 million) (Doria Medina 1986, cited in Morales and Sachs 1990), the result of the boom in cocaine consumption in the United States and the lax attitude of the Bolivian government—with the military directly involved in this industry.

The period witnessed a stronger support for the elite segment of the private sector, due to an alliance between members of the business community and the military regime (which inter alia resulted in industrialists occupying important positions in government), complemented by repressive measures against trade unions and labor. The elite in the private sector sought stability, business opportunities, and the control of the labor class—which had benefited from former regimes with increases in wages and labor legislation. Lobbies such as in agriculture strengthened their influence (emerging from Banzer's birthplace). Influence became a key feature in the relationship of elite firms with the state, while the bulk of the enterprise sector—those without influence—were effectively shut off from benefits of staying in the formal sector.

These elitist relationships between the state and private firms resulted in "large subsidies being vested to interest groups that supported the regime. Friends of the government, particularly in the military and among the private business community, were frequently favored with property rights over hitherto public land, with mining concessions, and, most importantly, subsidized credit" (Morales

---

American countries. In this sense, in Bolivia there was never a coherent and long-lasting policy to develop industrial sites. For an overview of other Latin American countries implementing the ISI, see Thorp 1998.

TABLE 12.2
Political and Economic Regimes in Bolivia, 1950–2000

Period	Political Phase	President	Ideology	Modality of Ascent to Power	Major Economic Measures	Average Fiscal Deficit (%)	Average Inflation Rate (%)	Average Growth Rate (%)
1952–56	MNR revolutionary government	Victor Paz Estenssoro	Nationalism	Revolution	Nationalization, land reform, tax incentives, subsidies to increase agricultural production and manufacturing, roads to connect the lower lands and increase agricultural production. Creation of more SOEs.		127.9 ↑	−2.0 ↓
1956–60		Herman Siles Suazo	Nationalism	Election	Stabilization package, price liberalization, exchange rate unification and trade liberalization, end of all subsidies, SOE's regulation so as to obtain only same benefits as PS		37.5 ↓	0.7 ↑
1960–64		Victor Paz Estenssoro	Nationalism	Election	Export diversification and import abandon, economic planification begins, plan to mechanize the mines		5.6 ↓	4.7 ↑
1964		Victor Paz Estenssoro	Nationalism	Election			10.1 ↓	4.8 ↑
1964–65	Military[a]	Rene Barrientos Ortuno	Right wing	Coup	Large subsidies credits, large investment in public sector, foreign direct investment in oil and mining		6.5 ↓	6.9 ↑
1965–66		Alfredo Ovando Candia Military	Right wing	Designated by the army	Continuation of policies		4.9 ↓	7.0 ↑
1966–69		Rene Barrientos Ortuno	Right wing	Election	Continuation of policies		6.2 ↑	6.0 ↑
1969		Luis Adolfo Siles Salinas	Center-right	VP elected	Continuation of policies		2.2 ↓	4.7 ↓
1969–70		Alfredo Ovando Candia	Nationalism	Coup	Nationalization of private oil company		3.0 ↑	5.2 ↑

Year	Leader	Orientation	Method	Notes			
1970–71	Juan Jose Torres G.	Populist	Coup	Nationalization of some private firms	1.4	3.7 ↑	4.9 ↓
1971–78	Hugo Banzer Suarez	Right wing	Coup	Credit subsidies, boom in exports of gas and tin, investment incentives for private firms, coca industry begins and expands rapidly, large subsidies to private sector	1.8 ↑	18.8 ↑	5.4 ↑
1978	Juan Pereda Asbun	Right wing	Coup		2.7 ↑	10.4	3.3 ↓
1978–79	David Padilla Arancibia	Right wing	Coup		3.8 ↑	15.0 ↑	1.8 ↓
1979	Walter Guevara Arze	Center	Designated by Congress		4.9 ↑	19.7 ↑	1.8
1979	Alberto Natusch Busch	Right wing	Coup		4.9	19.7	1.8
	Transition period. (Short military and congress appointed governments)						
1979–80	Lidia Gueiler Tejada	Center	Designated by Congress	Stabilization plan attempted but failed because of military overthrow		33.4 ↑	−0.55 ↓
1980–81	Luis Garcia Meza Tejada	Right wing	Coup	Major increase in coca industry and corruption	6.0 ↑	39.6 ↑	0.3 ↑
1981	Military Junta	Right wing	Designated by the army		5.6 ↓	32.1	0.3
1981–82	Celso Torrelio Villa	Right wing	Designated by the army		5.6	77.8 ↑	2.8 ↑
1982	Guido Vildoso Calderon	Right wing	Designated by the army		22.3 ↑	123.5 ↑	2.8
1982–85	Hernan Siles Suazo	Left-wing	Election	Hyperinflation, minimum wage increases, black markets	23.4 ↑	4471.7 ↑	−3.0 ↓

(continued)

TABLE 12.2 (*Continued*)

Period	Political Phase	President	Ideology	Modality of Ascent to Power	Major Economic Measures	Average Fiscal Deficit (%)	Average Inflation Rate (%)	Average Growth Rate (%)
1985–89		Victor Paz Estenssoro	Center-right	Election	Stabilization package, price liberalization, trade liberalization, reforms to smooth market mechanism, end of subsidies	7.7 ↓	75.0 ↓↓	1.8 ↑
1989–93		Jaime Paz Zamora	Center-right	Electiont	Privatization of small SOE's	4.3 ↓	14.7 ↓	3.9 ↑
1993–97		Gonzalo Sánchez de Lozada	Center-right	Election	Privatization of large SOE's. Establishment of regulatory framework Creation of private pension funds Banking Law Central Bank Law	3.2 ↓	8.8 ↓	4.4 ↑
1997–2001		Hugo Banzer Suarez	Center-right	Election	Judicial reform National dialogue Antidrug program	3.7 ↑	5.2 ↑	2.4 ↓
2001–2002		Jorge Quiroga	Center-right	Elected vice president. Assumed presidency after Banzer's resignation due to illness.	Proposed program for year 2001/2002: Implement poverty strategy Implement anticorruption program Implement emergency program for economic recovery	3.7[b]	3.7[b]	2.5[b]

Sources: Mesa, Mesa, and Gisbert 1998; Morales and Pacheco 1999; IMF 1998, 2001; World Bank 1994; authors' calculations.

Note: Upward arrow depicts an increasing trend over the period. A downward arrow indicates a decreasing trend over the period.
[a] Barrientos was democratically elected in a widely criticized election in 1966. He was a member of the armed forces and worked closely with them.
[b] Estimated.

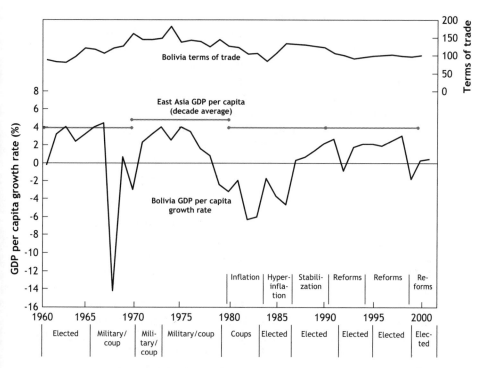

Figure 12.2. Bolivia GDP per capita growth rate and terms of trade. GDP base year = 1995. Data for 2000 is an estimate; 2001 is a projection.
Source: World Development Indicators. Nine East Asian countries included in each decade average: Terms of Trade (goods only) base year = 1995 (1995 = 100). Nine East Asian countries included in regional average for each decade.
Source: International Monetary Fund

and Sachs 1990, 183). Medium and small entrepreneurs, with no links to the government, were excluded from these incentive schemes. Anticompetitive practices were again prevalent, the result of the powerful influence of insiders. These practices, combined with the long-standing policies favoring capital-intensive extracting policies, implied little incentive for budding entrepreneurs, job seekers, or small and medium enterprises to be full participants in the formal economy, resulting instead in the evolution of the informal sector. By the early eighties the informal economy approached about one-half of GDP (Doria Medina 1986). These "crony" relationships between the economic elite and the state, and its particular financial manifestations, also had the deleterious effect of undermining the health of the financial sector: businessmen and bankers colluded to obtain subsidized, state-guaranteed credits, and borrowing from the state development banks and then defaulting on the loans was also common practice and resulted in perverse soft budget constraint mechanisms.

Democracy returned in 1982 but within a context of economic and political unrest. Debt buildup, coupled with domestic political instability, poor macroeconomic management, a very weak tax system, and poor export prospects, resulted in a lack of access to new sources of foreign loans after 1981. The government did not raise taxes or cut expenditures; instead it substituted domestic credit expansion for capital inflows, and a new inflationary process was under way (Morales and Sachs 1990). Inflation peaked in 1985 at an unprecedented (worldwide in a country not at war) annualized rate of 25,000 percent. The crisis pushed many firms into bankruptcy. Industrial output fell by almost 40 percent compared to its 1978 level. However, elite firms or individuals, with access to hard currency—for example, through special relations with the central bank and thus to subsidized foreign currency (then resold in the black market at 15 times its subsidized cost), let to the unproductive enrichment of a few who had preferential access to these rents. The Association of Private Entrepreneurs of Bolivia (CEPB) called for general strikes against the government.

In August 1985, a new government headed by the three-time former president Paz Estenssoro came into power. Only three weeks after the new administration took office, a stabilization package was introduced and, with this, a set of reforms that transformed radically the existing economic model, which the same president had introduced under state capitalism in 1952. The stabilization package was composed of several measures embodied in Supreme Decree 21060, which has become the axis of the economic policy since then.[10] The plan included immediate price and labor market liberalization, exchange rate unification on current and capital accounts and the free convertibility of foreign exchange, trade liberalization abolishing all import and export controls, and reduction of tariffs to a flat rate of 20 percent at first and further reductions subsequently. A radical reduction in the public deficit was implemented, the price of fuel was increased manyfold, layoffs in the public sector and a freeze in public sector wages and investment were carried out, and subsidies were ended.

The program had remarkable short-term results: inflation was controlled in 10 days and growth resumed by 1987, while international trade soared.[11] Labor unions opposed this austerity program, while import substitution industries opposed trade liberalization that once again exposed their inefficiency. Yet the government prevailed. The tax regime was also revamped (including introduction of a value-added tax) following stabilization, and far-reaching financial sector

[10] For a complete description of the stabilization package see Morales and Sachs 1990.
[11] For a description of the evolution of exports and imports see Cámara Nacional de Industrias 1997.

reforms were also implemented.[12] By the early 1990s it was already apparent that the stabilization reform package needed to be complemented by structural and social reforms.[13] In 1993, Gonzalo Sanchez de Lozada—the minister of planning and architect of the stabilization plan under the previous regime—became the fourth consecutive democratically elected president since the return to democracy in 1982. His government introduced an ambitious package of reforms: the five largest SOE's were privatized under the "capitalization" program,[14] the pension system was reformed (strongly linked to the capitalization program), a decentralization process was initiated, and an educational reform was launched. Aiming at autonomy from the political process, the government established a new regulatory framework, particularly for the privatized SOEs, via the superintendencies (water, telecommunications, financial institutions, etc.), as well as a General Superintendency to regulate the framework.[15]

In 1997 Hugo Banzer—who had come to power by a coup in 1971 and was a military dictator until 1978—became the fifth consecutive democratically elected president of the country since the return to democracy (table 12.2). During his tenure there were a number of additional reforms, such as the long overdue customs reform, and institutional streamlining of social programs, so to reduce political influence and achieve greater efficiency. The reforms in social programs were implemented via external donor pressure, since social funds have been a traditional source of corruption and patronage. Further, belatedly, participatory processes became a policy priority: this most recent period has witnessed the launch of consultative initiatives with civil society, to define national strategies and policies and allocation of financial resources that would be freed by the Highly Indebted Poor Countries (HIPC) debt reduction program for which Bolivia qualified.

---

[12] These included implementation of Basle accords on prudential regulation and supervision, minimum reserve requirements and equity capital. Supervision of the banks was transferred from the central bank to an independent Superintendency of Banks, and state-owned banks were closed. In 1995, the financial sector reform was completed when a new law governing the central bank was passed. Under this law, the central bank has the pursuit of price stability as its main objective and gains political and economic independence from the executive branch.

[13] For an analysis of the reforms and fiscal impact see World Bank 1994. For an overview of the reforms and principal objectives see Morales 2001; Morales and Pacheco 1999; IDB 1997. For a description of the effects of the reforms on the manufacturing sector see Cámara Nacional de Industrias (various) and Montano and Villegas 1993.

[14] The new scheme transferred ownership of 50 percent of the shares of the enterprise to a private firm in exchange for an investment commitment. The other 50 percent of the shares were transferred to all the citizen older than 21 as of 1995. These shares were allocated in special collective capitalization funds administered by private pension funds. The allocation of the 50 percent of shares to private enterprises was made by public tender and the winner determined by higher bid. The process achieved commitments exceeding U.S.$1.5 billion to be invested over an eight-year period.

[15] For details on the regulatory framework see Chavez 1997; Muller & Asociados 1997; Fundacion Milenio 1997c.

By 1998, the economic and political situation started to deteriorate as consequence of external and internal factors. In the external side, the effects of the Brazilian devaluation and the climate phenomena of "El Niño" and "La Niña" had a severe effect in the Bolivian economy. These costs were aggravated in the short term by the successful governmental efforts to reduce the cocaine industry, and by measures taken by customs to stamp out smuggling.[16] At the same time, political and economic mismanagement played a role; these led to a recession in 1999, and unemployment started rising rapidly, fueling an already charged political situation. Coupled with the extreme levels of poverty, serious internal conflicts arose—such as the riots in the third largest city, Cochabamba, following an increase in water tariffs, which brought a state of emergency. The conflict was finally resolved when the government passed a new law governing the tariff structure for water provision[17] and the private consortium that administered the water enterprise left the country.[18] The eradication effort by the government has also brought major unrest in the areas where coca is normally produced.[19]

Clearly, the economic and industrial development path of Bolivia has not been a dynamic one. The productive base has remained relatively undiversified, as suggested in figure 12.1. Primary commodities nowadays still account for the bulk of exports, in a fashion rather similar to 50 years ago. Foreign direct investment has increased over the past 15 years, but at U.S.$760 million in 2000, it is low in per capita terms. While significant macroeconomic reforms have taken place from the mideighties until the present, the Bolivian economy has grown at less than 3 percent per annum on average during this 15-year period of reforms, or at a mere one-half a percentage point per annum per capita. While external factors have not always been favorable to Bolivia, such performance is still disappointingly low: as seen in figure 12.2, in earlier decades Bolivia had enjoyed higher growth—and what Bolivia has managed to attain is only a fraction of what on average East Asian economies have managed in terms of per capita growth. This low rate of growth of the Bolivian economy has been insufficient to make a dent in poverty. At a per capita income of about US$1,000, which is a fraction of neighbors such as Chile or Argentina, one-half of Bolivia's populace lives on less than US$2 per day, and they exhibit some of the

---

[16] A study by Nogales (2001) estimates the reduction in smuggling at U.S.$538 million and in drug trafficking at U.S.$448 million for the years 1997 to 2001.

[17] *Financial Times;* Oxford Analytica 2001; Associated Press.

[18] The second set of large riots were observed in the highlands, in the western part of the country. A draft legislation pertaining irrigation in the countryside spurred massive protests and road blockades. Again, the protests resulted in violent crashes with the police and armed forces. The conflict was partially solved by an agreement between the peasant organizations and the government. Again, the government relented and increased salaries.

[19] Clashes between coca producers and the army had left several people dead, including members of the army.

highest rates of infant mortality in the world.[20] The dire economic realities in Bolivia are made starker by the vast inequalities in income and assets.[21]

While the reforms helped to create a more stable and competitive economy, the productive structure remained relatively undiversified and vulnerable to external shocks. The enterprise sector is still of the view that much of the official policy and institutional environment is not conducive to business development. In fact, much of the enterprise sector is unofficial. Estimates for informal manufacturing establishments run between 53,600 (Casanovas Sainz 1989) and 95,000 (Larrazabal 1997). A recent World Bank study (2001) suggests that nowadays the vast majority of manufacturing establishments and labor force are unofficial (i.e., they operate outside the law and do not have access to the institutional arrangements that enable economic units to realize economies of scale, encourage innovations, or improve the efficiency of factor markets). Further, a cross-country study assessing 69 countries in the midnineties placed Bolivia as one the economies with the largest share in the unofficial sector.[22]

Thus, a key tenet in this study is that the low productivity of much of Bolivia's enterprise sector is associated with widespread informality, in turn the result of official policies and institutional favoritism towards a small elite. As stated in the recent World Bank study: "A vast majority of Bolivians choose to operate informally because the existing institutions are designed to incorporate a privileged minority, consisting of those who can afford the high costs required to become and remain formal. On the other hand, the benefits of being formal are relatively low, because of the poor performance of the judiciary, government agencies, law enforcement and other public services."[23]

In August 2001, after four years in government and one year before his term expired, Hugo Banzer resigned the presidency, due to illness. By this time, important sectors of Bolivian society had already demanded his resignation, including the association of private entrepreneurs—a traditional ally of Mr. Banzer. The vice president, Jorge Quiroga, was sworn in as new president and appointed a new cabinet. In his inauguration speech he underscored three key objectives, namely, to jump-start the economy, to combat unemployment and poverty, and to fight corruption; and to do so he called for transparency in

---

[20] For a complete discussion of recent economic developments and sources of growth in Bolivia, see IMF 1998. For the effects of the structural adjustment program in poverty reduction see Vos and Mejia 1997.

[21] Illustrations are farmers in the high plains who still use oxen to plow fields. Hunters use bows and arrows in the jungle, and rural Indians live without electricity or potable water.

[22] Johnson, Kaufmann, and Zoido-Lobatón 1998. See section 6 below for further details.

[23] In Bolivia's report on constraints to enterprise (World Bank 2001, 6). The field study carried out in the cities of La Paz and El Alto reveals that the costs of complying with most of the legal requirements to start and to operate a business are extremely high, particularly for smaller businesses. Another key point made in this World Bank 2001 study is that court cases in Bolivia are costly, lengthy, and subject to corrupt influences.

government. He highlighted Bolivia's recently confirmed natural gas reserves, promising that an expected quantum leap in export proceeds would benefit the country's poorest—and pledging that corruption and mismanagement would not be an obstacle to proceeds reaching the poor.

In sum, from the perspective of the retired head of the entrepreneurs' association, Mr. Ramiro Calderón Sr., the Bolivian structural adjustment program has attained mixed results. Notably, the process has been undertaken by four different democratic governments, suggesting the broad consensus that the model has achieved. And these reforms transformed the Bolivian economy from "being one of Latin America's most interventionist republics to being one which is virtually a private economy" (Morales 2001, 41). Yet in spite of far-reaching macroeconomic reforms, the enterprise sector and the economy have not grown at a rate that permits a substantial increase in income per capita and a major reduction in poverty. Growth rates in Bolivia pale in comparison to rates attained in East Asia (see fig. 12.2), and also have been below rates in other Latin American countries such as Chile. Much of the enterprise sector operates unofficially and does not see the option of formality as beneficial. To understand some of the underlying public policy and institutional reasons for the persistence of an environment adverse to business and for the ascent of "unofficialdom" in the public sector, we rely on Mrs. Marta Vargas de Calderón, the historian and civil servant.[24]

4. THE EVOLUTION OF INFORMALITY IN THE PUBLIC SECTOR: MRS. MARTA VARGAS DE CALDERÓN'S HISTORICAL AND INSTITUTIONAL PERSPECTIVE

A History of Political Instability, 1952–85

Even by Latin American standards of political and economic instability, Bolivia has gone through a particularly tumultuous history. By one count, there were more than 190 changes of government between independence in 1825 and the early 1990s, more than one change of government a year. During the 1960s and 1970s there were "stable" military regimes, which implemented state-led capitalism that encouraged growth of the state apparatus. Between 1970 and 1978, public sector employment rose from 66,000 to almost 170,000. Political turmoil returned in 1978–82, when seven military and two civilian governments replaced each other in quick succession. The political decay reached a crisis proportion during the government of General Luis Garcia Meza.

---

[24] This section draws heavily from the analysis in the World Bank's Institutional and Governance Review report (World Bank 2000), and on the insights of the main author, Yasuhiko Matsuda.

Stability during the Revolutionary Regime, 1952–64.[25] After its defeat in the Chaco War (1932–36), Bolivia's traditional social fabric and its political and economic elite's ability to maintain their authority and legitimacy progressively weakened. "Between 1935 and 1952, Bolivia experienced five successful coups (1935, 1936, 1937, 1943, 1951); two successful urban insurrections (1946 and 1952); at least three large-scale bloody encounters between the army and labor groups (1942, 1947, 1950); and a brief civil war (1947)" (Malloy 1970, 323). The disintegration of the "old order" culminated in the MNR-led revolution in 1952, which introduced sweeping reforms including the nationalization of the large tin mines and agrarian reform, which legalized the peasants' seizure of hacienda lands, and introduction of universal suffrage. Labor, peasants, and indigenous groups were included in the broad governing coalition. Power relations with the military were changed through a large-scale purge of officers, reorganization of the military institution itself, and redefinition of its missions to include "civic actions" such as school construction and food distribution.

The Military Regime, 1964–78: Vested Interests Benefiting the Private Few. After the fall of Víctor Paz Estenssoro, General Barrientos ruled by decree for most of the next five years, until the dictator's death in a helicopter crash. During the next two years, coups and countercoups followed each other as different factions vied for power. In 1971, a coup led by Banzer put an end to this episode of political instability, and reasserted authoritarian control. Banzer continued to use the state as a source of patronage. Patrimonial use of state resources was not limited to dispensation of public jobs: the transfer of public resources to the private sector was done mainly through the state banking system.[26] As emphasized in the previous section (from Mr. Calderón's perspective), the regime's economic policies in the early seventies (and its repression of organized labor) benefited selected private businesses, while the rest of the private sector did not gain an institutionalized channel of preferential access: "With access structured through personal ties to Banzer, businessmen without those ties or those who sought to put forth sectoral- or class-wide concerns were left without any direct avenues for influencing policy making" (Malloy 1970, 67).

The Political Transition and Economic Crisis, 1978–82. By 1977, societal pressure on the Banzer regime to liberalize the political process stretched the regime's capacity to control political participation; elections were carried out, only to be thwarted by the military. During the next four years, seven military and two civilian governments replace each other in quick succession. The political

---

[25] For a detailed account of the political dynamics in the early postrevolutionary period, see Malloy 1970. For an excellent account on the political history of Bolivia, see Gamarra and Malloy 1990; and also Whitehead 1991.

[26] During the military dictatorship in the 1970s, for example, the state-owned Banco Agrícola de Bolivia (BAB) provided more than half of all agricultural credit in the country.

decay reached a crisis proportion during the government of the repressive and corrupt regime of General Luis Garcia Meza, with known ties to drug traffickers. After the fall of Garcia Meza, the Congress elected Hernán Siles Zuazo as president. Siles's selection had broad support from all key sectors in society, yet the scope of the economic management challenges meant that the government found itself unable to cope with the deteriorating economic conditions. Furthermore, the same political forces that negotiated Siles's election, mainly the Congress, organized labor, and even Siles's own vice president, obstructed the government's legislative agenda and even threatened to unseat him. Devoid of congressional support, the Siles administration relied on rules by decree. While the government negotiated several IMF standby programs, it faced strong opposition from organized labor, which forced the government to soften the content of the stabilization measures. The economy deteriorated further with inflation reaching more than 20,000 percent. Siles was forced out of power one year early, and new elections were called in 1985.

The Maturation of the Democratic Regime, 1985–97. Against this historical background, a major transformation of the Bolivian political economy began in the mid-1980s. First, through an interparty agreement ("pact") the newly elected government introduced the bold macroeconomic stabilization measures discussed in the previous section (which became a model for the region). Demonstrations by opposition groups were first controlled by declaring a state of siege, and more generally the authority of the state was reestablished from the chaotic years in the early 1980s. Since 1985, the transformation of the Bolivian political economy to a relatively stable multiparty democracy has been a remarkable accomplishment,[27] even as many of the institutional weaknesses and the informality in the public sector were not addressed.

Growing Informality in Public Administration since the Eighties. The extent and type of "informality" in the public sector has become a major source of institutional weakness, given the contradictions between the formal and the informal rules, which are resolved in favor of the latter (instead of having both sets of rules reinforce each other to produce predictable and desirable behavioral patterns). The prevalence of informal rules over formal institutions has impaired reform-minded policymakers.

While macroeconomic reforms and consolidation of the democratic political regime was taking place in the middle to late 1980s, structural and institutional reforms lagged behind, as did efforts to modernize the central administration and the delivery and quality of public services. The core of Bolivia's public sector has remained largely unreformed and suffers from deep institutional weaknesses. In 1990 the SAFCO (Financial Administration and Control System)

---

[27] Consider for instance how through this period several of Bolivia's neighbors have seen their democratic regimes falter because of the traditional political elite's inability to cope with their nations' political and economic governance (e.g., Ecuador, Peru, Venezuela).

Law, designed to turn the public sector into a modern, results-oriented institution, was promulgated, but with limited results so far. Throughout the recent period, public discontent with entrenched corruption and poor delivery of public services has increased pressure to reform public administration.

One of the principal formal-legal instruments for public sector modernization in Bolivia is the SAFCO legal framework for regulating public administration. But its implementation has been uneven at best, and thus it has not had its intended impact on the functioning of the Bolivian state bureaucracy, either in promoting operational efficiency and orientation toward results or in ensuring probity and accountability. Key reasons for subpar implementation have been (1) significant delays (often exceeding seven years since the law's promulgation) in implementing regulations; (2) limited commitment from the Ministry of Finance (which is in charge of issuing almost all regulations), with a focus instead on the traditional role of macrofiscal management, coupled with the weaknesses of central oversight bodies such as the comptroller, as well as in key institutions in the judiciary; (3) resistance from many public officials who did not welcome a rigorous system of accountability;[28] and, (4) lack of progress on public financial management due to a focus on narrow technical aspects, without paying attention to inadequate incentives, the latter in turn driven by institutional and political obstacles.[29]

Revenue Administration: Informality Resulting in Insufficient Public Revenue Mobilization. In spite of the efforts following the macrostabilization program, to date efforts to strengthen performance by the tax and customs agencies have fallen short of expectations. While domestic tax collections increased from about 1 percent of GDP to 7.8 percent of GDP between 1986 and 1992, and by 1995 were up to 10 percent, corruption is a serious problem in tax administration. And customs revenues have stayed constant at around 1 percent during the same period. The topography of the country's borders, high unemployment, and the government's poor supervisory capacity have made Bolivia a prime target for contraband, which has grown dramatically during the 1990s: in 1990, the Bolivian government lost about $109 million per year in revenue; by 1997, the estimated annual loss had risen to about $430 million (Valencia and Alcides Casas 1998, 68).

---

[28] Thus, for example, under SAFCO agencies' annual operational plans, which are meant to guide annual budgetary allocations, are not taken seriously by either the Ministry of Finance or the line agencies, and have become "rituals" to fulfill every year during the budget preparation cycle. Similarly, there is little evidence that the "individual" annual operational plans are used effectively as an instrument of performance evaluation (World Bank 2000).

[29] While SAFCO implementation has been supported by successive World Bank projects, it is evident that they have failed to achieve greater efficiency and accountability in the ways in which public officials manage the state's financial resources. The projects have emphasized technical aspects of information systems, paying little attention to altering the *incentives* for better financial management (World Bank 2000).

Furthermore, survey results indicate that both the Internal Revenue Agency and the Customs Agency are highly politicized and prone to corruption; the respondents from the Internal Revenue estimated that 75 percent of hiring is done for political reasons, while customs was ranked worst in terms of officials' perception of levels of corruption by agency. Evidence also suggests that customs posts are being bought by candidates to have access to illegal sources of revenue for personal enrichment. As we will review in the next empirical section, Bolivia's enterprise sector exhibits one of the highest levels of "unofficialdom," and, related, of underreporting of sales so as to avoid taxes. This, in turn is related to corruption. Finally, the revenue agency has also been used as a tool for political support, as in the case of a beer factory owned by a political party leader, which is millions of dollars in arrears in taxes—yet can continue operating unimpeded due to political support.

Informality in Public Expenditure Management. Informality is also evident in public financial management. Instead of annual budgets being one of the most important formal instruments guiding public administration, in practice they are not executed as approved by Congress. Examination of budget data during the first half of the nineties suggests that often up to 50 percent of the approved agency budgets were reallocated across agencies, far exceeding what may have been justified due to aggregate fiscal stringency needs. Compounding the credibility gap of the budget process and execution is the absence of information on agency transactions (making it difficult for any central oversight body to exercise control). The Treasury does not have timely information on budget execution during a fiscal year; often the comptroller does not audit line agencies' accounts because there is no financial statement to audit. As public officials like to say, "Everyone knows that the budget formulation is a 'salute to the flag' [i.e., paying lip service], but everybody has to go through this charade in order to get the budget allocation."

Informality in Personnel Management. Informality is also amply observed in public personnel management, such as the widespread use of "consultants" for line functions, as well as more generally the persistent problem of corruption within the public sector (details below). Survey evidence suggests other forms of informality in public personnel management also, including (1) outside political pressure, with the corresponding fear that refusal to go along with the pressure may result in the loss of job or salary; (2) deliberate destruction/concealment of agency-related information at the time of government change; and, (3) use of nonwage budget items (e.g., training) for salary supplements.

Deeper Causes of Informality: From Old Oligarchy to Political Capture. Identifying specific institutional weaknesses that contribute directly to the persistence of informality is only the first step of the diagnosis. The question is what motivates these informal behaviors in the first place. In the specific Bolivian context, one of the key reasons is found in the particular ways in which public bureaucracy is captured by political parties. The literature on Bolivia's political economy points to the pervasive practice of patronage and clientelism as a defining characteristic of the relationship between the broader political environment and public administration.

The key sources of patronage politics are (1) weakness of the private sector in generating gainful employment, providing an incentive to look to the public sector for employment; (2) politicians' incentives in obtaining electoral/political support by distributing public jobs and other types of rents; (3) politicians' incentives in controlling the government bureaucracy by placing "persons of confidence" in critical bureaucratic posts to ensure effective implementation of policies or doling out of favors and rents; and (4) the fragmented party system (which in turn reflects deep social divisions in the country). Such political fragmentation, coupled with the country's particular electoral institutions, results in an overwhelming tendency to produce coalition governments. Given the lack of party identity on the basis of clearly differentiated policy programs, parties negotiate coalition arrangements with explicit agreements for sharing state patronage. This practice, called *cuoteo político* (political quota), has been the basis for formation and sustenance of governing coalitions, and thus of democratic stability (World Bank 2000).

Throughout the decades of the sixties and beyond, the Bolivian political economy was characterized by the extensive use of public sector employment as a source of patronage to be distributed among the politically well connected. While patronage politics is by no means unique to Bolivia, it is unusually salient in the Bolivian economy.

Relatively stable coalition arrangements have also facilitated legislative passage of certain key reform measures in times of deep crisis, such as helping forge, during hyperinflation, a consensus on the macroeconomic stabilization program in the mid-1980s. Yet the cost was high: deteriorating public services at the microinstitutional level due to excessive politicization of the government bureaucracy and the resulting weak institutional capacity. State modernization, creating a cadre of highly professional civil servants and of a service-oriented approach in the public sector, all processes that take time and transcend political cycles, failed to evolve.

Aborted Civil Service Reform: Another Illustration of Institutional Weakness and Political Capture. There was at least recognition of the need to address the importance of creating a corps of technically competent, motivated public employees. The Civil Service Program (PSC) was born in 1992 and aimed to create a critical mass of around 2,500 employees. Yet by the end of 1997, less than 250 positions had been filled! Furthermore, turnover was high and retention was low, due to the highly politicized upper and lower levels of public personnel. In the event, the PSC itself became politicized and lost credibility. By 1998, with only 30 posts assigned to the PSC, it had ground to a halt.

Inadequate Decentralization Program: Continuation of "Clientelism" and Lack of Accountability. Another important institutional reform in Bolivia has been the decentralization and deconcentration of many public services, embodied in the Popular Participation Law (PPL), the Law of Municipalities, and the Administrative Decentralization Law (ADL). These reforms constitute part of an ongoing effort at shrinking the state and increasing popular participation in governmental decisions that directly affect citizens' lives. The PPL makes local governments responsible for considerable resources and public investment decisions and establishes mechanisms whereby local communities can monitor local government spending and hold their elected officials accountable for spending decisions. The ADL deconcentrates resources and operational responsibility to the prefectures, in an effort to increase public sector efficiency and tailor services to departmental needs. Yet the results of these reforms have been mixed. While some large cities have improved performance, the clientelistic culture of the central government has simply spread to much of the local level (note that prefects are named by the president). Further, inadequate human resource capacity at local levels has been a constraint (as illustrated by unprepared financial municipal statements). Finally, the administrative decentralization program did not shrink the overall size of the state, creating instead a bloated bureaucratic structure at the departmental level, hampering efficiency of local public service (World Bank 2000).

The Judiciary: Captured Legacy, Vested Interests, and Partial Reforms

Lack of Judicial Independence and Conflictive Judicial Reform. Through the first decades of the recently completed century, Bolivia's justice sector developed much like that of the rest of Andean South America. Under the civil code tradition (a mixture of Spanish and French influences) the judiciary was the weakest of the three branches of government, with a role confined to conflict resolution and rule enforcement. Despite a 1931 constitutional amendment reconfirming judicial independence, there were 16 massive purges of the judiciary (generally with each new government) between 1936 and 1982, which made courts subservient to the specific interests and partisan identifications of the government in power. With the opening of coalition democracy in 1982, the judiciary was not immune to patronage, and parties implemented means for dividing up judicial positions.

The government began judicial reform efforts in the early 1990s with changes in the constitution and supportive legislation, yet reform attempts have encountered stubborn resistance from entrenched interests inside and outside the judiciary—resulting in the slow implementation of such key institutions as the Judicial Council, the judicial career and training program, and the Constitutional Court. Progress was made in 1999 through revamping the Supreme Court, but the country must continue to press for full implementation of the proposed changes as well as others that are still in the planning stage.

Human Development Impaired by Political Capture and Patronage. In Bolivia, as in many countries, the Ministry of Education provides fertile ground for distribution of patronage. Survey respondents reported that nearly 50 percent of staff are hired for political reasons, while teachers are hired at the prefecture level, where politicization is shown to be even more rampant. Teaching posts are distributed based primarily on political affiliation rather than professional qualifications. The harmful effects of politicized personnel is compounded by the absence of effective budgetary oversight, resulting in low quality of Bolivian education. Despite increased budget allocations for education and some improvement in enrollment rates, by the early nineties still well over one-half the adult population was functionally illiterate, including many who finished primary and even secondary school. Recent test scores in language and math place Bolivian students well below the Latin American regional average, and repetition rates are over 85 percent. Basic health services are also woefully inadequate. Infant, child, and maternal mortality rates are among the highest in Latin America. Poor prenatal care prevails, while vaccination rates for children have remained stagnant or even worsened since the late eighties, as illustrated by the fact that the percentage of children with measles and polio vaccinations has dropped over the past decade.

The Problems of Patronage Politics: Government Capture by Party Politics. Patronage and clientelism have been a central feature of Bolivian politics. Under *clientelismo,* political criteria dominate the organization and management of the state bureaucracy and remain one of the most serious obstacles to effective functioning of the state. In a region where political parties have often been primarily vehicles to capture and circulate state patronage among the dependent middle classes, Bolivia stands out as an extreme case. Parties in Bolivia have exhibited a high degree of ideological flexibility, party loyalty has been low, and often the behavior of parties has been driven more by access to patronage than by constituting programmatically consistent governments (Gamarra and Malloy 1990, 399).

While the phenomenon itself is not unique to Bolivia (and it exhibits different variants in other regions of the world, as in the case of state capture by the oligarchy in some former Soviet economies), it is a major tenet here that capture of the state apparatus by political forces has significant implications for performance of the public sector and overall productivity of the economy. The effects of patronage politics on public sector performance are clear: the use of political over meritocratic and technical criteria for recruiting, selecting, and promoting public sector employees prevents development of professionalism in the public service and lowers efficiency and accountability of its operations.

Coalition Politics: "Captured" Democracy and the Power of Party Bosses. The dramatic political instability until the mid-1980s has been replaced with remarkable stability since then. Political actors have accepted the democratic "rules of the game," centered around political representation through officially registered political parties, which abide by constitutional means to reach and exercise power. Further, political parties have displayed abilities to arrive at negotiated settlements for power sharing, and the parties' adept use of coalitions as well as their respect for the independence of the Electoral Court (as an arbiter) illustrate that they are prepared to engage each other within established set of rules in a democratic setting. However, mistrust among parties and their "bosses" is strong, and thus maintenance of political coalitions (a must for the government to carry out its legislative agenda) is a difficult task. Parties are factionalized internally, depending more on the personalities of particular leaders than on well-developed internal organizations.

Further, party bosses can capture electoral politics. The closed-list proportional representation system, which had been used to elect all of the deputies until the 1997 elections and half of the deputies since then, tends to strengthen the influence of party leaders, who control selection of candidates and their position on party lists. This system provides an incentive for politicians to be more responsive to faction bosses, weakening electoral accountability. In Bolivia, Congress elects the president from the top two (three until the electoral reform in 1995) contenders. Since the return of democracy in 1982, no presidential candidate has won enough votes to be elected without a congressional runoff. This system of indirect presidential election, against the background of a fragmented party system based on a few strong personalities, has also encouraged coalition formation and constant negotiations among the powerful few before and after actual voting (Soberg Shugart and Carey 1992). The need to have an ally for the purpose of winning the presidency induces the major parties to seek compromise with potential coalition partners. And what keeps governing coalitions together is the careful sharing of patronage opportunities (World Bank 2000).

Yet in spite of this fractured and personalized political system, history has shown that in times of crisis, key reforms can take place. The traumatic hyperinflationary experience of the early eighties played a key role in forging consensus on macroeconomic issues: the major reforms in Bolivia have been led by teams of technocrats who have been relatively insulated from political interference.[30] Yet in spite of their role in furthering macroeconomic reforms, Bolivian technocrats (at least until recently) have had a much weaker institutional presence than in other countries such as in Chile or Mexico (where presidents and party leaders emerge from the technocracy).

In sum, the public sector in Bolivia has evolved within an environment conducive to unofficial behavior, consistent with personalized political party dynamics and the concomitant patronage and clientelism that have characterized

---

[30] The academic study that has emphasized this aspect most aptly is Conaghan, Malloy, and Abugattas's "Business and the 'Boys'" (1990). The term "boys" here refers to technocrats in government, originally borrowed from the famous "Chicago boys" associated with economic reforms under the Pinochet military regime in Chile. See World Bank 2000.

the government's relationship with the enterprise sector. Tellingly, Jorge Quiroga, the 41-year-old installed president as of August 2001, has urged the creation of a new constitution to minimize the monopoly of the old political parties and open up politics to average Bolivians. While this responds in part to the need to address the discontentment of Bolivia's indigenous farmers, it is also part of a broader constituency among a new generation of politicians intent in modernizing the polity—a daunting task given the entrenched interests of the still powerful old cadre of politicians—where the new president is likely to face major challenges even within his own party.

5. THE PERSPECTIVE OF THE NEW ENTREPRENEUR TODAY, MS. PATRICIA CALDERÓN-VALDES: ECONOMETRIC ANALYSIS OF THE FIRM'S BEHAVIOR AND PERFORMANCE

Complementing the historical overview of the previous two sections, drawn from the twin perspectives of the development of the enterprise and public sectors in Bolivia—both exhibiting a significant degree of "informality"—as recapped by the parents' generation, we move to the perspective of a modern-day entrepreneur, the daughter, Patricia. Given her rigorous statistical tooling, this section approaches the question from an empirical perspective. First it probes the causes of informality in Bolivia, and then the determinants of the firm's performance. It is based on recent empirical evidence. We start by drawing on an existing body of work on determinants of the unofficial economy worldwide. Then we present results from the empirical analysis of a large survey covering close to 10,000 enterprises in 80 countries.[31]

Determinants of Unofficial Enterprise: Brief Analytics and Worldwide Evidence

In considering the importance that unofficial enterprise can play in a misgoverned country, we draw from the framework utilized in Johnson, Kaufmann, and Shleifer (JKS) 1997 for the unofficial economy in transition, subsequently extended for 69 countries worldwide (Friedman et al. 2000). In the JKS model the firm makes a rational economic choice whether to operate officially or

---

[31] This survey is the World Business Environment Survey (WBES) undertaken by the World Bank, in collaboration with European Bank for Reconstruction and Development, Harvard University and the Inter-American Development Bank during 1999—2000. More details on this survey can be found at: http://www.worldbank.org/privatesector/ic/resources/ An interactive website, displaying survey results in a user-friendly format can also be found at the following address: http://info.worldbank.org/governance/wbes.

unofficially based on the incentives it faces; the latter are determined by the government provision (or lack thereof) of public goods (such as rule of law, honesty). The key prediction of the JKS model is the potential separation of economies into two distinct groups. In one, the government offers a combination of regulations, honest public administration, and public goods sufficiently attractive that most firms choose to stay in the official sector. In this group, government revenues suffice to provide the public goods, and the unofficial sector is small. In the other group, the government does not offer firms a sufficiently attractive combination of transparency, regulations, and public goods (including rule of law and a honest and efficient public administration) to keep them operating officially, and hence many firms end up in the large unofficial sector. Government revenues in these countries do not suffice to offer more public goods to firms operating in the official sector, and hence the unofficial sector wins the competition for firms.

The potential bifurcation of economies into those exhibiting a large or small share of unofficial activities and their divergent institutional and public finance outcomes matters for overall economic performance. As the official sector is better equipped to generate public goods, the overall growth performance of economies with a small unofficial sector is superior.[32] Further, the behavior of firms in the official and unofficial economies differs regarding perceived risk and thus investment behavior. Higher private investment in the official economy also positively affects long-term growth. Augmenting these conclusions, a model extension demonstrates that in addition to the lower public revenues collected in misgoverned settings, the rate of conversion of revenues into quality public goods (such as rule of law vs. military expenditures) is lower. In this quality-adjusted scenario the misgovernance-unofficial economy is fueled further, and growth is impaired through an additional channel.

Consistent with the work carried out in JKS and their related extensions, a central result is shown in figure 12.3, where the close relationship between corruption and the unofficial economy is established—and the econometric estimations indicate that such relationship is large and significant, controlling for other factors (Friedman et al. 2000). For the purposes of the current review, it is noteworthy that Bolivia both rates poorly in terms of corruption and exhibits one of the largest unofficial economies in the world.

Empirical Results from the Worldwide Enterprise Survey

Extending this earlier aggregate cross-country work, we undertook to probe the determinants of "unofficialdom" by utilizing a new firm-level data set from a

---

[32] On the nexus between the unofficial economy and overall growth, see also Loayza 1996.

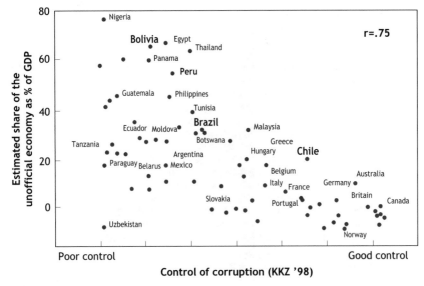

Figure 12.3. Unofficial economy vs. corruption: Cross-country evidence. Data on the unofficial economy is from various years during first half of the 1990s.
Source: Johnson, Kaufmann, and Zoido-Lobatón 1999

recent worldwide enterprise survey. This large survey covered close to 10,000 enterprises in 80 countries worldwide: the World Business Environment Survey (WBES), which was undertaken by the World Bank in collaboration with European Bank for Reconstruction and Development (EBRD), Harvard University, and the Inter-American Development Bank during 1999–2000. The coverage includes all regions of the world. Firms were asked a plethora of questions about their own characteristics and the obstacles they face, which were normally rated in an ordinal scale, with a few questions like growth of sales and extent of underreporting of official income, where a cardinal numerical figure was obtained (see below for glossary of variables used in this analysis with reference to each question in the survey).

First, based on this firm-level data set, we provide a relative cross-country perspective for Bolivia in terms of the environment for the enterprise sector. It is synthesized in figure 12.4, which does point to some major constraints identified by the entrepreneurial class, contrasts them with other factors, and also places Bolivia in a relative international standing.[33] We observe that Bolivia

---

[33] Given the inherent margin of error in these surveys, no precise country rankings can be derived, however. Thus, the graphical depiction of the relative standing of Bolivia ought to be interpreted with caution, illustrating in broad categorical terms whether the said obstacle is, relative to other countries, very large, middling, or lower —rather than an exact numerical ranking.

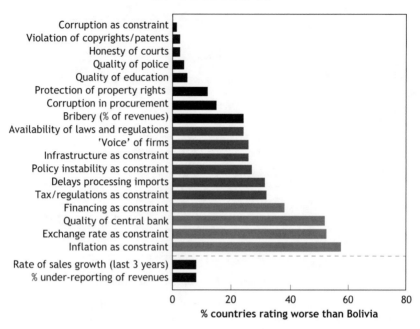

Figure 12.4. Institutional and governance assessment by firms (% countries rating worse than Bolivia—WBES)
Source: WBES, 2000

rates close to the top in the extent of "corruption as a constraint" and also very high in corruption in procurement, and in extent of bribery (measured in percentage of revenues paid in bribes annually), as well as in the poor quality of customs, in the extent of violation of patents/copyrights, compromised integrity of courts, and in poor protection of property rights (which furthermore, according to the survey, had not improved at all compared to three years prior to the survey). Its reported quality of education is low. Further, though this rating is not as low, firms in Bolivia are not of the view that they have much "voice" in terms of proper consultation and participation in the processes that affect them.[34] In terms of behavioral and performance outcome variables, it is also telling that Bolivia rates high in the extent of underreporting of revenues and of output growth. These results provide a conservative proxy for the extent of "unofficialdom" in Bolivia's enterprise sector, due to the tendency to overestimate in survey data the share of revenues officially reported by officially reg-

---

[34] A detailed glossary with the definitions of each variable following the question asked in the survey is presented in annex 1.

istered enterprises, and due to the fact that *unregistered* enterprises are not covered in this worldwide survey.[35]

By sharp contrast, the evidence from this data set suggests that neither the exchange rate, inflation, the quality of a key institution such as the central bank, nor even financing is found to be a major obstacle to enterprise in Bolivia nowadays in a comparative context. This evidence challenges the conventional notion that within a country with low overall institutional rating all institutional and governance characteristics would rate rather low. Instead, the results of the enterprise responses from Bolivia within the perspective of an 80-country firm-level survey are consistent with the historical account of the Calderón parents, contrasting the performance of different institutions within the country. Indeed, the data suggests that there is enormous variance, with institutions related to macroeconomic stability performing rather well, while many others exhibit significant weaknesses. The case for "localized" knowledge within a country is thus suggested.[36]

Do the factors that entrepreneurs in Bolivia identified as subpar matter for the firm's behavior, and particularly for their decisions to underreport revenues—that is, unofficial output? To answer this question, we first performed OLS regressions with this firm-level sample, including country effects. For reference, we show explicitly the Bolivia country effect in each regression in tables 12.3 and 12.4. The basic econometric specifications in table 12.4 present the various possible determinants of the unofficial economy behavior of registered firms. There are a number of policy-related variables that are significantly related to the firm's extent of underreporting of revenues based on this worldwide data set (such as macroeconomic, regulatory, and tax, as well as finance and governance-related, constraints). Yet the salient factors that fulfill both conditions, of rating low for Bolivia's case *and* of exhibiting econometric significance of the coefficient of the factor in explaining "unofficialdom," are corruption and property right protection, and related, the quality of courts. Further, we also note from table 12.3 that "voice" also matters to the enterprise sector. As noted, other significant variables in these worldwide regressions, such as those related to macroeconomic constraints, for Bolivia in particular they are not to be interpreted as an explanatory factor in hampering growth in the country, because they are not binding constraints—they rate very highly in a cross-country context (fig. 12.4).[37]

Overall, the literature treating corruption presents it as a negative factor in development (see Rose-Ackerman 1978; Klitgaard 1988; Shleifer and Vishny

---

[35] And indeed as noted in section 3, existing studies indicate that a very large share of the enterprise sector is not registered and operates fully informally (Doria Medina 1986; World Bank 2001).

[36] See Rodrik 2000, which makes a broad case for localization of knowledge.

[37] Although not shown here, we also run specifications interacting the Bolivia country effect with the policy variables, which did not turn out to be significant (while the separate policy effects significance remained largely unaltered).

TABLE 12.3
Underreported Revenues, Corruption, and Protection of Property Rights

Determinant	1	2	3	4	5	6	7	8
Country effect	2.12	6.08	5.98	6.11	2.37	2.66	2.15	6.08
	0.72	2.30**	2.37**	2.00**	0.80	0.87	0.73	1.99**
Business constraints								
Financing constraint	0.11	0.69	0.22	0.49	0.25	0.31	0.08	0.36
	0.29	2.21**	0.75	1.25	0.68	0.77	0.23	0.90
Inflation constraint	-0.28	0.14	-0.17	0.09	-0.21	-0.10	-0.20	0.04
	-0.65	0.36	-0.48	0.20	-0.48	-0.20	-0.46	0.09
Policy instability constraint	1.33	1.41	1.22	1.28	1.54	1.20	1.30	1.01
	3.05***	3.77***	3.53***	2.75***	3.62***	2.50**	2.95***	2.10**
Infrastructure constraint	0.84	0.78	0.68	0.70	0.95	0.72	0.88	0.55
	2.12**	2.31**	2.17**	1.62+	2.43**	1.70*	2.22**	1.27
Tax/regulatory constraint	0.92		0.91			1.52	0.90	1.09
	2.05**		2.55**			3.08***	2.00**	2.20**
Rule of Law								
Bribery (% of revenues)	0.28			0.29	0.29	0.29	0.28	0.28
	4.89***			4.53***	5.08***	4.78***	4.91***	4.38***
Quality of courts		0.29				-0.30		
		1.13				-0.94		
Protection property rights			0.22				-0.02	
			0.93				-0.07	
Copyrights violations				2.40				2.33
				6.79***				6.56***

Firm characteristics								
Private ownership	3.74	4.06	3.98	2.53	3.69	3.08	3.68	2.55
	2.66**	*4.05****	*4.28****	*1.59+*	*2.63***	*2.06***	*2.61***	*1.60+*
Small/medium size	2.91	4.38	4.52	2.37	2.93	2.94	3.07	2.35
	2.82***	*4.92****	*5.35****	*2.22***	*2.84****	*2.71****	*2.96****	*2.20***
De novo (since 1994)	0.57	1.69	1.26	0.62	0.61	1.01	0.56	0.58
	0.65	*2.18***	*1.80**	*0.64*	*0.69*	*1.04*	*0.63*	*0.60*
Exporter	−1.83	−1.40	−1.15	−1.70	−1.90	−2.01	−1.87	−1.58
	−2.22**	*−1.94**	*−1.70**	*−1.94**	*−2.30***	*−2.28***	*−2.25***	*−1.80**
Foreign investment	−4.30	−2.94	−2.97	−3.98	−4.33	−4.38	−4.09	−3.94
	−4.28***	*−3.28****	*−3.55****	*−3.72****	*−4.31****	*−4.05****	*−4.04****	*−3.68****
Adjusted R^2	.19	.16	.16	.20	.19	.18	.19	.21
Number of observations	3886	4762	5767	3212	3890	3214	3838	3208

Notes: The dependent variable is underreported revenues (in %, sample mean = 19%). From the survey, business constraints were rated on a scale from 1 to 4, where 1 implies "no constraint" and 4 "major obstacle". These include inflation, financing, infrastructure, tax/regulation, and policy instability constraints, as well as quality of courts, protection of property rights, copyright violations, and constraints to exercising "voice" of the firm. Bribery is expressed as percentage of revenues. Fixed country effects were used to account for differences across individual countries; only the Bolivian country effect is reported in the table.

+ Significant at 15% level.   * significant at 10% level.   ** significant at 5% level.   *** significant at 1% level.

TABLE 12.4

Firms' Underreporting of Revenues and Unpredictability of Corruption

Determinants	1	2	3	4	5	6	7	8	9	10	11	12
Bolivia country effect	9.74	10.28	10.88	9.24	3.62	10.20	5.04	5.24	6.12	8.07	2.72	8.68
	3.04***	*3.04****	*3.18****	*2.87****	*1.19*	*3.15****	*1.47+*	*1.54+*	*1.79**	*2.70***	*0.91*	*3.47****
Business Constraint												
Financing	0.98	0.58	0.74	0.98	-0.14	1.00	-0.08	-0.12	-0.12	0.66	0.12	0.59
	2.42**	*1.21*	*1.54+*	*2.41***	*-0.33*	*2.44***	*-0.16*	*-0.26*	*-0.24*	*1.77**	*0.32*	*1.94**
Inflation	0.21	0.35	0.45	0.31	-0.12	0.26	-0.48	-0.52	-0.47	0.27	-0.21	0.21
	0.46	*0.64*	*0.80*	*0.65*	*-0.24*	*0.55*	*-0.86*	*-0.94*	*-0.84*	*0.61*	*-0.47*	*0.57*
Infrastructure	0.87	1.35	1.21	0.86	0.40	0.86	1.06	1.25	1.14	0.85	0.80	0.61
	2.01**	*2.75****	*2.46***	*1.96***	*0.88*	*1.96***	*2.15***	*2.54***	*2.30***	*2.11***	*1.98***	*1.87**
Policy Instability	0.96	0.91	0.76	0.88	1.39	0.83	1.56	1.64	1.63	0.78	1.21	0.39
	1.96**	*1.62+*	*1.33*	*1.80**	*2.71****	*1.68+*	*2.80****	*2.97****	*2.93****	*1.73**	*2.70****	*1.07*
Tax/regulation	1.25	0.89	1.02	1.12	0.30	1.23	0.59	0.44	0.54	1.19	0.91	0.67
	2.51**	*1.45+*	*1.66+*	*2.20***	*0.55*	*2.41***	*0.98*	*0.74*	*0.88*	*2.57***	*1.96***	*1.74**
Corruption												
Bribery (% revenues)	0.21	0.22	0.21	0.21		0.22	0.25	0.25	0.25	0.26	0.28	
	3.47***	*3.48****	*3.30****	*3.45****		*3.46****	*3.94****	*4.00****	*4.04****	*4.44****	*4.86****	
Frequency of bribery					2.34							2.81
					6.96***							*13.83****
Corrupt service unpredictability			-0.07		0.73		0.29					
			-0.21		*2.33*		*0.85*					
Corrupt payment unpredictability		0.22						0.17	0.15			
		0.70						*0.57*	*0.47*			
Corrupt extra request unpredictability	-0.10			-0.08		-0.09						
	-0.38			*-0.30*		*-0.35*						

	(1)	(2)	(3)	(4)	(5)	(6)	(7)	(8)	(9)	(10)	(11)	(12)
"Kvetch" control												
Government inefficiency		1.24	1.27	0.71						0.88		0.66
		2.90	*2.98*	*1.93*						*2.60*		*2.35*
Government unhelpfulness					−0.55	0.12			−0.70		−0.35	
					−1.47	*0.33*			*−1.73*		*−1.07*	
Firm characteristics												
Private ownership	3.71	3.26	3.33	3.44	4.67	3.91	3.74	3.52	4.01	3.23	4.02	3.48
	2.44**	*1.94**	*1.96**	*2.26***	*3.00****	*2.54***	*2.14***	*2.03***	*2.30***	*2.31***	*2.81****	*3.53****
Small/medium size	2.95	2.71	2.57	3.04	3.90	2.91	3.44	3.58	3.50	2.56	2.94	3.15
	2.64**	*1.90**	*1.78**	*2.71****	*2.89****	*2.58****	*2.34***	*2.46***	*2.39***	*2.52***	*2.81****	*3.63****
De novo (since 1994)	0.24	0.90	0.78	0.29	0.06	0.31	0.85	0.97	1.02	0.43	0.66	0.26
	0.25	*0.84*	*0.73*	*0.30*	*0.06*	*0.31*	*0.80*	*0.92*	*0.96*	*0.48*	*0.73*	*0.36*
Exporter	−1.86	−0.79	−1.16	−1.69	−2.23	−1.79	−2.24	−1.87	−1.93	−0.94	−1.88	−0.89
	−2.07**	*−0.74*	*−1.07*	*−1.88**	*−2.19***	*−1.96***	*−2.03***	*−1.70+*	*−1.74**	*−1.13*	*−2.23***	*−1.28*
Foreign investment	−4.44	−4.75	−4.80	−4.57	−3.20	−4.51	−4.59	−4.72	−4.90	−4.36	−4.34	−3.03
	−4.03***	*−3.40****	*−3.39****	*−4.14****	*−2.46***	*−4.03****	*−3.21****	*−3.34****	*−3.45****	*−4.35****	*−4.23****	*−3.47****
Headquarters in capital/large city					0.45	−1.43		0.23	0.17	−1.14	−0.58	−0.24
					0.47	*−1.53+*		*0.22*	*0.16*	*−1.34*	*−0.67*	*−0.35*
Adjusted R^2	.19	.14	.14	.17	.13	.18	.13	.13	.13	.18	.18	.19
Number of observations	3276	2535	2505	3240	3776	3221	2737	2767	2726	3786	3959	5379

Notes: From the survey, business constraints were rated on a scale from 1 to 4, where 1 implies "no constraint" and 4 "major obstacle." These include inflation, financing, infrastructure, tax/regulation and policy instability constraints, as well as quality of courts, protection of property rights, copyright violations, and constraints to exercising "voice" of the firm. Bribery is expressed as percentage of revenues. Fixed country effects were used to account for differences across individual countries; only the Bolivian country effect is reported in the table.

+ significant at 15%;   * significant at 10%;   ** significant at 5%;   *** significant at 1%.

1994; Mauro 1997). However, in the theoretical literature some strands put forth more nuanced approaches, with equivocal results. In particular, two such strands that challenge the simple notion that corruption per se is an unambiguous negative are (1) the bribery as "grease" hypothesis, and (2) the "unpredictability of corruption" hypothesis. Under the "grease" hypothesis, the notion is that in an overregulated regime, bribery can be an efficiency-enhancing mechanism effectively deregulating privately, implying that corruption can play an efficiency-enhancing role where red tape is prevalent.[38] The main conceptual challenge to this notion, however, is that it presumes that the regulatory regime is exogenously given, while in reality often the same bureaucracy has an interest in making such red tape as complex as possible to maximize the potential for bribery.

Empirically, Kaufmann and Wei (1999) have shown that a higher incidence of bribery results in more (not less) time wasted with the bureaucracy, and in higher cost of capital for the firm. This challenges the "grease" hypothesis, the evidence supporting instead a "bribery as sand" hypothesis, emerging from a framework where there is endogenous joint determination of the optimal level of harassment by the bureaucrat and by bribe levels.

The second nuanced hypothesis in the corruption literature ("unpredictability" of corruption) posits that it is not corruption per se that has perverse effects, but its unpredictability (see, for instance, World Development Report 1997). In other words, in settings where corruption is predictable, the premise is that corruption does not have harmful effects compared to where the unpredictability of corruption is much higher. Predictability of corruption is characterized by both the bribe payer and the receiver knowing "what it takes" in payments required, to whom payment needs to be made, and the degree of certainty that the "service" from the official will be delivered.

This firm-level data set permits us to empirically evaluate these "nuanced" corruption hypotheses. First, the "grease" hypothesis predicts that a firm engaging in bribery tends to benefit from less red tape in the official economy and thus have less of an incentive to operate unofficially. The results in tables 12.3 and 12.4 point to the contrary, suggesting instead that the "sand" hypothesis is at work: higher levels of bribery are related to a significantly higher propensity to operate unofficially. And the bribery coefficient's magnitude is relatively large: an increase in bribery payment as share of revenue by two standard deviations increases the degree of underreporting of gross output by the firm by five percentage points (e.g. from 15 to 20 percent of gross revenues, and much more if it were calculated as share of net income).

Second, we can also test the "unpredictability of corruption" hypothesis through three separate questions in this survey: an uncertain "price" of the corrupt service, uncertainty whether other officials may subsequently request additional bribe payments, and uncertainty in the delivery of the "purchased" serv-

---

[38] For expositions of the "grease" hypothesis of bribery, see Huntington 1968; Leff 1964; Lui 1985.

ice. Yet as is reported in table 12.4, we find that controlling for other factors, there is no significant relationship between the degree of unpredictability of corruption, on the one hand, and the degree of underreporting of revenues by the firm, on the other. By contrast, the magnitude and significance of the level of corruption variables, proxied by the amounts of bribes paid or by the frequency of bribery, remain very high—irrespective of which (and if any) "unpredictability" of corruption component is used in the econometric specifications.

Whenever econometric work is performed based on survey data that contains an element of subjectivity or perception stemming from the nature of the firm's responses, we face the challenge of possible spurious correlation between the dependent and independent variables: firms that are doing well (performance measures often being the dependent variable) may have a "rosier" view of the obstacles to enterprises (the independent variables) than would be warranted from an objective standpoint. Conversely, firms who are performing poorly, or operate unofficially, may exaggerate the obstacles they find and understate the effectiveness of government policies and its provision of services.

This potential spurious correlation resulting from a possible tendency of firms to view many questions with the same subjective lens has been labeled the "kvetch" factor.[39] If these variables are indeed affected by some unobservable "common perceived view" factor across variables by the same firm (such as the propensity to gripe or "kvetch," or its converse, a tendency to gloat throughout the survey interview), then this measurement error would lead coefficient estimates to be biased, and the likelihood of observing spurious correlations among variables whose true underlined correlation is insignificant cannot be ruled out.

We have addressed this possible source of misspecification and bias through a two-prong approach. First, we identify from the survey possible "kvetch" control independent variables that fulfill the condition of being a public good provided by the government that is commonly encountered by all firms within a country, and thus it can be presumed that each firm's response's deviation from the country mean is a proxy for the extent of the firm's "kvetch" factor.

Given that the firm-level econometric specifications we perform included country effects, direct inclusion of the "universal" public good suffices as proxy of the kvetch effect, as the subtraction from the country mean is implicitly taken care of by the country effect dummies.

Then we identified four different "kvetch" control proxies, each one inserted separately in the set of econometric specifications: extent of government efficiency, extent of "helpfulness" by government, quality of public works, and quality of the postal service.[40] The first two proxies that we utilize in these

---

[39] For related econometric treatment of this potential "kvetch" perception bias in analyzing survey data based on an element of subjective assessment, see also Kaufmann and Wei 1999; Hellman et al. 2000.

[40] Admittedly, none of these is an ideal "kvetch control" proxy, since any such assessments of service provision, even if truly a public good, can always exhibit a measure of objective variance across

tests, of a generic nature, have the advantage of being less subject to enormous variations across different locations (within a city), while the two variables of specific infrastructure nature are less subject to preferential provision, or exclusion, by the government to a firm. In table 12.4 this was done with two different variables from the same survey instrument: the degree of government inefficiency as perceived by the firm, and also the firm's view on how helpful the government is to enterprise. Insofar as there is a significant "kvetch" factor, it would be picked up by these variables.

It is noteworthy that the control is significant for government efficiency, in contrast with the "government helpfulness" variable. Yet in all cases we find that inclusion of the control variables does not affect the magnitude or high significance of the other variables in the specifications, and in particular those earlier identified as key for Bolivia and elsewhere. We observe, for instance, in table 12.4, that the significance of the bribery variable remains unaltered. These results were also replicated with the other two "kvetch control" variables (not shown here), namely quality of public works and of postal services.

Determinants of Enterprises' Output Growth

What are the determinants of firm-level growth in general, and in particular, what appear to be the main obstacles to enterprise growth in Bolivia? Based on this same worldwide enterprise data set (WBES), and using the same approach as in the above analysis of the unofficial economy, our firm-level data permits us to undertake a preliminary investigation of the possible determinants of output growth by the firm. A question was asked to the firm regarding its growth in sales over the past year. We are aware of the likely noise in such a variable (which inter alia refers to a very narrow time frame, while the independent variables of interest are of a more structural nature in the longer term), and thus the results need to be interpreted with caution, in need of support from other empirical analysis. Nonetheless, given our broader overall inquiry into the economic performance of Bolivia, and the fact that some possible determinants appear to be significantly related to the growth of firms, within this broader context we present the results on determinants of the firm's output growth below.

As shown in table 12.5, the econometric results indicate that a number of key variables appear to matter significantly in terms of a firm's growth, notably

---

firms within the same country. Thus, not the full extent of the firm's assessment variance from the country mean can be assumed to measure the firm-specific "kvetch"; it may also measure the actual differential provision of such public service to firms. Thus, it is warranted to perform such a test with a number of such possible (admittedly imperfect) proxies with different qualities. At any rate, from the standpoint of addressing the omitted variable bias econometrically, McCallum (1972) and Wickens (1972) have shown that even an imperfect proxy is better than omitting an unobservable factor, on the criterion of asymptotic bias.

TABLE 12.5

Obstacles to Output Growth of Firms

Dependent Variable : Sales Growth 1997–1999 (sample 3-year mean = 12.3%)

Determinants	1	2	3	4	5
Country effect	−6.90	−8.91	−7.28	−9.22	−11.07
	−0.90	*−1.14*	*−0.94*	*−1.17*	*−1.32*
Business constraint					
Financing	−1.91	−2.09	−1.81	−1.95	−1.74
	*−1.99***	*−2.04***	*−1.87**	*−1.89**	*−1.55+*
Inflation	−2.96	−2.92	−2.83	−2.74	−3.24
	*−2.64****	*−2.44***	*−2.50***	*−2.27***	*−2.49***
Infrastructure	−0.07	0.36	−0.18	0.34	−0.04
	−0.07	*0.33*	*−0.17*	*0.31*	*−0.03*
Policy instability	−1.34	−2.04	−1.56	−2.32	−1.24
	−1.17	*−1.67+*	*−1.35*	*−1.88**	*−0.92*
Tax/regulations	0.50	0.33	0.40	0.26	0.27
	0.42	*0.27*	*0.33*	*0.20*	*0.19*
Rule of Law					
Bribery (% of	−0.65	−0.72	−0.65	−0.72	−0.71
Revenues)	*−4.52****	*−4.64****	*−4.49****	*−4.60****	*−4.06****
Availability of laws			0.35	−0.07	0.53
			0.50	*−0.09*	*0.66*
Copyrights violations					−1.66
					−1.66+
Quality of education		2.05		2.08	
		*2.38***		*2.38***	
Firm characteristics					
Private ownership	13.21	14.73	12.90	14.44	11.10
	*3.50****	*3.73****	*3.39****	*3.62****	*2.45****
Small/medium size	−6.57	−5.16	−6.90	−5.41	−7.07
	*−2.37***	*−1.78**	*−2.46***	*−1.85**	*−2.27***
De novo (since	10.12	11.69	10.09	11.70	12.41
1994)	*4.34****	*4.73****	*4.29****	*4.69****	*4.48****
Exporter	9.38	10.30	9.37	10.24	9.96
	*4.30****	*4.51****	*4.26****	*4.46****	*4.01****
Foreign investment	1.15	2.78	1.21	2.78	0.92
	0.43	*0.99*	*0.45*	*0.98*	*0.30*
Headquarters in	0.45	1.04	0.43	1.10	0.20
capital / large city	*0.20*	*0.44*	*0.19*	*0.47*	*0.08*
Adjusted R^2	.08	.08	.08	.08	.09
Number of observations	3,394	3,060	3,356	3,028	2,752

Notes: From the survey, business constraints were rated on a scale from 1 to 4, where 1 implies "no constraint" and 4 "major obstacle." These include inflation, financing, infrastructure, tax/regulation, and policy instability constraints, as well as quality of courts, protection of property rights, copyright violations, and constraints to exercising "voice" of the firm. Bribery is expressed as percentage of revenues. Fixed country effects were used to account for differences across individual countries; only the Bolivian country effect is reported in the table.

+ significant at 15%; * significant at 10%; ** significant at 5%; *** significant at 1%.

macroeconomic and financing constraints. Yet, as indicated, these are firm-level constraints not binding for Bolivia, relatively speaking, attesting to the far-reaching macroeconomic reforms in the country. By contrast, a very significant variable typically related to a firm's lower output growth performance world-wide, *and* which exhibits a low rating for Bolivia, is the extent of corruption and bribery. Furthermore, protection of property rights (including through the effective performance of the courts) matters significantly. Conversely, a variable such as "availability of laws and regulations" (which is not a strong feature in Bolivia) is not found to be significant in explaining a firm's output growth performance, consistent with the notion that the constraints are typically found in implementation, not in passing laws. The Bolivia country effect dummy suggests that even after accounting for all the obstacles to growth, Bolivia would not have been expected to grow as fast as the fastest performer in this sample (Latvia). The econometric specifications with interactive terms between Bolivia and the various obstacle variables did not yield any significant terms (column 6, table 12.5), suggesting that the slope of the coefficients for Bolivia is not significantly different than for the overall worldwide sample.

As in the previous analysis of the determinants of unofficial behavior by officially registered firms, for this investigation into determinants of the firm's output growth we also tested the validity of the "beneficial grease" and "un-predictability of corruption" hypotheses. Further, to address the possible bias due to the firm's "kvetch" factor, again we included two options to control for possible bias, namely government inefficiency and government helpfulness as viewed by the firm. As is seen in table 12.6, once again we found no empirical support to either the "grease" or "unpredictability" hypotheses: (1) bribery levels are significantly and negatively (not positively) related to the firm's output growth (supporting a "sand" hypothesis instead), (2) none of the components measuring unpredictability of corruption is significantly associated with a firm's sales growth, and, (3) the large magnitude and significance of the bribery level variable stays rather unchanged irrespective of inclusion of the various components of unpredictability of corruption.

The microeconomic perspective of the firm provides evidence on the extent to which corruption, property rights protection, and "voice" appear to matter both in the registered firm's decision to operate officially or unofficially—with a strong bias to the latter in Bolivia—and in output growth performance. These strong results contrast with the absence of evidence that lawmaking in itself matters, or that it is the unpredictability of corruption (as opposed to its overall prevalence) that ought to be the focus.

In summing up, Patricia Calderón, the young entrepreneur entrusted with this section of the analysis, underscored the importance that misgovernance plays in blocking entrepreneurial development in Bolivia. She noted, however, that it is important to transcend generalities and point to the particular dimensions of governance that are an acute challenge within Bolivia, distinguishing them from some policymaking areas where Bolivia is rather stellar. Those areas of governance weaknesses, she concluded, matter in explaining a firm's behavior and performance. To go deeper, she stated, it is paramount to recognize what had been suggested earlier in her mother's historical section: misgovernance is anchored in the dynamics of the public sector and relates to the nature of the "public goods" it provides, the degree of politicization of economic activity, clientelism, patronage, and associated corruption. Thus, for an integrated analysis, an empirical probe into these complex links within the public was needed, she said, turning to her brother Jose, responsible for this challenging task.

6. THE PUBLIC OFFICIAL PERSPECTIVE TODAY, BY JOSE CALDERÓN JR.: A MICROINSTITUTIONAL ANALYSIS OF DETERMINANTS OF PUBLIC SECTOR PERFORMANCE

While taking a different professional path than his entrepreneurial sister, Jose Calderón Jr., a fast-rising technocrat in the government, did not disagree with her rigorous assessment from the perspective of the firm, as presented in the previous section. Rather, Jose, an accomplished civil servant known for his technical know-how and integrity, sought to complement such firm-based analysis (as well as the twin industrial-governmental historical perspectives provided earlier by his parents), with an empirically rigorous analysis of the functioning of government institutions.

First, as background Jose Calderón Jr. sought an indication of how Bolivia, in terms of governance, placed in a cross-country context. Based on an existing set of worldwide aggregate governance indicators for six governance components and about 170 countries from 1998, as can be seen in figure 12.5, a comparison is suggestive of the insights that emerged from the firm-based analysis in the previous section, namely that compared with the rest of the world, Bolivia does face a significant governance challenge, and that the variance among various governance components is very large—with control of corruption, rule of law, and government effectiveness showing as clear weaknesses, while by contrast substantial progress has been attained in democratic processes and deregulation.

While Jose Calderón regarded a cross-country perspective as useful to get a general indication of particular governance challenges afflicting Bolivia, he knew that such an approach would not provide an in-depth analysis of the nexus between governance and public sector performance. First, from the historical account in section 3 above he was keenly aware that the various governance factors interact in complex ways, and he thought that the "vicious circles" used by political scientists such as Scott and de la Porta to analyze the bidirectional links between political clientelism and corruption in Italy, Mexico, and Spain were relevant for analyzing the challenge in Bolivia, since this approach recognizes

TABLE 12.6

Growth of Firms and Unpredictability of Corruption

Determinants	1	2	3	4	5	6	7	8	9
Bolivia country effect	-8.78	-13.33	-10.47	-12.52	-5.30	-7.79	-11.88	-9.55	-9.57
	-0.90	*-1.50+*	*-1.03*	*-1.18*	*-0.69*	*-0.80*	*-1.33*	*-0.95*	*-1.19*
Business constraints									
Financing	-2.58	-2.25	-3.18	-2.56	-1.82	-2.59	-2.20	-1.91	-2.28
	-1.99**	*-2.03***	*-2.25***	*-1.77**	*-1.87**	*-1.98***	*-1.97***	*-1.44*	*-2.24***
Inflation	-3.44	-2.57	-4.33	-4.46	-3.09	-3.59	-2.81	-3.51	-3.52
	-2.25**	*-1.99***	*-2.59***	*-2.59***	*-2.73****	*-2.34***	*-2.15***	*-2.24***	*-2.96****
Infrastructure	-0.34	0.49	0.24	0.62	-0.17	-0.41	0.41	0.02	0.34
	-0.25	*0.41*	*0.16*	*0.42*	*-0.16*	*-0.30*	*0.35*	*0.01*	*0.32*
Policy Instability	-1.86	-1.59	-2.35	-2.19	-1.32	-1.84	-1.54	-1.67	-1.62
	-1.23	*-1.20*	*-1.41*	*-1.28*	*-1.14*	*-1.20*	*-1.15*	*-1.08*	*-1.33*
Tax / Regulation	0.48	0.39	-0.20	-0.62	0.74	0.44	0.59	0.28	0.00
	0.30	*0.28*	*-0.11*	*-0.33*	*0.61*	*0.27*	*0.42*	*0.17*	*0.00*
Corruption									
Bribery (% revenues)	-0.65	-0.70	-0.71	-0.77	-0.63	-0.64	-0.68	-0.69	-0.72
	-3.83***	*-4.24****	*-3.84****	*-4.00****	*-4.39****	*-3.75****	*-4.11****	*-3.96****	*-4.62****
Corrupt service unpredictability					-0.39				-0.47
					-0.36				*-0.49*
Corrupt payment unpredictability	-1.22		-1.50			-1.21			
	-1.44		*-1.63+*			*-1.41*			
Corrupt extra request unpredictability		-0.07					-0.17		
		-0.09					*-0.22*		

"Kvetch" control									
Government inefficiency	0.89	1.03							0.59
	0.69	*0.78*							*0.63*
Government unhelpfulness			-1.32	-0.58	-1.52				
			-1.57+	*-0.51*	*-1.55+*				
Firm characteristics									
Private ownership	13.38	12.05	15.03	14.45	13.32	13.12	12.23	12.59	14.82
	2.79***	*2.84****	*3.00****	*2.83****	*3.51****	*2.72****	*2.87****	*2.58***	*3.82****
Small/medium size	-7.33	-7.46	-6.59	-6.71	-6.47	-7.28	-7.50	-7.36	-6.29
	-1.76*	*-2.37***	*-1.52+*	*-1.51+*	*-2.30***	*-1.74+*	*-2.35***	*-1.73+*	*-2.21***
De novo (since 1994)	8.05	12.51	10.69	11.05	9.84	7.55	12.29	8.33	12.16
	2.74***	*4.67****	*3.33****	*3.37****	*4.17****	*2.55***	*4.54****	*2.78****	*4.89****
Exporter	12.17	8.63	12.58	13.25	9.35	11.70	8.50	13.01	9.40
	4.03***	*3.49****	*3.98****	*4.10****	*4.23****	*3.85****	*3.41****	*4.23****	*4.17****
Foreign investment	1.99	2.76	3.24	3.30	0.81	2.00	2.43	1.85	1.63
	0.51	*0.90*	*0.77*	*0.77*	*0.30*	*0.51*	*0.79*	*0.46*	*0.59*
Headquarters in capital / large city	0.81	-0.71	0.31	0.88	0.44	0.73	-0.62	1.22	0.07
	0.28	*-0.28*	*0.10*	*0.28*	*0.20*	*0.26*	*-0.24*	*0.42*	*0.03*
Adjusted R^2	.08	.07	.08	.08	.08	.08	.07	.08	.08
Number of observations	2369	2744	2143	2114	3327	2336	2700	2340	3149

Note: From the survey, business constraints were rated on a scale from 1 to 4, where 1 implies "no constraint" and 4 "major obstacle". These include inflation, financing, infrastructure, tax/regulation, and policy instability constraints, as well as quality of courts, protection of property rights, copyright violations, and constraints to exercising "voice" of the firm. Bribery is expressed as percentage of revenues. Fixed country effects were used to account for differences across individual countries; only the Bolivian country effect is reported on the table.

*** significant at 1%;   ** significant at 5%;   * significant at 10%   + significant at 15%

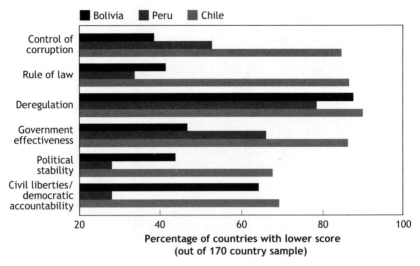

■ Bolivia ■ Peru ■ Chile

Figure 12.5. Aggregate governance indicators (ca. 1998)
Source: Kaufmann, Kraay, and Zoido-Lobatón 1999. For data set, sources of all individual variables used in the aggregate governance indicators, methodology of aggregation, as well as estimates of margins of error, at http://www.worldbank.org/wbi/governance.

that there is a joint determination of various endogenous components of governance.[41] Second, empirically he was to rely on a unique institutional data set for his country, namely an in-depth survey of 1,250 public officials in over 100 public institutions in Bolivia. Such a data set has been subjected recently to statistical analysis in Kaufmann, Mehrez, and Gurgur (KMG 2001), who address theoretically and empirically the relative importance of various determinants of public sector performance and governance.

In KMG, a model is developed that recognizes corruption, lack of transparency, and nondelivery of public services by individual public agencies as related but conceptually distinct concepts, all three of which constitute the key endogenous decision variables, simultaneously determined by the public official. The model characterizes a public official who maximizes his or her welfare subject to constraints: higher levels of corruption being subject to bargaining with the private agent (who tries to minimize the bribe payment) and to reputational costs; lower levels of transparency subject to internal rule-based constraints, and lower levels of public goods subject to lower official public service earnings or promotion prospects.

The model highlights the importance of public officials' incentive structure and behavior along these dimensions in determining the level and quality of

---

[41] Scott 1969, 1972; and for the account of de la Porta's writings, see Heywood 1997.

public goods provided. Further, and notwithstanding their treatment as exogenous variables, politicization (external negative influence on internal decision-making) and external "voice" (external positive feedback/checks and balances) also feature prominently in this framework, through an explicit effect on the incentives of public officials to settle for a lower governance/performance equilibrium (in the case of politiciz, tion), or for a higher equilibrium (in the case of more "voice")—in the joint determination of the levels of corruption, transparency, and service delivery (see fig. 12.A1 in the appendix). In addition to emphasizing the positive (negative) externalities of an honest (corrupt) public official, the model also integrates formally the importance of institutional norms.[42]

Indeed, under any circumstance the relationship between the various governance components (such as transparency), corruption, and service delivery is multidirectional. Governance factors, which may determine the rate of corruption, are in turn affected by corruption. Lack of transparency within an institution may result in a higher level of corruption, as a corrupt act is less likely to be exposed; conversely, corruption may lead to poor transparency, given the vested interests of those who engage in corrupt actions. When the link between "cause" and "effect" is not specified, the implications may be misleading. Thus, in contrast to conventional models, where the levels of corruption, transparency, or service delivery are determined by taking the level of the other two variables as given, in KMG the levels of these three key variables are endogenous and determined simultaneously. This requires addressing the issue of reverse causality; to do so we construct a model that identifies a specific equation for each one of these three variables, incorporating the causal effect of exogenous variables as well as other endogenous variables. Then, we estimate the system considering the effect of each endogenous variable on the others (2SLS). Further, we then consider the likelihood that the error terms of the endogenous variables may be

---

[42] For a description of the full formal model see Kaufmann, Mehrez, and Gurgur 2001. The joint determination of the three key decision variables by the public official extends the existing literature on corruption, inter alia by allowing for either a positive or negative a priori link between bribery and the level/quality of public service provision by the civil servant, and by explicitly introducing transparency as a separate endogenous factor in the model. A simple illustrative diagram synthesizing the model is included in annex 12.2. Derived from the model (analytical equations (9), (11), and (13) in KMG) we obtained a simultaneous system of equations (14) that can be estimated econometrically. Specifically, it implies the following system of equations:

$$\text{ServicePerformance} = h_1(\text{Corruption, Transparency})$$

$$\text{Corruption} = h_2(\text{ServicePerformance, Transparency})$$

$$\text{Transparency} = h_3(\text{Corruption, } \mathbf{X}_3)$$

Theoretically, the system can be estimated if the number of excluded variables is greater than the number of endogenous variables in each equation. The empirical task is to identify the variables that represent the variables/parameters of the model and then estimate the system using these variables.

correlated, and thus the 2SLS estimates may not be efficient, and thus perform a three-stage least square procedure (3SLS). Hence, the KMG model integrates the governance factors and public service delivery performance without imposing *ex ante* structure on the direction of causality.

Through this system of simultaneous equations, in KMG we then estimate the causes of poor governance, using the data set from detailed responses of public officials working in public sector agencies and municipalities in Bolivia. Based on an in-depth questionnaire with over 200 questions, specific governance characteristics were measured (and composites constructed) for each agency along the following three dimensions: (1) voice-related variables (internal transparency, citizen voice, politicization of agency); (2) formal public sector management (agency autonomy, rule enforcement, quality of rules, meritocracy, resource adequacy); and (3) individual public official variables (wage satisfaction, individual "ethical" values).

The public institutions surveyed include top executive branches (e.g., offices of the president and vice president); ministries (e.g., education, health, finance); line agencies (e.g., customs, tax, immigration); autonomous agencies (e.g., central bank); departmental institutions; and municipal governments. Each institution in the sample delivers services demanded by at least 5 percent of the population.[43] We utilize measures of governance and performance by the average response of all agents within the public agency.[44] The key variables used in the econometric analysis are presented in table 12.7.[45]

These variables, for which a definition glossary is given in table 12.8, are used to identify the various parameters of the model and for estimating these parameters using various methods, including ordinary least squares (OLS), two-stage least squares (2SLS), and three-stage least squares (3SLS).[46]

---

[43] Within each institution, a stratified random sample of at least 1 percent of all staff was selected at each of the following decision-making ranks: top management, middle management, and rank and file.

[44] Thus, the unit of observation in our analysis is a public agency.

[45] For a detailed description of the survey questions we used to construct each variable, see KMG.

[46] The rationale to estimate the model utilizing a 3SLS procedure emerges from the model (equation 14, see footnote 42). This model in KMG is identifiable, since in each equation the number of excludable variables is greater than the number of endogenous regressors. While the formal model in KMG points to a three-stage least squares (3SLS) econometric estimation procedure, we also argue that it is warranted to perform and present alongside such 3SLS specifications the full econometric results for OLS and 2SLS (as well as simple correlations). In the literature it is suggested that where there is endogeneity, a 2SLS or 3SLS instrumental variable technique is preferable to an OLS procedure, as the latter estimator is known to be biased and inconsistent. However, the choice of an estimator in a "small" sample remains a challenge in the literature, and in many empirical studies the OLS estimator is often found to be close to the 2SLS/3SLS estimator. Green (2000, 615) argues that "it is often found that the OLS estimator is surprisingly close to the structural estimator," while Nakamura and Nakamura (1985) show that the asymptotic bias of the OLS estimator will be smaller under reasonable assumptions (see also Heckman 1995, who points out

The KMG model thus yields the following set of econometric specifications:

$$ServicePerformance = \alpha_0 + \alpha_1 Bribery + \alpha_2 Transparency$$
$$+ \alpha_3 Decentralization + \alpha_4 WageSatisfaction$$
$$+ \alpha_5 RuleEnforcement + \alpha_6 IndividualValues$$
$$+ \alpha_7 Politicization + \alpha_8 ResourceEnvelope$$
$$+ \alpha_9 Meritocracy + \alpha Voice + \varepsilon_1$$

$$Bribery = \beta_0 + \beta_1 ServicePerformance + \beta_2 Transparency$$
$$+ \beta_3 Meritocracy + \beta_4 WageSatisfaction$$
$$+ \beta_5 RuleEnforcement + \beta_6 IndividualValues$$
$$+ \beta_7 Politicization + \beta_8 ResourceEnvelope + \varepsilon_2$$

$$Transparency = \chi_0 + \chi_1 Bribery + \chi_2 WageSatisfaction$$
$$+ \chi_3 RuleEnforcement + \chi_4 IndividualValues$$
$$+ \chi_5 Politicization + \chi_6 ResourceEnvelope$$
$$+ \chi_7 Voice + \chi_8 AgencyAutonomy + \chi_9 Education + \varepsilon_3$$

We estimate the system using four methods and present the results in table 12.8. First, we use simple correlation between the variables. Second, we estimate a linear least square of each equation separately. Third, we estimate the system using two-stage least square (2SLS) and finally we estimate the system using 3SLS.[47] In the main specifications shown here, we use the bribery index as a

---

the conditions under which the standard asymptotic approximations to the distributions of instrumental variables break down). Similarly, Monte Carlo studies suggest that the advantage of the system estimators in finite samples is more modest than the asymptotic results would suggest (Intriligator 1984).

[47] The instruments used in the first stage of the 2SLS and 3SLS estimations are the entire set of exogenous variables, since we used a system of equations model. The choice of adequate instruments for corruption and service delivery performance is not extensively addressed in the empirical literature on corruption (see, however, Bai and Wei 2000; Svensson 2000b; Kaufmann, Kraay, and Zoido-Lobatón 1999), and virtually nonexistent for transparency. In the context of 2SLS and 3SLS, two requirements for a variable to be used as a good instrument are that such instruments be correlated with the endogenous variable, but not be correlated with the error terms of these variables. In our context, the first requirement can be attained through instruments exogenous to the public officials themselves. The variables utilized as instruments are controlled by the institutions, such as constitution, parliament, and government, or determined at the ministry level. Agency autonomy, whether the agency is in a municipality or a central institution, civil service pay, meritocracy, existence of voice mechanisms, or existence and effectiveness of rule enforcement mechanisms are such variables. The first-stage regressions for the three endogenous variables yield high R^2 (0.55 for service delivery, 0.62 for corruption, and 0.78 for transparency), suggesting a high explanatory power of the instruments. Shea (1998) argued that R^2 can be a useful measure of relevance only in the case of univariate models and proposed a new R^2 measure when there are multiple endogenous variables. For each of the three endogenous variables, this statistic is also found to be around 0.71.

TABLE 12.7
Analysis of Bolivia's Public Agencies
Variable Description

Variable	Measure
Service performance	The average of three standardized service delivery indicators (if applicable): quality, quantity, and accessibility. The index is rescaled using the mean and standard deviation of national service, such that high numbers correspond to high performance in service delivery.
Bribery index	The average of two standardized bribery indicators: frequency of bribery, and bribe/official income ratio. The index is rescaled using the mean and standard deviation of corruption at the national level, such that high numbers correspond to high corruption.
Corruption index	The average of four standardized corruption indicators: frequency of bribery, bribe/official income ratio, percent of jobs purchased, and percent of budget diverted illegally. The index is rescaled using the mean and standard deviation of corruption at the national level, such that high numbers correspond to high corruption.
Transparency	Percentage of cases where the actions of the public officials and the decision making are transparent
Enforcement	Percent of the cases where rules, guidelines, regulations, and processes in the personnel, budget, and service management are strictly monitored and enforced
Meritocracy	Percent of the cases where the decisions on personnel management issues are based on level of education, or professional experience, merit, and performance.
Politicization	Percent of cases where decision on personnel, budget, and service management are free from political interference
Autonomous agencies	Central Bank, Bank and Finance Superintendence, Telecommunication Superintendence, Hierarchical Affairs Superintendence, Transportation Superintendence, National Comptroller, Electoral Court, Constitutional Tribune, Supreme Court, Ombudsman, Judicial Council
Resources	Percentage of cases where the physical, financial, and human resources of the agency are adequate
Values	The probability that if a public official were overpaid by an administrative error, the public official would return the money given that there is 100% chance of not getting caught and the superiors are doing the same without getting caught

(continued)

TABLE 12.7 *(Continued)*

Variable	Measure
Voice	An index representing the existence of consumer feedback and complaint mechanisms
Wages	The extent of satisfaction with the wages and other benefits
Decentralization	A dummy variable representing the municipal agencies

measure of graft, as presented in table 12.8. In addition to using the bribery variable, we also repeated the same procedure utilizing a composite corruption index instead, which is a broader index capturing illegal budget diversion and purchase of public positions, as well as including the frequency and level of bribery.[48]

From the main results summarized in the table, we first note that the outcomes of the simple correlations are substantially different from the controlled econometric estimations. This is suggestive of the large bias inherent in deriving policy advice from simple correlations. By contrast, we observe that the econometric results of the OLS, 2SLS and 3SLS specifications do provide similar estimates, with 3SLS results even more robust than the simpler specifications.

The main results, presented in table 12.8, indicate that (1) the *service delivery performance* depends negatively on the level of corruption and positively on external voice of users and on transparency; (2) *bribery and corruption* depends positively on the degree of politicization of the agency and negatively on internal transparency in the agency and on meritocracy (although the latter does not affect quality of public services directly), (3) *transparency* is affected positively by voice, and negatively by corruption and politicization; (4) where the agency is in the localities (such as a *municipality,* labeled as the decentralization variable), its performance in terms of quality of public service delivery is lower than for central agencies—although in some services they do provide more access to the poor; (5) the level of educational attainment by the staff of a public institution is also significantly associated with transparency in the agency; (6) although the formal model allowed for such effects, there is no empirical evidence that traditional *public sector management variables* such as civil service wage, availability of resources, and enforcement of rules have any significant direct effect on corruption; and, (7) the variable capturing individual *ethical values* is not significant either.[49]

---

[48] The results of the specifications utilizing a composite corruption index instead of the bribery variable are not shown here; see KMG.

[49] When there are several variables that are determined endogenously the *full* (general equilibrium) effect of a change in any of the exogenous variables can be significantly different from the *direct*

TABLE 12.8
Determinants of Performance of Public Agencies in Bolivia
OLS, 2SLS, and 3SLS Estimation Results

Variable	Model	Dependent Variable: Service Delivery				Dependent Variable: Bribery				Dependent Variable: Transparency			
		Simple Correlation	OLS	2SLS	3SLS	Simple Correlation	OLS	2SLS	3SLS	Simple Correlation	OLS	2SLS	3SLS
Service performance						-0.46***	-0.17 (-1.11)	0.65 (0.39)	0.78 (0.99)	0.72***			
Bribery		-0.46***	-0.29** (-2.27)	-0.27* (-1.78)	-0.24*** (-2.12)					-0.46***	-0.19 (-4.01)	-0.22* (-1.78)	-0.31** (-2.47)
Transparency		0.72***	0.30** (2.42)	0.40† (1.61)	0.45** (2.23)	-0.54***	-1.10** (-4.17)	-1.54** (-2.29)	-1.61*** (-2.62)				
Resource envelope	Z^*, f_1, f_2, f_3	0.62***	0.25** (1.92)	0.24† (1.59)	0.17† (1.54)	-0.39***	-0.08 (-0.41)	-0.10 (-0.65)	-0.11 (-0.74)	0.52***	-0.07 (-0.69)	-0.07 (-0.58)	-0.08 (-0.84)
Politicization	f_1, f_2, f_3	-0.332***	-0.06† (-1.41)	-0.04 (0.67)	-0.09 (-1.14)	0.40***	0.32** (2.49)	0.29** (2.12)	0.33** (2.35)	0.47***	-0.13** (1.99)	-0.13* (-2.40)	-0.13** (-2.21)
Wage satisfaction	f_1, f_2, f_3	0.13	0.13 (0.68)	0.03 (0.87)	0.11 (0.60)	-0.21**	-0.75† (-1.60)	-0.18 (-1.04)	-0.87† (-1.52)	0.32***	0.24** (1.98)	0.26* (1.76)	0.21† (1.52)
Rule enforcement	f_1, f_2, f_3	0.58***	0.13 (1.15)	-0.04 (-0.65)	-0.04 (-0.64)	-0.33***	-0.41 (1.30)	-0.28 (-1.19)	-0.21 (-1.12)	0.61***	0.24** (2.49)	0.20* (1.90)	0.21** (2.00)
Individual values	$g(.)$	0.03	0.01 (0.35)	-0.02 (-0.40)	-0.04 (-0.08)	-0.03	-0.06 (-0.68)	0.14 (0.81)	0.03 (0.69)	0.10	0.03 (0.75)	0.04 (0.95)	0.06 (1.22)

Variable									
Meritocracy	f_1, f_2	0.45***	−0.08 (−0.70)	0.06 (0.54)	0.14 (0.74)	−0.42***	−0.53** (−2.09)	−0.34* (−1.82)	−0.30** (−2.01)
Decentralization	$Z*$	−0.04	−1.87 (−1.19)	−3.67 (1.33)	−6.55** (−1.91)				
Voice	$Z*, T*$	0.68***	0.44*** (2.67)	0.41** (2.44)	0.39** (2.36)	0.72***	0.60*** (3.92)	0.58*** (3.15)	0.38*** (2.65)
Agency autonomy	$T*$					0.26***	−1.74 (0.65)	−2.17 (−0.70)	−2.45 (−0.67)
Education	$T*$					0.23**	3.89 (1.23)	2.75 (1.32)	4.19† (1.43)
Adjusted R^2		0.64	0.55	0.44	0.47	0.39	0.38	0.63	0.61
									0.55

Note: All variables are scaled from 0 to 100. Service performance index is the average of three standardized service delivery indicators (if applicable): quality, quantity, and accessibility. Bribery index represents the average of two standardized bribery indicators: frequency of bribery and bribe/official income ratio. The indices are re-scaled using the mean and standard deviation of national service quality and bribery, respectively such that high numbers correspond to high performance and high corruption. Number of observations in each public institution is chosen as the weight of each institution in the regression. Sample size is 89.

† Significant at 15 %; * significant at 10%, ** significant at 5%, *** significant at 1%.

These results also underscore the importance of focusing on the *high variance* that may prevail within a country, along two dimensions typically left to country-level aggregate analysis, which obscures the within-country variability containing much information at the local level: (1) variance across determinants of public sector performance, in terms of which factors are relevant and significant, and (2) governance quality variance across public institutions.

Indeed, as per results for Bolivia in table 12.8, and illustrated in the figure 12.6a–f, it is clear that voice- and transparency-related determinants may be more relevant in explaining performance of public agencies than conventional public sector management variables. Figure 12.6a–g illustrates determinants that are very significant, while by contrast, figure 12.6h, for wages, is one illustration of a variable often emphasized in traditional public sector management writings that the empirical evidence here suggests is nonsignificant.[50] Further, in this figure we can also observe that there is enormous variance in governance quality and performance *across institutions* within the country, backstopping the "localization of knowledge" notion emphasized in the previous empirical section on enterprise.

Indeed, Jose Calderón Jr., in ending his exposition to the rest of his family, stressed this particular finding of significant variability across public institutions in Bolivia, pointing to the need of unbundling the generic notions of policymaking, governance, and institutional quality, and of localizing knowledge. As a well-regarded and proud senior civil servant, who had colleagues, friends, and superiors with similar traits in the public sector, he concluded by stating that one ought to avoid generalizations such as "the public sector in Bolivia is totally corrupt and dysfunctional." Instead, he said, the focus ought to be in distilling the positive lessons of good performance and governance in some areas of policymaking (and from some well-performing agencies) for supporting

---

(partial equilibrium) effect. For example, an increase in voice will improve transparency, in turn reducing corruption, which will increase transparency even further. In order to estimate the full effect of policy variables, we draw from KMG's calculations of the reduced form equations using the estimates of the structural equations (i.e., incorporating the linkage between the various endogenous variables). The results (reported in full in KMG) indicate that the full effects of key variables are substantially larger than the partial effect that can be derived from single equation results as presented in table 12.8. In particular, the full effect of voice on corruption increases due to its effect on transparency, which has a significant impact on corruption, and the effect of politicization on corruption also becomes stronger because corruption causes less transparency that, in turn, leads to even higher level of corruption. And by contrast, the empirical estimates of the full effect based on this Bolivia survey suggest again that traditional public sector management factors, such as rule enforcement and government pay, or individual public official characteristics such as "ethical values," do not exert a significant impact on corruption.

[50] Due to space considerations, among nonsignificant variables, only wages are depicted in the figure; the absence of significance of the agency's resource envelope, agency autonomy, rule enforcement, and individual ethical values is explicit in table 12.9.

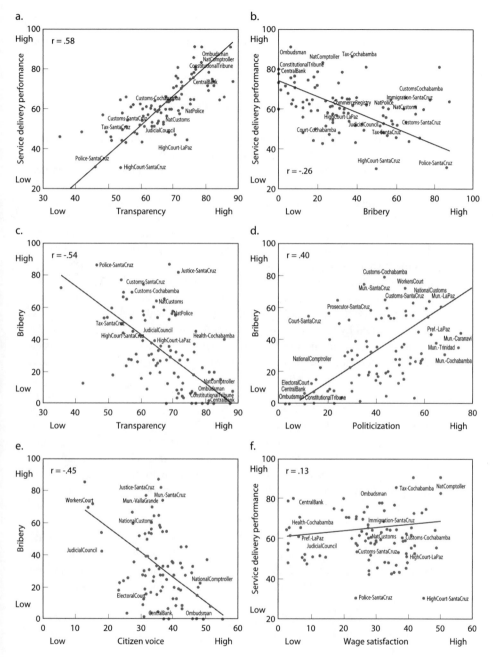

Figure 12.6. Performance and governance in Bolivia's public institutions. In the plotgrams above, each point represents a public sector (central, departmental, or municipal) agency in Bolivia. The fitted line is the predicted linear relationship between the dependent and the independent variables, which is calculated from the 3-equation model based on the 3SLS econometric estimates of the system as reported in table 12.8.

Source: Kaufmann, Mehrez, and Gurgur 2001

institutional reforms, so as to support the required revamping in those institutions afflicted by deep systemic weaknesses.

7. IMPLICATIONS AND CONCLUSIONS

For our inquiry into the Bolivian puzzle of strong and sustained macroeconomic reforms with tepid economic growth performance over the past 15 years we took an integrated approach, combining the following: (1) a two-pronged historical perspective from the twin standpoints of the evolution of the enterprise and government sectors over the past half-century; (2) an in-depth review of the literature on possible determinants of Bolivia's growth performance; (3) an empirical analysis of Bolivia's enterprise sector performance on the basis of a detailed firm-level survey conducted recently in over 80 countries, and (4) an empirical analysis of Bolivia's public agencies based on a survey of over 1,200 public officials in Bolivia working in over 100 institutions. As empirical background to the above, placing Bolivia in international perspective, we also utilized cross-country empirical evidence. The historical background sections, complemented by the review of the literature, provided a background to the evolution of Bolivia's political economy, helping frame key hypotheses tested in the subsequent econometric analysis with both data sets on enterprise and public officials.

We provided evidence on the ascent and entrenchment of "unofficialdom" in Bolivia: both the enterprise sector and the public sector were characterized by substantial unofficial and informal behavior. In the public sector this is in turn related to politics of patronage, of "clientelism," and of corruption, in an individual-centered political landscape, where public agencies have been hampered by entrenched politicization. In turn, politicization, patronage, clientelism, and corruption have defined a significant part of the relationship with the elite enterprise sector, while for the rest of the enterprise sector unofficialdom and informality have been the response to the absence of a level playing field—and the concomitant high costs of formality (including corruption), with the elite being the beneficiaries from remaining in the formal sector. Thus, it has been central to this inquiry to study the role that misgovernance in Bolivia has played in the lack of effective functioning of formal institutions in the public and private arenas.

In turn, the extent and particular manifestations of "unofficialdom" and misgovernance in Bolivia have had adverse consequences for its growth performance and thus significantly dampened the higher growth rate that Bolivia might have enjoyed in the aftermath of ambitious macroeconomic reforms boldly launched in the mid-1980s. In so doing, our work challenges some conventions, such as the notion that broad macroeconomic reforms can *suffice* to attain high growth rates. Instead we highlight the potentially key role that may be played by nontraditional institutional factors such as misgovernance, politicization of the government agencies, corruption, and "unofficialdom." Within the exploration of the effects of misgovernance on enterprise behavior and performance, we also found that there is no empirical support for either the beneficial "grease" hypothesis about bribery or the "unpredictability" of corruption hypothesis. The *extent* of corruption faced by a firm and experienced within a public institution does matter significantly and adversely for its performance.

More broadly, the methodological approach and findings of this study question the value of concentrating on a *country* aggregate as a relevant unit of empirical observation. The empirical evidence attests to the large variance in performance and governance across *institutions,* and also to the variance across policy and institutional factors within a country. This challenges the tendency to rank (or "grade") countries as if the within-country variance were low, obscuring the strengths and weaknesses that institutions in the country may have— in turn clouding our ability to provide properly prioritized and focused policy advice at the country level.

The Calderón-Vargas family gathered again during a break in August 2001, and reviewed the work they put together on Bolivia's low growth. They are relatively satisfied with the four key components of the work (the historical parts by the parents, the present-day empirically based research by their offspring), with the new evidence emerging, and with the integrated picture emerging from pulling such pieces together. The mother, Marta, always rigorously self-critical, is of two minds: with more time additional materials and further integration would have been possible, she says, yet at the same time she is of the view that the additional benefits are unlikely to alter the main results emerging from the analysis. Philosophically, she added:

> Let us keep in mind that whether we unveil this work tomorrow as is, or within a year after further work, a basic tenet will remain: while it is true that we have some insights regarding overlooked institutional areas that require priority, none of us can tell for sure what the optimal recipe is for Bolivia to grow stronger—not even the experts from the international financial institutions! Indeed, our review of the overall development field suggests that this is not specific to our country; there is simply no universally accepted truth on what are the most important factors in making a country grow. In part, the answers vary from setting to setting; in part, there are imponderable mysteries however deeply we study them.

"This means we need to have a modicum of modesty in concluding our work and in making use of it," she concluded.

"I agree," retorted the son Jose,

> yet as you hint, in our work we have pointed to a few areas that for too long have been neglected due to a combination of insufficient analytical and empirical analysis as well as vested interests for inaction, and in this process of working together

we have also challenged some conventions. We are making a strong case for focusing on political and institutional reforms that have not been accorded the priority they deserve ever since the major macroeconomic reforms of the eighties started. That message and rationale ought to be conveyed. Nowadays there may be a historical window of opportunity for Bolivia, with the imminent change in leadership—the passage from the old to the new.

Since Jose personally knew some of them from his professional work, he suggested he could contact some members of the new team in order to provide them with the key findings and messages from the analysis for possible use by the incoming administration.

Ramiro, the father, with his old sagacity and a tinge of skepticism, interjected.

We can do that, but let us keep some perspective; I have seen a number of promising new administrations come and go with dashed hopes. It is one thing to have the good rhetoric in all these speeches and statements of intention, or even to pass more laws and regulations and other such superficial measures seemingly to eliminate misgovernance by fiat. But as we have seen in our review and evidence, it is a rather different and politically courageous task to do what really matters: deep-seated political and institutional reforms. Lets face it, even very bright young leaders with a competent cabinet may find such task daunting, particularly when the political cycle is so short and the old guard is still entrenched.

Patricia, with her entrepreneurial practical-orientation, suggested then that they put together a brief memo to the authorities synthesizing the findings in their work, and outlining its implications in the form of policy recommendations. She asked her mother what she would suggest to present first in this set of recommendations.

Marta retorted by focusing on the need for *political reforms, and the de-politicization of public institutions.* She stressed the notion that the politicians' fortunes were still overly reliant on the *cuoteo político* system, yet was of the view that at present there was a real opportunity for reform with the new regime. Countervailing forces were likely to be present, however, because unless resolute action was taken early in the new administration, public discontent inherited from the outgoing government and with the existing political system might lead to serious deterioration of democratic institutions—akin to other Latin American countries currently in turmoil. Thus, a central institutional reform that needed to emerge was the transformation of the Bolivian state from a patronage-based system to a modern professional set of institutions providing quality public goods to the citizenry and enterprise, in turn key for sustained growth and alleviation of poverty.

Jose stressed that *voice, participation,* and *transparency* matter fundamentally. Voice and participation by the citizenry and by the enterprise sector were important to enhance accountability in public administration; in this context they agreed that it would be useful to deepen initiatives such as the National Dialogue and the Popular Participation reform, which has empowered (at least some of) the communities' ability to hold local governments accountable for their actions (World Bank 2000). In this context, Ramiro suggested that the government could put together a strategy of engaging the private sector and the media as supporters of the reform agenda, consulting with them more closely on reform implementation, and providing information on institutional performance of the public sector so that these societal actors could monitor progress in implementation and sustain constructive pressure.

All concurred that improved transparency and access to information by key government agencies was likely to be critical, particularly in the budgetary and public account institutions. Further, major transparency-related reforms were needed at the *local level,* where substantial weaknesses persist, and where many municipalities and local agencies are rife with corruption. Jose, from his perspective as a civil servant, thought it important to offer at least some concrete suggestions; initiatives such as holding public audiences for budgetary decision-making in the municipalities, web-based tools for transparent and competitive procurement, transparent access to public officials (and their dependents), asset and income declaration, public voting records of local councils, and the like.

In this context of municipal level misgovernance, Marta, drawing from her broader historical experience, pointed to the reforms at the local level in the United States following the widespread corruption related to clientelism and patronage in local political machines (e.g. Tammany Hall) in the late nineteenth and early twentieth centuries (Wiebe 1967; Scott 1969; Johnston 1979). In particular, she thought that one particular innovation dating a hundred years ago in the United States in response to such ingrained corruption at the local level could be of use in so many localities in Bolivia today, namely the movement to technocratize local level management ("manager movements") (Rehren 2001). She also was of the view that lessons could be learned also from the far-reaching anticorruption reforms introduced by a previous major in La Paz, and from the reversal of such reforms once he left office—which point to the need of civil society involvement in local administration so to both provide checks and balances and institutional continuity in local level reforms.

Patricia emphasized the need focus on a much improved framework for *protection of property rights* for enterprise, on the simplification of some regulatory procedures and delicensing, and measures to combat *bribery and corruption.* In this context, she underscored the fact that in spite of efforts in the right direction over the past three years, *judiciary reforms and the anticorruption program* were very much unfinished agendas, and that a bold re-launch in those two areas may be warranted. Without these reforms, she noted, the major challenge of "unofficialdom" of the enterprise sector was unlikely to be addressed, and that in turn would continue to dampen the growth prospects of Bolivia.

The Calderón-Vargas family decided to begin drafting a policy memo to the incoming administration, focusing on the above elements of political and institutional reforms, with emphasis on improved governance, voice, transparency, judiciary and local-level reforms, and on defining an anticorruption program that would emphasize institutional systemic reforms and complement efforts that were already ongoing—since the incoming president at the time, as outgoing vice president, had been entrusted previously with the responsibility of coordinating an anticorruption plan.

In writing the policy memorandum they were to frame such policy notes by pointing out in the introduction that they were not going to claim to have definitive answers in this complex field full of unknowns, yet they did know that nowadays the stakes were possibly higher than ever—not only because of the civil unrest of the recent past, but also due to the potential windfall or curse of the newly proven natural gas reserves. Given such a windfall, Bolivia's path could continue to deteriorate in the direction taken by Venezuela or Nigeria if misgovernance were not addressed. Conversely, under a much improved governance framework, involving institutional reform and including key institutional and political structures, countries like Chile or Botswana might be more fitting examples.

APPENDIX: GLOSSARY OF TERMS FOR VARIABLES IN EMPIRICAL ANALYSIS, AND BACKGROUND ECONOMETRIC RESULTS FROM WORLDWIDE BUSINESS SURVEY (WBES)

Dependent Variables

Underreported Revenues: "Recognizing the difficulties many enterprises face in fully complying with taxes and regulations, what percentage of total sales would you estimate the typical firm in your area of activity reports for tax purposes?" (%)
Sales Growth Rate: "Estimate of growth of your company's sales over the past three years" (%)

Independent Variables

"Voice" of the Firm: "In the case of important changes in laws or policies affecting my business's operation, the government takes into account concerns voiced either by me or by my business association." [1: always true . . . 6: never true]
Constraints in Financing, Policy Instability, Exchange Rate, Inflation, Corruption, Tax/Regulations (for each): Please judge on a four-point scale how prob-

lematic are the following factors for the operation and growth of your business. [1: no obstacle . . . 4: major obstacle]

Bribery: On average, what percentage of revenues do firms like yours typically pay per annum in unofficial payments to public officials? [percent]

Courts' Protection of Property Rights: "I am confident that the legal system will uphold my contract and property rights in business disputes": To what degree do you agree with this statement now? [1: fully agree . . . 6: fully disagree]

Availability of Laws: "In general, information on the laws and regulations affecting my firm is easy to obtain." [1: fully agree . . . 6: fully disagree]

Quality of Services: Please rate the overall quality and efficiency of services delivered by the following public agencies or services (education, judiciary/courts, public works, postal system, water, police, central bank). [1: very good . . . 6: very bad]

Copyright Violations: Please judge on a four-point scale how problematic the following practices of your competitors are for your firm. "They violate my (copyrights, patents, trademarks)." [1: no obstacle . . . 4: major obstacle]

Corruption in Procurement: When firms in your industry do business with the government, how much of the contract value must they offer in additional or unofficial payments to secure the contract? [1: 0 percent . . . 6: greater than 20 percent]

Corruption of Bank Officials: Please judge on a four-point scale how problematic is this financing issue for the operation and growth of your business. [1: no obstacle . . . 4: major obstacle]

Frequency of Bribery: "Thinking about government officials, it is common for firms in my line of business to have to pay some irregular 'additional payments' to get things done." [1: always true . . . 6: never true]

Corrupt Service Unpredictability: If a firm pays the required "additional payment," the service is usually also delivered as agreed. [1: always true . . . 6: never true]

Corrupt Payment Unpredictability: "Firms in my line of business usually know in advance about how much this 'additional payment' is." [1: always true . . . 6: never true]

Corrupt Extra Payment Unpredictability: If a firm pays the required "additional payment" to a particular government official, another government official will subsequently require an additional payment for the same service. [1: always true . . . 6: never true]

Government Inefficiency: How would you generally rate the efficiency of government in delivering services? [1: very efficient . . . 6: very inefficient]

Government Unhelpfulness: Please rate your overall perception of the relation between government and/or bureaucracy and private firms on the following scale. "All in all, for doing business I perceive the state as . . ." [1: very helpful . . . 5: very unhelpful]

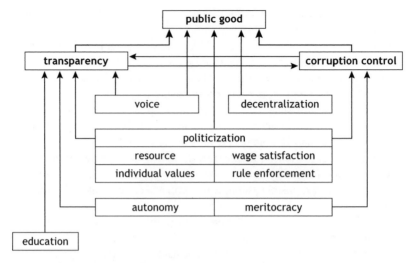

Figure 12.A1 on KMG model (from section 6). Determinants of public sector performance. The model's endogenous variables are Public (Goods) Service Provision, Corruption, and Transparency. The remainder are exogenous variables in the model.
Source: Kaufmann, Mehrez, and Gurgur 2001

REFERENCES

Bai, Chong-En, and Shang-Jin Wei. 2000. "The Quality of the Bureaucracy and Capital Account Policies." World Bank Policy Research Working Paper No. 2575. Washington, D.C.

Banco Central de Bolivia. 1967. *Boletín Estadístico.* No. 180. La Paz, Bolivia.

Barrera, F., and E. Lora. 1997. "A Decade of Structural Reform in Latin America: Growth, Productivity, and Investment Are Not What They Used to Be." Inter-American Development Bank Working Paper Green Series No. 350. Washington, D.C.

Batra, Geeta, D. Kaufmann, and Andrew H. W. Stone. 2001. "Voices of the Firms, 2000: Findings of the World Business Environment Survey." World Bank, Washington, D.C.

Cámara Nacional de Industrias de Bolivia. Various years.

Casanovas Sainz, Roberto. 1989. "Informalidad e Ilegalidad: Una Falsa Identidad." In *Informalidad e ilegalidad: Una falsa identidad,* ed. A. Péres Velasco, R. Casanovas, and H. Larrazabal. La Paz: Centro de Estudios del Desarrollo, Laboral y Agrario.

El Centro de Estudios del Desarrollo/Instituto Latinoamericano de Desenvolvimiento Economico e Social. 1977. *Fomento Industrial en América Latina.* Bogotá: Ediciones Internacionales.

Chavez, J. C. 1997. "Estado y Competitividad." In *Estudios de Milenio,* no. 9. La Paz: Fundación Milenio.

Conaghan, Catherine, James M. Malloy, and Luis A. Abugattas. 1990. "Business and the 'Boys': The Politics of Neoliberalism in the Central Andes." *Latin American Research Review* 25, no. 2: 3–30.

Cox, Gary, and Richard McKelvey. 1987. "Ham Sandwich Theorems for General Measures." *Social Choice and Welfare* 1:75–83.

Doria Medina, S. 1986. *La Economía Informal en Bolivia.* La Paz: Editorial Offset Boliviana.

Easterly, W., N. Loayza, and P. Montiel. 1996. "Has Latin America's Post-reform Growth Been Disappointing?" World Bank Policy Research Working Paper No. 1708.

Eder, G. J. 1968. *Inflation and Development in Latin America: A Case History of Inflation and Stabilisation in Bolivia.* Ann Arbor: University of Michigan Press.

Fisman, Raymond, and Jakob Svenson. 2000. "Are Corruption and Taxation Really Harmful to Growth? Firm Level Evidence." World Bank, Washington, D.C. Photocopy.

Friedman, E., S. Johnson, D. Kaufmann, and P. Zoido-Lobatón. 2000. "Dodging the Grabbing Hand: The Determinants of Unofficial Activity in 69 Countries." *Journal of Public Economics* 76, no. 3: 459–93.

Fundación Milenio. 1997a. "Fortalezas y Debilidades Institucionales de Organizaciones Empresariales." *Diálogos de Milenio,* no. 61. La Paz.

———. 1997b. "Identificación de las Ventajas Comparativas, Dinámicas, Efectivas y Potenciales del País." *Diálogos de Milenio,* no. 59. La Paz.

———. 1997c. *Informe Milenio Sobre la Economía,* no. 3. La Paz.

Gallup, John Luke, and Jeffrey D. Sachs, with Andrew Mellinger. 1999. "Geography and Economic Development." Center for International Development Working Paper No. 1.

Gamarra, E., and J. Malloy. 1990. "Bolivia: Revolution and Reaction." In *Latin American Politics and Development,* ed. Howard J. Wiarda and Harvey F. Kline. 3d ed. Boulder, Colo.: Westview Press.

Gisbert, T., J. Mesa, and C. Mesa. 1998. *Historia de Bolivia.* La Paz: Editorial Gisbert.

Gray-Molina, G., E. P. de Rada, and E. Yáñez. 1999. "Transparency and Accountability in Bolivia: Does Voice Matter?" Inter-American Development Bank Working Paper No. R-381, Washington, D.C.

Grebe, H. 1999. "Contribución para el Country Focus Bolivia." Photocopy.

———. 2001. "The Private Sector and Democratization." In *Towards Democratic Viability: The Bolivian Experience,* ed. John Crabtree and Laurence Whitehead. London: Palgrave.

Green, W. 2000. *Econometric Analysis.* Englewood Cliffs, N.J.: Prentice-Hall.

Gupta, Sanjeev, Hamid Davoodi, and Alonso-Terme. 1998. "Does Corruption Affect Income Inequality and Poverty?" IMF Working Paper No. WP/98/76.

Heckman, J. 1995. "Instrumental Variables: A Cautionary Tale." NBER Working Paper Series (U.S.) No. 185, September.

Hellman, J. S., G. Jones, and D. Kaufmann. 2000. "Seize the State, Seize the Day." World Bank Policy Research Working Paper No. 2444, Washington, D.C. http://www.worldbank.org/wbi/governance.

Hellman, J. S., G. Jones, D. Kaufmann, and M. Schankerman. 2000. "Measuring Governance, Corruption, and State Capture." World Bank Policy Research Working Paper No. 2312. Washington, D.C. http://www.worldbank.org/wbi/governance.

Heywood, Paul. 1997. "Political Corruption: Problems and Perspectives." Special issue of *Political Studies* 45.

Huntington, S. P. 1968. *Political Order in Changing Societies.* New Haven: Yale University Press.

Inter-American Development Bank (IDB). 1997. *Economic and Social Progress in Latin America: Latin America after a Decade of Reforms.* Washington, D.C.

International Monetary Fund (IMF). 1998. *Bolivia—Selected Issues.* Washington, D.C.

Instituto Nacional de Estadísticas. 1995. *Encuesta industria manufacturera 1994.* La Paz.

———. 1997. *Anuario estadístico 1996.* La Paz.

Intriligator, M. D. 1984. *Econometric Models, Techniques, and Applications.* Englewood Cliffs, N.J.: Prentice-Hall.

Johnson, S., D. Kaufmann, and A. Shleifer. 1997. "The Unofficial Economy in Transition." *Brookings Papers on Economic Activity* 1997, no. 2: 159–239.

Johnson, S., D. Kaufmann, and P. Zoido-Lobatón. 1998. "Regulatory Discretion and the Unofficial Economy." *American Economic Review* 88:387–92.

———. 1999. "Corruption, Public Finance, and the Unofficial Economy." World Bank Policy Research Working Paper No. 2169. Washington, D.C.

Johnston, Michael. 1979. "Patrons and Clients, Jobs and Machines: A Case Study of the Uses of Patronage." *American Political Science Review* 73:385–98.

Kaufmann, Daniel, A. Kraay, and P. Zoido-Lobatón. 1999. "Governance Matters." World Bank Policy Research Working Paper No. 2196, Washington, D.C. http://www.world-bank.org/wbi/governance.

Kaufmann, Daniel, G. Mehrez, and T. Gurgur. 2001. "Voice or Public Sector Management? A Model and Analysis Based on a Survey of Public Officials." World Bank, forthcoming.

Kaufmann, Daniel, and Shang-Jin Wei. 1999. "Does 'Grease Payment' Speed Up the Wheels of Commerce?" NBER Working Paper No. 7093, April. Also release as World Bank Policy Research Working Paper no. 2254.

Kiewiet, D. Roderick, and Mathew D. McCubbins. 1991. *The Logic of Delegation: Congressional Parties and the Appropriations Process.* Chicago: University of Chicago Press.

Klitgaard, Robert. 1988. *Controlling Corruption.* Berkley and Los Angeles: University of California Press.

Klitgaard, Robert, Ronald McLean-Abarroa, and Lindsay Parris. 2000. *Corrupt Cities: A Practical Guide to Cure and Prevention.* Oakland, Calif.: Institute for Contemporary Studies Press.

Larrazabal, H. 1997. "La Microempresa ante los Desafíos del Desarrollo, Encuentro Nacional Microempresa versus Pobreza ¿Un desafío posible?" Centro de Estudios para el Desarrollo, Laboral y Agrario, La Paz. Typescript.

Leff, N. H. 1964. "Economic Development through Bureaucratic Corruption." *American Behavioral Scientist* 8, no. 2: 8–14.

Loayza, Norman V. 1996. "The Economics of the Informal Sector: A Simple Model and Some Empirical Evidence from Latin America." *Carnegie-Rochester Conference Series on Public Policy* 45:129–62.

Lui, F. 1985. "An Equilibrium Queuing Model of Bribery." *Journal of Political Economy* 93, no. 4: 760–81.

Maddala, G. S. 1977. *Econometrics.* New York: McGraw-Hill.

Maddala, G. S., and Jinook Jeong. 1994. "On the Exact Small Sample Distribution of the Instrumental Variable Estimator." In *Econometric Methods and Applications,* vol. 1. Economists of the Twentieth Century. Cheltenham: Edward Elgar.

Malloy, James M. 1970. *Bolivia: The Uncompleted Revolution.* Pittsburgh: University of Pittsburgh Press.

Mauro, Paolo. 1997. "Corruption and Growth." *Quarterly Journal of Economics* 110, no. 3: 681–712.

McCallum, B. T. 1972. "Relative Asymptotic Bias from Errors of Omission and Measurement." *Econometrica* 40:757–58.

McCubbins, M., R. Noll, and R. Weingast. 1989. "Structure and Process, Politics and Policy: Administrative Arrangements and the Political Control of Agencies." *Virginia Law Review* 75:431–82.

Ministerio de Hacienda. 1963. *Boletín Estadístico.* No 88. La Paz.

Ministerio de Planificación y Coordinación. 1970. "Cuentas Nacionales 1950–1969." In *Revista de Planificación y Desarrollo.* La Paz.

Montano G., and C. Villegas. 1993. "Industria Boliviana: Entre los Resabios del Pasado y la Logica del Mercado." La Paz: CEDLA.

Morales, J. A. 2001. "Economic Vulnerability in Bolivia." In *Towards Democratic Viability: The Bolivian Experience,* ed. John Crabtree and Laurence Whitehead. London: Palgrave.

Morales, J. A., and N. Pacheco. 1999. "El retorno de los liberales." In *Bolivia en el siglo XX: La formación de la Bolivia contemporánea,* ed. Fernando Campero Prudencio. La Paz: Harvard Club de Bolivia.

Morales, J. A., and J. Sachs. 1990. "Bolivia's Economic Crisis." In *Developing Country Debt and Economic Performance,* ed. J. D. Sachs, vol. 2. Chicago: University of Chicago Press.

Muller & Asociados. 1997. *Bolivia Hacia el Siglo XXI: Oportunidades Para el Crecimiento.* La Paz: Soinpa.

Musgrave, R. 1977. *La Reforma Fiscal en Bolivia.* La Paz: Ministerio de Finanzas.

Nakamura, A., and M. Nakamura. 1985. "On the Performance of Tests by Wu and by Hausman for Detecting the Ordinary Least Squares Bias Problem." *Journal of Econometrics* 29:213–27.

Nogales, X. 2001. "Perspectivas de la Economía Boliviana, 2001–2005." Typescript.

Oficina de Estudios para la Colaboración Económica Internacional (OECEI). 1969. *Bolivia.* Sintesis Economica y Financiera, no. 2. Buenos Aires.

Oxford Analitica. 2001. Various reports.

"Patience Runs Out in Bolivia." 2001. *Economist,* April 19.

Rehren, Alfredo. 2001. "Clientelismo Político, Corrupción y Reforma del Estado en Chile." Paper prepared for Latin American Studies Conference, Washington, D.C., September 6.

Rodríguez, F., and Dani Rodrik. 2001. "Trade Policy and Economic Growth: A Skeptic's Guide to the Cross-National Literature." In *NBER Macroeconomics Annual 2000,* ed. Ben Bernanke and Kenneth S. Rogoff.. Cambridge: MIT Press.

Rodriguez Ostria, G. 1999. "Producción, mercancía y empresarios." In *Bolivia en el siglo XX: La formación de la Bolivia contemporánea,* ed. Fernando Campero Prudencio. La Paz: Harvard Club de Bolivia.

Rodrik, Dani. 1999. "Institutions for High-Quality Growth: What They Are and How to Acquire Them." Harvard University, October. Typescript.

———. 2000. "A Note on Analytical Country Studies on Economic Growth." Harvard University, September. Photocopy.

Romer, Paul M. 1993. "Two Strategies for Economic Development: Using Ideas and Producing Ideas." *Proceedings of the World Bank Annual Conference on Development Economics, 1992.* March.

Rose-Ackerman, Susan. 1978. *Corruption: A Study in Political Economy.* New York: Academic Press.

Sachs, Jeffrey, and Andrew Warner. 1995. "Economic Reform and the Process of Global Integration." *Brookings Papers on Economic Activity* 1995, no. 1: 1–118.

Scott, James C. 1969. "Corruption, Machine Politics, and Political Change." *American Political Science Review* 63:1142–58.

———. 1972. *Comparative Political Corruption.* Englewood Cliffs, N.J.: Prentice-Hall

Secretaria Nacional de Planificación y Coordinación. 1966. "Informe Monográfico Sobre la Industria Manufacturera Boliviana." La Paz.

Shea, J. 1998. "Instrument Relevance in Multivariate Linear Model: A Simple Measure." *Review of Economics and Statistics* 79, no. 2: 348–52.

Shleifer, Andrei, and Robert Vishny. 1994. "Corruption." *Quarterly Journal of Economics* 108 no. 3: 599–617.

Soberg Shugart, Matthew, and John M. Carey. 1992. *Presidents and Assemblies: Constitutional Design and Electoral Dynamics.* Cambridge: Cambridge University Press.

Svensson, Jakob. 2000a. "Foreign Aid and Rent Seeking." *Journal of International Economics* 51, no. 2: 437–61.

———. 2000b. "Who Must Pay Bribes and How Much? Evidence from a Cross-Section of Firms." World Bank Policy Research Working Paper No. 2486. Washington, D.C.

Thorp, R. 1998. *Progress, Poverty, and Exclusion: An Economic History of Latin America in the Twentieth Century.* Washington, D.C.: Inter-American Development Bank.

United Nations. 1958. "El Desarrollo Economico de Bolivia." In *Analisis y Proyecciones del Desarrollo Economico,* vol. 4. Santiago, Chile: United Nations Publications.

United States Agency for International Development (USAID). 1970. *Estadísticas Económicas.* No. 11. La Paz.

Valencia, Jose Luis, and Justo Alcides Casas. 1998. *Contrabando e informalidad en la economía boliviana.* La Paz: Fundemos.

Vos, R., H. Lee, and J. A. Mejía. 1997. "Structural Adjustment and Poverty in Bolivia." INDES Working Paper, Series I-3, Inter-American Development Bank, Washington, D.C.

Whitehead, L. 1991. "Bolivia since 1930." In *The Cambridge History of Latin America,* ed. Leslie Bethell, vol. 8. Cambridge: Cambridge University Press.

Wickens, M. R. 1972. "A Note on the Use of Proxy Variables." *Econometrica* 40:759–61.

Wiebe, Robert H. 1967. *The Search for Order: 1877–1920.* New York: Hill and Wang.

World Bank. 1994. *Bolivia: Structural Reforms, Fiscal Impacts, and Economic Growth.* Report No. 13067-BO. Washington, D.C.

———. 1997. *World Bank Development Report 1997: The State in a Changing World.* Oxford: Oxford University Press.

———. 2000. "From Patronage to a Professional State." Bolivia Institutional and Governance Review, vol. 1: Main Report, No. 20115-BO. Poverty Reduction and Economic Management Network, Latin America and Caribbean Region, Washington, D.C.

———. 2001. *Bolivia: Microeconomic Constraints and Opportunities for Higher Growth.* Washington, D.C.

World Bank Institute. 1999. *New Empirical Tools for Anti-corruption and Institutional Reform.* Washington, D.C. http://www.worldbank.org/wbi/governance.

CHAPTER 13

Fiscal Federalism, Good Governance, and Economic Growth in Mexico

MAITE CAREAGA AND BARRY R. WEINGAST

GOOD GOVERNANCE and appropriately designed institutions are now recognized as necessary for economic growth. Yet we know too little about this relationship. Why do some governments protect property rights, provide a stable macroeconomy, and have limited taxes and corruption, while others are corrupt kleptocracies that prey on their citizens?

In recent years, a new political economy literature has emerged that studies these questions by investigating the interaction of political institutions and economic performance.[1] Proponents of this approach provide a general if abstract answer to the above questions: A country's political and institutional framework determines whether government officials face incentives for good or bad governance. As Stiglitz (1998, 5) suggests, "misaligned incentives can induce government officials to take actions that are not, in any sense, in the public interest." Unfortunately, too little is known about how institutions systematically affect the incentives of government officials and what types of institutions lead to good governance and better economic performance.

We add to this new literature by exploring questions of governance and growth in the context of the global trend toward greater decentralization, particularly within developing countries. A long tradition in economics emphasizes the advantages of federalism for good governance. More recently, proponents of market-preserving federalism suggest that an appropriately structured decentralization fosters economic development.[2] Yet recent theory and evidence

The authors thank Lee Alston, Alberto Diaz-Cayeros, Rui de Figueiredo, James Fearon, Barbara Geddes, Stephen Haber, Robert Inman, Roger Noll, Yingyi Qian, Antonio Rangel, James Robinson, Gerard Roland, Jean-Laurent Rosenthal, Ernesto Stein, and William Summerhill for helpful comments and Juliana Bambaci for research assistance.

[1] See, for example, Acemoglu and Robinson 2000; Alesina and Drazen 1991; Alesina and Spolare 1997; Besley and Coate 1998; Bolton and Roland 1997; Cox and McCubbins 2001; Cremer and Palfrey, forthcoming; Dixit and Londregan 1995; Drazen 2000; Inman and Rubinfeld 1997; Jin, Qian, and Weingast 1999; Knack and Keefer 1995; Levy and Spiller 1994; North 1990; Persson and Tabellini 2000; Poterba and von Hagen 1999; Rodrik 1999; Roland 2001; Stiglitz 1998; Sturzenegger and Tommasi 1998.

[2] For the long-standing economists' argument, see Hayek 1939 and Tiebout 1956; for modern reviews, see Rubinfeld 1987 and McKinnon and Nechyba 1997. On market-preserving federalism, see McKinnon 1997; Montinola, Qian, and Weingast 1995; Weingast 1995; and Zhuravskaya 2000.

cast doubt on the assertion that decentralization promotes political and economic development. Many scholars suggest that federalism leads to more inflation or corruption; others emphasize that spillovers, common pool problems, and problems from soft budget constraints result in efficiency losses associated with decentralization.[3]

Following Shah (1997), our approach helps explain this puzzle about federalism by suggesting that there is not one kind of decentralization. Federal systems differ enormously in the ways they allocate money, power, and authority across levels of government. Some federal arrangements are therefore likely to foster corruption and inefficiency, while others foster economic growth.

We explore how variations in two institutional features—the fiscal system and electoral competitiveness—affect subnational government (SNG) performance. In particular, we study how variations in the distribution of locally raised taxes and increases in electoral competitiveness affect SNG choices. In our model, an SNG allocates its resources across two categories of policies: public goods that foster markets; and the public provision of private benefits, such as corruption and subsidies to interest groups, that hinder markets. Subject to its budget constraint, the SNG chooses between the two activities to maximize its utility, which is positively related to each type of policy. We define good governance as the provision by SNGs of market-enhancing public goods instead of nonproductive transfers and corruption. Good governance is therefore endogenous.

We analyze two comparative statics. The first concerns α, the proportion of locally generated taxes captured by the SNG: ceteris paribus, an increase in α increases good governance. The reason is that choosing public goods has two benefits: directly, it provides citizens with utility; indirectly it increases tax revenue and so relaxes the SNG's budget constraint. In contrast, corruption and nonproductive transfers benefit only those citizens receiving the rents.

The second comparative static concerns the degree of electoral competition. Ceteris paribus, electoral competition increases good governance. Although officials in all SNGs need political support to survive, those in an SNG that faces competition must appeal to the median voter, whereas those in noncompetitive SNGs do not need as strong appeals to voters.

Our first comparative statics result has an important implication for revenue-sharing systems that we call the *fiscal law of 1/n:* in a federation of n SNGs, where the central government collects and distributes all tax revenue (i.e., $\alpha = 0$), the indirect benefit for an SNG of fostering markets is on the order of $1/n$ that of a fiscal system in which SNGs are 100 percent financed through locally generated revenue (i.e., $\alpha = 1$) (see Inman 1988; Weingast, Shepsle, and

---

[3] See, e.g., Dillinger and Webb 1999; Garman, Haggard, and Willis 2001; Hzou 1998; Inman and Rubinfeld 1997; Jones, Sanguinetti, and Tommasi 2000; McKinnon and Nechyba 1997; Prud'homme 1995; Rodden 2000; Sanguinetti 1994; Stein 1998; Treisman 1999; and Wildasin 1997.

Johnsen 1981). The reason is that revenue sharing creates a common pool problem. Under complete revenue sharing, an SNG bears all the costs of providing a public good, but captures only 1/nth of the revenue benefits. The rest of the benefits are spread across other jurisdictions through the central government's division of the common pool. Therefore complete revenue-sharing systems greatly diminish an SNG's incentives to provide market-fostering public goods. We call revenue-sharing agreements in which SNGs give up their policy and fiscal autonomy *fiscal pacts with the devil* (FPWD) because they increase corruption, provide fewer public goods that enhance growth, and diminish citizen welfare.

We apply our approach to federalism in Mexico. Although twentieth-century Mexico always had a federal structure, the distribution of authority and fiscal resources among the levels of government (and therefore α) has changed over time. We identify four phases. During the first period, from the Revolution (1910–17) to 1940, the central government was unable to enforce parts of the constitution, allowing a variety of standard common pool problems. In the second period, 1940–80, the center became stronger and policed common pool problems. Indeed, early in this period, Mexico was characterized by market-preserving federalism, a type of federalism associated with economic growth (Weingast 1995). Yet Mexico continued to centralize, coaxing the states to join a revenue-sharing system. By 1980, Mexico was highly centralized, largely federal in name only. After the government achieved centralization, Mexico was characterized by the fiscal law of 1/n, producing efficiency losses. Of course the debt crisis and the collapse of oil prices also affected growth during this period. Finally, since 1994, Mexico has undergone some decentralization and liberalization. After 1994, both α and the degree of electoral competition increased. For this reason, Mexico offers a natural experiment of the isolated effects of α over good governance (until the late 1980s), and then of the combined effects of α and political competition (since 1994).

Consistent with our theory about federalism and good governance, Mexico's pattern of growth corresponds to these phases.[4] In the first, real GDP growth was slow, averaging 1.4 percent per year. In the second, often called the "Mexican Miracle," Mexico sustained four decades of rapid growth, 6.8 percent per year. In the third, growth slowed considerably to just 2.3 percent per year. In the last period, 1994–present, growth has improved somewhat: real GDP fell over 6 percent during the peso crisis (late 1994 and 1995), but then has grown at an average of 5.1 percent per year (1996–99).

We provide several types of evidence supporting our predictions for the case of Mexico. First, with respect to the differential willingness of states to join a fiscal pact that limits their ability to tax, our approach predicts that the more

---

[4] The quality of data from the early periods is poor, so these figures must be treated as approximate.

market-oriented states should be less likely to participate. We show that this holds in practice. Second, the theory predicts several changes in the behavior of SNG governance after they join the FPWD. Decreases in α should lead SNGs to spend more on rents and less on public goods. We provide some evidence of the changes in the patterns of expenditure after states joined the pact. The fiscal law of $1/n$ combines with the common pool problem created by revenue sharing to predict that state taxes should fall and total federal taxes should increase following the 1980 change in the fiscal system. We show that this happened.

Third, we calculate α as implied by the various revenue-sharing formulas used since 1980. The initial formula, made explicit in 1980 but employed previously, returned to states exactly what they contributed. Because the federal government also spent considerable sums in the states at this time, we calculate that α was on the order of .2. We also show that the current formula, dating from 1995, has somewhat better properties, allowing states to receive on the order of one-quarter of any increase in revenue generated in their state. We calculate our model's α in contemporary Mexico as .233. Fourth, the theory predicts that SNGs that face electoral competition have a stronger preference for providing public goods over rents. We provide evidence of good governance in municipalities that have become electorally competitive. Finally with respect to good governance and economic growth, we argue that increases in α and in electoral competition lead to better governance. We present evidence of the change in the rates of growth in Mexico as α and electoral competitiveness change.

Our approach contrasts with two normative rationales for federal revenue sharing. First, the traditional normative public finance perspective, relying on the assumption of a benevolent government that maximizes citizen welfare, argues that the federal revenue sharing allows the government to redistribute income, which a decentralized set of SNGs could not achieve on their own. Second, Persson and Tabellini (1993) argue that revenue sharing in federal systems provides a degree of social insurance against regional shocks. From a normative perspective, neither approach can be criticized. From a positive perspective, particularly in the developing world, these rationales often fail. Mexico's widespread corruption, its many antidevelopment policies, and the long-term diversion of public resources to maintain the party in power all question relevance of the benevolent government assumption. As we will show, Mexico's initial revenue-sharing scheme involved little redistribution and no social insurance: states received back from the center in proportion to their contributions. Although the Mexican system now contains some redistribution, it is a small portion of the total revenue shared with the states. Put simply, the normative rationales cannot explain why Mexico pursued fiscal centralization and revenue sharing.

An alternative hypothesis, more consistent with the facts in many developing countries, is twofold. First, revenue sharing qua FPWD allows the federal government to achieve a monopoly on taxes. The tax monopoly allows them to extract more revenue from citizens than can the SNGs in the aggregate. Capital and labor mobility, even if imperfect, limits the ability of SNGs to extract taxes from their citizens and firms. The federal government, with its monopoly on taxes, does not face this limit. Second, Mexican politicians used these funds to keep their dominant party in power for decades. Diaz-Cayeros, Magaloni, and Weingast (2000), for example, show that the dominant party used its control over fiscal resources to punish those areas that elected the opposition by withdrawing funds.

Our approach has implications for the larger question about the political foundations of good government. Appropriately structured federalism helps improve the incentives for resource allocation, particularly when corruption throughout and bad central government economic policies represent major problems hindering economic performance. Appropriately structured federalism decentralizes a range of decisions, taking a series of allocation decisions away from the federal government. This can have efficiency gains when the federal government is a major source of inefficient policy (Jin, Qian, and Weingast 1999; see also Brennan and Buchanan 1980). The key to capturing efficiency gains through decentralization, however, is getting the incentives for local government officials right.

The chapter proceeds as follows. Section 1 develops our theoretical framework. Sections 2 and 3 derive, respectively, the effects that revenue sharing and political competition have on good governance. Section 4 provides the background on federalism and electoral competitiveness in Mexico in Mexico. Section 5 provides evidence supporting our approach from the Mexican fiscal system, including the application of the fiscal law of $1/n$, and provides evidence to support the theory's predictions. Our conclusions follow.

1. A MODEL OF SNG CHOICE UNDER REVENUE SHARING

We begin by analyzing how fiscal incentives affect a subnational government's (SNG) decision making. We assume that government officials, whether elected or not, seek to advance their careers by remaining in office or, if they are part of a strong national party system, by enhancing their party's local reputation. Government officials pursue these career goals by attempting to generate political support. Democratically elected representatives must maintain the support of a majority of voters. For authoritarians, the percentage required to retain their office is undoubtedly lower than a majority, though it is also a substantial portion of the population.[5] We assume that government officials have two separate

---

[5] Students of comparative politics again and again emphasize the need of authoritarian governments to maintain sufficient support to remain in power. See for example Geddes 1999; Przeworski and Limongi 1997; Londregan and Poole 1996.

means of fostering political support. First, they may engage in corruption and provide politically generated rents to constituents. These rents may take a variety of forms, such as corrupt payments or various benefits derived from market intervention (e.g., local monopolies or anticompetitive regulations). Second, government officials may provide public goods that foster local economic growth, providing indirect benefits to constituents.

In what follows, we study how various fiscal arrangements affect political officials' tradeoff between pursuing rents and providing public goods. Assume that each of N (subnational) governments seeks to maximize the following utility function,

$$U_i = U_i(r, y), \tag{1}$$

where r represents the level of corruption and rents and y is the level of the (market-fostering) public good. The utility function is that of a representative constituent. For democratic local governments, the utility function is that of the median voter. By maximizing the median voter's utility function, the SNG assures enough support to survive. As noted, hegemonic SNGs also need to retain political support, though less support than those that face electoral competition, so we assume that these governments also have a representative constituent.

For simplicity, we drop the subscript i. We assume that $U(r, y)$ is increasing but at a decreasing rate in each variable; that is, $U_r > 0$, $U_{rr} < 0$, $U_y > 0$, $U_{yy} < 0$. We will also assume that $U_{ry} \geq 0$, indicating that the two means of providing political support do not interfere with one another; if at all, they actually help one another.

We also assume that the SNG faces a budget constraint. Its budget, B, is given by $B = T + \alpha\tau(y)$, where $T = T(\tau(y))$ represents the amount of fiscal transfers from the national government; $\tau(y)$ is the locally generated taxes as a function of the level of public good provided; and α is the proportion of locally generated taxes that the SNG may keep ($0 \leq \alpha \leq 1$). The public good, y, is assumed to affect positively the locally generated taxes; that is, $\tau_y > 0$.[6]

Finally, we have the SNG's budget constraint, which allows the SNG to spend its budget on r and y,

$$r + ay \leq B, \tag{2}$$

where a is the parameter representing the relative cost of a unit of y in terms of r (we normalize the price of r to 1). Substituting for B and rearranging terms yields $r = T + \alpha\tau(y) - ay$.

---

[6] Perhaps a more accurate formulation follows Haughwout and Inman (2000; Haughwout et al. 2000) and lets the size of the local economy, $E(y, r, \tau)$ be positively related to y and negatively related to r and τ, so that locally raised revenue is $\tau E(y, r, \tau)$. As the results are qualitatively similar, we use the simpler formulation.

To study the government's behavior, we use expression (2) for r and substitute back into (1). This yields the following maximization problem:

$$Max_y \quad U(T + \alpha\tau(y) - ay, y), \tag{3}$$

with first order conditions:

$$U_r(\alpha\tau' - a) + U_y = 0. \tag{4}$$

The first order conditions imply that the government's marginal rate of substitution between r and y, U_r/U_y, is given by

$$\frac{U_r}{U_y} = -\frac{1}{(\alpha\tau' - a)}. \tag{5}$$

To interpret the first order conditions, suppose that y had no effect on taxes; that is, $\tau' = 0$. Then we would obtain the standard result that at the optimum choice of r and y the marginal rate of substitution between r and y equals minus the ratio of the cost of r to the cost of y; that is, $U_r/U_y = 1/a$. In our problem, y affects the taxes, and hence the term in equation (5), $\alpha\tau'$, which adjusts the marginal rate of substitution. Intuitively, the adjustment term reflects y's positive effect on the budget, which leads the SNG to choose more y than otherwise. The specific amount of the adjustment in the marginal rate of substitution is given by $\alpha\tau'$.

To assure we have a maximum, we investigate the second order conditions. Under the assumption that $\partial^2 U/\partial r \partial y > 0$, these conditions hold. This ensures that an equilibrium exists and is characterized by a point.

We now turn to our principal question about how the SNG's behavior changes in response to the fiscal system. To begin, we investigate how a shift in α affects the SNG's choice of r and y. To do this, we derive the comparative statics results of α on (r^*, y^*), the SNG's optimal choice of r and y. We start with y^*. The first order conditions (4) give y^* as an implicit function of the exogenous parameters (a, α). By the implicit function theorem, we have for any exogenous parameter, x_i, that

$$\frac{\partial y}{\partial x_i} = -\frac{\dfrac{\partial F}{\partial x_i}}{\dfrac{\partial F}{\partial y}}, \tag{6}$$

where F is the left-hand side of the first order conditions (4).

To simplify, we know from the second order conditions that the denominator of (6) is negative for all x_i. Thus, to sign $(\partial y/\partial x_i)$, we have to sign the numerator; that is, sign $(\partial y/\partial x_i) = $ sign $(\partial F/\partial x_i)$. To calculate the effect of α on y^*, we differentiate (4) with respect to α. Given our assumptions, α is positive. *So increasing α, the SNG's share of locally generated taxes, has the effect of increasing the SNG's optimal level of y^*.*

The effect of α on r^* is more complicated. To calculate this, we first observe that the budget constraint yields $r^* = B(\tau(y, \alpha)) - ay^*$. Totally differentiating this equation and setting the other exogenous changes to 0 yields the following:

$$\frac{\partial r^*}{\partial \alpha} = (B_\tau \tau_y - a) \frac{\partial y^*}{\partial \alpha} + B_\tau \tau_a. \qquad (7)$$

Equation (7) has an interesting interpretation. First, since the first term on the right-hand side is negative and the second term is positive, $\partial r^*/\partial \alpha$ can either be positive or negative. Second, the response of r^* to an increase in α is negatively related to the $\partial y^*/\partial \alpha$. That is, the larger is the effect of α on y^*, the smaller is $\partial r^*/\partial \alpha$.

In sum, increasing α, the proportion of locally generated taxes retained by the SNG, increases the resources the SNG devotes to the market-fostering public good, y. The reason is straightforward: producing y has two benefits. As a direct benefit, more public goods make constituents better off and thus increase constituency support. As an indirect benefit, more y produces a healthier economy, thus more budget revenue, allowing the SNG to increase both r and y. The larger is α the greater the SNG's provision of the public goods and the lower is its reliance on rents to maintain political support.

We illustrate this effect in figure 13.1, which shows how $\tau(y)$ affects an SNG's choice of r and y. To make the case simple, we let the parameter a, giving the cost of y relative to r, equal 1. When $\alpha = 0$, indicating that the SNG captures none of the increase in locally generated taxes, $\tau(y)$, the SNG's budget line is then given by the straight line in figure 13.1, $r + y \leq T$. In this case, the SNG chooses the combination (r_o, y_o).

When the SNG captures a portion $\alpha > 0$ of $\tau(y)$, the budget curve shifts outward in a nonlinear fashion, as indicated on the figure. The shift makes the SNG's budget nonlinear because the budget increase, $\alpha \tau(y)$, increases as the SNG chooses more y. When $y = 0$, $r = T$ and the budget shift is zero; when $r = 0$, $y = T$ and the budget shift is largest.

This example shows how the effect of y on its budget induces the SNG to substitute r for y. In the figure, r decreases somewhat from r_0 to r_1, while y increases from y_0 to y_1. Per our comparative statics result, the effect of α on y is larger than the effect on r. This reflects the fact that y not only increases U directly but shifts out the budget line.

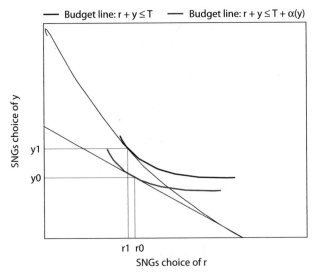

Figure 13.1. SNGs choice of *r* and *y*

2. APPLYING THE MODEL: THE ECONOMIC AND POLITICAL EFFECTS OF REVENUE SHARING

Federal systems around the world employ a range of revenue-sharing schemes. To investigate the incentive effects of revenue sharing, we compare two tax and revenue schemes. In the first, the SNG raises all its own money, so that $T = T_0$ and $\alpha = 1$. In the second, the national government captures all locally generated revenue, possibly combining this with other revenue, and then divides the pool among all the SNGs. In the simplest scheme, the national government collects all the revenue from all SNGs and then divides this revenue among n SNGs so that each receives $1/n$ of the total common revenue pool. Because the government takes all locally generated revenue from all SNGs and then returns $1/n$ of the total to each, $\alpha = 1/n$.

The Fiscal Law of 1/n and FPWD

We compare the effects of these two fiscal systems using equation (5), $U_r/U_y = -1/(\alpha \tau' - a)$. The term in the (right-hand side) denominator tells us, in comparison with the case where y has no effect on the SNG's revenue, how much the SNG's choice of y shifts the marginal rate of substitution at the optimum toward y for a given $\alpha > 0$. When the SNG keeps all locally generated revenue, $\alpha = 1$, so the shift in the marginal rate of substitution is the full τ'. Next we calculate the shift when the SNG keeps none of its locally generate revenue and receives all its revenue from the common pool, P, created by the revenue from all SNGs. In this case, the SNG's budget is given by $B = T$, where $T = [P-\tau(y)]/n + \tau(y)/n$. The last equation says that the total transfer, T, can be divided into two portions: first, the SNG's share of the revenue raised in all other SNGs; and second, its share of the tax revenue raised in its own jurisdiction, $\tau(y)/n$. This implies that, when revenue from all SNGs goes into a common pool P, $\alpha = 1/n$. This yields that the shift in the marginal rate of substitution is τ'/n.

From this analysis we derive the *fiscal law of 1/n*: When the SNG raises all of its taxes, it chooses more y because it captures all the subsequent increase in revenue due to τ'; in contrast, under revenue sharing, it captures only τ'/n. In short, the relative effect of an increase in y^* under the complete revenue-sharing scheme is $1/n$ the magnitude of the increase when the local governments captures all the locally generated revenue. Under the revenue-sharing scheme, the SNG must share nearly all the revenue increases (i.e., $(n-1)/n$ of the increase) with the other SNGs, while it retains only $1/n$ of the revenue increase. In contrast, when an SNG captures all its locally generated taxes, it keeps 100 percent of any increase in taxes from increasing y. For federal systems with many SNGs—Mexico with 32 states, Russia with 89 regions, or the United States with 50 states—the disincentive to invest in public goods can be large.

To illustrate the nature of the shift, we calculate an example. We let the relative cost parameter, $a = 1$, the number of SNGs be 32, and $\tau(y) = y/4$. If there were no shift due to $\tau(y)$, that is, if $\alpha = 0$, then the marginal rate of substitution between r and y at the optimum (r^*, y^*) is given by $U_r/U_y = -1$. Under the fiscal arrangement where the SNG gets to keep all its revenue, $\alpha = 1$, the shift in the marginal rate of substitution is given by $\alpha \tau'$, which equals ¼ in this example. This implies that the SNG's marginal rate of substitution at the optimum is

$$\frac{U_r}{U_y} = -\frac{1}{1 - 1/4} = -\frac{4}{3}.$$

In this case, the shift in the marginal rate of substitution produced by the effect of y on local taxes accruing to the SNG is a full ⅓.

Under the fiscal arrangement where the SNG keeps none of its revenue, but the federal government shares all collected SNG revenue equally among n SNGs, $\alpha = 1/n$. Given $n = 32$, then the SNG's marginal rate of substitution at the optimum is

$$\frac{U_r}{U_y} = -\frac{1}{(1 - 1/4)*(1/n)} = -\frac{128}{127}.$$

In the common pool case, the shift toward y induced by $\tau(y)$ is just 1/127.

To summarize the effect in this example, consider the base case where y has no effect on the budget. Then the shift in marginal rate of substitution away from the base case when $\alpha = 1$ is a full $1/3$, and is more than 42 times the shift when $\alpha = 1/n = 1/32$.

Many parts of the world during the middle to late twentieth century exhibited a trend toward greater fiscal centralization. In Argentina and Mexico, for example, the national government made a political deal with its SNGs in which the SNGs gave up important aspects of their taxing authority in exchange for the national government's providing greater revenue. National governments were able to offer this exchange in part because they gained monopoly authority over taxes. As Hayek (1939) and Tiebout (1956) noted long ago, competition among SNGs for tax base limits their ability to tax: too high a tax rate induces mobile factors to move to other jurisdictions. The national government faces no such constraint because it can impose the same tax laws across all SNG jurisdictions. Thus, when the SNGs give up their tax authority to the national government, the national government can set taxes at higher rates than allowed by SNGs facing competitive pressures.

We call this agreements *fiscal pacts with the devil* for two reasons. First, revenue-sharing agreements typically require that SNGs give up their policy and fiscal autonomy. Second, these pacts induce the SNG to substitute nonproductive transfers, such as corruption and rent seeking, for public goods. The tradeoff between r and y represents SNG's tradeoff between corruption, rent seeking, and market intervention, on the one hand, and economically productive activities on the other. The simple model above shows that, holding constant for all other proclivities toward corruption and market intervention, the fiscal system affects an SNG's incentives to foster markets. Put simply, the stronger an SNG's fiscal incentives—as measured in terms of the proportion of locally generated taxes it captures—the less corrupt and more promarket oriented the government. All this is generated simply by government officials pursuing their rational goal of political survival.

The model predicts that countries whose fiscal system primarily finances SNGs through revenue sharing should have higher rates of corruption than countries whose SNGs are primarily self-financing.

3. APPLYING THE MODEL, PART 2: THE EFFECTS OF POLITICAL COMPETITION ON GOOD GOVERNANCE

We now investigate how electoral competition systematically affects local leaders' preferences. As noted, all SNGs need some level of political support in order to survive. Maintaining political support in localities where the government faces political competition requires greater attention to public goods provision than in areas where the government retains monopolistic control of elections.

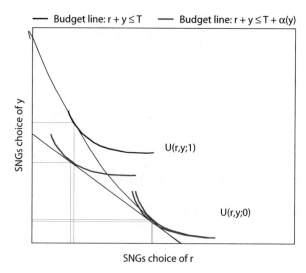

Figure 13.2. SNGs choice of *r* and *y*

This is because an SNG that faces competition must appeal to the median voter, while a hegemonic SNG does not need to.

We model the difference between competitive and hegemonic SNGs as a shift in the representative voter's utility function that they must satisfy. As shown in figure 13.2, the utility function for localities without competition, $U(r,y;0)$, is systematically lower (prefer more r, ceteris paribus) than the representative utility function for localities facing competition, $U(r,y;1)$. Along the flat budget line, $\alpha = 0$, the two types of leaders make different choices between r and y, with the SNG facing greater competition choosing more y and less r than the leader who does not face competition.

To study how the fiscal incentives work differently in these two localities, we examine the shift in SNG choice when we increase α a fixed amount from $\alpha = 0$. Preferences of SNGs without competition are in the lower right of the figure. In this region, the fiscal leverage associated with an increase in α from $\alpha = 0$ is small. In the figure, this SNG provides a tiny increase in resources devoted to corruption and a slightly larger amount to public goods. In contrast, the preferences of leaders from a locality with a high degree of competition are in the upper left. In this region, a shift in α affords the SNG significant leverage, and it uses the increase in fiscal resources to provide approximately 40 percent more public goods. There is also a small increase in corruption and rent seeking.

In sum, political competition makes SNG leaders more sensitive to constituent interests. The model predicts that political competition combines with the fiscal effect to give local leaders greater incentives to provide public goods.

4. HISTORICAL BACKGROUND ON FISCAL FEDERALISM
AND ELECTORAL COMPETITIVENESS IN MEXICO

We present here the general trends in twentieth-century Mexico with respect to fiscal federalism and electoral competitiveness.

Fiscal Federalism

Although the Mexican constitution of 1917 established a decentralized fiscal system, revenue collection and expenditure became very centralized over the second half of the twentieth century. We divide the evolution of the Mexican fiscal system into four periods. The first period covers the end of the Revolution to the late 1940s. States retained full fiscal authority, but the center was too weak to police the common market, and the system suffered from various common pool problems. The second period covers 1947 until end of the 1970s. The federal government slowly centralized fiscal power by coaxing all the states to enter a revenue-sharing pact. The third period, covering 1980 to 1994, began with the establishment of a formula to allocate federal revenue among the states; all the states were in the FPWD and it was a period of great centralization. Finally, the fourth period covers from 1994 to the present. We discuss these periods in turn.

Period 1: 1917–47. The victors of the Revolution (1910–17) drafted a constitution with the aim of restoring political order and financial stability. The constitution granted exclusive taxing powers over strategic areas to the federal government and forbade the states from levying taxes that would obstruct the emergence of a national market. Yet the constitution failed to achieve these objectives. Well into the 1940s, the fiscal system remained chaotically decentralized as the Mexican federal system exhibited significant common pool problems. The states levied unconstitutional and overlapping taxes; they also erected internal trade barriers; and the federal government proved unable to police the constitution or the common market (Margain 1971; Islas 1997; Diaz-Cayeros 1999). To illustrate, in 1940 the three levels of government levied 80 separate taxes on industry and commerce and 32 on capital (*Presidencia de la Republica* 1998). Exacerbating these problems, "corruption was rampant in every tax administration" (Islas 1997, 17). The result was too many taxes, protectionism that hindered interstate commerce, and corruption.[7]

---

[7] According to Diaz-Cayeros (1999, 48), "The constitution prohibited taxes that would hinder interstate trade, but this was systematically violated. Local governments relied on immobile assets or on transactions that were easily measured. Producers had few exit options due to the state of physical infrastructure and the financial system. This state of anarchy hindered economic growth but politicians were unable to solve the collective dilemma."

In the 1920s and 1930s leaders and interests in many states realized that there existed efficiency gains to improving cooperation among the states (Diaz Cayeros 1999). However, consistent with the two dilemmas of federalism (de Figueiredo and Weingast 2000), the states failed to cooperate in the construction of a national market for two reasons. First, it was hard for states to trust one another because each had incentives to defect, and most states retained the necessary resources to restart a war. This is evidenced by the smoldering civil war that persisted well into the 1930s. Second, it was hard for states to trust the federal government as a neutral enforcer of the national market (Diaz-Cayeros 1999).

Period 2: 1947–1970s. Two contradictory forces were at work during the second period. First, in the initial phase of centralization, the federal government reduced the ability of the states to overgraze the commons. The political result was a federal system closer to market-preserving federalism (Montinola, Qian, and Weingast 1995; Weingast 1995). The economic result was greater economic efficiency, as witnessed by sustained growth commonly known as the "Mexican Miracle."

However, by coaxing state after state to join the FPWD after 1947, the federal government progressively compromised the states' ability to exercise independent policy and fiscal autonomy. By the end of the second period, fiscal pacts with the devil had significant political effects beyond their direct economic effects. By agreeing to these pacts, the states abdicated their right to tax several important areas of economic activity in exchange for revenue transfers and investment projects from the federal government. In addition, the states would cease to collect unpopular local taxes.[8] By centralizing tax collection and expenditure, the federal government increased its revenue and control over policymaking.

The federal government induced the states to join an FPWD through economic and political carrots and sticks. First, the federal government offered the carrots of additional revenue for states and exciting political careers to the state officials. Second, the federal government provided two sorts of sticks: first, it would collect federal taxes in the state used for the revenue-sharing pool regardless of whether the state joined the pact; and second, the PRI's system of rotation for political officials destroyed the ability of representatives to develop independent relationships with their constituents.

In 1947 the federal government created a new, voluntary, and contractual tax coordination system. States that joined would get more revenue in exchange for their authority to tax in the areas decreed exclusively federal. States that did not

---

[8] According to Islas Torres (1997), federal officers argue that states lack the political courage to raise their own taxes. "Appointments of tax collectors are often politically motivated and those selected are often not committed to the task or are strongly influenced by political pressures, such that relatives of the local authorities or powerful '*caciques*' do not pay their taxes at all" (Islas Torres 1997, 27).

join could continue levying taxes in these areas, but they would continue to bear the cost of the federal taxes without receiving any revenue.

Between 1947 and 1952, 11 states joined this system: 4 under the control of the federal government: the Federal District and the territories of Quintana Roo and North Baja California and South Baja California; and 7 voluntarily: Aguascalientes in 1949; Morelos, Querétaro, and Tlaxcala in 1950; Michoacán and Sinaloa in 1951; and San Luis Potosí in 1952.

The next step in the fiscal centralization occurred in 1953 with the first Law of Fiscal Coordination (LFC). As with the previous agreement, the LFC was a contractual arrangement between two levels of government. The LFC's intent was to coax the still reticent states to join the revenue-sharing system. This law also declared the income tax exclusively federal; and the center committed to share a proportion of it with the states. This carrot was sufficiently attractive to induce 7 more states to join: Colima, Yucatán, Hidalgo, Campeche, Tabasco, Puebla, and Guerrero. Nonetheless, for the next two decades, 14 states remained outside the system.

In 1972, the federal government increased the sales tax by 1 percent, sharing the increase with the states. The additional revenue induced even the most reticent states to comply with the voluntary tax coordination system (*Presidencia de la Republica* 1997, 88).

The federal government completed its program of fiscal centralization in 1980, when it issued a new LFC. In exchange for greater centralization of tax authority, states received increased and supposedly less arbitrary transfers that would be regulated by a formula.[9] Prior to 1980 the central government shared with the states a portion of two specific taxes (the sales tax and income tax); since then it has shared a proportion of a larger set of taxes. The 1980 law also markedly increased the proportion of revenue that the central government transferred to the states.

Period 3: 1980–94. The third period of Mexican federalism starts with the 1980 reforms. This new system completed the centralization of tax authority and established a formula to provide transparency to the assignation of the Transfers Fund. Stability was not established, however, as the central government altered the formula frequently: in 1981, 1983, 1984, 1988, and 1990.[10]

Period 4: 1994–Present. Since 1994, population and revenue raised in a state are accorded equal weight (45.17 percent each) in the distribution of funds. We

---

[9] The new law also introduced two big changes in the revenue-sharing system. First, it created the value-added tax (*impuesto al valor agregado*, IVA), replacing a vast number of municipal and state taxes on production and services. Second, the law established the National System of Fiscal Coordination (SNCF). Under SNCF the federal government agreed to share with the states and municipalities a portion of the *Recaudacion Federal Participable* (RFP).

[10] We analyze two of these formulas in section 5; appendix 13.1 summarizes the various changes in the formula.

analyze this formula in section 5. Moreover, the fiscal constraints on the national government have allowed some freedom to emerge for lower governments, particularly municipalities.

Electoral Competition

Between its formation and the late 1980s, the PRI controlled nearly all elected and appointed offices at all levels of government. This began to change after the fraud-ridden and highly contested presidential elections of 1988.[11] In 1988, opposition parties governed only 39 of the 2,419 municipalities (1.6 percent of the population); by May 1999, these parties governed 583 municipalities (46 percent of the population). In 1988 all 32 states had a PRI governor; by May 1999 10 states (32 percent of the population) had opposition governors, including the Federal District. Similarly, in 1988 the PRI had the necessary supermajorities to legislate in all matters in all the nation's legislative assemblies; by May 1999, the PRI had this level of control in only 2 of the 34 assemblies. The opposition's success deepened in the 2000 presidential elections, where for the first time a party other than the PRI won the presidency.

These changes were brought about by different political and economic developments: the fiscal changes discussed above in combination with the international debt crisis and the fall in oil prices in the early 1980s, the breakdown of the elite coalition in the PRI and a split of the party in 1986, several electoral reforms of which the last (1996) was approved by all the parties represented in congress. This is not the place to analyze the sources of these changes, but for the purposes of this chapter, after 1988 electoral competition had become a reality in many municipalities and states.

5. EMPIRICAL EVIDENCE ABOUT MEXICO'S FISCAL PACTS WITH THE DEVIL

In this section, we provide five pieces of evidence from Mexico to support the predictions of our model: we account for why different states joined the FPWD at different times; we provide evidence about changes in the spending and taxing behavior of states after entering the FPWD; we calculate α from the different revenue-sharing formulas used after 1980; we provide evidence of the changes in good governance with the emergence of political competition; and we support our hypothesis of the of changes in the rate of growth as α changed.

---

[11] The following data comes from Lujambio 2000.

Explaining Which States Delayed Joining the FPWD

Given that all Mexican states faced the same carrots and sticks for joining the FPWD, what explains the differential willingness to enter these agreements? Fourteen states, the Federal District, and two territories (these latter three governed directly by the federal government) joined in the late 1940s and early 1950s. In contrast, 14 states waited over two decades to join, in 1972. Our theory predicts that the more market-oriented states are likely to be the last to join. The reason is that, ceteris paribus, the marginal effect of public goods on local tax revenues differs across states.

To test our hypothesis, we investigate the relationship between when states joined the FPWD and various economic indicators. The analysis reveals that, per our predictions, the richer and more market-oriented states on average joined later. For example, the average per capita state income of states joining in the 1940s and 1950s was approximately 5,600 pesos in 1970; whereas for the states that joined in 1972, it was approximately 16,000 pesos, roughly three times higher. Similarly, states that joined later had far more exports. At present, we only have export figures for 1998, so this figure is only indicative. States that joined the FPWD early averaged exports of $1.2 billion in 1998, whereas those joining late averaged exports of $4.4 billion, a factor of roughly 3.7 times larger.

To obtain more systematic evidence, we used logit analysis. To create the dependent variable, we divided states into those who joined early and late. We used two independent variables, state GDP per capita in 1970 and state exports in 1998.

The results are reported in table 13.1. They show that GDP per capita is a statistically significant determinant of the decision to join early. In contrast, the other variable, exports in 1998, is not statistically significant (perhaps because our data for this variable is for a date so much later than when these states made their decisions to join). The overall performance of the logit is also good. For example, it correctly predicts 74.2 percent of the cases, which outperforms the null model's correctly predicting 54.8 percent of the cases.

The evidence supports our theory. On average, states with higher per capita income joined later.

The Impact of the FPWD on Governance

We have argued that, by breaking the relationship between the provision of local public goods (more broadly, good government) and state revenue, FPWD diminished state officials' incentives to foster a prosperous economy. After joining the FPWD, states should thus substitute away from public goods to nonproductive expenditures, such as corruption.

TABLE 13.1
Logit Analysis of When States Joined the FPWD

Independent Variable	Estimated Coefficient (*t* statistic)
Constant	−2.36*
	(2.47)
GDP/capita	0.25*
	(2.02)
Exports	−.075
	(.44)
Number of observations	31
Percent correctly predicted	74.2
Log Likelihood	
Initial	−21.5
Convergence	−15.2

* significant at the .05 level.

Table 13.2 provides some modest evidence of an increase in rents over public goods after the states all joined the FPWD. The table shows the percentage growth of employment in the government and in the economy. In the period 1910–70, public sector employment was 1.2 percent of total employment; by 1970–83 it had become 20 percent. Consistent with our theory about subnational governments under the FPWD, public employment in municipalities and states grew even faster than federal employment, and at a time when policy responsibly

TABLE 13.2
Rate of growth of Employment in the Public Sector compared with the Economy

	1910–70	1970–75	1975–83	1970–83
% growth of total employment	243	118	127	151
% growth of government employment	958	348	185	647
% growth of federal government employment	1142	350	182	639
% growth of municipal and state government employment	505	339	203	690
Ratio of public sector/total employment	1.2	4.8	14	20.4

Source: Calculated by authors with data from Zaid 2000.

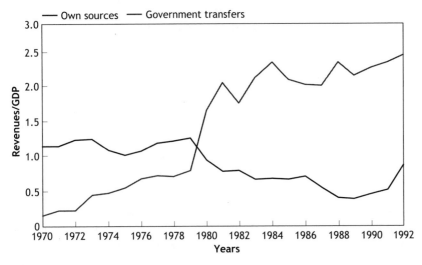

Figure 13.3. State revenues as a percentage of GDP
Source: Islas Torres 1997

shifted to the federal government. Although some of the public sector growth represents an increase in public services, some of it reflects politicians offering jobs to supporters as part of the PRI's extensive patronage system. Indeed, *aviadores* are common throughout the public sector in Mexico: people on the payroll who never show up to work but receive their checks.

Our theory also makes several predictions about tax collection following the FPWD. First, it predicts that state taxes should go down after accepting an FPWD. As α decreases, states have incentives to substitute towards nonproductive expenditures; as shown in section 1, tax collection effort should also fall, so locally raised revenue should fall. Second, we argue that the federal government created the system in part to capture a central monopoly on taxes, allowing it to extract greater resources from the economy. In other words, our theory predicts that total federal taxes should rise following the FPWD. We discuss these predictions in turn.

Ideally, we could use time series data on state taxes to investigate how taxes fared before and after each state joined the FPWD. Such data is difficult to obtain. Instead, we look at the behavior of all states following the 1980 changes. As suggested above, this date represents a watershed year in the fiscal system, as state dependence for revenue on the federal government increased dramatically.

The effect of the 1980 changes on state taxes is easily seen in figure 13.3. In the decade prior to 1980, state taxes averaged a little above 1 percent of GDP. Over the next decade, state taxes fell continuously so that, by the end of

TABLE 13.3
State Taxes as a Proportion
of Total Revenue (percent)

1970–72	45
1973–80	29
1981–94	3
1994–99	2

Source: Institute Nacional de Estadística Geografía y Informática.

the decade, they were below 0.5 percent of GDP.[12] The figure also shows the incentive of "bribe" aspect of the revenue system: the fall in locally generated taxes is more than compensated by the rise in revenue sharing.

Another way to measure the fiscal impact is to assess the proportion of revenue raised by a state from its own taxes. The ideal data set would cover the entire period, so we could see the differential impact of the early FPWD on both types of states (early and late joiners). Unfortunately, we have data only from 1970 onwards.

The data reveal significant changes following both the 1972 and 1980 centralizations. Per our theory's predictions, state taxes as a proportion of total state revenue fell dramatically after 1972: from 45 percent prior to 1972 to 29 percent for the rest of decade (table 13.3). This proportion fell again dramatically after 1980, to 3 percent, remaining slightly lower in the late 1990s.

We now turn to our second prediction—that federal taxes exhibit a greater rise than the decrease in state taxes. Systematic data for all the different federal taxes is hard to obtain. Nonetheless several indicators are consistent with our theory. First, consider the change in the federal taxes after the fiscal changes in 1980 (see fig. 13.3). Federal taxes in 1980 were approximately 15–16 percent of GDP, with oil revenue representing approximately half of the total. The 1980 law imposed a new value-added tax, generating new revenues of between 2 and 3 percent of GNP. This represents an increase in nonoil revenue on the order of one-quarter to one-third. Similarly, collection of the income tax (created in 1972, the year of the final FPWD) increased 22 percent every year since its creation.

A final illustration concerns the federal sales tax. When states joined the FPWD in 1972, the sales tax became exclusively federal, and the states outside this agreement stopped collecting this tax. At this time, the federal government also increased the rate of the federal sales tax to 4 percent. Even so, collection

---

[12] A recent econometric study, for example, claims that after 1980, for every peso given through transfers, state treasuries reduced their own tax revenue by 17 cents (Gutierrez and Islas 1995, 139).

TABLE 13.4
Effects of FPWD on the Collection of the Federal Sales Tax
(millions of pesos)

Year	Projected Collection[a]	Total Collection	Unanticipated Increase (%)[b]
1973	6.0	7.6	26
1974	6.8	10.6	55
1975	10.2	17.4	95
1976	11.7	28.7	170

Source: Escamilla de León 1999.

[a] Based on the prevailing tendency in the previous presidential term.
[b] Between projected and actual.

of the sales tax increased far more than was projected based on the conditions of the previous presidential administration (see table 13.4). Four years later, in 1976, actual receipts were over two and one-half times anticipated receipts.

In short, the evidence supports both of our theory's predictions about the changes in tax revenue.

Calculating "α" and the Incentive Effects in Mexico's Revenue-Sharing Formula

We now investigate incentive effects of the various formulas employed in Mexico's revenue-sharing system after 1980. In particular, we calculate the marginal retention rate, α, for three of the formulas employed over the period.

Analysis of the 1980 Formula. We begin with the formula used in 1980,

$$R_i = \frac{Ai}{\sum A_j},$$

where R_i is the revenue share allocated by the formula to state i from the common pool, P, where $P = \sum_j A_j$, and A_j is the amount of revenue raised in state j. The formula says that a state's revenue share, R_i, is the fraction of the total revenue pool represented by the share of taxes raised in its state.

Our theory yields several implications about this revenue-sharing formula. First, the formula provides good incentives on the portion of revenue allocated by formula: a state captures 100 percent of any increase in local revenue flowing into the pool. Second, because only a small portion of funds spent in localities is allocated by this formula, the incentive effects of the centralized fiscal system are actually much worse. In 1980, the amount of funds spent by the federal government in the states on local projects was approximately four times that allocated by the revenue pool. Thus, the funds allocated by formula are on the order of only one-fifth of those spent locally, implying that α is on the order of .2. Third, the negative effect on locally generated taxes is likely to be larger in the more market-oriented states. The reason is that in these states the effect of public goods on locally generated revenue is likely to be larger.

The 1980 formula involves no redistribution to poorer states. Remarkably, each state puts in A_i and receives back A_i. To see this, notice that state i's share of the total pool, P, is $R_iP = (A_i/\sum_j A_j)P$. Substituting for P, yields that each state gets back A_i.

These results for the revenue-sharing formula in use in 1980 demonstrate that the purpose of this FPWD and this revenue scheme cannot be redistribution. Because each state gets back the same amount that it puts in, the purpose of revenue sharing must be political and not redistributive.

Analysis of Current Formula (1995–Present). Mexico's current formula for distributing revenue dates from 1995 and has three components. The formula allocates 45.17 percent of the revenue pool on the basis of population; 45.17 percent by a formula, analyzed below; and 9.66 percent in inverse proportion to the other two criteria.

The component based on population is simple to analyze. A state with a proportion, q_i, of the population receives $.4517q_i$ of the total pool. The formula entitles a state of average population (3.125 percent of the total) to receive $.4517*.03125P = .014P$. This also implies that, if a state changes its policies so that it increases its revenue by x percent, this component entitles the average state to $.014x$, or about 1.4 percent of the increase.

We analyze the 45.17 percent of total revenue allocated by formula. It implies several different effects. After 1980 the federal government attempted to give states an incentive to improve their collection of tax revenue. The 1995 formula does this in a clever if complicated way.

Since 1995, Mexico has used the following formula (F1) for distributing 45.17 percent of the pool based on revenue collection:

$$R_{it+1} = \frac{R_{it}(A_{it}/A_{it-1})}{\sum_j R_{jt}(A_{jt}/A_{jt-1})} \tag{F1}$$

where R_{it} is state i's share of the total revenue in time t; A_{it} is the proportion of revenue pool, P, raised in state i in time t; and the total revenue pool, P, is given by $P = \sum_j A_{jt}$.

The incentive effects of this portion of the formula are good: the formula returns any increase in tax revenue contributed to the common pool. Mathematically, this is easily shown since $\partial R_{it}/\partial A_{it} = 1$. Intuitively, this can be seen by considering what happens when one state raises its tax collections by x percent, assuming that the revenue from all other states remains constant. The numerator of the formula becomes $(1 + x)*R_{it}$, and the denominator becomes $\sum_j R_{jt} +$ $x*R_{it}$. Suppose that state i produces 5 percent of total revenue and that it increases collections by 10 percent (i.e., $x = .1$). Then the numerator becomes $1.1*.05 = .055$; and the denominator becomes $.95 + .1*.05 = 1$. So a 10 percent increase in locally generated revenue leads to a 10 percent increase allocated by the formula. To summarize, the formula says that, holding constant for the behavior of other states, if state i increases its revenue, this year over last year, then next year it will receive nearly the full increase. Of course, this formula applies only to 45.17 percent of the total pool.

We now investigate the impact of the formula as a whole on a state's marginal incentives. Thus, if state i increases its collections by x percent, the overall formula has three independent components that affect state i's portion of the increase. First, by the population component, state i with population proportion q_i receives back a portion of their gain from the common revenue pool of $.4517q_i*x$. For a state with the average population of .03125, this implies that state i receives back 1.4 percent of the gain. The second component is by the complex formula F1, which grants state i 45.17 percent of the gain. The third component, based on inverse of population, grants a state with the average population an additional 0.3 percent x.

Thus, for a state with the average population, an increase of x percent of revenue translates into three components of gain: $.4517x$, $.014x$, and $.003x$, for a total increase of $.466x$. Of course, the overall formula represents only half of all federal revenue spent in the states. This implies that, at the margin, each state keeps a little less than one-quarter (.233) of any increase in locally generated revenue.

Analysis of the 1991 Formula. As indicated in the appendix, the revenue-sharing formula evolved in the early 1990s. The difference between these formulas and that initiated in 1994 is solely the weights accorded the three portions allocating funds based on population, revenue collection, and the inverse of the first two. As shown in table 13.4, the weights changed in each year from 1991 to 1994.

The analysis of the 1994 formula can readily be applied to these earlier formulas. The 1991 formula is perhaps the most interesting of the group. This formula allowed states to capture 72.29 percent of their revenue collection. Recalling that the revenue allocated by formula is about half that spent by the federal government in the states at this time, the 1991 formula implied a higher α than the 1994 formula, on the order of .37. As table 13.4 reveals, the proportion allocated by revenue collection systematically decreased from 1991 to the present formula analyzed above so that α decreased from approximated .37 in 1991 to .23 in 1994.

Implications of the Revenue-Sharing Formula. Over the 1980s and early 1990s, Mexico changed its formula for distributing revenue from the common

TABLE 13.5
Change in the Ratio of State Expenditures
(Late Joiners to Early Joiners) after 1980

	Period	
	1970–80	1980–94
Ratio (late to early)	4.17	2.16

pool. Throughout this period, the system provided poor incentives for improving tax collection and promoting local growth.

Unfortunately (from the incentive point of view), the revenue going into the pool and thus covered by the three-part formula just analyzed is only a portion of total funds spent by the central government in the states and localities. The amount of discretionary money given states under other categories—earmarked funds referred to as federal investment—far exceeds that given in this category. In 1982, federal investment in the states on average exceeded transfers by a ratio of four to one. In the late 1990s, federal investment approximately equaled transfers. Further, due to Mexico's centralization, including the FPWD, states have many fewer policy options.

In terms of the theory in section 1, a marginal factor of 100 percent on approximately 20 percent of all revenue raised spent in the states (in 1982) yields an α of just .2. Given the comparative statics in section 1, this implies that Mexican states in the early 1980s faced very low fiscal incentives to produce market-fostering public goods. In recent years, the formula has changed, but the situation has not improved markedly. We calculated that the proportion of revenue returned to each state by the formula was .466. The revenue transferred to the states allocated by the formula is now about one-half of all revenue transferred to the states. Taken together, these two observations imply that, in present-day Mexico, α, the marginal revenue return from expenditures fostering local economic prosperity, is $.466*.5 = .233$.

We do not have the figures on total federal spending in the states prior to 1980, hence the implied α is hard to assess for the earlier period. Yet the data in figure 13.3 and table 13.5 bear on this issue. Federal taxes and spending in the states increased after 1980. With respect to state taxes: prior to the final FPWD in 1972, states raised 45 percent of their own revenue; this proportion fell to 29 percent for the period 1973–80, and then dramatically fell again, to 3 percent for the period after the 1980 fiscal changes. These figures are average revenue raised, while α is the marginal revenue collection. Nonetheless, the systematic changes in 1972 and in 1980, dramatically increasing federal taxes and lowering state taxes, suggest that α fell significantly.

The Effects of Political Competition in Municipal Government

Our theory predicts that SNGs, which face electoral competition, have a stronger preference for providing public goods over rents. In order to isolate the effects of political competition from those of changes in α, we investigate the changes in municipalities after 1988, when electoral competition became a reality but α remained constant. The findings accord with our theory.

A voluminous case study literature has emerged in the last few years that studies the changes in government operation in municipalities in Mexico.[13] Many analysts say that these changes amount to a "new municipal governance." Ward (1995) summarizes the general trends of change in municipal governance observed in these case studies. First, recruitment patterns for both nominations to elected office and appointments have moved from a clientelistic system to one based on the skills, experience, and local popularity of the prospective officers. Second, municipalities have increased their tax collection efforts and have greatly diminished the dependence on federal and state transferences, financing a high portion of their expenses with municipal taxes. Third, the political agenda of municipalities has moved from being concerned only about the provision of basic services, to focusing on promoting rule of law and markets, including modernizing the police, promoting cleaner markets and slaughterhouses, building highways, paving streets, and engaging in urban planning. Fourth, because political competition implies that their political careers depend more on the popular perception of their job than on the leadership of their parties, municipal presidents have become more autonomous from their parties and from the corporatist organizations to which traditional PRI administrations had very strong bonds.

These changes are more pronounced in the richer and more urbanized municipalities that have more administrative capacity and possibilities to generate their own income. The changes are stronger in Panista (that is, run by the National Action Party, or PAN) cities in the North and the rich Bajío region. The export orientation of many of these areas also increases the demand for the good governance necessary to promote growing markets.

The fiscal experience of the municipalities electing the opposition PAN in the 1980s and 1990s accords with our theory. Diaz-Cayeros, Magaloni, and Weingast (2000) show that municipalities that defect from the PRI by electing the opposition pay a substantial fiscal penalty in terms of lower revenue transfers from the PRI-controlled state and federal governments. Our theory helps explain how the PAN survived despite the PRI's fiscal punishment. As a market-

---

[13] See for example Rodríguez and Ward 1992, 1995, 1999; Merino 1994; Ziccardi 1995; Cabrero Mendoza 1995, 1996; Garza Villarreal 1998; and Guillén López 1995, 1996.

oriented municipality opted out of the PRI fiscal system to take control of local public goods provision, its revenue increased along with the local economy. In combination with lowering levels of corruption, enhanced delivery of public goods and services greatly increased local citizens' willingness to pay taxes and new user fees. For localities that elected PAN governments, local tax revenue grew quickly to replaces losses from the state and federal governments. Rodríguez (1995, 166) reports of Ciudad Juárez, for example, that "Over the course of only a few years [after electing the PAN], the ratio of state to local revenues . . . changed from around 70 percent *state* funding to over 70 percent *local* funding." In particular, during the first year of the Panista government, 1984, local revenue increased 300 percent.

Moreover, per our theory, the changes in behavior of municipal governments are not just associated with the new opposition governments. These changes can also be seen where the PRI municipal governments face political competition. As with the opposition governments, PRI governments facing competition are forced to improve services and the fiscal system.

The Effects of Revenue Sharing on Economic Growth

We argue that revenue-sharing pacts motivate local politicians to reduce efficiency and increase corruption, and therefore dampen economic growth. Mexico's FPWD seems best interpreted as helping the center create political power and rents rather than enhancing efficiency. Our theory has several predictions about the impacts of changes in α on growth in Mexico. In the first period (1917–40) common pool problems slowed down growth. In the second period (1947–80) the ability of the center to police the common market brought about major efficiency improvements. However, by coaxing states to join the FPWD, the center also compromised growth in those states. Growth was dampened in the third period (1980–94). Since 1994, increases in both competition and in α have boosted growth. The figures discussed in the introduction bear out this pattern: growth averaged 2.3 percent per year from 1980 to 1993, increasing to 5.1 percent from 1996 to 1999.

To study the effects of the fiscal changes on economic growth, we created a sample of five states that joined the FPWD early and five that joined late. The fiscal system treated these states differently, with significant effects on growth. The sample included the early joiners Aguascalientes, Campeche, Guerrero, Michoacán, and Puebla; and late joiners: Chihuahua, Durango, México, Nuevo León, and Zacatecas.

As noted above, late-joining states were richer. For expenditures, expenditures in late-joining states averaged 647 million pesos per year (1970–72), while those joining early averaged 178 million, a ratio of about 3.6 (late to early). Similarly, late joiners had larger state GDPs. For the year 1970, early joiners aver-

TABLE 13.6
Average Real State GDP Growth Rate, by Group and Period
(percent per year)

	1970–80	1980–93
Early joiners	6.6	3.0
Late joiners	7.5	1.7

aged 7.5 billion pesos GDP, while for late joiners the figure is 18.1 billion pesos, about 2.4 times larger.

As we have already noted, two major events occurred in the early 1980s that affected these patterns: the change in the fiscal system, resulting in greater centralization; and the exogenous economic shocks caused by the international debt crisis and by collapsing oil prices. Given the data we have, we cannot separate the effects of these two changes.

The first major change is the relative growth of state expenditures among the early joiners. We have calculated the ratio of state expenditures (late to early joiners) for the two periods, 1970–80; and 1980–94. This calculation is reproduced in table 13.5. The data reveal a dramatic change in expenditures: the ratio of expenditures (late to early joiners) falls by nearly a factor of one-half after 1980. Because nearly all state expenditures after 1980 were financed through the federal revenue-sharing system, the new tax system clearly gave disproportionately more revenue to the early joiners.

We next turn to the state GDP growth rates. By separating the states into the two sets of early and late joiners, we are able to assess the differential impact of the two changes (changes in the fiscal system; and exogenous economic shocks) across the two sets.

The data show that real state GDP growth rates for the late joiners is somewhat larger than for the early joiners in the early period, 7.5 percent versus 6.6 percent per year respectively (table 13.6). The data also show that the growth rates of both groups fall dramatically after 1980, as is well known. The fall, however, is much larger for the late joiners: average GDP growth per year is 3.0 percent for the early joiners, while only 1.7 percent for the late joiners.

The change in growth rates is consistent with the FPWD hypothesis: growth rates should fall more in states joining later. Moreover, the smaller fall for the early joiners is consistent with the evidence from the data on expenditures (and hence redistribution). Because the early joiners get proportionately more transfers under the revenue-sharing scheme, they are likely to grow at a greater rate (assuming that some of the revenue is spent on public goods!). Of course, there are many alternative hypotheses about why state GDP growth rates should fall. Perhaps the debt crisis and the oil shock hit the richer states harder. Nonetheless, the fact that growth rates for the late joiners fall more than for the early joiners is consistent with our hypothesis.

6. CONCLUSIONS

In this chapter, we examine how political institutions affect good governance. Our context is fiscal federalism. We show that different forms of decentralization have markedly different effects on governance, as indicated by the incentives of SNGs to foster local economic prosperity.

The theory examines how SNGs make tradeoffs between providing public goods that foster markets and nonproductive expenditures, such as rent seeking, transfers to interest groups, and corruption. The analysis shows that revenue sharing greatly reduces a state's incentive to produce public goods. When an SNG raises the lion's share of its revenue, it has the possibility of recouping the costs of providing market-fostering public goods through the increased revenue generated. When an SNG derives most of its funds from a revenue-sharing system, increases in revenue from providing public goods go into the common pool, shared among all states. Because an SNG bears all the costs of providing public goods but receives only a portion of the return, it will provide a much lower level of public goods.

In comparison with engaging in corruption or rent seeking, providing public goods generates two sources of value for an SNG. Because citizens value public goods, these goods generate direct utility for citizens. Public goods have an indirect value as well: providing public goods generates more tax revenue, thus relaxing the SNG's budget constraint.

The model yields a comparative statics result. The greater the proportion of locally generated revenue captured by the SNG, the more the SNG substitutes public goods provision for corruption. We showed that a major consequence of this result is the *fiscal law of 1/n:* the indirect effect of fostering greater SNG choice of public goods in a complete revenue-sharing system is $1/n$ that of a fiscal system in which SNGs capture all locally generated revenue. The reason is that in revenue-sharing systems that allocate revenue independent of contributions, nearly all the increased revenue from providing additional public goods goes into the common pool, implying that the SNG receives only on the order of $1/n$ of the increase. Revenue-sharing systems therefore greatly diminish an SNG's incentive to provide market-fostering public goods; they also increase corruption and rent seeking.

Consistent with this result is the following pattern among federal systems. During the United States' rise from a small economy on the periphery of the developed world in the late eighteenth century to become the richest nation by the early twentieth century, states depended almost exclusively on their own sources of revenue. So too do provinces in modern China (see Jin, Qian, and

Weingast 1999, although this has changed somewhat in the late 1990s). Iaryc-zower, Saiegh, and Tommasi (2000) suggest that this characteristic also held in Argentina during its high-growth phase in the latter part of the nineteenth century and early twentieth century. In contrast, this condition fails for modern Argentina, India, Mexico, and Russia.

We applied our framework to Mexico, whose federal system has gone through four phases since the Revolution in the early twentieth century, each with different implications for efficiency and growth. In the first federal phase, the absence of central control fostered common pool problems as states overgrazed the commons. Too weak a center allowed competitive taxation of businesses, state corruption, and internal trade barriers, resulting in significant efficiency losses. In the second phase, beginning in 1940, the federal government rationalized taxation, removed burdensome taxes, established the common market, and generally policed common pool problems. States maintained several independent sources of revenue. High growth ensued for the next 30 years, resulting in a period known as the "Mexican Miracle."

In the third phase of Mexican federalism (after 1980), the central government worked in tandem with the ruling political party, the PRI, to centralize power, authority, and finances. Gradually, the central government coaxed the states into giving up their policy and taxation authority in exchange for revenue and attractive career alternatives for politicians. Growth stalled substantially during the third phase.[14] The theory implies that Mexico's present revenue-sharing scheme is characterized by the fiscal law of $1/n$.

Our analysis of the various revenue-sharing formulas employed by the central government bears out the theory. The initial formula returned almost exactly the same revenue to the states as they put in. The purpose of this formula could not be either of the principal normative rationales for revenue sharing—redistribution or insurance against shocks—there was none. All the formulas employed by the central government since 1980 exhibit aspects of the fiscal law of $1/n$.

This chapter also analyzed the central government's method of coaxing the states to join the fiscal pact with the devil. These pacts forced states to toe the national party line, greatly reducing their ability to pursue policies independent of the center. The central government accomplished this by a series of carrots and sticks. On the cost side, the federal government collected its tax revenue in each state regardless of whether they joined the revenue collection system. On the benefit side, states obtained greater revenue if they joined the federal system. The center's incentives implied that retaining policy freedom forced states to have higher taxes and lower revenue.

---

[14] Of course, this third phase of Mexican federalism also coincided with the onset of the international debt crisis, which had deep effects on Mexico.

In closing, we speculate on a larger question. Our emphasis on the costs of revenue sharing forces us to ask why the Mexican government created this system. The answer, we argue, is that Mexico's dominant ruling party, the PRI, created this system to help preserve its power. First, the revenue-sharing system afforded the PRI, via its control of the federal government, a near monopoly on taxes. This allowed them to extract greater total revenue from the economy than could the states acting independently. Second, the PRI used this revenue to solidify constituent support. Nearly all empirical investigations of Mexico's expenditure programs show that they are used to help the PRI win elections rather than to address the policies to which they are nominally associated (see Diaz-Cayeros 1997; Diaz-Cayeros, Magaloni, and Weingast 2000; Magaloni 2000; and Molinar Horcasitas and Weldon 1994). Third, the system helps the PRI keep its officials in line with the party. By reducing the policy and fiscal authority of states, the PRI made it difficult for SNG officials to simultaneously defect from the system and create an independent source of political power. Finally, following Diaz-Cayeros, Magaloni, and Weingast (2000) and Fiorina and Noll (1978), we argue that this system provides citizens with the incentive to accept it. The reason is that, acting alone, citizens in a given locality cannot affect the system and yet face direct punishment. Yet electing the opposition means that the center punishes them, as the PRI withholds fiscal resources. The "tragic logic" of modern Mexican political economy is that the PRI's system at once accomplished two goals: It skimmed a large portion of social resources used to ensure its own survival; and it provided citizens with the incentive to go along (Diaz-Cayeros, Magaloni, and Weingast 2000).

The model has implications beyond the study of Mexico. Our approach shows that good governance requires the appropriately designed political institutions. For government officials to implement policies that increase social surplus, they must have incentives to pursue these policies instead of transferring resources to private groups or engaging in corruption (see also Persson and Tabellini 2000, among others). We showed that fiscal institutions affect how political officials make the tradeoff between the provision of public goods and corruption. Greater fiscal reliance of SNGs on their own resources induces them to provide more public goods and less corruption. The model shows that the degree of corruption and inefficiency is in part endogenous to the fiscal system.

When central government policies are a major impediment to economic growth, the appropriately structured decentralization can enhance government performance. First, as is well known, appropriately structured decentralization creates competition among jurisdictions, forcing them to attend to the inefficiencies, rent seeking and corruption associated with their policymaking. Second, it diminishes the "one size fits all" problem observed by Hayek (1939). Third, as we have shown in this chapter, fiscal decentralization also provides SNGs with the incentive to foster local economic prosperity.

In this work, we join a growing group of scholars who emphasize that good governance is a function of political institutions. Our exploration of the effects of the fiscal system on SNG decision making demonstrates how fiscal institutions affect their decisions to foster markets or engage in corruption. Put simply, greater revenue self-reliance allows SNGs the ability to capture greater revenue from enhancing markets and thus biases their choices in favor of market-fostering public goods over corruption.

APPENDIX: CHANGES IN THE ALLOCATION CRITERIA OF THE MEXICAN REVENUE-SHARING FORMULA SINCE 1980

The following is a summary of various changes since 1980 in the criteria utilized by the Mexican federal government to share revenue with the states.

- In 1980 the Transfers Fund was allocated among the states solely on the basis of the proportion of federal taxes raised in each state.

- In 1981, each state received the same nominal amount as in the previous year, and the increase in the Transfers Fund (i.e., Transfers Fund 1981—Transfers Fund 1980) was distributed among the states, taking into account the collection effort of each in the current year.

- In 1983 the formula again assigned each state the same nominal amount as the previous year, plus a proportion of the increase in the Transfers Fund, taking into account their collection efforts of the year with respect to the past two years.

- In 1984, the central government attempted to stimulate the collection of the value-added tax (IVA). Since the reform of 1980, states were responsible for collecting the IVA and for sending a portion to the federation. In this year, the formula allowed each state to keep 30 percent of the IVA it collected, plus an amount similar to that received by each the year before, modified a bit by general collection effort of the past year.

- In 1990 the federation took IVA collection away from the states and made transfers based on three criteria: population, tax collection effort, a small part inversely related to population. During the next four years, the federal government tinkered with the relative weight of the three criteria. Table 13.A1 shows the percentage of the Transfers Fund that was distributed by the three assignations criteria in the years 1991 to 1994.

- Since 1994, 45.17 percent of the Transfers Fund has been distributed according to state population; 9.66 percent in inverse per capita relation; and 45.17 percent according to a formula that awards the states the same nominal

TABLE 13.A1
Weights in the Distribution Criteria of the Transfer Fund by Year

Year	% Distributed by Population	% Distributed by Formula Based on Revenue Collection	% Distributed in Inverse to the Other Two Criteria
1991	18.05	72.29	9.66
1992	27.10	63.24	9.66
1993	36.15	54.19	9.66
1994–present	45.17	45.17	9.66

Source: Presidencia de la Republica 1998.

amount as the previous year, plus a proportion of the increase in the Transfers Fund, taking into account their collection efforts of the year with respect to the past two years.

- Since 1991, the revenue-sharing formula has been the same, consisting of three components: population, revenue raised in the state, and a category representing the inverse of the other two. However, the weights of the categories changed. Table 13.A1 shows the weights accorded to the categories since 1991.

REFERENCES

Acemoglu, Daron, and James A. Robinson. 2000. "Why Did the West Extend the Franchise? Democracy, Inequality, and Growth in Historical Perspective." *Quarterly Journal of Economics* 115, no. 4: 1167–99.

Alesina, Alberto, and Allan Drazen. 1991. "Why Are Stabilizations Delayed?" *American Economic Review* 81:1170–88.

Alesina, Alberto, and Enrico Spolare. 1997. "On the Number and Size of Nations." *Quarterly Journal of Economics* 112, no. 4: 1027–56.

Bailey, John. 1995. "Fiscal Centralism and Pragmatic Accommodation in Nuevo Leon." In *Opposition Government in Mexico,* ed. Victoria E. Rodríguez and Peter M. Ward. Albuquerque: University of New Mexico Press.

Besley, Timothy, and Stephen Coate. 1998. "Sources of Inefficiency in a Representative Democracy: A Dynamic Analysis." *American Economic Review* 88, no. 1: 139–56.

Bolton, Patrick, and Gerard Roland. 1997. "The Breakup of Nations: A Political Economy Analysis." *Quarterly Journal of Economics* 112, no. 4: 1057–90.

Brennan, Geoffrey, and James M. Buchanan. 1980. *The Power to Tax.* Cambridge: Cambridge University Press.

Cabrero Mendoza, Enrique. 1995. *La nueva gestión municipal en México: Análisis de experiencias inovadoras en gobiernos locales.* Mexico City: Centro de Investigación y Docencia Económicas.

———. 1996. *Los dilemas de la modernización municipal: estudios sobre la gestión hacendaria en municipios urbanos de México.* Mexico City: Centro de Investigación y Docencia Económicas.

Cao, Yuanzheng, Yingyi Qian, and Barry R. Weingast. 1999. "From Federalism, Chinese Style, to Privatization, Chinese Style." *Economics of Transition* 7, no. 1: 103–31.

Cornelius, Wayne A., Ann L. Craig, and Jonathan Fox, eds. 1994. *Transforming State-Society Relations in Mexico: The National Solidarity Strategy.* La Jolla: Center for U.S.-Mexican Studies, University of California, San Diego.

Cornelius, Wayne A., Todd A. Eisenstadt, and Jane Hindley. 1999. *Subnational Politics and Democratization in Mexico.* La Jolla: Center for U.S.-Mexican Studies, University of California, San Diego.

Cremer, Jacques, and Thomas Palfrey. Forthcoming. "Federal Mandates by Popular Demand." *Journal of Political Economy.*

Cox, Gary, and Mathew D. McCubbins. 2001. "Institutions and Public Policy in Presidential Systems." In *Presidents, Parliaments, and Policy,* ed. Stephan Haggard and Mathew D. McCubbins. Cambridge: Cambridge University Press.

de Figueiredo, Rui, and Barry R. Weingast. 2000. "Self-Enforcing Federalism: Solving the Two Fundamental Dilemmas." Working paper, Hoover Institution, Stanford University.

Diaz-Cayeros, Alberto. 1997. "Political Responses to Regional Inequality: Taxation and Distribution in Mexico." Ph.D. diss., Duke University.

———. 1999. "Do Federal Institutions Matter? Rules and Political Practices in Mexico." Working paper, Centro de Investigacion para el Dessarrollo, A.C. Mexico.

Diaz-Cayeros, Alberto, and Beatriz Magaloni. 2000. "From Authoritarianism to Democracy: The Unfinished Transition in Mexico." Working paper, Stanford University.

Diaz-Cayeros, Alberto, Beatriz Magaloni, and Barry R. Weingast. 2000. "Democratization and the Economy in Mexico: Equilibrium (PRI) Hegemony and Its Demise." Working paper, Stanford University.

Dillinger, William, and Stephen B. Webb. 1999. "Fiscal Management in Federal Democracies: Argentina and Brazil." World Bank Working Paper No. 2122.

Dixit, Avinash, and John Londregan. 1995. "Redistributive Politics and Economic Efficiency." *American Political Science Review* 89:855–66.

Drazen, Allan. 2000. *Political Economy in Macroeconomics.* Princeton: Princeton University Press.

Escamilla, Sergio. 1999. "Análisis de Incentivos de la Ley de Coordinación Fiscal de 1990." Instituto Technologico Autónomio de México. Typescript.

Fiorina, Morris P., and Roger G. Noll. 1978. "Voters, Bureaucrats, and Legislators: A Rational Choice Perspective on the Growth of Bureaucracy." *Journal of Public Economics* 9:239–54.

Garman, Christopher, Stephan Haggard, and Eliza Willis. 2001. "Fiscal Decentralization: A Political Theory with Latin American Cases." *World Politics* 53:205–36.

Garza Villareal, Gustavo. 1998. *La Gestión Municipal en el Area Metropolitana de Monterrey 1989–1994.* Mexico City: Instituto de Investigaciones Sociales, UNAM.

Geddes, Barbara. 1999. "What Do We Know about Democratization after Twenty Years?" *Annual Review of Political Science* 2:115–44.

Guillen López, Tonáhtiu. 1995. *Municipios en transición: Actors sociales y nuevas políticas de gobierno.* Mexico City: Ford Foundation.

————. 1996. *Gobiernos municipales en México: Entre la moderniozación y la tradición política.* Mexico City: El Colegio de la Frontera Norte, Porúa.

Gutiérrez, Jéronimo, and Alberto Islas. 1995. "Federalismo Fiscal: Una comparación internacional y reflexiones sobre el caso do México." B.A. thesis, Instituto Tecnológico Autónomo de México.

Haughwout, Andrew, and Robert P. Inman. 2000. "Fiscal Policies in Open Cities with Firms and Households." NBER Working Paper No. 7823.

Haughwout, Andrew, Robert P. Inman, Steve Craig, and Thomas Luce. 2000. "Local Revenue Hills: A General Equilibrium Specification with Evidence from Four U.S. Cities." NBER Working Paper No. 7603.

Hayek, Friedrich A. 1939. "The Economic Conditions of Interstate Federalism." *New Commonwealth Quarterly* 5:131–49. Reprinted in *Individualism and Economic Order* (Chicago: University of Chicago Press, 1948).

Hzou, Heng-fu. 1998. "Fiscal Decentralization and Economic Growth: A Cross-Country Study." *Journal of Urban Economic* 43:244–57.

Iaryczower, Matias, Sebastian Saiegh, and Mariano Tommasi. 2000. "Coming Together: The Industrial Organization of Federalism." Working paper, Universidad de San Andres, Argentina.

Inman, Robert P. 1988. "Federal Assistance and Local Services in the United States: The Evolution of a New Federalist Fiscal Order." In *Fiscal Federalism: Quantitative Studies,* ed. Harvey S. Rosen. Chicago: University of Chicago Press.

Inman, Robert P., and Daniel L. Rubinfeld. 1997. "The Political Economy of Federalism." In *Perspectives on Public Choice Theory,* ed. Dennis C. Mueller. Cambridge: Cambridge University Press.

Islas Torres, Alberto. 1997. "The Political Economy of Fiscal Decentralization: The Case of Mexico." M.S. thesis, Department of Political Science, Massachusetts Institute of Technology.

Jin, Hehui, Yingyi Qian, and Barry R. Weingast. 1999. "Regional Decentralization and Fiscal Incentives: Federalism, Chinese Style." Working Paper 99-013, Hoover Institution, Stanford University, March.

Jones, Mark P., Pablo Sanguinetti, and Mariano Tommasi. 2000. "Politics, Institutions, and Fiscal Performance in a Federal System: An Analysis of the Argentine Provinces." *Journal of Development Economics* 61, no. 2: 305–33.

Knack, Stephen, and Philip Keefer. 1995. "Institutions and Economic Performance: Cross-Country Tests Using Alternative Institutional Measures." *Economics and Politics* 7 (November): 207–27.

Kraemer, Moritz. 1997. "Intergovernmental Transfers and Political Representation: Empirical Evidence from Argentina, Brazil, and Mexico." Inter-American Development Bank Working Paper No. 345, January.

Levy, Brian, and Pablo T. Spiller. 1994. "Institutional Foundations of Regulatory Commitment: A Comparative Analysis of Telecommunications Regulation." *Journal of Law, Economics, and Organization* 10:201–46.

Londregan, John, and Keith T. Poole. 1990. "Poverty, the Coup Trap, and the Seizure of Executive Power." *World Politics* 42:151–83.

————. "Does High Income Promote Democracy?" *World Politics* 49:1–30.

Lujambio, Alonso. 2000. *El poder compartido: Un ensayo sobre la democratización mexicana.* Mexico City: Oceano.

Magaloni, Beatriz. 2000. "Institutions, Political Opportunism, and Macroeconomic Cycles: Mexico, 1970–1998." Working paper, Stanford University.

Margain, Hugo. 1971. "El Sistema Tributario en Mexico." In *Mexico, 50 años de Revolución.* Mexico City: Fondo de Cultura Económica.

Merino, Mauricio. 1994. *En Busca de la democracia municipal: La participación ciudadana en el gobierno local mexicano.* Mexico City: COLMEX.

McKinnon, Ronald I. 1997. "Market-Preserving Fiscal Federalism in the American Monetary Union." In *Macroeconomic Dimensions of Public Finance,* ed. Mario I. Blejer and Teresa Ter-Minassian. New York: Routledge.

McKinnon, Ronald I., and Thomas Nechyba. 1997. "Competition in Federal Systems: Political and Financial Constraints." In *The New Federalism: Can the States Be Trusted?* ed. John Ferejohn and Barry R. Weingast. Stanford, Calif.: Hoover Institution Press.

Molinar Horcasitas, Juan, and Jeffrey A. Weldon. 1994. "Electoral Determinants and Consequences of National Solidarity." In *Transforming State-Society Relations in Mexico: The National Solidarity Strategy,* ed. Wayne Cornelius, Ann L. Craig, and Jonathan Fox. La Jolla: Center for U.S.-Mexican Studies, University of California, San Diego.

Montinola, Gabriella, Yingyi Qian, and Barry R. Weingast. 1995. "Federalism, Chinese Style." *World Politics* 48:50–81.

North, Douglass C. 1990. *Institutions, Institutional Change, and Economic Performance.* Cambridge: Cambridge University Press.

Oi, Jean. 1999. *Rural China Takes Off: Institutional Foundations of Economic Reform.* Berkeley and Los Angeles: University of California Press.

Parikh, Sunita, and Barry R. Weingast. 1997. "A Comparative Theory of Federalism: India." *Virginia Law Review* 83, no. 7: 1593–1615.

Persson, Torsten, and Guido Tabellini. 1996. "A Federal Fiscal Constitution: Risk Sharing and Redistribution." *Journal of Political Economy* 104:979–1009.

———. 2000. *Political Economics: Explaining Economic Policy.* Cambridge: MIT Press.

Poterba, James M., and Jurgen von Hagen. 1999. *Fiscal Institutions and Fiscal Performance.* Chicago: University of Chicago Press.

Presidencia de la Republica. 1998. Typescript.

Prud'homme, Remy. 1995. "On the Dangers of Decentralization." *World Bank Research Observer* 10, no. 2: 201–20.

Przeworski, Adam, and Fernando Limongi. 1997. "Modernization: Theories and Facts." *World Politics* 49:155–83.

Riker, William H. 1964. *Federalism.* Boston: Little, Brown.

Robinson, James C. 1999. "Why Did the West Extend the Franchise? Growth, Inequality, and Democracy in Historical Perspective." *Quarterly Journal of Economics* 115: 1150–71.

Rodden, Jonathan. 2000. "The Dilemma of Fiscal Federalism: Hard and Soft Budget Constraints around the World." Working paper, Massachusetts Institute of Technology.

Rodríguez, Victoria E. 1995. "Municipal Autonomy and the Politics of Intergovernmental Finance: Is It Different for the Opposition?" In *Opposition Government in Mexico,* ed. Victoria E. Rodríguez and Peter M. Ward. Albuquerque: University of New Mexico Press.

————. 1997. *Decentralization in Mexico: From "Reforma Municipal" to "Solidaridad" to "Nuevo Federalismo."* Boulder, Colo.: Westview Press.

Rodríguez, Victoria E., and Peter Ward. 1992. *Policymaking, Politics, and Urban Governance in Chihuahua: The Experience of Recent Panista Government.* Austin: Lyndon B. Johnson School of Public Affairs, University of Texas.

————. 1999. *The New Federalism and State Government in Mexico: Bringing the States Back In.* Austin: University of Texas Press.

————, eds. 1995. *Opposition Government in Mexico.* Albuquerque: University of New Mexico Press.

Rodrik, Dani. 1999. "Institutions for High-Quality Growth: What Are They and How to Acquire Them?" Working paper, Harvard University.

Roland, Gerard. 2001. *Transition and Economics: Politics, Markets, and Firms.* Cambridge: MIT Press.

Rubinfeld, Daniel. 1987. "Economics of the Local Public Sector." In *Handbook of Public Economics,* ed. A. J. Auerbach and M. Feldstein, vol. 2. New York: Elsevier.

Saez, Lawrence. 1998. "A Comparison of India and China's Foreign Investment Strategy toward Energy Infrastructure." *Journal of Developing Areas* 32 (winter): 199–220.

Sanguinetti, Pablo J. 1994. "Intergovernmental Transfers and Public Sector Expenditures: A Game-Theoretic Approach." *Estudios de Economia* 21, no. 2: 179–212.

Shah, Anwar. 1997. "Balance, Accountability, and Responsiveness: Lessons about Decentralization." World Bank Working Paper No. 2021.

Shirk, Susan. 1993. *The Political Logic of Economic Reform in China.* Berkeley and Los Angeles: University of California Press.

Stein, Ernesto. 1998. "Fiscal Decentralization and Government Size in Latin America." In *Democracy, Decentralization, and Deficits in Latin America,* ed. Kiichiro Fukasako and Ricardo Hausmann. Washington, D.C.: Inter-American Development Bank–Organisation for Economic Cooperation and Development.

Stiglitz, Joseph. 1998. "Distinguished Lecture on Economics in Government: The Private Uses of Public Interests: Incentives and Institutions." *Journal of Economic Perspectives* 12, no. 2: 3–22.

Sturzenegger, Federico, and Mariano Tommasi. 1998. *Political Economy of Reform.* Cambridge: MIT Press.

Tiebout, Charles. 1956."A Pure Theory of Local Expenditures." *Journal of Political Economy* 64:416–24.

Treisman, Daniel. 1999. "Decentralization and Inflation: Commitment, Collective Action, or Continuity?" Working paper, UCLA.

Ward, Peter M. 1995. "Policymaking and Policy Implementation among Non-PRI Governments: The PAN in Ciudad Juarez and in Chihuahua." In *Opposition Government in Mexico,* ed. Victoria E. Rodríguez and Peter M. Ward. Albuquerque: University of New Mexico Press.

Weingast, Barry R. 1995. "The Economic Role of Political Institutions: Market-Preserving Federalism and Economic Development." *Journal of Law, Economics, and Organization* 11:1–31.

————. 2000. "The Comparative Theory of Federalism." Working paper, Hoover Institution, Stanford University.

Weingast, Barry R., Kenneth A. Shepsle, and Christopher Johnsen. 1981. "Political Economy of Benefits and Costs: A Neoclassical Approach to Distributive Politics." *Journal of Political Economy* 89:642–64.

Weldon, Jeffrey. 1997. "The Political Sources of *Presidencialismo* in Mexico." In *Presidentialism and Democracy in Latin America,* ed. Scott Mainwaring and Matthew Soberg Shugart. Cambridge: Cambridge University Press.

Wildasin, David E. 1997. "Externalities and Bailouts: Hard and Soft Budget Constrains in Intergovernmental Fiscal Relations." Vanderbilt University. Photocopy.

Willis, Eliza, Christopher Garman, and Stephan Haggard. 1998. "The Politics of Decentralization in Latin America." Working paper, University of California, San Diego.

Zaid, Gabriel. 2000. *La economia presidencial.* Mexico City: Oceano.

Zhuravskaya, Ekaterina V. 2000. "Incentives to Provide Local Public Goods: Fiscal Federalism, Russian Style." *Journal of Public Economics* 76:337–68.

Ziccardi, Alicia. 1995. *La Tarea de Gobernar: Gobiernos locales y demandas ciudadanas.* Mexico City: Instituto de Investigaciones Sociales, UNAM.

Part IV

ECONOMIC GROWTH
WITHOUT SOCIAL DEVELOPMENT

The Political Economy
of Growth without Development

A CASE STUDY OF PAKISTAN

WILLIAM EASTERLY

PAKISTAN is an intriguing paradox. It has a well-educated and entrepreneurial Diaspora who thrive as small business owners in industrial economies, skilled workers in Gulf States, and high officials in international organizations. The professional elite within Pakistan is at a similar level to those in the industrialized world. Pakistan benefited from $58 billion of foreign development assistance (in 1995 dollars over 1960–98), 22 adjustment loans from the IMF and the World Bank (not counting the adjustment loan each is making in the years 2000–2001), a lucrative Cold War alliance with the United States, and multiple government development programs. Pakistan is the third largest recipient of official development assistance in the world over 1960–98 (India and Egypt are one and two). If it had invested all the official development assistance from 1960 to 1998 at a real rate of 6 percent, Pakistan would have a stock of assets equal to $239 billion in 1998, many times the current external debt. The World Bank alone provided $20 billion in loans from 1952 to 1999 (in 1995 dollars). Pakistan is blessed with fertile cropland watered by rivers that flow down from the Himalayas; it inherited the world's largest irrigation system from the British at independence. It has even had per capita economic growth—on average 2.2 percent per year from 1950 to 1999. Pakistan's tripling of its per capita income over this period, and the concomitant poverty reduction, was an important achievement while many low-income countries were stagnating. Pakistan's PPP per capita income was higher than a third of the world's countries by 1999.

I am grateful for comments by Reza Baqir, Parvez Hasan, Ishrat Husain, Ambar Narayan, Dani Rodrik, Tara Vishwanath, and by participants in seminars at Lahore University of Management Sciences, the Sindh Ministry of Finance, the Government of Pakistan/World Bank Poverty Reduction Workshop in Islamabad, the Harvard Kennedy School Workshop on Analytical Growth Narratives, and for data helpfully provided by Ambar Narayan and Ahmad Jamshidi. I have benefited from conversations with Mohsin Khan and Shahid Yusuf. I alone am responsible for any errors. Views expressed here are solely those of the author and not to be taken as views of the World Bank or its member countries.

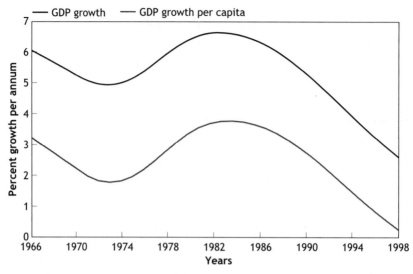

Figure 14.1. Pakistan's smoothed growth series

Yet after all this, social indicators like infant mortality and female primary and secondary enrollment in Pakistan are among the worst in the world. Female literacy ranges from 41 percent in urban Sindh to 3 percent in rural Northwest Frontier Province and Balochistan, with a nationwide average of 29 percent. Despite a major effort to increase services under a donor-supported eight-year-long campaign called the Social Action Program, Pakistan is only spending two dollars per capita on health. In contrast, the government is able to find the money for big-ticket items like nuclear weapons and the $1.2 billion six-lane expressway between Lahore and Islamabad (with traffic less than 10 percent of capacity). Pakistan is also more corrupt, more politically unstable and violent, less respectful of human rights, and less democratic than the benchmark for its level of income.

One possible consequence of the imbalance between Pakistan's growth and its other aspects of development is that growth itself has now decelerated sharply, with a decline of 4 percentage points in the permanent component of GDP growth by the end of the 1990s compared to its peak in the 1980s (figure 14.1). At the end of the 1990s, the permanent component of GDP per capita growth is estimated to be near zero.

Several recent political economy models could shed light on Pakistan's growth without development. The dominance by an elite that does not support human capital investment in the masses is a theme in several theoretical models in the literature. In a paper presenting the model most relevant for this chapter, Bourgignon and Verdier (2000) argue that an "oligarchy" will oppose widespread education because educated peoples are more likely to demand political power, that is, democracy. Even if the country is already "democratic," more educated peoples will be more likely to be politically active and thus more likely to vote for a redistribution of income and power away from the "oligarchy." Hence, the oligarchy will resist mass education even in a democratic society. Acemoglu and Robinson (1998) also feature an equilibrium with concentration of power among the elite and low human capital accumulation among the majority. Gradstein and Justman (1997) in related work find that the same conditions (such as inequality) that work against democracy also work against publicly funded education.

Galor and Moav (2000) have a story that relates investment in schooling by the elite to factor endowments. At an early stage of development, when labor and land are abundant and capital is scarce, there will be a low return to investing in mass education. This is assuming that skill is complementary to physical capital but not complementary to land. In a point very important for the Pakistani case, Galor and Moav note that large landowners would have little incentive to tax themselves to pay for schooling for the masses. As development proceeds and physical capital rises, the return to skills increase and industrial capitalists are willing to invest in mass education so as to gain a skilled labor force to complement their physical capital. Pakistan appears stuck at the early stage of development where land is abundant relative to physical capital and ownership of the land is highly concentrated.

As far as the low human capital of women, Galor and Weil (1996) develop a model in which factor endowments again determine education choices. If physical capital increases, the importance of "brain" versus "brawn" rises, and women's relative wages rise. This induces them to substitute education and labor force participation for child-rearing, lowering fertility, which in turn feeds back into more physical capital per capita. The economy may have multiple equilibria—one with high fertility, low women's education, physical capital scarcity, and low output per capita, and another with low fertility, high women's education, and high output per capita. Pakistan appears stuck in the first equilibrium. We also could imagine a political economy model of the gender gap that was a variant of the Bourguignon and Verdier (2000) theory. A male power elite could decide to keep women uneducated so that women would not have the skills necessary to petition for more equal treatment.

The second type of political economy approach stresses the link between ethnic fractionalization and poor public service and institutional outcomes. Alesina, Baqir, and Easterly (1999) find that more ethnically diverse U.S. cities and counties devote less resources to education and other public goods than more ethnically homogeneous cities and counties. Easterly and Levine (1997) found that ethnically diverse countries invest in less schooling and infrastructure. Goldin and Katz (1999) find lower public support for higher education in states with more religious-ethnic heterogeneity. Goldin and Katz (1997) likewise find lower high school graduation rates in states that have higher religious-ethnic diversity. Miguel (1999) likewise finds lower primary school funding in more ethnically diverse districts in Kenya.

Political economy approaches also link ethnic diversity to poor institutions. Mauro (1995) and La Porta et al. (1998) find that ethnic diversity predicts corruption and poor quality of government services. Alesina, Baqir, and Easterly (2000) find a link from ethnic diversity to bloated government payrolls in U.S. cities. Easterly, Ritzen, and Woolcock (2001) find that high inequality and high ethnic diversity both predict poor-quality institutions.

Pakistan's social backwardness for its level of income is an interesting case study of these predictions. Scholars argue that Pakistan has both elite domination and ethnic diversity. A case study approach can yield detailed insights in addition to what can be derived from cross-country regressions.

The study of Pakistan's social backwardness is itself not new. It has been noted in just about every one of the copious books and reports written by Pakistani economists, outside scholars, and international organizations (referenced below). This chapter will go further by documenting in much more detail the social (and importantly, the institutional) lag, by studying its evolution over time, by examining intracountry patterns, by reviewing the past history of government and aid programs to correct the social lag, and by analyzing the political economy of the social lag.[1]

INCOME WITHOUT DEVELOPMENT

Pakistan's social backwardness is all the more startling because not only is it low relative to income, but low after years of excessive public spending that led to a very high public debt-to-GDP ratio (101 percent of GDP in 2000) (Government of Pakistan 2001). Pakistan's high public debt (figure 14.2) and social backwardness may have contributed to poor creditworthiness ratings by international credit risk agencies, even compared to other countries of similar income levels (table 14.1). This in turn may have contributed to Pakistan's poor record at attracting private capital in the 1990s (table 14.1 again).

Pakistan has poor health, education, and fertility indicators for its level of per capita income.[2] Table 14.2 shows the lag in health indicators in Pakistan. Compared to other countries at this income, Pakistan has 36 percent lower births

---

[1] A recent example of analyzing growth without development is the self-explanatory article "Poverty Reduction without Human Development in Pakistan" by Joekes et al. (2000).

[2] Most of the differentials described here remain significant if one controls for a "South Asia effect" or a "Muslim effect." It is also possible that PPP per capita income (the concept used here) is overestimated for Pakistan, although that seems less credible given that there has been a threefold increase in income over the last half-century according to independently estimated growth statistics.

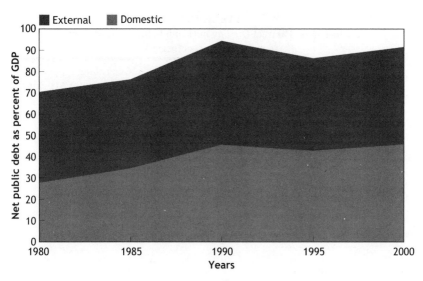

Figure 14.2. Pakistan's net public debt as percentage of GDP

attended by trained personnel, 11 percentage points higher babies born with low birthweight, 42 percent lower health spending per capita, 1.6 percent of GDP less in public-health spending, 27 excess infant deaths per thousand, 19 excess child deaths per thousand, and 23 percentage points less share of population with access to sanitation.

Table 14.3 shows the lag in education indicators. Relative to other countries at its level of income, Pakistan has 20 percentage points fewer of its elementary school–age children enrolled in primary school. This gap is explained entirely by the 40 percentage points fewer of elementary school–age girls who attend primary school. Similarly, the 14-percentage-point shortfall in secondary

TABLE 14.1
Coefficient on Pakistan Dummy in Regression of Indicators
of Private Financial Creditworthiness on per Capita Income

Variable	Coefficient	*t*-statistic
Euromoney creditworthiness rating (1–5 scale) 1998	−0.52	−7.05
International Country Risk Guide (1–5 scale) 1998	−0.76	−8.51
Institutional Investor (1–5 scale) 1998	−0.20	−2.59
Foreign direct investment/GDP (%), 1990s	−1.58	−3.36
Gross private capital inflows/GDP (%), 1990s	−4.23	−3.96

TABLE 14.2

Coefficient on Pakistan Dummy in Health Indicator Regressions
(*t*-statistic below coefficient)

Variable	Controlling for per Capita Income for Matching Time Period
Births attended by trained personnel, 1998	−36.537
	−18.54
Percent low birthweight 1990s	11.630
	17.62
log(health spending per capita PPP$ 1990s)	−0.558
	−8.13
Public health spending as percent of GDP 1996	−1.616
	−7.38
Infant mortality 1998	27.430
	11.55
Under-5 mortality 1998	18.954
	3.91
Hospital beds per 1000 1990s	−1.568
	−8.64
Percentage of population with access to sanitation 1990s	−23.732
	−10.43
Percentage of rural population with access to sanitation 1990s	−25.071
	−8.86
Percentage of urban population with access to sanitation 1090s	−17.232
	−7.33

enrollment is explained mainly by a 20-percentage-point shortfall for females. Tertiary enrollment is also abnormally small, although equally split between males and females.

Twenty-four percentage points more of Pakistan's population is illiterate than is normal for a country of its income level, reflecting excess illiteracy of 32 percentage points for females and 16 percentage points for males. Public spending on education is 1.4 percentage points lower than the benchmark for income level. There are nearly five additional students per teacher in Pakistani schools than its income level would predict.

Demographic indicators are also out of line in Pakistan. Although population growth is not unusually high for Pakistan's income level, there is excess fertility

TABLE 14.3
Coefficient on Pakistan Dummy in Education Indicator Regressions
(*t*-statistic below coefficient)

Variable	Controlling for per Capita Income for Matching Time Period
Gross primary enrollment, 1990s	−20.843
	−7.87
Female	−40.502
	−14.36
Male	−2.194
	−0.84
Gross secondary enrollment, 1990s	−13.602
	−9.72
Female	−20.471
	−13.43
Male	−9.030
	−6.20
Gross tertiary enrollment, 1990s	−5.644
	−9.09
Female	−5.543
	−7.91
Male	−5.590
	−9.07
Illiteracy rate, 1990s	24.420
	13.64
Female	32.177
	15.73
Male	16.294
	10.30
Daily newspapers per 1,000 people, 1995	−14.079
	−2.46
Public spending on education as percentage of GDP, 1990s	−1.367
	−7.55
Pupil/teacher ratio, 1989–97	4.629
	3.67

TABLE 14.4
Coefficient on Pakistan Dummy in Demographic Regressions
(*t*-statistic below coefficient)

Variable	Controlling for per Capita Income for Matching Time Period
Population growth, 1997	0.144
	0.81
Contraceptive prevalence	−21.023
	−12.87
Fertility, 1998	0.628
	6.83
Urbanization, 1997	−5.142
	−4.03
Female proportion of population, 1999	−2.058
	−21.30

of 0.6 childbirths per woman. Twenty-one percentage points fewer married women of childbearing age use contraceptives than is typical for a country of Pakistan's income level. Pakistan is more rural than the typical country of its development level (table 14.4). Finally, there is the well-known phenomenon of "missing women," which is also present throughout South Asia and China. Pakistan has a lower female proportion of population than normal—presumably reflecting the consequences of various forms of gender discrimination (see World Bank 2001). Girls between the ages of one and four had a 66 percent higher death rate than boys in the 1990s (Tinker 1998, 6).

Another indicator of a society's development is the quality of its institutions. Table 14.5 shows Pakistan's performance relative to its income level on a number of governance indicators. Pakistan fares worse on all six dimensions of governance measured by Kaufmann, Kraay, and Zoido-Lobatón (1999b): less government effectiveness, more graft, more political instability and violence, more regulatory burden, less rule of law, and less democratic voice and accountability. Other independent assessments give a similar picture of Pakistan's poor governance. Compared to other countries of its income level, it is less democratic, according to Freedom House (which is interesting, because these ratings were done when Pakistan did have an elected government in power).

Pakistan has more abuses of human rights than other countries of its income level according to the Humana Institute. The 1998 U.S. State Department re-

TABLE 14.5
Coefficient on Pakistan Dummy in Governance Regressions
(*t*-statistic below coefficient)

Variable	Controlling for per Capita Income for Matching Time Period
Governance as of 1997–98[a]	
Government effectiveness	−0.471
	−6.82
Graft	−0.454
	−7.24
Political instability and violence	−0.257
	−2.80
Regulatory burden	−0.146
	−2.21
Rule of law	−0.446
	−6.43
Voice and accountability	−0.274
	−3.74
Other political indicators for longer periods	
Freedom House Political Liberties, 1972–98 (from 1 for best to 7 for worst)	−0.468
	−2.86
Humana Institute Human Rights Index (from 0 to worst to 100 for best), average of 1986 and 1992	−13.785
	−6.93
Defense spending/GDP, 1972–98	3.313
	8.55

[a] Kaufmann, Kraay, and Zoido-Lobatón 1999b indicators, ranging from approximately −2.5 to 2.5, a positive number indicating a better outcome.

port on human rights (U.S. Department of State 1999) cited examples such as a death sentence for blasphemy imposed on a Christian and a Shi'a Muslim (although these have so far not been carried out). According to the same report, "police committed numerous extrajudicial killings and tortured, abused, and raped citizens."

The Pakistani government spends 3.3 percentage points of GDP more on defense than other countries of its income level. It is interesting that the overspending on defense is roughly equal to the sum of the underspending on health and education as a percentage of GDP (see below for a political economy explanation of this pattern). The statistics in table 14.5 may help explain the poor social performance, but they in turn need to be explained by fundamental political economy factors.

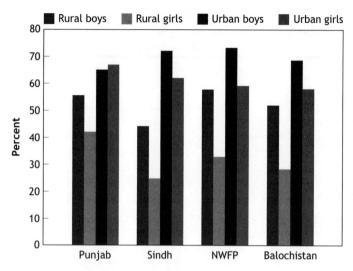

Figure 14.3. Net primary school enrollment

UNDERDEVELOPMENT ACROSS REGIONS AND CLASSES

Although the national averages of indicators are informative, they conceal significant regional and urban/rural inequality. The lag of rural areas is very important, as 64 percent of Pakistan's population lives there. Figure 14.3 shows the rural/urban variation in net primary enrollment rates, ranging in Sindh, for example, from 24 percent for rural girls to 62 percent for urban girls.[3] Figure 14.3 also shows that the gender gaps in primary enrollment vary across regions, with both rural and urban gender gaps smaller in Punjab than in other regions.

Figure 14.4 shows similar variation in secondary school enrollment across regions and across the urban/rural divide. Nine percent of rural Sindhi girls are enrolled in middle school, in contrast to 47 percent of urban girls in Sindh. Balochistan and Northwest Frontier Province (NWFP) also show low rural enrollment for girls, while the gender and rural/urban gaps are somewhat less pronounced in Punjab.

Figure 14.5 shows that contraceptive prevalence is lower in NWFP and Balochistan than other provinces. Similarly figure 14.5 shows that attendance of trained personnel at childbirth is much lower in rural areas.[4] Punjab had a better urban/rural balance than the other provinces.

[3] The source of all the regional urban/rural by gender data is the 1998——99 Pakistan Integrated Household Survey (PIHS).
[4] The PIHS data seem to imply a higher national average for attendance at childbirth than was apparent from the cross-country data used for table 14.1. Perhaps this is due to a broader definition of what are "trained personnel."

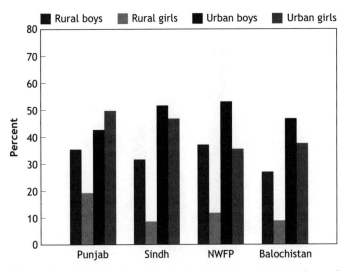

Figure 14.4. Net secondary school enrollment by region, gender, and urban/rural classification

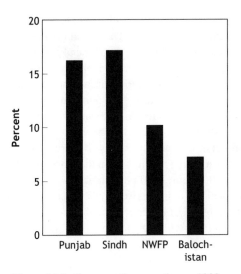

Figure 14.5. Contraceptive prevalence, 1998–99 (percentage of currently married women aged 15–49)

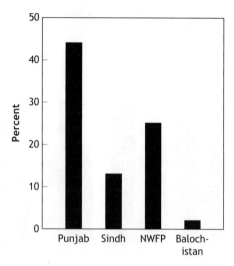

Figure 14.6. Percentage of rural households
with access to drainage, 1998–99

Figure 14.6 shows gaps of 40 percentage points across regions in rural access
to sanitation (in this case drainage). Five percent of rural residents of Balochistan have access to drainage.

How does the social lag relate to poverty within Pakistan? Not surprisingly,
material poverty is connected to the other social gaps documented in this chapter. The illiterate, especially the rural illiterate, have a far higher poverty rate
than the more educated (figure 14.7). The causation here no doubt runs in both
directions, but the picture is consistent with one of an educated elite who do not
wish to invest in the human capital of the majority.

Data on educational attainment shows further evidence for this story. The education gap between the rich elite and the poor majority is startling. Table 14.6
shows various education statistics on Pakistan by income level, using data on
household surveys from Filmer (2001). There is a gap of nine years in median
educational attainment between the richest 20 percent and the poorest 40 percent, which is close to being the highest in the world for Filmer's sample. The
typical member of the poorest 40 percent has *no* schooling. The shortfall of
Pakistani educational enrollment is explained—in the numerical sense—by the
lower class being shut out of education.

The class gap interacts with the gender gap, so that two-thirds of rich males
have attained ninth grade, compared to 2 out of every 100 poor females. (Rich
and poor are again defined as richest 20 percent and poorest 40 percent.) These
gaps appear at every level of educational attainment, not just ninth grade. In
fact, the gender/class gap is even larger for attainment of first grade (table 14.6).
The idea of dominance by a rich male elite is definitely borne out by the data.

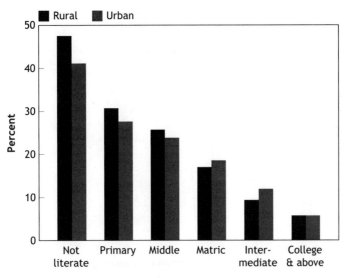

Figure 14.7. Poverty incidence, 1998–99, by level of education and location

GROWTH WITHOUT DEVELOPMENT

How did Pakistan wind up with such low levels of social well-being for its income level? Could this have reflected simply poor initial conditions, such as might have been due to underinvestment in the social sector under British colonial rule? In this section, I consider two exercises. First, I consider countries that were at the same income level as Pakistan at the beginning of the period and compare the subsequent evolution of per capita income and social indicators. I generally find that Pakistan grew much more than other low-income

TABLE 14.6

Educational Gaps in Pakistan by Income Class, Gender, and Location, 1990–91

	Richest 20 percent	Poorest 40 percent
Median grade attained, 15- to 19-year-olds	9	0
	Rich male	Poor female
Percentage of 15- to 19-year-olds who attained grade 9	61%	2%
Percentage of 15- to 19-year-olds who attained grade 1	92%	12%

Source: Filmer 2001.

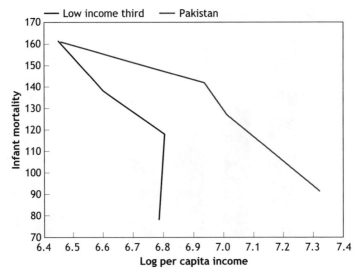

Figure 14.8. Path of income and infant mortality, low income third and Pakistan, 1960–98

countries (which in itself is an impressive accomplishment), but unfortunately achieved the same or less social progress. Second, I consider countries that grew at about the same rate as Pakistan, regardless of initial income level, and compare indices of per capita income and social indicators with the initial year set to equal unity. I find that other moderate growers achieved more social progress than Pakistan for a given amount of growth.

Figures 14.8 and 14.9 illustrate these two approaches for per capita income and infant mortality. Figure 14.8 shows that Pakistan had about the same infant mortality rate as other countries of its income level in 1960.[5] Over the succeeding four decades, Pakistan grew much more rapidly than other low-income countries, but had less improvement in infant mortality. Figure 14.9 shows indices (with 1960 = 1.0) of per capita income and infant mortality for the control group that had the same growth rate as Pakistan.[6] In the moderate-growth control group, infant mortality declined by 73 percent from 1960 to 1998. In

---

[5] In all of the control groups of "income level at same level," I take the third of the sample ordered by income centered around Pakistan in the initial year. I then plot the median income and infant mortality for that group of countries over the succeeding decades. Pakistan is always at the same level of income as the control group at the beginning of the period by construction.

[6] Again, I choose the control group as the third of the sample ordered by growth centered around Pakistan. I then plot the index of per capita income and infant mortality, set to 1 in the initial year. By construction, the index of per capita income will reach the same point at the end of the period in the control group as in Pakistan.

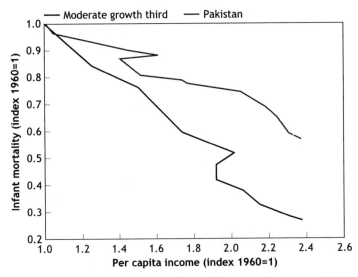

Figure 14.9. Path of income and infant mortality, moderate growth third and Pakistan, 1960-98

Pakistan, the same amount of growth resulted in a decline in infant mortality of 43 percent.

Figures 14.10 and 14.11 illustrate the same approaches for female illiteracy. Figure 14.10 shows that Pakistan already had higher female illiteracy at the same initial income level as the control group (the starting point for this data is 1970). Over the next three decades, income grew more in Pakistan, but female illiteracy improved less. Figure 14.11a shows indices for per capita income and female illiteracy (1970 = 1.0) for the control group that had the same growth rate as Pakistan. The moderate-growth control group achieved a reduction of female illiteracy of about 60 percent, while the same amount of growth in Pakistan yielded a decline in female illiteracy of about 20 percent. The gap between female and male illiteracy actually increased with rising per capita income in Pakistan, while it declined sharply in other comparably growing countries (figure 14.11b).

THE SOCIAL ACTION PROGRAM

The slow record of improvement in social indicators is particularly disappointing because for the past eight years the government and international donors have been making a concerted effort to improve them. This effort, known as the Social Action Program (SAP), has cost $8 billion over 1993–98, 25 percent of

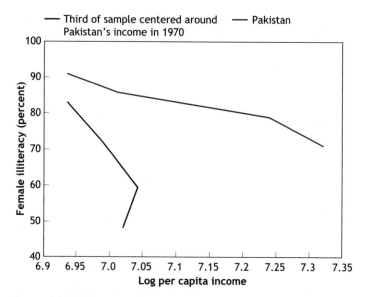

Figure 14.10. Female illiteracy and per capita income, third of sample centered around Pakistan and Pakistan, 1970–98

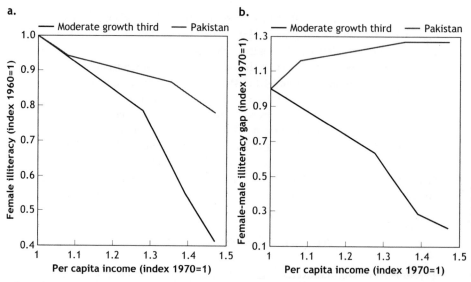

Figure 14.11a. Path of income and female illiteracy, moderate growth third and Pakistan, 1970–98

Figure 14.11b. Path of income and female-male illiteracy gap, moderate growth third and Pakistan, 1970–98

which was put up by foreign donors. The program aimed at improving outcomes in health, education, family planning, and rural water supply and sanitation.

The data seem to indicate that the Social Action Program failed. Primary school enrollment actually declined slightly over the 1990s. The total net primary enrollment rate fell to 40 percent in 1998–99 from around 46 percent in 1990–91. The share of the private sector in primary schooling has risen significantly, reflecting parents' discontent with the quality of government schools. Net secondary enrollment remained static at about 16 percent in the 1990s. The rural/urban gap for middle school enrollment increased during the decade as a result of modestly increasing rates in urban areas and declining rates in rural areas.

Infant mortality did decline, as we saw in figures 14.9 and 14.10, but by a smaller amount than with countries with comparable initial income or growth. Expanding immunization was a major goal of the SAP with a target of universal coverage (over 90 percent) by the end of 1990s. This goal was not reached, as less than 50 percent of one-year-olds were fully immunized by the end of the decade. Between 40 and 50 percent of health clinics reported stock-outs of at least two essential medicines in the most recent quarter at the time of the 1999 survey.

Contraceptive prevalence increased from 7 percent in 1990–91 to 17 percent in 1998–99. Fertility is declining in both rural and urban areas. The percentage of deliveries conducted by qualified personnel in Pakistan increased from 45 percent in 1990–91 to 61 percent in 1998–99. The share of pregnant women visiting a health facility for prenatal consultations has increased slightly over the 1990s, though it remains less than one-third of all pregnant women, and the increase is only in urban areas. On the other hand, the percentage of women receiving a tetanus toxoid vaccination decreased in both Punjab and Sindh in the 1990s, with a greater fall in rural areas.[7] The percentage of rural households connected to a drainage system decreased from 37 percent in 1990–91 to 33 percent in 1998–99.

The Social Action Program monitored compliance with guidelines for recruitment, procurement, absenteeism, and site selection. In 1998–99, compliance with the guidelines ranged from 81 percent for site selection, to 62 percent for recruitment, to 50 percent for procurement. The compliance rate on absenteeism was only 30 percent.

The Social Action Program aimed at increasing government spending on the social sectors. This objective failed, as the government first increased slightly then decreased the amount spent on SAP (table 14.7).

Total government spending on health and education, measured either as a percentage of GDP or constant dollars per capita, remained flat or declined slightly after the initiation of SAP (figure 14.12). Given the high dropout rates

---

[7] Results on tetanus toxoid are not available for other provinces.

TABLE 14.7
SAP Spending as Percentage of GDP

1992 to 93	1.70
1993 to 94	1.72
1994 to 95	1.88
1995 to 96	2.05
1996 to 97	2.35
1997 to 98	1.69
1998 to 99	1.60

in the early grades, part of this spending is being wasted on students who do not stay in school long enough to acquire functional literacy. Government spending on health of two dollars per capita and on education of eight dollars per capita is surely inadequate for expanding these services to a broader range of the population. It's not so much that "social action" failed, as it was that it was never really tried.

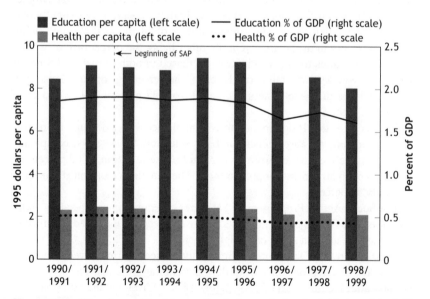

Figure 14.12. Education and health spending before and after the initiation of the SAP in 1992–93

Past Social Reform Attempts

The Social Action Program is only the latest of many government and foreign aid programs to try to improve Pakistan's social lag. Pakistan's founding father, Mohammad Ali Jinnah, sent a message to the first education conference, held in November 1947 shortly after independence, saying, "the future of our state will and must greatly depend on the type of education we give to our children." A commission on national education in 1959 called for universal and compulsory education. It stressed education of women in particular, since "unless a mother is educated, there will never be an educated home or an educated community" (UNESCO 1987, 7–8). The five-year plan in 1959 called for "a universal system of free and compulsory primary education by about 1975."

In 1965, the government's five-year plan aimed "greatly to increase enrolment at the primary level in order that universal primary education may be achieved as early as possible." The long-run plan in 1965 aimed to achieve by 1985 "universal literacy" (Government of Pakistan 1965, 17, 189). (Actual literacy in 1985 would turn out to be 24 percent.)

Bhutto nationalized private schools in the 1970s, eroding their quality. They were finally reprivatized in the early 1990s. Bhutto also established a national textbook board, which Burki (1999) blames for the continuing abysmal quality of textbooks. Nevertheless, the Education Policy of 1972 called for universal primary education for boys by 1979 and girls by 1984 (boys' primary enrollment in 1979 turned out to be 52 percent, and girls' primary enrollment in 1984 was 31 percent).

The World Bank in a 1977 study sounded the alarm about school quality: "Even the few children fortunate enough to reach school often have no books, pencils or paper . . . the roofs leak or have collapsed without funds for repair, thus crowding two classes and two teachers into the same room. Teachers, especially in rural areas, are often absent" (World Bank 1977, 6).

The World Bank in 1984 noted that the Pakistani government planned to launch a "program of mass literacy," noting that "progress in recent years has been disappointing" (103). Quality issues continued to fester, as a 1986 National Education Commission found that "large numbers of teachers are under-educated, under-trained, under-paid, and most important of all undervalued" (Bhatti et al. 1986, 12). A Harvard/USAID survey in 1988–89 found that about 20 percent of primary schools had no school building, meaning that classes were held outside under a tree (a 2001 World Bank study of Punjab Province found similar proportions of "shelterless" schools). Classes were canceled if it was too hot, too cold, or if it rained. The survey found that 60 to 70 percent of the students had no textbooks at the beginning of the year, although this was reduced to about 30 percent by the end of the year. The textbooks were hard to understand and contained numerous errors (Warwick and Reimers 1995, 34, 37,

82). The 2001 World Bank study of Punjab Province found that the allocation for teaching materials came to only 36 cents per pupil.

A 1996 World Bank study pointed out again the low literacy and enrollment rates in Pakistan. But it hopefully noted that "efforts to improve schooling have been increasing," with a "growing emphasis" on basic schooling for rural residents, and a focus on "improved schooling quality" (8–9). Instead, as we have seen, enrollment rates declined in the 1990s, especially in rural areas. Quality did not improve, as flight from public to private schools continued. In Punjab Province in 1999, only 41 percent of the highly selective group that made it to tenth grade passed the matriculation exam.

As one study put it, there have been many education "reforms and commissions on reform" (by one account there were 11 national education commissions between 1947 and 1993 [Farooq 1993, 6–7]), but education has remained "unabashedly elitist" (Library of Congress 1994). Total adult literacy remains at only 45 percent at the start of the new millennium.

Women's and mothers' issues have also featured in many government and aid programs. Notwithstanding the subsequent poor record on controlling fertility, the government had noted the need to reduce birthrates as long ago as the First Five Year Plan in 1955–60. Fertility rates did not begin to decline until the mid-1980s, and then—as we have seen—at a rate that lagged behind the rise of income. The redressing of gender inequality has also long been a feature of government plans. As a government document put it, "toward the close of the 1970's, women development issues were considered urgent [and] became one of the priority objectives of the government" (World Bank 1989, xxi). Again in 1989, the government of Pakistan was "committed to redressing this waste of human and development potential," that is, low female human capital (World Bank 1989, xiii). The 1996 World Bank report, done in collaboration with the government of Pakistan's Planning Commission, noted efforts toward "more equal distribution of basic schooling," "particularly for girls" (World Bank 1996, 8). Still at the end of the 1990s, female primary enrollment was the same as it was at the beginning of the decade. A critical indicator of maternal welfare, the percentage of low birthweight babies, has remained stuck at about 27 percent over the past two decades. Similarly, the low share of females in the population, a critical indicator of female health status, has not changed over the past four decades.

A nationwide campaign for improvement in health began as long ago as the second five-year program in 1960–65. The Third Five Year Plan in 1965–70 aimed at increasing "the supply of medical personnel in rural and semi-urban areas" and promoted "active participation by local communities." The government started the decentralized system of basic health units to serve the rural population in the early 1970s (World Bank 1996, 8). These units have never really functioned effectively due to missing medicines, absenteeism of medical staff assigned to the units, and unfilled posts for doctors. A USAID study in 1980 rather defensively concluded that "the lack of interest within the Government of Pakistan in social sector investments helps to explain the poor performance of recently funded AID projects in health" (26). The SAP in the 1990s was meant to revitalize this system, but a recent review based on data through 1999 concluded that basic health units were still missing essential medicines, underfunded, understaffed, and undervisited.[8]

The Third Five Year Plan noted in 1965 that "a programme for the complete eradication of malaria has been in progress since 1960–61." The campaign was expected to take five to seven years (Government of Pakistan 1965, 248). Instead, both the percentage of the country area affected by malaria and the percentage of the population living in such areas was higher in 1994 than it was in 1966 (or in 1946).[9] Pakistan today is still at an early phase of the epidemiological transition; 40 percent of the burden of disease continues to consist of communicable infectious diseases.

The military government that took power in 1999 soon thereafter announced a plan of devolution of authority for social services to the district level, in the hope that district-level officials would be held more accountable for service delivery than higher-level officials. It is too soon to tell whether this plan will be effective. Devolution is another idea that has been tried before: the military governments of Ayub Khan in the 1960s and Zia Ul Haq in the 1980s also tried to strengthen local governments, without succeeding in eliminating Pakistan's social lag. The First Five Year Plan in 1955 planned to "decentralise school administration, giving greater degree of financial authority to the district education officers, . . . and constituting local school management committees" (UNESCO 1987, 10). The SAP in the 1990s resuscitated these ideas, but without much success.

The SAP review in 2000 concluded that inadequate resources, lack of trained staff, absenteeism, inadequate and unreliable supplies of key inputs needed to maintain service quality, faulty construction, and weak monitoring all contributed to the continuing disappointment in social progress.

Part of the problem throughout Pakistan's history is that foreign donors placed a relatively low emphasis on social progress compared to overall GDP growth as a measure of success. Pakistan's lack of social progress did not prevent the World Bank's touting Pakistan as a success story in 1985 in a publication entitled *Pakistan and the World Bank: Partners in Progress.* Figure 14.13 shows that the social sector (defined to include education, health, nutrition, and population policy) had a miniscule share in World Bank lending to Pakistan until recently (and even in the 1990s was still only 22 percent of lending). This

---

[8] A review of the largest province, Punjab, found that 50 percent of clinics reported that they ran out of more than two essential drugs during October–December 1999.

[9] Data from the Center for International Development at Harvard (available online at http://www2.cid.harvard.edu/ciddata/).

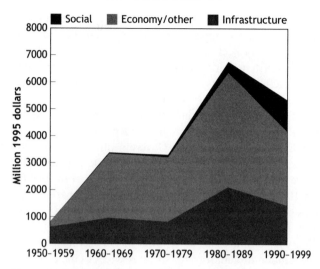

Figure 14.13. World Bank lending to Pakistan by decade and sector

probably reflects some combination of low demand from the Pakistani government (which I will explore in the next section) and the donors' emphasis on building things and directly supporting manufacturing and agriculture. In any case, foreign aid and government social programs are not a success story.

The Political Economy of Growth without Development

Why didn't Pakistani growth result in social and political development? Why is the social crisis so pronounced in Pakistan for its level of income? Why was the large volume of aid so ineffective? At the beginning, I noted the paradox of the highly educated Pakistani Diaspora in the West and the troubled, poorly educated society at home. I hypothesized that political economy models of elite dominance and ethnic division could help explain this paradox.

Pakistani economist Ishrat Husain puts forward a persuasive formulation of the effects of elite dominance: "The ruling elites found it convenient to perpetuate low literacy rates. The lower the proportion of literate people, the lower the probability that the ruling elite could be displaced" (Husain 1999a, 359). In a famous statement, the chief economist of the planning commission, Mahbub ul Haq, alleged in the 1960s that 22 families controlled 66 percent of the industrial wealth and 87 percent of banking and insurance (Husain 1999a, 19). The rural areas are dominated by the large "feudal" landowners, whom Gazdar (2000) classifies as belonging to a high "caste." Landowners have been prominent in virtually all Pakistani government coalitions. Their power is so great that they were long able to block direct taxation of agricultural income, depriving the state of an important revenue source.[10] The Economist Intelligence Unit estimates that the "rural gentry" captured 70 percent of the seats in local elections in December 2000.[11] Landowners have formed an alliance with the military leadership, who have in turn played a prominent role in Pakistani politics.

It is notable anecdotally that rural/urban and gender gaps are very high in Sindh, where "feudal" landlords are commonly thought to still be predominant in rural areas (Talbot 1998, 37). The rural/urban and gender gaps are much less in Punjab, by contrast, which is thought to be less "feudal" except in its southwestern extremity. By the same token, the severe social backwardness of rural areas all over the country, which explains much of Pakistan's overall lag in social indicators for its income level, is consistent with the story that landowners oppose human capital accumulation.

To explore more the relationship of the elite to public schooling services, Gazdar (2000) performed a careful survey of primary schools in selected rural locales. In a sample of 125 schools surveyed with surprise visits, a quarter of the schools were not open at the time of the visit (Gazdar 2000, 46). There were several cases where the teacher was a relative of the landowner and, thus protected, did not bother to show up for classes. The schools were sometimes used as a personal building by the landowner. Only a quarter of the schools had electricity, and only half had a latrine (Gazdar 2000, 50). There were no teachers present at all in 19 percent of the schools, and only one teacher was present in 35 percent of the sample (Gazdar 2000, 51). The researchers on the Gazdar team classified only 38 percent of the schools as "functional," according to a minimalist criterion (Gazdar 2000, 55). There was an association between high "caste" status and participation in schooling (Gazdar 2000, 112, 115).

In a case study of the Sanghar district in rural Sindh, Gazdar gives specific examples of landlord interference with schooling:

> In both these villages (in different areas of Sanghar), there were school buildings but no functioning schools. In AR Sammat1 the building was in a cluster of four homes, all belonging to a local landlord family, who had connections with a bigger landlord of the area. This building was being used as a farm shed, and for keeping goats. In Y Baloch2, the school was located in the middle of fields, and did not appear to have a connection at all with any of the surrounding settlements. Y Baloch2 was the name of a powerful large (deh level) landlord. The school was used here too as a farm shed, and one of Y Baloch2 employees was taking a nap there at the time of the visit. (2000, 71)

---

[10] Talbot 1998, 37–38. The government is introducing an agricultural income tax as of this writing (June 2001), but it is too soon to tell how effective it will be at mobilizing revenue from landlords.
[11] http://wb.eiu.com/report_full.asp?valname=CRBPK2&title=Country+Report+Pakistan#7.

In another village described by Gazdar:

There are 28 families in this village, which is about half a kilometre from the metalled road, though much further from any main or link road. The village is unique in the sample in that it is organized around the landlord's manor. There are four homes belonging to one branch of an extended Sammat2 family who are the sole landlords. Their land ownership is in the hundreds of acres. . . . The Sammat2 home is a towering pukka mansion, and is equipped with modern amenities. . . . Other homes are clustered around 50 meters away, and are all mud and thatch structures. . . . The conditions of the tenant homes are very poor, and the attitude of the Sammat2 towards the tenants is high-handed. . . . The tenant families, nevertheless, speak frankly about their exploitation, and state openly that they would not be exploited if they were educated. There is a government school in the village, but it does not function because the teacher remains absent. The school was established and building constructed under the Iqra scheme in 1986. According to a Bheel respondent, the only benefit they have of the school was that they could sleep in the building when it rained and their own roofs leaked. None of the tenant children go to school. The children of the Sammat2 all go to private school in a nearby town, and are driven to school and back in a jeep. (2000, 72)

The elite enforces their preferences on underinvestment in human capital by keeping social service delivery highly centralized, with all decisions on allocation of resources taken at the top. In Pakistan, it is the provinces that are responsible for social service delivery. For Punjab's population of 73 million, for example, the provincial government in Lahore makes the decisions on how many textbooks and medicines will make it to some remote rural backwater. The national government in Islamabad, in turn, largely determines the province's resources through transfers of taxes collected at the national level.

A variant of "the elite keeping the masses uneducated so as to keep power" hypothesis is that the male elite in a highly patriarchal society are reluctant to invest in women's education, since that is likely to lead to demand by women for increased power and equality. As we have seen above, Pakistani women are discriminated against in both health (as indicated by their low share of total population) and education. This discrimination may reflect some exogenous ideological and religious currents as well as political economy determinants.[12] The gender gap in turn may be feeding other social gaps. There is a negative association between mothers' education and the mortality rate of their children, both at the micro and macro levels. There is also a negative association between women's education and fertility, in both the household survey and cross-country data sets (World Bank 2001, 79–83). Lower women's rights are also associated with more corruption across countries (World Bank 2001, 94–95).

---

[12] As Noman (1997, 37) puts it, "ideological puritanism" led to "social and private subjugation of women."

The second political economy hypothesis is that division into linguistic, religious, or regional factions has also inhibited public provision of social services in Pakistan. Pakistan has a troubled political history. An anomalous feature of nationalism in Pakistan is that the cultural and geographical homeland of the "Pakistan idea" in British India lay outside the boundaries of what is today Pakistan (Talbot 1998, 130). Ironically, significant areas of what is today Pakistan supported other parties—including the Indian Congress Party—rather than the Pakistan-founding Muslim League in preindependence elections. For example, the Muslim League won only 1 of 86 seats set aside for Muslims in 1937 elections in Punjab (Burki 1986, 16). Only shortly before partition did the northwest Muslim-majority provinces embrace the idea of Pakistan. Even so, Pakistan became a nation of "disparate ethnic groups who had never previously coexisted except under colonialism" (Talbot 1998, 18). The way the British rushed independence contributed to the panicky migration of some 6 million Hindus from Pakistan to India and 8 million Muslim refugees from India to Pakistan and extensive communal violence that left 500,000 dead (Talbot 1998, 41; Bell-Fialkoff 1996). The failure of the British to resolve the dispute over Kashmir (a Muslim-majority state with a Hindu prince) prior to independence would poison the relationship with India forever after.[13]

The death of the unifying founder figure Jinnah soon after independence was an additional blow to the formation of strong national leadership. The remaining Muslim League leaders had their political base mainly in areas that were now in India (Library of Congress 1994). The division between West Pakistan and Bengali-speaking East Pakistan further complicated the launching of the national community at independence.

One indicator of polarization is the alternation of power between feuding factions of the elite, with governments rarely completing their terms of office. From independence to 1958, Pakistan had seven successive nonmilitary appointed governments. Then it had a secular military dictator, Ayub Khan, a violent breakup of East and West Pakistan, then a socialist democratic (but nevertheless autocratic) regime under the Sindhi landowner Z. A. Bhutto. Many Pakistani economists today trace the roots of the decay of the professional civil service to Bhutto's politicizing civil service appointments in the 1970s (Husain 1999b, 27). Next came an Islamic military dictator, Zia ul Haq (who executed Bhutto). The spillover of weapons and refugees from the war in Afghanistan further destabilized Pakistani politics. (The United States was happy to use Pakistan as a conduit for arms to the Afghans fighting the Soviets, but left Pakistan in the lurch once the Soviets left.) Zia died in a plane crash in what probably was an assassination. The nation returned to democracy, with an alternation in

---

[13] So politically salient is the Kashmir issue that during both of my two visits to Pakistan, Kashmir was on the front page of Pakistani newspapers every day of my visit.

power between the populist regime of Bhutto's daughter Benazir and the Muslim League regime of the Punjabi industrialist Nawaz Sharif. Each party leader out of power wound up in court charged with corruption, while the party in power often resorted to extraconstitutional means to hold on to it. Finally today there is another military regime (under which both Benazir Bhutto and Nawaz Sharif are in exile and banned from politics [Husain 1999a, xiii; Burki 1986, 37–101]).

The political instability has made Pakistan's successive governments more like Mancur Olson's (2000) "roving bandit," who loots only for today. The governments are not like Olson's "stationary bandit" who invests in his victim's future prosperity so he can continue fleecing him. The political polarization and instability may help explain the poor quality of government institutions documented above.

Part of the root of the factionalism lies in ethnolinguistic diversity. There are many different linguistic groups—although Urdu is the national language, it is spoken as the native tongue by only 8 percent of the population. Others out of the 20 languages spoken by fractions of the population include Punjabi (48 percent), Sindhi (12 percent), Siraiki (a variant of Punjabi, 10 percent), Pashto (8 percent), and Balochi (3 percent).

Before the secession of East Pakistan, of course, there was even more linguistic polarization. A contentious issue in the first quarter-century of Pakistan's existence was whether Bengali (spoken by East Pakistanis) was to be a second national language along with Urdu. When the East Pakistanis resorted to civil disobedience over this and other autonomy issues in 1971, the West Pakistani army responded with a campaign of rape and murder against the largely defenseless population. Scholars estimate that the army killed between 1.2 and 3 million Bengalis in 1971, and something like 10 million Bengalis fled their homes. Bangladesh finally won its independence with help from India.[14]

Another division is between native inhabitants of the region that became Pakistan and the Muslim immigrants (the *muhajirs*) that came from India at the time of partition.[15] The president of Pakistan accused the second Benazir Bhutto administration of extrajudicial killings of *muhajir* militants in Karachi when he dismissed her in 1996 (Talbot 1998, 17, 410). Balochis tried to secede in the 1970s under Bhutto senior, but Bhutto and the army responded with a campaign of mass murder of Balochis (continuing violence that dated back to 1958) (Harff 1992). Finally, there is polarization between different variants of Islamic belief and non-Muslim minorities, and the debate over the degree to which the Pakistani state should be secular or Islamic. The move towards increased Islamicization of society under Zia (beginning in 1979) may have ex-

---

[14] Various estimates by Fein (1992), Charny (1999), Rummel (1997).
[15] Library of Congress Pakistan page: go to http://lcweb2.loc.gov/frd/cs and select *Pakistan*.

acerbated other divisions by leading to a more exclusive definition of "Islamic." As the Library of Congress puts it, "Disputes between Sunnis and Shia, ethnic disturbances in Karachi between Pakhtuns and *muhajirs,* increased animosity toward Ahmadiyyas, and the revival of Punjab-Sindh tensions—can all be traced to the loss of Islam as a common vocabulary of public morality."[16] Husain concurs: "Every conceivable cleavage or difference: Sindhi vs. Punjabi, Mohajirs vs. Pathans, Islam vs. Secularism, Shias vs. Sunnis, Deobandis vs. Barelvis, literates vs. illiterates, Woman vs. Man, Urban vs. Rural—has been exploited to magnify dissensions, giving rise to heinous blood baths, accentuated hatred, and intolerance" (1999a, 396).

Polarized societies find it difficult to agree on what is a public good, and even if they compromise, each faction will value it less than would a citizen of a society with more homogeneous values. Examples in Pakistan might be disagreements about the role of Islam in the public schools, or disagreement about whether English or Urdu should be the language of instruction. (English was used in the schools until Zia instituted Urdu in the early 1980s; English was brought back in the private schools in the late 1980s and early 1990s.) The Harvard/USAID survey found that even in the Urdu schools, there were translations by students into local languages such as Baluchi, Punjabi, Pushto, and Sindhi (Warwick and Reimers 1995, 39). A further schism in education is between the Western-style schools and the *madrassahs* that focus mainly on religious instruction in Urdu and Arabic (Burki 1999). In both education and health, the access of women to these services, and the role women play in delivering the services, has been a divisive issue.[17] The result of such polarization over public services is that less public services are provided. Pakistan is the poster child for the hypothesis that a society polarized by class, gender, and ethnic group does poorly at providing public services.

An interesting exception to the general underprovision of public goods is the abundant supply of one national public good: military defense. Real defense spending more than doubled from 1980 to 2000, while real development spending decreased in absolute terms over the same period (Government of Pakistan 2001). One of the few things all factions can agree on is animosity towards India over the disputed province of Kashmir. Hence, it is easy for the military to justify a large investment in the army and advanced weaponry (the testing of a nuclear device set off widespread popular celebrations in Pakistan). The political and military leadership may exploit the Kashmir grievance as a distraction from its poor performance in other areas.

Polarized societies also find it difficult to agree on a common set of institutions to restrain rent seeking. An example in Pakistan is how successive governments

---

[16] Go to http://lcweb2.loc.gov/frd/cs and select *Pakistan,* then *Politicized Islam.*
[17] Noman 1997 (37) attributes part of the poor human capital performance of Pakistan to the divisive debate on role of women in society.

(starting with Bhutto senior if not earlier) have politicized the high-quality civil service inherited from the British. The poor institutions in turn reinforced poor public service delivery, aggravating the social lag.

The two political economy hypotheses of elite domination and ethnic factionalism fit the realities of Pakistani society, confirming cross-sectional results in the growth literature. One area for further investigation might be to examine how the two types of polarization interact—if the Pakistani elite was divided into factions, how did it manage to keep power from the poor majority? There were some attempts to co-opt the masses in the populist governments of Z. A. Bhutto and Benazir Bhutto, which we could think of as one section of the elite using the poor majority as a weapon against another section of the elite. However, the powerful position of the army and the landlords has prevented any passing of decision making to the illiterate majority. Each segment of the elite is powerful enough by itself to exclude the majority from power, even when it is feuding with another segment.

One Last Econometric Check on Hypotheses

One way to check on the ethnic divisions and inequality story is to introduce measures of ethnic divisions and inequality into the regressions of human capital on per capita income and the Pakistan dummy. The significance and magnitude of the Pakistan dummy when one controls for Pakistan's ethnic divisions and inequality will help assess whether these factors explain the poor social outcomes.

One piece of evidence that is not consistent with the inequality story should be mentioned before doing this exercise. Pakistan has a fairly low Gini coefficient by comparison with the rest of the sample: it was only in the twentieth percentile in the 1990s. It similarly ranks low on inequality by the land Gini (the thirty-first percentile). Yet virtually all country-level analyses of Pakistan stress the great divide between the elite and the poor majority.[18] It may be that the concentration of power and social status ("high caste") among the elite is more important than the actual material divide between the elite and the masses. It may also be that the skewed distribution of education (the near world-record gap of nine years of schooling between the richest 20 percent and the poorest 40 percent mentioned earlier) is a more important dimension of inequality than income.

Table 14.8 shows that controlling for ethnic diversity and inequality generally renders the Pakistan dummy insignificant. The educational inequality variable

---

[18] Having paid visits to both elite and poor households, I can anecdotally vouch for the "great divide" thesis.

(absolute difference in years of schooling between top 20 percent and bottom 40 percent) generally outperforms the income Gini in both having the "right" sign and significance and rendering insignificant the Pakistan dummy.[19] The coefficients on ethnic diversity and inequality are not themselves consistently significant, as the sample size is small and collinearity is a problem. However, there are some important significant results confirming that polarization inhibits human capital accumulation, controlling for per capita income. The Pakistan dummy is almost always insignificant when controlling for ethnic diversity and educational inequality. The results are uneven but supportive of the hypothesis that Pakistan's poor level of human capital investment for a given level of income is related to its high degree of ethnic and class polarization.

CONCLUSIONS

The political economy of growth without development helps us understand why Pakistan has resisted treatment by many well-intentioned government and donor programs. The Pakistan case illustrates the principle that the social payoff to foreign aid is low in a polarized society.[20]

The legacy of that failure is a lag in Pakistan's social indicators behind countries of comparable income, and there are serious inequities across rural/urban, provincial, and gender divides. The poor social indicators in turn lower the productive potential of the economy and its ability to service its high debt, not to mention the loss in human welfare from having achieved so little social and political progress.

Another puzzle to study in future research is why the low human capital indicators did not prevent a respectable growth rate of 2.2 percent per capita over 1950–99. It may be that a certain degree of development and growth was attainable with a skilled managerial elite and unskilled workers, but over time this strategy ran into diminishing returns, as human capital did not grow at the same rate as the other factors. This is consistent with the slowdown in growth from the mid-1980s to the present, but this requires more study to confirm. This interpretation is supported by some of the evidence of the cross-country growth regression literature.[21] Agricultural growth may have also been possible with the

---

[19] The relationship between the education gap and the enrollment ratio variables is partly mechanical, in that an extremely large gap makes it arithmetically impossible for enrollment to attain very high levels.

[20] Svensson 2000 finds that foreign aid tends to go into corruption in societies polarized along ethnic lines.

[21] Barro 1998 finds initial health and education to affect subsequent growth, and Kaufmann, Kraay, and Zoido-Lobatón 1999a find corruption, political instability, and other measures of government dysfunction to lower growth.

TABLE 14.8

Testing Pakistan Human Capital Dummy Controlling for Ethnic Divisions and Inequality
(*t*-statistics below coefficient)

Variable	Coefficient on Income	Coefficient on Pakistan Dummy	Coefficient on Ethnic Fraction-alization	Coefficient on Income Gini	Coefficient on Education Gap	R^2	Number of Observations
Primary enrollment	11.82 5.26	−8.46 −1.71	−0.01 −0.17	1.10 3.89		0.447	80
Primary enrollment	25.19 4.50	−6.58 −0.61	0.07 0.65		−3.90 −1.93	0.480	36
Female primary enrollment	13.59 5.92	−26.32 −5.35	−0.06 −0.91	1.25 4.26		0.530	79
Female primary enrollment	28.17 4.70	−18.63 −1.57	0.01 0.05		−5.26 −2.36	0.546	35
Male primary enrollment	10.31 4.62	9.07 1.73	0.05 0.74	0.99 3.40		0.347	79
Male primary enrollment	23.06 3.91	3.94 0.40	0.13 1.22		−2.46 −1.33	0.355	35
Secondary enrollment	24.73 13.25	−22.82 −7.43	0.00 0.03	−0.63 −2.86		0.819	80
Secondary enrollment	23.64 7.39	−5.68 −0.78	−0.02 −0.20		−1.57 −1.09	0.644	36
Female secondary enrollment	25.91 13.03	−27.14 −8.48	−0.06 −0.87	−0.50 −2.16		0.814	79
Female secondary enrollment	24.86 6.64	−8.39 −1.30	−0.10 −1.38		−2.07 −1.58	0.692	35
Male secondary enrollment	23.24 12.01	−18.94 −5.73	0.04 0.54	−0.71 −3.14		0.797	79
Male secondary enrollment	24.97 7.49	−4.10 −0.48	0.03 0.30		−1.41 −0.86	0.593	35
Illiteracy	−15.24 −8.47	18.55 4.67	0.05 0.91	−0.55 −2.52		0.621	61
Illiteracy	−22.50 −6.44	−7.34 −0.83	−0.06 −0.60		6.73 4.11	0.676	36
Female illiteracy	−15.79 −7.56	24.07 5.37	0.09 1.40	−0.72 −2.90		0.599	61
Female illiteracy	−23.29 −6.47	−4.14 −0.44	−0.02 −0.18		7.48 4.34	0.649	36

(*continued*)

TABLE 14.8 *(Continued)*

Variable	Coefficient on Income	Coefficient on Pakistan Dummy	Coefficient on Ethnic Fraction-alization	Coefficient on Income Gini	Coefficient on Education Gap	R^2	Number of Observations
Male illiteracy	−12.32	13.32	−0.02	−0.32		0.546	61
	−6.74	3.13	−0.31	−1.38			
Male illiteracy	−18.93	−10.89	−0.12		6.07	0.651	36
	−5.18	−1.33	−1.44		4.03		
Pupil-teacher ratio	−8.35	7.62	0.02	0.30		0.618	76
	−6.57	2.48	0.46	1.83			
Pupil-teacher ratio	−12.24	−8.36	0.04		2.62	0.497	36
	−3.78	−1.54	0.52		2.58		
Newspapers	85.12	−49.04	−0.58	−3.12		0.608	79
	7.80	−2.52	−1.49	−2.67			
Newspapers	22.70	8.67	−0.04		−1.93	0.588	35
	4.23	2.16	−0.62		−1.77		
log(public health spending per capita)	1.13	−0.48	−0.01	0.00		0.875	74
	12.72	−2.85	−2.41	−0.16			
log(public health spending per capita)	0.79	−0.36	−0.01		0.01	0.658	31
	4.61	−1.26	−3.19		0.21		
Infant mortality	−28.36	20.46	0.17	−0.22		0.820	81
	−11.63	4.44	2.34	−0.79			
Infant mortality	−37.74	23.97	0.05		0.67	0.731	36
	−8.36	5.11	0.51		0.63		
Under-5 mortality	−49.19	3.37	0.33	−0.65		0.769	77
	−9.74	0.32	2.34	−1.12			
Under-5 mortality	−80.85	18.06	0.10		0.86	0.770	35
	−8.58	1.54	0.45		0.34		
Access to sanitation	22.30	−21.72	0.01	0.35		0.646	74
	9.45	−4.18	0.11	1.26			
Access to sanitation	21.44	2.68	0.18		−5.73	0.416	35
	4.71	0.35	1.43		−3.33		
Access to sani-tation, rural	23.41	−31.20	0.05	−0.24		0.542	66
	6.41	−4.17	0.36	−0.57			
Access to sani-tation, rural	15.55	5.90	0.19		−6.09	0.273	35
	2.53	0.70	1.31		−3.11		

landlord elite taking advantage of the immense potential of the irrigation network and the green revolution, using only unskilled agricultural laborers. But agricultural growth may also have run into diminishing returns, as irrigated land and human capital did not grow at the same rate as other factors of production.

On the other hand, Pakistan could be taken as a supporting case for the proposition that per capita income growth is possible without commensurate human capital accumulation, at least as measured by the enrollment and educational attainment statistics (Pritchett 1999; Benhabib and Spiegel 1994).[22]

The bottom line is that Pakistan made little social progress for given rates of per capita income and growth relative to comparator groups, lowering the welfare of the population compared to that under more broadly based development. Pakistan is an interesting illustration that growth alone is not enough for broader development under circumstances of high social polarization. It may help us understand why economic growth is not always reliably associated with social and institutional progress (see Easterly 1999).

REFERENCES

Acemoglu, Daron, and James Robinson. 1998. "Why Did the West Extend the Franchise? Democracy, Inequality, and Growth in Historical Perspective." MIT Department of Economics Working Paper. http://web.mit.edu/daron/www/qje_kuz6.pdf.

Alesina, Alberto, Reza Baqir, and William Easterly. 1999. "Public Goods and Ethnic Divisions." *Quarterly Journal of Economics* 114 (November): 1243–84.

———. 2000. "Redistributive Government Employment." *Journal of Urban Economics* 48, no. 2: 219–41.

Barro, Robert. 1998. *Cross-Country Determinants of Growth*. Cambridge: MIT Press.

Bell-Fialkoff, Andrew. 1996. *Ethnic Cleansing*. New York: St. Martin's Press.

Benhabib, J., and M. Spiegel. 1994. "The Role of Human Capital in Economic Development: Evidence from Aggregate Cross-Country Data." *Journal of Monetary Economics* 34:143–73.

Bhatti, Mukhtar A., Mian Muhammad Afzal, Mahmood-ul-Hassan Nadeem, et al. 1986. *Primary Education Improvement: Desired Measures*. Islamabad: National Education Council.

Bourguignon, François, and Thierry Verdier. 2000. "Oligarchy, Democracy, Inequality, and Growth." *Journal of Development Economics* 62, no. 2: 285–313.

Burki, Shahid Javed. 1986. *Pakistan: A Nation in the Making*. Boulder, Colo.: Westview Press.

———. 1999. "Crisis in Pakistan: A Diagnosis of Its Causes and an Economic Approach to Resolving It." Lectures in Development Economics, No. 9, Pakistan Institute of Development Economics.

Charny, Israel W., ed. 1999. *Encyclopedia of Genocide*. 2 vols. Santa Barbara, Calif.: ABC-CLIO.

---

[22] Krueger and Lindahl 1999 challenge this view.

Easterly, William. 1999. "Life during Growth." *Journal of Economic Growth* 4, no. 3: 239–75.

Easterly, William, and Ross Levine. 1997. "Africa's Growth Tragedy: Policies and Ethnic Divisions." *Quarterly Journal of Economics* 112, no. 4: 1203–50.

Easterly, William, Jo Ritzen, and Michael Woolcock. 2001. "Social Cohesion, Institutions, and Growth." World Bank. Photocopy.

Farooq, R. A. 1993. *Education System in Pakistan: Issues and Problems.* Islamabad: Asia Society for Promotion of Innovation and Reform in Education.

Fein, Helen, ed. 1992. *Genocide Watch.* New Haven: Yale University Press.

Filmer, Deon. 2001. "Educational Attainment and Enrollment Profiles: A Resource 'Book' Based on an Analysis of Demographic and Health Survey Data." Development Research Group, World Bank. http://www.worldbank.org/research/projects/edattain/edbook.htm.

Galor, Oded, and Omer Moav. 2000. "Das Human Kapital." Brown University. http://www.econ.brown.edu/fac/Oded_Galor/.

Galor, Oded, and David N. Weil. 1996. "The Gender Gap, Fertility, and Growth." *American Economic Review* 86, no. 3: 374–87.

Gazdar, Haris. 2000. "State, Community, and Universal Education: A Political Economy of Public Schooling in Rural Pakistan." Asia Research Centre, London School of Economics, October.

Goldin, Claudia, and Lawrence Katz. 1997. "Why the United States Led in Education: Lessons from Secondary School Expansion, 1910 to 1940." NBER Working Paper No. 6144, August.

———. 1999. "The Shaping of Higher Education: The Formative Years in the United States, 1890 to 1940." *Journal of Economic Perspectives* 13, no. 1: 37–62.

Government of Pakistan. 1965. Planning Commission. *The Third Five Year Plan, 1965–70.* June.

———. 2001. Debt Reduction and Management Committee, Finance Division. *A Debt Burden Reduction and Management Strategy.* March.

Gradstein, Mark, and Moshe Justman. 1997. "Democratic Choice of an Education System: Implications for Growth and Income Distribution." *Journal of Economic Growth* 2, no. 2: 169–83.

Harff, Barbara. 1992. "Recognizing Genocides and Politicides." In *Genocide Watch,* ed. Helen Fein. New Haven: Yale University Press.

Husain, Ishrat. 1999a. *Pakistan: The Economy of an Elitist State.* Karachi: Oxford University Press.

———. 1999b. "The Political Economy of Reforms: A Case Study of Pakistan." Lectures in Development Economics No. 10, Pakistan Institute of Development Economics.

Joekes, S., N. Ahmed, A. Ercelawn, and S. A. Zaidi. 2000. "Poverty Reduction without Human Development in Pakistan: Money Doesn't Buy You Everything." *Development Policy Review* 18, no. 1: 37–62.

Kaufmann, Dani, Aart Kraay, and Pablo Zoido-Lobatón. 1999a. "Governance Matters." Working paper, World Bank.

———. 1999b. "Aggregating Governance Indicators." Working paper, World Bank.

Krueger, Alan B., and Mikael Lindahl. 1999. "Education for Growth in Sweden and the World." NBER Working Paper No. 7190, June.

La Porta, Rafael, Florencio Lopez-de-Silanes, Andrei Shleifer, and Robert Vishny. 1998. "The Quality of Government." NBER Working Paper No. 6727, September.

Library of Congress. 1994. *Pakistan: A Country Study.* May. http://lcweb2.loc.gov/frd/cs/pktoc.html.

Mauro, Paolo. 1995. "Corruption and Growth." *Quarterly Journal of Economics* 110, no. 3: 681–712.

Miguel, Ted. 1999. "Ethnic Diversity and School Funding in Kenya." Harvard University, November. Photocopy.

Noman, Omar. 1997. *Economic and Social Progress in East Asia: Why Pakistan Did Not Become a Tiger.* Oxford: Oxford University Press.

Olson, Mancur. 2000. *Power and Prosperity: Outgrowing Communist and Capitalist Dictatorships.* New York: Basic Books.

Pritchett, Lant. 1999. "Where Has All the Education Gone?" World Bank. Photocopy.

Rummel, R. J. 1997. *Death by Government.* New Brunswick, N.J.: Transaction.

Svensson, Jakob. 2000. "Foreign Aid and Rent-Seeking." *Journal of International Economics* 51, no. 2: 437–61.

Talbot, Ian. 1998. *Pakistan: A Modern History.* New York: St. Martin's Press.

Tinker, Anne. 1998. *Improving Women's Health in Pakistan.* Washington, D.C.: World Bank.

UNESCO. 1987. *Universal Primary Education for Girls: Pakistan.* Bangkok: Principal Regional Office for Asia and the Pacific.

United States Agency for International Development (USAID). 1980. *Review of United States Development Assistance to Pakistan, 1952–1980.* Washington, D.C.

U.S. Department of State. 1999. Bureau of Democracy, Human Rights, and Labor. "Pakistan Country Report on Human Rights Practices for 1998." http://www.state.gov/www/global/human_rights/1998_hrp_report/paki stan.html.

Warwick, Donald P., and Fernando Reimers. 1995. *Hope or Despair? Learning in Pakistan's Primary Schools.* Westport, Conn.: Praeger.

World Bank. 1977. *Educational Issues in Pakistan: A Sector Memorandum.* August. Washington, D.C.

———. 1984. *Pakistan: A Review of the Sixth Five Year Plan.* Washington, D.C.

———. 1989. *Women in Pakistan: An Economic and Social Strategy.* Washington, D.C.

———. 1996. *Pakistan 2010 Report: Policy Options for Sustained Growth into the Next Century, in Collaboration with the Planning Commission, Government of Pakistan.* Washington, D.C.

———. 2001. *Engendering Development: Through Gender Equality in Rights, Resources, and Voice.* Policy Research Report. Oxford: Oxford University Press.